D1190452

Foreign Relations of the
United States, 1969–1976

Volume XII

Soviet Union
January 1969–
October 1970

Editor　　　　　　Erin R. Mahan

General Editor　　Edward C. Keefer

United States Government Printing Office
Washington
2006

DEPARTMENT OF STATE PUBLICATION 11375

OFFICE OF THE HISTORIAN

BUREAU OF PUBLIC AFFAIRS

r
JX 233
.A3
1969-1976
VOL. 12

0 07809779

For sale by the Superintendent of Documents, U.S. Government Printing Office
Internet: bookstore.gpo.gov   Phone: toll free (866) 512-1800;   DC area (202) 512-1800
Fax: (202) 512-2250 Mail: Stop IDCC, Washington, DC 20402-0001

ISBN 0-16-076698-2

Preface

The *Foreign Relations of the United States* series presents the official documentary historical record of major foreign policy decisions and significant diplomatic activity of the United States Government. The Historian of the Department of State is charged with the responsibility for the preparation of the *Foreign Relations* series. Under the direction of the General Editor of the *Foreign Relations* series, the staff of the Office of the Historian, Bureau of Public Affairs, researches, compiles, and edits the volumes in the series. Secretary of State Frank B. Kellogg first promulgated official regulations codifying specific standards for the selection and editing of documents for the series on March 26, 1925. These regulations, with minor modifications, guided the series through 1991.

Public Law 102–138, the Foreign Relations Authorization Act, which was signed by President George H.W. Bush on October 28, 1991, established a new statutory charter for the preparation of the series. Section 198 of P.L. 102–138 added a new Title IV to the Department of State's Basic Authorities Act of 1956 (22 USC 4351, et seq.).

The statute requires that the *Foreign Relations* series be a thorough, accurate, and reliable record of major United States foreign policy decisions and significant United States diplomatic activity. The volumes of the series should include all records needed to provide comprehensive documentation of major foreign policy decisions and actions of the United States Government. The statute also confirms the editing principles established by Secretary Kellogg: the series will be historically objective and accurate; records should not be altered or deletions made without indicating in the published text that a deletion has been made; the published record should omit no facts that were of major importance in reaching a decision; and nothing should be omitted for the purposes of concealing a defect in policy. The statute also requires that the *Foreign Relations* series be published not more than 30 years after the events recorded, a requirement that the Office of the Historian is striving to meet. The editors are convinced that this volume meets all regulatory, statutory, and scholarly standards of selection and editing.

Structure and Scope of the Foreign Relations Series

This volume is part of a subseries of volumes of the *Foreign Relations* series that documents the most important foreign policy issues and major decisions of the administrations of Richard M. Nixon and Gerald R. Ford, 1969–1972. When all volumes are published, the subseries will contain 41 print volumes and 16 electronic-only volumes. These 57 volumes will document all aspects of foreign policy during the 8-year period. More volumes are allocated to the first Nixon administration than the Nixon-Ford administration, with the issue that is covered determining the beginning and ending dates of the volume. For example, the volume on Chile culminates with the overthrow of President Salvador Allende in September 1973, and the first volume on energy covers 1969–1974, ending with the post-oil embargo Washington Energy Conference. Two volumes cover the 1969–1976 period, South Africa and European Security. This volume, *Foreign Relations, 1969–1976*, Volume XII, documents U.S. policy towards the Soviet Union during the first 22 months of the Nixon administration. This is a short time span, but a period of burgeoning conflicts and major initiatives. The volume culminates with the resolution of the crisis over the Soviet construction of a nuclear submarine base at Cienfuegos in Cuba.

Focus of Research and Principles of Selection for Foreign Relations, 1969–1976, Volume XII

The scope of this volume is different from previous volumes on the Soviet Union and reflects a reexamination of how the Office of the Historian should present documentation on U.S. relations with its major opponent in the Cold War, the Soviet Union. In the past, volumes on the Soviet Union primarily documented U.S.-Soviet bilateral relations, and much of the documentation on U.S.-Soviet global confrontation and/or cooperation was found in other *Foreign Relations* volumes. On the advice of the Advisory Committee on Historical Diplomatic Documentation, the Office of the Historian revised its approach. In *Foreign Relations, 1961–1963*, Vol. V, Soviet Union, the editors made a concerted effort to use editorial notes to highlight key instances of U.S.-Soviet conflict or collaboration in other volumes in the subseries. The publication of an additional volume, VI, on Kennedy-Khrushchev exchanges also sought to broaden the coverage of U.S.-Soviet relations. This volume continues the trend and is the first of three volumes documenting the first Nixon administration's global confrontation, competition, and cooperation with the Soviet Union.

The Nixon administration presented a pressing argument to look at the U.S.-Soviet relationship in its broadest, global context. President Nixon created a secret, private channel of dialogue and negotiation between the President's Assistant for National Security Affairs, Henry A. Kissinger, and the Soviet Ambassador in Washington, Anatoly F. Dobrynin. The documentary record of the establishment and early use of that channel is presented in its entirety in this volume. In his relations with Moscow, President Nixon insisted on linkage of other issues with improvements in U.S.-Soviet relations. This volume highlights U.S.-Soviet interaction in the negotiations for a Middle East settlement, the role that the United States expected the Soviet Union to play in ending the Vietnam war, challenges to the U.S.-Soviet relationship in light of the Sino-Soviet border dispute, and the concern over Soviet strategic nuclear developments, such as the SS–9, in beginning Strategic Arms Limitation Talks. This expanded interaction between the two superpowers required a redesign of *Foreign Relations* coverage of the Soviet Union. The number of documents printed and the scope of their content were greatly expanded. There are five volumes for the Soviet Union within the Nixon-Ford subseries, 1969–1976, three of which document the crucial first Nixon administration. These volumes document U.S.-Soviet relations worldwide and more accurately reflect the global nature of the Cold War.

These changes do not mean that documentation on U.S.-Soviet competition and cooperation is not in other *Foreign Relations* volumes of the subseries. The Soviet Union volumes are the core documentary account of U.S.-Soviet conflict and cooperation during this period of the Cold War. They are the volumes to consult first, but with the exception of providing a complete documentary record of the Kissinger-Dobrynin backchannel, this volume in many ways serves as a guidepost to fuller coverage of topics where U.S.-Soviet interests intersect. In the end, of course, the *Foreign Relations* series must be viewed and used as an integrated publication of many volumes. The Soviet Union volumes—with their extensive use of extracts and editorial notes highlighting and summarizing relevant related material in other volumes in the subseries that impact on U.S-Soviet relations—emphasize the core issues of the Cold War, as seen through the prism of U.S.-Soviet global relations. This volume on the Soviet Union provides a summary account of U.S.-Soviet worldwide confrontation, competition, and cooperation during the 22 months it covers, and directs the reader to *Foreign Relations* volumes in which other aspects of U.S.-Soviet relations are covered, such as the Strategic Arms Limitation Talks, U.S.-Soviet negotiations for a Middle East peace settlement, U.S.-Soviet discussions on a negotiated settlement in Southeast Asia, U.S-Soviet negotiations over Germany and Berlin, U.S. monitoring of the Sino-Soviet border dispute, and U.S.-Soviet interaction in South Asia. The preponderance of memoranda generated by Henry Kissinger and his NSC staff also reflects the central role that the President's Assistant for National Security Affairs played in the formulation of policy toward the Soviet Union.

Editorial Methodology

The documents are presented chronologically according to Washington time. Memoranda of conversation are placed according to the date and time of the conversation, rather than the date the memorandum was drafted. Documents chosen for printing are authoritative or signed copies, unless otherwise noted.

Editorial treatment of the documents published in the *Foreign Relations* series follows Office style guidelines, supplemented by guidance from the General Editor. The documents are reproduced as exactly as possible, including marginalia or other notations, which are described in the footnotes. The editors have supplied a heading for each document included in the volume. Spelling, capitalization, and punctuation are retained as found in the original text, except that obvious typographical errors are silently corrected. Other mistakes and omissions in the documents are corrected by bracketed insertions: a correction is set in italic type; an addition in roman type. Words or phrases underlined in the source text are printed in italics. Abbreviations and contractions are preserved as found in the original text, and a list of abbreviations is included in the front matter of each volume.

Bracketed insertions are also used to indicate omitted text that deals with an unrelated subject (in roman type) or that remains classified after declassification review (in italic type). The amount and, where possible, the nature of the material not declassified has been noted by indicating the number of lines or pages of text that were omitted. Entire documents withheld for declassification purposes have been accounted for and are listed with headings, source notes, and number of pages not declassified in their chronological place. All brackets and ellipses that appear in the original text are so identified in footnotes.

The first footnote to each document indicates the document's source, original classification, distribution, and drafting information. This note also provides the background of important documents and policies and indicates whether the President or his major policy advisers read the document.

Editorial notes and additional annotation summarize pertinent material not printed in the volume, indicate the location of additional documentary sources, provide references to important related documents printed in other volumes, describe key events, and provide summaries of, and citations to, public statements that supplement and elucidate the printed documents. Information derived from memoirs and other first-hand accounts has been used when appropriate to supplement or explicate the official record.

The numbers in the index refer to document numbers rather than to page numbers.

Advisory Committee on Historical Diplomatic Documentation

The Advisory Committee on Historical Diplomatic Documentation, established under the Foreign Relations statute, reviews records, advises, and makes recommendations concerning the *Foreign Relations* series. The Advisory Committee monitors the overall compilation and editorial process of the series and advises on all aspects of the preparation and declassification of the series. The Advisory Committee does not necessarily review the contents of individual volumes in the series, but it makes recommendations on issues that come to its attention and reviews volumes, as it deems necessary to fulfill its advisory and statutory obligations.

Presidential Recordings and Materials Preservation Act Review

Under the terms of the Presidential Recordings and Materials Preservation Act (PRMPA) of 1974 (44 USC 2111 note), the National Archives and Records Administration (NARA) has custody of the Nixon Presidential historical materials. The requirements of the PRMPA and implementing regulations govern access to the Nixon Presidential historical materials. The PRMPA and implementing public access regulations require NARA to review for additional restrictions in order to ensure the protection of the privacy rights of former Nixon White House officials, since these officials were not given the opportunity to separate their personal materials from public papers. Thus, the PRMPA and implementing public access regulations require NARA formally to notify the Nixon Estate and former Nixon White House staff members that the agency is scheduling for public release Nixon White House historical materials. The Nixon Estate and former White House staff members have 30 days to contest the release of Nixon historical materials in which they were a participant or are mentioned. Further, the PRMPA and implementing regulations require NARA to segregate and return to the creator of files private and personal materials. All *Foreign Relations* volumes that include materials from NARA's Nixon Presidential Materials Staff are processed and released in accordance with the PRMPA. Of the five U.S.-Soviet volumes in the Nixon-Ford subseries, this is the only volume that does not contain transcripts of the Nixon presidential recordings because the audio system used by President Nixon did not begin until February 1971.

Declassification Review

The Office of Information Programs and Services, Bureau of Administration, conducted the declassification review for the Department of State of the documents published in this volume. The review was conducted in accordance with the standards set forth in Executive Order 12958, as amended, on Classified National Security Information and other applicable laws.

The principle guiding declassification review is to release all information, subject only to the current requirements of national security, as embodied in law and regulation. Declassification decisions entailed concurrence of the appropriate geographic and functional bureaus in the Department of State, other concerned agencies of the U.S. Government, and the appropriate foreign governments regarding specific documents of those governments. The declassification review of this volume, which began in 2001 and was completed in 2003, resulted in the decision to withhold no documents in full, excise a paragraph or more in 3 documents, and make minor excisions of less than a paragraph in 14 documents.

The Office of the Historian is confident, on the basis of the research conducted in preparing this volume, and as a result of the declassification review process described above, that the documentation and editorial notes presented here provide an accurate and comprehensive—given limitations of space—account of the Nixon administration's complex policy towards the Soviet Union, 1969–October 1970.

Acknowledgments

The editors wish to acknowledge the assistance of officials at the Nixon Presidential Materials Project of the National Archives and Records Administration (Archives II), at College Park, Maryland. Special thanks are due to John Haynes of the Library of Congress who facilitated access to the Kissinger Papers. The editors were able to use the Kissinger Papers with the permission of Henry Kissinger. The Central Intelligence Agency and Department of Defense provided full access to their records.

Erin R. Mahan collected the documentation for this volume, made the selections, and annotated the documents under the supervision of the General Editor, Edward C. Keefer. Susan C. Weetman coordinated the declassification review. Vicki E. Futscher and Aaron Marrs did the copy and technical editing. Do Mi Stauber prepared the index.

Marc J. Susser
The Historian
Bureau of Public Affairs

November 2006

Contents

Sources

Sources for the Foreign Relations Series

The 1991 *Foreign Relations* statute requires that the published record in the *Foreign Relations* series include all records needed to provide comprehensive documentation on major U.S. foreign policy decisions and significant U.S. diplomatic activity. It also requires that government agencies, departments, and other entities of the U.S. Government engaged in foreign policy formulation, execution, or support, cooperate with the Department of State Historian by providing full and complete access to records pertinent to foreign policy decisions and actions and by providing copies of selected records. U.S. foreign policy agencies and Departments—the Department of State, National Security Council, Department of Defense, Central Intelligence Agency, and the Nixon Presidential Materials at College Park, Maryland—have complied fully with this law and provided complete access to their relevant records. In addition, Henry Kissinger and Eliot Richardson have allowed the editors access to their private papers at the Library of Congress. These papers are a key source for the Nixon-Ford sub-series of *Foreign Relations.*

Research for *Foreign Relations* volumes is undertaken through special access to restricted documents at the Nixon Presidential Materials Project, the Library of Congress, and other agencies. While all the material printed in this volume has been declassified, some of it is extracted from still-classified documents. The Nixon Presidential Materials staff is processing and declassifying many of the documents used in this volume, but they may not be available in their entirety at the time of publication.

Sources for Foreign Relations, 1969–1976, Volume XII

The Nixon Presidential Materials, presently housed at the National Archives and Records Administration at College Park, Maryland, are the single most important source of documentation for those interested in US-Soviet relations during the first Nixon administration. The Nixon Presidential Materials are scheduled to be transferred to the Nixon Presidential library in Yorba Linda, California over the next few years.

Foreign policy research in the Nixon Materials centers around the National Security Council (NSC) Files, which include the President's Trip Files, Subject Files, Country Files for each country, occasional topical files related to certain countries, backchannel messages, presidential correspondences, Agency Files, NSC staffers' Name Files, and Kissinger's Office Files. The NSC files contain about 1,300 archive boxes of materials. In particular, the President's Trip Files which contain records of the Kissinger-Dobrynin private channel; Country Files for the USSR, Middle East, Vietnam, and Cuba; and NSC Unfiled Materials; contain the most important documentation of high-level policy making for this volume.

There are several collections in the NSC Files that contain scattered, but often valuable, documentation on the evolution of U.S. policy towards the Soviet Union. They include the Subject Files, Agency Files, Alexander M. Haig Chronological Files, and Harold Saunders Files, which contain extensive information on the Middle East negotiation process. The Subject Files include documentation such as Kissinger (HAK)/Richardson Meetings and Kissinger (HAK)/Sisco Meetings. The Agency Files cover bureaucratic relations between the NSC and various U.S. and international agencies. Kissinger's Office Files overlap considerably with the Kissinger Papers at the Library of Congress (discussed below) and with other NSC files in the Nixon Presidential Materials such as the Country Files for the USSR. The documentation on the Presidential transition, from November 1968 to January 1969, in the NSC Files, Kissinger Office Files, is a unique collection.

Also part of the Nixon Project, NSC Files, are the NSC Institutional Files (H-Files) that contain documents distributed prior to each meeting of the National Security Council, Special Review Group, Senior Review Group, and Washington Special Actions Group, and other NSC sub-groups, along with detailed minutes of most of these meetings. Instead of debating only US-Soviet relations, most of these meetings touched upon US-Soviet interaction in multiple regional conflicts. Other important collections in the H-Files that highlight the Soviet Union are the files on the National Security Study Memoranda (NSSMs) and National Security Decision Memoranda (NSDMs).

Besides the NSC Files, the Nixon Materials include the White House Central Files, which include Staff Member and Office Files, Subject files and Name files. Within the Central Files are the White House Special Files, a Confidential File which also includes Staff Member and Office Files, Subject Files, and Name Files. The White House Central Files generally contain few materials on Soviet policies and were therefore of little value for this volume. The White House Special Files are marginally more valuable. The most important resource in the White House Central Files is the President's Daily Diary, which lists all those who met with the President at the White House or while he was traveling. The Diary also indicates telephone calls to and from the President and has a daily record of "Presidential Movements."

The 303/40 Committee record and subject files of the Nixon Intelligence files provide information on covert operations policy. The 303 Committee (later called the 40 Committee) officially approved covert operations, and its records contain agendas and minutes for 303 and

40 Committee meetings as well as documents submitted by various agencies to the Committee.

The Henry A. Kissinger Papers located in the Manuscript Division of the Library of Congress largely replicate documentation found in other collections, especially the NSC Files at the Nixon Presidential materials. The editor found the most useful parts of the Kissinger papers for this volume to be the Chronological Files, Memoranda of Conversations, Memoranda for the President, and a collection of documents organized by country under the Geopolitical Files heading. Since this volume was compiled, copies of the most important source—the Kissinger Telephone Conversation Transcripts—have been deposited at the Nixon Project at the National Archives. Although the citations in this volume refer to Kissinger Papers, copies of the transcripts as organized in the original collection are available to the public at the National Archives.

The Department of State, Department of Defense, and the Central Intelligence Agency, which were strong bureaucratic players in past Soviet volumes, play a much reduced role under President Nixon and Henry Kissinger, who concentrated policy in their own hands. There are far fewer Department of State documents that play a key role in policy decisions towards the Soviet Union, since the Secretary of State and his Department were essentially excluded from key policy decision-making on the Soviet Union. The one exception is the early Assistant Secretary of State Sisco-Ambassador Dobrynin talks on the Middle East. Still, some of the Department of State's Central Files most useful for other discussions between U.S. diplomats in the field and Soviet officials are POL US–USSR, POL 1 US–USSR, and POL 1 USSR.

The Central Intelligence Agency records are valuable for intelligence on Soviet policy generally and Soviet policies towards specific regions. The editor selected primarily CIA records on general Soviet policies. Collections under CIA custody of value are the DCI Helms and DCI Executive Registry Files. The Department of Defense and Secretary of Defense Melvin Laird were key players concerning Soviet strategic capabilities, but they were not part of the inner circle on U.S.-Soviet policy run out of the White House. When key memoranda from Secretary of Defense Laird are printed, they are almost always from the Nixon Presidential Materials, NSC Files. Department of Defense files used in this volume are listed below. At the Ford Library, there is a collection of documents that cover Laird's tenure as Secretary of Defense. His staff chose these Laird Papers at the end of his term as Secretary of Defense with a view to documenting his major decisions, but few of these materials document general Soviet policies. Defense related records that were not available at the time that this volume was researched, but that deserve mention as potential sources, are the Official Records of Chairman of the Joint Chiefs, General Earle G. Wheeler, RG 218, at the National Archives.

This *Foreign Relations* volume covers a period for which there were no White House Presidential tape recordings. Their absence places a premium on the Kissinger telephone transcripts and the Haldeman Diaries to provide the contemporary and impromptu records behind the more official documentation of cables, memoranda, and memoranda of conversation.

The following list identifies the particular files and collections used in the preparation of this volume. The declassification and transfer to the National Archives of the Department of State records is in process, and most of these records are already available for public review at the National Archives.

Unpublished Sources

Department of State

Central Files. See National Archives and Records Administration below.

Lot Files. For lot files already transferred to the National Archives and Records Administration at College Park, Maryland, Record Group 59, see National Archives and Records Administration below.

National Archives and Records Administration, College Park, Maryland

Record Group 59, Records of the Department of State

Central Files

DEF 1 US, general US defense policy; national security
DEF 1 US–USSR, US–USSR Defense relations
POL CZECH, general political affairs of Czechoslovakia
POL 15–2 GER W, Western Germany's legislature
POL 1 US, general US policy
POL 1 USSR, general political affairs of the USSR
POL USSR 7, Visits and meeting of Soviet leaders
POL 15–1 USSR, head of state, USSR
POL US–USSR, general US–USSR relations.
POL 1 US–USSR, general US–USSR relations
POL 17 US–USSR, diplomatic and consular relations between the US and USSR
POL 27–14 ARAB–IS, the Arab-Israeli dispute and ceasefire

Lot Files

Office Files of William P. Rogers, Entry 5439 (formerly S/S Files: Lot 73 D 443)
    Official and personal files of Secretary of State Rogers, including correspondence, speeches, statements, and chronological and alphabetical files, 1969-1973.

S/S Presidential Transition Files: Lot 71 D 228
    Transition books prepared by the Department for the Nixon administration, December 1968

Records of Joseph Sisco, Entry 5405 (formerly Sisco Files, Lot Files 74 D 131)
    Personal files of Joseph Sisco, 1951-1976

Nixon Presidential Materials Project

National Security Council Files
    Agency Files
    Alexander M. Haig Chronological Files
    Backchannel Files
    Country Files
    Harold Saunders Files
    Name Files
    NSC Secretariat, Unfiled Materials
    Presidential Correspondence
    Presidential/HAK Memoranda of Conversation
    President's Daily Diary
    President's Trip Files
    Staff Files
    Subject Files
    Henry A. Kissinger Office Files: Administrative and Staff Files, November 1968-January 1969, Country Files

National Security Council Institutional Files (H-Files)
    National Security Council Meetings
    National Security Council Minutes
    Senior Review Group Meetings
    Senior Review Group Minutes
    Washington Special Action Group Minutes
    Policy Papers, National Security Decision Memoranda Study Memoranda
    Under Secretaries Committee Files

White House Central Files
    Staff Member and Office Files: President's Daily Diary

Central Intelligence Agency

DCI (Helms) Files: Job 80–BO1285A, files of Director of Central Intelligence Richard Helms

DCI Files: Jobs 79R01012A, 79T01159A, 80R01621R, files of the Deputy Director for Intelligence and the Intelligence Directorate

DDO Files: Jobs 79480A, 7901440A, 8000037, files of the Deputy Director for Plans and the Directorate for Plans

DCI Executive Registry Files: Jobs 80B01086A, 80M00165A, 80M01048A, 80R01284A, 80R01580R, 86B00269R, Job 93–T01468R, executive files of the Director of Central Intelligence

National Intelligence Council (NIC) Files: Job 74–R1012A, intelligence memoranda, national intelligence estimates and special estimates

Library of Congress

Papers of Henry A. Kissinger
    Chronological File
    Geopolitical File
    Memoranda of Conversations
    Memoranda to the President
    National Security Council, 303 Committee, 1969-1970
    Senior Review Group Meetings, Washington Special Actions Group
    Meetings
    Telephone Records

Papers of Eliot Richardson

National Security Council

Nixon Intelligence Files
    303/40 Committee Files
    Subject Files

Washington National Records Center, Suitland, Maryland

Record Group 330, Records of the Office of the Secretary of Defense

OASD/ISA Files: FRC 330 2 6308 and FRC 330 72 6309

    Top secret and secret subject decimal files of the Assistant Secretary of Defense for International Security Affairs, 1969

OSD Files: FRC 330 75 0089 and FRC 330 75 0103

    Secret and top secret subject decimal files of the Office of the Secretary of Defense, Under Secretary of Defense, and their assistants, 1969

OSD Files: FRC 330 76 0067 and FRC 330 76 0076

    Secret and top secret subject decimal files of the Office of the Secretary of Defense, Under Secretary of Defense, and their assistants, 1970

Secretary Laird's Staff Meetings: FRC 330 76 0028

    Minutes of Secretary of Defense Melvin Laird's morning staff meetings, 1969–1973

Published Sources

Documentary Collections

Council on Foreign Relations. *Documents on American Foreign Relations,* 1969–1972. New York: New York University Press, 1972.

Current Digest of the Soviet Press, 1969–1970.

Haldeman, H.R. *The Haldeman Diaries: Inside the Nixon White House: The Complete Multimedia Edition.* Santa Monica, CA: Sony Electronic Publishing Co., 1994.

U.S. Arms Control and Disarmament Agency. *Documents on Disarmament,* 1969-1970. Washington, D.C.: U.S. Government Printing Office.

U.S. Department of State. *Bulletin,* 1969-1972.

U.S. National Archives and Records Administration. *Public Papers of the Presidents of the United States: Richard Nixon,* 1969–1970. Washington, D.C.: U.S. Government Printing Office, 1969, 1970.

Memoirs

Beam, Jacob. *Multiple Exposure: An American Ambassador's Unique Perspective on East-West Issues.* New York: W.W. Norton, 1975.

Haig, Alexander M. Jr. *Inner Circle: How America Changed the World.* New York: Warner Books, 1992.

Johnson, U. Alexis. *The Right Hand of Power.* Englewood Cliffs, NJ: Prentice-Hall, 1984.

Kissinger, Henry A. *White House Years.* Boston: Little, Brown, and Company, 1979.

Nixon, Richard M. *RN: The Memoirs of Richard Nixon.* New York: Grosset & Dunlap, 1978.

Smith, Gerard. *Disarming Diplomat: The Memoirs of Ambassador Gerard C. Smith, Arms Control Negotiator.* New York: Madison Books, 1996.

_____. *Doubletalk: The Story of SALT I.* New York: Doubleday, 1980.

Abbreviations and Terms

ABM, anti-ballistic missile
ACDA, Arms Control and Disarmament Agency
AF, Bureau of African Affairs, Department of State
AG, Attorney General
AID, Agency for International Development
ARA, Bureau of Inter-American Affairs, Department of State

CIA, Central Intelligence Agency
CINCLANT, Commander in Chief, Atlantic
CL, classified
Comite, committee
CPR, Chinese People's Republic

DCI, Director of Central Intelligence
DCID, Director of Central Intelligence Directive
DCM, Deputy Chief of Mission
DDC, Office of the Deputy Director for Coordination, Bureau of Intelligence and Research, Department of State
DDCI, Deputy Director of Central Intelligence
D/DCI/IC, Deputy to the Director of Central Intelligence for the Intelligence Community
D/DCI/NIPE, Deputy to the Director of Central Intelligence for National Intelligence Programs Evaluation
DDI, Deputy Director for Intelligence, Central Intelligence Agency
DDO/IMS, Deputy Director for Operations/Information Management Staff, Central Intelligence Agency
DD/P, Deputy Director for Plans, Central Intelligence Agency
DG, Director General of the Foreign Service, Department of State
DIA, Defense Intelligence Agency
D/INR, Director, Bureau of Intelligence and Research, Department of State
DIRNSA, Director, National Security Agency
Dissem, dissemination
DOD, Department of Defense

E, Bureau of Economic Affairs, Department of State
EA, Bureau of East Asian and Pacific Affairs, Department of State
ELR, Elliot L. Richardson
EOB, Executive Office Building
ESC, European Security Conference
EUR, Bureau of European Affairs, Department of State
Exdis, exclusive distribution

FDP, Free Democratic Party of Federal Republic of Germany
FRG, Federal Republic of Germany
F.R., Federal Register
FSO, Foreign Service Officer
FSR, Foreign Service Reserve officer
FSS, Foreign Service Staff officer
FY, fiscal year
FYI, for your information

G, Deputy Under Secretary of State for Political Affairs
GA, General Assembly
GS, General Schedule
GVN, Government of (South) Vietnam

H, Office of the Assistant Secretary of State for Congressional Relations
HAK, Henry A. Kissinger
HEW, Department of Health, Education, and Welfare

IG, Interdepartmental Group
IG/EUR, Interdepartmental Group for Europe
INR, Bureau of Intelligence and Research, Department of State
INR/DDC, Office of the Deputy Director for Coordination, Bureau of Intelligence and Research, Department of State
INR/IL, Intelligence Liaison, Bureau of Intelligence and Research, Department of State
IO, Bureau of International Organization Affairs, Department of State
IRBM, intermediate-range ballistic missile
IRG, Interdepartmental Regional Group
ISA, Office of International Security Affairs, Department of Defense

JCS, Joint Chiefs of Staff
J/PM, Office of the Deputy Assistant Secretary of State for Politico-Military Affairs
JRC, Joint Reconnaissance Center

K, Kissinger

L, Legal Adviser of the Department of State

MBFR, Mutual and Balanced Force Reductions
ME, Middle East
MFN, Most Favored Nation
MIRV, Multiple Independently Targetable Re-entry Vehicle
MR, Memorandum for the Record
Mtg, meeting

NASA, National Aeronautics and Space Administration
NATO, North Atlantic Treaty Organization
NCO, Non-Commissioned Officer
NEA, Bureau of Near Eastern and South Asian Affairs, Department of State
NIE, National Intelligence Estimate
NIPE, National Intelligence Programs Evaluation
NIRB, National Intelligence Resources Board
Nodis, no distribution (other than to persons indicated)
Noforn, not releasable to foreign nationals
NPT, Non Proliferation Treaty
NSC, National Security Council
NSC/OCB, National Security Council, Operations Coordinating Board
NSDM, National Security Decision Memorandum
NSSM, National Security Study Memorandum
NVA/VC, North Vietnamese Army/Viet Cong

OASD/ISA, Office of the Assistant Secretary of Defense for International Security Affairs
OAS, Organization of American States

OMB, Office of Management and Budget
OSD, Office of the Secretary of Defense

P, President
Para, paragraph
PDB, President's Daily Brief
PFIAB, President's Foreign Intelligence Advisory Board
PM, Bureau of Politico-Military Affairs, Department of State
PM/ISP, Office of International Security Policy and Planning, Bureau of Politico-Military Affairs, Department of State

RG, Record Group; Review Group
RMN, Richard M. Nixon
RN, Richard Nixon

S, Office of the Secretary of State
SAC, Strategic Air Command
SALT, Strategic Arms Limitation Talks
SecDef, Secretary of Defense
Secto, series indicator for telegrams from the Secretary of State while away from Washington
Septel, separate telegram
SFRC, Senate Foreign Relations Committee
SNIE, Special National Intelligence Estimate
SOV, Soviet; Office of Soviet Union Affairs, Bureau of European Affairs, Department of State
SOVGOV, Soviet Government
S/PC, Planning and Coordination Staff, Department of State
SPD, Social Democratic Party of Federal Republic of Germany
SRG, Senior Review Group
S/S, Executive Secretariat, Department of State
SVN, South Vietnam

TASS, Telegraphnoe Agentsvo Sovietskogo Soiuza (Telegraph Agency of the Soviet Union)
Tosec, series indicator for telegrams to the Secretary of State while away from Washington
TS, Top Secret

U, Office of the Under Secretary of State
UNGA, United National General Assembly
USC, Under Secretaries Committee
USG, United States Government
USIA, United States Information Agency
USIB, United States Intelligence Board
USIS, United States Information Service
USSR, Union of Soviet Socialist Republics
USUN, United States Mission to the United Nations

VC/NVA, Viet Cong/North Vietnamese Army
VP, Verification Panel

WSAG, Washington Special Action Group

Persons

Aldrich, George H., Acting Deputy Legal Adviser, Department of State, from January to October 1969; thereafter, Deputy Legal Adviser
Atherton, Alfred L., Jr., Deputy Assistant Secretary of State for Near Eastern and South Asian Affairs from March 1970
Anderson, Admiral George, USN, Member of PFIAB

Beam, Jacob D., Ambassador to the Soviet Union from April 1969 to January 1973
Behr, Colonel Robert, USAF, Member of the Operations Staff for Scientific Affairs, National Security Council
Brandt, Willy, West German Foreign Minister until October 1969; thereafter, West German Chancellor
Brezhnev, Leonid T., Secretary General, Communist Party of the Soviet Union
Buchanan, Patrick, Special Assistant to the President, from 1969

Chernyakov, Yuri N. Soviet Chargé d'Affaires
Cleveland, Harlan, U.S. Permanent Representative on the Council of the North Atlantic
Cline, Ray S., Director, Office of Intelligence and Research, Department of State, from October 1969

Davis, Jeanne W., Director, NSC Staff Secretariat, from 1970 to 1971
Dobrynin, Anatoliy F., Soviet Ambassador to the United States
Dubs, Adolph, Country Director, Office of the Soviet Union, Bureau of European Affairs, Department of State

Eagleburger, Lawrence S., Member of the National Security Council staff from 1969 to 1970
Eban, Abba, Minister of Foreign Affairs of Israel
Ehrlichman, John D., Counsel to the President from January to November 1969; Assistant to the President for Domestic Affairs from November 1969 to May 1973
Eliot, Theodore L., Jr., Special Assistant to the Secretary and Executive Secretary of the Department of State from August 1969 to September 1973

Garthoff, Raymond L., Deputy Director, Bureau of Politico-Military Affairs, Department of State
Gromyko, Andrei A., Foreign Minister of the USSR

Haig, Brigadier General Alexander M., Jr., USA, Senior Military Assistant to the Assistant to the President for National Security Affairs from January 1969 to June 1970; Deputy Assistant to the President for National Security Affairs from June 1970 to January 1973; Army Vice Chief of Staff from January 1973
Haldeman, H.R., Assistant to the President from January 1969 to April 1973
Helms, Richard M., Director of Central Intelligence until February 1973
Hillenbrand, Martin J., Assistant Secretary of State for European and Canadian Affairs from February 1969 to April 1972
Holdridge, John, Member of the National Security Council staff from 1970 to 1972
Hughes, Thomas L., Director, Bureau of Intelligence and Research, Department of State, until August 1969
Hyland, William, member of the National Security Council staff from 1970 to 1972

Irwin, John N. II, Under Secretary of State from September 1970

Jarring, Gunar, Special Representative of the United Nations Secretary General to the Middle East from November 1967

Johnson, U. Alexis, Under Secretary of State for Political Affairs from February 1969 to February 1973

Kennedy, Colonel Richard T., USA, member, Planning Group, National Security Council Staff

Kissinger, Henry A., Assistant to the President for National Security Affairs from January 1969 to January 1973

Kosygin, Alexei N., Chairman of the Council of Ministers of the USSR

Korniyenko, Georgy, Chief of Soviet Foreign Ministry's American Desk and Soviet Middle East negotiator

Kuznetsov, Vasily V., First Deputy Minister of Foreign Affairs

Ky, Nguyen Cao, Vice President of the Republic of Vietnam

Laird, Melvin R., Secretary of Defense

Latimer, Thomas, Member of the National Security Council Staff, Office of the Assistant to the President

Lord, Winston, Member of the National Security Council Planning Staff

Malik, Yakov Alexandrovich, Permanent Representative of the Soviet Union to the United Nations

Meir, Golda, Prime Minister of Israel from March 1969

Moorer, Adm. Thomas H., USN, Chief of Naval Operations until July 1970; thereafter, Chairman of the Joint Chiefs of Staff

Moose, Richard, Member of the National Security Council staff

Murphy, Franklin, Member of the President's Foreign Intelligence Advisory Board

Murphy, Robert, Member of President's Foreign Intelligence Advisory Board

Nasser, Gamal Abdel, President of the United Arab Republic

Nixon, Richard M., President of the United States

Nguyen Van Thieu, President of the Republic of (South) Vietnam

Nutter, G. Warren, Assistant Secretary of Defense for International Security Affairs from March 1969

Packard, David, Deputy Secretary of Defense

Podgorny, Nikolai V., President of the Presidium of the Supreme Soviet of the USSR

Read, Benjamin H., Special Assistant to the Secretary of State and Executive Secretary of the Department of State until February 1969

Riad, Mahmoud, Foreign Minister of the UAR

Richardson, Elliot L., Under Secretary of State from January 1969 to June 1970; Secretary of Health, Education, and Welfare from June 1970

Robinson, Rembrandt C., Joint Chiefs of Staffís Liason at the National Security Council

Rogers, William P., Secretary of State

Saunders, Harold H., Member of the National Security Council staff

Sedov, Boris, Second Secretary of the Embassy of the USSR

Semenov, Vladimir S., Soviet Deputy Minister of Foreign Affairs

Shakespeare, Frank, Director, U.S. Information Agency, from February 1969

Sisco, Joseph J., Assistant Secretary of State for International Organization Affairs until February 1969; thereafter, Assistant Secretary of State for Near Eastern and South Asian Affairs

Smith, Gerard, Director, U.S. Arms Control and Disarmament Agency, from February 1969

Sonnenfeldt, Helmut, Member of the National Security Council Staff from January 1969

Stans, Maurice, Secretary of Commerce from January 1969

Swank, Emory C., Deputy Assistant Secretary of State for European Affairs from June 1969 to September 1970; Ambassador to Cambodia from September 1970

Thant, U, Secretary-General of the United Nations

Thieu, see Nguyen Van Thieu

Thompson, Llewellyn E., Jr., Ambassador to the Soviet Union until March 14, 1969

Toon, Malcom, Acting Deputy Assistant Secretary for European Affairs

Vaky, Viron P., Acting Assistant Secretary of State for Inter-American Affairs, January to May 1969; member of the National Security Council Staff from May 1969

Vinogradov, Vladimir M., Soviet Deputy Foreign Minister

Zamyatin, Leonid M., Director General, TASS or Chief of the Press Department, Soviet Foreign Ministry

Ziegler, Ronald, Press Secretary to the President of the United States

Note on U.S. Covert Actions

In compliance with the *Foreign Relations of the United States* statute that requires inclusion in the *Foreign Relations* series of comprehensive documentation on major foreign policy decisions and actions, the editors have identified key documents regarding major covert actions and intelligence activities. The following note will provide readers with some organizational context on how covert actions and special intelligence operations in support of U.S. foreign policy were planned and approved within the U.S. Government. It describes, on the basis of declassified documents, the changing and developing procedures during the Truman, Eisenhower, Kennedy, Johnson, Nixon, and Ford Presidencies.

Management of Covert Actions in the Truman Presidency

The Truman administration's concern over Soviet "psychological warfare" prompted the new National Security Council to authorize, in NSC 4–A of December 1947, the launching of peacetime covert action operations. NSC 4–A made the Director of Central Intelligence responsible for psychological warfare, establishing at the same time the principle that covert action was an exclusively Executive Branch function. The Central Intelligence Agency (CIA) certainly was a natural choice but it was assigned this function at least in part because the Agency controlled unvouchered funds, by which operations could be funded with minimal risk of exposure in Washington.[1]

The CIA's early use of its new covert action mandate dissatisfied officials at the Departments of State and Defense. The Department of State, believing this role too important to be left to the CIA alone and concerned that the military might create a new rival covert action office in the Pentagon, pressed to reopen the issue of where responsibility for covert action activities should reside. Consequently, on June 18, 1948, a new NSC directive, NSC 10/2, superseded NSC 4–A.

NSC 10/2 directed the CIA to conduct "covert" rather than merely "psychological" operations, defining them as all activities "which are conducted or sponsored by this Government against hostile foreign states or groups or in support of friendly foreign states or groups but which are so planned and executed that any US Government responsibility for them is not evident to unauthorized persons and that if uncovered the US Government can plausibly disclaim any responsibility for them."

---

[1] NSC 4–A, December 17, 1947, is printed in *Foreign Relations,* 1945–1950, Emergence of the Intelligence Establishment, Document 257.

The type of clandestine activities enumerated under the new directive included: "propaganda; economic warfare; preventive direct action, including sabotage, demolition and evacuation measures; subversion against hostile states, including assistance to underground resistance movements, guerrillas and refugee liberations [*sic*] groups, and support of indigenous anti-Communist elements in threatened countries of the free world. Such operations should not include armed conflict by recognized military forces, espionage, counter-espionage, and cover and deception for military operations."[2]

The Office of Policy Coordination (OPC), newly established in the CIA on September 1, 1948, in accordance with NSC 10/2, assumed responsibility for organizing and managing covert actions. The OPC, which was to take its guidance from the Department of State in peacetime and from the military in wartime, initially had direct access to the State Department and to the military without having to proceed through the CIA's administrative hierarchy, provided the Director of Central Intelligence (DCI) was informed of all important projects and decisions.[3] In 1950 this arrangement was modified to ensure that policy guidance came to the OPC through the DCI.

During the Korean conflict the OPC grew quickly. Wartime commitments and other missions soon made covert action the most expensive and bureaucratically prominent of the CIA's activities. Concerned about this situation, DCI Walter Bedell Smith in early 1951 asked the NSC for enhanced policy guidance and a ruling on the proper "scope and magnitude" of CIA operations. The White House responded with two initiatives. In April 1951 President Truman created the Psychological Strategy Board (PSB) under the NSC to coordinate government-wide psychological warfare strategy. NSC 10/5, issued in October 1951, reaffirmed the covert action mandate given in NSC 10/2 and expanded the CIA's authority over guerrilla warfare.[4] The PSB was soon abolished by the incoming Eisenhower administration, but the expansion of the CIA's covert action writ in NSC 10/5 helped ensure that covert action would remain a major function of the Agency.

As the Truman administration ended, the CIA was near the peak of its independence and authority in the field of covert action. Although the CIA continued to seek and receive advice on specific projects from the NSC, the PSB, and the departmental representatives originally del-

---

[2] NSC 10/2, June 18, 1948, printed ibid., Document 292.

[3] Memorandum of conversation by Frank G. Wisner, "Implementation of NSC–10/2," August 12, 1948, printed ibid., Document 298.

[4] NSC 10/5, "Scope and Pace of Covert Operations," October 23, 1951, in Michael Warner, editor, *The CIA Under Harry Truman* (Washington, D.C.: Central Intelligence Agency, 1994), pp. 437–439.

egated to advise the OPC, no group or officer outside of the DCI and the President himself had authority to order, approve, manage, or curtail operations.

NSC 5412 Special Group; 5412/2 Special Group; 303 Committee

The Eisenhower administration began narrowing the CIA's latitude in 1954. In accordance with a series of National Security Council directives, the responsibility of the Director of Central Intelligence for the conduct of covert operations was further clarified. President Eisenhower approved NSC 5412 on March 15, 1954, reaffirming the Central Intelligence Agency's responsibility for conducting covert actions abroad. A definition of covert actions was set forth; the DCI was made responsible for coordinating with designated representatives of the Secretary of State and the Secretary of Defense to ensure that covert operations were planned and conducted in a manner consistent with U.S. foreign and military policies; and the Operations Coordinating Board was designated the normal channel for coordinating support for covert operations among State, Defense, and the CIA. Representatives of the Secretary of State, the Secretary of Defense, and the President were to be advised in advance of major covert action programs initiated by the CIA under this policy and were to give policy approval for such programs and secure coordination of support among the Departments of State and Defense and the CIA.[5]

A year later, on March 12, 1955, NSC 5412/1 was issued, identical to NSC 5412 except for designating the Planning Coordination Group as the body responsible for coordinating covert operations. NSC 5412/2 of December 28, 1955, assigned to representatives (of the rank of assistant secretary) of the Secretary of State, the Secretary of Defense, and the President responsibility for coordinating covert actions. By the end of the Eisenhower administration, this group, which became known as the "NSC 5412/2 Special Group" or simply "Special Group," emerged as the executive body to review and approve covert action programs initiated by the CIA.[6] The membership of the Special Group varied depending upon the situation faced. Meetings were infrequent until 1959 when weekly meetings began to be held. Neither the CIA nor the Special Group adopted fixed criteria for bringing projects before the group;

---

[5] William M. Leary, editor, *The Central Intelligence Agency: History and Documents* (The University of Alabama Press, 1984), p. 63; the text of NSC 5412 is scheduled for publication in *Foreign Relations, 1950–1955*, The Intelligence Community.

[6] Leary, *The Central Intelligence Agency: History and Documents*, pp. 63, 147–148; *Final Report of the Select Committee To Study Governmental Operations With Respect to Intelligence Activities, United States Senate*, Book I, *Foreign and Military Intelligence* (1976), pp. 50–51. The texts of NSC 5412/1 and NSC 5412/2 are scheduled for publication in *Foreign Relations, 1950–1955*, The Intelligence Community.

initiative remained with the CIA, as members representing other agencies frequently were unable to judge the feasibility of particular projects.[7]

After the Bay of Pigs failure in April 1961, General Maxwell Taylor reviewed U.S. paramilitary capabilities at President Kennedy's request and submitted a report in June that recommended strengthening high-level direction of covert operations. As a result of the Taylor Report, the Special Group, chaired by the President's Special Assistant for National Security Affairs McGeorge Bundy, and including Deputy Under Secretary of State U. Alexis Johnson, Deputy Secretary of Defense Roswell Gilpatric, Director of Central Intelligence Allen Dulles, and Chairman of the Joint Chiefs of Staff General Lyman Lemnitzer, assumed greater responsibility for planning and reviewing covert operations. Until 1963 the DCI determined whether a CIA-originated project was submitted to the Special Group. In 1963 the Special Group developed general but informal criteria, including risk, possibility of success, potential for exposure, political sensitivity, and cost (a threshold of $25,000 was adopted by the CIA), for determining whether covert action projects were submitted to the Special Group.[8]

From November 1961 to October 1962 a Special Group (Augmented), whose membership was the same as the Special Group plus Attorney General Robert Kennedy and General Taylor (as Chairman), exercised responsibility for Operation Mongoose, a major covert action program aimed at overthrowing the Castro regime in Cuba. When President Kennedy authorized the program in November, he designated Brigadier General Edward G. Lansdale, Assistant for Special Operations to the Secretary of Defense, to act as chief of operations, and Lansdale coordinated the Mongoose activities among the CIA and the Departments of State and Defense. The CIA units in Washington and Miami had primary responsibility for implementing Mongoose operations, which included military, sabotage, and political propaganda programs.[9]

President Kennedy also established a Special Group (Counter-Insurgency) on January 18, 1962, when he signed NSAM No. 124. The Special Group (CI), set up to coordinate counter-insurgency activities separate from the mechanism for implementing NSC 5412/2, was to confine itself to establishing broad policies aimed at preventing and resisting subversive insurgency and other forms of indirect aggression in friendly countries. In early 1966, in NSAM No. 341, President Johnson assigned responsibility for the direction and coordination of

---

[7] Leary, *The Central Intelligence Agency: History and Documents*, p. 63.

[8] Ibid., p. 82.

[9] See *Foreign Relations, 1961–1963*, vol. X, Documents 270 and 278.

counter-insurgency activities overseas to the Secretary of State, who established a Senior Interdepartmental Group to assist in discharging these responsibilities.[10]

NSAM No. 303, June 2, 1964, from Bundy to the Secretaries of State and Defense and the DCI, changed the name of "Special Group 5412" to "303 Committee" but did not alter its composition, functions, or responsibility. Bundy was the chairman of the 303 Committee.[11]

The Special Group and the 303 Committee approved 163 covert actions during the Kennedy administration and 142 during the Johnson administration through February 1967. The 1976 Final Report of the Church Committee, however, estimated that of the several thousand projects undertaken by the CIA since 1961, only 14 percent were considered on a case-by-case basis by the 303 Committee and its predecessors (and successors). Those not reviewed by the 303 Committee were low-risk and low-cost operations. The Final Report also cited a February 1967 CIA memorandum that included a description of the mode of policy arbitration of decisions on covert actions within the 303 Committee system. The CIA presentations were questioned, amended, and even on occasion denied, despite protests from the DCI. Department of State objections modified or nullified proposed operations, and the 303 Committee sometimes decided that some agency other than the CIA should undertake an operation or that CIA actions requested by Ambassadors on the scene should be rejected.[12]

The effectiveness of covert action has always been difficult for any administration to gauge, given concerns about security and the difficulty of judging the impact of U.S. initiatives on events. In October 1969 the new Nixon administration required annual 303 Committee reviews for all covert actions that the Committee had approved and automatic termination of any operation not reviewed after 12 months. On February 17, 1970, President Nixon signed National Security Decision Memorandum 40,[13] which superseded NSC 5412/2 and changed the name of the covert action approval group to the 40 Committee, in part because the 303 Committee had been named in the media. The Attorney General was also added to the membership of the Committee. NSDM 40 reaffirmed the DCI's responsibility for the coordination, control, and conduct of covert operations and directed him to obtain policy approval from the 40 Committee for all major and "politically sensitive"

---

[10] For text of NSAM No. 124, see ibid., vol. VIII, Document 68. NSAM No. 341, March 2, 1966, is printed ibid., 1964–1968, vol. XXXIII, Document 56.

[11] For text of NSAM No. 303, see ibid., Document 204.

[12] *Final Report of the Select Committee To Study Governmental Operations With Respect to Intelligence Activities, United States Senate*, Book I, *Foreign and Military Intelligence*, pp. 56–57.

[13] For text of NSDM 40, see *Foreign Relations*, 1969–1976, vol. II, Document 203.

covert operations. He was also made responsible for ensuring an annual review by the 40 Committee of all approved covert operations.

The 40 Committee met regularly early in the Nixon administration, but over time the number of formal meetings declined and business came to be conducted via couriers and telephone votes. The Committee actually met only for major new proposals. As required, the DCI submitted annual status reports to the 40 Committee for each approved operation. According to the 1976 Church Committee Final Report, the 40 Committee considered only about 25 percent of the CIA's individual covert action projects, concentrating on major projects that provided broad policy guidelines for all covert actions. Congress received briefings on only a few proposed projects. Not all major operations, moreover, were brought before the 40 Committee: President Nixon in 1970 instructed the DCI to promote a coup d' etat against Chilean President Salvador Allende without Committee coordination or approval.[14]

Presidential Findings Since 1974 and the Operations Advisory Group

The Hughes-Ryan amendment to the Foreign Assistance Act of 1974 brought about a major change in the way the U.S. Government approved covert actions, requiring explicit approval by the President for each action and expanding Congressional oversight and control of the CIA. The CIA was authorized to spend appropriated funds on covert actions only after the President had signed a "finding" and informed Congress that the proposed operation was important to national security.[15]

Executive Order 11905, issued by President Ford on February 18, 1976, in the wake of major Congressional investigations of CIA activities by the Church and Pike Committees, replaced the 40 Committee with the Operations Advisory Group, composed of the President's Assistant for National Security Affairs, the Secretaries of State and Defense, the Chairman of the Joint Chiefs of Staff, and the DCI, who retained responsibility for the planning and implementation of covert operations. The OAG was required to hold formal meetings to develop recommendations for the President regarding a covert action and to conduct periodic reviews of previously-approved operations. EO 11905 also banned all U.S. Government employees from involvement in political assassinations, a prohibition that was retained in succeeding executive orders, and prohibited involvement in domestic intelligence activities.[16]

---

[14] *Final Report of the Select Committee To Study Governmental Operations With Respect to Intelligence Activities,* United States Senate, Book I, Foreign and Military Intelligence, pp. 54–55, 57.

[15] Public Law 93–559.

[16] Executive Order 11905, "United States Foreign Intelligence Activities," *Weekly Compilation of Presidential Documents,* Vol. 12, No. 8, February 23, 1976.

Soviet Union, January 1969–October 1970

Initial Contacts, January–April 22, 1969

1. Memorandum of Conversation[1]

Washington, January 2, 1969.

PARTICIPANTS

Boris Sedov, Counselor, Soviet Embassy
Henry A. Kissinger

Boris Sedov, officially counselor of the Soviet Embassy, but in fact a member of Soviet intelligence,[2] called on me today at his request. He had asked to see me during the previous week, but the meeting was delayed because of my trip to Key Biscayne.[3]

---

[1] Source: National Archives, Nixon Presidential Materials, NSC Files, Box 725, Country Files, Europe, USSR, Contacts With the Soviets Prior to January 20, 1969. Secret; Nodis. The meeting was held at the Pierre Hotel, headquarters for the Nixon transition team. On January 31 Kissinger sent Secretary of State Rogers copies of his memoranda of conversation with Sedov on January 2 and his earlier conversation on December 18, 1968, at the Soviet Embassy. Kissinger reminded Rogers that President Nixon asked that the copies be closely held. (Ibid.) Kissinger's memorandum to Nixon on his December 18, 1968, meeting with Sedov is printed in *Foreign Relations, 1964–1968*, volume XIV, Soviet Union, Document 335.

[2] Sedov's activities as an officer of the Soviet Committee for State Security (KGB) were closely monitored by FBI Director J. Edgar Hoover, who provided Kissinger with periodic updates. On June 11, after learning that Sedov informed a Lebanese American citizen with ties to the KGB of his contact with the President's Assistant for National Security Affairs, Kissinger informed Under Secretary of State Richardson that "In view of [Sedov's] continuing activity, I believe it would be appropriate, through discussions with the Soviet Ambassador, to request that Sedov be returned to the Soviet Union. If such action cannot be accomplished through this procedure, it would appear that persona non grata action against Sedov may have to be taken without further delay." (Library of Congress, Manuscript Division, Kissinger Papers, Box CL 1, Chronological File) Additional FBI information on Sedov is in the National Archives, Nixon Presidential Materials, NSC Files, Box 242, Agency Files, FBI, Vol. II.

[3] On December 28, 1968, Kissinger met with Nixon's senior appointees at Key Biscayne, Florida.

Sedov began by saying that the Soviet Embassy had given a copy of their Middle East note to Ellsworth on December 30[4] because I had warned Sedov against "surprises," and because the Embassy wanted to deal with the President-elect on the basis of complete frankness.

Sedov then read the attached communication. I copied it and read it back to him (he made a few corrections).

I then asked Sedov about the meaning of the phrase: "The Soviet leadership would do their utmost . . . to ensure ratification by states of the non-proliferation treaty."[5] Did it mean that the USSR would try to create an atmosphere in which ratification of the treaty would be possible in the United States, or was it proposing joint action with the US to secure ratification by third parties. Sedov replied that both meanings were intended. I said we were studying the problem.

Sedov then asked about strategic arms talks. I repeated my observation of December 18, 1968, that we did not believe that political and strategic issues could be completely separated. The Nixon Administration wanted to see more progress in Vietnam and the Middle East before committing itself to strategic arms talks. *Sedov asked whether the Soviet overture on the Middle East could be seen as a sign of good faith along the lines of my communication of December 18.* I said we would have to study it.

Sedov then turned to Vietnam. He asked whether my mutual withdrawal proposal was the policy of the new Administration.[6] I replied that we were studying all realistic options. Sedov then said that he considered the proposal the best way to solve the Vietnam war. Did he understand correctly that I required that there be no violent upheaval during the period of withdrawal? I said this was correct. He asked how long a time I had set—in my own mind—for withdrawal. I replied three–five years, although this was obviously subject to negotiation. I added

---

[4] On December 30, 1968, Soviet Chargé Yuri Tcherniakov gave Robert Ellsworth, an assistant to President-elect Nixon, two notes outlining a Soviet plan for a political settlement in the Middle East. The documents given to Ellsworth were almost identical to those Tcherniakov handed to Secretary of State Dean Rusk the same day. A text of the Soviet notes given Rusk is in *Foreign Relations, 1964–1968*, volume XX, Arab-Israeli Dispute, 1967–1968, Document 374. The memorandum of conversation between Ellsworth and Tcherniakov and the Soviet notes given Ellsworth are in the National Archives, Nixon Presidential Materials, NSC Files, Kissinger Office Files, Box 1, HAK Administrative and Staff Files—Transition, Robert Ellsworth.

[5] Ellipses in the source text. On July 1, 1968, the Treaty on the Non-Proliferation of Nuclear Weapons was opened for signature in Washington, London, and Moscow. On March 5, 1970, after the United States and 81 other nations signed the treaty, it entered into force. (21 UST 483)

[6] Sedov is referring to Kissinger's views expressed in "The Viet Nam Negotiations," *Foreign Affairs*, Vol. 47, No. 2 (January 1969), 211–234. Kissinger later discussed the article in *White House Years*, pp. 234–235.

that as long as American soldiers continued to be killed in Vietnam with Soviet weapons it was difficult to speak of a real relaxation of tensions.

Sedov said that the Soviet Union was very interested that the inaugural speech contain some reference to open channels of communication to Moscow. I said that all this would be easier if Moscow showed some cooperativeness on Vietnam. Sedov replied that he would try to have an answer by January 10.

Tab A

Notes of a Conversation[7]

Washington, January 2, 1969.

Notes on Conversation with Boris Sedov, January 2, 1969

Tcherniakov (of the Soviet Embassy) delivered the memo on the Middle East to Ellsworth because of its official nature and my absence.

The following is the verbatim text of Sedov's statement to me:

1. Moscow has carefully watched the election campaign which, though a US internal affair, has world-wide significance.

2. Moscow does not have the pessimistic view expressed in many parts of the world in connection with the accession of the Republicans to power.

3. It is not true that Moscow makes its attitude dependent on which party is allegedly more to the right.

4. The key concern of Moscow is whether statements of great powers are animated by a sense of reality.

5. Moscow noted with satisfaction Mr. Nixon's cable to President Podgorny[8] to the effect that the American and Soviet people work together in a spirit of mutual respect and on the basis of special responsibility for the peace of the world. This wish is considered an

---

[7] Kissinger summarized his conversation with Sedov in a memorandum to Nixon on January 4 and made three recommendations: "1) that when next I see Sedov I repeat to him substantially what I told him at our first meeting; 2) that some reference to open communications be included in your inaugural address; 3) that we wait until January 17 to tell Sedov of the reference in the inaugural address so that we can see what further message he brings us first." Nixon initialed his approval of all three recommendations. (National Archives, Nixon Presidential Materials, NSC Files, Kissinger Office Files, Box 66, Country Files, USSR, Soviet Contacts) In his inaugural address, Nixon stated, "Let all nations know that during this administration our lines of communication will be open." The address is in *Public Papers: Nixon, 1969*, 1–4.

[8] Not found.

encouraging sign of the interest of the American side to proceed further in the solution of those problems outlined in bilateral contacts.

6. On the other hand, Moscow is very worried by statements that there is a desire on the part of the US to operate from a "situation of strength." If this theory dominates, and if a new round of armaments starts, the USSR is capable and willing to match the US effort. The world will be reduced to the worst days of the cold war.

7. Moscow realizes that there are theoretical and practical differences between our two countries. These should not interfere with gradual achievement of agreements on a number of problems. That of disarmament is in the first place.

8. To achieve this goal, it is necessary to develop mutual trust. On the part of Moscow, it is willing to make important steps in this direction, but it wishes that the new Administration act in the same spirit.

9. The Soviet leadership will do their utmost to find ways of solving at least some important problems of disarmament, and to ensure ratification by states of the non-proliferation treaty.

10. The US and USSR must find a way to disarmament, or the consequences will be extremely dangerous for in this connection one always has to keep in mind that disarmament is specifically a Soviet-US problem.

11. The Soviet leadership is determined to continue a policy of peaceful coexistence.

12. Mr. Nixon's statement of November 11 to continue keeping open channels to the USSR did not pass unnoticed in Moscow. Great attention was paid to the part where Mr. Nixon, speaking of President Johnson's foreign policy, confirms his desire to keep open channels of communication to Moscow.

13. It goes without saying that the future of Soviet-American relations would be favorably affected by settlement of Vietnam problem, a political solution of the situation in the Middle East, a realistic approach to the situation in Europe as a whole, and the German problem in particular. (Oral comment: The Soviet Union has special interests in Eastern Europe.)

14. Moscow hopes that even before the inauguration Nixon indicates interest in betterment of relations with the Soviet Union. (inaugural address)

2.   Briefing Paper[1]

Washington, January 14, 1969.

ISSUES IN US-SOVIET RELATIONS REQUIRING EARLY DECISION

A number of matters concerning either directly or indirectly our relations with the USSR will need prompt attention after January 20. They are of sufficient importance to the whole nature of this relationship that, ideally, it would be preferable for us to clarify our general purposes and interests before we take further action. However, as a practical matter a hiatus in US-Soviet relations will be hard to arrange and probably even undesirable because important events should not be permitted to unfold without our exerting influence upon them.

Consequently, pending a more thoroughgoing reexamination of our Soviet policy, we should get some general guidelines—relating perhaps more to style than substance—and take such early decisions as we must in conformity with them.

Without here engaging in extensive supporting argumentation, I suggest three broad guidelines:

1. Although for several reasons there are special, indeed unique features in the US-Soviet relationship, we should establish a scale of priorities in which relations with our allies normally take precedence.

2. We should take account of the obviously special position of the USSR in world affairs by maintaining diplomatic contact with it; but our approach should be one of aloofness. If we judge that there are issues on which our interests intersect, the Soviets will presumably discern them also. There is no automatic net advantage in our assuming the initiative or in our becoming deeply engaged with the Soviets in all such cases. Certainly, and in line with point 1 above, when important interests of other states are also at stake, US-Soviet bilateralism must be tempered by due regard to those interests. Moreover, commonly held views that certain problems can be coped with only through intimate US-Soviet collaboration require reexamination. In any event, great zeal in approaching the Soviets or in responding to their overtures should be avoided as a general rule, certainly at the outset of the Administration.

3. We have no interest in deliberately seeking crises with the USSR or even in striking out on policy paths that we judge would carry some substantial risk of crises. But we might encounter a Soviet attempt to

---

[1] Source: National Archives, Nixon Presidential Materials, NSC Files, Kissinger Offices Files, Box 3, Transition Files, Staff Reports. Confidential. Drafted by Sonnenfeldt.

test the new Administration in some confrontation. In that case, we must stand our ground—or help an ally do so, if that should be the testing ground.

Apart from these general aspects of our approach, we should arrive at a more or less coherent posture with respect to the Soviet occupation of Czechoslovakia.[2] Such measures in the realms of contacts and protocol as we took to convey our indignation have now probably outlived their purpose (though we should not in any case return to some of the excessive comraderie that occasionally occurred in the past). But two general points should be conveyed clearly to the Soviets through the various channels available: (1) That any instance of direct and gross Soviet intervention in Czechoslovak internal affairs is bound to retard establishment of a business-like relationship with us; and (2) that while the US recognizes the special and sensitive nature of Soviet relations with countries that are immediately adjacent to it and part of its alliance system, we will not let the USSR control the character and pace of our relations with these countries. In our approach we should be guided by the proposition that we should not be reluctant to compartmentalize our affairs with the USSR if that suits our interests, but we should not cooperate in the obvious Soviet effort to make the outside world accept total Soviet hegemony in Eastern Europe and to make the conduct of our policy toward Eastern Europe subject to Soviet sanction.

Middle East

The Soviets have lately given us a number of documents[3] on an Arab-Israeli settlement; they involve essentially a phased scheme for implementing the November 1967 UN resolution[4] and, in the latest (December 30) version, display some movement, evidently with UAR concurrence, in the direction of agreement between the parties and a package approach in which the first step occurs only after the scheme as a whole has been settled.

As always the reasons for the Soviet initiative are open to speculation. They may reflect genuine Soviet concern with the explosiveness of the present situation. In any case, the new Administration inherits

---

[2] On the night of August 20–21, 1968, 200,000 Warsaw Pact forces invaded Czechoslovakia; see *Foreign Relations, 1964–1968*, volume XVII, Eastern Europe, Documents 80–97.

[3] See footnote 4, Document 1.

[4] Security Council Resolution 242, adopted on November 22, 1967, among other things, called upon the Secretary-General to designate a special representative to the Middle East "to establish and maintain contacts with the States concerned in order to promote agreement and assist the effort to achieve a peaceful and accepted settlement." (UN doc. S/RES/242 1967) The text is in *Foreign Relations, 1964–1968*, volume XIX, Arab-Israeli Crisis and War, 1967, Document 542.

an active US-Soviet exchange of communications in this area, rather than a state of acute US-Soviet crisis. In this respect, Soviet moves on the Middle East fit into other post-Czechoslovak, pre-January 20 efforts by the USSR to damp down open hostility toward us and, indeed, to engage us diplomatically.

Nevertheless, there remain fundamental issues in controversy between ourselves and the USSR in the Mediterranean and adjacent regions, not least a continuing Soviet effort to project power and influence there to our detriment.

Plainly, the US must remain in touch with the Soviets on the Middle East (1) because it may be one (though not the only) way of preventing renewed large-scale hostilities with a potential for a direct US-Soviet military clash, and (2) because the Soviets have great influence in the Arab country (UAR) that is the key to any tranquilization of Middle East tensions and dangers. Moreover, in the exchanges with us the Soviets have over time inched away from some of the most rigid Arab positions. But US-Soviet dialogue should not be the only means by which we seek to cope with the dangers of the region. Any settlement, partial, temporary or complete, requires the assent of the parties. So-called imposed settlements are not likely to be viable; moreover the implication of US-Soviet condominium (itself of questionable viability over any length of time) that an imposed solution would carry would gravely damage our alliance relationships elsewhere. It would involve, in addition, a basic restructuring of our relationship with Israel which cannot be lightly undertaken.

US-Soviet dialogue should therefore be largely refocussed on the future of the Jarring mission[5] and its function in dealing with the parties. The British and French—also recipients of parallel Soviet overtures—should be urged to channel matters in the same direction. Four-power roles at this stage should be largely confined to influencing or assisting the parties in narrowing differences. We should not let ourselves become Israel's negotiating agent, nor accept the USSR as the agent of the Arabs. Consequently, we should not rely solely or even chiefly on the Soviets as intermediaries between ourselves and the Arabs.

---

[5] On November 23, 1967, UN Secretary-General U Thant informed the Security Council of the appointment of Gunnar Jarring, the Swedish Ambassador to the Soviet Union, as Special Representative to the Middle East as authorized under UN Resolution 242. (UN doc S/8259) Jarring's initial efforts were summarized in a report made by Secretary-General U Thant to the UN Security Council on January 5, 1971. (*Public Papers of the Secretaries-General of the United Nations*, Vol. VIII: U Thant, 1968–1971, pp. 514–525) Extensive documentation on the Jarring Mission is in the National Archives, RG 59, Central Files 1967–69, POL 27 ARAB–ISR.

In considering resumption of diplomatic relations with the UAR, we will have to think about the implications of present Soviet use of Egyptian air base facilities for operations against the Sixth Fleet. At the very least we should probably tell both the Soviets and the UAR that we are aware of these operations and that they could be a source of future trouble.

Strategic Weapons Talks (Tactics)

The motivation and the interplay of political forces that went into Soviet agreement last year to opening the strategic arms talks[6] were complex. Among the considerations that played a role was probably a desire to exert some influence against certain new weapons decisions by the US. If so, the Soviets may seek to get the talks underway soon after inauguration.

In the US, both inside the government and outside, much of the sense of urgency about getting these talks begun stemmed from a judgment that the present moment in time was unusually propitious, and also unusually crucial, in seeking to curb US-Soviet arms competition. There is no need to rehearse here the rationale for the US initiative; it has been well and amply presented and whatever one may think about some of it, the general case for US-Soviet talks in this field is persuasive.

Nevertheless, the incoming administration will wish to make its own assessment of the present and prospective strategic balance and set its own objections for any direct dealings with the USSR on this subject. Moreover, there is a real need to take our European allies more completely into our confidence about the direction in which we would like to see the strategic relationship develop. The Germans, in particular, need to be reassured that whatever we do—be it by some form of arrangement with the Russians or through unilateral decisions—will not ignore the strategic "threat" against Western Europe.

The process of internal US review and interallied consultation will take some time and dictate some delay in the opening of formal US-Soviet talks. The Soviets should be informed of these reasons for delay. Since the US has in the exchanges of the past two years already given the Soviets some indication of its approach (at least under the previous Administration) the Soviets should be encouraged to give

---

[6] Shortly before the invasion of Czechoslovakia, the Soviet Union informed the United States that it was prepared to begin strategic missile talks between special representatives of their countries in Geneva on September 30, 1968. As a result of the Soviet invasion of Czechoslovakia, the United States delayed the opening of talks but never formally answered the Soviet communication proposing the beginning of such negotiations on September 30.

some indication of theirs. Whatever the eventual changes of formal or explicit agreement, it will be desirable to draw the Soviets into conversation on strategic issues. If the opportunity arises (though we need not soon go out of our way to seek it) we should engage in such conversation. Our purpose, whatever the pros and cons or the practicality of specific agreements, should be to learn more about the processes of interaction that operate in the US-Soviet military relationship and to induce similar awareness on the part of the Soviets.

Berlin Bundesversammlung (March 5)[7] and German Issues

The Soviets some time ago gave us, the British and the French a relatively mild complaint and warning about the Bundesversammlung. The tone and content of these oral démarches and subsequent Soviet talks with the Germans suggest that the Soviets have not yet reached a decision about their course of action. They have obviously set up a basis for harassment or worse; or they may also try to argue or bargain the Western powers and/or the Germans out of holding the meeting. There are several other possibilities or combinations. In any case, we are on record as approving the meeting if the Germans want to hold it. Consequently we should avoid extensive argument with the Soviets before the meeting date and we should delay a rejection of the Soviet démarche until shortly before March 5. Since our response will presumably be the first policy statement to the Soviets on German issues by the new Administration we should use the occasion not only to rebut the specific Soviet complaint but to set forth a more general affirmation of the legitimacy of the FRG's role in safeguarding West Berlin's viability and of the responsibility of the Western allies for ensuring that that role conforms to four power agreements as we interpret them. Because of difficulties with the French we can probably do no more than to affirm these principles in general. We do need to give fresh thought to the future of Berlin and some time after the Bundesversammlung hurdle has been crossed should look toward inter-allied consultations.

Meanwhile, we cannot ignore the danger of Soviet and East German harrasment and the possibility that Berlin may become an early testing ground of the administration's conduct in a crisis. Contingency plans should be promptly examined and if necessary updated and revised.

There are signs that a Soviet-FRG dialogue on various matters, including non-use of force, is being reviewed. At the procedural level we should ensure promptly that the Germans keep us fully informed and consult on issues involving our interests. We must recognize, however,

---

[7] See Document 3.

that consultations are a two-way street and that German candor will in some measure reflect our own readiness to engage in meaningful consultations.

Summitry

We may soon get Soviet soundings about an early top level meeting. Soviet reasons for seeking such encounters in the past have been varied (including inter alia, Khrushchev's hankering for the limelight, a general impulse to deal with the head of the other superpower sometimes on the assumption that he may be more "reasonable" than his subordinates, considerations of prestige relating to internal Soviet politics, hopes of generating concern among our allies or in Peking, expectations of settling some specific issue, etc. etc.). American Presidents have had their own impulses and objectives, some not wholly dissimilar from those animating the Soviet leaders.

A broad exchange of views in which the President sets forth his approach directly to one or more of the members of the Soviet collective has some virtue and should probably be considered some time during the first year of the Administration. (Experience with the specific agreements made at summits with the Soviets has been less than encouraging, however, and it is not advisable to look to this device for that purpose.) High-level meetings with our major allies and perhaps with one or two important neutrals should have precedence over a summit with the Soviets and any overtures from Moscow should be handled accordingly.

Romania, Yugoslavia

The outgoing Administration is on record with several public and private statements about the grave situation that would arise if the USSR invaded Romania or Yugoslavia. Contingency planning has been underway within the US government and at NATO for some time. Although tensions in the Balkans have subsided, the potential for Soviet moves against Romania and Yugoslavia continues to exist. Whatever we may or may not find it possible to do in the event, and whatever short and long-term problems the Soviets would create for themselves if they did move against these two countries, the US retains a basic interest in the preservation of their present status of independence (or relative autonomy in the case of Romania).

Both countries, though to different degree, have indicated that they regard their network of foreign relations and contacts as one form of insurance against possible Soviet attack. Given the limited and highly unpleasant options available to us in the event of a Soviet attack, we have a substantial interest in strengthening now such deterrents as may be operating on the Soviets. The new Administration should be responsive to overtures from Bucharest and Belgrade on the question of economic relations and should be prepared to engage in political consultations with them. The Yugoslavs, who have greater freedom of maneuver than the Romanians, have already indicated their interest in regular consultations and we should agree.

---

3.   Editorial Note

On January 22, 1969, Secretary of State William Rogers sent President Richard Nixon a memorandum recommending a U.S. reply to the Soviet protest over the holding of the West German Federal Assembly (Bundesversammlung) in Berlin on March 5 to elect the President of the Federal Republic of Germany. The United States, Great Britain, and France had given permission for the Bundesversammlung to meet in Berlin and agreed that it did not violate the status of Berlin under international agreements. Since the founding of the Federal Republic of Germany, three of the four Federal Assemblies had taken place in Berlin (1954, 1959, 1964) without incident. Rogers expressed concern about possible Soviet-East German interference with access to Berlin. He also stated "that prohibiting the Federal Assembly in Berlin if the FRG wanted to hold it there would have serious damaging consequences: it would undermine German confidence in the Allies, have a bad effect on Berlin morale, [and] encourage the Soviets to proceed further on the course of trying to sever the vital ties between the FRG and Berlin." (National Archives, Nixon Presidential Materials, NSC Files, Box 681, Country Files, Europe, Germany, Vol. I)

Two days later, the President's Assistant for National Security Affairs Henry Kissinger forwarded Rogers' memorandum to Nixon and recommended that the President approve the draft text of the reply to the Soviets but delay transmission of the note "for some three weeks to minimize the likelihood of a further exchange with the Soviets; but that if the Germans prefer early delivery we abide by their wish on this matter." On January 28, 1969, Kissinger notified Rogers of Nixon's approval. (Ibid., RG 59, Central Files 1967–69, POL 15–2 GER W)

4.   National Security Study Memorandum 9[1]

Washington, January 23, 1969.

TO

The Secretary of State
The Secretary of Defense
The Secretary of the Treasury
The Director of Central Intelligence

SUBJECT

Review of the International Situation

The President has directed the preparation of an "inventory" of the international situation as of January 20, 1969. He wishes the review to provide a current assessment of the political, economic and security situation and the major problems relevant to U.S. security interests and U.S. bilateral and multilateral relations. In order to put this review into effect he wishes to consider responses to the attached set of questions along with other material considered relevant. The review should include a discussion, where appropriate, of the data upon which judgments are based, uncertainties regarding the data, and alternative possible interpretations of the data.

The responses should be forwarded to the President by February 20, 1969.[2]

Henry A. Kissinger

Attachment

THE U.S.S.R.

I. General

1. How do the Soviets see their position in the world vis-à-vis the United States?

---

[1] Source: National Archives, Nixon Presidential Materials, NSC Files, NSC Institutional Files (H-Files), Box H–129, NSSMs, NSSM 9. Secret. Also ibid., NSC Files, Box 364, NSSMs 1–42. Secret.

[2] The eight-volume response dated February 19, 1969, which was based on papers generated by multiple agencies and included 150 pages on the Soviet Union and Eastern Europe in volume I, is in the National Archives, Nixon Presidential Materials, NSC Files, NSC Institutional Files (H-Files), Box H–129, NSSM 9. On March 6, Halperin sent Kissinger a memorandum outlining how NSSM 9 should be used. Halperin suggested having the NSC staff review the eight-volume response for the purposes of "NSSMs to the bureaucracy requesting additional policy and information studies" and

2. Is there a general trend toward greater assertiveness in Soviet foreign policy or toward more concentration on internal affairs?

3. What bearing does the military balance have on US/Soviet relations? What factors tend to promote Soviet efforts at cooperation with the US; what factors impel the Soviets toward confrontation with us?

4. Are there special factors operating one way or the other at the moment?

II. Military

  A. Strategic Forces

1. What is the inventory of deployed Soviet strategic offensive and defensive forces as of January 1969? How are these forces likely to develop over the next 1–3–5–10 years in the absence of a US-Soviet limitation agreement? What technological changes seem likely over this time period? What is the extent and significance of increasing Soviet military presence far from the USSR?

2. How much do we know about current Soviet doctrines, plans, and procedures relating to the structure, basing and deployment, command and control, and use of strategic offensive and defensive forces? Which organizations control what particular offensive and defensive programs and forces? How do we get our information about Soviet strategic forces? What are the "hard" and "soft" areas of our information?

  B. General Purpose Forces

1. How has the Czechoslovak crisis affected the pattern of deployment, state of readiness and supply, and numerical levels of Soviet General Purpose Forces? Have manning and equipping levels of ground forces changed? Are these short or long-term effects?

2. What is the Soviet capability to deploy and support ground, naval, and air forces (a) in the Mediterranean, (b) in the Middle East, (c) in Africa and Asia? What trends are likely in the next 1–3–5 years regarding each of these areas?

3. What are present Soviet doctrines, plans, inventory levels, and deployments for non-strategic nuclear weapons? What future trends may be discerned?

III. Political

1. What are the sources of our information and the basis for our assessment of Soviet intentions and objectives? What are the "hard" and "soft" areas of our information?

"a Presidential review of the international scene later this spring." Kissinger initialed his approval to "HAK will outline at staff meeting."

2. From the perspective of the Soviet leadership, what challenges does the US appear to present? What threats to Soviet interests or to Soviet security?

3. What do we know of Soviet desires for a Summit?

4. What is the status of US-Soviet negotiations on opening consulates? What is the status of negotiations on chancery sites, leased lines, fisheries? What is the status of cultural exchanges with the US?

5. Apart from the possible release of Ivanov,[3] what possibilities are available for gestures toward the Soviets?

6. What is the role of "wars of national liberation" in current Soviet political-military doctrine and policy? Has this role been modified since Khrushchev's famous speech of 1961?[4]

7. By what means does the USSR currently influence and/or control the policies of its East European allies? How are the relationships between Moscow and the several East European governments and communist parties likely to be modified as a result of the Czechoslovak crisis?

8. What is the extent and strength of the relationship between Moscow and the various Communist parties of the non-Communist world? Has the crisis affected relationships with Communist parties in other regions? To what extent is competition with Peking a factor?

9. What are the forces within the USSR tending to promote internal political and economic liberalization? What elements oppose liberation? How strong are these factors? How is their balance likely to be affected (a) by US actions or policies, (b) by other external sources? How is their balance likely to be reflected in Soviet foreign and military policies?

10. How do the Soviets see the future of their relations with principal West European countries? How do they see the future of NATO?

IV. Economic

1. How rapidly is the Soviet economy growing? What trends are likely over the next 1–3–5–10 years? What are the likely effects of these trends on Soviet foreign and military policies?

---

[3] Igor Ivanov, a former employee of Amtorg, a Soviet trading cooperation in the United States, was serving a 20-year sentence for espionage. His appeal was under consideration by the Supreme Court. Before leaving office, President Lyndon Johnson reviewed his clemency appeal and decided it was inadvisable to intervene at that juncture in the judicial process. The Nixon administration was considering permanent deportation in lieu of Ivanov serving out his sentence.

[4] On January 6, 1961, in a speech at the Moscow Meeting of World Communist Leaders, Soviet Premier Nikita Khrushchev promised support for "wars of national liberation," defined as those "which began as uprisings of colonial peoples against their oppressors [and] developed into guerrilla wars."

2. How useful and how effective are existing Western controls on the export of strategic goods (a) to the USSR, (b) to other East European countries? In which areas do our COCOM partners disagree with the US positions and what is the basis of their disagreement? How useful, and how effective, are limitations on the extension of credit?

3. What is the existing pattern of trade between the USSR and (a) the West as a whole, (b) the US? What would be the economic and political effects on enlargement of this existing pattern of trade, or other significant modifications of it? Are there goods which, if traded between the US and USSR, would create a significant threat to US security? Noting Kosygin's remarks to McNamara about truck production, arc there any initiatives in the trade field which the US should consider?

V. Foreign Military and Economic Assistance Programs

1. What are the principal objectives of the Soviet Government in providing military/economic aid to the LDCs?

2. What strains and burdens do these programs place upon the Soviet economy?

3. What are Soviet attitudes with regard to the provision of sophisticated weapons (surface-to-surface missiles, supersonic fighters, special radar, etc.) to the LDCs?

4. What degree of influence has the USSR acquired as a result of these programs?

5. What politico-military risks does the USSR incur as a result of its military assistance program? Is the Soviet leadership cognizant of these risks? What will be the pattern of resource allocation over the next 1–3–5 years?

---

5.   **Editorial Note**

The National Security Council held its second meeting on January 25, 1969, from 9:30 a.m. to 2:20 p.m., and Vietnam was the primary topic. For the Vietnam portion of the meeting, see *Foreign Relations, 1969–1976*, volume VI, Vietnam, January 1969–July 1970, Document 10. Near the end of the meeting, a brief discussion of the Soviet Union's role in encouraging a peace settlement in Vietnam was raised in the context of "linkage":

"The President then asked where our contact with the Soviets is at present. Secretary Rogers said the Soviet Ambassador here in Washington but also the Soviet Ambassador in Paris. The President stated, 'I would like to get some recommendations on getting to the Soviets. In a tactical sense, we need a solution to bridge the gap but we also need strategic help in making Hanoi change its policy, a sort of carrot and stick approach. These efforts should be centered here in Washington. Talking on the strategic arms issues is certainly the carrot. We should get planning started on this immediately.' " (National Archives, Nixon Presidential Materials, NSC Files, NSC Institutional Files (H-Files), Box H–109, NSC Meeting Minutes, Originals, 1969)

---

6.   National Security Study Memorandum 10[1]

Washington, January 27, 1969.

TO

The Secretary of State
The Secretary of Defense
The Director of Central Intelligence

SUBJECT

East-West Relations

The President has directed that a study be prepared on the nature of US-Soviet relations, on US interests and objectives with respect to them and on the broad lines of appropriate US policies. The study should incorporate alternative views and interpretations of the issues involved. It should include summary statements of the conceptions and policy lines of the previous administration.

The study should include the following:

1. a characterization of US-Soviet relations in their broadest sense;
2. a discussion of Soviet perceptions of these relations and of Soviet interests and objectives as we understand them, including such indications as there are of differences, vacillations and uncertainties among Soviet decision-makers;
3. a discussion of US interests and objectives, short, medium and longer term;
4. a brief description of the broad lines of policy that we have hitherto pursued;
5. a recommended US approach to East-West relations.

The President has directed that the NSC Interdepartmental Group for Europe perform this study.

---

[1] Source: Library of Congress, Manuscript Division, Kissinger Papers, Box CL 316, NSSM Studies, March 1969–June 1970. Confidential. A copy was sent to the Chairman of the Joint Chiefs of Staff.

The paper should be forwarded to the NSC Review Group by February 6, 1969.[2]

Henry A. Kissinger

---

[2] The paper on "East-West Relations" is printed as Document 18 but was never discussed. A handwritten note on this NSSM reads: "Result: Overtaken by specific policy decisions."

---

7.   **Memorandum From Helmut Sonnenfeldt of the National Security Council Staff to the President's Assistant for National Security Affairs (Kissinger)[1]**

Washington, January 28, 1969.

SUBJECT

    Soviet Attitude toward New Administration

You may wish to show the President the attached Intelligence Note prepared by the State Department on reactions to the first days of the new administration.[2]

The report makes the following points.

1. The Soviet response to the new administration remains *cautiously optimistic*, and Soviet media obviously have been instructed to *avoid personal attacks on the President.*

2. By contrast, Soviet *comment on other administration figures such as Secretaries Rogers and Laird has been mixed*, indicating that editors are more free to criticize their public statements.

3. In an apparent effort to impress us with the seriousness of their desire for good relations, the Soviets have *invoked the sanction of Lenin on the need for friendly US-Soviet relations.*

---

[1] Source: National Archives, Nixon Presidential Materials, NSC Files, Box 709, Country Files, Europe, USSR, Vol. I. Confidential. Sent for information. Drafted by Donald R. Lesh, NSC staff officer responsible for Europe and sent through Eagleburger. On January 29, Lesh wrote a related memorandum to Kissinger on "Further Reports of Serious Kosygin Illness," in which he explained that Premier Kosygin was seriously ill with a liver ailment. (Ibid.)

[2] Attached but not printed was a January 27 Intelligence Note from Hughes, entitled "Moscow's Attitude Toward the New Administration—Cautious Optimism."

4. The Zamyatin press conference on January 20[3] indicating Soviet readiness to talk about strategic weapons limitation was probably designed to *pressure the new administration to agree to early negotiations,* and to indicate SALT as the preferred topic for opening the bilateral dialogue.

5. The total impression is that the Soviets are *eager to create the atmosphere of détente;* it is worthy of note that they fostered such a honeymoon in the early days of the Kennedy and Johnson administrations too. Only their subsequent performance will show how far the Soviets are prepared to go on substance.

Owing to the six to seven hour time differential, substantive comment in Soviet and East European media on the President's press conference yesterday[4] did not begin until late last night (radio) and early this morning (press). FBIS summaries are only becoming available during this afternoon. The first Soviet report on TASS International Service was brief and factual; from Warsaw initial treatment was scanty but factual, with the comment that the President's remarks appeared to signal a harder line on Communist China than had been expected; from Budapest comment on the press conference also was restrained, brief, and factual. By tomorrow morning more authoritative analyses from both Western and Eastern Europe will no doubt be available.

Donald R. Lesh[5]

---

[3] Not further identified.

[4] President Nixon held a press conference on January 27; for text, see *Public Papers: Nixon, 1969,* pp. 15–23.

[5] Lesh signed for Sonnenfeldt above Sonnenfeldt's typed signature.

---

8.   **Notes From Lunch Between the Assistant to the President (Ellsworth) and the Soviet Chargé (Tcherniakov)**[1]

Washington, January 29, 1969, 1–2:40 p.m.

NB: The following narrative is not a chronological account but is organized according to significant topics.

---

[1] Source: National Archives, Nixon Presidential Materials, NSC Files, Box 709, Country Files, Europe, USSR, Vol. I. No classification marking. In a January 29 covering memorandum to Kissinger, Ellsworth stated that he was "addressing it to you rather than the President because I do not want to introduce this material into the regular mechanism."

I. Ambassadors.

I asked when Ambassador Dobrynin would be returning to Washington. T. said Dobrynin had become ill after his arrival in Moscow and on January 7 had entered a sanitarium where the treatment takes 30 days. Therefore, T. expects Dobrynin to arrive back in Washington around February 10.

He stated that when Dobrynin arrives in Washington he will probably have visited personally with the leaders, Kosygin and Brezhnev. T. stressed that this is unusual—most Ambassadors on their home leaves do not even get to talk to Minister Gromyko, but Dobrynin almost always has personal conversations with Kosygin and Brezhnev. In addition, Brezhnev is in the same sanitarium as Dobrynin, so the two might have better-than-ordinary opportunities for private chats. The sanitarium is in a place whose name begins with a "B." It is just outside Moscow.

T. asked when President Nixon might be selecting a man to go to Moscow as U.S. Ambassador, and I replied (in accordance with explicit instruction on this point by Kissinger) that Mr. Nixon would be selecting his Ambassador to Moscow within two weeks.

II. Missile Talks.

I opened the subject of missile talks early in the lunch, with the observation that both T. and Dobrynin had had conversations from time to time with me in the past on the general subject of talks between the two countries; that I had emphasized, in such past talks, Mr. Nixon's awareness of the special responsibilities of the United States and the U.S.S.R.; that Mr. Nixon, in his acceptance speech at Miami and in his Inaugural address, had said we moved from an era of confrontation to an era of negotiation; that I had always stressed Mr. Nixon's view that talks on various subjects are interrelated.

I stated further that President Nixon approaches the question of talks with the Soviet Union in the following spirit: that talks on complicated and important matters such as these must always be conducted in a precise, businesslike, and detailed manner; that Mr. Nixon's background and life as a political man and lawyer in the United States, as well as his extensive international experience, have made it natural and imperative for him to place the greatest importance on semantic and substantive precision in international discussions; and that his news conference on Monday was only the most recent example of this attitude.

I stated that the President has reached no decision to have talks on missiles or any particular subject; that he is looking for evidence of general political movement in many areas. I stated that, while such a decision is under consideration, the President intends not to engage in any kind of arms escalation.

T.'s response to this will be embraced within the concluding section (VII) of this memorandum.

III. The Middle East.

With regard to the Middle East, and in response to my observation that the Middle East would be an area in which the President would look for political movement in connection with his overall consideration of a decision whether or not to commence talks, T. made the point that his own government has only limited influence over the principal Arab states involved, i.e., Egypt, Jordan and Syria (although Syria is not as significant a factor as Egypt and Jordan). In the case of Egypt, for example, he made the point that Egypt is a defeated nation and there is a limit to how far Colonel Nasser can be pushed without destroying him from the standpoint of the internal Egyptian situation.

IV. Non-Proliferation Treaty.

T. brought up the NPT, saying that he felt it was unfortunate the Johnson Administration had delayed the matter. In accordance with instructions from Kissinger, I stated the President would have a political problem with regard to ratification of the NPT if there should be further Soviet talk about Article 53 of the United Nations Charter or if the Soviet Union should make an issue of the West German meeting scheduled to be held in West Berlin on March 6.[2]

T.'s response to this will be embraced within the concluding section (VII) of this memorandum.

V. Vietnam.

I stated that it was President Nixon's intention to end the war in Vietnam, one way or another. I repeated this four times during the course of the lunch.

Each time I mentioned this point, I supplemented it with the observation that President Nixon could not end the war in Vietnam on a basis which would be interpreted as a disadvantageous conclusion from the point of view of the United States, after President Nixon's predecessor had fought and been eliminated from the political scene in America for his pains.

I mentioned also that the Administration is aware of the assistance the Soviet Union has put into the Paris negotiation situation, and

---

[2] Article 53, one of the "enemy states" clauses of the UN Charter, permitted the assertion of a unilateral right to intervene in West German affairs. The term "enemy state" applied to any state which during World War II had been an enemy of any signatory of the Charter. (A Decade of American Foreign Policy, pp. 117–139) For information on the West German Bundesversammlung meeting on March 6, see Document 3.

appreciates it; further, that it is hoped the Soviet Government will be able to continue its positive efforts in this area.

T. responded on this whole area at great length and with substantial sophistication. Essentially, his point is that the Saigon regime is a small minority regime, that the basic problem in Vietnam is an indigenous Vietnamese problem, that the Soviet Government has limited influence over the NLF, and that in the final analysis there was going to have to be some kind of temporary, provisional coalition set up in South Vietnam which will include the NLF in some way. I responded by referring to various statements in President Nixon's news conference of Monday, January 27, and in general said these were matters that T. and I could not dispose of at the lunch today.

I want to emphasize that T. expanded on these matters in great length and in detail.

VI. Stalinism.

T. spent a substantial portion of time, and great energy, being defensive about the Stalin era. He described how "upbeat" conditions were for Soviet citizenry in the middle and late '30's and how unrealistic are the current popular portrayals of that era by Western writers (as well as Solzhenitsyn's portrayal).

He particularly stressed that he had noticed in the press a report that President Nixon has on the table by his bed in the White House a book entitled "The Great Purge"[3] or something to that effect, and he explicitly asked me to either throw the book away or tell the President it is not worth reading. (I said I doubted if the press knows what is on the table in the President's bedroom.)

In response to pressing questions by me, he was very explicit in stressing the importance of the proposition that:

(1) such books do not accurately portray conditions in the Soviet Union in the 1930's or whenever they pretend to be set; and,

(2) even if such books may be taken (*arguendo*) (within artistic license) as reflections of reality, such reality should not be perceived as a relevant guide or comparison to present conditions.

VII. Talks.

Toward the end of the luncheon period, T. said in passing that he could assure me quite officially that his government is prepared to commence talks on limiting offensive and defensive missiles, on Vietnam, on Europe, and on the Middle East. As soon as it was appropriate

---

[3] Reference is to Robert Conquest's *The Great Terror: Stalin's Purge of the Thirties* published in 1968.

to do so in the conversation, I went back to that statement, quoted it to him, cited to him a statement that had been made to me by Ambassador Dobrynin in my home on Sunday evening, November 24,[4] to the same effect and asked T. if I was to understand his government is now prepared to start simultaneous talks on all these subjects immediately. T. sparred over the question of the meaning of the word "simultaneous"—did it mean simultaneous in place as well as time, and did it mean simultaneous in a sense which would imply an interrelationship to the extent that the substance of one subject would be a condition for talks on the substance of another?

I replied that, as I had said earlier, Mr. Nixon had always had the view that talks on various subjects are always interrelated and must be understood as taking place in context with each other.

T. emphasized that his government was always highly sensitive to any suggestion that one subject matter was being used to "blackmail" the Soviet Government on another subject—that Walt Rostow had been quite crude in his approach to the interrelationship of different subjects and that Dobrynin had received such severe backlash from the Kremlin when he reported one Rostow episode along this line that he, Dobrynin, had simply not reported other Rostow episodes. T. indicated that he would be unwilling to suggest any such proposal or idea to his government, but expressed the belief that his government would, in fact, agree to the simultaneous commencement of talks on all the listed subjects with the understanding that all should be considered within an interrelated context.

And then, I asked him if he would be willing to participate with me in preparing a memorandum which would more precisely describe the conditions that could surround such talks and an exact list of the topics for discussion in such talks.

He agreed that he would do that if I would give him three or four days. He will be back to me within three or four days for further conversation.[5]

---

[4] No record of this conversation was found.

[5] No record of a further conversation was found.

9.   **Editorial Note**

On February 1, 1969, the National Security Council met to discuss the Middle East. President Richard Nixon listened to briefings by Director of Central Intelligence Richard Helms and by Chairman of the Joint Chiefs of Staff General Earle Wheeler. According to minutes of the meeting, Helms described Soviet interests in the region as follows: "USSR has leapfrogged Northern Tier. Soviet naval expansion—steadier, more effective than Khrushchev's rather opportunistic move to put missiles in Cuba." Nixon asked, "You talk about USSR's 'measured, effective plan.' Does this emanate from military strategy or something that just happens? Do they have a meeting like ours here today, decide on policy and then execute it? Or do they just muddle along?" Helms replied, "Highest level decision. Considered policy."

General Wheeler's briefing on the significance of the Soviet fleet and U.S. contingency plans for conflict in the region generated the following comments and queries from Nixon: "I understand your contingency plan is based on intelligence estimate that local conflict [is] main possibility. I agree that US–USSR conflict remote, but what if one of Arab countries where Soviet fleet present is attacked?" Wheeler replied, "Possibilities we are examining: U.S. attack on Soviet bases in Siberia; sink one Soviet ship in Mediterranean; seize Soviet intelligence trawler."

Nixon then asked, "Could you consider what we could do indirectly through the Israelis? Seems to me Soviet naval presence is primarily political. Therefore, we must be prepared for a less-than-military contingency." Wheeler responded, "Primarily political. But Soviet presence in ports puts a Soviet umbrella over those ports. In a tenuous sense, fleet therefore does have military use." (National Archives, Nixon Presidential Materials, NSC Files, NSC Institutional Files (H-Files), Box H–109, NSC Meeting Minutes, Originals, 1969)

On February 3, 1969, Kissinger sent Nixon a follow-up memorandum that summarized the policy recommendations made at the NSC meeting the day before. Kissinger urged that "we should particularly concentrate on U.S.-Soviet arrangements which could slow the pace of the Near Eastern arms race and serve as a restraining influence on the nations in the area—at least arrangements which would assure U.S.–U.S.S.R. disengagement if hostilities break out again." Kissinger then layed out the pros and cons of a two-power dialogue with the Soviets as opposed to the advantages and disadvantages of the four-power (Great Britain, France, United States, Soviet Union) approach recommended by the French:

"1. The *pros* are:

"a. This reflects the power realities in the Middle East, and the Russians have assured us that they consider this the primary channel, even though they have accepted the four-power proposal. If there is to be a general settlement, only the USSR has the necessary leverage with Nasser to produce it, and only we come close to having the necessary influence with Israel.

"b. Each of us could consult directly with these parties while negotiating and yet retain the desirable UN umbrella by turning over our product to Jarring.

"c. It would be easier to position the Middle East on the U.S.–USSR agenda—particularly to establish the linkage to strategic arms talks—in a two-power context.

"d. It would also position the Middle East into the whole context of East-West relations with maximum control and linkage to other negotiations such as those on force limitations.

"2. The *cons* are:

"a. It might give the USSR credit for any settlement and enhance its position in the area to our detriment. The counters to this point are that all the Arabs know only the U.S. can move Israel; that settlement which has even a remote chance of Israeli acceptance would have enough elements unpalatable to the Arabs so that the Russians would not win popularity by pushing it; and that the U.S. can hold its own in peaceful competition with the USSR so should be willing to accept passing credit to the USSR, if any, for the sake of a settlement that would help us more than Moscow.

"b. We have no strong evidence that the Soviets want the kind of basic peace settlement we have been seeking. Although their intent is debatable, they seem to be aiming at a limited accommodation to reduce the possibility of a sudden crisis with dangerous and unforeseeable consequences. Limited accommodation would leave enough unsettled grievances for them to use in keeping the Arabs dependent on their support. If the Soviets are not sincere, we risk walking into a propaganda trap. The counters to this are that the Soviets are the ones who have persistently pushed this dialogue, that they have already moved toward our position and that we will never know their real position until we pin them down in negotiation.

"c. Israel will object to our negotiating their fate with anyone, though they are likely to react somewhat less sharply to the two-power than to the four-power approach. Agreement directly between them and the Arabs is fundamental to their position—and, they believe, to ours. They hold that a lasting settlement cannot result unless the parties themselves develop one they can live with. If we went down either the two-power or the four-power track, we would have to cope with vociferous Israeli charges that our position had weakened, that we had been taken in by Soviet blandishments and that, worst of all, we had undercut their position by compromising on the central point in that position."

In telling the President where to go from here, Kissinger wrote: "If you chose to follow the two-power course—either by itself or with the four-power track as an adjunct—you would have a choice between waiting for the USSR to respond to the U.S. note of January 15 and framing our own proposal and taking it to them. The advantage of waiting would be to test their seriousness. The last U.S. note asked them to clarify some obvious ambiguities in their December 30 [1968] note. But if we are going to wait, we should probably find a way to let Moscow know we are awaiting their reply. The advantages of taking the initiative would be to get our own plan on the table, to seize the propaganda initiative and to give the Arabs the impression that you are serious about wanting a just settlement. Of course, we must consider this in connection with other initiatives we plan with Moscow." (Ibid.)

On February 4, when the National Security Council met again to discuss the Middle East, Kissinger circulated his memorandum on policy recommendations. According to minutes of the meeting, Nixon asked Kissinger to "talk about how we meld 2-power and 4-power [talks]." Kissinger replied, "Intimate relationship among all these things. On overall settlement, I'll concentrate on 4-power and 2-power approaches. Other two options have little support—let Jarring go by himself or US mediation." Kissinger then outlined the pros and cons from his February 3 memorandum. President Nixon concluded the discussion about the various approaches to a Middle East settlement with the following remarks: "Don't be in any hurry to have anything done on the four-power front. At UN go to the two-power forum. Start talking with Soviets. Harmful if we give impression that four-power forum [is] where things will be settled. Main value as umbrella." (Ibid.)

During a February 6 news conference, Nixon announced a five-pronged U.S. approach toward a Middle East settlement: "We are going to continue to give our all-out support to the Jarring mission. We are going to have bilateral talks at the United Nations, preparatory to the talks between the four powers. We shall have four-power talks at the United Nations. We shall also have talks with the countries in the area, with the Israelis and their neighbors, and, in addition, we want to go forward on some of the long range plans, the Eisenhower–Strauss plan for relieving some of the very grave economic problems in that area." (*Public Papers: Nixon, 1969*, pages 68–69)

10.   Letter From President Nixon to Secretary of State Rogers[1]

Washington, February 4, 1969.

Dear Bill:

I have been giving much thought to our relations with the Soviet Union and would like to give you, informally, my ideas on this central security problem. My purpose in doing so is not to prejudge the scheduled systematic review by the National Security Council of our policy options with respect to the USSR, but rather to set out the general approach which I believe should guide us in our conduct as we move from confrontation to negotiation.

1. I believe that the tone of our public and private discourse about and with the Soviet Union should be calm, courteous and non-polemical. This will not prevent us from stating our views clearly and, if need be, firmly; nor will it preclude us from candidly affirming our attitude—negatively if warranted—toward the policies and actions of the Soviet Union. But what I said in my Inaugural address concerning the tone and character of our domestic debates[2] should also govern the tone and character of our statements in the international arena, most especially in respect of the Soviet Union.

2. I believe that the basis for a viable settlement is a mutual recognition of our vital interests. We must recognize that the Soviet Union has interests; in the present circumstances we cannot but take account of them in defining our own. We should leave the Soviet leadership in no doubt that we expect them to adopt a similar approach toward us. This applies also to the concerns and interests of our allies and indeed of all nations. They too are entitled to the safeguarding of their legitimate interests. In the past, we have often attempted to settle things in a fit of enthusiasm, relying on personal diplomacy. But the "spirit" that permeated various meetings lacked a solid basis of mutual interest, and therefore, every summit was followed by a crisis in less than a year.

---

[1] Source: Library of Congress, Manuscript Division, Kissinger Papers, Box CL 215, "D" File. Secret. Kissinger sent this letter to the President on February 4 for his signature and reminded him that they had cleared the draft that morning. (Ibid.) An identical letter to Secretary of Defense Laird was included for Nixon's signature. (Ibid.) The letter to Laird is in *Foreign Relations, 1969–1976*, volume I, Foundations of Foreign Policy, 1969–1972, Document 10.

[2] The passage in Nixon's inaugural address reads: "In these difficult years, America has suffered from a fever of words; from inflated rhetoric that promises more than it can deliver; from angry rhetoric that fans discontents into hatreds; from bombastic rhetoric that postures instead of persuading. We cannot learn from one another until we stop shouting at one another—until we speak quietly enough so that our words can be heard as well as our voices." (*Public Papers: Nixon, 1969*, pp. 1–4)

3. I am convinced that the great issues are fundamentally interrelated. I do not mean by this to establish artificial linkages between specific elements of one or another issue or between tactical steps that we may elect to take. But I do believe that crisis or confrontation in one place and real cooperation in another cannot long be sustained simultaneously. I recognize that the previous Administration took the view that when we perceive a mutual interest on an issue with the USSR, we should pursue agreement and attempt to insulate it as much as possible from the ups and downs of conflicts elsewhere. This may well be sound on numerous bilateral and practical matters such as cultural or scientific exchanges. But, on the crucial issues of our day, I believe we must seek to advance on a front at least broad enough to make clear that we see some relationship between political and military issues. I believe that the Soviet leaders should be brought to understand that they cannot expect to reap the benefits of cooperation in one area while seeking to take advantage of tension or confrontation elsewhere. Such a course involves the danger that the Soviets will use talks on arms as a safety valve on intransigence elsewhere. I note for example that the invasion of Hungary was followed by abortive disarmament talks within nine months.[3] The invasion of Czechoslovakia was preceded by the explorations of a summit conference (in fact, when Ambassador Dobrynin informed President Johnson of the invasion of Czechoslovakia, he received the appointment so quickly because the President thought his purpose was to fix the date of a summit meeting).[4] Negotiation and the search for agreement carry their own burdens; the Soviets—no less than we—must be ready to bear them.

4. I recognize the problem of giving practical substance to the propositions set forth in the previous paragraph. Without attempting to lay down inflexible prescriptions about how various matters at issue between ourselves and the USSR should be connected, I would like to illustrate what I have in mind in one case of immediate and widespread interest—the proposed talks on strategic weapons. I believe our decision on when and how to proceed does not depend exclusively on our review of the purely military and technical issues, although these are of key importance. This decision should also be taken in the light of the prevailing political context and, in particular, in light of progress

---

[3] Reference is to the Soviet use of force in Hungary on October 24, 1956. Disarmament negotiations between the Western powers and the Soviet Union began in London on March 18, 1957.

[4] The evening of August 20, 1968, Dobrynin informed Johnson of Warsaw Pact military intervention in Czechoslovakia. The day before, Soviet leaders had invited Johnson to Leningrad, and on August 21, the White House had intended to announce the summit. A memorandum of Johnson's August 20 meeting with Dobrynin is in *Foreign Relations*, 1964–1968, volume XVII, Eastern Europe, Document 80.

toward stabilizing the explosive Middle East situation, and in light of the Paris talks. I believe I should retain the freedom to ensure, to the extent that we have control over it, that the timing of talks with the Soviet Union on strategic weapons is optimal. This may, in fact, mean delay beyond that required for our review of the technical issues. Indeed, it means that we should—at least in our public position—keep open the option that there may be no talks at all.

5. I am, of course, aware that the Soviets are seeking to press us to agree to talks and I know also of the strong views held by many in this country. But I think it is important to establish with the Soviets early in the Administration that our commitment to negotiation applies to a range of major issues so that the "structure of peace" to which I referred in the Inaugural will have a sound base.

Sincerely,

RN

---

11.   **Memorandum From the Ambassador to the Soviet Union (Thompson) to Secretary of State Rogers**[1]

Washington, February 7, 1969.

I had lunch with Henry Kissinger today. While there the President sent for both of us and chatted with us while having his lunch at his desk. The following are the highlights:

I urged that we proceed as rapidly as possible to set up arrangements for strategic missile talks with the Soviets although obviously not until he returned from his European trip.[2] I argued briefly with the President and at greater length earlier with Henry that we not attempt to tie the start of talks with political concessions from the Soviets. I thought that to so do might have the opposite effect than the one we intended. I got the impression that the President was inclined to agree. I also suggested that we drop the idea of agreeing to a set of principles before starting the talks.

I told the President I thought we should be careful not to feed Soviet suspicions about the possibility of our ganging up with Commu-

---

[1] Source: National Archives, RG 59, Office Files of William Rogers: Lot 73 D 443, Box 4, White House Correspondence, 1969. Secret.

[2] On February 23 Nixon left for an 8-day visit to Europe on his first foreign trip as President.

nist China against them. In reply to his question I said I was not referring to his public statements on this matter as the Soviets would understand that we would pursue our national interests. Rather I was thinking of any hints or actions that indicated something was going on under the table. As a specific example I mentioned the possible shifting of our talks with the Chinese in Prague from the present location which the Soviets have doubtless bugged to our respective Embassies. (I understand the Chinese have turned this down.)

The President referred to the importance of close understanding between you and Kissinger. I gathered that both he and Henry were disturbed by press reports of [friction] between the Department and the NSC staff.

The President said he was not fanatical about the idea of summit talks. Nevertheless he thought that summit talks with the Soviets would eventually take place and asked for my thoughts on timing. I said I thought it was important to proceed first with one or two important problems. Ratification of the Non-Proliferation Treaty would be useful but I thought it would also be wise at least to have started the Missile talks. If they succeeded, this would create a favorable atmosphere—if they got stuck perhaps the President could resolve the difficulty on his level.

In this connection I said I thought some changes in the Soviet leadership were quite possible before the year was out.

The President asked if I would help in the planning of any eventual summit meeting with the Soviets and I said I would be happy to do so.

In my earlier talk with Henry I said that if Missile talks with the Soviets were set, I thought this would diminish the likelihood of the Soviets stirring up trouble in Berlin over the meeting there of the Bundesversammlung.[3]

The President said he had not met Ambassador Dobrynin. I said I thought the top Soviet leaders had confidence in his judgment and that he had never deceived me, unless he in fact knew about the missiles in Cuba, which I did not think was the case. The President asked if there was any reason why he should not see Dobrynin after the forthcoming European trip. I said I thought it was quite proper. He said he might ask him to an informal lunch.

The President referred to a talk we had in Moscow in 1967 when I told him the Soviets were prejudiced against him. He asked what their present attitude was. I said that they had been relatively correct in their attitude during the election campaign and since. They had

---

[3] See Document 3.

been impressed by his conduct of the campaign and had referred favorably to his remarks about negotiations. They were, however, always suspicious and would be examining carefully his first moves in the field of foreign affairs.

L. W. Thompson[4]

---

[4] Printed from a copy that bears this typed signature.

---

12.   Editorial Note

On February 13, 1969, at 2:45 p.m., Secretary of State Rogers met with Soviet Ambassador Dobrynin at the Soviet Ambassador's request. Dobrynin was under instructions from his government to seek an appointment with President Nixon to express formally its views on U.S.-Soviet relations and receive the Nixon administration views of the relationship. When Rogers asked whether the Soviet suggestion for a meeting was urgent, Dobrynin responded that he hoped one could be arranged within the next couple of days. (Memorandum of conversation, February 13; National Archives, RG 59, Central Files 1967–69, POL US–USSR) A summary of Rogers' conversation with Dobrynin on February 13 was included with the President's evening reading and is printed as Tab B to Document 13.

On February 15, Haldeman described preparations for the President's first meeting with Dobrynin:

"Big item was meeting planned for Monday with the Soviet Ambassador. Problem arose because P wanted me to call Rogers and tell him of meeting, but that Ambassador and P would be alone. I did, Rogers objected, feeling P should never meet alone with an Ambassador, urged a State Department reporter sit in. Back and forth, K disturbed because Ambassador has something of great significance to tell P, but if done with State man there word will get out and P will lose control. Decided I should sit in, Rogers said OK, but ridiculous. Ended up State man and K both will sit in, but P will see Ambassador alone for a few minutes first, and will get the dope in written form. K determined P should get word on Soviet intentions direct so he knows he can act on it. May be a big break on the Middle East. K feels very important." (*Haldeman Diaries: Multimedia Edition*, February 15, 1969)

Kissinger's recollection, related in his *White House Years* (page 141), of the decision to exclude Rogers from the first meeting with Dobrynin is as follows: "Procedurally, Nixon wished to establish his dominance over negotiations with the Soviet Union; in his mind, this required the exclusion of Rogers, who might be too anxious and who might claim credit for whatever progress might be made. Substantively, he wanted to begin the linkage approach at his own pace. Nixon sought to solve the Rogers problem in his customary fashion by letting Haldeman bear the onus (and no doubt Haldeman laid it off on me). Haldeman told the Secretary of State that the best guarantee for not raising expectations was for Rogers to be absent from the meeting. Attendance by Rogers would convey a sense of urgency contrary to our strategy; it might lead to an undue sense of urgency."

Also on February 15, Kissinger wrote Nixon a memorandum describing a message from Dobrynin that was conveyed to him through the head of the American section of the Institute of World Politics in Moscow during a reception the previous evening at the Soviet Embassy:

"1. While in Moscow he had stayed in the same sanatorium with Brezhnev, Podgorny, and Kosygin.

"2. He carried a message, personally approved by the top leadership, for you, which he would prefer to deliver to you without any diplomats present. He himself would come alone.

"3. The Soviet leaders were full of goodwill and eager to move forward on a broad front.

"4. Dobrynin would like to conduct his conversations in Washington with some person you designate who has your confidence, but who was not part of the diplomatic establishment.

"5. The Soviet leaders were reluctant to accept conditions on the ground that they had to show their good faith. However, if we wanted simultaneous progress on several fronts at once, they were ready to proceed on the basis of equality.

"6. They were especially prepared to proceed on a bilateral basis with discussions on the Middle East. They would prefer to do this, however, outside the UN framework. We could designate a trusted official at our Embassy in Moscow and they would designate a very high official in the Foreign Ministry. Alternatively, you could designate somebody you trusted here and Dobrynin would be prepared to conduct conversations.

"7. They were prepared to answer questions on other outstanding topics, such as Vietnam, and to talk on any other political problem on our mind." (National Archives, Nixon Presidential Materials, NSC Files, Box 340, Subject Files, USSR Memcons Dobrynin/President 2/17/69)

13.   Memorandum From the President's Assistant for National Security Affairs (Kissinger) to President Nixon[1]

Washington, February 15, 1969.

SUBJECT

Soviet Ambassador Dobrynin's Call on You

Dobrynin has just returned from Moscow after an absence of several weeks; he will presumably have a message from the Soviet leaders. *If it is a written message of any substance—he may provide a translation—I recommend that you not react on the spot, but tell him it will be studied and answered in due course.*

Whether written or oral, *Dobrynin's line* will probably be

(1) to assure you of Soviet desires to do business, especially on strategic weapons,
(2) to express concern that we are not sufficiently responsive to the conciliatory stance displayed by the Soviets since January 20,
(3) to leave an implication that we should not pass up the present opportunity, and
(4) to establish a direct channel between you and the Russian leaders.

I recommend that *your approach* should be

(1) to be polite, but aloof;
(2) to show willingness to be responsive when they have concrete propositions to make, but not to let the Soviets force the pace merely by offers to talk without indications of substance;
(3) to convey concern that a Berlin crisis could throw a shadow over our relations;[2]
(4) to make clear that we believe progress depends on specific settlements, not personal diplomacy. Summits should come at the end of careful preparation.[3]

You should be aware that Dobrynin is a friendly and outgoing individual who has long enjoyed close personal contact with leading American officials.

While he is a member of the Soviet Central Committee and has some access to the top Moscow leaders, he is not part of the in-group that makes decisions.

---

[1] Source: National Archives, Nixon Presidential Materials, NSC Files, Box 340, Subject Files, USSR Memcons Dobrynin/President 2/17/69. Confidential; Nodis. Sent for action.

[2] See Document 3.

[3] Nixon underlined most of this paragraph.

His reports probably do carry weight in Moscow, but his bosses also seem to run a check on his reporting through the sizeable KGB establishment in their Embassy here.

Dobrynin speaks English quite well, but his comprehension is imperfect; consequently, important points must be made in simple words and relatively slowly.

I attach:

—recommended talking points (Tab A)
—Secretary Rogers' account of his own conversation last Thursday (Tab B)

Tab A

Talking Points Prepared by the National Security Council Staff[4]

Washington, undated.

TALKING POINTS

I. Strategic Weapons Talks

1. We are reviewing the subject as part of our priority examination of all our major security problems.

2. We have noted Soviet expressions of readiness to begin talks.

3. We believe that negotiations that go to the very heart of our (and their) interests should bear a proper relationship to the crucial issues that endanger peace. Our reading of history indicates that almost all crises have been caused by political conditions, not by the arms race as such. We have no preconditions, but believe one cannot engage in mutually beneficial arms talks while major crises fester in which we and they might be pitted against each other.[5] You are thinking especially of the Middle East and Vietnam. We think it would be dangerous if arms talks dulled our efforts to cope with threats to the peace.

---

[4] On February 15, Rogers also sent Nixon a memorandum of talking points for his meeting with Dobrynin, which were similar but more detailed than those printed as Tab A. (National Archives, Nixon Presidential Materials, NSC Files, Box 709, Country Files, Europe, USSR, Vol. I)

[5] Nixon underlined these sentences and also highlighted and checked this paragraph.

II. Berlin

1. Any crisis there now would be artificial; we see no justification for it and have no interest in confrontation.

2. We do have a vital interest in the integrity and viability of the city.[6]

3. We know of no infringement on Soviet interests by any actions in the Western sectors of the city on the part of any of our allies.

4. You are going to Berlin to affirm our interests and our responsibilities.[7]

5. (Optional if Conversation Warrants) A crisis[8] now would place a heavy burden on our[9] relations.

III. Middle East

1. We recognize that the Soviet Union has interests in the region. So have we. The legitimate interests of all deserve to be safeguarded. Efforts to promote one's own interests and ambitions at someone else's expense will lead to confrontation not settlement.

2. We have no desire to get drawn into the wars and conflicts of the area; we assume the Soviet Union has no such desire either.[10]

3. We are prepared to participate constructively in talks that give promise of leading somewhere.[11] Talks for talks' sake may simply embolden those who favor recourse to force.

4. We are convinced that there can be no progress, nor faith in the process of negotiation unless it is understood by all that all the parties in the Middle East acquire tangible guarantees of their security.

IV. Vietnam

1. We seek an honorable peace for all concerned; we have no wish to humiliate Hanoi and do not intend to see Saigon or ourselves humiliated.[12]

2. You will not be the first President to lose a war; therefore you intend to end the war one way or the other.[13] (This is deliberately ambiguous.)

---

[6] Nixon underlined this sentence.

[7] Nixon visited West Berlin on February 27 as part of his 8-day trip to Europe. For his remarks on arrival at Tempelhof Airport in West Berlin, see *Public Papers: Nixon, 1969,* pp. 153–155.

[8] Nixon underlined this word.

[9] Nixon underlined this word.

[10] Nixon underlined most of this sentence.

[11] Nixon underlined this sentence.

[12] Nixon underlined the second part of this sentence.

[13] Nixon underlined the second half of this sentence and highlighted and checked this paragraph.

3. Vital interests of the United States and the Soviet Union are not in conflict in Vietnam. We do, between us, have a responsibility to keep it that way. Which is another way of saying we both have an interest in getting the war ended.[14]

4. We would like to see the Soviet Union exert its influence on its friends in Hanoi, who depend heavily on Soviet support, though we recognize, of course, the delicacy of its position. But if that fails, we do not exclude that others who have an interest could be enlisted to bring about progress toward a settlement.[15]

Tab B

Department of State Submission for the President's Evening Reading[16]

Washington, February 13, 1969.

SUBJECT

Call by Soviet Ambassador Dobrynin

In response to his request, I received Ambassador Dobrynin this afternoon.[17] He came specifically to inform me that he was under instructions from his government to seek an appointment with you, at your convenience, but hopefully within the next day or two. He gave no indication that he was carrying a message but merely stated that he had been asked by his government to convey to you its current views on the most important international issues. He planned to tell you how the Soviet Government presently views U.S.-Soviet relations and how these relations might develop in the future. Your views on the questions raised, he said, would be appreciated. I said I would be in touch with him as soon as I had any information to pass on.

I took advantage of his call to express our concern over the possibility of another Tet offensive[18] as well as our concern over developments involving Berlin. Ambassador Dobrynin seemed unaware of

---

[14] Nixon underlined most of this paragraph.

[15] Nixon underlined most of this sentence.

[16] Confidential. Drafted by Adolph Dubs (EUR/SOV) on February 13.

[17] February 13.

[18] Reference is to the possibility of a 1969 North Vietnamese and Vietcong offensive in South Vietnam during the Tet lunar holidays in February 1968. Nixon underlined "Tet offensive" and "developments involving Berlin" in this sentence.

any danger signals in Viet-Nam. He simply repeated his government's position that the Soviet Union would continue to be helpful with respect to the negotiations on Viet-Nam, assuming that the U.S. accepted the equality of all participants in those negotiations.

On Berlin, he was at pains to underline that the U.S. should not misread developments there. The Soviet Union did not wish to do anything to jeopardize relations with the U.S. What was happening with respect to Berlin was merely a reaction to the FRG decision to convene the Bundesversammlung there. He added that the Soviet Union did not want Berlin and that it was not asking that the East Germans should get it. At the same time, the Soviet Union is not prepared to give West Berlin to the FRG. Ambassador Dobrynin also underlined that actions taken by East Germany were not in any way related to your planned visit to Berlin.

With respect to the Middle East, he indicated that the Soviet Government evidently does not intend to reply formally to the previous Administration's last communication on that subject. He said that the Soviets were prepared to discuss this matter in detail both bilaterally and in a Four-Power context. Discussions could take place in New York, Moscow and here.

Ambassador Dobrynin also said that the Soviet Union remained ready to initiate discussions on the limitation of offensive and defensive missile systems. He thought it unfortunate, however, if this matter were to be linked with progress on other issues.

I emphasized during the course of the conversation that we hoped the Soviet Union would be helpful with respect to Viet-Nam and that the Soviet Government should advise East Germany to play Berlin in a low key.

14.   Memorandum of Conversation[1]

Washington, February 17, 1969, 11:45 a.m.–12:45 p.m.

SUBJECT

Ambassador Dobrynin's Initial Call on the President

PARTICIPANTS

U.S. Side:
The President
Mr. Henry A. Kissinger, Asst. to the
President for National Security Aff.
Mr. Malcolm Toon, Acting Deputy
Assistant Secretary for European Affairs

Soviet Side:
H.E. Anatoliy F. Dobrynin,
Soviet Ambassador

The President greeted Ambassador Dobrynin in the Fish Room and escorted him into his office for a brief private chat. Ambassador Dobrynin told the President privately that, before his departure from Moscow last week, he had spent two days at a government dacha outside Moscow with Brezhnev, Kosygin and Podgorny and the message that he carried was based on his talks with the leadership. The President should understand, therefore, that what he had to say on substantive issues was an accurate reflection of the views of the leadership.

After Mr. Kissinger and Mr. Toon joined the President, the President gave the floor to Ambassador Dobrynin.

Dobrynin said that his government had noted with interest President Nixon's statement that his Administration looked forward to an era of negotiations, not confrontation. He could assure the President that the Soviet Government shared this view and was prepared to do its part to see to it that the period that lies ahead was truly one of negotiations and not confrontation. This was on the understanding, of course, that the issues to be negotiated and the subjects to be discussed would be by mutual agreement, that negotiations would not be pursued simply for their own sake but for the purpose of bringing about constructive results. Past experience indicated the importance of beginning negotiations as soon as possible. Delay could be harmful, and it was important therefore to recognize the desirability of moving ahead at an early date. The Ambassador had been instructed by his government to ascertain precisely what the President had in mind by negotiations—specifically what issues the President felt should be the subject of negotiations and when, where, and at what level these should

---

[1] Source: National Archives, RG 59, Central Files 1967–69, POL 1 US–USSR. Secret; Nodis. Drafted by Toon. The conversation was held in the Oval Office at the White House.

take place. So far as the Soviet Government was concerned, negotiations and an exchange of views on various subjects and at various levels could take place simultaneously. It was not excluded that at an appropriate time discussions could be carried on at the Summit level.

The President asked Ambassador Dobrynin what he meant by his statement that negotiations on various issues could be carried on simultaneously.

Dobrynin referred to the President's remarks at his first press conference concerning the Middle East situation and the arms race.[2] The Soviet Government was prepared to use its influence on parties directly involved in the Middle East situation to help arrive at a solution of the problem. Depending on the President's views, talks on the Middle East problem could take place in New York or Washington and also in Moscow, either with the American Embassy there or with a special emissary, if the President desired to send one. With regard to the so-called arms race, the Soviet Government was prepared to reach agreement on limitation and subsequent reduction of both offensive and defensive strategic missiles. As the President was aware, certain aspects of this question had already been discussed with the previous Administration. Both sides had agreed on the desirability of early initiation of talks on the missile problem, although there had not been full agreement on a procedural aspect, which Ambassador Dobrynin understood related to the level at which the talks should begin. In any case, he was instructed by his government to inform the President that the Soviet side was prepared to begin talks now and to ascertain from the President his ideas on where, when, and at what level talks might begin. The Soviet Government was not pressing for an early reply but, in its view, discussions of the arms control problem as well as the Middle East problem were worth pursuing and could be carried on simultaneously. Certainly, the Soviet Government was under no illusion that the solutions to either problem could be achieved overnight, but it felt that a beginning should be made. While other subjects might be discussed, and in this respect Ambassador Dobrynin was prepared to hear our own suggestions either through Mr. Kissinger or the State Department, it was his government's view that the two subjects he had

---

[2] During Nixon's first press conference on January 27, the President was asked where he stood on starting missile talks with the Soviets. He replied that he preferred "to steer a course between those two extremes" of waiting until there was "progress on political settlements" and moving forward without such political talks. "What I want to do is to see to it that we have strategic arms talks in a way and at a time that will promote, if possible, progress on outstanding political problems at the same time—for example, on the problem of the Mideast and on other outstanding problems in which the United States and the Soviet Union, acting together, can serve the cause of peace." A full text of the conference is in *Public Papers: Nixon, 1969*, pp. 15–23.

mentioned—the Middle East and the arms control—were among the most important which should engage our early attention.

The President thanked Ambassador Dobrynin for his forthright statement of the Soviet Government's position. The President wished to make clear that his Administration began its tasks with a fresh viewpoint and with an eye to the future. Since Ambassador Dobrynin referred to a possible Summit meeting, the President wished to make clear that he shared the view that at some point a meeting of Heads of Government might be useful. The President felt, however, that such meetings must be based on a carefully prepared agenda and be preceded by adequate preparatory work on the issues to be discussed and possibly on which agreements might be reached. Without adequate preparations, Summit meetings could be harmful, since expectations of results might not be met. The President did not believe in a Summit meeting simply for the sake of bringing together the Heads of Government. Some specific purpose must be served, and the President felt strongly that we should now discuss at lower levels the principal issues before us so that ultimately when there should be a Summit meeting it would have constructive results.

Secondly, the President wished to set forth in a completely candid way his view of the relationship between the two super powers, as they are now commonly referred to. We must recognize that there are basic differences between us. This has been true historically of the relationship between great powers, and it is equally true now. We both have a responsibility to moderate these differences, to see to it that they do not result in a sharp confrontation, and in the President's view the most effective way of doing this was to keep the lines of communication open. This is the task of diplomacy—to recognize that great powers will differ and to insure that differences be resolved by peaceful means.

Finally, the President wished to stress the importance of eliminating those areas of friction where our own fundamental interests are not involved. We know from history that great powers can be drawn into a confrontation with each other as a result of actions by other nations. The President felt, for example, that it would be the height of folly to let the parties directly involved in the Middle East conflict bring about a confrontation between Moscow and Washington. It is particularly for this reason that the President attached great importance to an exchange of views, either bilaterally or in a multilateral forum on the Middle East situation.

The strategic arms problem involves primarily the United States and the Soviet Union, although both sides, of course, must consult, as necessary, with their Allies. The President wished to make clear his views on the relationship between strategic arms talks and progress on political issues. It was not his view that the initiation of such talks must be conditioned on the settlement of larger political issues. We both recognize that the principal purpose of strategic arms talks is peace, but there is no guarantee that freezing strategic weapons at the present level alone would bring about peace. History makes clear that wars result from political differences and political problems. It is incumbent upon us, therefore, when we begin strategic arms talks to do what we can in a parallel way to de-fuse critical political situations such as the Middle East and Viet-Nam.

Ambassador Dobrynin asked if his understanding was correct that the President favored simultaneous discussion of the problems which the President had mentioned. The Ambassador recognized, of course, that it might not be possible to discuss all problems at the same time, and he was not pressing the President to set the exact time for beginning arms talks. He wanted simply to clarify his own understanding of the linkage between arms talks and negotiations on political issues. His government, of course, would be interested in having a more precise idea as to when the President would be prepared to begin an exchange of views on the missile problem, even if preliminary and at the level of experts.

The President replied that it was his hope that we would soon be able to decide the question of timing. First, of course, the Administration would wish thoroughly to examine the whole problem and our position on it. This would probably have to await his return from Europe. In any case, as Ambassador Dobrynin was aware, Mr. Gerard Smith had just recently been appointed Director of the Arms Control and Disarmament Agency[3] and he was now engaged in reviewing our entire position on arms control issues.

With regard to the Middle East situation, the President wished to review the question of modalities for our bilateral discussions with Ambassador Yost and others. The President is gratified to learn that the Soviets are prepared to do what they can to cool the situation, and certainly the President himself would do everything in his power to bring this about.

On Viet-Nam the President recognized that the Soviet position was somewhat more delicate than our own since the Soviets were not directly involved in the problem. The President knew, however, that the Soviet Government has an interest in terminating the conflict and had played a helpful role in getting the Paris talks started. For our part, we are prepared to go "the extra mile" in Paris, but the Soviets should understand clearly that the American public will not tolerate endless

---

[3] Nixon submitted Smith's name to the Senate for confirmation on January 31; he was confirmed on February 7.

discussions there. The Administration's determination is to bring the conflict to an end, one way or another. We hope that the Soviets will do what they can to get the Paris talks off dead-center.

Dobrynin said he would like to speak briefly of the Soviet position on the Paris talks. The Soviet Government had welcomed their initiation and it was their view that if all participants in the Paris talks would face realities and treat each other on an equal basis, then the Soviets might be in a position to play a constructive role. Dobrynin said that he agreed generally with the President's statement that progress in one area is bound to affect progress in other areas. He thought, however, that it was useful to make a beginning and it would be wise not to begin with the most difficult issues. Often small steps can have influence.

The President said that he wished to make clear that it was not his view that agreement on one issue must be conditioned by settlement of other issues. The President wished to express his conviction, however, that progress in area is bound to have an influence on progress all other areas. The current situation in Berlin is a case in point. If the Berlin situation should deteriorate, Senate approval of the Nonproliferation Treaty would be much more difficult. The President wished to make clear that he favored early ratification of the treaty and he is optimistic that the Senate will act favorably in the near future. We should bear in mind, however, that just as the situation in Czechoslovakia had influenced the outlook for the treaty last fall, so would the situation in Berlin now have an important bearing on the Senate's attitude. Ambassador Dobrynin had mentioned the desirability of making progress on some issues, even if settlement of other issues should not be feasible. The Non-Proliferation Treaty is just such an issue. If we can move ahead on this it would be helpful in our efforts on other issues. The only cloud on the horizon is Berlin and the President hoped that the Soviets would make every effort to avoid trouble there.

Dobrynin said that the situation in Berlin did not stem from any action taken by the Soviets. The President would recall that a meeting was scheduled in Berlin last fall and the Secretary of State had discussed the problem with the Ambassador, urging him to persuade his government to avoid any action in connection with this meeting which might possibly result in unpleasantness in and around Berlin. The Ambassador said he would not wish his remarks to be recorded but he felt the President should know that his Government had used its influence to insure that the situation remained calm. There was no confrontation then, and Ambassador Dobrynin saw no need for a confrontation between us in the present situation.

The President hoped that there would be no trouble in Berlin and he welcomed Ambassador Dobrynin's assurances on this point. The

Soviets should understand that we are solidly behind the integrity of West Berlin, and we will do whatever is necessary to protect it. He had noted in the press references to the "provocative nature" of his visit to Berlin. The President wished to assure Ambassador Dobrynin that these stories were totally without foundation and that his visit to Berlin was a perfectly normal action for any United States President to take in connection with a visit to Europe.

The President concluded the discussion by pointing out to Dobrynin that the United States and the Soviet Union have all the power necessary to maintain peace in the world. If we play our role effectively, peace will be maintained. We do ourselves and others disservice, however, if we pretend that we agree on all the basic issues. We should rather insure that our differences do not lead to confrontation, that we are not drawn into confrontation by actions of others. We should recognize that diplomacy can play a vital role in insuring that this does not happen.

---

15.   Note From Soviet Leaders to President Nixon[1]

Moscow, February 17, 1969.

The attention has been paid in Moscow to President Nixon's statements in which he set forth his views on questions of peace and international cooperation.

As is known, the Soviet Union pursues and will pursue the policy of peace. We are prepared to develop relations of peaceful cooperation with all states which on their part strive for the same end, and we think that if both the Soviet Union and the United States in their actions proceed from exactly that principle basis, thereby there will be created the widest opportunities for mutual agreement and Soviet-American cooperation in solving the urgent international problems. We would like to particularly stress here, that although the great powers

---

[1] Source: National Archives, Nixon Presidential Materials, NSC Files, Box 340, Subject Files, USSR Memcons Dobrynin/President 2/17/69. No classification marking. On January 31, Sedov told Kissinger that the Soviets were "considering putting out 'something' to indicate they will not use the NPT as an excuse for intervening in the domestic affairs of others" and that they "are also putting together a 'package' on their views re political settlement. Dobrynin may bring this back with him about February 15." (Ibid., RG 59, Central Files 1967–69, POL 1 USSR) This note was the "package" promised Kissinger and given him by Dobrynin on February 17. The date is handwritten on the note.

bear special responsibility for preserving peace, in their intentions and actions they—like all other participants of international intercourse—must respect the inherent rights of other states, big and small, for sovereign and independent development, they must proceed from the real situation existing in the world. If you agree with such understanding of major principles of our relations, we on our part can fully subscribe to your statement to the effect that "after a period of confrontation, we are entering an era of negotiation".

That is what we would like to say to the President right now in order to exclude any misunderstanding on the American side of our approach to one or another question.

We do not see any other principle basis on which the Soviet-American relations could be built in the present world.

We are deeply convinced that if such approach be followed then despite all differences of views, social and political systems and of state interests there can be no such situation that would lead with fatal inevitability to direct confrontation between our countries.

All this, of course, presumes a certain level of confidence and mutual understanding that should also be present in searching ways to solving urgent world problems. It implies, of course, not only formal agreements but also opportunities provided by parallel or complementary actions including those based on the principle of "mutual example" and so on.

We are convinced that by their mutual efforts the USSR and the USA together with other states could achieve a situation when international negotiations would serve first of all the purpose of preventing conflicts rather than finding ways out of them after peace and international security had already been endangered. It is of particular significance also because there are a lot of temptations to set our countries against each other. It may cause additional complicating elements in the process of development of Soviet-American relations which is not simple even as it is.

At present there has accumulated a number of big international problems which are under discussion now, and the peoples have been waiting for a long time for their solution in the interests of consolidation of peace.

First. We believe that all possible efforts should be made to have the Treaty on non-proliferation of nuclear weapons start effectively operating. This is a question of war and peace of the future. The Treaty that had been worked out to a considerable degree due to the joint efforts of the USSR and the USA has not been signed yet by a number of states and this, naturally, strengthens the positions of the opponents of the Treaty and casts doubts upon the possibility of solving the problem of non-proliferation. If, however, a number of nuclear states grow the risk of new conflicts will increase with most dangerous consequences for universal peace.

In Moscow, there is readiness to continue consultations with the U.S. Government to work out coordinated measures on securing the signing of the Treaty by a maximum number of states and its earliest entering into force.

Second. It is believed in Moscow that the termination of the war in Vietnam providing the Vietnamese people with the opportunity to solve their internal affairs by themselves without any interference from outside will not only eliminate the most dangerous hotbed of war tension in the world, but also will serve as a convincing proof of a real possibility for settling even most acute and difficult problems. It is hardly doubtful that the political settlement of the Vietnam conflict on the basis of respect for legitimate national aspirations of the people of that country and the complete withdrawal of the American troops from the territory of Vietnam will affect in a most positive way the Soviet-American relations.

The Soviet Government welcomed the beginning of the Paris talks aimed at the political settlement of the Vietnam problem and it thinks that these talks should continue. We would like the talks to bring about positive results. This will be possible, of course, only if there is a realistic appraisal of the political forces acting in Vietnam and the recognition of their right for equal position in the negotiations. If the Paris negotiations develop in such a direction we shall render them all and every support.

Third. Great anxiety is caused by the tense and unsettled situation in the Middle East. We have already presented to President Nixon our views on the causes of the situation created there that may lead to most undesirable consequences not only for the states of this area but far away outside it. The Soviet Government seeking for durable peace and security in this area with due regard for legitimate rights and interests of the Arab states—victims of aggression, put forward a concrete plan for the settlement there which fully corresponds to the spirit and content of the resolution unanimously adopted by the Security Council on November 22, 1967.[2] President Nixon has been informed about this plan.

We proceed from the necessity, on the one hand, that the Arab territories occupied by Israeli troops be liberated, and, on the other hand, that the existence of Israel as an independent state be guaranteed. If the government of Israel considers these principles unacceptable for the political settlement of the conflict then it means that Israel continues to follow aggressive and expansionist aims and remains on an ad-

---

[2] See footnote 4, Document 2.

venturist position. Neither Israel nor anyone else can have any reason to expect that the Arab countries and the states supporting them will agree with such Israeli policy.

We are confident that if the Soviet Union and the United States combining their efforts with the efforts of other states concerned make full use of their possibilities and influence in order to find just and lasting settlement in the Middle East it will also greatly contribute to the general relaxation of international tensions. We are ready for the exchange of views on the bilateral basis with the U.S. Government on the problems of the Middle East with the aim of achieving the necessary agreement on the settlement of the conflict. We said that before. But for some reasons not depending on the Soviet side such exchange of views didn't get due development. We also declare our readiness for the exchange of views on the problems of the Middle East among the four powers—permanent members of the Security Council—the USSR, the USA, France and Great Britain.

Fourth. We are strongly convinced that the following premise has a first-rate importance for the character and prospects of the relations between the USSR and the USA: that is, whether both our countries are ready to proceed in their practical policies from the respect for the foundations of the post-war structure in Europe, formed as a result of the Second World War and the post-war development, and for the basic provisions, formulated by the Allied powers in the well-known Potsdam Agreements. There is no other way to peace in Europe but to take the reality into consideration and to prompt the others to do the same. It's impossible to regard the attempts to undermine the post-war structure in Europe otherwise than an encroachment on the vital interests of our country, of its friends and allies—the socialist countries.

At one time, and in particular in 1959–1963, when the Soviet and U.S. Governments were discussing the complex of German affairs, we were not far apart in understanding of that with regard to some important problems.[3]

The Soviet Union regards with particular watchfulness certain aspects of the development of the F.R.G. and its policy not only because the past German invasion cost us many millions of human lives. President Nixon also understands very well that revanchism begins not when the frontier marks start falling down. That's the finale, the way to which is leading through the attempts to gain an access to the nuclear weapons, through the rehabilitation of the past, through the provocations similar to those which the F.R.G. commits from time to time with regard to West Berlin.

---

[3] Kissinger wrote "what?" in the margin of this paragraph.

It became almost a rule that the F.R.G. stirs up outbursts of tensions around West Berlin, which didn't and doesn't belong to it, involving the Soviet Union, the USA and other countries into complications. It's hardly in anyone's interests to give the F.R.G. such a possibility. Anyhow the Soviet Union can't let the F.R.G. make such provocations.

We would like the President to have complete clearness and confidence that the Soviet Union has no goals in Europe other than the establishment of the solid foundations of security in this part of the world, of the relations of détente between the states of East and West.

Fifth. If we agree that we should aim not at the collision between the USA and the USSR but on the contrary—at the elimination of the war threat, then the containment and curtailing of the arms race and first of all of the rocket—nuclear arms race is necessary. As you know, Mr. President, the stockpiles of nuclear weapons already at the disposal of the USSR and the USA, are more than enough to bring down a catastrophe upon the whole mankind, and this places special responsibility upon the USSR and the USA before all peoples of the world.

A significant step in the field of the containment of the arms race and the reduction of a war threat could be made as it is believed in Moscow through the achievement of an agreement between the USSR and the USA on the limitation and subsequent reduction of strategic arms, both offensive and defensive.

In the course of the exchange of views on this question which has already taken place between the Governments of the USA and the USSR we agreed with the proposal of the American side that the general objectives in this field should be primarily the achievement and maintenance of a stable U.S.-Soviet strategic deterrence by agreeing on limitations on the deployment of offensive and defensive strategic armaments and also the provision of mutual assurance to each of us that our security will be maintained, while at the same time avoiding the tensions, uncertainties and costs of an unrestrained continuation of the strategic arms race.

It was also agreed that the limitation and reduction of the strategic arms should be carried out in complex, including both the systems for delivering offensive strategic weapons and the defensive systems against ballistic missiles, and that the limitation and reduction of these arms should be balanced in such a way that neither side could obtain a military advantage and that the equal security for both sides be assured.

The Soviet Government confirms its readiness to continue the exchange of views with the U.S. Government on the questions of containment of the strategic arms race.

Sixth. It would seem that broad and full-scale relations between the USSR and the USA in the field of international policy should be accompanied by an adequate scope of their bilateral relations. The mutually advantageous potentialities which exist in this area also speak for the development of connections and cooperation between our countries in most various fields, such as science, technology, economy, culture. The extent of the realization of these potentialities depends, of course, on the general political atmosphere in our relations.

If the U.S. Government is of the similar opinion then it could be possible to specifically look upon the opportunities existing now for the further development of the Soviet-American bilateral relations, to determine the succession of things to be done and to proceed with their implementation. As some of the examples, there could be mentioned possibilities for combined efforts in solving urgent problems of medicine, in space research in exploration and exploitation of the World ocean, in creation of the universal satellite communication system, etc.

As a whole, it is possible apparently to speak not only about usefulness but also about real feasibility of a constructive dialogue between the USSR and the USA on the wide range of questions. Indeed, it is in this sense that in Moscow there were taken President Nixon's statements about the vital importance of the relations between the USSR and the USA for the cause of peace and general security, about the necessity to eliminate a possibility of military conflict between our countries and about the preparedness for negotiations with the USSR at all levels.

The thoughts on the above mentioned questions as well as on other questions which President Nixon may wish to express will be considered in Moscow with full attention.

16.   Memorandum From the Acting Deputy Assistant Secretary of State for European Affairs (Toon) to the President's Assistant for National Security Affairs (Kissinger)[1]

Washington, February 18, 1969.

You have asked for my personal assessment of the meeting today with Dobrynin.[2] The following views represent precisely that—my personal assessment—and I have not discussed them with any of my principals here.

1. What Dobrynin told the President privately is extremely important. What he had to say to the President was clearly the considered view of the collective leadership—not just Kosygin but Brezhnev and Podgorny as well.

2. His remarks indicated clearly that the leadership is anxious to press on with the missile talks. This may be because they are under considerable pressure to assign more resources to the military if in fact we go ahead with our ABM program. They may hope by an early start of the missile talks to delay decisions here and thus to cope with the pressures on them from their own military.

3. It is obvious that the leadership was intrigued with the President's reference to "negotiations, not confrontation" but is uneasy as to the real meaning of linkage between arms control talks and political issues. The Soviets may have suspected that the President, by his reference to linkage, was reverting to the posture of the early Eisenhower years when we attempted to condition progress in arms control on the German issue. I think as a result of the conversation today the Soviets now have a clearer understanding as to the President's view—i.e., that progress on Viet Nam and on the Middle East or lack of progress in these areas must inevitably influence what is possible in the arms control field.

4. On Viet Nam, it seems to me that Dobrynin was trying to make clear that we must deal with the NLF if there is to be any progress at Paris.

5. On Berlin, I think the President's remarks were useful in that they conveyed to Dobrynin our concern lest tough action by the East Germans result in a nasty situation and a confrontation with us. I am

---

[1] Source: National Archives, RG 59, Central Files 1967–69, POL 1 US–USSR. Secret; Nodis. In a covering memorandum for the record, Toon wrote, "After consultation with Mr. Kissinger and Mr. Ziegler, I called Dobrynin to inform him that the White House would make a brief statement on his call on the President, identifying the participants in the meeting, and indicating that the meeting was a constructive one. I told Dobrynin that there would be no reference to the fact that Ambassador had met privately with the President."

[2] The meeting was on February 17; see Document 14.

not sure, however, that Dobrynin understands clearly that a blow-up in Berlin would seriously affect the outcome of NPT as well as our own decision to proceed with missile talks. Perhaps we should follow this up with a further meeting in the Department, probably toward the end of the President's tour when we may have a clear understanding as to the action contemplated by the other side. My own view is that there will not be serious problems around Berlin until the President departs that city but that we can probably expect unpleasantness immediately after his departure.

Since it is widely known that Dobrynin called on the President and because of the traditional suspicion on the part of our Allies as to what goes on between us, I think it important for us to get the President's permission to summarize the talk in the NAC or at least convey a summary to the more important of our Allies on a more restricted basis.[3]

Hastily

Mac

---

[3] On February 22, the Department sent telegram 28290 to Harlan Cleveland, U.S. Permanent Representative on the Council of the North Atlantic Treaty Organization, authorizing Cleveland "to convey to NAC at earliest opportunity following highlights of conversation between President and Dobrynin." A summary of the meeting followed. (National Archives, RG 59, Central Files 1967–69, POL US–USSR)

---

17.   Memorandum From the President's Assistant for National Security Affairs (Kissinger) to President Nixon[1]

Washington, February 18, 1969.

SUBJECT

Analysis of Dobrynin Message

1. I am attaching the memorandum of conversation with Dobrynin (Tab A)[2] as well as the analysis of the note-taker and a member of my staff (Tab B).[3] They did not see the note.[4]

---

[1] Source: National Archives, Nixon Presidential Materials, NSC Files, Box 340, Subject Files, USSR Memcons Dobrynin/President 2/17/69. Secret; Sensitive; Eyes Only. Sent for information.

[2] Attached and printed as Document 14.

[3] Attached and printed as Document 16.

[4] Document 15.

2. My reaction to the note is as follows:

a. The tone of the document is extraordinarily forthcoming. The Soviet approach is, as far as I can see, totally non-ideological—even anti-ideological. The arguments are posed strictly in terms of national interests and mutually perceived threats, without even the usual ritual obeisance to Marxist-Leninist jargon.

b. The document advances the dialogue between the Soviet Union and the United States beyond mere détente and into the realm of overt Soviet-American cooperation in the solution of outstanding international problems and the maintenance of peace.

3. The gist of the paper is that the Soviets are prepared to move forward on a whole range of topics: Middle East, Central Europe, Vietnam, Arms Control (strategic arms talks), cultural exchange. In other words, we have the "linkage." Our problem is how to play it.

4. The document is vague about specific proposals. However, the following aspects deserve mention:

Vietnam. There is no reference to the usual Soviet claims of American aggression. They ask for "equal position" for all parties in the negotiating. We could probe what they mean.

Middle East. The document links Israeli withdrawal to a guaranteed existence for Israel. These are not posed as successive actions; rather they appear parts of a negotiated settlement, to be enforced by the sanctions of the Great Powers. Of course the Soviet statement leaves many loose ends, such as navigation rights in Suez, freedom of the Straits of Tiran, refugee problems, etc., but if one wishes to place the most generous possible construction on the Soviet statement, one could conclude that these points would follow agreement on the two basic tenets. Here, as in the case of Vietnam, there is great vagueness on specifics, but a positive tone of accommodation and mutual interest. It also offers specific negotiations.

European Settlement. Here the statement comes close to offering a deal recognizing the status quo. There is not the slightest mention of the Brezhnev doctrine of "Socialist sovereignty"[5]—presumably because the Soviets reason it applies only within their half of Europe, which we would agree must not be disturbed. They add a particularly clear expression of Soviet disinterest in further expansion in Europe and hope for détente. They add that we were close to agreement in 1959–63. We might probe what they have in mind.

---

[5] A term applied in the West to the Soviet justification for its occupation of Czechoslovakia in August 1968. In a speech on November 11, 1968, Brezhnev declared that a threat to Socialist rule in any state of the East European bloc constituted a threat to all and therefore "must engage the attention of all the Socialist states."

SALT. The line of seeking limitation and subsequent reduction of strategic arms, both defensive and offensive, has been used before, but not, so far as I know, advanced so strongly in the context of "mutual assurance that our security will be maintained." As they have repeated often before, the Soviets here reiterate their readiness to sit down to talk as soon as we wish.

5. The question then is what the Soviets are up to. There are two schools of thought.

The first is based on the notion that while the US-Soviet relationship is basically antagonistic and competitive, there are many areas where our interests overlap and where there is opportunity for at least tacit cooperation. The main common interest is in survival and, hence, in the prevention of war. This common interest, in turn, is held to make arms control a central issue in US-Soviet relations since the arms race is seen as a major source of potential conflict. Consequently, in this approach every effort should be made to engage the Soviets in negotiations wherever common interests occur, and especially on arms control. Moreover, every effort must be made to insulate these areas of common interests from those areas where our interests clash. It is argued, indeed, that arms control talks, even if they are not immediately successful, can serve as a firebreak to prevent confrontations from getting out of hand and spilling over into our whole relationship. It is fair to say that these are the principles on which the last Administration sought to operate, though it recognize, of course, there are limits beyond which a compartmentalization of our relations with the USSR became infeasible and counter-productive. (The invasion of Czechoslovakia was one of the limiting points.)

A rather different approach is one that holds that an excessively selective policy runs into the danger that the Soviets will use the bait of progress in one area in order to neutralize our resistance to pressure elsewhere. It holds that precisely because we remain in an antagonistic relationship the erection of firebreaks may encourage the Soviets to be more adventurous. Moreover, in this view, there is an essential connection between crises and confrontations; unless there is progress on a fairly broad front to mitigate confrontations, there is little prospect of real reduction in tensions. This view also holds that arms per se rarely cause wars (at least as long as they are kept in relative balance) and that the arms control agreements that have been reached have had singularly little effect in reducing areas of conflict and confrontation.

My own view tends toward the latter approach, and I might add that the Soviets, with their Marxist training, have little difficulty in grasping its meaning—although they have become quite skilled in conducting a policy of selective tension and selective accommodation.

I believe the current Soviet line of conciliation and interest in negotiations, especially on arms control but also on the Middle East, stems in large measure from their uncertainty about the plans of this Administration. They are clearly concerned that you may elect to undertake new weapons programs which would require new and costly decisions in Moscow; they hope that early negotiations would at least counteract such tendencies in Washington. (I doubt that there is much division on this point in the Kremlin, though there may well be substantial ones over the actual terms of an agreement with us.) In a nutshell, I think that at this moment of uncertainty about our intentions (the Soviets see it as a moment of contention between "reasonable" and "adventurous" forces here), Moscow wants to engage us. Some would argue that regardless of motive, we should not let this moment of Soviet interest pass, lest Moscow swing back to total hostility. My own view is that we should seek to utilize this Soviet interest, stemming as I think it does from anxiety, to induce them to come to grips with the real sources of tension, notably in the Middle East, but also in Vietnam. This approach also would require continued firmness on our part in Berlin.

---

18.   **Paper Prepared for the National Security Council by the Interdepartmental Group for Europe**[1]

Washington, February 18, 1969.

EAST-WEST RELATIONS

I. U.S.-Soviet Relationships

Despite our intensive efforts to analyze and understand Soviet behavior, we are still far from a complete understanding of how major

---

[1] Source: National Archives, Nixon Presidential Materials, NSC Files, NSC Institutional Files (H-Files), Box H–020, NSC Meeting, Strategic Issues—East/West Relations 2/19/69. Confidential. Sent under a February 18 covering memorandum from Richard M. Moose of the National Security Council staff to the Vice President, Secretary of State, Secretary of Defense, Director of OEP, Chairman of the Joint Chiefs of Staff, Director of Central Intelligence, and the Under Secretary of State. The memorandum stated that "The NSC Meeting on Wednesday, February 19, will be devoted to continuation of a discussion of Strategic Issues and—time permitting—to a discussion of East-West Relations." The minutes of the meeting do not include the latter topic. This paper on East-West Relations was a response to Document 6 and reflected revisions from the NSC Review Group. No record of a Review Group meeting discussing it has been found. A 3-page summary was also prepared for the NSC. (Ibid., Box H–109, NSC Meeting, Strategic Issues—East/West Relations 2/19/69)

foreign policy decisions are made in the Soviet Union or how our own behavior influences Soviet decisions. Moreover, in seeking to characterize the nature of the Soviet-American relationship, we are confronted with difficult problems of evaluating our own, as well as Soviet, interests in various parts of the world. Because of these uncertainties, a number of different views exist as to the most appropriate way to characterize Soviet-American relations as a guide to U.S. policy. There appear to be, however, three basic alternative views of the Soviet-American relation.

1. Mutual Antagonism with Minimal Cooperation

Those who take this approach emphasize the basic ideological hostility between the U.S. and the Soviet Union. They point to the Soviet invasion of Czechoslovakia, the Brezhnev Doctrine of Limited Sovereignty,[2] and the Soviet assertion of special rights to intervene in Germany,[3] as evidence that no form of major accommodation with the Soviet Union is likely to be achievable. They believe that the Soviets are primarily interested in spreading their own influence and in undermining the influence and prestige of the United States.

Western military strength and the cohesion of the NATO alliance is emphasized by proponents of this view. They would view measures such as the Non-Proliferation Treaty as a Soviet effort to split the alliance and as a move that weakens NATO flexibility in nuclear arrangements. Proponents of this view would urge other nations in the world to refrain from diplomatic relations and trade and aid relationships with the Soviet Union. They would urge American military assistance programs where necessary to prevent (or, at least, parallel and thereby hope to counterbalance) Soviet involvement, for example, in India and Pakistan or Nigeria.

Those who hold this position accept the fact that the United States and the Soviet Union share an overriding concern with preventing a nuclear war. Some of them argue that this interest is essentially self-regulated in that both sides pull back before a nuclear confrontation. Others hold that the Soviets use mutual fear to make us flinch in face of pressure. However, they do not believe that meaningful agreements even on nuclear matters can be based on this common interest. Specifically they are highly suspicious of efforts to negotiate arms control arguing that the Soviets will use arms control negotiations as a cover for their aggressive political behavior and use arms control agreements as a way of catching up to the United States or even lulling it into accepting inferiority.

---

[2] See footnote 5, Document 17.

[3] See footnote 2, Document 8.

2. Détente

Advocates of this position tend to emphasize common Soviet-American interests. They argue that despite Soviet rhetoric, ideology is no longer the basic motivating factor in Soviet external behavior and that both countries have an interest in maintaining the status quo in Central Europe. They believe that both have limited interests in the rest of the world, and emphasize the need to avoid a confrontation with each other.

Proponents of this view would emphasize efforts at Soviet-American accommodation. They would have pushed forward efforts at a Non-Proliferation Treaty with less regard than was shown for the concerns of our allies. They would seek to negotiate arrangements with the Russians in such areas as the Middle East and India and Pakistan even though such agreements might pave the way for increased Soviet involvement and influence in those areas.

While recognizing the need for a military deterrent against the Soviet Union, proponents of this view would urge a scaling down of our own efforts on the grounds that this could lead to Soviet reciprocation, and would not threaten our security.

In considering these two options, the Review Group believed that neither of them was an adequate basis for policy. The first option understates the possibilities for agreement with the Soviet Union and the extent to which there is a perception of at least certain limited common interests between the two countries. The Group, at the same time, felt that Soviet policy and behavior had not yet evolved—if it ever will—to the point that the second option could now be a basis for policy. Thus, the Group felt that the only realistic choice was a third option—which is essentially the one successive U.S. Administrations have taken—with the real differences of view arising within the scope of that approach. This middle option may be described as follows:

3. Limited Adversary Relationship (Strong Deterrent with Flexible Approach)

This view is based on the assumption that there will continue to be an underlying hostility between the United States and the Soviet Union. This hostility arises in part from the continuing Soviet commitment to an ideology which supports their wish to see the world evolve in a way radically different from our own preferences. The hostility also derives from clashes on political issues primarily involving clashes of interest in the Middle East and elsewhere.

At the same time there are elements of shared concerns which make possible certain kinds of accommodation. The dominant common interests is in avoiding a nuclear war. This requires active Soviet-American collaboration to damp down potentially explosive situations in the Middle East, in the Indian sub-continent and elsewhere. Reduction of the likelihood of a nuclear clash would also be enhanced by arms control arrangements seeking to limit and then reduce strategic forces on both sides.

Proponents of this view agree that a strong U.S. nuclear deterrent and a continuing strong NATO are necessary in order not to tempt the Soviets into military or diplomatic adventures.

U.S.-Soviet interests and relations in the third world area seen as partly competitive and partly cooperative. In some cases, such as most of Africa, both Soviet and American interests are sufficiently modest that neither we nor they are fundamentally concerned about the role of the other. In other cases, as in the Middle East, we have competing interests, but these are mixed with a common desire not to permit others to drag us into a direct confrontation.

The Review Group noted that while there appears to be a consensus among officials working on Soviet-American problems on this broad view of U.S.-Soviet relations, there is a wide spectrum of differences both about specific issues and about general policy lines. Although views fall across the entire spectrum, it is possible to characterize two distinct policy emphases consistent with the limited adversary perspective of the U.S.-Soviet relationship.

II. Alternative Policy Approach Based on Limited Adversary Relationship

1. Emphasis on Accommodation While Maintaining the Deterrent

Advocates of this position would emphasize the search for accommodation with the Soviet Union while maintaining the U.S. deterrent.

They would argue that negotiation of a strategic arms control agreement with the Soviet Union is sufficiently important that a major effort should be made to insulate the search for such an agreement from other political issues, while acknowledging that major Soviet threats and acts of aggression such as the invasion of Czechoslovakia create a climate in which strategic talks could not go forward. They would argue that the current climate in which we are talking to the Russians about the Middle East and in which they appear to be cooperative about seeking a Vietnam settlement is a sufficient basis for proceeding with talks.

With regard to possible conflict between allied concerns and negotiations with the Soviet, advocates of this position would argue that although we would consult with our allies, we should not permit them to have a veto on our actions provided we ourselves are convinced they are consistent with allied interests. The U.S. posture during the Non-Proliferation Treaty negotiations, in essence, followed the pattern recommended by this Group in contrast to others who argued that we did not pay sufficient attention to allied concerns.

Those who take this approach view the third world as an area for substantially greater Soviet-American cooperation than has been the case. They would emphasize the virtual absence of vital Soviet or American interests in most, if not all, of the third world. According to this approach no effort would be made to discourage other countries from increasing their contacts, both political and economic, with the Soviets since such contacts would be viewed as largely inevitable and in many cases as potentially helpful. In the Middle East, for example, an effort would be made to work out a Soviet-American understanding even if this involved pressure by each on its allies and even if it appeared to sanction a major Soviet role in the area.

U.S. relations with Eastern Europe and with China would at least to some degree be subordinated to concerns about Soviet reaction. Thus, we would not seek to frighten the Soviets with the prospect of a Chinese-American rapprochement and would counsel our allies to be sensitive to Soviet concerns in their dealing with Eastern Europe.

2. Emphasis on Deterrence While Seeking Limited Accommodation

Advocates of this view would emphasize the continuing areas of hostility with the Soviets and the need to take these fully into account in designing possible measures of accommodation.

Following this approach we would insist upon greater progress in political areas before being prepared to move ahead with strategic talks and we would not proceed with such talks until our allies have been fully consulted and had given their agreement to proceeding even if this procedure should impose substantial delays.

Efforts to improve relations with the Soviet Union in general would proceed only after full allied consultation. We would be concerned not only with our perception of allied interests but their own perception of these interests as well. For example, proponents of this position would have taken much greater account of the German argument that the Non-Proliferation Treaty was essentially a Soviet effort aimed at obtaining concessions from Germany without reciprocal Soviet concessions to the Federal Republic.

In the third world this approach would emphasize continuing competition while not excluding areas of possible accommodation. Thus, in many areas of the world we would urge governments to reduce or at least not expand their contacts with the Soviets and warn against the dangers of accepting Soviet aid. Without ruling out joint efforts to damp down areas such as the Middle East we would keep conflicting Soviet-American interests in the area very much in mind and perhaps make an effort to devise settlements which reduce Soviet influence.

In the case of relations with China and Eastern Europe we would proceed with whatever actions seem justified on their own merits, with secondary consideration to the possibility that we would antagonize the Soviet Union. We might introduce deliberate ambiguity in our policies designed to increase Soviet apprehensions.

III. Specific Issues

Although a number of officials would quite consistently advocate one of these two policy approaches, most officials have views somewhere in between; and differences arise with regard to specific matters of style as well as specific policy issues. The Review Group felt that differences on several questions were particularly worthy of attention. These include:

(1) The question of whether useful political progress with the Soviets is made by increasing Soviet concerns or providing them with reassurance, e.g. with regard to China and Eastern Europe.

(2) The relative priority to be given to efforts at accommodation with the Soviets versus efforts at strengthening the NATO alliance and fully consulting with our allies.

(3) Policy toward countries in the third world.

(4) The advantages and disadvantages of relating arms control negotiations to other political issues.

1. Possibilities for Political Progress with the Soviet Union

The essential argument here is whether or not progress on political issues with the Soviet Union is more likely if we provide assurances to the Soviets, or if we seek to increase their sense of concern by raising the possibility that we will act in ways contrary to their interests unless they come to some agreement with us. The dispute arises in part from our imperfect understanding of Soviet decision-making and the forces which determine Soviet behavior.

In dealing with the Soviet Union should we generally emphasize reassurance about our intentions?

Arguments for:

(1) Such reassurance would accurately reflect our motives since we are not out to challenge basic Soviet national interests.

(2) Progress on major issues will be possible only through mutual understanding that in certain areas neither side will seek to undercut the other.

(3) Deliberately fostering Soviet concern about our intentions may increase the danger of misunderstandings and possible conflicts.

(4) U.S. pressures could play into the hands of the more hostile elements in the Soviet Union. We could generate counter-pressures that will be contrary to our objectives.

Arguments against:

(1) It is a bad negotiating tactic generally to reassure the other side. We could appear overeager for agreements and over-ready to make concessions.

(2) The Soviets are likely to make concessions only if they are confronted with alternatives which they perceive to be considerably worse.

This general issue arises in a number of specific forms. For example, some argue that Soviet cooperation on Far East matters, including Vietnam, depends on convincing the Russians that we are not seeking to a deal behind their backs with the Chinese. It is suggested that the Russians' primary concern is limiting Chinese influence in the area and that they are reluctant to deal with us as they fear that we may expose our contacts with them in an effort to seek an understanding with the Chinese. Others argue that only the fear of a Chinese-American rapprochement will lead the Russians to be cooperative in the Far East. European policy encounters the same difference of opinion. Will progress come from assuring the Russians that we have no inimical designs on Eastern Europe, or will it come from U.S. support of tendencies toward autonomy and liberalization in Eastern Europe? Another area where this general issue arises is arms negotiations. For example, should we proceed with deployment of an ABM system as a bargaining counter in order to induce the Soviets to negotiate in earnest? Or should we reassure the Soviets by holding up deployment?

2. Accommodation vs. Deterrence

All advocates of a limited adversary relationship favor a combination of deterrence and accommodation. They disagree on the relative emphasis to be put on each. There are two central issues: atmospherics and allied consultation.

a. Should we emphasize an atmosphere of accommodation with the Soviets?

Arguments for:

(1) Agreement to cultural exchanges with the Soviets and employment of a positive style and tone in our statements generally improves the political atmosphere and lessens tension.

(2) Such a framework makes it easier for the Soviets and our own public to accept political agreements which are in our mutual interest.

Arguments against:

(1) Atmospherics are essentially irrelevant; concrete actions are what count.

(2) Such atmospherics may be harmful since the Soviets will feel less need for agreements (as sanction for their actions) if they detect a general sense of détente.

(3) Excessive emphasis on an atmosphere of accommodation could generate false euphoria in the U.S. and allied countries, making it more difficult to obtain public acceptance in our country and among our allies of burdens of defense and alliance cohesion.

b. Should we have full allied consent before proceeding to major agreements with the Russians?

Arguments for:

(1) We should not jeopardize relations with our allies who may be suspicious of our motives and fear a U.S.-Soviet "condominium" at their expense.

(2) Failure to get our allies on board would make many agreements with the Soviets unstable at best.

(3) Complete cooperation in advance with our allies would make it much harder for the Soviets to drive wedges between us and our friends.

(4) Being forthcoming with our allies on our relations with the Soviets should encourage our allies to be more helpful to us on other issues.

Arguments against:

(1) Our allies are split, with some favoring an emphasis on accommodation and others opposing it. It is extremely difficult to reconcile the interests and opinions of fourteen diverse nations and achieve consensus.

(2) Attempting to obtain full consent of our allies will greatly complicate our negotiations with the Soviets and slow down progress.

(3) Our allies do not give us a veto on their own dealings with the Soviet Union on Eastern Europe. They really desire only a decent respect for their views, not a decisive voice in our own policies.

(4) While our allies will always complain and interpose objections if we ask them, they are prepared to see us go ahead with the Soviets, provided we do not ask them to share the onus for our actions.

3. Policy Towards Third World

All of those who accept the basic option of a limited adversary relationship believe that in some third world areas Soviet involvement is not sufficiently detrimental to U.S. interests that we should seek actively to combat it, and all agree that we should seek limited understandings with the Soviets in some cases.

There are, however, differences in regard to the general presumptions of U.S. policy.

Should we generally oppose Soviet involvement in the third world and advise other countries to avoid increased aid and trade relations?

Arguments for:

(1) Greater Soviet involvement will come at the expense of U.S. or allied influence and will erode support in the third world for our various policies.

(2) Larger Soviet influence in the third world could threaten specific U.S. interests such as treaty relationships, base arrangements, trade positions, investment prospects, etc.

(3) The larger the Soviet presence in the third world, the greater the chance for direct confrontation with us through conflict of interest or miscalculation.

(4) Soviet presence in, or assistance to, third world nations is self-serving and is unlikely to contribute to our general objective of the orderly political and economic development of the poor nations.

Arguments against:

(1) Increased Soviet involvement in the third world is natural and inevitable for a great power.

(2) In most cases there is little that we can do to counter greater Soviet involvement. Attempting to oppose it only causes strains both with the Soviet Union and with third world countries.

(3) The poorer nations need all the assistance they can get from industrialized nations. Soviet involvement serves to lessen our economic burdens.

(4) Cooperation with, rather than opposition to, the Soviets in the third world can prevent misunderstandings. Furthermore, it could help to improve our overall bilateral relationships, increase mutual trust, and make it easier to reach agreements on more fundamental questions such as Europe on security and arms control.

(5) Soviet influence can help to counter what we consider even more inimical influences in certain areas of the world, e.g., China in Asia or Cuba in Latin America.

We must weight these various considerations in choosing whether to: (a) generally oppose Soviet involvement in the third world; (b) generally welcome, or at least acquiesce in, such involvement; or (c) not adopt any general policy line and treat each issue on its merits.

4. Arms Control and Political Matters[4]

a. Should we establish an explicit relationship between arms control matters and political matters?

---

[4] This section repeats the discussion previously included in the Strategic Balance Paper. The section is more extensive than those dealing with other issues because the subject has been more fully considered in the meetings of the Review Group. [Footnote

Arguments for:

(1) Strategic arms limitations, unlike previous arms control agreements, go to the very heart of our security interests. It is unrealistic to expect both sides to agree to and abide by an agreement while basic issues such as Berlin and the Middle East which could lead to a direct U.S.-Soviet confrontation continue to fester. The U.S. should not be prepared to cooperate with the Soviets on some matters while they are seeking to build their influence at our expense.

(2) Arms control agreements, at least in the past, have not led to détente and have on occasion preceded Soviet moves which increased tension (e.g., Test Ban followed by Soviet involvement in Vietnam). The Soviets may believe the arms control agreements take the risk out of lower level pressures and conflicts.

(3) Arms competition, on the other hand, does not preclude political cooperation and relative détente, and Soviet-American arms competition itself has not contributed markedly to the danger of war.

(4) The Soviets have in the past used arms talks as political and psychological regulators; we should not permit them to do so. The Soviets may be hoping that the talks on strategic arms will slow our programs while they proceed with their own buildup. If we want a satisfactory agreement and political cooperation, we should not appear too eager for negotiations.

(5) Unless the Soviets change their conduct, particularly in regard to Berlin and Germany, our allies will view arms control negotiations as an indication that we consider our relations with the Soviets paramount and are willing to sell out their interests.

Arguments against:

(1) Negotiations with the Soviet Union on limiting strategic weapons are matters of the highest political importance in contrast to previous arms control matters and can create the climate for successful negotiations on other political matters.

(2) The common Soviet-American interests in reducing the likelihood of nuclear war is so widely perceived and accepted not only in the United States and the Soviet Union but throughout the world that the necessary political consensus to effect such agreements can be obtained even in the absence of negotiations on other issues. Provided we consult with them in advance and obtain a limit on Soviet

---

in the source text. A 21-page paper on "Strategic Policy Issues" was prepared for the NSC meeting on February 19. (National Archives, Nixon Presidential Materials, NSC Files, NSC Institutional Files (H-Files), Box H–020, NSC Meeting, Strategic Issues—East/West Relations 2/19/69)]

MR/IRBMs, our allies will not view the agreement as contrary to their interests.

(3) While the current Soviet leadership is clearly anxious for the talks to begin, there are many in the Soviet leadership who oppose the talks and who will take efforts by the U.S. to link the talks with other political matters as an effort at political blackmail. Even the majority group which favors the talks appears to believe that they are in the interest of both countries and they are unlikely to make political concessions to get the talks started.

(4) There is a significant possibility of negotiating an arms control agreement which both reduces the likelihood of general war and freezes the current relative strategic force postures. Because the Soviets believe that they will have to spend very large sums to prevent us from increasing our advantage, they may be prepared to accept a freeze. These two objectives—reducing the likelihood of general war and freezing our relative strategic force postures—are matters of the highest political importance which should be pursued immediately whether or not negotiations on other political matters are going forward.

b. If we decide to emphasize the connection between arms control and other issues, what form should it take?

There are several possibilities:

(1) Insist on only a very general linkage such that major aggressive acts rule out strategic talks. This was the policy of the previous administration in declining to go forward with the talks after the Soviet invasion of Czechoslovakia. The Soviet's willingness to proceed may also have depended on the halting of the bombing of Hanoi by the United States.

The arguments for this position are essentially the same as the arguments against establishing any linkage at all with the added point that certain very major events can so affect the domestic and foreign political climate as to make talks inadvisable.

(2) Insist that discussions on arms control and other political matters proceed in parallel. This would mean that we would have preliminary arms control talks as we have preliminary talks on other matters such as Vietnam and the Middle East; that we would proceed to serious negotiations about detailed substantive positions only if we proceeded to such negotiations on other political matters and that we would sign agreements only if Soviet behavior in regard to other issues was reasonably cooperative. Under this approach we would need to decide whether the current discussions with the Soviet Union on Vietnam and the Middle East were sufficient to justify corollary discussions on strategic talks or whether we would want to have discussions on other political matters underway or see changes in Soviet conduct.

The arguments for this position are essentially the arguments for a linkage listed above with the following added points:

—discussions proceeding in parallel are sufficient to create the necessary climate of negotiation rather than confrontation to permit arms control talks to go forward successfully.

—the successful negotiation of agreements on matters such as the Middle East and Vietnam depend largely on matters beyond the control of either the United States and the Soviet Union. Thus, the test should be our judgment that the Soviets are using their influence in a constructive way and not whether agreements can in fact be reached with all the parties.

(3) Insist upon concluding successful negotiations on other matters before opening arms control talks.

The arguments for this position are:

—Arms control agreements do not in themselves reduce the likelihood of war. In the absence of a political settlement, they are mere gimmickery.

—Following a political settlement, arms control agreements can and should be negotiated in an effort to reduce budgets.

---

19.   Talking Points Prepared by the National Security Council Staff for President Nixon[1]

Washington, February 19, 1969.

EAST-WEST RELATIONS

Opening

1. It is particularly timely to discuss this subject:

—my upcoming European trip.
—Middle East explorations with the Soviets.
—the possibility of strategic talks with the Soviets.
—possible heating up of the Berlin situation.

2. We might focus the discussion on:

—What is the most realistic characterization of the US-Soviet relationship?

---

[1] Source: Library of Congress, Manuscript Division, Kissinger Papers, CL 312, Meetings, National Security Council, February–March, 1969. Confidential. Similar talking points were also prepared for Kissinger. (Ibid.) Time did not permit discussion of East-West relations at the NSC meeting on February 19.

—What US policy emphases should flow from this characterization?

—What should I stress on my European trip?

—What are the implications of relating strategic talks to progress on other political issues?

3. You may wish to highlight your conversation with Ambassador Dobrynin.

Briefing

If time permits, Dick Helms is ready with a 15-minute briefing on trends in the Soviet leadership as they affect Soviet foreign policy.

Discussion

1. Call on Dr. Kissinger to lead off the discussion.

2. Secretary Rogers may wish to give his general views.

Conclusion

You may wish to conclude the meeting by presenting to the NSC your views on East-West relations based on the talking points on the next page.

Additional Studies

You may wish to direct additional studies on:

A. Policy Toward Eastern Europe.

B. East-West relations as an issue in NATO and in our relations with major allies.

C. Policy guidelines, including difficulties, for implementing the approach of linking strategic talks to political matters.

D. The U.S.-Soviet-Chinese triangular relationship.

Attachment[2]

Washington, undated.

MASTER TALKING PAPER ON EAST-WEST RELATIONS

(All the leaders you are meeting are interested in your view of East-West relations and in your plans for dealing with the USSR. Several have asked about our "conception." Europeans have conflicting worries: on the one hand they fear our dealing with the Soviets behind their backs ("condominium"); on the other, they worry that we might

---

[2] Secret.

draw them into excessive risks and load on them responsibilities that they are not prepared to carry. Lately, they have wondered about the significance and implications of your public statements connecting missile talks with progress on other issues. Among some, who sense a big US push for across-the-board settlements with the USSR, these statements have raised the condominium spectre. The Europeans also want to know how we propose to consult with them on East-West matters generally, and on missile talks particularly. The French, especially, would like to engage in bilateral consultations rather than through NATO. The others want to consult through NATO but maintain bilateral channels as well. None of them want us to make formal proposals to the Soviets on arms control without having been consulted. The Germans and, to a lesser degree, the Italians have painful memories of the early NPT negotiations in which they feel, justifiably, that they were confronted with a fait accompli.)

I. Our Basic Approach.

A. We have said that we are entering an era of negotiation. We see this as a complex and extended process and recognize that there will remain substantial elements of confrontation.

B. By negotiation we mean a serious engagement of the issues, not simply meetings for meetings' sake. In general, we believe that high-level or other official conferences with the Soviets should be well prepared in advance and should offer promise of concrete progress.

C. We think the allies should attempt to concert their approaches as much as possible; Soviet incentive to negotiate seriously is reduced if they think they can maneuver among the allies and divide them.

D. In negotiating we want to proceed on a basis of a sense of military security. I have used the word "sufficiency": in its broadest sense, this means forces that are strong and varied enough to deter not only Soviet attack but also gross pressures which the Soviets might be tempted to try if they calculated that confidence in our capabilities and resolve was eroding. But neither in what we say nor what we do, would we want to force the pace of armaments.

II. Relationship Between Arms Talks and Political Issues.

A. Wars and crises generally result not from the level of arms—not, at least, when these levels are in relative balance—but from clashing interests, ambitions, and purposes. For this reason I am skeptical about singling out arms as an exclusive subject for negotiation.

B. Indeed, at various times in Western relations with the East, the Soviets have tended to use the bait of arms talks, or actual talks, as a means of regulating crises they themselves created. (Examples: abortive disarmament talks after Hungary, early exchanges on non-proliferation in the midst of the Cuban missile crisis, etc.)

C. Moreover, it is difficult to get public understanding for arms talks at moments of crisis (e.g., the invasion of Czechoslovakia had negative impact on NPT and on feasibility of opening SALT talks).

D. In addition, the problem of strategic weapons goes to the core of the security of ourselves and our allies (and, for that matter of the Soviets); it cannot therefore be isolated from the other great issues that impinge on security and peace.

E. We are not establishing rigid linkages between arms control and other issues. But we do believe that there has to be progress in coping with the volatile issues (notably the Middle East and Vietnam) before one can get very far on strategic weapons. We recognize that the Soviets are not controlling factors in these situations; but they do have influence and we know that at various times that influence has been exerted in directions away from, rather than toward, settlements. If that were to happen again it would not be compatible with progress on arms control.

III. Consultations with Allies.

A. We seek intimate concert with our allies on anything as crucial to the interests of all of us as the control of strategic weapons.

B. We have no rigid feelings about the means and the forum.

C. We know that different allies may approach the issues from different vantage points. We want to give these full weight.

D. We will make no proposal to the Soviets unless we have first discussed them with the allies.

E. If negotiations should get underway, there will be a practical problem of consultation. What suggestions do the Europeans have?

F. We assume the allies will take the same approach to consultation in connection with their own negotiations with the USSR.

20.   Memorandum From the President's Assistant for National Security Affairs (Kissinger) to the Acting Executive Secretary of the Department of State (Walsh)[1]

Washington, February 21, 1969.

SUBJECT

  Circular Guidance to all Mission Chiefs on Administration's Approach to East-West Relations

Please circularize our Mission Chiefs abroad along the following lines:

1. The President plans to explain his general approach to East-West relations in the course of his conversations with European leaders.[2]

2. President will draw on following points, of which Mission Chiefs should be aware for their own guidance and conversations on this subject:

Basic Approach:

1. We have said that we are entering an era of negotiation. We see this as a complex and extended process and recognize that there will remain substantial elements of confrontation.

2. By negotiation, we mean a serious engagement of the issues, not simply meetings for meetings' sake. In general, we believe that high-level or other official conferences with the Soviets should be well prepared in advance and should offer promise of concrete progress.

3. We think the allies should attempt to concert their approaches as much as possible; Soviet incentive to negotiate seriously is reduced if they think that they can maneuver among the allies and divide them.

4. In negotiating, we want to proceed on a basis of sense of military security. We have used the word "sufficiency" in its broadest sense; this means forces that are strong and varied enough to deter not only Soviet attack but also gross pressures which the Soviets might be tempted to try if they calculated that confidence in our capabilities and resolve was eroding. But neither in what we say nor what we do, would we want to force the pace of armaments.

---

[1] Source: National Archives, Nixon Presidential Materials, NSC Files, Box 340, Subject Files, USSR Memcons Dobrynin/President 2/17/69. Secret.

[2] On February 23 Nixon left for an 8-day visit to Europe; texts of remarks made on various occasions during his trip are in Department of State *Bulletin*, March 24, 1969, pp. 249–271.

Relationship between Arms Talks and Political Issues:

1. Wars and crises generally result not from the level of arms—not, at least, when these levels are in relative balance—but from clashing interests, ambitions, and purposes. For this reason, we are skeptical about singling out arms as an exclusive subject for negotiation.

2. Indeed, at various times in Western relations with the East, the Soviets have tended to use the bait of arms talks, or actual talks, as a means of regulating crises they themselves created. (Examples: abortive disarmament talks after Hungary, early exchanges on non-proliferation in the midst of the Cuban missile crisis, etc.)

3. Moreover, it is difficult to get public understanding for arms talks at moments of crisis (e.g., the invasion of Czechoslovakia had negative impact on NPT and on feasibility of opening SALT talks).

4. In addition, the problem of strategic weapons goes to the core of the security of ourselves and our allies (and, for that matter of the Soviets); it cannot therefore be isolated from the other great issues that impinge on security and peace.

5. We are not establishing rigid linkages between arms control and other issues. But we do believe there has to be progress in coping with the volatile issues (notably the Middle East and Vietnam) before one can get very far on strategic weapons.

6. We recognize the Soviets are not controlling factors in these situations; but they do have influence and we know that at various times that influence has been exerted in directions away from, rather than toward, settlements. If that were to happen again, it would not be compatible with progress on arms control.

Our policy on consultations with other governments, especially allies, is broadly as follows:

We will consult intimately on anything as crucial to the interests of other governments as the control of strategic weapons. More generally, we will consult on subjects that plainly affect the interests of other governments because we wish to give full weight to the points of view of other governments concerned. On major issues, we will make no proposal to the Soviets unless we have first discussed them with allies, especially those having direct concern. Consultations will be maintained during, as well as before, any negotiations. We are open to suggestions regarding means and forum for consultations. We assume that the allies will take a similar approach to consultation in connection with their own negotiation with the USSR.

21.   National Intelligence Estimate[1]

NIE 11–69   Washington, February 27, 1969.

BASIC FACTORS AND MAIN TENDENCIES IN CURRENT SOVIET POLICY

Note

This paper considers in broad perspective the principal factors which underlie the USSR's external policies at present and its aims and intentions with respect to certain key areas and issues. As such, while it suggests the limits within which Soviet policies are likely to operate, it does not estimate likely Soviet conduct and positions in detail. In view of the intimate interaction between Soviet and American policies, this could not be done in any case without specific assumptions about American policy and actions.

Principal Observations

A. Ideology in the Soviet Union is in a certain sense dead, yet it still plays a vital role. This paradox explains much about the nature of Soviet society and the USSR as a world power today. While the regime's doctrines now inhibit rather than promote needed change in the system, the leaders continue to guard them as an essential support to their rule. They also view developments at home and abroad mainly within the conceptual framework of the traditional ideology. This fact will continue to limit the possibilities of Soviet-American dialogue.

B. Changes in the system and the society have probably made collective leadership of the Party Politburo less vulnerable to new attempts to establish a personal dictatorship. This seems particularly true so long as the men who now comprise the leadership remain. Nevertheless, a crisis within the present leadership, accompanied by high domestic tensions and greater unpredictability of external policy, could occur at any time without warning. If stability of the leadership continues, a relatively deliberate, bureaucratically compromised manner of decisionmaking will also continue.

---

[1] Source: Central Intelligence Agency, NIC Files, Job 79–R1012A, NIEs and SNIEs. Secret. Controlled Dissem. A note on a cover sheet indicates that the Central Intelligence Agency and the intelligence organizations of the Departments of State and Defense and the National Security Agency participated in the preparation of this estimate. The Director of CIA submitted this estimate with the concurrence of all members of the USIB, except the Assistant General Manager of the Atomic Energy Commission and the Assistant Director of the Federal Bureau of Investigation, who abstained because the subject was outside their jurisdiction.

C. The Soviet leaders face severe problems at home. A decline in the rate of economic growth is tightening the perennial squeeze on resource allocation. Dissidence and alienation in the professional classes is of growing concern to the Soviet leaders. Generally speaking, however, they are not at this time constrained by domestic problems from continuing the general line of foreign policy they have followed in recent years.

D. The leadership believes that the USSR's net power position in the world, as affected by both military and political factors, has improved in the years since the Cuban missile crisis. But this is qualified by instability in its main security sphere in Eastern Europe and by increased strains in the Soviet economy and society. This appraisal by the Soviet leaders probably argues for continuing an external policy of cautious opportunism and limited pressures, perhaps with some increased watchfulness against the development of uncontrolled risks.

E. There is a tendency in Soviet foreign policy to give increased weight to geopolitical considerations as against the traditional conception Moscow has had of itself as the directing center of a world revolutionary movement. This is evident in the concentration of diplomatic and aid efforts in recent years on countries around the southern periphery of particular strategic interest to the USSR. It is seen also in the guidance given to most Communist parties to pursue moderate tactics, which are now more compatible with Soviet foreign policy interests.

F. Soviet aims to bring about a European settlement which would secure the USSR's hegemony in Eastern Europe, obtain the withdrawal of US forces, and isolate West Germany have suffered a severe setback because of the action taken to suppress Czechoslovakia's attempt to follow an independent course. For the present, the Soviets are unlikely to be responsive to any new Western initiatives to promote a European settlement, unless the West seems willing to contemplate recognition of the Soviet sphere in Eastern Europe and of the division of Germany.

G. The Soviets have a double concern in the Middle East at present: to keep their risks under control and to do this in such a manner as to avoid diminishing the influence they have won with the Arab States. Should renewed hostilities occur, the USSR might be drawn into assisting the defense of the Arabs, but it would not want to run the political and military risks of joining in attacks on Israel or actually threatening its survival. At that stage, the Soviets would probably collaborate tacitly with the US to control the situation.

H. Beginning as an attempt to move into the vacuum left by the end of Western colonialism, Soviet policy in Asia in recent years has been geared increasingly to the containment of China. Nevertheless, the Soviets still act in particular situations, including Vietnam, basically on the premise that the Soviet-American relationship in Asia is competitive. The major risks which may eventually arise from the growth of Chinese power, however, may persuade them to move toward some tacit collaboration.

I. Through the inducements to reach a strategic arms limitation agreement with the US are probably stronger at this time than ever before, Moscow's policy-bureaucratic argument over this issue is not resolved. The Soviets probably hope that talks themselves, even if no agreement is reached, will ease the pressures of the arms race by slowing US decisions on new programs.

J. Even though the Soviet system appears ripe for change because it is now poorly suited to managing a complex industrial society, its rulers remain tenacious in defending their monopoly of power and acutely fearful of adaptive change. The wider involvement of the USSR in world affairs and possible shifts in world power relations may eventually generate stronger pressures for change. Short of this, the outlook is for chronic tensions in Soviet-American relations, perhaps caused more frequently by events over which neither side has much control.

DISCUSSION

Basic Factors Underlying Soviet Policy

Ideology

1. Qualified observers are heard to say, "Ideology is dead in the USSR," while others equally qualified assert, "Ideology remains dominant in Soviet political and policy." Taken literally, neither statement is valid. But understood as half-truths, both not only say something important about Soviet reality but are also compatible with each other. The paradox that ideology is in some sense dead but still plays a vital role explains much about the nature of the USSR as a society and as a world power today.

2. Marxism-Leninism is a dead ideology in the sense that it has become a calcified scripture, is seen as boring or irrelevant by most of the Soviet population, is cynically manipulated by the political elite, and inhibits rather than promotes needed social change in the USSR. It remains a major factor, however, because in the main it continues to provide the conceptual framework within which Soviet internal and external policies are formulated. It is the semantical prism through which the Soviet leaders view the problems and development of their own system. More important, it conditions profoundly the way in which they interpret the aims and conduct of non-Communist societies. With respect to the US, in particular, it underlies the fearful and hostile "set" of Soviet attitudes which so greatly limits the flexibility needed for resolving conflicts of interest.

3. Some observers have thought at various times that all this was changing, that doctrinal politics was giving way inevitably to pragmatic politics. Such opinions have proved premature. The basic and often overlooked reason is that ideology performs a vital political function in the Soviet system: it serves as the regime's badge of legitimacy. Without the claim that it was the embodiment of a historically predestined process of revolutionary social advance, all the crimes and deprivations which this regime has inflicted on a long-suffering people might not have been borne. Force alone, without buttressing from doctrinal rationalizations which claimed high moral purpose, probably would not have been enough to give the Soviet regime the authority it needed. From the beginning, moreover, ideological rigor has been used as a weapon to preserve the unity of a fractious Party and to suppress nonconforming elements inside and outside it. In Russian conditions and against the background of Russian history, ideology has proved to be an important tool in making effective the rule by force and repression of the small political sect which seized power in 1917 and has held it by tyrannical methods since.

4. Today the Soviet leadership remains as sensitive as ever to any hint of challenge to its ideological pretensions. In fact, during the last several years it has grown more rigid and conservative in this respect. The reasons for this are complex. They begin simply with the temperament of the bureaucratic collective which now governs. Then, social change has produced a larger educated class and in particular a technical elite which is less disposed to think ideologically or to accept ritualistic formulas of the old kind. Further, the ideological as well as political authority of the Soviet leadership has been sharply challenged by the nationalist-inspired deviations which have appeared in China and Eastern Europe since Stalin's death. Finally, the effort to isolate the population and also Party members from alien influences, on which the preservation of the regime's ideological authority depends, has grown more difficult; there has been increased exposure to the outside world in a number of ways, partly as a consequence of the development of communications.

5. The consequence is that the men who now govern the USSR feel themselves on the ideological defensive. They believe that if they retreat on this front the whole structure of their power will crumble. This concern lies behind their intensified repression of dissidents in recent years and their cautious restoration of Stalin's reputation; it figured strongly in their use of force against the Czechoslovak reform movement. Short of the appearance of new leadership, and possibly not then, this mood of fearful conservatism is unlikely to change. It will affect adversely the tone of Soviet-American relations and thus the possibilities of the more constructive dialogue which must be the prelude to any significant improvement in those relations.

Stability and Stress in the Domestic System

6. *The Leadership.* To the surprise of some students of the Soviet system, collective leadership—the sharing of power by a dozen or so top leaders in the Politburo, the Party's supreme executive organ—has endured since the fall of Khrushchev in October 1964. While collectivity has always been the declared principle on which the system was supposed to operate, the dictatorship of one man has been the rule during much of the Soviet history. Some have concluded that the failure of Khrushchev to consolidate himself in such a role and the evident fact that Brezhnev, despite the prominence conferred by the title of General Secretary, does not have it now, means that the age of dictators has passed in the USSR.

7. Persuasive considerations argue for this view. The dynamics of other revolutions suggest that the heroic figures of the first generation give way to men of more limited capacity whose temper is more bureaucratic. The men who now comprise the top echelon, who have spent their entire lives in the apparatus, appear to be of this stripe. Moreover, the enormous growth of state and economic institutions, and the far greater complexity of the issues posed as Soviet society has developed, make the simplistic methods of an earlier time inapplicable. Collective, i.e., bureaucratic, decisionmaking seems the normal mode in the USSR today.

8. Yet tensions arising from the attempt of individual leaders to enlarge their power are evident from time to time, and it cannot be doubted that the classic form of power struggle seen in the past persists behind the façade of collectivity. The system remains one of men and not of laws. Therefore, it is impossible to rule out new attempts by individual leaders to establish themselves in the role of dictator, together with the arbitrary measures, increased social tensions, and unpredictability of policy which would inevitably accompany such attempts. At a minimum, there will be leaders who will strive to establish ascendancy over their colleagues, and thus, as Khrushchev appeared likely to do for a time, to reduce collectivity in effect to a mere form.

9. If such developments were to occur, they would probably result from some major setback at home or abroad, from a deadlock over some vital issue of policy whose resolution was urgent, or simply from an accumulation of unsolved problems. A new personal dictatorship would require the emergence of some commanding personality clearly superior to his colleagues in the skills of the power game, though the appearance of a man of such dimensions is entirely a matter of chance. On the whole, while it is not at all implausible to believe that attempts to displace collective leadership will be made, it appears unlikely that such attempts will be successful in the conditions that now obtain in the political system and the society. This seems particularly true so long as the men who now comprise the leadership remain.

10. A breakdown in the apparent stability of the present collective, even short of an attempt by one man to displace or dominate it, is always possible, however. The result might be a change in the composition of the leadership and a shift of direction on some major aspect of policy. It is impossible to say what circumstances might precipitate such a development or to predict the event itself. The principal members of the Politburo are old enough to be subject to sudden health hazards; sooner or later the need to coopt new members might unhinge the delicate balance of power within that group. Domestic issues which are always key ones and are now serious, combined with the kind of contentious problems now being encountered by Soviet policy abroad, most conspicuously the setback in Czechoslovakia, could bring a leadership crisis at any time.

11. This threat of instability overhanging the top leadership does not arise from a mere constitutional imbalance, like the weakness of the executive under the Fourth Republic in France, and the consequent instability of cabinets. It is due, despite the existence of a constitution on paper, to the disregard of constitutional restraints which could confer legitimacy on the system and its procedures. Thus the matter of succession to leadership has been on each occasion a struggle for raw power as in a gang. Similarly, the role of the Party in relation to society and its institutions, including government organs, is an arbitrary one, uncontrolled by law. The Party purports to be merely an instrument for political inspiration and guidance, but in fact Party men under direction from the top exercise a power of intervention at all levels and in every institution. The result is a sense throughout the society that power is wielded arbitrarily and unjustly. In this atmosphere, individuals withhold their voluntary cooperation and the ability of authority to deal efficiently with many problems is reduced.

12. If the collective leadership continues without major ructions, policy and decisionmaking will be of the cautious and deliberate kind seen in recent years. This does not mean that decisions do not get made or that policy is wholly without initiative. It does mean that significant moves are likely to come under the pressure of events, and normally will be less sweeping or erratic than they were under Khrushchev, for example.

13. *Sources of Strain.* The problems facing the Soviet leadership at present are severe. One of the major ones is the perennial dilemma of all modern governments: how to allocate inadequate resources among the primary goals of policy—military strength and security, economic development and growth, consumption and welfare. The Soviet system continues to be able to apply proportionately greater resources to public purposes than non-Communist industrial states can. But it is trying to sustain a world power competition with the US on an economic base half that of the US. While this has been managed by

reliance on a highly-centralized and inflexible command economy, the resulting strains are serious and have been increasing. In the USSR as elsewhere, decisions affecting the allocation of resources are made at the margin, and the margins have been narrowing.

14. Both a reflection and a source of increasing strain has been a decline in the economy's rate of growth. This decline was owing to a combination of factors: with growing technological complexity, growth rates per unit of investment have fallen off, particularly in industry; the resources drain of major military and space programs in this decade has been substantial; concessions to popular demands for material improvement, especially in food and housing, were thought necessary. The result has been a slow decline in the rate of growth of investment in industry. This, along with the drop in productivity of investment, has led to a significant decline in the rate of growth in industrial output.

15. The response of the Soviet leaders has been to introduce economic reforms aimed at raising the still low levels of productivity in industry and agriculture. The program laid down in 1965 and still being implemented seeks to do this by providing greater autonomy and incentives for enterprises. The measures were not only partial but were largely frustrated in practice and the gains so far have been insignificant. While much more radical departures, amounting in effect to a change in the nature of the system, would be necessary to get results, the resistance of the Party and the vast state bureaucracy precludes change of this magnitude. Moreover, the Soviet leaders fear, as was demonstrated most recently in Czechoslovakia, that moves to free the economy from central control give rise rapidly to demands for freedom in every aspect of society, including politics. This they seem less ready than ever to face, and so their economic dilemmas will remain and sharpen.

16. Social strains have led the leaders to give steady attention and increased resources to meeting expectations for an improved level of life, even at the cost of investment in other sectors traditionally of high priority. Thus a multiplicity of goals makes decisions harder, especially under collective leadership; perhaps there has also been some loss of will and ruthlessness on the part of the ruling elite. Yet the leadership does not appear to regard the material discontents of the masses as an actual threat, and it is probably right in this.

17. What it evidently does fear is the striking increase in recent years of manifestations of dissidence among intellectuals. It is easy enough to threaten and imprison a handful of activist writers and artists, and this is being done, but these brave few represent the leading edge of an alienation that is far broader, especially in the educated professional class. These people resent the frustration of hopes for

greater freedom which arose in the decade after Stalin's death, they fear the neo-Stalinist tendencies which are evident, and they are contemptuous of the narrowness and mediocrity of the present leaders.

18. No one can say for sure what the scope of such alienation really is, but that it is wider, deeper, and less passive than formerly seems clear. What the regime fears is the erosion of respect for its authority among leading elements of the society which might, in certain unforeseeable circumstances, combine with and activate the chronic discontents of the masses to produce a genuine challenge. While no such challenge seems imminent, occupants of the Kremlin probably always remind themselves that in Russia anarchy has usually lurked close beneath the surface of tyranny. In any case, barring a change of leaders, the outlook is for a careful but steady repression of liberalizing forces, and a continuing effort to wall out external sources of infection.

19. A threat to the political leadership stemming from the military establishment is sometimes predicted by Western analysts. Clearly the military leaders do have larger influence on decisions, partly because the leadership is a collective. Their role has also increased because the resources given to defense since World War II have grown greatly, and because decisions affecting defense are now more technically complex. Even though some military leaders might try to influence the outcome of a leadership crisis, the increased bureaucratic weight the military now enjoy is unlikely to persuade them that they could replace the Party in running the country. Probably most military men believe that the attempt would nowadays involve grave risks to national security. Should the Party regime be seriously weakened or collapse, however, the military leadership probably would intervene, but in such circumstances they would be acting primarily out of concern for national security. Such a development now seems remote.

20. *Implications for External Policy.* As in other states, there is a linkage in the USSR between internal and external policies. Since preoccupation with the regime's security at home is high, risks abroad are normally weighed carefully. It is worth noting, however, that in the years of Khrushchev's real ascendancy (1957–1962), when internal tensions were reduced and confidence in the domestic outlook was generally rising, there was a tendency toward more assertiveness and risk-taking abroad, though this was obviously due also to Khrushchev's own temperament.

21. The present leaders are evidently aware that successes on the international scene can help to ease internal stresses and that setbacks abroad are dangerous to them at home. While they are not inclined, therefore, to be adventurous in foreign policy, they have shown a will to advance opportunistically under conditions of controlled risk, with

a preference for moving into vacuums rather than for direct confrontations. The exception to this generally deliberate approach is their own security zone in Eastern Europe where, as in Czechoslovakia last summer, after some hesitation, they finally moved with brutal assertiveness. This action was primarily defensive, however, and the leading motive for it was precisely a fear for the eventual security of the Soviet regime itself.

22. Generally speaking, the present leadership conducts its foreign policies in such a manner as to impose no special handicaps on itself internally, and the domestic problems described above do not now prevent it from doing abroad what it wants to do. Apart from occasional grumbling over foreign aid expenditures, which are not in fact very heavy, on the whole the policies which have brought greater Soviet influence abroad, for example in the Middle East and South Asia, are probably a plus for the regime. But whenever Soviet policies encounter setbacks, and especially if they appear to heighten risks of war, as in the Arab-Israeli conflict of June 1967, stresses on the home front are sharply increased. This is one of the major reasons for a foreign policy of limited risks.

Soviet Perception of the Balance of Power

23. Intense preoccupation with the balance of power—what they call "the relation of forces"—is characteristic of the Soviet leaders. This springs from Marxism-Leninism itself, which is a doctrine concerned primarily with the analysis of power relations in society and the techniques for manipulating them. It also reflects the long years of "encirclement" when the Soviet leaders constantly perceived external threats aimed at the very existence of their regime.

24. In calculating power relationships the Soviets weigh a variety of factors. They give great weight to military power, perhaps as much for its political-psychological effects, i.e., its support to political warfare, as for its direct utility. In measuring the strength of other states, they also attach great importance to economic trends, to the degree of internal unity or division, and to the capacities of leaders and their will to confront risks. They are sensitive to the ebb and flow of opinion in other countries, not for reasons of sentiment, but because it may register shifts of attitude toward power relations and can thus actually affect those relations.

25. Viewed in such terms, the Soviet leaders evidently feel that their position has improved since the low point of the Cuban missile crisis in 1962. Nevertheless, not everything has come up roses. They have substantially bettered their relative strength in strategic weapons, and have acquired conventional capabilities which, in certain areas beyond the Bloc periphery, would permit them to intervene in a limited way. But in strategic weapons the US is now moving to new generation

systems which will demand further strenuous efforts—and added economic burdens—if the Soviets wish to keep pace. Meanwhile, the US has sustained improved rates of economic growth for some years as Soviet growth has declined, and visions of "overtaking and surpassing" have vanished, even from propaganda. On the positive side, the world influence of the US has suffered because of Vietnam, its alliances have been strained, and it has been wracked by internal discords at a time when Soviet influence and presence in Asia and the Middle East have grown. But then the USSR's position in Eastern Europe has become more complicated, Czechoslovakia was a disaster in world opinion, the disarray in the Communist movement has deepened, and there have even been important setbacks to Soviet influence in the Third World, as in Indonesia and Ghana.

26. As the Soviet leaders look at the world scene today, they probably feel that they can allow themselves no more than a measured optimism, tinged with real concern for the long-term outlook in Eastern Europe and for the growing severity of their problems at home. This does not mean that the total relation of forces, as viewed from Moscow at present, results in a conclusion that the USSR is overextended and must retrench. On balance, it probably argues for continuing policies of cautious opportunism and limited pressures, perhaps with some increased watchfulness against the development of uncontrolled risks. The Soviet leaders feel able to assert, moreover, as they have for some years, that their relative power justifies their claim to a world role equal to that of the US.

Soviet Policies on Major Current Issues

Some General Tendencies

27. Despite what was said in the opening section of this paper about a retreat to ideological conservatism internally, the USSR's foreign policy under the present leaders has been marked generally by a decline in ideological emphasis and by what appears to be a primary concern for geopolitical considerations, of the sort normal in any great power. This is seen most notably in the concentration of diplomatic and aid efforts on the USSR's southern periphery and in the virtual abandonment of the appeals for revolutionary brotherhood which accompanied Soviet entry into the Third World in the 1950's. A parallel shift has been discernible also in the Soviet approach to Europe, and even intermittently in a more business-like if still harsh tone in dealings with the US.

28. Whatever Soviet rhetoric may still say, Moscow tends to act more like world power than like the center of the world revolution. This has come about less by choice than by inadvertence and necessity. Possessed of global military strength in the nuclear age, the Soviet

leaders wish the USSR to be recognized as a responsible global power. They have come to understand that under modern conditions even their security may rest partly on their ability to influence rather than to overthrow non-Communist governments. Compared with the 1950's, the outlook for Communist revolutionary advance in the world as a whole seems far more complicated and much less promising. Finally, the transformation of China from ideological ally to great power enemy has evidently had a profound effect on the USSR's view of the world and thus on its policies.

29. The effort to preserve Moscow's leadership of the International Communist Movement goes on, but the motives have changed. Now this is desired primarily to preserve the Soviet security sphere in Eastern Europe and the party's domination at home, to counter Chinese action against Soviet interests everywhere, and to insure that Communist parties around the world serve rather than prejudice Soviet great power interests. The Soviet leaders may still believe that they are moving on the traditional double track—a state policy and a revolutionary policy—but their advice to Communist parties everywhere to moderate revolutionary tactics suggests otherwise.

30. One consequence of the more geopolitical emphasis in Soviet policy is the assignment of lesser priority to some areas. Latin America and Africa seem to be so regarded at present. Soviet diplomacy and propaganda are active and opportunities are taken in these areas, especially for trade and arms sales, but efforts and expectations are clearly reduced from what they were at the beginning of the 1960's. The troubled relationship with "socialist" Cuba and several disappointments in Africa and Asia have presumably brought about this change. Castro is probably carried today as a somewhat painful legacy of a more innocent phase, before the Soviets discovered their error in coopting as reliable Communists the often vigorous but "ideologically weak" revolutionaries they encounter in less developed countries.

31. The tendencies described here do not mean that the USSR is no longer a thrusting and ambitious power concerned to enlarge its world position. They do suggest that in practice the Soviets place somewhat less emphasis on their pretensions to be a revolutionary power with a universal mission. They are inclined to set priorities for their efforts in various areas in accordance with a more traditional view of Russian security interests and also with a more realistic view of the possibilities for expanding their influence. This does not ease US problems in coping with Soviet power; it may in some ways make the USSR a more formidable opponent. And, because the Soviet leaders are committed to a basically forward policy and have shown that they sometimes fail to appraise risks accurately, the possibility of crisis by miscalculation remains.

The Enduring Confrontation in Central Europe

32. However active they have been in other areas in recent years, the Soviets have always been clear that their security and their aspirations to a world role rest in the first instance on their position in Europe. This is based on holding Eastern Europe as an ideological and security buffer, and they have worked doggedly to consolidate, and to get international recognition for their hegemony there. With that went the long campaign to win final acceptance from the Western Powers of the division of Germany and the persistent effort to isolate and contain the Federal Republic, the revival of whose economic and political influence, the Soviets believe, would undermine their control of Eastern Europe. That nothing in this basic pattern has changed is shown clearly by their action in Czechoslovakia last summer.

33. A more forward kind of Soviet diplomacy in Europe, which gave a clue to long-range Soviet hopes for the area, had emerged in 1966–1967. Taking advantage of US involvement in Vietnam and the consequent strains in US relations with Europe, of de Gaulle's withdrawal from NATO, and of desires for détente in Western Europe, the Soviets tried to promote moves toward a European settlement without the US. At the time, they probably had in mind no more than a preliminary probe to stimulate West European interest in such an approach. But the outcome they look for eventually was made clear: dissolution of NATO and withdrawal of US forces, recognition of the status quo in Eastern Europe and in Germany, bilateral understandings between the USSR and Western European states which would in effect neutralize them, and general European support for the political isolation of West Germany. Fragmentation, not unity, in Europe is what the Soviets think serves their interests.

34. Czechoslovakia has buried such Soviet hopes, probably indefinitely, for what Moscow faces now is tantamount to a general crisis in its Eastern European sphere. Even if the Czechoslovaks are finally brought to heel and a responsive regime is restored, deep fissures in the Bloc system will remain. Nationalist frustration, resentment of economic dependence and stagnation, desire for renewed contact with the West will continue to plague all these regimes in one degree or another; serious instability is possible in several. Within their present premises, which include fear of radical change in Eastern Europe because it may generate pressures for the same in the USSR, the Soviets have no lasting solution. Sooner or later, they may be driven to use force again.

35. Against this background, the USSR is not likely for the present to be very responsive to new Western initiatives for a European settlement, whether these involve regional arms control, new security arrangements, or a revised approach to the German problem. Of course,

if the West seemed willing to contemplate recognition of the Soviet sphere in Eastern Europe and of the division of Germany, the Soviet attitude would be different. But assuming that the West would not abandon the principle of eventual self-determination in Germany in some form, and that the tendency of its proposals would be to promote freer East-West contacts in Europe, the Soviets would see only danger in them. In fact, such proposals might contribute to prolonging the USSR's present embarrassment over its relations with Eastern Europe.

The Middle East

36. When the Soviets, with their arms sales to Egypt in 1955, moved into the vacuum left in the Middle East by the collapse of the Western colonial system, they almost certainly did not anticipate the kind of situation in which they are now so heavily involved. Their aims were to diminish the Western presence, to increase strains in the Western Alliance, and ultimately to establish themselves as the pre-eminent power in the region. They hoped to do these things by developing the natural alliance they saw between themselves and "the progressive forces of national liberation," which they also imagined could be led under Soviet influence to take the "socialist road." They had no very profound understanding of the forces at work in the Arab world, nor of the depth of the Arab-Israeli conflict. Their opportunism in this case did win them great influence and a military presence in an area they clearly regard as of strategic importance to them, but it has also brought risks and burdens.

37. In the immediate situation in the Middle East, the USSR has a double concern: to contain risks and at the same time to avoid any undue prejudice to its influence with the Arabs. Even if it were possible for Soviet-Western collaboration to impose a stable settlement, the Soviets would probably believe that their influence with the Arabs would suffer, since it has been built largely on implicit support of radical Arab hostility to Israel. The more recent Soviet moves for diplomatic collaboration with the Western Powers probably reflect concern that eventually the risks could become less controllable, especially because of the increasing role of Arab terrorist organizations which the Arab States themselves cannot control. Soviet tactics evidently aim now at persuading the US to influence Israel toward moderating its claims sufficiently to permit diplomatic processes to work and some defusing of tensions to occur. But the Soviet leaders do seem to recognize that some pressure on their own clients, which could damage the USSR's standing with the Arabs, will also be needed. Perhaps awareness of the possibility of Israel's early acquisition of nuclear weapons gives the Soviets an added incentive to try to move the Arabs toward a reduction of tensions.

38. If a general settlement could be achieved, the Soviets would expect to gain certain advantages. Opening of the Suez Canal would shorten their shipping route to Asia and would facilitate Soviet maritime operations in the Indian Ocean. Their part in bringing about a settlement might constitute implicit acceptance by the Western Powers of their right to a decisive voice in the affairs of the area. But to achieve a general settlement, the Soviets would have to bring such great pressure to bear on the Arabs to make concessions that they would risk losing the position of influence they have won. This they are very unlikely to do. That is why their present diplomatic activity is probably undertaken only with a view to containing the risks in the present situation rather than in any expectation of actually bringing about a lasting settlement.

39. If violence mounts further and formal hostilities resume, the Soviets will face harder choices. They might then be drawn into assisting the defense of the Arab States; this could happen because Soviet ships and aircraft are present intermittently at UAR bases and large numbers of Soviet advisors serve with Egyptian combat units. But the Soviets would not want to run the political and military risks of joining in attacks on Israel itself or actually threatening its survival. While they may not rate the likelihood of a direct involvement with the US as very great at present, it does not appear that what is at stake for them in the area would justify risks of this magnitude. At that stage, they would probably move further toward tacit collaboration with the US to contain the situation.

Asia

40. The Soviets have pursued a variety of aims in the arc from Japan to the Indian subcontinent, though it is not clear that they have operated on the basis of any grand strategic conception for the area. They have sought, as elsewhere, to move into the vacuum left by the end of Western colonialism, using trade, the supply of arms, and their "anti-imperialist" credentials as principal instruments of influence. They have given priority to efforts to deny use of the area to US military power. They have tried to maintain their leadership of the Communist parties there and to guide them in ways compatible with Soviet foreign policy interests. And increasingly over the last several years, their policy has been geared to the containment of China as an ideological and great power competitor.

41. Soviet political and material support to North Vietnam since 1965 has also been intended to serve aims of policy. The Soviet leaders have wanted to see a setback for US power in Vietnam which would limit the future US role in Asia. But they also wanted this to be achieved by tactics which would limit political and military risks to themselves and maximize their own rather than Chinese credit for the success.

Thus, though they have had only modest leverage in Hanoi, they have evidently used it, not toward ending the war, but to influence the Vietnamese to rely more on the political element in their mix of political-military tactics. The Soviets brought propaganda and diplomatic pressure to bear on the US in order to promote negotiations under conditions Hanoi would accept. Now that negotiations are in train, the USSR will want to help them succeed, but not in ways which would prejudice its future relations with Hanoi. If the North Vietnamese accede to a settlement short of their original aims, however, the Soviets will not stand in the way and will adapt their policy accordingly.

42. The Vietnamese episode illustrates the basically competitive nature of the Soviet-American relationship in Asia. Where circumstances require, as in India, they will permit some tacit parallelism to operate, but they will not convert it into active collaboration. In Southeast Asia, they appear to be positioning themselves for continued competition whatever the outcome in Vietnam; they are unlikely to participate in the efforts for regional organization and development which the US has in view. Their attitudes on the Indonesian debt case and on the Asian Development Bank show their preference for unilateralism over cooperation. In Korea, they do not now encourage the North to adopt an adventurous course, but neither are they willing to pay any political price to restrain the North Koreans. As the Soviets see it, cooperation with the US in Asia would compromise their own aims; they will entertain moves in that direction only when it seems necessary to contain major risks to their security and interests.

43. If Chinese power becomes more menacing, this might provide the occasion for a change in this general Soviet stance in Asia. The Soviets probably do not anticipate a major threat to themselves in the near term, and may still have some slight hope for the revival of "healthy" forces in Chinese communism. But Moscow is clearly concerned for the longer future. The Soviet leaders have given signs, moreover, that they fear not only the growth of Chinese military power but the possibility of an eventual rapprochement between China and the US. This they would see as a major and unfavorable shift in the relation of forces which they should do all they could to prevent. In the long run, therefore, events may compel fundamental revisions of Soviet policy. The Chinese factor seems more calculated to bring this about than any other.

Arms Control

44. The Soviet leaders have reasons at this time, perhaps more than ever before, to entertain a serious approach to arms control. As indicated in earlier paragraphs, the burdens of the arms race have been substantial in recent years, and a change in priorities would contribute in some degree to forestalling economic and social strains which otherwise

are likely to become more serious, and in time, perhaps even critical. In the field of strategic nuclear weapons their buildup over the last several years has given the Soviets a better relative position than they have ever had. Even apart from the added economic pressures they would face, the Soviets may not be confident that as the US moves to more advanced systems, they will be able to maintain the pace technologically. They could think that stabilization in the near future would give them more security than they are otherwise likely to have. They might also reason that, to support the kind of competitive foreign policy they are pursuing in distant areas, greater emphasis on appropriate conventional forces would serve them better than additional strategic nuclear strength.

45. However persuasive such considerations might be to some elements of the regime, the reasons which others will find to oppose a genuine effort to obtain a strategic arms limitation agreement will also carry great weight. Grounds for mistrust of US intentions, fear of ideological compromise or penetration, concern about misunderstanding on the part of allies and clients will all be urged. The influence of the military establishment will generally work against a positive approach, though some elements might, in the interests of other force components, welcome a halt to the strategic weapons buildup. Given the climate of opinion ordinarily surrounding so highly charged an issue, the chances of a positive approach emerging would not be great, were it not for the serious dilemmas which prolongation of the arms race would invoke.

46. What signs there are indicate that the policy-bureaucratic struggle over this issue was not resolved by the decision to begin strategic arms talks with the US, but in fact seems to be continuing. It is likely that the decision was agreed to on the basis that the Soviet approach would be exploratory, and that even if no agreement was reached, some US decisions might be slowed down and time gained. The fact that the move was opposed earlier, however, suggests that some people in Moscow believe that, once the talks get started, they may acquire a momentum of their own which would propel the USSR into an unsound agreement.

47. Given the complexity of the issues, of course, the actual Soviet position will be precipitated, like that of the US, only in the process of negotiation. As usual, and perhaps more so because of disagreement in Moscow, the Soviets will leave the initiative for developing concrete proposals largely to the US. They will expect the negotiations to be prolonged, and will try to make them so if there are signs of domestic political pressures on the US side to postpone arms decisions or to make greater concessions to Soviet views. They will insist on an agreement which, whatever its actual content, registers at least implicitly their

right to equality in strategic power. Acknowledgment of this is, in fact, one of the principal political gains they would expect to get out of the talks.

Prospects for Change in the USSR

48. The Soviet system described in this paper is one which, in view of its situation at home and abroad, might be judged to be ripe for change. But it is also a system within which resistance to change is very strong. Even though the totalitarian Party regime is in many ways poorly suited to managing the complex industrial society which the USSR has become, it retains great tenacity and vigor in defending its monopoly of power. Its conservative instincts and fear of adaptive change are acute.

49. Nobody can foresee what will finally happen to a system as rigid as this as it comes under the increasing pressures generated by the further development and modernization of the society. The ruling group might succeed for a long time in simply containing such pressures, even at the price of some stagnation. Some Western observers assume that there will be change of a gradualist and relatively benign sort, because the holders of power will consent by a series of pragmatic steps to a diffusion of power to groups and institutions other than the Party. Others believe that, against the background of Russian political experience and the Party's own history, it is more plausible to expect that change in the system can come only under conditions of severe political instability and disorder, perhaps even accompanied by violence in one degree or another. In any case, the USSR's future role as a world power, and the degree of uncertainty and danger its policies cause, will be greatly affected by what happens to the internal system in the years ahead.

50. With the wider involvement of Soviet policy in many parts of the world where it was not active until recently, external forces may come to play a larger role in generating pressures for change inside the USSR. A more realistic view of the forces at work in other societies might replace the doctrinaire conceptions which have governed Soviet thinking. Further major setbacks to the USSR's position in Eastern Europe or developments affecting Chinese power and policy, especially if these involved a change in China's relations with the US, might compel radical shifts in Soviet policy which would have serious repercussions on the internal system. On the other hand, it is difficult to imagine successes which Soviet power might have externally which would have any more than temporary effect in easing internal strains.

51. Without significant change in the nature of the internal system, the external policies which are so largely determined by it will not alter much either. There may be a further diminution of the ideological input to foreign policy in favor of greater concentration on the

USSR's great power interests, but this would not decrease competitiveness and hostility toward the US and might even increase them. And the US will continue to have very limited means for influencing these attitudes directly. Short of unexpected early change in the Soviet system, therefore, the outlook is for basic hostility and chronic tensions in Soviet-American relations for a considerable period. As in the past, such tensions will rise and fall depending on events, but more frequently than in the past, these may be events in one area or another over which neither side has much control.

---

22.   Editorial Note

On March 3, 1969, the President's Assistant for National Security Affairs Henry Kissinger sent President Nixon a memorandum covering recent intelligence information about a Sino-Soviet border clash of March 2:

"The Soviets have accused the Chinese of violating their border and killing border guards in an attack on a post on the Ussuri River. A protest note has been sent which states that any provocative actions on the border will be rebuffed and resolutely cut short by the USSR. The shooting incident was the first of its kind, although there have been previous instances of border provocations by the Chinese." (National Archives, Nixon Presidential Materials, NSC Files, Box 3, President's Daily Briefs)

Over the next few weeks, Kissinger continued to inform the President about the Sino-Soviet border incidents. Although clashes had occurred periodically, this spate of border incidents revealed an intensity and frequency that worried U.S. policymakers. On March 12, Kissinger wrote the following "information item" to the President:

"Developments arising from the March 2 Sino-Soviet border incident in the Far East continue to be revealed [*less than 1 line of source text not declassified*]. Both the Soviets and the Chinese have conducted border reconnaissance flights during this period with some evidence that the Soviets have violated the border on at least two occasions— [*less than 1 line of source text not declassified*] by a light attack bomber and [*less than 1 line of source text not declassified*] by a helicopter. [*less than 1 line of source text not declassified*], a Chinese helicopter operating along the border drew a reaction from a Soviet fighter aircraft. No hostile intent was detected and both aircraft remained within their respective airspaces. In addition, [*less than 1 line of source text not declassified*] the Soviets violated Chinese airspace in the Vladivostok area." (Ibid.)

On March 15, Kissinger wrote the following in a memorandum to Nixon:

"The Soviets today charged that Chinese troops tried to invade Soviet territory in the Far East yesterday and today, and had killed Soviet troops. The clashes took place on and near Damansky Island, scene of a clash on March 2." (Ibid.)

The CIA's Office of Current Intelligence prepared an extensive chronology of Sino-Soviet border incidents for the *CIA Bulletin*, which was disseminated widely to U.S. Government officials. An annex of the *CIA Bulletin*, released on March 18, 1969, provided a chronology of events from March 2–16 from both the Soviet and Chinese perspectives. (Central Intelligence Agency, Job 93–T01468R, Executive Registry Files, Box 3, Sino-Soviet Border January–July 1969)

On March 20, Richard Sneider, NSC Operations Staff officer for East Asia, sent Kissinger a Department of State Intelligence Note titled "Sino-Soviet Border: Has Peking Bitten Off More Than It Can Chew?" The covering memorandum summarized the note as follows:

"You may find the attached Intelligence Note of interest. Prepared by INR in the Secretary of State, it describes the decreasing bluster in Peking's handling of the crisis, and suggests that the Chinese have realized that they are in a very bad 'face' situation. They cannot dislodge the Soviets from Chenpao Island without an unacceptable risk of escalation, and that they will have to eat their earlier threats of crushing retribution if the Soviets persisted in 'armed provocation.' The report concludes that, typically, the Chinese Communists are not likely to retreat and thus acknowledge defeat, nor are they likely to mount a real military challenge to the USSR. They will probably maintain enough activity to conceal the fact that their bluff has been called, as they have done by shelling Quemoy on alternate days for ten years after the subsidence of the offshore island crisis." (National Archives, Nixon Presidential Materials, NSC Files, Box 709, Country Files, Europe, USSR, Vol. I)

23.   Memorandum From the President's Assistant for National Security Affairs (Kissinger) to President Nixon[1]

Washington, March 6, 1969.

SUBJECT

Conversation with Ambassador Dobrynin, Lunch, March 3

Ambassador Dobrynin opened the conversation by saying that the Soviet Union noted the President's trip to Europe with interest. Except for some phrases in Berlin, it had found nothing objectionable. He asked whether these phrases indicated any new commitment to German unification. I replied that the purpose of the Berlin speech[2] was to emphasize existing American commitments, not to undertake new ones. I also told him that we viewed any harassment of Berlin with the utmost gravity. Dobrynin replied that the only concern of the Soviet Union was to prevent a change in the status quo in Berlin and elsewhere in Europe. The Bonn government had deliberately created a provocation. I replied that a clear precedent existed so that one could hardly talk of provocation.[3]

Dobrynin then said that Moscow had noted his conversation with the President as well as the lunch with me with "much satisfaction." Moscow was ready to engage in a "strictly confidential exchange on delicate and important matters" with the President using the Dobrynin–Kissinger channel. The exchange will be kept very secret. Moscow "welcomes an informal exchange."

Moscow had noted "with due attention" my comment at the previous meeting that the United States had no interest in undermining the Soviet position in Eastern Europe. He was authorized to assure me that in its turn, the Soviet Union had no intention of undermining the status quo in Western Europe. The Soviet Union was interested that the United States acted on the basis of the actual conditions in Europe.

---

[1] Source: National Archives, Nixon Presidential Materials, NSC Files, Box 489, President's Trip File, Dobrynin/Kissinger, 1969, Part 2. Secret; Nodis. The memorandum indicates the President saw it. This conversation, like most meetings between Kissinger and Dobrynin, was private and occurred without interpreters or secretaries.

[2] For the passages of Nixon's speech that concerned the Soviets, see *Foreign Relations, 1969–1976*, volume XL, Germany and Berlin, 1969–1972. The text of the speech is in *Public Papers: Nixon, 1969*, pp. 156–158.

[3] On March 5, West German federal elections took place in West Berlin without harassment of access routes by either the Soviets or East Germans. This Bundesversammlung was the fourth to occur in Berlin without incident.

I asked whether that meant that the Soviet Union did not care about formal recognition of Eastern Germany. Dobrynin replied that this was correct. I added that for us it was essential to get the access procedures to Berlin regularized. Dobrynin suggested that there had been many positive developments in the negotiations of 1963 to 1969 crisis that might be re-examined. He refused to specify what those were but said he would go over the record and give me some indication later. He urged me to do the same, indicating that Moscow's attitude was "positive."

Turning to the Middle East, Dobrynin quoted Moscow as saying: "We are prepared to discuss with Mr. Kissinger how bilateral talks can be organized, when and how to start them and how to relate them to four power combination." Moscow had a slight preference for conducting the conversations in the Soviet capital; alternatively, it was willing to conduct them in Washington. New York was a definite third choice. Dobrynin stressed that the Soviet Union was very seriously concerned about the Middle East and willing to discuss *all* the elements of the UN Resolution.[4] He asked whether the United States was willing to envisage Israeli troop withdrawal. I said if there were proper guarantees for the new frontiers, it would certainly have to be talked about. Speaking privately, I added that it seemed to me improbable that Israel would be prepared to withdraw to its pre-1967 frontiers. Dobrynin replied that Moscow understood this. The Soviet Union was willing to discuss every aspect of the Middle East, including guarantees. However, he added, this was one of the "important and delicate" subjects that should be discussed in the Dobrynin–Kissinger channel. He then repeated that the subjects Moscow was willing to discuss were frontiers, guarantees, communications, waterways and refugees. Dobrynin indicated that he thought that the real negotiation would have to be bilateral United States-Soviet Union and that he regarded the four-power meeting in New York as largely window-dressing. He added "we are willing to discuss *any* question including those that concern Israel."

Turning to Vietnam, Dobrynin said that Moscow had noted our previous conversation. He inquired whether I was aware of Zorin's call on Lodge,[5] which indicated Soviet good will. However, the Vietnam issue was a delicate matter for the Soviet Union since it was not the only power involved. He thought the Soviet Union could be most

---

[4] See footnote 4, Document 2.

[5] The specific meeting is unclear. Between January 1 and the time of this meeting, Soviet Ambassador Valerian Zorin met several times with the Nixon administration's chief Vietnam Peace Talks negotiator in Paris, Henry Cabot Lodge.

helpful if we had a concrete proposition to make and not one in the abstract.

Dobrynin asked me about the German attitude toward the NPT and whether the Soviet reassurance was enough to get German ratification.[6] I told him in my judgment, if the Soviet Union could give the Germans some reassurance on Article 2,[7] either through us or directly, it would ease the problem of signature considerably.

I then explained to Dobrynin our decision on ABM,[8] which he noted with intense interest and about which he asked a number of very intelligent questions. We agreed to meet again within a week.

(*Note:* The quotes were taken down during the conversation.)

---

[6] The President underlined "the NPT" and "ratification" and highlighted the paragraph.

[7] Article 2 of the NPT obligated non-nuclear-weapon states not to receive the transfer, either directly or indirectly, of nuclear weapons or devices and not to manufacture or seek assistance in the manufacture of nuclear weapons or devices. (21 UST 483) On January 28, Kissinger sent Nixon a memorandum prepared by Spurgeon Keeny, Assistant Director of ACDA, that outlined the provisions and problems of the NPT. (National Archives, Nixon Presidential Materials, NSC Files, Subject Files, Box 366, Non-Proliferation Treaty Through March 1969)

[8] Nixon decided to move forward with the construction of an anti-ballistic missile defense system, which he believed was a crucial bargaining chip in forthcoming Soviet arms control talks. On March 14, the White House issued a press release; for text of the "Statement on Deployment of the Antiballistic Missile System" see *Public Papers: Nixon, 1969*, pp. 216–219.

---

24.   Memorandum of Conversation[1]

Washington, March 8, 1969, 10 a.m.

SUBJECT

  Middle East

PARTICIPANTS

  Anatoliy F. Dobrynin, Soviet Ambassador
  The Secretary
  Malcolm Toon, Acting Deputy Assistant Secretary

---

[1] Source: National Archives, RG 59, E 5405, Records of Joseph Sisco (Lot Files 74 D 131 and 76 D 251), Box 27. Secret; Nodis. Drafted by Toon. The memorandum is part I of IV. A notation on the memorandum indicates the President saw it.

The Secretary briefly described the President's trip to Europe[2] and told Dobrynin that the Middle East problem had been one of the principal subjects of discussion, particularly with the British and the French. In response to Dobrynin's specific inquiry, the Secretary said that the French position initially had been a piecemeal approach but it seemed now to be closer to our own position in the sense that the French now recognize the need for working out an overall settlement before Israeli withdrawal.

The Secretary said that we felt it would be desirable to have quiet bilateral talks with the Soviets, and it was his view that we should begin these talks in Washington and perhaps at a later date they could be continued in Moscow.

Dobrynin said that the Soviet preference, of course, would be Moscow, but he felt that his Government would agree with the Secretary's suggestion. After some discussion it was agreed that Mr. Sisco would meet with Ambassador Dobrynin on Friday, March 14.

The Secretary suggested that the talks might proceed on the basis of the Soviet December 30 plan[3] as well as our own proposals which are now in the process of preparation. The Secretary pointed out that these private bilateral talks should not be considered a substitute for Four-Power talks in New York. It was his feeling that such talks among the Four Powers might begin the following week. As the Secretary saw it, the principal purpose of the Four-Power talks should be to provide support for the Jarring mission since there seemed to be general agreement among the Four Powers that it was essential that Ambassador Jarring continue his efforts to bring the parties directly involved together. The Secretary felt that Four-Power meetings in New York should be private, and this was also the view of the British and French. Dobrynin said that the Soviets also would favor private talks, and he felt that there would be no objection to the timetable set forth by the Secretary.

There was a brief discussion of the Soviet December 30 plan, with the Secretary pointing out that some points needed clarification. For example, it was not clear from the text of the plan that the Soviet position on freedom of navigation extended to the Suez Canal as well as the Gulf of Aquaba. Dobrynin said that he felt that paragraph 2 of the Soviet plan was a clear statement of the Soviet position, and the subsequent specific reference to the Gulf of Aquaba, did not mean that the Soviets did not favor freedom of navigation in Suez for all parties as well.

---

[2] See footnote 2, Document 11.
[3] See footnote 4, Document 1.

The Secretary made clear that we cannot persuade Israel to enter into any agreement which would not provide the Israelis with the security that they seek. While it is true, as Dobrynin pointed out, that the Soviets stand for the continued existence of the State of Israel, the Arab position is much less clear. Arab leaders continue to state publicly their desire to destroy Israel, and so long as this attitude persists it is not likely that the Israelis would be prepared to withdraw their forces from areas they now occupy.

Dobrynin pointed out that there can be no peace in the Middle East so long as Israel insists rigidly on its own requirements. A peace settlement must respond to the interests of all parties. So far as Israel's security is concerned, this could be satisfied by a Security Council guarantee or a Four-Power guarantee. Dobrynin pointed out that the Soviet position is flexible on this question.

It was agreed that these and other points of substance could be explored more thoroughly in the private bilateral talks which would begin Friday, March 14.

25.   Editorial Note

During their March 8, 1969, conversation (see Document 24), Secretary of State William Rogers and Soviet Ambassador Anatoliy Dobrynin also discussed recent developments in Vietnam, including the possibility of U.S. retaliation for North Vietnamese attacks on South Vietnamese cities. Rogers raised the option of engaging in private talks with North Vietnam and four-party talks among the United States, Republic of Vietnam, Democratic Republic of Vietnam, and National Liberation Front on political issues. Dobrynin stated that he considered this an important change in U.S. policy and he would report it to Moscow. A memorandum of their conversation is in *Foreign Relations, 1969–1976*, volume VI, Vietnam, January 1969–July 1970, Document 32.

Later that evening, from 6:25 to 7:10 p.m., Henry Kissinger spoke on the telephone with President Nixon, who was in Key Biscayne, Florida, about a number of issues including Vietnam. Kissinger complained to President Nixon about Rogers' volunteering four-party talks to Dobrynin: "We weren't saying we didn't want to discuss political questions. I think, myself, we would have wound up, in this first testing period, in a weak position in a tough sequence of events. My concern is they will now feel free to press us along in these private talks." Nixon responded, "We can't be boxed in where we are at the mercy of the fact that we can't hit the north and we can't have private talks. We will have no bargaining position." Kissinger stated that after 4 weeks of pressing publicly for military and political talks, the North Vietnamese had achieved that and "they can go to private talks and string them out." Nixon suggested that Kissinger "can cut that down by making clear to the Soviets and I will say so in my press conference, there will be no compromise on this coalition government [within South Vietnam]." Kissinger suggested that, "I don't believe it will be easy for you to attack Cambodia while private talks are going on and not much is being done in South Vietnam." Nixon replied that, "My point is if, while the private talks are going on and they are kicking us, we are going to do something." Nixon and Kissinger returned to the Rogers–Dobrynin conversation. Nixon stated that "There is not going to be any de-escalation. State has nothing to do with that. We are just going to keep giving word to Wheeler to knock hell out of them." Kissinger suggested that, "If they hit us again, we must refuse to have private talks for another week." The President stated: "We cannot tolerate one more of these without hitting back. We have already warned them. Presumably they have stopped. If they hit us again, we hit them with no warning. That is the way we are going to do it. I can't tolerate argument from Rogers on this. You warn once. However, if they don't hit us, we are screwed." (Library of Congress, Manuscript Division, Kissinger Papers, Box 359, Telephone Records, 1969–1976, Telephone Conversations, Chronological File, 3–13 March 1969)

On March 9, Haldeman described Kissinger's reaction to Rogers' conversation with Dobrynin:

"K called me early in great distress because Rogers had reversed United States policy in his talks with Dobrynin yesterday. K feels it is disastrous and is really upset, but will spend today developing recovery plan and come down tomorrow to see P. K feels the policy question is so serious that if continued he'll have to leave. Can't preside over destruction of Saigon government. Feels we have great chance to take hard line and Rogers gave it away. . . . K felt Rogers, (by alluding that we would stop the private talks with the North Vietnamese) had given Dobrynin the stance that the U.S. wasn't fully backing the Thieu government, K also felt this would lead to the destruction of Saigon, and was against current policy." (*Haldeman Diaries: Multimedia Edition*) (Ellipsis in the source text)

On March 10, Kissinger sent Nixon a memorandum following up on their telephone conversation 2 days before and recommending remedial steps to counter the Dobrynin–Rogers discussion. This memorandum is printed in *Foreign Relations, 1969–1976*, volume VI, Vietnam, January 1969–July 1970, Document 35.

26.   **Memorandum From the Acting Executive Secretary of the Department of State (Walsh) to the President's Assistant for National Security Affairs (Kissinger)**[1]

Washington, March 15, 1969.

SUBJECT

The President's Meeting with Ambassador Beam on March 20, 3:00 p.m.[2]

Ambassador Beam is in Washington on consultation prior to assuming his duties as Ambassador to the Soviet Union.[3] He plans to arrive in Moscow on March 31. The Ambassador will be taking up his new post at a time when several positive developments are in train in US-Soviet bilateral relations. Specifically:

(1) We are completing final arrangements with the Soviets on an exchange of chancery sites in Washington and Moscow and hope to reach formal agreement in the latter part of April.

(2) We hope to negotiate with the Soviets this summer on the reciprocal establishment of consulates in Leningrad and San Francisco.

(3) We expect to hold talks soon with the Soviets on peaceful uses of nuclear explosives.

Soon after his arrival in Moscow, Ambassador Beam will be calling upon a number of high Soviet officials, who will be anxious to learn what our latest position is on strategic arms limitations talks, the Middle East, Vietnam, and an eventual Summit meeting. The President may

---

[1] Source: National Archives, RG 59, Central Files 1967–69, POL 17 US–USSR. Confidential. Drafted by Gifford D. Malone (EUR/SOV) on March 14, and concurred in by Thompson Buchanan (EUR/SOV), Dubs, Toon, and Beam.

[2] According to the President's Daily Diary Nixon met with Beam and Kissinger on March 20 from 3:08–3:50 p.m. No substantive record of the meeting has been found. (National Archives, Nixon Presidential Materials, White House Central Files) On March 18, Kissinger sent Nixon a memorandum of talking points with 6 tabs: a copy of Nixon's letter to Rogers and Laird of February 4 (see Document 10), a draft letter to Kosygin (see Document 28), supplementary explanatory oral instructions for Beam, press guidance for Ziegler and Beam, draft letters to the major West European allies, and instructions to USNATO for briefing the North Atlantic Council. Beam describes the meeting in *Multiple Exposure*, p. 218, as follows: "Kissinger was present at my farewell talk with the President when we went over the draft letter to Kosygin. I was told to treat our talk with great secrecy. Since Secretary of State Rogers was away, I naturally left a memorandum for him reporting on what I had been doing, a step which I understand caused great annoyance to the White House staff." No record of Beam's memorandum to Rogers has been found.

[3] On March 13, the U.S. Senate confirmed Beam as Ambassador to the Soviet Union.

wish to discuss these subjects with Ambassador Beam with a view to the Ambassador's subsequent discussions with Soviet officials.

A biographic sketch of Ambassador Beam is enclosed.[4]

Robert L. Brown[5]

---

[4] Attached but not printed.

[5] Deputy Executive Secretary Robert L. Brown signed for Walsh.

---

27.   Memorandum From the President's Assistant for National Security Affairs (Kissinger) to President Nixon[1]

Washington, March 19, 1969.

SUBJECT

Memorandum of Conversation with Ambassador Dobrynin, March 11, 1969

Dobrynin called me about 7:00 p.m. to ask whether I could see him that evening or the next morning. I agreed to drop by the Soviet Embassy about 9:00 p.m. Dobrynin was extremely cordial. He met me together with Mrs. Dobrynin and, after some social conversation about their daughter, they both mentioned that Mrs. Dobrynin was hoping to call on Mrs. Nixon soon.

Dobrynin then handed me a brief message[2] from Kosygin to the President acknowledging his good wishes on his birthday. He also handed me a copy of a note which the Soviet Union proposed to hand to the Germans the next day, designed to meet some of the German concerns about the NPT. Dobrynin said that the note had been influenced by some of our suggestions and was given to us simply for our information and as a token of their good faith. (An analysis of the note is attached at Tab A.)[3]

---

[1] Source: National Archives, Nixon Presidential Materials, NSC Files, Box 489, President's Trip Files, Dobrynin/Kissinger, 1969, Part 2. Secret; Nodis.

[2] Not found.

[3] Attached but not printed.

Dobrynin then told me that he had been extremely pleased by his conversation with the Secretary of State.[4] There had been real progress toward four-power talks on Vietnam, including political topics. I told him that this was a little premature. The Secretary of State had described what would be the end result, but I was sure that our position was to continue to discuss withdrawals on a bilateral basis with the DRV. Political questions should be handled by Saigon and the NLF. Dobrynin said the NLF found it difficult to go into a forum with its mortal enemy. Hanoi told Moscow that they wanted a four-power meeting so that all the participants could work on the GVN in order to make it more adaptable. I said that I had correctly interpreted your thinking and I could not go beyond that. The initial contacts would have to be bilateral.

I then said the President was determined to end the war in Vietnam one way or the other. There was no intention to humiliate Hanoi. We recognized they had sacrificed a great deal and we would be generous. At the same time, we had certain conditions that had to be satisfied. I repeated that you were determined to end the war one way or the other. Dobrynin smiled and said you would find it difficult to escalate—there just were not very many things we could do militarily that would not cost us more than they were worth. I said, we shall see.

Dobrynin then asked me what I thought of the Sino-Soviet dispute, especially the fight along the Ussuri River.[5] I said we regarded it primarily as a problem for China and the Soviet Union and we did not propose to get involved. Dobrynin became very emotional and said China was everybody's problem. He asked whether we would try to take advantage of the Soviet Union's difficulties. I said that he had probably seen enough of the President to recognize that the President was not playing for petty stakes. We had offered serious negotiations to the Soviet Union; we meant to pursue them. At the same time, if the Soviet Union tried to embarrass or humiliate, we would take appropriate countermeasures without much fanfare. However, my presence

---

[4] See Document 25.

[5] On March 11, at approximately 10 p.m., Kissinger spoke on the telephone with Nixon and summarized his earlier conversation with Dobrynin. Kissinger reported that "Dobrynin asked how we evaluated that Chinese clash. I told him we think it is their problem. We don't presume to give them advice. We won't play any little games. We try to settle things, but if threatened, we will do what we have to. Obviously, this is much on their minds." Nixon stated that "Sometimes events which we could not have foreseen may have some helpful effect—who knows." Kissinger responded, "If one evaluates accounts of events, we gained more from that clash than we lost through Saturday's conversation [between Rogers and Dobrynin]." Nixon then stated, "It must have shook the North Vietnamese." Kissinger agreed that "It must be a warning to Hanoi it can happen again." (Ibid.)

in his apartment in such informal circumstances indicated the seriousness with which the President took Soviet-American relations. Dobrynin then gave me a gory account of the atrocities committed by the Chinese. He spent about fifteen minutes describing the military situation. I listened politely but made no comment.

At the end, Dobrynin asked me whether I was willing to meet him on a purely social basis to see some color slides of the Soviet Union. I told him yes.

28.   Letter From President Nixon to Chairman of the Council of Ministers of the Soviet Union Kosygin[1]

Washington, March 26, 1969.

Dear Mr. Chairman:

I should like to use the occasion of Ambassador Beam's assumption of his duties as my Ambassador in Moscow to share with you my thoughts on the future of relations between our two countries.

First of all, I should like to assure you that Ambassador Beam has my complete confidence and is fully familiar with my views. You may be certain that he will communicate to me promptly and in complete confidence any views that you and your colleagues may wish to convey to me at any time.

Because of the awesome power our two countries represent we, as heads of government, carry the gravest responsibilities for the peace and safety of the world. I am prepared to explore with you and your colleagues every available avenue for the settlement of international problems, particularly those that involve the danger of confrontation or conflict. I am determined to see us enter an era of negotiations and to leave behind the tensions and confrontations of the past.

I am encouraged by the contacts that have already been initiated by our two governments on the problems of the Middle East. It is essential that both our countries exert a calming influence on this situation which,

---

[1] Source: National Archives, Nixon Presidential Materials, NSC Files, Box 433, Backchannel Files/Backchannel Messages, Beam Instructions, 3/26/69 (Amb to Moscow). No classification marking. The date is handwritten. This letter was attached to a March 26 covering memorandum from Kissinger to Beam, which is not printed. Also attached but not printed were instructions from Nixon for Beam to use when he delivered the letter to Kosygin. On April 22, Beam presented the letter to Kosygin; see Document 40.

as the past has shown, is fraught with profound dangers for peace not only in the immediate area in question but for the rest of the world. I believe that no outside power must seek advantages in this area at the expense of any other; on the contrary it is, in my view, the duty of all outside powers, especially the great powers, to help create conditions in which the opposing sides can find a solution that protects their essential and legitimate interests, as foreseen in the Security Council resolution of November 1967. I believe that the willingness of our two countries to exert a responsible and beneficial influence in the Middle East is an essential element in building the confidence that must be the basis of serious and productive negotiations.

I am aware of the constructive role which your government has played at certain stages of the search for a peaceful settlement of the Vietnam conflict. I am aware also of the great influence which you possess in North Vietnam by virtue of your military support to that country. In the spirit of candor which I hope will mark communications between us, I would ask you to continue using that great influence in the direction of peace. For peace is what I am striving to achieve, patiently and in a spirit of conciliation. The effort toward peace cannot of course be confined exclusively to the conference table; it must be reflected in Vietnam itself. As Commander in Chief I am responsible for the safety of American troops and I must also meet solemn commitments to the Government of the Republic of South Vietnam. But my country has demonstrated its readiness for moderation that takes into account the legitimate concerns of the Government of North Vietnam. Moderation, however, must be mutual and I believe that you can be influential in that direction. In any event, it is my conviction that the era of negotiation which I believe we both wish to embark upon would be seriously burdened if the day of peace in Southeast Asia cannot be brought closer.

I believe, Mr. Chairman, that our responsibilities also require the avoidance of crises and the removal of threats to peace in Europe. I was disturbed by the recent flare-up of tensions in Berlin. As I pointed out to your Ambassador, my country is committed to the integrity of West Berlin; it is committed also to fulfilling the obligations and exercising the rights stemming from four-power agreements. Here as elsewhere, unilateral attempts to change the existing situation to the advantage of one side would place obstacles on the road to peace. I believe that any change must be the result of agreement and should improve on the unsatisfactory aspects of the existing situation. If you have suggestions that would make the situation in Berlin mutually more satisfactory, I would, of course, be interested in hearing them.

More generally with regard to Europe, I would hope that there, too, negotiation rather than confrontation will mark our future relations. I am conscious of the great suffering endured by the Soviet people in the past because war was carried to your soil across your

Western frontier. It is undoubtedly the responsibility of the Soviet Government to ensure that such a disaster does not occur again. At the same time, I am bound to say that last year's events in Czechoslovakia produced a profound shock in American opinion. Our commitments to our European allies are solely for defense and for the production of their legitimate security interests. This should not be an issue between us.

As countries with the largest arsenals of modern weapons in the world, we carry a special responsibility for the control of armaments. The era of negotiation to which I have referred must clearly include efforts toward disarmament. I am confident that progress toward the solution of the great political problems that engage our interests can be matched by progress toward curbing competition in arms; for there can be no doubt that such competition, especially if unrestrained, is utterly wasteful and would not, ultimately, enhance anyone's security. I can assure you that my decisions in this area will be guided solely by the principle of "sufficiency," that is, by the principle that our military strength will be only that which is required to ensure the safety of this country and meet the commitments to our allies. We base this on the assumption that you will adhere to a similar policy for your country. Military requirements depend, among other things, on the crises and dangers that confront us in the world. As the dangers recede, I am convinced so can the levels of arms in our arsenals. These are the simple and, I believe, realistic principles that will guide me in negotiations on disarmament. It is my sincere hope that in the years of my Administration you and we can increasingly cooperate so that the burden of arms that our people bear can be lessened.

If I may sum up the approach to our relations that I have sought to convey to you in this message, it is simply that I intend to safeguard the interests of my country with due regard to the interests of yours; that in this spirit we should join together, wherever and whenever possible, to curb the dangers and eliminate the sources of conflict. I would like to remain in frequent and candid communication with you through our Ambassadors and otherwise; my representatives stand ready, and indeed have already begun, to explore with you the whole range of issues that confront us and the means to make our relations increasingly cooperative and constructive.

Sincerely,

Richard Nixon

29.   Memorandum From the President's Assistant for National Security Affairs (Kissinger) to President Nixon[1]

Washington, undated.

SUBJECT

Conversation Between Senator Percy and Ambassador Dobrynin

Senator Percy had a long conversation over lunch with Ambassador Dobrynin on March 27. The Senator provided us a copy of his account of the talk and asked that I inform you that he had followed up on your suggestion about seeing Dobrynin. I already have acknowledged Percy's letter.[2]

The Percy–Dobrynin conversation was wide-ranging and substantive; a full text of the Senator's memorandum is at Tab A.

I consider the following points of special interest:

1. *Estimate of You.* Dobrynin agreed that you were taking a firm, but not rigid, line on world problems, and that you were approaching their solution with a knowledgeable, open, and reasonable attitude.

2. *Consular Relations.* Dobrynin stated there was "every reason" to have consulates in each of our countries in addition to those planned for San Francisco and Leningrad, and said that the Soviets "would have no objection" to others being opened.

3. *Bilateral Trade.* In this area, according to Dobrynin, "America always puts politics ahead of good sound economics," and he was not optimistic about trading opportunities between the US and the USSR for that reason.

4. *Comments on Secretaries Rogers and Laird.* Dobrynin said he had followed the recent testimonies of Secretaries Rogers and Laird[3] closely. He found the positions taken by Secretary Rogers "responsible," but

---

[1] Source: National Archives, Nixon Presidential Materials, NSC Files, Box 725, Country Files, Europe, USSR, Memcons, Dobrynin/Percy, March 1969. Confidential. Sent for information. Nixon wrote "Note page 2" on the memorandum.

[2] On April 3, Kissinger wrote Percy and acknowledged receipt of his memorandum of conversation. Kissinger informed Percy that "You covered a lot of ground, and we are studying your account of the talk with great interest. I will advise the President that you have taken his suggestion, as requested, and will give him a summary of the key points of your conversation." Kissinger provided a summary to Nixon in an undated memorandum drafted by Lesh on April 2. (Ibid., Box 709, Country Files, Europe, USSR, Vol. II)

[3] On March 27, Rogers testified before the Senate Committee on Foreign Relations. Extracts of his testimony concerning U.S. preparations for Strategic Arms Limitation

objected strongly to Secretary Laird's assertion that the Soviet leadership was attempting to develop a pre-emptive first strike capability against the US. Dobrynin said that "even taking into account the fact that we know he is trying to sell the American people and the Congress on an ABM system that is not very popular, he is going to extremes."

In contrast, Dobrynin added, the Soviets had "not wanted to poison the Russian people against the Nixon Administration," and had not printed critical comments, "hoping for the best."[4] But he said that "time may be running out" on that policy.

5. *Disarmament.* There is a growing feeling in Moscow, according to Dobrynin, that the United States is not really interested in disarmament talks with the Soviet Union. He commented that the Johnson Administration had been ready to sit down for strategic arms talks,[5] and it was difficult to understand why—if the Nixon Administration were equally interested in such talks—it should take up to six months more to prepare the US position. He also warned that no preconditions could be set if disarmament talks were to be held. The Soviets, Dobrynin asserted, were ready to begin discussions with us tomorrow.[6]

6. *Vietnam.* A US decision to resume bombing of North Vietnam would be "very foolish," in Dobrynin's judgment, since it would only unite the North Vietnamese more solidly, and require both the Chinese and the Russians to step up their levels of assistance.

7. *Middle East.* Dobrynin saw no evidence that the situation would improve in the near future; "it is filled with danger and there can be more serious outbreaks." He pushed for successful four-power talks to lessen the dangers.

By way of comment, I would note that in the past few days Soviet Deputy Foreign Minister Kuznetsov has *not* taken as hard a line as

---

Talks are in *Documents on Disarmament, 1969*, pp. 138–139. On March 20–21, in nationally televised hearings, Laird testified before the International Organization and Disarmament Subcommittee of the Senate Foreign Relations Committee and declared that the Soviet Union had begun a nuclear forces build-up aimed at eliminating U.S. defenses in a single blow. Laird supported his assertion with information about the SS–9, a Soviet intercontinental ballistic missile (ICBM). He stated that the SS–9 threat could be countered only with an anti-ballistic missile (ABM) system. Extracts of Laird's testimony are ibid., pp. 125–131.

[4] In an Intelligence Note of March 27 entitled "Soviet Style Honeymoon for President Nixon," Thomas L. Hughes, Director of Intelligence and Research, informed Rogers that US-Soviet relations have been "notably restrained in its public treatment of the new administration, and has maintained an almost complete moratorium on personal criticism of the President." (National Archives, RG 59, Central Files 1967–69, POL US–USSR)

[5] See footnote 6, Document 2.

[6] Nixon highlighted this paragraph and wrote in the margin, "H.K.—maybe we are better off on this line than we thought."

Dobrynin did with Senator Percy on topics such as the ABM decision and strategic arms limitation talks.

Tab A

Memorandum From Senator Charles Percy to the President's Assistant for National Security Affairs (Kissinger)

Washington, March 27, 1969.

TO

    William Rogers, Secretary of State
    Melvin Laird, Secretary of Defense
    Richard Helms, Director of Central Intelligence
    J. Edgar Hoover, Director of Federal Bureau of Investigation
    Henry Kissinger, Assistant to the President

On May 27, 1968, I had lunch alone with Ambassador Dobrynin at the Soviet Embassy, at his invitation, and there was a productive discussion. Last week I invited Ambassador Dobrynin to my home in Georgetown for luncheon. We met at 1:00 PM, Thursday, March 27, 1969, and talked until 3:30 PM. Following are summary statements that represent, to the best of my recollection, the position and attitude taken on various questions. Ambassador Dobrynin is extremely articulate. He is very skilled, however, in talking a great deal, seemingly in response to a question without ever directly answering the question. It was necessary on several occasions to repeat a question in a different way three or four times in order to get a more direct response.

President Nixon

Percy: Do you feel that the answer I gave to your question last May, "Is there a new Nixon?", was accurate and that he does appear to be a man who has a broad-gauged view of world problems and, though firm, is not what you consider rigid "hard line" and would approach the solution to problems with a knowledgeable, open and reasonable attitude?

Dobrynin: Yes, the description was not only accurate but coincided with my own feelings. But of course we have had no real opportunity to negotiate or work together yet.

Consular Treaty

Percy: I was pleased to see the Soviet suggestion that a consulate be opened in one Soviet and one American city. Do you envision others being opened?

Dobrynin: There is every reason to have additional consulates and we would have no objection to others being opened.[7]

Bilateral Trade

Dobrynin: What is the outlook for expanding trade between the Soviet Union and the United States? We would like to do more business with your country and it would benefit both economies. It is rather ridiculous for us to ship vodka to Denmark and have them rebottle it and sell it to the United States when we could sell it direct. When the Italians assured us that they could purchase $30 million of machine tools for the Fiat factory being built in Russia from the United States, we were highly skeptical and we were proven right. America always puts politics ahead of good sound economics and I am not optimistic about trading opportunities between our two countries.

Percy: You have asked whether most favored nation treatment could be extended to the Soviet Union and indicated that you feel no real trade of significance compared with what went on for instance in 1930 could be carried on without such treatment. I would have to say the chances would not be good for extension of this position to the Soviet Union under the present circumstances. However, normalizing East-West relationships has to be approached step by step and I would suggest that it might be practical to consider extending MFN treatment to some other eastern European country such as Czechoslovakia, putting it on the same basis as Poland and Yugoslavia, which would at least be a step in this direction.

Dobrynin: This sounds logical though I cannot see why Americans are so afraid of trading with the Soviet Union.

Percy: It is directly related to the threats to American security and the security of other nations. For instance, if the Administration were to propose MFN being extended to the Soviet Union today, the first opposition would come from those who would talk about the amount of war materials being supplied to North Vietnam by the USSR to kill American boys in South Vietnam and that nothing can be done to just strengthen an economy with this the end result. You have mentioned automobile manufacture but you also have indicated that an agreement to manufacture trucks would be most interesting from your standpoint. The provision of technical assistance for the mass production of trucks would be directly related to the kind of military assistance that you would be providing to North Vietnam.

Dobrynin: We do not like to think we need technical assistance as we are capable of making anything we want to make. But it does stand

---

[7] Nixon highlighted this paragraph.

to reason that we can benefit from mass production techniques. But if we do not make agreements with the United States we can always make agreements with European countries. The machine tools that the United States would not furnish for the Fiat factory are all obtainable in Western Europe and these countries sell freely to us and are glad to have the business.

Leadership Relationships

Percy: I sat in on part of Secretary William Rogers' testimony[8] before the Foreign Relations Committee today and brought you a copy of the full text of his comments.

Dobrynin: Yes, I watched part of his testimony on television and his positions were responsible. However, I am concerned about the very strong reaction in Moscow among our leadership against statements made by your Defense Secretary Melvin Laird. I tried to picture the average American sitting in front of his television set watching Laird talk about the Soviet intention to make a first strike on the United States, thus depicting us as the worst kind of people. Even taking into account the fact that we know he is trying to sell the American people and the Congress on an ABM system that is not very popular, he is going to extremes.[9] After all, the leadership in Moscow is only human and I am concerned about their reactions to this kind of talk. I spent thirty days back home in January and spent many days at a resort thirty miles from Moscow where Brezhnev, Kosygin, and Podgorniy came with their families and we all skied together cross country. I know their wives and their children and I know their reactions as human beings. They do not like to be put in the position of appearing to plot millions of deaths or used this way for the purpose of selling an American defense program. I am concerned about their reaction as they have not formulated their judgment on the Nixon Administration and have tried to hold back any judgments that might be premature. In fact, we have not wanted in any way to poison the Russian people against the Nixon Administration and have not printed critical comments, hoping for the best. But time may be running out on this.[10]

Disarmament

Percy: When in your judgment should talks get under way on disarmament, how long will they take do you think, and what do you foresee as the end result?

---

[8] See footnote 3.

[9] Nixon underlined and highlighted this sentence.

[10] Nixon underlined and highlighted this sentence.

Dobrynin: There is a growing feeling in Moscow that the United States is really not interested in disarmament talks.[11] The Johnson Administration was ready to go ahead with these talks, in fact anxious to do so, and a set of principles had been laid down for such discussions. Then certain advisers to Johnson started to attach all sorts of conditions to these talks involving such issues as Vietnam. We said that we would be glad to talk about Vietnam or any other subject the United States wished to discuss, but would not make agreements in advance. We were not particularly anxious to have a summit meeting with an administration that had only a few months left in office but were willing to do so. But it never came about.

With the Nixon Administration we are ready to have talks on disarmament tomorrow. We would also be willing to discuss any other subject with the Administration, but as recently as two weeks ago we were told that such talks could be held within a period of "up to six months." This did not reassure Moscow that the United States was serious about wanting talks. The Nixon Administration said that it needed time to prepare for such talks. But look at the amount of time it has been putting into appearing before Congress and on television to try to sell an ABM system. It has also put in a lot of time analyzing such a system and coming up with a program. This same amount of time could have been put into preparing for disarmament talks that certainly should not take six months if America considered them important. It is a matter of priorities and the United States may not think this is an important subject, at least that is the impression they give.

Percy: The President may consider disarmament talks less meaningful when we both possess the power to annihilate each other—even were production stopped at the present level—if we leave unresolved serious political difficulties that could bring about conflict.

Dobrynin: We are always willing to talk about the problems of Vietnam or the Middle East or any other subject the United States wishes to discuss, but preconditions cannot be established if disarmament talks are to be held.[12]

Percy: Does the USSR feel that it requires an ABM directed against China?

Dobrynin: Let me ask you how you regard China and what your relationships should be with China.

Percy: In my opinion it is dangerous to regard China as an "outlaw" nation, and we should try to bring her within the community of

---

[11] Nixon underlined and highlighted this sentence.

[12] Nixon underlined the last clause of this sentence.

nations providing she will meet acceptable standards of conduct. But China has shown no inclination to act as a civilized member of society. She has steadily reduced her level of diplomatic contact with the rest of the world, and it will be interesting to see how long she lets Canada, where a good trading relationship could be built, cool its heels on its suggestion for diplomatic recognition. We have had one irrational ruler in our lifetime, Adolf Hitler, and it is always possible that we could have another.

Dobrynin: China's actions against us on the border have been an interesting case in point. They selected an unoccupied island which complicated our military options. Had we moved across the water to their side, they would have screamed that we were invading them, and yet they were able to raid, withdraw and be in a position of challenging and even embarrassing the mighty Russian Army.

Percy: Going back to disarmament, let me ask for your reaction to a purely personal suggestion. What would you think of a mutual moratorium by Russia and the United States on the emplacement of missiles and nuclear warheads? Acceptable verification means are available. Today there is a rough parity between the United States and the Soviet Union. We do not know how long disarmament talks would take to complete and, during the process of negotiation, an extensive build-up of missiles by one side or the other might upset the balance. This would seem, therefore, an excellent time for a joint moratorium. It might provide an improved atmosphere for the talks and the talks would have a better chance to succeed.

Dobrynin: Such a proposal could certainly be considered but to even consider it we would have to get talks under way and I see no real inclination to do this.

Percy: In his testimony this morning Secretary Rogers said that talks could begin within a few months.

Dobrynin: I do not know what your definition of "few" is. All I know is that I was told up to six months and that does not appear to me as though there is any real desire to get talks under way.

Percy: I am not a spokesman for the Administration and in fact regretfully find that I differ sometimes with its judgments. However, I will convey your impressions to the appropriate parties and it would be my own hope that talks could be gotten under way soon. However, the events in Czechoslovakia made it impossible to hold talks heretofore and talks could be set back again if there were other unfortunate happenings in that area.

Vietnam

Percy: I do believe it would be important to bring Vietnam into the context of our talks since one act of easing tensions should relate to another. I am deeply disturbed by the lack of progress in the Paris talks. There are, of course, some in this country who would withdraw from South Vietnam regardless of the consequences, though I believe they are very few in number. There are many more who feel that the cessation of bombing by the United States has been used by the North Vietnamese only to build up their own forces and has enabled them to undertake another offensive which has cost many American lives. There would be a strong body of support for the President ordering a resumption of bombing in the North, particularly to cut off supply lines. There are many who would support very heavy bombing on the basis that representations to us have been betrayed and that the North Vietnamese are making no serious effort to find the basis for a negotiated political settlement.

Dobrynin: This would be very foolish, in my judgment. First of all, it would be ineffective as has been proved by all of the past bombing done by the United States in North Vietnam. It merely unifies the North Vietnamese and requires a greater level of support by both China and ourselves.[13] As soon as you bomb near China, she intensifies her efforts. And were we called upon to provide a stepped-up level of aid to a Socialist country, we could not possibly fail to respond if we were to remain credible in the eyes of other Socialist countries.[14] The bombing of concentrated urban areas in World War II failed to conquer a people or defeat them. That could only be done by land armies. Of course if you intend to invade North Vietnam with your land forces that would require a minimum of one million men and would call for an equal or greater response by the Chinese Army. Where would all of this get you? You already have a great problem with world opinion. It is difficult to convince people—the average person—that you are not a warlike nation. One of the greatest difficulties I have when I go home is with my father and his friends. I have been in the United States now going on my eighth year. My father is a plumber, he works with his hands, he is a simple man and so are his friends. But they are worried about the intentions of the United States.

There are many Russians who believe that the United States is going to wage war on the Soviet Union. All that our government would have to do is say that we are going to cut back on housing, on consumer goods and other forms of civilian production, and we are going to double our output of armaments. We can do anything that we feel we have to do and the Russian people will fully support us and back us up.

---

[13] Nixon underlined this sentence.

[14] Nixon underlined most of this sentence.

You must take into account that the military in the Soviet Union does not have anywhere near the power and influence that it has in the United States. Your Secretary of Defense sits in the Cabinet, and he consults with the President more than almost any other top official. Your military interests are strong in the Congress. This condition simply does not exist in the Soviet Union. The head of our military is not even a member of the Politburo and only infrequently sits in on major political discussions affecting national policies.

Percy: On the other side of the scale you must take into account, and the world should take into account, that the United States has not used its power for the expansion of its own territories, and our government must take into account in its planning the fact that the Soviet Union is building either five or 25 megaton ICBM's which do not enhance the peace. Why is such explosive power of this magnitude needed? There is talk that the Soviet Union is orbiting nuclear explosives, and this is understandably disconcerting to our average citizen.

Middle East

Percy: Before we finish we should at least have a word of the Mideast. It is important to find a basis for settlement not only because of the danger for the nations directly involved, but also because we must try to avoid situations which could bring our own two nations into dangerous confrontation.

Dobrynin: I cannot see the situation improving in the near future. It is filled with danger and there can be more serious outbreaks. We must do the best we can to lessen the danger through successful four-power talks which will be getting under way. I agree with you that the situation is dangerous and we must act positively to lessen this danger.

On departing, Ambassador Dobrynin suggested that we get together again after the Easter recess. The conversation was cordial and relaxed throughout. On his arrival he was greeted by Loraine and our children who were home from school on Easter vacation, and he was extremely gracious to them. I highly recommend an informal home atmosphere for relaxed discussions when an exchange of views, rather than hard negotiating, is the purpose of the meeting.

Charles H. Percy

30.   **Memorandum From the President's Assistant for National Security Affairs (Kissinger) to President Nixon**[1]

Washington, March 30, 1969.

SUBJECT

The Mid-East Talks with the USSR So Far

What We Have Done So Far

Joe Sisco has seen Dobrynin four times now, three this past week.[2] The discussion has proceeded along three tracks: (1) attempts to clarify each other's position on the main issues listed in the November 1967 UN resolution; (2) Soviet answers to US requests for clarification of the Soviet plan laid out in Moscow's December 30 note;[3] (3) clarification of our working paper distributed Monday for discussion among the four powers. The next session will be April 2.

Much of the discussion has taken place in highly liturgical language—"just and lasting peace," "secure and recognized boundaries," "agreement between/by the parties," "binding agreement." These are the words of the November 1967 UN resolution and of the argument since over its interpretation. They are the words in the working paper we have surfaced in the Four-Power talks. What follows is an effort to identify the real issues behind those words, which are hard to pin down without talking about concrete proposals—something we are not yet prepared to do, partly because of Israel's strong objection to that procedure.

Common Ground Established

We seem agreed on some of the more general principles:

1. The aim is a *real settlement* ("just and lasting peace"). Dobrynin has now said that Moscow does not want just another armistice. The test will come when we get down to details, but this point is worth establishing in view of Israel's concern that Nasser just wants to buy Israeli withdrawal at the cheapest price to get ready for the next round.

---

[1] Source: National Archives, Nixon Presidential Materials, NSC Files, Box 653, Country Files, Middle East, Sisco Middle East Talks, April–June 1969. Secret; Nodis. The memorandum is not initialed by Kissinger. A copy was sent to Halperin on April 2. A virtually identical copy of this memorandum was sent to Kissinger on March 28 by Saunders, which indicates that he was the drafter. (Ibid., Box 649, Country Files, Middle East, Middle East Negotiations, March 27–May 31, 1969)

[2] Saunders summarizes these meetings in Document 38.

[3] See footnote 4, Document 1.

While the Soviets may figure that even a reasonable settlement will leave them enough tension to exploit, their present position seems to leave us room to press for specific arrangements to make the terms of settlement as secure as possible.

2. The Near Eastern *parties must participate* ("agreement"). Dobrynin says Moscow is thinking of a settlement agreed to *by* the Arabs and Israelis. While big-power talks may constitute pressure, the "question of imposing a settlement does not arise." This point is worth establishing because the Arabs believe that all we have to do is say the word and Israel will withdraw. Even de Gaulle's thinking contains this theme. But the USSR seems to recognize the dilemma we share—we must move our clients by persuasion rather than by dictat.

3. A related point is that any US-Soviet views must go to the parties *through Jarring,* at least officially. Unlike de Gaulle who sees a possible role for the four powers independent of the UN, we and Moscow seem agreed on the desirability of keeping a formal UN buffer between us and the parties to avoid having to absorb all the shock of their reaction ourselves. This, of course, assumes continued exchanges between the parties and Jarring.

4. Agreement should be reached on all issues listed in the UN resolution *as a package.* While we are not yet clear on the exact sequence for implementing the elements in the package, Moscow recognizes the practical fact that the Israelis will not withdraw until its security and recognition are guaranteed. This is an important shift from the 1967 Soviet argument that Israel must withdraw *before* other issues could be negotiated.

5. *Israel has a right to exist* as an independent state. This is not new in the Soviet position, but it is important as the one major point on which it differs with Cairo.

Remaining Issues

While there are also differences on a number of secondary points, the important issues at this point are these:

1. *Peace*—What kind of relationship will exist between Arabs and Israelis after a settlement? Moscow has circulated (December 30) a specific sequence of agreements and implementing steps for arranging Israeli withdrawal. We have not, because we must try to meet some of Israel's requirement that these specifics be worked out by the Arabs and Israelis themselves. Therefore, we have chosen to describe our position in terms of a set of carefully worded principles, though behind these we have in mind staff studies of each major element of a settlement.

The issue is this: The farther we can go now in defining precisely the obligations of each side, the more certain we can be of Soviet motives. It is easy for Dobrynin to say Moscow wants a real settlement. It is important for us to close as many loopholes for future exploitations as possible, though frankly this is difficult as long as we keep ourselves from talking specifics. So we keep pressing Dobrynin to define the relationship which will exist between Arabs and Israelis after a settlement.

The importance of the issue is that the long-run position of the US in the Middle East will thrive almost in proportion to the degree to which tensions are reduced. While Moscow profits from exploiting divisions—Arab-Israeli, radical-moderate—the US has interests in all these camps (friends and political interests in Jordan and Israel, oil in Iraq and Saudi Arabia) and can pursue a coherent policy only when tension is at a manageable level, as it was between the late 1950's and early 1967.

The practical elements of the issue are:

a. *Controlling fedayeen.* The US is concerned that the Arab governments—more UAR, Syria, Iraq than Jordan—will sign an agreement and then stand back while the fedayeen violate it. Dobrynin discounts this possibility; he says the fedayeen will dry up when Israel withdraws. We remember how mounting terrorist activity in 1966–67 started the sequence of events that led to war. We also recall that we (and apparently the USSR) were powerless to stop this activity. Convinced that no big-power guarantees can police this, we believe it is crucial that the governments on the ground—the only ones capable of rolling up the terrorists at the source—commit themselves to stop it, at least as an organized movement. We want to be as precise as we can because we have no reason to trust Nasser or the Syrians; after all it was our tacit 1957 understanding with Nasser that he renounced in closing the Straits of Tiran in 1967.

b. *Enforcing the peace.* The only practical measure of the intentions of the Arabs and Soviets is to determine what they will commit themselves to in the way of policing for demilitarized zones and guarantees for free navigation and any other rights which are part of the agreement. Again, we have done staff work on these issues, but it will be difficult to draw Dobrynin out further until we are prepared to get specific. Dobrynin is hard to disagree with when he says Moscow can go no further in defining "peace" than to point out that the collection of practical arrangements worked out on each of the major issues will define the Arab-Israeli relationship that will exist. We have said much the same to the Israelis ourselves.

We have two choices:

a. Continuing our efforts to persuade both the Soviets and French to define more precisely how they see the relationship between Arabs and Israelis after a settlement. Both Dobrynin and the Quai[4] have essentially told us this is no longer a fruitful exercise. They seem to have gone as far as they will until we are ready to talk in terms of the specific collection of arrangements that would define the situation after a settlement.

b. Surfacing our own specific views on the various elements of a settlement. We have numerous staff studies and a working-level document putting these together into an illustrative peace plan. We have carefully avoided getting specific for fear that the Israelis would refuse to go further with us. The time may have come for us to face the decision to begin surfacing specific proposals. This may be the difference between continuing a diplomatic holding action largely on Israel's behalf and trying to turn this exercise into one that could have a chance of producing results.

The *main risk* of surfacing our own plan now is that of Israeli refusal to cooperate. We are familiar with strong Israeli objection to the Four-Power talks. They are still with us because we have stopped short of breaching their basic principle that the Arabs and Israelis must reach the settlement themselves. It can be argued that they need us and in the end will come along. That may be true, but there is a large amount of go-it-alone thinking in the Israeli mood now.

The *advantage* would lie in the possibility of getting a real negotiating process started.

2. *"Secure and recognized boundaries"*—To what lines must Israel withdraw? In the working paper we have circulated we say that any changes in the pre-war lines should be confined to those required for mutual security and should not reflect the weight of conquest. But again, we have stopped short of expressing our views on where the lines might be drawn, and we are arguing principle.

The issue is this: Israel is determined to redraw Israel's boundaries to enhance its security. As Eban says, if this is to be the final map of Israel, Israel wants to draw it right this time. The Arabs, of course, regard any boundary change as Israeli conquest and Arab humiliation. We have frankly resisted all insistence for return to pre-war boundaries mainly because we knew we could not force Israel out of Jerusalem.

The importance of the issue: The basic fact is that we know that Israel is determined to change the lines and we cannot dissuade her. In a longer range vein, while we have no interest in supporting Israeli expansionism, the future stability of the area will depend on remov-

---

[4] The French Ministry of Foreign Affairs is located at Quai d'Orsay in Paris.

ing as many points of friction and Israeli fear as possible. Israel's militancy is directly related to its sense of insecurity.

The practical elements of the issue are:

a. *The US* has no stake in where the lines are drawn. Our only real criteria are (a) that the parties be willing to live with them (that would allow for fair exchanges) and (b) that points of future frictions (such as the divided fields and haphazard lines under the old armistice regime) be minimized. We do not see topography as the sole guarantor of security, as many Israelis do, and we are ahead of others in thinking about alternative means of guaranteeing security. We are more concerned, for instance, about control of Sharm al-Shaikh, and we seem to have thought a lot harder about the practical problems involved in policing DMZ's.

b. *Positions of UK, France, USSR.* Our concept of what reasonable boundaries might look like does not differ greatly from British, Soviet and French views. The USSR talks of border rectifications in terms of a few kilometers, but they might be moved further if some reciprocal exchange could be arranged (e.g. Gaza to Jordan).

c. *Jerusalem.* One reason we have stuck so hard against "return to June 5 lines" is our conviction that no one could force Israel out of Jerusalem. The USSR has no stake of its own there but must support strong Arab claims. There is, therefore, a premium on working out some mixture of Jordanian and Israeli presence in the city.

d. *Israel's position* apart from Jerusalem, is furthest from ours on the West Bank and Sharm al-Shaikh. We have not come up yet with satisfactory alternatives to Israel's plans for these areas. We are ignoring the Golan Heights.

There seem to be *two ways of handling the issue:*

a. We could go on much as we have been and say to the Israelis: "If we could get such-and-such commitment on 'peace' from the Arabs, would you then reveal your territorial requirements to Jarring?" This is what Jarring has been trying to do, and the Israelis would probably continue to refuse unless that such-and-such included direct Arab-Israeli contact. However, one added wrinkle might be to try our hand at eliciting Soviet support in arranging some sort of *secret meeting* with the UAR to satisfy Israeli requirements.

b. We could go to the Israelis and say: "If we could get such-and-such practical arrangements from Nasser or Hussein (demilitarized zones, etc.) would you withdraw to these boundaries?" This would require US to *put a detailed US plan on the table* at least with the Israelis. So far we have refused to do this, arguing with Dobrynin and others that only the parties themselves can draw the proper lines (especially on the West Bank). That has been part realism (the parties do know the terrain better than we) and partly defense (we know Israel will be tough to move especially without an Arab bargaining partner).

The *main obstacle* to the second course, again, is Israeli insistence on negotiating their own arrangements directly with the Arabs. A secondary problem is that the people on the ground really do have a better sense than we of what boundaries make sense.

3. *"Agreement between the parties"*—How much direct negotiation between the parties can we achieve? In the diplomatic shorthand, the argument is over whether there must be agreement "between" or "by" the parties. It is possible to achieve agreement of both sides without its being arrived at by contact between them, but again we have had to cope with Israeli insistence on direct negotiation. In our working paper we have actually supported indirect negotiations to start but have said that, as a practical matter, we believe direct contacts will be necessary at some point.

The issue is twofold: (a) The Israelis require some kind of direct negotiation for political purposes, and we think at some point it would be a lot more efficient for local experts to work out their own arrangements. (b) We were the middle-man in 1957, and we got badly burned. Therefore, we would like to see Nasser take greater responsibility for bailing himself out this time.

The importance of the issue is mainly tactical, partly substantive. The overriding point is that some degree of direct negotiation is necessary to bring Israel along. We have also argued that the arrangements are more likely to stick if the Arabs strike their bargain directly with Israel and accept responsibility for it. But if Israel were not insisting on direct contact, we probably would not.

The practical elements of the issue are:

a. *The Israelis* insist on a direct confrontation. We must take this into account, even if we do not wholly share their reasoning.

b. The *USSR* and *France* believe a direct meeting non-essential, if not impossible. Dobrynin says Jarring could do the whole job.

c. The *UAR* refuses in principle, but we have indications that Nasser might agree to some sort of meeting under Jarring toward the end of the process.

The only *way to handle this* is for us to go on insisting in the Four-Power forum that there must be a meeting under Jarring at some point. We judge that this is essential to bring the Israelis along, and we cannot really accept the Arab point that they absolutely cannot meet with Israel. The problem is to devise a formula which will permit direct contact as part of the phasing of implementation (see below). However, the problem might also be met by attempting to arrange secret UAR-Israeli contacts (as suggested above). In either case, we would have to develop more concrete suggestions.

4. *"Binding agreement" or "contractual agreement"*—How can the implementation of various elements of the agreement be phased and enforced so as to let each party feel he is giving up at each stage an advantage commensurate to what his adversary is giving up? We have staff studies on the possible legal forms of agreement and on the guarantees that might stiffen enforcement of the agreement, but we have not surfaced any of these.

The issue is (a) that Israel is being asked to give up something concrete in return for Arab promises on paper and (b) that the Arabs refuse to negotiate with the pistol of Israeli occupation at their heads. The question is how to assure Israel that the Arabs will make good if it withdraws all the way. The question is equally how to assure the Arabs that Israel will not just stop its withdrawal half-way on some pretext.

The importance of the issue is twofold: First is the question, again, of maximizing those elements in the agreement which will persuade Israel that the obligations the Arabs assume are binding—that the costs of not meeting them as defined in the settlement will be great enough to deter the Arabs from violation. *Second* is the tactical need to structure the implementation in such a way as to satisfy each side at each stage that it is getting as much as it is giving up.

The *practical elements of the issue* are:

a. The *nature of the agreement.* We hold no brief for a peace treaty, but we do want some international instrument we can point to in case of violation. In 1967, we had no written undertaking from Nasser which might justify US or international action to hold him to his agreement to leave the Straits of Tiran open to Israeli shipping.

b. *Phasing its implementation.* Dobrynin has suggested that an initial declaration of intent and then a set of agreed documents covering all elements of a settlement be deposited with the UN as Israeli withdrawal begins and that they go into effect on the last day of withdrawal. Dobrynin recognizes the practical requirement for achieving agreement on all issues before withdrawal. We have countered that the agreements must be binding—i.e. in effect—before withdrawal can begin. However, we recognize that some compromise formula is necessary here.

c. *Guarantees.* The Israelis want an Arab signature on a contract, and the Arabs may go as far as to sign a joint document of some sort, though not a peace treaty. But we feel that the self-enforcing provisions that are written into the agreement (e.g. automatic penalties for violation) and the international guarantees that may supplement it will contribute far more to making the agreement binding than signatures on a treaty, which have psychological value in Israel but little practical value.

The practical *way to handle this* is to concentrate discussion on (a) the forms an agreement might take and (b) the ways of phasing implementation. These are practical problems susceptible of practical solutions if other conditions can be met. But we have to be able to begin talking specifics to get to them.

One Issue Not Yet Addressed

Although we and Moscow agree that we should work through Jarring, we have not yet really worked out in detail how we will relate our bilateral conclusions, the Four-Power conclusions, Jarring and our bilateral contacts with Cairo, Amman and Jerusalem. In part, we have not done this because we needed to see first how much common ground we might find to work from. While we may wish to try one or two Four-Power meetings to get a similar feel for them, we now need to be more precise about how all these relate.

General Conclusions From the Soviet Talks So Far

1. We and the USSR are closer than we might have expected on the substance of a settlement. While we have yet to get specific enough to determine how far the Soviets are prepared to go, our greatest differences seem to grow more out of the positions of our respective clients than out of our own particular interest in one form of arrangement over another. Moscow may well have decided that even the best possible settlement will leave enough residual tension for it to exploit.

2. The main point of disagreement relates to how we get from here to there, and we are handicapped by our unwillingness so far to surface concrete ideas. We both recognize the need. Moscow is working hard to achieve for the Arabs a face-saving legal fiction which makes it appear that the Arabs have committed themselves to nothing until the Israelis have withdrawn. But the effort to achieve this fiction feeds natural suspicion that Moscow is trying to build escape hatches into the settlement for later Arab use. We are trying to argue Dobrynin toward our position without being able to surface practical suggestions of our own.

Operational Conclusions

1. The recurrent theme in this paper is (a) that we do not yet have a fully developed position and (b) that to the extent we have developed one, we have not surfaced it for tactical reasons. This suggests that we need:

—an agreed government position on the terms of a settlement;
—an agreed position on the tactics of presenting that position.

2. We also need a clearer position now on how to relate the Two-Power and Four-Power talks and on how to relate both to Jarring. The

Sisco–Dobrynin channel seems a useful one. Its usefulness suggests that we should use the four-power talks mainly to divert attention from the US–USSR channel. We can also use it to discipline the French and as an inducement to the Soviets, who may want to deal more with us than with the others.

3. While we have so far avoided the worst dangers of an unprepared position, the whole burden of the talks could still fall on us—for producing all the substantive proposals and for bringing the Israelis around. One essential aim for us in the Four-Power forum is to draw the others into sharing the practical problem of moving Israel. If we are expected to deliver Israel, we must make it clear that they are expected to deliver the Arabs.

4. A good definition of an equitable settlement is one that will make both sides unhappy. If so, we must have Soviet help, and the Soviets must share the blame for pushing an unpalatable solution.

Recommendation:

That you authorize NSC consideration of (1) a specific plan and set of objectives for relating the US-Soviet talks, the Four-Power talks and Jarring's continuing mission; (2) a paper considering the advantages and disadvantages of surfacing concrete proposals of our own on the elements of a settlement; (3) a detailed statement of what those proposals might be.[5]

Attached (Tab B)[6] is a tabular presentation of the positions of the Four Powers on each of the major issues.

---

[5] There is no indication that Nixon approved or disapproved any of the options.

[6] Attached but not printed.

31.   Memorandum of Conversation[1]

Washington, April 1, 1969, 3:40–4:30 p.m.

SUBJECT

General; U.S.-Soviet Relations

PARTICIPANTS

U.S.S.R. Participants
Vassily V. Kuznetsov, First Deputy Minister of Foreign Affairs
Anatoliy F. Dobrynin, Ambassador to the United States
Yuri N. Chernyakov, Minister-Counselor
Alexander I. Zinchuk, Deputy Chief of USA Division, MFA

U.S. Participants
William P. Rogers, Secretary of State
Martin J. Hillenbrand, Assistant Secretary for European Affairs
Malcolm Toon, Deputy Assistant Secretary
Adolph Dubs, Acting Director of Soviet Union Affairs
William D. Krimer, Interpreter

Mr. Kuznetsov expressed his thanks to the Secretary for having given him the opportunity of visiting him in spite of the Secretary's very busy schedule. He first wanted to convey Foreign Minister Gromyko's best regards to the Secretary. Mr. Gromyko had not been very well recently, having fractured several bones in his wrist in an accident, but he was better now. For a period of three weeks he had been unable to carry out his functions.

The Secretary replied with a request to convey his best wishes to Mr. Gromyko, whom he had met in 1959 on the occasion of Mr. Khrushchev's visit to Camp David.[2] He said that he admired the Foreign Minister for having lasted in his office continuously since 1957.

Mr. Kuznetsov went on to express the condolences of his government on the sad occasion of the loss of such a great man as former President Eisenhower.[3] The Soviet people had known him as a man

---

[1] Source: National Archives, Nixon Presidential Materials, NSC Files, Box 725, Country Files, Europe, USSR, Memcons, Kuznetsov/Dobrynin/Secretary Apr 69. Secret. Drafted by Krimer on April 2. The meeting was held in the Secretary's office. The memorandum is part I of III; parts II and III, brief discussions of the Middle East and the NPT respectively, are ibid. All three parts are attached to an April 2 covering memorandum from Acting Executive Secretary Walsh to Kissinger. On April 3, the Department sent telegram 50635 to Moscow, which summarized the three part-conversation. (Ibid., RG 59, Central Files 1967–69, POL US–USSR)

[2] Soviet Premier Nikita Khrushchev made an official visit to the United States, which included a trip to Camp David, Maryland, September 15–27, 1959. Rogers served as Attorney General under President Eisenhower.

[3] Eisenhower died on March 28.

who had made great contributions to the common cause of achieving a victory over fascist Germany at the time when he had been the Allied Supreme Commander. The Soviet Government had therefore immediately decided to send a delegation to the funeral. In this connection Mr. Kuznetsov recalled that our two countries had been allies in those days, when the world situation had been extremely difficult. At that time we had managed to find a good understanding on very complex problems and resolve them in the interests of mankind. Today the situation was also difficult and today, too, it was most important to create understanding and confidence between the Soviet Union and the United States. The Soviet Government wanted to do everything in its power to create a situation in which a better understanding and confidence between the two countries would lead to a solution of important international problems in the interests of our peoples and all humanity. He emphasized that his government wanted to achieve this goal and said that therefore any initiative from the American side would be welcomed.

The Secretary thanked Mr. Kuznetsov for his remarks and for the fact that the Soviet Government had sent a high-ranking delegation to the funeral. General Eisenhower had always spoken in glowing terms of his wartime experiences with Soviet soldiers. It was a fact that there was a common bond between the Russian people and the American people, as well as great friendship between them. The Secretary referred to his brief conversation with Mr. Kuznetsov of the day before, when Mr. Kuznetsov had said that when he had dealt with American engineers only, his relations had been friendly indeed, and that his difficulties only started when he began to deal with diplomats. As the Foreign Minister knew, the Secretary had already informed Ambassador Dobrynin that we were anxious to proceed to establish better relations between our two countries. The best time to do so in his view, was the time when a new administration came to office. We wanted to talk to Soviet representatives with an open mind about many things. As the Minister knew, we were now already discussing problems of the Middle East on a bilateral basis; we would appreciate everything the Soviet Union could do to help us achieve a peaceful settlement of the Vietnam conflict; in the months ahead we wanted to go ahead with talks on arms limitation. Although we were not attaching any conditions to any of these subjects and were willing to deal with each of them separately, it is self-evident that a reduction of tensions in one area would also be helpful to produce results in others. The Secretary thought that the time had come to have far-reaching talks on the many problems facing us. Our two countries had a special responsibility with respect to maintaining the peace. It was clear that in the absence of good relations between our two countries we incur the possibility of a conflict which could destroy mankind. The Secretary was therefore looking forward to working with Mr. Kuznetsov, with the Foreign Minister and with the excellent Ambassador in Washington.

Mr. Kuznetsov said that he was glad to hear this. He thought the present moment was one when we faced many important international problems awaiting solution. If we were to do nothing to improve the situation, it was quite natural that it would deteriorate. He shared the Secretary's views that there was no need to attach conditions to the efforts to reach agreement on any problem. He knew that some people took the position that it was first necessary to build up confidence so as to be able to proceed to a solution of problems. He did not agree with such a position, for how could there be any confidence without forward movement? He felt that confidence would improve as a result of progress in the solution of important problems. He referred to the time when he had worked with Ambassador Lodge, when it sometimes appeared that there was no progress on disarmament because of this same vicious circle. He therefore agreed with the Secretary that we should not place any conditions requiring progress on one problem before proceeding to another; this would unnecessarily complicate the situation. We should explore all possibilities and where we could proceed we should then find common language.

The Secretary pointed out that from a point of view of improving the relations between our two countries difficulties were often caused by polemics. Speaking for the new administration he said that the President and he were determined to be very careful and not say anything that could be interpreted as being belligerent, since this would not be conducive to good relations. He hoped that it would be possible within the framework of the Soviet system to respond in kind in their press and public statements.

Mr. Kuznetsov replied that as far as the Soviet leaders were concerned, they, too, had been careful not to say anything bad in their statements beyond the usual explanations of Soviet policy. But he was sorry that he could not say the same about some of the leaders of the United States. Last night he had had a brief but heated discussion with Defense Secretary Laird. He had brought up some of Secretary Laird's arguments in favor of going ahead with Safeguard, which had been presented during the Congressional hearings. Secretary Laird had said that the Soviet Union had the intention of attacking the United States with a first strike. This was, of course, not true. The Soviet Union was actively pursuing all possible ideas leading to disarmament, arms reduction and the stockpiling of explosive materials. The Soviet Union was striving for peace and was therefore willing to consider all suggestions to resolve international problems and to improve the world situation.

The Secretary replied that he did not think Secretary Laird had spoken of Soviet intentions, but rather of Soviet capabilities, bearing the SS–9 in mind. Certainly he (Secretary Rogers) had given no such indication in his testimony.[4]

Ambassador Dobrynin remarked that within the context of Secretary Laird's testimony the impression had been created that he regarded the Soviet Union as the most aggressive nation in the world. The Ambassador did not know of a single article in the Soviet press which had attacked the President, although Secretary Laird was criticized because of the impression he had created.

The Secretary said that the less top officials said anything that could be interpreted by the public as being belligerent, the better it would be for the relations between our two countries. We now had the opportunity of making progress in these relations and the President and he were determined to be very careful in their statements so as not to impede this progress.

Mr. Kuznetsov noted with satisfaction that the President had told him last night that he appreciated the responsible attitude displayed by the Soviet leadership since he had taken office.

---

[4] See footnote 3, Document 29.

---

32.   Memorandum From the President's Assistant for National Security Affairs (Kissinger) to President Nixon[1]

Washington, April 3, 1969.

SUBJECT

Memorandum of Conversation with Ambassador Dobrynin, April 3, 1969

Dobrynin called me about 3:30 p.m. to ask whether he might come by for fifteen minutes this afternoon. I received him at 4:30 p.m. and he stayed for an hour.

Dobrynin began the conversation by saying that he had been instructed by the highest level of the politburo to give me an advance indication of a note that was going to be presented at the State Department

---

[1] Source: National Archives, Nixon Presidential Materials, NSC Files, Box 489, President's Trip Files, Dobrynin/Kissinger, 1969, Part 2. Secret; Nodis. The memorandum was not initialed by Kissinger.

tomorrow morning.[2] This note in effect presents the Budapest Declaration of the Warsaw Pact nations, and asks for a European Security Conference. (I am sending you a separate memorandum on this.)[3] Dobrynin asked me for my views. I told him a European Security Conference which excluded the United States would meet with strong opposition. Dobrynin said that Moscow has no intention of prescribing the membership; if one of our allies proposed United States participation, Moscow would agree. (This represents a major change in Soviet policy.)

However, it soon became clear that the note was just a pretext. Dobrynin turned the conversation to Vietnam and asked me what I thought of developments. I said we were very relaxed, we knew what we were doing and would not be deflected by public protest. Dobrynin asked me whether we had "any intention of expanding the war." I replied that I had always told him that the President was determined to end the war one way or the other. He could be sure that I did not speak idly and that I hoped Hanoi kept Moscow fully informed of everything that was going on. Dobrynin said: "You know we do not have any advisers at the headquarters in South Vietnam." I replied: "Well, I hope they keep you informed of everything that goes on."

Dobrynin then asked how I visualized the relationship between a military and political settlement. I decided to play fairly tough and said that we would probably want to discuss military issues first. (I did this to preserve the option of the Vance mission[4] and to have our willing-

---

[2] On April 4, during a meeting from 2:30 to 3:30 p.m., Dobrynin presented the Appeal on European Security issued by the Warsaw Pact countries at Budapest on March 17 to Under Secretary of State Elliot Richardson, who was accompanied by Special Assistant Morton Abramowitz, and Dubs. (Memorandum of conversation; ibid., NSC Files, Box 725, Country Files, Europe, USSR, Memcons, Dobrynin/Richardson) Since 1968 Warsaw Pact members had urged the convening of a conference on European security. The proposed agenda included an agreement renouncing the use or the threat of force, and trade and technical exchanges.

[3] See Document 33.

[4] According to Kissinger's memoirs, "the proposed mission involved linking the opening of SALT talks with an overall settlement in Vietnam." Kissinger further recalls that on March 18, he met with Cyrus Vance, who served as Deputy Chief of the U.S. delegation to the Paris peace talks until February 19, to ask him whether he would go to Moscow to discuss strategic arms limitations and to meet secretly with a DRV negotiator. Vance would discuss a political and military settlement for Vietnam, including a cease-fire, mutual troop withdrawal, and guarantees for NLF non-violent participation in South Vietnam's political life. Under the Vance proposals, South Vietnam would be free and independent, but after 5 years there would be negotiations for reunification with the North. No record of their meeting has been found.

In early April, Kissinger pressed Nixon to authorize the Vance mission. Although the President was lukewarm about its prospects for success, he permitted Kissinger to broach it with Dobrynin during this meeting. The Vance mission, however, never took off. Kissinger explains in his memoirs, "Yet no reply was ever received from Moscow— no rejection, no invitation, not even a temporizing acknowledgment." (Kissinger, *White House Years*, pp. 266–268)

ness to discuss political matters within that framework serve as a concession.) I added that we could understand it, however, if after the military issues were settled, Hanoi would make their application dependent on progress towards a political settlement. Dobrynin pretended that this was a major concession and said it put a new complexion on things. He said we had to understand that the NLF was reluctant to risk itself in a forum with the GVN since it considered the GVN determined to destroy it. Dobrynin asked whether I saw any chance of replacing Thieu and Ky. I said no, but we were willing to consider safeguards for the NLF after a settlement. Dobrynin said this was all terribly complicated. The NLF did not insist on a coalition government. It would settle for a peace cabinet (without Thieu and Ky) which would safeguard its members.

Dobrynin then returned to the problem of escalation. I told him it would be too bad if we were driven in this direction because it was hard to think of a place where a confrontation between the Soviet Union and the United States made less sense. I added that it seemed to me our interests in Vietnam were quite compatible. Dobrynin replied: "Our interests in Vietnam are practically identical. We might want a slightly more neutral South Vietnam than you, but it is not an issue of consequence."

Dobrynin then turned to China. He referred to a news story that I was in charge of a policy review of Communist China and asked what conclusions we had reached. I said we had reached no conclusions but the President's thinking was well expressed to Kuznetsov when he said the Soviet Union and the United States still had the power to order events but that they might not have that power much longer.[5] Dobrynin said this was quite right. He added that he hopes things will get better after a while. I said that looking at the problem from a sheer political point of view, I thought China would be a major security concern of the Soviet Union no matter who governed it. Dobrynin then said that it seemed to many in the Soviet Union that Formosa could well be an independent state. I did not respond. Dobrynin said he might want to get together in two weeks to review the entire international situation.

Comment:

Dobrynin seemed very insecure when speaking about Vietnam. All of this suggests to me that maybe the Vance mission is our best hope.

---

[5] For Nixon's view expressed to Kuznetsov by Rogers, see Document 31.

33.   Memorandum From the President's Assistant for National Security Affairs (Kissinger) to President Nixon[1]

Washington, April 4, 1969.

SUBJECT

Soviet Initiative for a European Security Conference

The Soviets and East Europeans are currently pushing, diplomatically and through propaganda, an "appeal" adopted by the Warsaw Pact countries in Budapest on March 17 which proposes an early conference on European security. Ambassador Dobrynin today delivered a copy to Elliot Richardson.[2] (You will recall that Prime Minister Rumor[3] raised the subject with you on April 1.)

The appeal has aroused interest in the West because it almost completely is devoid of the polemical attacks on the US and the Federal Republic which normally appear in Communist declarations of this sort. There are no really significant new substantive proposals on how to go about getting a European settlement in this document—its main concrete proposition is that officials from interested European states should meet to arrange a conference and its agenda. Its main theme is that if the present status quo is recognized in Europe, especially by the Federal Republic, there could then be extensive east-west cooperation on economic and technical matters and military alliances could be abolished.

On the face of it, the appeal excludes the United States from participation in the proposed conference. But in the past when this criticism was levelled against their European security proposals, the Soviets have indicated that they are prepared to see a US role. They have maintained this line privately in the present instance, too.

Soviet Objectives

There has been speculation about the reasons why this appeal should have been issued at this time. The timing may be connected with the impending NATO meeting: the Soviets may hope that the trend toward better cohesion in NATO after Czechoslovakia and as a result of your European visit can be halted or reversed by a conciliatory proposition from them. Beyond this tactical motivation, the Soviets may in fact be interested in restoring some of the east-west con-

---

[1] Source: National Archives, Nixon Presidential Materials, NSC Files, Box 392, Subject Files, Soviet Affairs. Secret. Sent for information.

[2] See footnote 2, Document 32.

[3] Marianno Rumor, Prime Minister of Italy.

tacts, including economic ones, that were disrupted by their invasion of Czechoslovakia. Since the document makes a number of demands on the FRG—including recognition of East Germany, the Oder-Neisse Line and the "special status" of West Berlin, as well as renunciation of nuclear weapons—the Soviets may have wanted to lay the groundwork for renewed political contacts with Bonn. The obverse side of that coin is, as it always has been, an effort to isolate the Federal Republic by picturing it is the main obstacle to a European settlement if it fails to meet Communist demands.

Another motivation that may have played a role relates to Soviet efforts to consolidate the Warsaw Pact: this is the first major document in some time that all the East Europeans, including Romania, have been willing to sign.

Our Attitude

Although I do not believe that in and of itself this "appeal" does anything to advance the prospects of a European settlement, I believe we should not give it a negative response. Rather, we might use it in our effort to impress on the Soviets the need to talk concretely about the issues that exist between us.

What we have said about the inutility and, indeed, dangers of holding grandiose conferences at this stage should hold true in this case also; but we need not rule out eventual meetings, after the necessary spadework has been done to ensure that they get somewhere.

I do not believe that we should make an issue of our attendance at such meetings. Anyone who is serious about making progress on European problems knows that we must be a party; we should not make the Soviets think that they are doing us a favor if they agree to such an obvious fact of life.

I do believe that in the context of a constructive response we should make clear that

(1) in our view a real settlement in Europe is incompatible with gross intervention in the domestic affairs of other countries, and

(2) cannot be based on discrimination against Germany, since this would undermine any settlement from the beginning.

All of this, of course, looks very far into the future. But I think it would be desirable for us to be in a positive if cautious posture on this range of issues. This, judging from discussions at NATO, is also the position of our allies in Europe.

34.   Telegram From the Embassy in the Soviet Union to the Department of State[1]

Moscow, April 7, 1969, 1640Z.

1447. Subject: Initial Call on Gromyko.

Ref: State [*Moscow*] 1401 (Notal).[2]

1. Gromyko received me cordially this afternoon at Foreign Ministry for about 45 minutes. He said that Marshal Chuikov and Dep-FonMin Kuznetsov had conveyed report of their conversation with President Nixon at recent White House reception and that Soviets welcome and agree with President's thought that a "great deal depends on US and USSR." Soviets fully associate themselves with this view and believe there are grounds for optimism for future conversations and negotiations. I replied we earnestly hoped to carry on continuous and rational discussion of matters of mutual and world interest.

2. Principal substantive points of conversation were Middle East and NPT. With respect to former, Gromyko had little new to offer. He said that he was pleased that in four bilateral talks in Washington discussions had proceeded to get away from generalities and down to specifics. He also stressed that Soviets are in full agreement with us that understanding on a "package" settlement must be reached first; then it can be implemented in phases. He said that both Israelis and Arabs have too many suspicions and suggested we should both help to eliminate ill-founded ones.

3. I introduced subject of synchronized ratification of NPT along lines para 2 reftel.[3] Gromyko indicated Soviets much preoccupied with this question and that final decision not yet taken. Trend of his observations was nevertheless rather negative. He argued that Socialist countries (for whom USSR implicitly responsible) had signed treaty but that position of FRG (for whom US implicitly responsible) far from clear.

---

[1] Source: National Archives, RG 59, Central Files 1967–69, POL US–USSR. Confidential. Repeated to Bonn, London, Prague, USMISSION Geneva, USMISSION NATO, and USUN.

[2] In telegram 1401 from Moscow, April 14, the Embassy informed the Department that Beam planned to make his initial call on Gromyko on April 7 and intended "to make some mention of Czechoslovakia at least to extent of saying U.S. reaction to summer crisis is well known and that we are following current developments with concern." (Ibid., POL CZECH)

[3] The reference is an error. Beam is apparently referring to telegram 51269 to Moscow, April 3. (Ibid.)

He said USSR would face "intolerable" situation if it ratified agreement and FRG did not. I countered with arguments that our synchronized ratification would, on contrary, encourage action by FRG and other countries, and that Bonn faces delicate internal political situation vis-à-vis NPT which is only aggravated by Soviet anti-FRG propaganda and by Soviet statements such as that concerning alleged right of intervention under Articles 53 and 107 of UN Charter.[4] With reference to statement by Gromyko that Charter provisions are a fact, I said important question was to devise tactics to promote FRG signature, Gromyko thought Bonn is looking for pretext to defer action but seemed somewhat impressed by argument that whole NPT may stand or fall on ratifications of nuclear powers.

4. (*Comment:* While high level here may already have taken fairly adamant preliminary stand against ratification of NPT before FRG acts, argument that we must ratify jointly to encourage signature of other countries in addition to FRG such as Japan and India may still carry some weight.)

5. I did not raise Czechoslovak question since believe more opportune occasion will occur shortly.

6. Other particulars in septels.

Beam

---

[4] See footnote 2, Document 8.

35.   Talking Points[1]

Washington, undated.

TALKING POINTS ON VIETNAM FOR DISCUSSION WITH SOVIET AMBASSADOR DOBRYNIN

1. I plan to utilize the following points in discussing efforts to resolve the Vietnam conflict:

a. The President has just completed a thorough going review of the Vietnam situation in its fullest world-wide context.

b. The President is convinced that it is in no one's interest to have an outcome that would encourage Mainland China's aggressive drive.

c. The President has therefore decided that he will make a major effort to achieve a reasonable settlement.

d. The President views this point in history with the utmost gravity, especially since he is eager to move into an era of conciliation with the Soviet Union on a broad front. He is willing to begin talks on strategic arms limitations. He has agreed not to threaten the status quo in Europe. He is willing to consider meetings at the highest levels.

e. However, the President believes that an acceptable settlement to the Vietnamese conflict is the key to everything. Therefore, concurrently, the President proposes to designate a high-level representative to meet with a North Vietnamese negotiator at any location, including Moscow, designated by the Soviet Union to seek agreement with a designated North Vietnamese negotiator on a military as well as a political settlement. The President visualizes that this negotiation would be conducted distinct from the existing Paris framework in order to avoid the sluggish and heretofore cumbersome mechanisms that have evolved in Paris.

---

[1] Source: National Archives, Nixon Presidential Materials, NSC Files, Box 489, President's Trip Files, Dobrynin/Kissinger, 1969, Part 2, Vol. I. Top Secret; Sensitive. An April 12 covering memorandum from Kissinger to Nixon stated: "Attached are the talking points I propose to use in discussions with Soviet Ambassador Dobrynin Monday evening. These points lay out the main thrust of our proposal together with the conditions that we would attach to a settlement in principle of the conflict." Nixon initialed his approval on the covering memorandum and added the following insertion: "Willing to discuss broad *relaxation* of *trade* restrictions." An earlier draft prepared for Kissinger contained the following sentences not in the final version presented for Nixon's approval: "He will not be the first American President to lose a war, and he is not prepared to give in to public pressures which would have that practical consequence. . . . These measures could not help but involve wider risks. U.S.-Soviet relations are therefore at a crossroad. The President views this point in history with the utmost gravity, especially since he is eager to move into an era of conciliation with the Soviet Union on a broad front." (Ibid., Box 340, Subject Files, USSR Memcons Dobrynin/Kissinger) (Ellipsis in the source text)

f. The President will give this peace effort just six weeks to succeed. (*Handwritten insert by RN:* "perhaps 2 months is more realistic.")

g. The President will ask nothing of the Soviet Union inconsistent with its position as a senior communist power. He expects that nothing will be asked of the U.S. inconsistent with its world-wide obligations.

h. If this negotiation is successful, the President will conclude that the major danger to war is being removed and he would expect progress in many areas.

i. The President is prepared to repeat this proposition to the Soviet Ambassador personally if there is any interest in the Kremlin.

j. Our proposal to Hanoi will be conciliatory embracing both political and military measures for ending hostilities.

2. The object of the Vietnam negotiations would be as follows:

a. *Definition of Objective:* To reach prompt agreement with the North Vietnamese on the general shape of a political-military settlement, specifically:

(1) *Military*—Agreement that there will be mutual withdrawal of all external forces, and a ceasefire based on a mutual withdrawal.

(2) *Political*—(a) Agreement that guarantees the NLF freedom from reprisals and the right to participate fully in the political and social life of the country in exchange for agreement by NLF and DRV to forego further attempts to achieve their political objectives by force and violence, and (b) agreement that there will be a separate and independent SVN for at least five years.

(*Handwritten note by RN:* "a date for new elections.")

(3) *Mechanism for supervising and verifying the carrying out of the settlement.* The agreement with the DRV should not attempt to spell out the manner in which the general principles agreed to will be implemented. That should be left for Paris.

3. If the special U.S. and North Vietnamese negotiators can achieve an agreement in principle, the negotiations would shift back to Paris for final implementation. The whole process should be completed before the end of August. If the special talks prove unsuccessful, it is difficult to visualize the progress which we both seek and the outlook for improved U.S.-Soviet relations would be seriously jeopardized.

4. The President realizes that this proposal represents a most complex and difficult choice for all parties concerned, but because we are at a most significant crossroad, he is convinced that extraordinary measures are called for. Because they are extraordinary, he would anticipate that Ambassador Dobrynin would wish to discuss them in detail with his government.[2]

---

[2] "RN" appears on the approve line.

36.   Memorandum From the President's Assistant for National Security Affairs (Kissinger) to President Nixon[1]

Washington, April 15, 1969.

SUBJECT

Memorandum of Conversation with Dobrynin April 14, 1969

After an exchange of pleasantries and a somewhat lengthy discussion of the Middle East (reported separately),[2] the discussion turned to Vietnam. I asked Dobrynin whether he had had any reaction from Moscow to our last conversation.[3] He said he had not, but that he was aware of a conversation Zorin had had with Lodge.

I then said that the President had wished me to convey his thoughts on Vietnam to Moscow. We had followed the discussions in Paris with great interest and considerable patience. As Lodge had already pointed out to Zorin, it was very difficult to negotiate when the other side constantly accused us of insincerity, when every private meeting so far had been initiated by us, and when every proposition was put forward on a take-it-or-leave-it basis. The President had therefore decided to make one more direct approach on the highest level before drawing the conclusion that the war could only be ended by unilateral means. The President's personal word should be a guarantee of sincerity. After showing Dobrynin the talking points and the President's initials, I read them to him.[4] He took copious notes, stopping every once in a while to ask for an explanation. When I said we wanted to have the negotiations concluded within two months, Dobrynin said that if this proposal was feasible at all, we would be able to tell after the first week of negotiations whether they would lead anywhere.

---

[1] Source: National Archives, Nixon Presidential Materials, NSC Files, Box 489, President's Trip Files, Dobrynin/Kissinger, 1969, Part 2, Vol. I. Secret; Nodis. A handwritten notation on the first page reads, "Back from the President, 4/16/69." On April 10, Kissinger and Dobrynin set up their April 14 meeting for 8:30 p.m. at Kissinger's house. According to a transcript of the telephone conversation, "Dobrynin ventured the guess that HAK must be very busy these days and HAK said this is a hectic period. HAK said last time they met they talked about getting together next week and asked what his schedule was—Dobrynin said 'give me a time and and I'll tell you.'" After scheduling their meeting, "HAK mentioned that he lives alone so can't offer Dobrynin dinner. Later in conversation Dobrynin said he would be delighted to see how bachelors live." (Library of Congress, Manuscript Division, Kissinger Papers, Box 359, Telephone Records, 1969–1976, Telephone Conversations, 1969)

[2] See Document 37.

[3] See Document 32.

[4] See Document 35.

When I got through, Dobrynin asked whether I was saying that unless the Vietnam war was settled, we would not continue our discussions on the Middle East and not enter the talks on strategic arms. I replied that we were prepared to continue talking but that we would take measures which might create a complicated situation.

Dobrynin said that whatever happens in Vietnam, the Soviet leaders were eager to continue talking. He then asked whether these new measures might involve Soviet ships. I replied that many measures were under intensive study. In dealing with the President, it was well to remember that he always did more than he threatened and that he never threatened idly.

Dobrynin then said he hoped we understand the limitations of Soviet influence in Hanoi. We had to understand that while the Soviet Union might recommend certain steps, it would never threaten to cut off supplies. He could tell me that the Soviet Union had been instrumental in helping to get the talks started. Moreover, Communist China was constantly accusing the Soviet Union of betraying Hanoi. The Soviet Union could not afford to appear at a Communist meeting and find itself accused of having undermined a fellow Socialist country. On the other hand, the Soviet Union had no strategic interest in Southeast Asia. The chief reasons for its support of North Vietnam have been the appeals of a fellow Socialist country. I could be sure that the President's proposal would be transmitted to Hanoi within 24 hours. Dobrynin added that often Soviet messages were never answered by Hanoi so he could not guarantee what the reply would be or indeed if there would be a reply.

Dobrynin then said that the North Vietnamese were using the following agreement with Moscow and he stressed that Moscow did not necessarily agree with it: The Saigon Government was composed of individuals committed to the destruction of the NLF. The NLF would not enter a political confrontation in which the administrative apparatus was in the hands of people who sought to destroy them. The NLF would not insist on participating in the Government but it would insist that the Government be broadened and that Thieu and Ky be removed. Dobrynin repeated that he was simply stating Hanoi's arguments, not endorsing them.

I replied that I was familiar with Hanoi's arguments since they were being made to us as well. Nevertheless, the best policy for the NLF would be to work out guarantees for its political participation *after* a settlement of the war. They would certainly find us forthcoming.

Dobrynin reiterated Moscow's desire to stay in negotiations with us whatever happened in Vietnam. He told me many anecdotes of Stalin as well as of Molotov. He added that the Soviet Union had intended to send Marshal Zhukov to Eisenhower's funeral but Zhukov had recently had two strokes and was partially paralized. He then asked whether we understood that Communist China was attempting to produce a clash between the Soviet Union and the United States. If the war in Vietnam escalates, it would only service Communist China's interest. I replied that this was the precise point the President had tried to make to Kuznetsov on the occasion of the Eisenhower funeral. It was, therefore, incumbent on the Soviet Union to help us remove this danger. We felt that in this period, the great nuclear powers still have the possibility of making peace.

As he was preparing to leave, Dobrynin asked me whether he could read over the talking points once more. I handed them to him and he read them slowly and carefully. He departed saying "this has been a very important conversation."

---

37.   Memorandum From the President's Assistant for National Security Affairs (Kissinger) to President Nixon[1]

Washington, April 15, 1969.

SUBJECT

  Memorandum of Conversation with Dobrynin April 14, 1969

After an exchange of pleasantries, Dobrynin said that Moscow had asked him to talk to me about the situation in the Middle East. Moscow was prepared to come to an understanding on the Middle East as rapidly as possible. On the other hand, Moscow's feeling was that we were proceeding too abstractly. The principles put forward by Joseph Sisco were all very well, but the key issue was the location of the frontiers and other matters. He felt that we should put forward a proposal which would be kept in strictest confidence and the Soviet Union would see whether they could turn it into a joint offer to both sides. I replied that we did not want to be in a position where we had to make all the proposals, deliver all the parties and take all the criticism. Dobrynin said

---

[1] Source: National Archives, Nixon Presidential Materials, NSC Files, Box 489, President's Trip Files, Dobrynin/Kissinger, 1969, Part 2, Vol. I. Secret; Nodis. A handwritten notation on the first page reads: "Back from the President, 4/16/69."

that the Soviet Union would do a great deal to make an agreement but "you have to be specific." For example, the U.S. constantly asked for a contractual agreement. However, it had never stated what it understood by a contractual agreement. "Why don't you write out a paragraph that tells us exactly what you want Nasser to say and if we agree with it, we will try to get them to accept it." Similarly, he said it was impossible for the Soviet Union to know what we had in mind about troop withdrawals. The U.S. spoke of border rectification but we had given no indication of where the frontier was to be. He added that "the Soviet Union did not care about Golan Heights or the Gaza Strip. Indeed, whether the borders were 30 miles east or west is of no difference to us as long as both sides agree." I told him that Sisco was likely to produce a scheme within the next two weeks. If it presented any difficult problems, I suggested Dobrynin get in touch with me.

We then turned to discussions on Vietnam.[2]

---

[2] See Document 36.

---

38.   **Memorandum From Harold Saunders of the National Security Council Staff to the President's Assistant for National Security Affairs (Kissinger)**[1]

Washington, April 18, 1969.

SUBJECT

The Dobrynin–Sisco Talks

You asked for a short summary of each of the Sisco–Dobrynin talks.

On March 4, Dobrynin suggested the US–Soviet talks to Sisco. (Tab A)[2] Initial arrangements were made on March 8 by Secretary Rogers and Dobrynin. (Tab B)[3]

---

[1] Source: National Archives, Nixon Presidential Materials, NSC Files, Box 725, Country Files, Europe, USSR, Sisco–Dobrynin Talks, Part I, April 1969. Secret; Nodis.

[2] Attached but not printed at Tab A is telegram 33865 to Moscow, March 5.

[3] Attached but not printed at Tab B is telegram 36425 to Moscow, March 8.

First Meeting—March 18 (Tab C)[4]

The meeting dealt mainly with points on which the US and USSR already agreed such as working for a lasting peace, no imposition of a settlement, achieving a settlement through Jarring, a package settlement, and an agreed settlement. There was some disagreement on whether the settlement would be agreed *by* or *between* the parties and on the method of setting borders and ensuring an Arab commitment to peace.

Second Meeting—March 24 (Tab D)[5]

Sisco tried to draw out Dobrynin on a contractual peace and Dobrynin tried to draw out Sisco on withdrawal. Sisco presented the US working paper to Dobrynin.

Third Meeting—March 25 (Tab E)[6]

Sisco explained the US working paper in detail.

Fourth Meeting—March 26 (Tab F)[7]

Dobrynin discussed Soviet ideas on withdrawal and recognized the need for a package settlement. He suggested a system of declarations and phased withdrawal. He also asked some questions about the US working paper which he found somewhat one-sided.

---

[4] Attached but not printed at Tab C is telegram 4215 to Moscow, March 19. On March 19, Sisco spoke twice on the telephone with Kissinger about his meeting the day before with Dobrynin. According to a transcript of the 12:45 p.m. conversation between Kissinger and Sisco, "K asked how meeting with Dobrynin had gone—S said it is a beginning and once K has seen cable, he would like his reactions." (Library of Congress, Manuscript Division, Kissinger Papers, Box 359, Telephone Records, 1969–1976, Telephone Conversations, 1969) At 3:50 p.m. the same afternoon, after Kissinger returned from seeing Dobrynin at a luncheon for the Czech Ambassador, Kissinger and Sisco spoke again on the telephone. According to a transcript of their conversation, "K said he had given Dobrynin no comfort at all but said whatever S did had his full backing." Kissinger and Sisco then discussed Middle Eastern issues in general terms. Before hanging up, "S said we have to keep telling Dobrynin what it is we want and in every meeting with him S will hit the same theme. S said it was a very interesting discussion but he doesn't expect any quick results." (Ibid.)

[5] Attached but not printed at Tab D is telegram 46143 to Moscow, March 25.

[6] Attached but not printed at Tab E is telegram 46317 to Moscow, March 26.

[7] Attached but not printed at Tab F is telegram 47123 to Moscow, March 27. On March 26, at 5:45 p.m., Sisco and Kissinger spoke on the telephone about the former's session earlier that day with Dobrynin. According to a transcript of their conversation, "S said this procedure will go on another couple of weeks then we will have to face decision—do we really then try to develop a more detailed 'plan' which we would try out on Israelis and then try out on Russians. K asked what S thought. S said he did not want to make any judgments—told K to think about it." Sisco also told Kissinger that he hoped they could find at least 30 minutes each week to talk about the Middle East. Kissinger promised that he would have his secretary set aside the time. (Library of Congress, Manuscript Division, Kissinger Papers, Box 359, Telephone Records, 1969–1976, Telephone Conversations, 1969)

Fifth Meeting—April 2 (Tab G)[8]

In answer to Dobrynin's questions of the previous meeting, Sisco discussed US ideas on special arrangements for Sharm el Shaykh and Gaza, demilitarization, Jerusalem and a peace treaty.

Sixth Meeting—April 3 (Tab H)[9]

Dobrynin said the USSR wants a permanent peace, asked about the talks with Fawzi,[10] agreed that Arab and Israeli positions are hardening, and said the USSR has no interest in giving guarantees as part of the peace settlement. Sisco—speaking personally—thought it might be possible to work out a practical US-Soviet plan.

Seventh Meeting—April 11 (Tab I)[11]

Sisco, again speaking personally, suggested that the US-Soviet talks be directed towards working out a preliminary US-Soviet agreement to be given to Jarring for the parties. Dobrynin again pressed for a clear US statement on withdrawal. They met again yesterday. I will give you a more detailed report on that meeting when we have the full record. But Dobrynin did seem to commit himself to the idea of a single document—in contrast to the earlier idea of parallel documents—such as the Israelis want.

Eighth Meeting—April 17 (Tab J)[12]

Hal's memorandum reviewing this latest meeting is at Tab J.

Ninth Meeting April 22 (Tab K)[13]

Memorandum reviewing this meeting is at Tab K.

---

[8] Attached but not printed at Tab G is telegram 50983 to Moscow, April 3.

[9] Attached but not printed at Tab H is telegram 51229 to Moscow, April 3.

[10] The morning of April 3, Rogers met with Dr. Mahmoud Fawzi, Nasser's adviser on foreign affairs. According to telegram 51229 to Moscow, "Sisco said two principal topics [were] touched upon: (a) UAR desire to have Four Powers move ahead; and (b) indication that current UAR reaction to US working paper not as negative as public statement by Nasser on March 27."

[11] Attached but not printed at Tab I is telegram 56630 to Moscow, April 13.

[12] Tab J is telegram 59898 to Moscow, April 18, summarizing the eighth meeting. Also attached but not printed is telegram 59897 to Moscow, April 18, which lists U.S. questions about the Soviet note on the Middle East of December 30, 1968; Soviet replies of April 17, 1969, to those U.S. questions; and Soviet questions of April 17 about the U.S. interpretation of UN Security Council Resolution 242 of November 22, 1967.

[13] Attached at Tab K but not printed is telegram 62563 to Moscow, April 28, summarizing the ninth meeting. After this paragraph, Lawrence Eagleburger handwrote, "Tenth meeting being summarized. I'll bring it to K[ey] B[iscayne] on Friday." The summary of the meeting has not been found.

Tab J

Memorandum From Harold Saunders of the National Security Council Staff to the President's Assistant for National Security Affairs (Kissinger)

Washington, undated.

SUBJECT

Latest Sisco–Dobrynin Conversation (April 17)

Sisco's April 17 discussion with Dobrynin was a concrete step forward, in contrast to the more nebulous exchanges in the past few meetings.

Dobrynin dropped the general discussion of the main elements of the UN resolution and came in with written answers to some of our earlier questions, indicating that they represented a decision made at the highest level of the Soviet government. In return, Dobrynin presented five written Soviet questions to us.

An analysis of the Soviet answers suggests some shifts in the Soviet position:

1. More important, the Soviets seem to be talking for the first time about a *single document* as the instrument for recording the final agreement. [Holding this out to the Israelis would make our job a little easier with them.][14]

2. They seem to recognize the need to address *such issues as boycotts and blockades* in defining obligations. [These are the sorts of issues Eban addresses when he spells out what would be required if belligerency were terminated.]

3. They state flatly that they are not talking of "some kind of truce but of a *complete cessation of the state of war* and the settlement of all questions connected therewith." [This is less than the commitment to "peace" Israel wants but it also looks like less than an effort to leave loopholes for later aggression against Israel.]

On the negative side, the Soviet answers specifically advise against raising the question of direct negotiations. We have been thinking that being able to provide a meeting under Jarring would make it easier for us to bring the Israelis along. They also envision smaller DMZ's than we do.

---

[14] Brackets in this and following two paragraphs are in the source text.

The Soviet questions try to pin us down on how much negotiating room we plan to leave the Israelis on where the boundaries are drawn, on what kinds of international guarantees we have in mind and on our specific ideas about Gaza, Sharm al-Shaykh and refugees.

Conclusions: The Soviets continue to move in our direction on procedural issues. This helps because these are important to Israel. The Soviets may be a lot tougher when we try to enlarge their view of DMZ's or discuss what will amount to infringements or UAR sovereignty to police demilitarization or free navigation. In any case, we do seem now to be in a reasonable negotiation with the full engagement of the top echelons in the Kremlin.

Tab K

Memorandum From Harold Saunders of the National Security Council Staff to the President's Assistant for National Security Affairs (Kissinger)

Washington, April 23, 1969.

SUBJECT

Sisco–Dobrynin Meeting on April 22

The latest Sisco–Dobrynin meeting was probably the least productive of the series, mainly because both were waiting for the decision on making our position more specific.

Joe opened the meeting by expressing concern at the firefights on the Suez Canal. He told Dobrynin we would discuss the matter with Israel and asked if the Soviets were prepared to talk to the Egyptians. Dobrynin hedged, but said he would take note of U.S. concern.

Most of the meeting was taken up by replies to questions Dobrynin had asked at the previous meeting. Before replying, Joe explained that his answers would not go beyond what we had said before but are not our last word. We were considering these questions in connection with a possible substantive document.

He made the following points, which you know by heart, in the answers:

1. We feel that the parties should accept the resolution and implement all its provisions. We put the emphasis on agreement between the parties.

2. We see two kinds of guarantees of a settlement. We feel that arrangements on the ground such as demilitarized zones are the most

important, and that outside guarantees should be supplementary and cannot take the place of agreements between the parties.

3. We have reached no definite conclusion about the future of Gaza.

4. A refugee settlement must respond to the requirements for justice for the refugees, but must also take into account Israeli security concerns. Each refugee should have a choice among (1) returning to Israel to live under Israeli law, (2) compensation and resettlement in the country where he now resides, and (3) compensation and resettlement in other countries. Refugees from the 1967 war would return home. We feel that not many refugees would choose to live in Israel. We have no definite conclusions on the machinery to implement this plan.

5. Sharm al-Shaykh is important because of its location and is a difficult problem because the Israelis are unwilling to trust anyone else with keeping the Straits of Tiran open, and the UAR will not accept an Israeli presence there. We feel this has to be worked out by the parties, but are not ruling out any solution.

Because neither side was ready to add anything more, the date of the next meeting was left open.

You should be aware that State has informed the British Embassy of the possibility of a joint Soviet-U.S. paper on the Near East. It was necessary to do so to lessen British pressure for raising the idea of a multilateral document soon in the four-power talks. The British feel that this knowledge will allow the Foreign Office to slow the pace in New York.

Comment: We have exhausted the Sisco–Dobrynin channel unless we can come up with something more specific to say to the Soviets.

39.   Oral Statements by the Ambassador to the Soviet Union (Beam)[1]

Moscow, April 22, 1969.

Oral Statements Made by Ambassador Jacob D. Beam to Soviet Premier Alexei Kosygin April 22, 1969[2]

1. In handing over his written message the President has asked me to say that his purpose was to set forth his general approach to our relations. Explorations and negotiations on the specific issues should, he feels, be carried on through our Ambassadors and other representatives, as the case may be, rather than through formal written communications. He would like to keep our contacts as confidential as possible and feels that written messages may reduce our flexibility in dealing with complex and sensitive issues. This does not of course exclude our reducing to writing any understandings reached.

2. With regard to the Middle East, we share your assessment that our bilateral talks in Washington have brought our views somewhat closer. We see these talks as a vehicle for helping the parties to narrow the differences between them. We hope therefore that these talks as well as the wider discussions in New York will provide useful support to Ambassador Jarring in his further efforts with the parties. The President is mindful of the fact that Soviet flexibility is limited by your relations with the Arab countries, just as our own position must take into account the interests of the countries involved. However both of us

---

[1] Source: National Archives, RG 59, Central Files 1967–69, POL US–USSR. Secret; Nodis. These oral statements by Beam were an enclosure to airgram A–446 from Moscow, April 23. In transmitting his oral statements, Beam wrote: "It will be noted that since the question of a 'summit meeting' did not arise, I did not use the pertinent portion of the original instruction furnished me under cover of Mr. Henry Kissinger's transmission slip of March 26." For Kissinger's memorandum, see footnote 1, Document 28.

[2] On April 21, the day before Beam's meeting with Kosygin, Sonnenfeldt sent Kissinger a memorandum with the subject: "Ambassador Beam Requests Updating of Instructions for Use in Conversation with Kosygin." Sonnenfeldt attached telegram 168 from Moscow in which Beam asked whether his instruction should be updated on the Middle East and NPT. Sonnenfeldt's memorandum added the following: "In his conversation with Podgorny, Beam stated that 'on the vital questions of disarmament we were undertaking a basic review which we hoped would enable us in a few weeks to make contact with the Soviets.' I do not know of any basis for such a statement in any of the Ambassador's instructions of which I have knowledge." Kissinger handwrote the following at the bottom of this memorandum, which was later crossed out: "I never saw Podgorny cable. This is the sort of cable I should see. There is no basis for this statement." (National Archives, Nixon Presidential Materials, NSC Files, Box 709, Country Files, Europe, USSR, Vol. I) No record of Beam's telegram reporting his conversation with Podgorny has been found.

must be prepared to accept certain burdens if negotiations are to succeed. The President continues to hope that progress toward a viable settlement will improve chances of placing restraints on outside military assistance to countries of the region; indeed, the President remains ready to discuss such restraints even under present circumstances.

3. With regard to Vietnam, the President recognizes the sensitivity of the Soviet position due to your relations with China and your position in the communist movement. We have no intention to exploit whatever constructive influence the Soviets may be able to exert on Hanoi for any other purpose than the establishment of peace.

4. The United States Government was appreciative of efforts by Soviet vessels in the Sea of Japan in searching for possible survivors of our aircraft which was shot down by the North Koreans.[3] The shootdown of our aircraft is only the most recent example of developments in the area which lead to increased tension and which must be a source of concern to the Soviet Government as well as to us. We hope the Soviet Union will do what it can to restrain the North Koreans from such irresponsible acts since we believe it to be in our mutual interest to avoid further exacerbation of tension in the area.

5. More specifically on China, we have been concerned by the deterioration in Sino-Soviet relations. We have no interest in seeing these two countries in conflict and certainly have no intention to exploit their present difficulties. We do hope over the long run to achieve some normalization in our relations with China and were disappointed by the aborting of the Warsaw talks. If these talks resume, or other contacts eventuate with the Chinese, we will continue, as did the previous Administration, to keep the Soviets informed.

6. As regards Berlin and Germany, we would welcome any improvement in Soviet-German relations. We think German signature of

---

[3] On April 14, a North Korean aircraft shot down a U.S. Navy EC–121 of Fleet Air Reconnaissance Squadron One over the Sea of Japan. The North Koreans claimed that the U.S. plane had violated its air space, had attempted to escape, and was then shot down approximately 80 miles at sea. On April 15, Rogers and Kissinger spoke on the telephone about registering some type of diplomatic protest over the EC–121 shootdown. According to a transcript of their conversation, "R said he was going to have Dobrynin in at 12:00. K said President does not want any protest to anyone. R said he was not going to protest—he wanted to talk to Dobrynin about helping to save the men." Kissinger added that he "thinks the President is inclined to play this in low key and to say nothing to anyone until we know where we are headed." (Library of Congress, Manuscript Division, Kissinger Papers, Telephone Records, Box 359, 1969–1976, Telephone Conversations, 1969)

On April 17, at 9:25 a.m., Nixon and Kissinger spoke on the telephone about the shootdown. According to a transcript of their conversation, "President and K discussed idea of formal protest—decided should not be done with Soviets." (National Archives, Nixon Presidential Materials, NSC Files, Box 434, Korea, EC–121 shootdown, North Korea Reconnaissance, Vol. II, Haig)

the Non-Proliferation Treaty will assist this and we hope that the Soviets will be able to give Chancellor Kiesinger any help you may consider feasible to enable him to get the treaty adopted. Meanwhile as we have told Ambassador Dobrynin and Deputy Foreign Minister Kuznetsov in Washington, we believe early completion of the ratification process by the major nuclear powers, including simultaneous deposit of instruments of ratification, would be helpful in bringing about the widest possible endorsement of the treaty which we both seek. On Berlin, we are prepared to examine any way to improve the present unsatisfactory situation, and the President believes from his recent talks with the Germans that they are prepared to do so too. But this cannot be done under pressure. Perhaps some quiet exchanges would show the way.

7. On strategic arms talks, it should be stressed that we are not deliberately stalling; we are seriously reviewing our position, something the President feels he is obligated to do as head of the new Administration. We are not setting pre-conditions. But we want the talks to succeed once they begin and for that reason we feel that prospects for progress will be better in the context of generally improved US-Soviet relations. If you have some substantive ideas to convey to the President through me, he would be interested.

8. The President has asked me to inform you that he has given instructions to the members of the Administration to avoid harsh words about the USSR. The President will, of course, state our views but he sees nothing gained by "shouting." At the same time the residue of suspicion of the USSR remains in the US and events like those in Czechoslovakia had a profound shock effect. We should cooperate to preserve the present low key in our discourse with and about each other.

9. We believe our relations will improve as we gain a better understanding of each others' aspirations, problems, and concerns. It is for this reason that the United States Government strongly supports a free flow of information and ideas between our two peoples. We would hope that we could work toward this objective by expanding by mutual agreement the exchange program which we have carried on for a number of years. Both sides should do what they can to remove existing barriers to the free flow of information and in this connection it is our hope that in due time the Soviet authorities will find it possible to cease jamming the Voice of America which was reimposed after the events of last summer.

10. The President has asked me to say that he fully understands your concern for your security and your desire to have friendly countries on your borders. We have no wish to complicate your relations with your neighbors, communist or otherwise. It is the President's judgment—he has been seeking to act on that judgment in our relations

with our allies—that the maintenance of a hegemonial relationship by a great power over less powerful countries is self-defeating. It is the President's feeling, without attempting to give you advice, that this judgment applies to your situation as well. We will applaud whatever you can do to achieve normal, friendly relations with all your neighbors.

---

40.   Telegram From the Embassy in the Soviet Union to the Department of State[1]

Moscow, April 22, 1969, 1610Z.

1693. Subject: Delivery of President's Letter to Kosygin. Ref: State 061671.[2]

1. Accompanied by DCM Swank, I was received by Chairman Kosygin for a one hour forty minute talk this afternoon at three P.M. when I delivered to him the President's letter of March 26.[3] In order to facilitate translation I had earlier in the day given Kornienko of FonMin who was present at the talk a copy of the President's letter as well as a full version of the President's instructions for my oral presentation.[4] Kosygin said he had been unable to read the letter because of his preoccupation with current CEMA meeting. He was nevertheless probably acquainted with its contents since translations were on his desk. Wishing doubtless to reserve his considered reply he confined himself to stating the Soviet view which was particularly rough on the South Vietnamese Govt. I responded on a number of points with citations from the President's letter.

2. In welcoming me as Ambassador of "a great country" Kosygin noted that Soviet people are in general well disposed to American people, esteem their science and technology, and respect them. He observed that our relations have had their ups and downs but that despite accumulated and inherited difficulties he hoped for close cooperation with US and improved relations.

---

[1] Source: National Archives, RG 59, Central Files 1967–69, POL US–USSR. Secret; Nodis. Beam's description of his meeting with Kosygin on April 22 is in *Multiple Exposure*, pp. 219–220.

[2] Telegram 61671 to Moscow, April 2, provided instructions for Beam's oral presentation to Kosygin. (National Archives, RG 59, Central Files 1967–69, POL US–USSR)

[3] Document 28.

[4] See Document 39.

3. In concurring with these remarks, I noted that differences in our economic organization and social systems are likely to persist but that it is nevertheless in our mutual interest to limit dangers of world in which we live. I observed that President Nixon is a close student of international affairs and is especially interested in the USSR. I also noted that the President desires we engage in continuing and rational talks about bilateral and world problems through all feasible channels, including possibly reciprocal visits of important officials. I said that as stressed in President's letter we are interested in having productive and practical discussions on concrete problems and are hopeful that this approach to our relations will bring positive results.

4. Kosygin said that he would be preoccupied for several days with the CEMA summit meeting, which he described as a "search for ways to achieve improved economic cooperation" among Socialist countries. He also commented in passing that "contrary to reports in Western press" this meeting is totally unrelated to the "Chinese question."

5. Kosygin then stated that he hoped our two governments could find constructive solutions to outstanding problems in a businesslike atmosphere free of sensationalism. He said he thought it might be wise to identify problems to which we should seek solutions, and he then brought up in turn NPT, Middle East, Vietnam and Europe.

6. On NPT, Kosygin observed that treaty represents a joint effort which should now be brought to a conclusion. He suggested that we concert efforts to see that "certain countries" do not interfere with realization of objectives of treaty. I observed that if all three nuclear powers do not ratify treaty it may prove impossible to induce signature and ratification by other powers. Kosygin did not react to this remark nor did he indicate attitude of SovGov to our proposal for joint ratification.

7. On Middle East, Kosygin said vigorously that USSR desires "greatly" to cooperate with US in reaching a settlement. He commented that by "uniting our strengths" we could achieve such a settlement. He said that he would not go into detail on this subject but wished to observe that aggressors should be punished, not encouraged. He also referred to circles in United States who seek an "unbalanced" (that is, a pro-Israel) solution. In my answering remarks, I said that President Nixon believes both our countries must be willing to accept burdens of bringing peace to area. I also noted that we have been encouraged by talks now underway and hope they will eventually assist Jarring's mission.

8. Kosygin expressed himself at greater length and with most vehemence on subject of Vietnam. Emphasizing that he speaking for himself and not on behalf of Hanoi. His main target was the Thieu govt, which he repeatedly characterized as a corrupt puppet regime lacking popular support, dictatorial in character and unrepresentative of

people of South Vietnam. He criticized lack of progress in Paris talks, comparing them to unfruitful US-Chinese talks in Warsaw and referring somewhat sardonically to "formal" proceedings which had not yet got to heart of matter. He said that Soviet policy is still directed to objective of stopping the war and added that he is convinced this is also objective of Vietnamese. He said he was also prepared accept judgment that US shares this objective. It was therefore imperative for progress to be made toward a settlement since another interested power, and he mentioned China by name, could potentially use its influence against a settlement and in manner to increase tensions throughout Southeast Asia. He stressed that those interested in reaching a settlement must seek some practical "informal" approach to problem but admitted that he could not now identify such an approach.

9. In my response I remarked that I regretted to note that our interpretations of situation in Vietnam were so far apart. I stated that the Republic of Vietnam has a democratic strong govt with substantial international recognition. I also read aloud to Kosygin portion of President's letter stressing his desire to achieve peace and his hope that Soviet influence can be brought to bear to this end. (It is obvious that Kosygin's remarks offer little new on subject of Vietnam, but is equally apparent that he is concerned that talks in Paris are not making progress and that he views Chinese role in area as both unpredictable and sinister.)

10. On Europe, Kosygin said he wished to confine himself to a brief restatement on Soviet position. He asserted that the USSR seeks to avoid tension in area, citing recent diminution of tensions in Berlin, but emphasized SovGov absolutely firm in position that it will not tolerate any revision of "results of World War II." He called Soviet obligations in this respect "sacred." I said that I would not address myself to European questions since I believed President's letter covered subject adequately.

11. In conclusion, Kosygin asked me to transmit to President interim message that Soviet leaders wish to establish relations with United States on a basis of honesty and realism. He said that Soviet leaders believe it important that Soviet and American peoples achieve satisfaction of knowing that they are not threatened by the other. Each side possesses an enormous arsenal. In our approach to mutual relations there is no room for insincerity. He asked me to extend personal greetings to the President and to tell him that in due course he will answer his letter, which he would also of course share with Brezhnev, Podgorny and entire leadership. He said he regretted he had been unable to receive me immediately following my presentation of credentials but press of business had interfered.

12. Although I can hardly report that Kosygin has as yet made much movement away from standard Soviet positions, he was inter-

ested and serious in reciprocating the President's approach to negotiation. He was genial throughout and laughed when I told him I could have made his day brighter by describing at great length the South Vietnam Government's growing achievements.

13. We are informed that Soviet media will confine publicity of meeting to usual brief statement that I was received at my request and that conversation touched on questions of mutual interest. We do not plan to go beyond that in comments to press here.

Beam

Establishment of the Kissinger–Dobrynin Channel; Dialogue on the Middle East; and the Sino-Soviet Dispute, April 23–December 10, 1969

41. Memorandum From Harold Saunders of the National Security Council Staff to the President's Assistant for National Security Affairs (Kissinger)[1]

Washington, May 2, 1969.

SUBJECT

Authorization for Next Step in Sisco–Dobrynin Talks

Sisco has revised his approach in the light of our comments and Barbour's recommendation that we go to the USSR first.

This is a lot closer to your position—let the USSR make the first big concessions and defer a confrontation with the Israelis until we can give them those concessions, if any, to consider.

Joe has a tentative appointment with Dobrynin Monday[2] but will, of course, delay until he hears from us. Now that we have moved him this far, I see no tactical reason to delay further once you are satisfied this is close enough to the President's view.

Recommendations:

1. That you send the attached memo to the President.[3]

2. That you at least authorize me to show Sisco informally, before he sees Dobrynin, contents of the draft NSDM[4] I sent you earlier in the week if you feel it represents the President's views.[5]

---

[1] Source: National Archives, Nixon Presidential Materials, NSC Files, Box 653, Country Files, Middle East, Sisco Middle East Talks, April–June 1969. Secret; Nodis.

[2] Sisco met with Dobrynin on May 6; see footnote 2, Document 44.

[3] Attached but not printed. In this May 3 memorandum, seen by the President, Kissinger described the principal changes decided at the NSC meeting on April 25, which included the following: "We would not, therefore, have one big consultation with Israel before giving our ideas to Dobrynin. Instead, Sisco would try pieces of our proposal out on Dobrynin first, and then—hopefully after negotiating the best possible Soviet response—he would bring Rabin up to date. This would give us a chance of avoiding one sharp Israeli reaction, while still keeping our promise to consult with them." Nixon initialed his approval for Kissinger to tell Rogers to proceed on the basis laid out in the memorandum. The minutes of the April 25 NSC meeting are in *Foreign Relations, 1969–1976*, volume XXIII, Arab-Israeli Dispute, 1969–1972.

[4] Not found. Kissinger wrote the marginal comment, "Tell Sisco no NSDM because of sensitivities."

[5] Kissinger initialed his approval of both recommendations.

42.   Memorandum of Conversation[1]

Washington, May 5, 1969.

SUBJECT

SALT

PARTICIPANTS

Soviet Ambassador Dobrynin
Llewellyn E. Thompson

My wife and I had the Dobrynins to dinner alone last night to show them our new house and to receive a mounted photograph of Kosygin which he had informed me he had been asked to transmit.

In an after dinner conversation with the Ambassador alone we discussed the strategic arms talks. He said that the Soviet leadership had been disturbed by the speculation in the American press to the effect that because of economic pressure the Soviet Government was eager for the talks to begin and that over a month ago he had been instructed not to raise the question of talks on his own initiative with anyone and had not done so. When I said I was optimistic that we could reach agreement he replied that he had thought so too but had changed his mind. He thought that as a result of the delay in starting the talks and the attempt to charge the Soviets with building for a first strike he thought that there was great suspicion and distrust in Moscow of our purposes.

I explained at some length the thoroughness of the review the U.S. Government was undertaking of the problem and Dobrynin said that he could understand this but indicated he had not convinced Moscow. In this connection he mentioned the leak of the Packard study which added to the difficulty and said that this was something that even he could not understand.

---

[1] Source: National Archives, RG 59, Central Files 1967–69, DEF 1 US–USSR. Secret; Nodis. Drafted by Thompson on May 6. Copies were distributed to Rogers, Smith, Kissinger, Laird, and the Embassy in Moscow. On May 8, Kissinger sent Nixon a copy of this memorandum of conversation with a covering memorandum that reads: "I particularly draw your attention to the third paragraph on page 2 which indicates that Ambassador Thompson—under instructions—told Dobrynin that we 'hoped to be in a position to discuss the matter of date and place' for SALT before Secretary Rogers left for the Far East. This conversation took place *before* you had made your decision on how to proceed with SALT." Kissinger's covering memorandum and copy of the memorandum of conversation between Thompson and Dobrynin are stamped "the President has seen" and are ibid., Nixon Presidential Materials, NSC Files, Box 725, Country Files, Europe, USSR, Memcons, Thompson/Dobrynin.

He asked whether in the talks we would propose a reduction or a freeze, whether we would go for parity or insist upon superiority and how we would define strategic.

I began my reply by saying that the whole question of our position at the talks was under review and I could therefore only give him my personal views. I thought it would be foolish of both of us to go for parity in every category as this would probably amount to escalation since one of us in each case would have to destroy weapons or systems which would be difficult as a way to reach a first agreement, although reductions could be considered later. I did think that our position would be based on an overall balance between us.

I evaded answering his question on our definition of strategic weapons but did mention that in the case of airplanes this was very difficult. He observed that in the present situation airplanes were not very important.

On the matter of delay I said the Secretary had asked me to tell him that he hoped to be in a position to discuss the matter of date and place with him before he left on his trip the beginning of next week. Dobrynin expressed his hope this would be possible.

I tried to draw Dobrynin out on the Soviet position in the talks. He said he had been familiar with the position that had worked out for the previously proposed talks. He said this position laid down general principles and objectives but did not go into specifics. He explained that this would be done after the talks had opened and they had a better idea of what kind of agreement we had in mind. I had earlier mentioned that one reason for the considerable time we were taking to develop our position was that the President liked to have several options explored in depth. He said the Politburo did not normally operate in this way. Papers usually come to the Politburo in a form that enabled issues to be decided by a yes or no. Of course the members had to do a lot of homework on the agenda before the meeting. He said an agenda might have as many as sixty items on it. On a complicated issue like SALT the members could not be expected to form opinions on all the specific issues that might theoretically arise in the talks but the delegation could get instructions on these as they came up.

At one point Dobrynin asked if the problem of Communist China would affect our position in the talks. I said my guess was that we would have an open mind on this and would give careful consideration to any points they might wish to raise. I said he would be aware from the discussion in our press that one argument for an ABM system was that it would be useful against a Chinese attack even though such an attack in the foreseeable future would be irrational. He inquired when we thought the Chinese Communist would have ICBMs.

When I hesitated in replying he suggested not until in the 1970s and I said I thought this was our view.

One interesting remark by Dobrynin was that my job as Ambassador had been easier than his. I had only to convince the Secretary and the President of a given position. In his case although Brezhnev was the boss, even if he and Kosygin accepted his position, if the other members of the Politburo did not agree that position would not be adopted. Therefore on his trips to Moscow for consultation he had to talk to all of the Politburo members and convince a majority of them in order to put across his point of view. I pointed out that in the case of the President he had Congress to consider. He admitted that this was true but thought the President could prevail in most cases where it was important to him.

I started to raise the question of Vietnam but at this point the ladies came in and his wife insisted on their going home as the hour was late.

Before parting Dobrynin said he needed something to show that the Nixon Administration sincerely wanted to enter into an era of negotiation with the Soviet Union and in that connection even a small step in advance would help. It was for that reason he had raised with the Secretary the matter of their opening a consulate in San Francisco in return for one for us in Leningrad. I gathered he had done this without specific instruction to do so.

---

43.   **Editorial Note**

During their conversation on May 5, 1969 (see Document 42), Ambassador Llewellyn Thompson and Soviet Ambassador Anatoliy Dobrynin also discussed "Suspected Advanced Weapons Related Facilities in China (SAWRF)." A memorandum of conversation of their meeting, with this subject title, was sent only to Under Secretary of State for Political Affairs U. Alexis Johnson and Director of Central Intelligence Richard Helms. During this conversation with Dobrynin, Thompson informed him of the U.S. discovery of approximately 15 SAWRF along the Mongolian border in the neighborhood of the Chinese missile and atomic test range and asked whether the Soviet Ambassador was aware of their construction. Thompson described Dobrynin's response as follows:

"Dobrynin gave me the impression he had already heard of these installations as he did not seem at all surprised at my raising the subject. He asked how large they were. When I said I simply did not recall what our estimate of size was he pressed me further and asked if they were around a mile long. I said my guess was that a quarter or eighth of a mile was more like it. He asked about width of the internal structure and I said I could only recall that they were narrow—perhaps about six feet. In reply to his question I said the orientation of the facilities appeared to be random. Dobrynin said he would get in touch with his Government about the matter." (Central Intelligence Agency, DCI Files, Job 80–M01044A, Box 1, Folder 12)

On May 20, Dobrynin gave Thompson a reply from Moscow about the SAWRF in China, which Thompson passed verbatim to Helms in a memorandum:

"Adjacent to the border of Mongolia there are in the construction stage several launching pads of semi-subterranean type. There are 28 launching pads there altogether. In the area of Peking and to the south of it there are several launching pad complexes of the same type under construction with direction of fire to the South East." (Ibid.)

---

44.   Memorandum From Harold Saunders of the National Security Council Staff to the President's Assistant for National Security Affairs (Kissinger)[1]

Washington, May 8, 1969.

SUBJECT

Sisco–Dobrynin Meeting, May 6

In his talk with Dobrynin on Tuesday, Sisco presented part of our proposed preliminary Arab-Israeli agreement.[2] He told Dobrynin that we feel efforts should concentrate on an Israel-UAR settlement, but that this didn't mean we were disregarding other aspects of the settlement. (Dobrynin said Moscow insisted that a UAR settlement could not be considered separately.)

---

[1] Source: National Archives, Nixon Presidential Materials, NSC Files, Box 725, Country Files, Europe, Sisco–Dobrynin Talks, Part II, May 1969. Secret; Nodis. Sent for information.

[2] A summary of the May 6 Sisco–Dobrynin session was transmitted in telegram 71012 to Moscow, May 7. Included in this telegram is the partial text of the draft U.S. proposal that Sisco gave Dobrynin. (Ibid.)

Sisco said we wanted a joint document for which both the US and USSR would take the credit and the blame. He asked for an intensive effort and said he was willing to meet every day. Dobrynin had no problems with Sisco's procedural suggestions, but said he would have to check with Moscow.

Sisco explained the following US proposals: —a settlement would be based on the UN resolution,[3] the settlement would be a package, a formal state of peace would exist, all claims or states of belligerency would end including terrorist raids, and the parties would agree to abide by the UN charter in settling future disputes. These are points 1, 2, 3, 6, 7 of our draft document; 4 and 5 deal with withdrawal and borders.

Dobrynin did not comment directly on any single item. He said Moscow would have to examine our entire document before giving a positive reply, and what Sisco had given him so far left out the key issues for the entire settlement—borders and withdrawal. Dobrynin felt that the US may have misunderstood the Soviet position on borders. They want withdrawal to pre-war lines, but have no objections if the parties want to change their borders. So far, the US document reflected the views of only one side—the Israelis—and if there is no more substance in our other points, Dobrynin thinks we will be back where we were two months ago.

Although Dobrynin seemed to be taking a harder line than usual towards our proposals, he may just have wanted to make it clear that the USSR will want to put its own ideas into the preliminary agreement instead of making minor changes in the US plan.

They are meeting again today (Thursday). I will have a fuller report on this meeting when you get back to Washington.[4]

On Wednesday, Sisco went over much the same ground with Rabin.[5] Rabin feels that the points so far surfaced are generally negative, do not spell out what peace is, and contain no positive Arab obligation to peace. (Comment: Joe rebutted by pointing to a number of such obligations, including that to control the fedayeen.) He also felt that the entire approach demonstrated that the four power and two power talks are designed to avoid negotiations between the parties.

---

[3] UN Resolution 242; see footnote 4, Document 2.

[4] See Document 46.

[5] Sisco met with Rabin on May 7. In telegram 71862 to Moscow, May 8, the Department reported on their discussion. (National Archives, Nixon Presidential Materials, NSC Files, Box 725, Country Files, Europe, Sisco–Dobrynin Talks, Part II, May 1969)

Sisco also briefed the British and French on the meeting with Dobrynin, and told them that we welcome their comments. Neither had any immediate reaction.

45.   Memorandum of Conversation[1]

Washington, May 8, 1969, 12:10 p.m.

SUBJECT

NPT and SALT

PARTICIPANTS

Soviet Ambassador Anatoly F. Dobrynin
The Secretary
Mr. Joseph J. Sisco, Assistant Secretary for Near Eastern and South Asian Affairs
Mr. Malcolm Toon, Acting Deputy Assistant Secretary for European Affairs

The Secretary asked Ambassador Dobrynin to stop in for a brief chat after his meeting with Mr. Sisco. The Secretary told the Ambassador that before his departure on the Far East trip[2] he wished to discuss with him his current thinking with regard to NPT and SALT.

NPT

The Secretary asked when the Soviets would be prepared to respond to our proposal for joint action in ratification of the Treaty. Dobrynin said that he had been informed by Moscow this morning that Ambassador Beam had been given some information by Deputy Foreign Minister Kuznetsov with regard to Soviet ratification plans.[3]

---

[1] Source: National Archives, Nixon Presidential Materials, NSC Files, Box 709, Country Files, Europe, USSR, Vol. II. Secret; Nodis. Drafted by Toon. On May 9, the Department sent telegram 73688 to Moscow summarizing Rogers' conversation with Dobrynin and added: "In view of this development and because we continue to feel that joint action is desirable from several points of view, we do not contemplate at this juncture any further move in ratification process." (Ibid.)

[2] Rogers left Washington on May 12 for a 17-day trip to the Far East to confer with Asian leaders. Rogers' press statement and details of his itinerary are in the Department of State *Bulletin*, May 19, 1969, pp. 433–434.

[3] Beam met with Kuznetsov on the morning of May 8 and received the following oral statement: "In connection with the question posed by the American side concerning the desirability of a simultaneous ratification by the Soviet Union and the United States of the treaty on the non-proliferation of nuclear weapons, I can inform you that the Soviet government has decided to approve the treaty and to transmit it to the Supreme Soviet of the USSR for ratification. Of course, the completion of the process

Ambassador Dobrynin's understanding on the basis of the cable he received was that the Soviets now intended to begin the ratification process. Mr. Toon added that according to Ambassador Beam's reporting telegram, Kuznetsov had also said that his Government had not yet decided when the final act of ratification should take place.

The Secretary said that the President was interested in holding joint ceremonies both here and in Moscow which might be covered on world-wide television through a Telstar hookup. It was not the Secretary's intention to press the Soviets to fix a date now for such joint ceremonies, but he did feel if we could reach agreement in principle, leaving the date open, it would be helpful to us in our planning. It was the President's view that joint action by our two countries would give momentum to the NPT and might encourage reluctant non-nuclear countries to sign. Ambassador Dobrynin said he would report the Secretary's remarks to Moscow.

SALT

The Secretary told Dobrynin that he hoped to see him again immediately after his return from his Far East trip in order to discuss modalities for beginning the strategic arms talks, including date, place, and the level of negotiations. He wondered how soon after a specific proposal were put to Dobrynin his Government would be able to react. Dobrynin said that this was difficult for him to answer at this time, and indicated that it would be helpful now if the Secretary could give a more specific indication as to his own ideas on modalities, particularly timing. The Secretary said that on timing he was not really able to go beyond what he said before—i.e., early summer. With regard to place, the Secretary understood that Geneva had been suggested informally as a suitable location and he assumed that this would not give the Soviets a problem. Dobrynin said that the question of place, he felt, was secondary and while he could not give a definitive answer, he believed that Geneva might be an acceptable location. The important thing, however, was to fix an opening date and he would look forward to his talk with the Secretary when he returned from the Far East.

---

of ratification of the treaty by the Soviet Union will greatly depend on the accession to the treaty of countries possessing potential possibilities to produce nuclear weapons, especially the Federal Republic of Germany." Beam reported on his conversation with Kuznetsov in telegram 1963, May 8. (National Archives, Nixon Presidential Materials, NSC Files, Subject Files, Box 366, Non-Proliferation Treaty April 1969–Mar 70)

46.   Memorandum From Harold Saunders of the National Security Council Staff to the President's Assistant for National Security Affairs (Kissinger)[1]

Washington, May 10, 1969.

SUBJECT

Sisco–Dobrynin Meeting, May 8

At their meeting on Thursday, Sisco presented more of our preliminary document, and Dobrynin again emphasized that no comment was possible until the Soviets have the complete document.[2]

Dobrynin said that if he were in Moscow he would recommend against a reply at this time. Moscow will have to consult with the Arabs, and the one-sided fragments presented so far in the US "striptease" would only bring a negative reaction from Cairo. Sisco said we have consulted with the Israelis.

Sisco gave Dobrynin the following points (at the previous meeting he gave him 1, 2, 3, 6 and 7):

8 and 9—Mutual recognition of sovereignty, territorial integrity, territorial inviolability and political independence.

11—Freedom of navigation in the Gulf of Aqaba and the Suez Canal.

12—The refugee settlement including an option for repatriation with an agreed ceiling on the number to be allowed into Israel. Dobrynin commented that it would be hard to put this contradiction into a document, but Sisco said this might be done with an informal understanding worked out by Jarring. Dobrynin also suggested that there be a specified time period for implementing the refugee solution.

13—The final accord would enter into force when signed by both parties. Dobrynin said the USSR envisaged implementation stretched over a period of time although the obligations would exist from the beginning.

Sisco confirmed that points 4, 5 and 10 and the preamble—which the US has not presented—deal with withdrawal, boundaries, and demilitarization.

Sisco briefed Argov on the above Thursday afternoon. Sisco's third and final meeting with Dobrynin in this round takes place Monday morning.

---

[1] Source: National Archives, Nixon Presidential Materials, NSC Files, Box 725, Country Files, Europe, Sisco–Dobrynin Talks, Part II, May 1969. Secret; Nodis.

[2] In telegram 72809 to Moscow, May 9, the Department provided a full account of the Sisco–Dobrynin session on May 8. (Ibid.)

Comment: So far, little Soviet reaction. It is interesting, however, that in New York last Thursday Malik said he hoped we had noted two important steps the USSR had taken toward us in the past week:

1. They have opened the door to border changes and delineation of permanent boundaries;
2. They circulated a public document (letter to U Thant) calling for observance of the cease-fire on the Suez Canal.

We will know more only when Moscow reacts to our full proposal. This will probably take several days following Sisco's Monday presentation.

---

47.   Memorandum From Harold Saunders of the National Security Council Staff to the President's Assistant for National Security Affairs (Kissinger)[1]

Washington, May 14, 1969.

SUBJECT

Sisco–Dobrynin Talk, May 12

At their meeting on Monday, Sisco gave Dobrynin the rest of our preliminary agreement:[2]

Point 4. The parties would agree on secure and recognized boundaries, and Israel would agree that the former Egypt-Palestine border is not necessarily excluded as the future boundary. There would also be an agreed timetable. Sisco explained that in raising the possibility of withdrawal to pre-war borders this had something for the UAR, and the need to agree gave something to Israel.

Tied to this point is the question of Sharm al-Shaykh which Israel feels it needs to keep the Gulf of Aqaba open. Sisco told Dobrynin that this is a critical point to which the parties must find an answer. The US does not want to return to 1967 when Nasser broke commitments obtained by the US and closed the straits.

---

[1] Source: National Archives, Nixon Presidential Materials, NSC Files, Box 725, Country Files, Europe, Sisco–Dobrynin Talks, Part II, May 1969. Secret; Nodis.

[2] In telegram 75822 to Moscow, May 13, attached but not printed, the Department provided a full account of the meeting. Also attached but not printed is telegram 75035, May 12, which summarizes the meeting.

Point 5. The status of Gaza would be worked out among Israel, Jordan and the UAR under Jarring. Sisco said the three countries ought to be able to work out a satisfactory solution.

Point 10. The areas from which Israel withdraws would be demilitarized. Arrangements would be worked out under Jarring for demilitarization and guaranteeing freedom of navigation. Dobrynin said that it was unrealistic to demilitarize all areas vacated. He could not accept Sisco's idea that the greater the DMZ the more likely Israel would be to withdraw. Also one cannot talk about only one side's security.

The Preamble which calls for the inadmissibility of the acquisition of territory by war, the need to establish a just and lasting peace, and negotiations under Jarring. Sisco explained that we see this as meaning that there must be direct negotiations at some point. Hypothetically, if both parties accept the US-Soviet document there would only be specific details to work out. Dobrynin asked about Jarring's role, and Sisco said the talks would be under his auspices and he would decide when direct and indirect negotiations would take place.

Sisco closed by reiterating that we are interested in a truly combined enterprise with the Soviets. He said we have no assurance Israel will accept the document, and its success or failure would depend on whether the USSR can get the UAR to make the necessary commitments and concessions. Even if negotiations begin, we and the Soviets would have to remain ready to help.

Dobrynin's preliminary impression was that the US had left out the most important question—withdrawal and boundaries. All of Israel's demands are clearly stated, but not points important to the Arabs. The UAR reaction will be negative. The USSR is trying to meet US and Israeli wishes, but has not gotten anything on boundaries in two months.

Dobrynin asked about the four-power talks in New York. Sisco answered that they should continue, but the primary emphasis should be in Washington. The talks in New York should concentrate on refugees and guarantees.

They agreed tentatively that their next meeting would be May 19 or 20.

Sisco briefed the British Tuesday and the French Wednesday afternoon.

48.   **Memorandum From the President's Assistant for National
        Security Affairs (Kissinger) to President Nixon**[1]

Washington, May 14, 1969.

SUBJECT

Your Meeting with Ambassador Dobrynin

Dobrynin will be coming in to see me at 11:00 a.m., today. I suggest you ask Dwight to call us to your office at about 11:30.[2]

I will have gone over your Vietnam speech with him in some detail,[3] so I suggested that you keep your meeting brief and tough, avoiding any discussion of the particulars of the speech. Nor do I think you should give him any opportunity for rebuttal remarks. If you fail to reply to his arguments, he will take it as acquiescence; if you do reply, you will be drawn into unnecessary disputation. I would *not* thank him for anything the Soviet Union did in Vietnam. Their contribution is too nebulous.

The following are suggested talking points:

—As you know, I will make a Vietnam speech tonight. The speech has been painstakingly prepared, and is the product of many months of intensive personal study and thought.

—The proposals I will make tonight set forth what I consider to be the general principles of a settlement that both sides can accept.

—If we can end this war, it will encourage friendly cooperation between our two countries. I am willing to move forward on a broad front including talks at the highest levels and expansion of trade. But an end of the war in Vietnam is the key.

—If we cannot end this war, we will continue to maintain as close relations with the Soviet Union as possible, but clearly the ending of the Vietnamese war will be our overriding concern.

—As Henry told you earlier, a failure to achieve a reasonable Vietnam settlement can only mean that we will have to take whatever steps are necessary to bring it to a successful conclusion. We are determined to end this war one way or another.

—We both know how this would affect relations between our two countries.

---

[1] Source: National Archives, Nixon Presidential Materials, NSC Files, Box 489, President's Trip Files, Dobrynin/Kissinger, 1969, Part 2. Secret; Sensitive. A notation on the memorandum indicates the President saw it.

[2] No record of this meeting has been found.

[3] A text of Nixon's address to the nation on Vietnam is in *Public Papers: Nixon, 1969,* pp. 369–375.

**49.   Memorandum From Harold Saunders of the National
        Security Council Staff to the President's Assistant for
        National Security Affairs (Kissinger)[1]**

Washington, May 21, 1969.

SUBJECT

Sisco–Dobrynin Meeting, May 19

Sisco talked with Dobrynin both May 19 and 20. Moscow is still considering our formulations and, according to Dobrynin, discussing them with "people involved in the area" so little was accomplished. (Tab A)[2]

However, Dobrynin said an Egyptian would be in Moscow soon for consultation—Joe had the impression it might be Nasser but didn't ask. He asked for clarification on two points:

1. Dobrynin said a package settlement should cover all the countries, but so far only a UAR-Israel settlement had been discussed. He asked what we planned for Jordan. Sisco told him that we feel the best place to begin is with the UAR, but we doubt that an Egyptian settlement can be implemented without a Jordanian settlement. We are not trying for a separate UAR-Israel settlement, but cannot give specific ideas on a Jordan settlement now. [The Russians know the Egyptians will object to what they believe is our policy of trying to split them off from Jordan.][3]

2. Dobrynin said the US has departed from the positions Secretary Rusk took when he met Gromyko in New York last fall. Moscow would be puzzled by this, and Dobrynin asked for an explanation. Sisco said he would review the record.

What is happening here is that Rusk, in talking with Gromyko and UAR Foreign Minister Riad last fall, was more specific on withdrawal. We have, for bargaining purposes, been less specific. The Russians in December must have told the UAR they thought they could produce US agreement to full Israeli withdrawal from the Sinai. They obviously sent Dobrynin back to find out whether we're just bargaining or have changed our substantive position, since they're now getting ready to talk with the Egyptians about our proposals. Sisco, in replying (Tab

---

[1] Source: National Archives, Nixon Presidential Materials, NSC Files, Box 725, Country Files, Europe, Sisco–Dobrynin Talks, Part II, May 1969. Secret; Nodis.

[2] Attached but not printed at Tab A is telegram 79805 to Moscow, May 20.

[3] Brackets in the source text.

C),[4] simply said there was "no deviation" in principle "between general views expressed in the past and the present proposals. This will leave the Russians to conclude that our present formulation is not our last word if the Russians can produce the right concessions from the UAR.

Just for your background, Secretary Rusk saw Gromyko on October 6, 1968, but little that he said on the nature of an Arab-Israeli settlement was specific enough to conflict with our current proposals. The Soviets may be thinking more of Rusk's "Seven Points" which he gave to Egyptian Foreign Minister Riad on November 2 and Gene Rostow gave to Dobrynin on November 8 (Tab B).[5] Even these were just tossed off by Rusk in a conversation as illustrative and weren't intended as a definitive statement of policy.

The main changes in our position as the Russians would see them are:

1. Rusk talked about Israeli withdrawal from the UAR to the old international border. We are still thinking along these lines, but as you know have avoided being that specific about a return to pre-war borders in talking with the Russians.

2. Rusk took the position, as we do now, that the refugees would have the option of returning to Israel, but we have now added restrictions by Israel such as an upper limit on the number of returnees.

3. Rusk suggested a non-removable international presence at Sharm el Sheikh. Our current position is that any arrangements must be worked out by the parties.

4. Rusk's "Seven Points" were not intended as an exposition of our entire position and there was much less emphasis on peace than in our current proposal. This is not a change in our position but Dobrynin may feel it is.

It will probably be 2–3 weeks before we have a complete Russian response to our proposals.

Dobrynin said the USSR attaches importance to the talks, is prepared to continue, and will give us their comments but he couldn't estimate when this would be.

Sisco told Dobrynin that the Israeli attitude towards the talks is negative, and it would help if we could get a positive Soviet reaction on the UAR attitude towards peace.

---

[4] Attached but not printed at Tab C is telegram 80620 to Moscow, May 21, which provides a full account of the Sisco–Dobrynin session of May 20.

[5] Attached but not printed at Tab B are telegram 269827 to Moscow, November 9, 1968; telegram 7544 from USUN, November 3, 1968; and a memorandum of conversation between former Secretary of State Dean Rusk and Gromyko, October 6, 1968.

Sisco also brought up the Suez Canal incidents, and told Dobrynin that although the situation seemed to be cooling, we were concerned with the Israeli attitude and their message to the UAR that they could not accept a continuation of the incidents.

50.   Memorandum From Helmut Sonnenfeldt of the National Security Council Staff to the President's Assistant for National Security Affairs (Kissinger)[1]

Washington, May 22, 1969.

SUBJECT

Memorandum to the President on Soviet Developments—Comment on our Policy

Attached, pursuant to your instruction, is a memorandum to the President on Soviet developments (Tab A).

In this general connection, I understand that the President at the May 21 NSC meeting[2] made a series of negative decisions on East-West trade issues. I have only been intermittently involved in the preparatory work for the NSC meeting, so that I am not familiar with the factors and considerations that led up to this rather major decision in the area of East-West relations.

But I consider it unfortunate that the Executive appears to have surrendered a flexible instrument of policy vis-à-vis the East. I have never believed that our trade (and cultural) policies will have more than marginal impact on the evolution of Soviet policy. On the other hand, I find it surprising that we should want to let the Soviets (and, for that matter, the North Koreans and North Vietnamese) control our policy toward all the Communist states of Eastern Europe. I believe that the policy of treating different Communists differently, if pursued without

---

[1] Source: National Archives, Nixon Presidential Materials, NSC Files, Box 710, Country Files, Europe, USSR, Vol. V. Secret; Sensitive.

[2] A NSC meeting on U.S. trade policy toward Communist countries was held in the Cabinet Room of the White House from 10:26 to 11:30 a.m. on May 21. (Ibid., White House Central Files, President's Daily Diary) No record of this meeting has been found. On May 28, National Security Decision Memorandum 15 on East-West trade was issued as a result of this meeting. For NSDM 15, see *Foreign Relations, 1969–1976*, volume IV, Foreign Assistance; International Development; Trade Policies, 1969–1972, Document 299.

illusion and grandiose expectations, is a wise one. But there is little, if anything, that we can do in practice to implement it if we deprive ourselves of just about the only instrument we have for doing so.

If the intention is to hold out lush vistas of trade as an incentive for the Soviets to cross the threshold of "sufficient progress" it is doubtful that we will be successful. The Soviets are unlikely to consider the potential economic benefits of sufficient interest to warrant political concessions; and since our present policy supports their own efforts to rebuild a monolith in Eastern Europe, they will hardly be inclined to pay us in order to get us to give it up.

More fundamentally, I find disturbing the apparent decision, as I understand it, to withhold a "generous" Eastern trade policy until there is "sufficient progress" in our "overall relations" with the Communists.

It seems to me that this implies a concept of our relations with the Soviets that can lead us into serious difficulty. The notion that there is some definable threshold between insufficient and sufficient progress—between confrontation and negotiation—is unrealistic. The prospect is for a highly mixed relationship with elements of both. The attached paper attempts to sketch some of the reasons why this is so.

If we think of our relations with the Soviets in terms of milestones and thresholds, we run the risk of arbitrarily proclaiming great new eras of cooperation—much as President Johnson did for subjective reasons of his own in connection with the most marginal housekeeping agreements or with a summit of the most dubious achievement—when in fact little that was fundamental had changed. We should not forget President Eisenhower's experience with his speech of April 16, 1953,[3] in which he established certain litmus paper tests for Soviet good behavior. After the Soviets had met some of them (like the Austrian peace treaty) it nevertheless turned out that we were small, if any, distance farther along in improving "overall relations."

In sum, rather than conditioning our minds and hopes to a vision of a relationship with the Soviets that is moving in one consistent direction of progress, we should anticipate that SALT and pepper will mark these relations for a long time to come. If the past is any guide at all, the landmarks we are likely to pass will not be ones of progress in overall relations as much as lines we draw in our own imagination for reasons and purposes and at moments of our own choosing. And the path along which these kinds of landmarks are posted is likely to lead to disillusionment or worse.

---

[3] Eisenhower's address, "The Chance For Peace," was delivered before the American Society of Newspaper Editors. (*Public Papers: Eisenhower, 1953*, pp. 179–188)

Tab A

Memorandum for President Nixon[4]

Washington, May 22, 1969.

SUBJECT

The View from Moscow

If one had to summarize the view from Moscow in a word, it would be "uncertainty." Whether considering their internal situation or surveying the external scene, the Soviet leaders must see a number of problems and issues that are increasingly difficult and complex. Even if the collective leadership were disposed to be more decisive, which it is not, there are too many variables that impinge on their calculations and over which they have only limited control and influence.

A case might be made that the several pressures and uncertainties with which Soviet leaders must cope may dispose them to seek quiescence in their relations with us. Yet, for the most part these pressures cut several ways, leading the Soviets into policy lines that impede improved relations with us.

China

This problem is at the center of Soviet preoccupation because it affects almost every other area of decision. The build-up which the Soviets have made in the Far East will, by the end of this year, have created stronger ground forces than the USSR has in Eastern Europe; this has been and will be extremely costly, especially as the Russians create tactical nuclear capabilities along the China border. This is an entirely new aspect to the traditional squeeze on Soviet military-economic resources, and one which Moscow should logically want to alleviate.

Yet the Soviets find it difficult to cope with the China problem. The results of the Chinese party congress offer little hope for the future, if Lin Piao[5] actually does succeed Mao. Moreover, any forceful move greatly complicates the situation in Europe, in the international communist movement, and above all, would seem to call for a much more stabilized relationship with the US and the West in general.

---

[4] Secret. Kissinger sent this memorandum to Nixon on May 24, suggesting that the paper "points up the many conflicting strands in current Soviet behavior." A note on Kissinger's covering memorandum reads, "9/15, Ret[urned] and no indication that Pres has seen."

[5] Lin Pao was Minister of Defense of the People's Republic of China and Vice Chairman of the CCP Central Committee (Politburo).

There are significant barriers, however, to moving very far in this direction.

Eastern Europe

The Soviets would prefer a tight, cohesive, ideologically orthodox Warsaw Pact. But the two recent "summit" meetings exposed once again the enormous problems of recreating such an alliance, without provoking the gravest crises; meanwhile, Rumania remains determined to create an independent position, and receives aid and comfort from Tito, whose relations with Moscow are deteriorating.

Much the same applies to the international communist movement, which will gather in Moscow on May 29 to prepare for the grand conclave of June 5. The Soviets would like, of course, to lay down a new "general line" on major issues—the imperialist threat, the Chinese, the "Brezhnev doctrine,"[6] the character of the international movement, etc. But sharp clear positions are almost certain to provoke a showdown with the dissident parties. So the result is likely to be a compromise which will settle very little.

And in the background is Czechoslovakia. The situation there is, of course, improved from the Soviet viewpoint. But they are not out of the woods by any means. To the extent that Husak[7] seeks to conciliate Moscow and consolidate his own position, he courts popular resistance. Yet if and as he succeeds, his strong personality and sharp nationalist sentiments may confront Moscow with yet further problems.

The net result is that the Soviets are reluctant to see a significant relaxation of tension in Europe, despite propaganda exercises such as the Budapest Appeal,[8] since they are concerned that the centrifugal forces already at work might be accelerated.

Western Europe

At the same time, the Soviets recognize the attraction of "détente" politics in the West, and still intend to play this line. The uncertainties created by de Gaulle's withdrawal,[9] however, probably have upset all

---

[6] The Brezhnev Doctrine applied in the West to the Soviet justification for its occupation of Czechoslovakia in August 1968. In a speech on November 11, 1968, Soviet Premier Leonid Brezhnev declared that a threat to Socialist rule in any state of the East European bloc constituted a threat to all and therefore "must engage the attention of all the Socialist states."

[7] Gustáv Husák was First Secretary of the Czechoslovakian Communist Party.

[8] Warsaw Pact nations issued the Budapest Appeal on March 17, calling for cooperation among all European countries and a conference on European security. For text, see *Documents on Disarmament, 1969,* pp. 106–108.

[9] French President Charles de Gaulle resigned in April 1969.

Soviet calculations. They have already evidenced some concern over possible departures from the Gaullist line by Pompidou.[10]

The principal Soviet concern, however, is whether the political weight of Bonn does not automatically gain as de Gaulle leaves the scene. Relations with Bonn, in any case, have been ambiguous. The Soviets are tempted to promote a "dialogue," especially while the SPD is in the Grand Coalition, and even open up the Berlin question. Recent trade overtures and agreements with German industry also point in this direction. Any extensive dialogue, however, creates problems for Moscow's relations with East Germany and Poland. Moreover, the NPT issue is a source of tensions between Bonn and Moscow. While the Soviets have now decided to start the ratification process, they will still withhold the final steps until the Germans sign, which probably means after the German elections. Thus, the issue may become acrimonious and an issue in German politics in which the Soviets will try to involve themselves. It may also complicate relations with us.

Middle East

On the Middle East, the Soviets have recognized the explosiveness of the situation and the need for a breathing spell; hence their interest in the four-power discussions and their fairly flexible approach. But the question remains whether they believe a breather is all that is necessary, or that a more durable settlement is required. In the latter case, they would have to consider the cost to their position in the Arab World of trying to reach a mutually acceptable compromise. It is unlikely that they have faced the hard decisions on the Middle East, since they do not seem to share our concern over the recent deterioration of the situation.

Vietnam

A similar ambiguity seems to characterize the Soviet position on Vietnam. In Paris they have been stonewalling and of no visible help in the talks. Recently, however, there were some signs—in remarks by Kosygin to Beam—that they might again take a more active role in private talks; perhaps this was conveyed to Le Duc Tho[11] when Kosygin saw him.

The Soviets are probably still basically of two minds on Vietnam, however. On the one hand, they could see the virtue in further stalling, in expectation that domestic pressures in the US will force new concessions in Paris. On the other hand, they may recognize that Vietnam

---

[10] George Pompidou succeeded de Gaulle as President of France in April 1969.

[11] Le Duc Tho was a member of the Politburo of the Democratic Republic of Vietnam and Special Adviser to the DRV Delegation to the Paris Peace Talks on Vietnam.

casts a shadow over relations with the US and may stand in the way of proceeding on other issues. The Soviets may also be concerned that the lack of progress in Paris vindicates the Chinese criticism and reduces Moscow's influence in Hanoi. But Vietnam is still a critical issue over which the Soviets have limited leverage and no compelling incentive to exert pressures on North Vietnam.

The US

Apparently, the uncertainties over Vietnam and the Middle East are reinforced by doubts over relations with the US. The Soviets have been notably patient about the SALT talks and fairly calm in their criticism of the US ABM decision. They have also been moderately positive in evaluating the new American administration. And Brezhnev in his keynote speech on May Day seemed restrained.

At the same time, the Soviets may have suspicions that the US is improving its military position and attaching "preconditions" to arms control talks.

SALT

That there is a greater uncertainty seems to be reflected in evidence of a debate over military affairs. The military seem to be arguing among themselves over weapons programs, including ABMs, and with the civilians over who should have the last word on professional military decisions. Civilian control is almost certainly not in danger, but concessions to military pleading, say for new weapons programs, may affect the political leaders' attitude toward SALT.

Internal Pressures

These issues have been sharpened by the need to begin preparations for the new Five Year Plan (1971–75). The Soviets are not facing an acute economic crisis; nor are they faced with simple choices of guns versus butter. The problems are more complex. The main one is how to increase the rate of investment for future growth, which is almost certain to decline further if investment rates are not increased.

Eventually, enough political leaders may conclude that they should cut into the military pie, which is probably exactly what the marshals fear and are trying to head off in their contentious articles of late.

While it can be argued that economic pressures push the Soviets in the direction of a détente with the United States, social dissidence and internal unrest draw the Soviet leaders into an increasingly repressive, authoritarian mode of behavior. Some very ugly features of the Soviet leadership are more and more apparent. Historically, such trends in internal affairs are linked to a more defensive but militant attitude toward the outside world.

The Outlook

All of the foregoing does not add up to a crisis. Nor does it suggest a more belligerent, forward policy abroad. Probably the leadership will continue to manage, rather than solve, its principal problems, and do so in the businesslike fashion which has characterized the collective in Moscow since they assumed power.

From our standpoint, this may offer some opportunities. If the Soviet leaders seem to be temporizing and are rather uncertain, then there may be room for the US to influence decisions, especially on the critical issues—the Middle East, Vietnam, and disarmament.

From the standpoint of the Kremlin, however, there may be those who are impatient with a leadership which seems increasingly tired. A change at the top, before the party congress next spring could be one outcome. Another could be the development of a new "general line" after the Communist conference, which is the next major landmark which should provide us with considerable material for a better view of Moscow's foreign policy direction.

---

51.   Memorandum From the President's Assistant for National Security Affairs (Kissinger) to President Nixon[1]

Washington, May 28, 1969.

SUBJECT

Kosygin's Reply to Your Letter of March 26[2]

Kosygin's letter—handed to Ambassador Beam by Gromyko in Kosygin's absence (he is in Afghanistan) today—is on the whole calm and unideological in tone.[3] It is clear that the Soviet leaders want to

---

[1] Source: National Archives, Nixon Presidential Materials, NSC Files, Box 765, Presidential Correspondence, Kosygin. Secret; Nodis. Sent for action. Nixon wrote "A very shrewd and very depressingly hard line letter. There is *no* conciliation in it except style!" on the first page of the memorandum.

[2] Nixon's letter to Kosygin is Document 28.

[3] In *Multiple Exposure* (p. 221), Beam describes the letter: "An interesting feature was that the reply raised the later, much-publicized issue of 'linkage.' Apparently answering some earlier Kissinger remarks about the crucial importance of finding solutions for Vietnam and arms control, Kosygin's letter declared it would be inadvisable to make the solution of one problem depend upon the solution of another, since this procedure might postpone a general improvement of U.S.-Soviet relations or of the international situation as a whole, and could create a vicious circle."

maintain a dialogue with you and that they remain interested in keeping our relations on an even keel.

However, while the tone is civil and constructive, I detect no substantive concessions. But none were to be expected in this general sort of communication, just as your own letter contained general considerations rather than specific new offers of substance.

As was to have been expected, Kosygin argues against linking various issues too closely, although he recognizes a certain interrelationship. In principle, this is not too different from your position, and I see no need for arguing this issue further with the Soviets. We should simply continue to apply our conception in practice.

On specific issues, Kosygin's most important points are

—continued relaxation on SALT, with a bare reference simply stating that they await our views. He failed to pick up your suggestion that he give you any substantive views he may have. This bland posture is probably due (1) to their desire not to seem too eager and (2) their wanting to watch the outcome of our domestic debates to see whether we might be forced into unilateral "restraint";

—a rather more demanding position on South Vietnam, with, in effect, a proposition that we get rid of Thieu and set up a "temporary" coalition. On the other hand, Kosygin makes no demands for US troop withdrawals, as Zorin has been doing in talks with Lodge. Kosygin offers to "facilitate" a political settlement but this seems to be contingent on the changes in South Vietnam he asks for. I see nothing particularly hopeful in this;

—on the Middle East, Kosygin supports the present US-Soviet talks and the four-power conversations in New York but offers no change in substance. (Gromyko told Beam they are studying Sisco's recent suggestions.) As was to be anticipated he urges you to use influence on Israel. He maintains the position that arms control in the Middle East must await a political settlement;

—on Berlin, he insists that the FRG is to blame for any trouble but picks up your suggestion to exchange views on improving the situation; while we might explore the matter in a low key to Dobrynin, I doubt that this is a good time to rush into any full-scale talks. Following the German election, we might raise the issue with the new government in Bonn and then consider whether and how to follow up with Moscow;

—on Europe, he bears down hard on the demand that the FRG sign the NPT and appears to rule out Soviet ratification until then. He asks us to press the Germans and other countries allied with us (presumably meaning Japan and, by Soviet definition, Israel);

—he takes pro forma exception to the comments in your letter to Czechoslovakia;

—on China, Beam had orally told Kosygin that we did not seek to exploit Sino-Soviet difficulties; Gromyko now replies that they will not exploit our troubles with China either and, rather enigmatically, suggests that in general US-Soviet relations should be based on long-range considerations and on a whole range of factors, rather than just China.

I believe that this exchange of letters has served your purpose of putting on record your basic approach to our relations with the Soviet Union and that for the moment nothing is to be gained by pursuing it further. Other channels are open on pending issues.

A translation of Kosygin's letter is at Tab A; for your reference, your letter of March 26 and Beam's oral presentation of April 22 are at Tabs B and C respectively.[4]

Since we gave the NATO allies the gist of your letter of March 26, I believe we should give them a very brief account of the reply. If you agree, I will ask the State Department to have Ambassador Cleveland inform the Permanent Representatives by means of the text at Tab D.[5]

Recommendation:[6]

1. That no written reply be made to Kosygin's letter.

2. That I inform Dobrynin that you have read Kosygin's letter, that you believe we should now pursue matters of common interest through existing channels, that you do not plan at this time to make a written reply.

3. That you approve the text at Tab D for use at NATO to inform the allies of Kosygin's letter.

Tab A

Letter From Chairman of the Council of Ministers of the Soviet Union Kosygin to President Nixon[7]

Moscow, May 27, 1969.

Dear Mr. President:

I and my colleagues have attentively familiarized ourselves with your message, and also the additional considerations conveyed by Ambassador Beam.

---

[4] Beam's oral presentation is Document 39.

[5] Attached but not printed.

[6] President Nixon initialed his approval of recommendations 1–3.

[7] Secret; Nodis.

We have received with satisfaction confirmation by you of the idea of the necessity of entering into an era of negotiations and of readiness to examine any possible path for the settlement of international problems, in particular of those which are connected with the danger of a clash and of conflicts.

This accords with our opinion, already expressed earlier to you, on the importance of achieving a situation in which negotiations would serve first of all to avert conflicts, and not to seek for ways out of them after peace and international security have been placed in jeopardy.

Such a task is completely feasible if our two countries with their resources and influence will act in the direction of maintaining and consolidating peace, with due consideration of each other's fundamental interests and without setting themselves against third countries. At the same time it is important not to permit anyone to exert pernicious influence on Soviet-American relations.

The achievement of mutual understanding in this matter is all the more necessary since our countries must take into account the character and degree of influence on the international situation also of other forces. From this point of view much that can be done now, given mutual desire, and setting aside complicating (kon yunturnye) questions, may turn out with the passage of time either to be fully unattainable of much more difficult and complex.

As far as can be judged by your statements, in principle we have with you a common understanding in this regard. It is a matter now, perhaps, of embarking on the practical realization of such an understanding, on a search for ways and means of resolving concrete problems which burden international relations at the present time and are fraught with great dangers for the future.

In this regard, it seems to us, that, taking into account the complexity of each of these problems by itself, it is hardly worthwhile to attempt somehow to link one with another. Although it is indisputable that progress in solving each problem taken individually would facilitate the solving also of other problems, it would be unjustified in our view to draw from this a conclusion about the advisability of making the solution of one problem dependent on the solution of any other problem or of postponing in general their examination until there is some sort of general improvement in Soviet-American relations or in the international situation as a whole. Such a posing of the question would inevitably lead to the emergence of a vicious circle and would in no way facilitate the solving of problems which have become ripe for this.

We have already transmitted to you through Ambassador Dobrynin our observations on a number of international problems and on questions of Soviet-American bilateral relations. In connection with your message we would like in addition to express the following thoughts.

(1) As facts show, the situation in the Near East is becoming more and more exacerbated by virtue of the *continuity* lack of settlement of the conflict in this region. Without going into a detailed discussion of this question here, with which our representatives are now occupied, I would only like to emphasize our conviction that in the working out of any plans for a Near Eastern settlement, the strict observance of the main principle is necessary—aggression must not be rewarded. Without this there can be no firm and lasting peace in the Near East.

As we understand it, the Government of the USA assesses seriously the situation which has been created, and therefore we hope that it will devote efforts to exert the necessary influence on Israel, which stubbornly does not wish to take a realistic position and which ignores the dangerous consequences of its annexationist course.

For our part, we intend to continue, in the framework of a bilateral Soviet-American exchange of views and of the consultations of the representatives of the four powers in New York, to use every opportunity to secure real progress in the matter of a just settlement of the Near Eastern conflict in conformity with the November 22, 1967, Security Council Resolution.[8]

As regards the question raised by you about limiting outside military assistance to countries of the Near East, in principle we advocate the limitation of an unnecessary arms race in the Near East and we assume that appropriate steps in this direction would not contradict the interests of countries of this region. We believe that this question could be examined on a practical plane after the realization of a political settlement, including the withdrawal by Israel of its troops from occupied Arab territories.

(2) It causes regret and concern to us that real progress in the direction of a political settlement in Vietnam still has not been noted in the negotiations in Paris.

The Soviet Union, just as earlier, is ready to facilitate such a settlement. However, I will say frankly: the American side itself is complicating the possibility of rendering this assistance by its obviously unrealistic position in such a fundamental question as the question of the South Vietnamese Government. If one admits the hopelessness of a military way to the solution of the Vietnam problem and one expresses the desire to stop the armed conflict, then it would seem self-evident that the present Administration in Saigon must give way to a government which reflects the actual disposition of political forces in

---

[8] See footnote 4, Document 2.

South Vietnam. Together with the question of creating in South Vietnam a temporary coalition government is, without question, a decisive one. It has now become completely obvious already that if one strives for a halt in the war in Vietnam then it is impossible to continue to bank on the present Saigon Administration.

(3) We fully share the view on the necessity of averting crises and of eliminating threats to peace in Europe. In this connection we attach special importance to the understanding with the Soviet Government, expressed earlier by you Mr. President, that the foundations of the post-war system in Europe should not be changed, inasmuch as this could cause great upheavals and the danger of a clash among great powers.

For our part, we are not interested in the creation of tension in Europe, including West Berlin. If such tensions emerges from time to time, then the responsibility for it is borne by those forces in Western Germany which oppose the foundations of the post-war system in Europe, which attempt to undermine these foundations, and in particular which come out with totally unjustified claims with respect to West Berlin. There are no objections from our side to an exchange of opinions proposed by you concerning ways of improving the present unsatisfactory situation with West Berlin.

We, Mr. President, are not at all against an improvement also of Soviet-West German relations. And the practical steps which have been undertaken by us in this direction are obviously known to you. Unfortunately, however, in the FRG the understanding still has not apparently matured that its relations with other countries, including those with the USSR, cannot be developed apart from the general foreign policy course of Bonn. And the fact that this course still is based on these which are contrary to the goals of strengthening European security and world peace is confirmed in particular by the attitude of the FRG toward the treaty on the non-proliferation of nuclear weapons. After all, it is precisely the stubborn refusal of Western Germany to accede to the treaty—with whatever contrived pretext it fortifies itself—which greatly impedes its entry into force. We hope that the United States is using its influence in order to secure the most rapid accession to the treaty by the FRG and by a number of other countries allied with the USA. As regards the ratification of the treaty by the Soviet Union, the matter is not up to us (to za nami delo nye stanet).

(4) With regard to concrete times for the beginning of talks on the limitation and curtailment of strategic—both offensive as well as defensive—armaments, we await your views on this matter.

(5) We take note of your assurances, Mr. President, that you fully understand our concern about our security and that the USA does not want to complicate the relations of the USSR with its neighbors—both Communist as well as with others. In light of your assurances,

the mention in your message of events in Czechoslovakia is all the more incomprehensible. As we have already noted earlier, these events concern first of all Czechoslovakia itself, and also its relations with other participating states of the Warsaw Pact and their security, including the security of the USSR, and they do not in any way affect the state interests of the USA.

In conclusion, I would like once again to stress our readiness to develop relations with the USA in a constructive plane on the basis of mutual confidence and frankness. In this connection, we consider useful the practice which has developed of a confidential exchange of views on topical international problems and on questions of Soviet-American relations. In this regard we agree with you, Mr. President, that in different situations—depending on the character of the questions and on other considerations—one must apply different forms and utilize various channels for such an exchange of views.

With respect,

A. Kosygin

---

52.   **Memorandum From the President's Assistant for National Security Affairs (Kissinger) to the President's Assistant for Domestic Affairs (Ehrlichman)**[1]

Washington, June 5, 1969.

SUBJECT

Comment on Suggested Invitation to Khrushchev

I am afraid Bill Safire is being optimistic when he calculates that his suggestion has one chance in a hundred of working out.[2] I do not

---

[1] Source: National Archives, Nixon Presidential Materials, NSC Files, Box 709, Country Files, Europe, USSR, Vol. II. No classification marking. Sent for information. Drafted by Lesh on June 2. Sent under a covering memorandum from Sonnenfeldt to Kissinger with the recommendation that he sign it. Kissinger signed the memorandum; an invitation to Khrushchev was apparently never issued.

[2] On May 28, William Safire, speechwriter to President Nixon, sent the following message to Haldeman and Ehrlichman: "Here is a far-out thought with a chance in a hundred of working out. We are planning some kind of reunion celebrating the 10th anniversary of the Kitchen Conference on July 24. What about approaching the Soviet[s] about inviting Khrushchev? Not so wild as it sounds—they might just go along if it suits their interests." (Ibid.)

think there is any chance that the Soviets would permit Khrushchev to come to the US for a reunion of the participants of the 1959 "Kitchen Debate,"[3] and in fact I recommended against sending an invitation, for the following reasons:

1. Khrushchev is close to being an un-person in the USSR. In a great advance over past Soviet practices, he is still alive and is fed and housed in comfort. But he is a political pariah, allowed one brief and closely guarded public appearance each November to vote in his local district elections. Knowing Khrushchev's penchant for oratory, the Soviets would never permit him to travel abroad, especially to the US.

2. Furthermore, since Khrushchev was deposed by a coup in 1964, it would be diplomatically unwise either to ask the current Kremlin leaders—who were his deposers—to let him come to Washington, or to circumvent them by asking Khrushchev directly. (As you may know, the present leaders have bridled at previous attempts by prominent Americans to contact Khrushchev.)

In general I recommend that you place the major emphasis in your plans on the tenth anniversary of the first US national exhibit in Moscow and the President's trip to the Soviet Union, rather than on the "Kitchen Debate" per se. While we look back on the episode with a certain nostalgia, the Soviets do not regard the Nixon–Khrushchev encounter as one of the high points in Soviet-American relations. In fact the "Kitchen Debate" was associated in the past with a strong anti-Nixon line in the Soviet press—now conveniently forgotten. Because of these overtones, the Soviets might not even let Ambassador Dobrynin participate unless we characterize the occasion as commemorating the President's trip as a whole (rather than only the "Kitchen Debate").

---

[3] Nixon attended the American Exhibition in Moscow in July 1959. During a stop in the model kitchen at the Exhibition, Nixon and Khrushchev had an impromptu debate, over the relative merits of each nation's economic system. Nixon's description of the "Kitchen Debate" is in *RN: The Memoirs of Richard Nixon*, pp. 208–209.

53.   Memorandum From Harold Saunders of the National Security Council Staff to the President's Assistant for National Security Affairs (Kissinger)[1]

Washington, June 10, 1969.

SUBJECT

Sisco–Dobrynin Meeting, June 9

The Soviets have not completed their reply to our paper,[2] but Monday's Sisco–Dobrynin meeting[3] confirmed that the Soviets are having serious talks with the Egyptians about it.

Dobrynin said that the UAR has made a devastating critique of our proposals. The Soviets are, however, still in the middle of intensive discussions with the Arabs, with Gromyko, Semenov—Sisco's Soviet equivalent—and Semyushchin—who was here helping Dobrynin— arriving in Cairo on Tuesday. Dobrynin hoped he could give us the Soviet response by the end of June or perhaps even by June 20.

There was a general discussion of the four power talks in New York in the course of which Dobrynin said that Moscow is interested in a joint communiqué if the text is good but otherwise sees no need for it. Apparently they don't regard it as vital to their talks with the UAR. Dobrynin asked if the US is interested in a recess after the communiqué is issued, but Sisco gave him a non-committal answer.

Sisco briefed Dobrynin in general terms on the Israeli and Jordanian reaction to the peace efforts.

---

[1] Source: National Archives, Nixon Presidential Materials, NSC Files, Box 653, Country Files, Middle East, Sisco Middle East Talks, April–June 1969. Secret; Nodis.

[2] Reference is to "A Preliminary Document Which it is Suggested Be Used By The Governments of Israel and the UAR Under Ambassador Jarring's Auspices as a Basis for Concluding a Final Binding Accord Between Them on a Just and Lasting Peace in Accordance with Security Council Resolution of November 22, 1967," which Sisco advanced in installments beginning May 6 in talks with Dobrynin. (National Archives, Nixon Presidential Materials, NSC Files, Box 711, Country Files, Europe, USSR, Vol. VI) Printed in *Foreign Relations,* 1969–1976, volume XXIII, Arab-Israeli Dispute, 1969–1972.

[3] In telegram 93698 to Moscow, June 10, the Department provided a summary of the Sisco–Dobrynin meeting of June 9. (National Archives, Nixon Presidential Materials, NSC Files, Box 653, Country Files, Middle East, Sisco Middle East Talks, April–June 1969)

54.   Intelligence Note From the Director of the Bureau of
       Intelligence and Research (Hughes) to Secretary of State
       Rogers[1]

No. 452   Washington, June 11, 1969.

SUBJECT

   USSR–MIDDLE EAST: Gromyko Probably in Cairo to Clear New Soviet Position
   for US–USSR Talks on Middle East

   A Soviet Embassy source in Washington has intimated that
Gromyko's visit to Cairo which began June 10 is connected with the
Sisco–Dobrynin discussions on the Arab-Israeli settlement problem and
that it will enable the Soviets to make a new presentation to the US in
the near future. There is other good evidence as well that this is the
main purpose of Gromyko's trip. Although the evidence is sketchy regarding the extent of Moscow's optimism, it seems likely that Moscow
in sending Gromyko was confident that the consultations would produce a useful position which the Soviets could take in Washington, and
that the trip does not signify Soviet consternation over a totally negative UAR attitude toward further Soviet settlement talks with the West.

   Purpose of the Trip. Egyptian media have noted that the Soviet Ambassador in Cairo called on Nasser on May 17 and on UAR Foreign
Minister Riad on May 10 and 19 to discuss the US-Soviet and the Four
Power talks on the Middle East, and there is every reason to believe
that such consultations have continued since then. The authoritative
Cairo newspaper *Al Ahram* on June 10 stated that Gromyko was coming to Cairo for "important political talks on the Middle East crisis,"
and a Western wire service on June 11 cited "officials" as saying that
Gromyko briefed Riad June 10 on the US-Soviet and Four Power talks.
It is also noteworthy that the four other Soviet officials who accompanied Gromyko to Cairo are all Middle East experts from the USSR Foreign Ministry. The group includes Deputy Foreign Minister Semenov,
who has been extensively involved in international discussions since
1967 relating to the Jarring mission, and Deputy Near East Division
Chief Semyoshkin, who was in Washington on temporary duty from
March to May to take part in the Sisco–Dobrynin talks.

   Moscow Reasonably Sure Gromyko Will Succeed. From recent indications the Soviets appear to want and expect the US-Soviet and Four
Power discussions on the Middle East to continue. Our estimate is that

---

[1] Source: National Archives, RG 59, Central Files 1967–69, POL USSR 7. Secret;
Limdis.

Moscow in recent weeks succeeded in obtaining through the Soviet Ambassador in Cairo assurances that Nasser—perhaps grudgingly—recognized the utility of ongoing great power efforts, regardless of his expectations as to the outcome, and that Nasser conceded that the Soviets would need periodically to take a fresh approach. The Soviet Embassy source in Washington, in linking the Gromyko trip to the Sisco–Dobrynin talks, went further, saying that the US had given the Soviets a statement of US views, to which the Soviets were preparing a reply. If so, the purpose of Gromyko's trip would be to clear the new Soviet stand with the Egyptians.

The Cairo press has indicated UAR displeasure over the position taken by the US in the US-Soviet discussions on the Middle East. It seems likely that the Egyptians would not agree with any Soviet proposal to take the US position as a point of departure for working out a new Soviet stand. On the other hand, the Egyptian authorities would have trouble defending the view with Gromyko that the Soviets should reject US views out of hand and should only reiterate existing Soviet positions, as this obviously would end the US-Soviet discussions. Soviet-Egyptian differences undoubtedly exist, since otherwise Gromyko's trip would be unnecessary. But these differences probably concern how far the Soviets should go toward US views in their next presentation in the Washington discussions, and not whether the Soviets should take any fresh position at all. As long as Gromyko is able to obtain Egyptian acquiescence on a new Soviet position for use with the Americans which will contain enough movement to keep the bilateral talks going, Moscow would probably consider the trip a success.

---

55.   Telegram From the Department of State to the Embassy in France[1]

Washington, June 12, 1969, 2346Z.

96244/Todel 2840. 1. Dobrynin saw Secretary afternoon June 11 prior to his departure Moscow on urgent consultation orders. Secretary raised Viet-Nam with Dobrynin stressing our disappointment that

---

[1] Source: National Archives, Nixon Presidential Materials, NSC Files, Box 177, Paris Talks/Meetings, Paris Meetings, May–June 1969, State Nodis Cables/Habib Calls. Secret; Nodis; Paris Meetings/Plus. Drafted by Toon, cleared by Walsh, and approved by Rogers. Repeated to Moscow and Saigon.

there had been no progress in Paris in beginning private talks by the GVN and NLF on political issues. Secretary reminded Dobrynin of his conversation in March when he made clear that private talks on political issues could be bilaterally between GVN and NLF or in four-power forum.[2] Our only reservation was with regard to private talks between US and NLF which we could not accept. This remained our position and Secretary hoped that the Soviets would do what they could to get talks underway.

2. Dobrynin said that he understood position of NLF (which he referred to throughout conversation as Provisional Revolutionary Government) to be that there could be no discussion with GVN unless Saigon prepared to agree to coalition government beforehand. Secretary told Dobrynin that if NLF position was that precondition to talks was removal of Thieu and Ky, this was totally unacceptable. As President had made clear, composition of Saigon Government must be determined by electoral process, and Secretary saw no reason why arrangements for elections including appropriate supervision could not be proper subjects for discussion in Paris in private talks, either bilaterally or with four. Secretary could not understand how composition of possible coalition government could be fixed before views of electorate known. Dobrynin rejoined that in NLF view free choice impossible in presence foreign military forces and while Saigon committed to continuation of war. Secretary said if NLF felt this way, adequate guarantees free elections could be discussed in Paris, and he saw no reason why Soviets themselves could not play role in supervisory process. Dobrynin reiterated NLF position on coalition government and said that NLF felt strongly that Thieu and Ky knew their political future depended on continued presence of US forces and continuation of war, and it was for this reason that they were opposed to commitment to coalition. Secretary firmly rejected this thesis and said that, if other side genuinely interested in peace, moves to replace US forces could be reciprocated by North Vietnamese, and Soviets and their allies could move to get Paris talks off dead center. Secretary reminded Dobrynin of past indications from Zorin and Oberemko to US counterparts in Paris of NLF willingness to discuss questions relating to political settlement in Viet-Nam and said that other side seemed to be raising new and unacceptable preconditions for such discussions.

Rogers

---

[2] See Document 25.

56.   Memorandum From the President's Assistant for National Security Affairs (Kissinger) to President Nixon[1]

Washington, June 13, 1969.

SUBJECT

Memorandum of Conversation with Ambassador Dobrynin, June 11, 1969

Dobrynin had requested the appointment to inform me that he had been recalled to Moscow for consultations. Dobrynin opened the conversation by saying that he had been impressed by the deliberateness and precision of the Administration. We had moved one step at a time towards first establishing a general atmosphere, then into the Middle East talks, then beginning some discussion on Vietnam and only when the main outlines were set did we offer to have the SALT talks. We had not been stampeded at any point. He had reported accordingly to his government. He said the Soviet Union preferred to deal with careful planners since they were much more predictable.

Dobrynin then turned to Vietnam. I told him that we were following a very careful policy. We had our moves for the next few months fully worked out. I reminded him of what the President had said when we gave him an advance copy of the Vietnam speech. He should not be confused by the many statements that he heard. We were not interfering with much that was being said. But the President reserved the final decision on essential items. Dobrynin replied that he had noticed that we moved on about the schedule we had given him a month ago.

Dobrynin then asked about our ideas for settling the war in Vietnam. He inquired especially on our views on a coalition government. I said that he and I were both realists. He knew very well that in order to bring about a coalition government we would have to smash the present structure of the Saigon Government while the NLF remained intact. This would guarantee an NLF victory sooner or later. We would never accept that. We would agree to a fair political contest—not to what the President had called a disguised defeat.

Dobrynin made no effort to defend Hanoi's position. He replied that Hanoi was very difficult. He said I could be sure that the Soviet Union had transmitted our discussion of April and added a recom-

---

[1] Source: National Archives, Nixon Presidential Materials, NSC Files, Box 489, President's Trip Files, Dobrynin/Kissinger, 1969, Part 1. Secret; Nodis. The memorandum indicates the President saw it. Kissinger prepared a memorandum of conversation with Dobrynin on June 11, an identical copy of which he sent to Rogers on June 24. The June 11 memorandum of conversation is a less complete version of this memorandum sent to Nixon. (Ibid.)

mendation. However, Hanoi believed that they knew their own requirements better than the Soviet Union. I said, on the other hand, the Soviet Union supplied 85% of the military equipment. Dobrynin asked whether we wanted the Soviet Union to give Hanoi an ultimatum. I said it was not for me to tell the Soviet Union how to conduct its relations with its allies. I said that we were determined to have the war ended one way or another. Hanoi was attempting to break down the President's public support. It was too much to ask us to hold still for that. I added that what we needed was some strategic help, not just negotiating devices for settling particular problems as has been the case until now. Dobrynin, who was very subdued, said I could be sure that they are looking into the question.

Dobrynin then asked me about US-Soviet relations in general. I said that while some gradual progress was possible even during the Vietnam war, a really massive change depended on the settlement of the Vietnam war. Dobrynin said we always seem to link things. I replied that as a student of Marxism he must believe in the importance of objective factors. It was an objective fact that Hanoi was trying to undermine the President. It was an objective fact that we had to look to every avenue for a solution. Dobrynin then said supposing the war were settled, how would you go about improving relations.

I called his attention to the President's offer of increased trade and I also suggested the possibility of a summit meeting. I said that they could count on the same careful preparation for a summit meeting that characterized all the President's efforts. One possibility would be to have a meeting at which the major issues were discussed together with a precise agenda for dealing with them, to be followed by periodic meetings to resolve them. In this way we might reach a stage in which war between the two major nuclear countries would become unthinkable, and other countries which might be emerging could not disturb the peace of the world. I added this should help the Soviets with some of their allies. Dobrynin said that they had no problem with any of their allies. I replied that China was still a Soviet ally. Dobrynin emphatically said China is not an ally; it is our chief security problem. He was very intrigued by the suggestion of a summit meeting and I added that there was no prospect of it without a settlement of the Vietnam war.

Dobrynin then turned to the Middle East. He said the Soviet Union was very interested in a settlement—Sisco was always speaking in the abstract about secure and recognized borders. The Soviet Union was perfectly willing to discuss a rectification of the borders even if it did not promise to agree right away. Gromyko was in Cairo to try to see how much give there was in the Egyptian position. I said that if Vietnam were settled, we could certainly give more top level attention to the Middle East.

Dobrynin returned to the theme of US-Soviet relations and asked what he could tell his principals when he returned. I said that everything depended on the war in Vietnam. If the war were ended, he could say that there was no limit to what might be accomplished. You would like to be remembered as a President who ensured a permanent peace and a qualitative change in international relations. Dobrynin asked whether we were expecting a change in the Moscow leadership. I replied that we had no intention of playing domestic politics in the Kremlin. Dobrynin said: "Don't believe your Soviet experts; they understand nothing."

Dobrynin then asked whether I might be willing to come to Moscow sometime very quietly to explain your thinking to Kosygin and Brezhnev. I told Dobrynin that this would have to be discussed with you but that if it were for the right issue, you would almost certainly entertain the proposition.[2]

---

[2] This paragraph was omitted from Kissinger's June 11 memorandum of conversation.

---

57.   Memorandum From the President's Assistant for National Security Affairs (Kissinger) to the Ambassador to Moscow (Beam)[1]

Washington, June 16, 1969.

Dear Jake:

I appreciated your letter of June 2.[2] I will of course be interested in anything of substance that might develop in connection with Humphrey's visit. Your ideas for handling the visit strike me as just right.[3]

---

[1] Source: National Archives, Nixon Presidential Materials, NSC Files, Box 710, Country Files, Europe, USSR, Vol. III. Personal and Confidential. Drafted by Sonnenfeldt on June 7. A handwritten notation indicates the memorandum was sent to the Department of State for dispatch on June 16.

[2] Beam wrote Kissinger to tell him about an upcoming visit to the Soviet Union of former Vice President Hubert Humphrey. (Ibid.)

[3] Beam stated his ideas as follows: "I shall try to meet him on arrival and perhaps arrange a small luncheon party with his hosts. I imagine that the Soviets will try to keep him out of our clutches and that it would not be appropriate for me to insist that I accompany him in his talks, since he is a private citizen. I shall try to get hold of him to get some briefing before his departure. He will doubtless stop by the State Department and it will be interesting to see how he plans to handle the ABM question. I hope he will remain fairly well committed on Vietnam." (Ibid.)

Your point about seeing the top Foreign Ministry officials from time to time is well taken and it should certainly be possible to supply you with material to take up with them. As you know, and as I mentioned to Boris Klosson[4] when he stopped in last week, we would like to see more of our business with the Soviets done at your end. We are giving this some thought and it may be that in connection with SALT something along these lines will develop.

I have read your telegrams with interest and was especially impressed with your recent analyses of the Soviet leadership picture. Your judgment on that subject from time to time will be most helpful here. And, of course, whenever you have comments on how we are handling our relations with your hosts, I will value them.

With warmest regards,

Henry A. Kissinger[5]

---

[4] On June 3, at 4 p.m., Kissinger met with Klosson, who was on his way to Moscow to become Minister-Counselor. Talking points prepared by Sonnenfeldt for that meeting are ibid., Vol. II.

[5] Printed from a copy that indicates Kissinger signed the original.

---

58.   Telegram From the Department of State to the Embassy in the Soviet Union[1]

Washington, June 18, 1969, 0031Z.

99315. 1. Soviet Chargé Tcherniakov called at his request on the Secretary afternoon June 17 to deliver what is in effect the Soviet counter-proposal[2] to US formulations on Middle East settlement provided to the Soviets last month in Sisco–Dobrynin talks.[3]

---

[1] Source: National Archives, Nixon Presidential Materials, NSC Files, Box 649, Country Files, Middle East, Middle East Negotiations, June 1969. Secret; Nodis; Noforn. Drafted by Atherton on June 17; cleared in substance by Sisco, Walsh, and Swank; and approved by Sisco. Repeated to Amman, USINT Cairo, Tel Aviv, London, Paris, and USUN.

[2] The oral statements made by Tcherniakov and the official U.S. Government translation of the Soviet text on the "Basic Provisions" of a Middle East settlement are in *Foreign Relations, 1969–1976*, volume XXIII, Arab-Israeli Dispute, 1969–1972.

[3] For a summary of the nine exploratory discussions held between Sisco and Dobrynin March–April, see Document 38.

2. In preliminary comments, Tcherniakov said Soviet Government had considered US proposals contained in draft preliminary accord and accompanying oral comments by Sisco as well as views exchanged in US-Soviet and four power meetings. Soviet Government, guided by desire to secure just and lasting peace in Middle East on basis of Security Council Resolution 242, had prepared new plan for peaceful political settlement of Middle East problem.

3. We are giving new Soviet document urgent and detailed study. Our tentative impression, however, is that it represents very little movement and consists largely of a recasting of December 30 Soviet plan[4] plus some modifications given to Sisco orally by Dobrynin, including specifically provision for deposit with UN of agreed and irrevocable document or documents covering all aspects of a settlement before Israeli withdrawal begins. Soviet document does not provide for direct negotiations between parties at any stage, does not include specific affirmation of establishment of state of peace and calls for complete withdrawal by Israel to pre-June 5, 1967 lines with all its neighbors. In prepared oral statement commenting on this document Tcherniakov noted among other things that on the whole it reflects Soviet views and that, if agreement is reached with USG, Soviets will need to obtain final consent from Arab side.

4. Following foregoing presentation, Tcherniakov said he was instructed to propose that venue of US-Soviet talks be moved to Moscow. Secretary said we would study Soviet document carefully. Re moving bilaterals to Moscow, Secretary noted that we had earlier informed Dobrynin we might be willing to hold some of talks there. We would consider this suggestion and give Soviets our reply after we had completed study of document Tcherniakov had delivered.

Rogers

---

[4] See footnote 4, Document 1.

59.   Memorandum From Helmut Sonnenfeldt of the National Security Council Staff to the President's Assistant for National Security Affairs (Kissinger)[1]

Washington, June 18, 1969.

SUBJECT

Comment on Arthur Burns' Report on Sino-Soviet Feelings

Dr. Burns' report of his conversation with a Soviet economist (Tab A)[2] simply confirms what we have long known: that the Soviets are terribly uneasy about their potentially explosive dispute with Red China, and are pathologically suspicious of anything that smacks of Sino-American collusion.

We know that the Soviets are in a nervous state of mind, but they apparently feel they need security more than they need friends—one piece of evidence being their brutal suppression of nascent liberalism in Czechoslovakia.

---

[1] Source: National Archives, Nixon Presidential Materials, NSC Files, Box 710, Country Files, Europe, USSR, Vol. IV. Limited Official Use. Sent for information.

[2] Tab A is attached but not printed. On June 13, Burns wrote a memorandum to President Nixon describing his luncheon meeting with Anatoly Shapiro, a Russian economist at the Institute of World Economics in Moscow. Burns reported Shapiro's fears about the U.S. attitude toward Sino-Soviet differences as follows: "If [Shapiro] is really right that the Russians are fearful that sentiment in this country, including that of our government, is favorable to the Chinese Communists, this would suggest that the Russians are in a nervous state of mind and that they feel they need friends. All this is highly speculative on my part, and I'm merely passing on what I learned for what little it may be worth."

60.   Memorandum From Harold Saunders of the National Security Council Staff to the President's Assistant for National Security Affairs (Kissinger)[1]

Washington, June 20, 1969.

SUBJECT

The Soviet Counterproposal on the Middle East

The two documents the Soviet Chargé gave Rogers June 17 are at Tab A.[2] One is the actual Soviet counterproposal; the other is the oral explanation he made. At Tab B[3] is our document for comparison. Sisco is working up a memo[4] for the President on where we go now, but here are my first thoughts.

You should know that Sisco has told Rabin we have the Soviet reply but will not be in a position to give it to him until we have our position on it thoroughly worked out. State, if asked by the press, will say we have a reply but refuse to comment on it.

I. *Analysis of the Soviet paper* shows some movement but not a great deal:

A. *On the positive side:*

1. *Phasing.* It reaffirms the idea of a package settlement—all elements of the settlement to be agreed before Israeli withdrawal begins. There is some slight movement in that previously *after* Israeli withdrawal the agreement went into effect with the signing of a document, although preliminary documents were deposited with the UN before withdrawal. Now, the final, signed document is to be deposited *before* withdrawal begins, and will be binding and irrevocable immediately.

2. *Nature of agreement.* It talks about "a final and mutually binding understanding"—closer to what Israel wants than the Soviet December 30 plan's "time schedule for withdrawal" and "agreed plan" for implementing the UN Resolution. It also accepts a document signed by the parties.

3. *UN forces.* The previous Soviet position was never clearly spelled out, but they are now willing to put UN troops in Gaza and Sharm el-Sheikh on a fairly extended basis. Previously the troops seemed destined

---

[1] Source: National Archives, Nixon Presidential Materials, NSC Files, Box 649, Country Files, Middle East, Middle East Negotiations, June 1969. Secret; Nodis. Sent for information. The memorandum bears the handwritten comment, "HAK has seen, 7/7."

[2] Attached but not printed; see footnote 2, Document 58.

[3] Tab B is the document cited in footnote 2, Document 53.

[4] See Document 63.

to stay only during the withdrawal itself. They also include a long proposal for making the UN force less vulnerable to expulsion (although they talk only of a temporary period of "up to 5 years" after which the UN forces could be thrown out on several months' notice).

4. *Recognition of Israel.* The Arabs would "respect and recognize Israel's sovereignty, territorial integrity, inviolability and political independence . . . and right to live in peace in secure and recognized borders without being subjected to threats or use of force."[5] This would, of course, be mutual and doesn't represent much change in the official Soviet position of the past twenty years, but it may indicate that they think they can get the Arabs to agree to this. The December 30 Soviet document did refer to "appropriate documents concerning" sovereignty and territorial integrity, but the current version is much more explicit.

5. *Waterways.* It affirms Israeli passage through the Straits of Tiran and the Suez Canal, though it does not provide for any concrete means of enforcing this other than the UN force at Sharm el-Sheikh.

6. The Soviets have used our language in a few places where it doesn't hurt them.

B. On the negative side:

1. *Direct negotiations.* The Soviets have done their best to exclude direct negotiations. They refer to "contacts through Jarring" while we called for "representatives to meet promptly" under him. The Soviets have repeated, almost verbatim, a long section from their December 30 plan which is, in effect, a formula for getting a final agreement without the kind of negotiations the Israelis insist on.

2. *Peace.* The Soviets cut our proposal for acknowledgment by both sides that a formal state of peace exists. This is important to the Israelis. More specifically, they have eliminated the Arab obligation to control the fedayeen. They also dropped our effort to end Arab sanctions against Israel.

3. *Borders.* The Israelis would withdraw to pre-war lines. This is now a "premise" from which the parties would work rather than the immutable fact of December 30. But it still turns aside our effort to create a situation for border changes to be negotiated. It concentrates on working out the timetable for Israeli withdrawal. Because of their position on withdrawal, the Soviets have not made any attempt to address the question of special arrangements for Jerusalem.

4. *Gaza* would apparently revert to UAR control. There would be a UN force and "the situation in this area which existed in May of 1967 shall be restored."

---

[5] Ellipsis in the source text.

5. *Refugees.* Israel would carry out the "decisions of the UN" on the refugees. This presumably means unrestricted repatriation. This rejects our efforts to restrict return.

6. *Demilitarized zones.* It provides for small ones (not the whole Sinai) on both sides of the border (which Israel rejects).

7. The Syrians and withdrawal from the Golan Heights have been included in the settlement, but the Soviets are still ambiguous on this. In some places they are talking only about the Arabs who agree to a settlement.

II. Reflections on the Soviet position:

A. It leaves open the possibility that the Soviets are happy with the present no-peace, no-war situation.

B. It leaves unanswered our basic question whether the Soviets and UAR are willing to pay any serious price for Israeli withdrawal.

C. It leaves enough room for further talk to keep the discussion going (Sisco says "barely enough").

D. It may reflect the view that our talks help modestly in stabilizing the situation in the Near East so the Soviets want to keep them going for whatever damping effect they have without any real intent to press the Arabs any further.

E. However, this is still just the first round, and we cannot assume with certainty that there is no further give in the Soviet position.

III. The impasse that remains is that:

A. The Soviets and UAR still refuse to negotiate with Israel on the basis that all occupied territory is negotiable. They are not going to state more forthrightly their willingness to make peace in this document (both have said more elsewhere) until we tell them we are not trying to parlay Israel's conquests into a permanently expanded map of Israel.

B. The Israelis want significant changes in their borders at key places. They believe peace with Nasser is impossible and even if he said he wanted peace, they would doubt him and still want their own control over key spots. They want to be left alone with the Egyptians so that the Egyptians will have to face up to the realities of Israeli power and accept Israeli terms.

C. In short, the Arab governments are willing to recognize Israel in its pre-war borders but not yet to sign off on the Palestine issue for the Palestinians. Because the Israelis believe they will still be under attack, they aren't willing to settle for pre-war borders.

IV. The issues now posed for us are:

A. Should we break off the talks with the Russians?

1. Yes.

a. Their response shows very little give on points crucial to us.

b. We don't want to play into their hands. If they're just trying to string the talks along to keep the no-peace no-war situation alive but safer, we have no interest in playing that game.

c. Breaking off might shake them up.

2. No.

a. Their response isn't all bad.

b. We couldn't have expected them to go too much further in this first exchange.

c. Hard bargaining so far has brought them a long way from their position six months ago. We owe it to ourselves to keep at it.

B. Should we go back to the Russians with revisions to their document to try to improve it somewhat before we consult Israel?

1. The argument against is that the Russians probably won't give much more until we get specific about territories.

2. The argument for is that their paper doesn't give us much to work with in approaching the Israelis. The Israelis will just regard the present response as clear vindication of their argument that the Soviets (and Arabs) don't want peace. We have to make at least one more try with Moscow before tackling them.

C. Shall we go ahead now and state our position on borders?

1. Yes.

a. It's essential to further movement. It is plain from Dobrynin's comments to you and from the USSR reply, that the Soviets are not likely even to consider serious concessions until we are willing to break down and state a concrete position on borders.

b. We don't really agree with Israel's territorial ambitions (as we understand them), so why should we bear the stigma of holding out for them.

c. We do want to move this situation closer to a settlement. We can hold out for awhile longer—hard to say exactly how long—but there's little question that prolongation of the current impasse works against us.

2. No.

a. We have no indication that the UAR is ready to sound convincing enough on its desire for peace to give us what we need to persuade the Israelis to state a firm position on borders. The USSR in New York and Egyptians privately have said they are willing to end twenty years of war but their formal response is not enough for the Israelis (if, indeed, anything would satisfy them).

b. There's no reason why we should give in first. Nasser lost the war and until he is willing to make peace without obvious purpose of evasion, there is no reason why we should pay any price to get his territory back for him.

D. If we state a position, should it be Israel's or ours?

1. We could go to the Israelis now and tell them it's time for them to be specific about borders.

   a. The argument against this is that the Israelis are adamant in saying they won't surface their position until the Arabs sit down to negotiate. We have very little chance of beating them down on this.
   b. The argument for is that the time has come to make a real try to find out what the UAR will pay to get its land back and Israel either has to go along or bear the onus for blocking a reasonable effort—an onus we will share.

2. If they won't agree, we could go ahead and surface our own position for bargaining purposes. Roughly this might be return to the old international border; Gaza under UN administration for a transition period (with the idea of its going to Jordan); UN presence at Sharm el-Sheikh, perhaps with joint patrols; demilitarization, perhaps to the Mitla pass with a token area on the Israeli side.

   a. The argument against this is that we will not be speaking for Israel.
   b. The argument for is that we will at least get away from the stigma of supporting what most people regard as unreasonable Israeli demands. Telling the Israelis we were going ahead might—though the odds are probably against it—smoke out an Israeli position.

E. Should we lay aside this document for the moment and try a different tack? One possibility is to say quite straightforwardly to the Soviets: We are prepared to press on Israel the territorial settlement outlined above *provided* the Soviets can deliver the Arabs for direct negotiations with a clear-cut statement of their willingness to make peace and control the fedayeen. We can't guarantee a positive Israeli response, but if they will try in Cairo, we will try in Jerusalem. If they don't want to try, we will stick to our present formulation.

1. The argument against this is that Russians don't negotiate this way. This gives away our hand too easily.
2. The argument for is that we won't get anywhere until we get down to the territorial question. This might be a way of doing it without committing ourselves formally to a territorial position.

V. My tentative recommendation is that we:

A. Try one more round with the current paper, giving the Russians a counter document revised to put some of our language on peace back in.

B. Only then consider stating a position on territories, but if we feel it necessary to discuss boundaries at the end of this next round, do it first via the alternative stated above (IV–E).

61.   **Memorandum From the President's Assistant for National Security Affairs (Kissinger) to President Nixon**[1]

Washington, June 26, 1969.

SUBJECT

Diplomatic Exploitation of the Sino-Soviet Schism—Comment on Pat Buchanan's Suggestions

Pat Buchanan has relayed a suggestion that the US recognize Albania and promote West German contact with Communist China, as a means of making the Soviets nervous over a possible US/Chinese deal. He suggests that this might lead the Soviets to offer us something in return for our agreement to continue to cooperate in isolating China. (Tab A)[2]

I basically agree with attempts to play off the Chinese Communists against the Soviets in an effort to extract concessions from or influence actions by the Soviets. Any effort of this kind, however, is replete with complexities.

The specific moves Pat suggested pose such problems:

1. *Recognition of Albania*—Our problem here is that the Albanians could well react to any US initiative with loud and public vituperation. When we took the small step two years ago of allowing Americans to travel to Albania, the Albanian Government reacted with shrill hostility and announced that they would not allow Americans in. Since then, Czechoslovakia and the Brezhnev doctrine may have made them somewhat less inclined to slam doors in the face of contacts, but Chinese pressure and their own desire to maintain the pose of anti-imperialist purity might serve to make them turn down any US initiative. The proposed initiative would risk a scolding from the Albanians, and would make our friends nervous, without creating the appearance of a Sino-US deal.

2. *Increased West German trade and diplomatic contact with China*—The FedRep already competes with Japan as the biggest exporter to China. It has reasons of its own (the East German question) for not wanting diplomatic contact. To have the desired effect on the Russians

---

[1] Source: National Archives, Nixon Presidential Materials, NSC Files, Box 392, Subject Files, Soviet Affairs. Confidential. Sent for information. The memorandum indicates the President saw it. Nixon wrote "I agree" in the upper righthand corner of the first page.

[2] Tab A, a June 13 memorandum from Buchanan to the President passing on these suggestions from "a George Washington University professor in the Sino-Soviet Department," is attached but not printed.

we would openly have to urge the Germans to take this action. This would be inconsistent with our current UN policy and could trigger a general swing toward recognition of Communist China.

It would in turn prejudice our relations with the Republic of China and with serious repercussions throughout Asia.

There may well be opportunities to profit from rising Sino-Soviet tensions. We are looking seriously at the possibilities. The problems cited above make clear how delicate an operation it would have to be. We should need to be very clear as to precisely what we want from the Soviets—or the Chinese—and how our course of action would relate to them and to the other countries which would be affected.

---

62.   **Telegram From the Department of State to the Embassy in the Soviet Union**[1]

Washington, July 1, 1969, 0035Z.

108202. For Ambassador.

1. Purpose of this message is to bring you up to date re our current thinking on how to handle next steps in US-Soviet bilaterals on Middle East. Soviets, as you know, have proposed we move talks to Moscow. We believe there are political and psychological as well as practical advantages in maintaining pattern of Soviets talking to us in Washington, and therefore do not favor change of venue.

2. On other hand, when Soviets agreed to open talks here, we said we would keep open mind about having some discussions in Moscow. Our thinking, therefore, is to tell Soviets that in response to their proposal USG is prepared to send Asst Sec Sisco to Moscow for few days to hold a round of talks with FonMin officials prior resuming discussions with Dobrynin here. Subject your views, Sisco would hope at minimum to see Gromyko and Semenov and, of course, Dobrynin.

3. In Moscow talks Sisco would have three main aims in mind: (a) To have broad-ranging general discussion in which he would explain in depth rationale and basic principles underlying our approach

---

[1] Source: National Archives, Nixon Presidential Materials, NSC Files, Box 649, Country Files, Middle East, Middle East Negotiations, June 1969. Secret; Priority; Nodis; Noforn. Drafted by Atherton, cleared by Swank and Hornblow, and approved by Sisco. Repeated to London, Paris, and USUN.

to Arab-Israel settlement. From such an exchange he would hope we might also get better feel of Soviet intentions and strategy, although we realize difficulties this poses. (b) To engage Soviets in brief discussion of Middle East arms control problem. While Soviet response is probably predictable, we believe that for the record this subject should not be omitted in such a general exchange with Soviet Government. (c) To present our counter suggestions to Soviets' June 17 document[2] and explain in detail rationale behind it.

4. Sisco, accompanied by Atherton (NEA) and Walter Smith (INR), would hope to depart Washington Monday, July 7, stopping for consultations with British and French July 8 and 9 and arriving Moscow July 10. He would plan remain in Moscow through Monday, July 14, leaving following day for direct return to Washington.

5. Foregoing plan has been cleared by Secretary, but awaiting final White House approval, and you should make no approach to Soviets at this time. Meanwhile would appreciate soonest your comments on proposed schedule and substantive approach outlined above as well as your suggestions re how publicity should be handled if trip materializes. Our own thinking is that best way to minimize undue speculation and expectations is for announcement to be made along following lines: When U.S.-Soviet talks began in Washington, it was agreed that there might be some talks in Moscow as well. Assistant Secretary Sisco is now proceeding to Moscow for brief round of talks as part of continuing U.S.-Soviet discussions on Middle East. He will stop in London and Paris for consultation with British and French Governments enroute and will return to Washington in about one week's time.

Rogers

---

[2] See footnote 2, Document 58.

63.   **Memorandum From the President's Assistant for National Security Affairs (Kissinger) to President Nixon**[1]

Washington, undated.

SUBJECT

Middle East—Reply to Soviet Counterproposal

The attached memo from Secretary Rogers[2] seeks your approval of Joe Sisco's going to Moscow to present our counter to the Soviet counterproposal on the draft framework for a UAR-Israel settlement.

It is our judgment that we should not break off these talks now. While the Soviet response contains less than we had hoped, it does offer some refinements to work with. We may want to give them a negative reaction for effect, but on balance it seems worth trying another round.

If you share this judgment, the attached proposal contains two principal issues for your decision:

1. *How to handle our position on the Israel-UAR border.* In our first document, we left this to be negotiated by the parties, with the proviso that the pre-war border was not excluded as a solution. The Secretary's proposal would have us go back to the Soviets with substantially the same position, but this time with a fallback position we could use as bait to get them to be more forthcoming on direct negotiations and the substance of a peaceful relationship between Israel and the UAR.

The fallback position proposed is that Israel would agree on returning to the pre-war border "assuming agreement on the establishment of demilitarized zones and on practical arrangements for guaranteeing freedom of navigation through the Straits of Tiran." This formulation is designed to leave room for an Israeli position at Sharm al-Shaikh short of permanent annexation.

---

[1] Source: National Archives, Nixon Presidential Materials, NSC Files, Box 649, Country Files, Middle East, Middle East Negotiations. Secret; Nodis. Sent for action. A July 2 covering memorandum from Saunders to Kissinger reads, "Here is the Sisco memo you said you would try to get the President to focus on in Florida." On July 12, Haig sent both Saunders' and this memorandum to Saunders with the following explanation: "As you know, this memorandum was handled over the telephone by Henry with the President and as a result, per the President's instructions, Henry told Sisco he could proceed with the trip to Moscow to present our counter to the Soviet counterproposal with the provision that he could not modify our position beyond a few verbal changes. Specifically the fall-back position was not approved."

[2] Attached but not printed.

The arguments for authorizing the fallback position are:

a. Until we change our position on territories, we can not expect significant movement from the Arabs, and hence the Soviets, on direct negotiations, peace and binding commitments—the subjects most important to the Israelis. Since the situation is becoming rapidly worse (this is subject to debate), we have to do all we can to achieve a settlement.

b. We are going to have to come out eventually for the pre-war border between Israel and the UAR, at least in principle.

—The chances for a lasting peace are poor if the Israelis keep part of the UAR.

—The last four US Presidents have guaranteed territorial integrity in the Near East on the basis of the 1948 lines. They may have been thinking mainly of Israel, but the guarantee applies equally to Egypt (and Jordan).

c. If we do not try to bring Israel along on the territorial question, our prestige and influence in the Arab world will be hurt badly. Even if we fail in the attempt we might insulate ourselves from some of the consequences by trying.

The arguments against authorizing the fallback position now are:

a. It is too early in our talks with the Russians to give away our trump card. If we judge that the pressure for a settlement is greater on them than on us, they—not we—should be making the first concessions.

b. We have to be extremely careful about getting too far ahead of the Israelis. They say that they must have a position at Sharm al-Shaikh and overland access to it. Whether we accept that view or not, we have to deal with it as the position of the party holding the upper hand on the ground. Even though the proposed fallback is drafted to leave room for what we see as the Israeli position, if we are going to become Israel's lawyer we want to be more certain than we are now that they will buy this.

c. At the least, this attempt would further increase strains in our relations with Israel. They reacted strongly to our previous mention that the pre-war border was not excluded.

Conclusion. I do not believe we should play our trump card on this round. I could see telling Sisco to come back with a candid assessment of what this fallback might buy. But I would not at this stage give him authority to commit us in any way to the fallback language. That puts us too far ahead of Israel and gives away our position without any return. I think the Russians—not we—should be setting the bait. (Although I do not presume to speak for them, I gather that the fallback proposal is included largely under pressure from Charlie Yost and that Richardson and Sisco are not enthusiastic about it.)

Recommendation: That we *not* authorize State to commit us to the fallback language now but tell Sisco to put himself in a position to give us his estimate of what this would buy.

Approve

End the above sentence before "but"

Sisco may use the fallback

2. *Whether to send Joe Sisco to Moscow.* Secretary Rogers recommends a brief visit to deliver our counter-draft, to talk with Soviet officials other than Dobrynin and to brief Ambassador Beam. The Russians have asked us to resume the talks in Moscow. He would stop in London and Paris on the way.

Arguments for:

a. The principal argument, in my view, is to give us a chance to get behind Dobrynin and try to get some sense of how much give there is in the Soviet position.

b. A quick trip by Sisco would meet the Russians part way without, in my view, costing us very much.

c. This would provide a chance to brief our embassy in Moscow, which now has very little depth on the Mid-East.

Arguments against:

a. Even a quick trip would put the spotlight on Moscow and increase Soviet stature in the Near East. We have no reason to run to them. The Israelis are making this argument vigorously.

b. The Israelis will be even less happy with talks in Moscow than in Washington. They regard the USSR as their prime enemy, and they have no representation there.

c. The Soviets may not be satisfied by a quick trip.

Conclusion: The one argument that appeals to me is making a try at seeing what the Soviet position behind Dobrynin looks like. We may not learn much at all, but talking to three or four specialists might give us a more three-dimensional picture than we get from Dobrynin alone.

Recommendation: That you authorize Sisco to go to Moscow as proposed.

Approve

Disapprove

There are some lesser changes in our paper of which you might wish to be aware, though I do not believe they require your approval:

1. In the preamble and other places we have adopted some *Soviet wording* where it does not alter our substantive position.

2. We have agreed substantially to the Soviet concept of a *timetable* for withdrawal to go into effect under UN supervision after final agreement on overall terms. The difference between us and the Soviets on this point has been that they have tried to use the "timetable" idea to avoid direct negotiations. We have now accepted this part of their plan, but only in the context of negotiations.

3. While not closing off options for the future of *Gaza,* we have mentioned UN administration as a choice. Although this is to be decided by the parties, the Israelis are likely to object to anything specific we say about a solution.

4. We have included a reference to clearing the *Suez Canal,* as withdrawal proceeds. The Israelis could object in that this conceivably could open the canal before the other parts of the agreement became absolutely final. But we feel that once Israeli troops pull away from the Canal, the UAR will be free to do what it wants anyway.

5. We have slightly altered our position on *demilitarized zones.* Our original position was that all of Sinai would be a DMZ and all details would be worked out by the parties. We have now left an opening for Egyptian troops along the Canal itself—this would put them only a few miles closer to Israel—and have defined more clearly our concept of administration in the DMZ's—the return of Egyptian civil administration.

6. On the *refugees* we have changed our position from calling for an upper limit on the total number of repatriates to calling for an annual limit. In theory this leaves the way open for the eventual repatriation of all the refugees and so will be less pleasing to the Israelis and more pleasing to the Arabs, although it will satisfy neither. Our guess is that so few refugees will want to live in Israel that a limit is unnecessary.

The document holds the line on the points we feel are vital:

1. Our plan still calls for a settlement negotiated directly between the parties.

2. We are still talking about peace and binding commitments.

3. We are still calling for irrevocable guarantees of navigation satisfactory to the Israelis.

4. We are still calling for a commitment to end terrorism, whether government or private.

5. We still call for Arab recognition of Israeli sovereignty.

6. We are still trying to work out a UAR-Israel settlement first, although acknowledging that we will have to have a Jordan settlement before the UAR settlement becomes effective. The Soviet paper specifically kept the door open for an overall Arab-Israeli settlement which we shy away from because it includes the Syrians who are still talking about destroying Israel and have rejected all of the peace efforts of the past two years.

64.   National Security Study Memorandum 63[1]

Washington, July 3, 1969.

TO

> The Secretary of State
> The Secretary of Defense
> The Director of Central Intelligence

SUBJECT

> U.S. Policy on Current Sino-Soviet Differences

The President has directed a study of the policy choices confronting the United States as a result of the intensifying Sino-Soviet rivalry and the current Soviet efforts to isolate Communist China.

The study should consider the broad implications of the Sino-Soviet rivalry on the U.S., Soviet, Communist Chinese triangle and focus specifically on alternate U.S. policy options in the event of military clashes between the Soviet Union and Communist China.[2]

The study should also examine alternative policy approaches in the event of continued intensification of the Sino-Soviet conflict short of a military clash.

The President has directed that the paper be prepared by an ad hoc group chaired by a representative of the Secretary of State and including representatives of the addressees of this memorandum and the Assistant to the President for National Security Affairs.

The study should be submitted to the NSC Review Group by August 15.[3]

Henry A. Kissinger

---

[1] Source: National Archives, Nixon Presidential Materials, NSC Files, NSC Institutional Files (H-Files), Box H–155, NSSM Files, NSSM 63. Secret. A copy was sent to the Chairman of the Joint Chiefs of Staff.

[2] Since the outbreak of Sino-Soviet military clashes along the Ussuri River, the CIA and DIA provided periodic intelligence updates of continued hostilities. (Central Intelligence Agency, Executive Registry Subject Files, Job 93–T01468R, Box 2–4)

[3] A draft study was submitted on September 3 and discussed at a meeting of the WSAG on September 4. The final version was completed on November 10; see Document 101.

65.   Memorandum From the President's Assistant for National Security Affairs (Kissinger) to President Nixon[1]

Washington, July 10, 1969.

SUBJECT

Gromyko's Foreign Policy Speech

Soviet Foreign Minister Gromyko spoke at length to the semi-annual session of the Supreme Soviet in Moscow today. We have a TASS summary but no verbatim text yet.[2]

From the summary, it appears that Gromyko's language was temperate and on the whole positive as regards relations with the US. In terms of content, however, I can detect no advance on such matters as the Middle East, Vietnam, Europe and arms control.

Gromyko mentions Romania several times in the context of its membership in the Warsaw Pact and the socialist camp, along with the other bloc countries. In effect, he reaffirms the "Brezhnev doctrine" albeit in less provocative words than the original formulation last year.

The pre-occupation with China is very prominent; his words are a mixture of threats to "rebuff" provocations and expressions of interest in better relations in the long term.

On SALT, he carefully describes the forthcoming talks as an exchange of views rather than negotiations; he does not refer to an opening date. (There are indications that we may get a response fairly soon and that it will be in terms of early or mid-August.) He also notes what you have said about a well-prepared summit but leaves it at that.

All told, in my judgment, this speech leaves Soviet policy where it has been; but the temperate tone on relations with us and, especially, on arms talks will probably be cited—as the Soviets undoubtedly intended it to be—by Administration opponents as justifying "restraint" on our part.

---

[1] Source: National Archives, Nixon Presidential Materials, NSC Files, Box 392, Subject Files, Soviet Affairs. Confidential. Sent for information. A notation on the memorandum indicates the President saw it. Another copy is ibid., Box 710, Country Files, Europe, USSR, Vol. III.

[2] A full text of Gromyko's speech is in *The Current Digest of the Soviet Press*, vol. 21, August 6, 1969, pp. 6–10.

Whatever the Soviets' real view of your Romanian visit,[3] Gromyko shows no direct reaction, beyond, of course, affirming the essence of the "Brezhnev doctrine."

Ron Ziegler and the State Department spokesman will say, if they are asked for comment, that we have seen the accounts of Gromyko's speech and that as far as US-Soviet relations are concerned you and the Secretary of State have previously stated our attitude.

Attached is the summary of the Gromyko speech (Tab A).[4]

---

[3] Nixon visited Romania August 2–3, the first trip of a U.S. President to a Communist East European nation. In *White House Years,* Kissinger describes the Soviet response to Nixon's decision, which was announced on June 28, as follows: "The Soviets also reacted—in a manner that made clear they understood the significance of the visit. The planned attendance of Brezhnev and Kosygin at the rescheduled Romanian party conference was canceled." (p. 157)

[4] Tab A, an extensive summary of the speech as taken from the TASS International Services in English, July 10, is attached but not printed.

---

66.   Memorandum From Director of Central Intelligence Helms to Secretary of State Rogers[1]

Washington, July 14, 1969.

SUBJECT

Gromyko's Review of Current Soviet Foreign Policy

1. The key to Gromyko's address of 10 July[2] lies in the classified instruction[3] cabled over his signature to Soviet embassies around the world four weeks earlier. That lengthy document announced that

---

[1] Source: Central Intelligence Agency, Executive Registry Files, Job 80–R015080R, Box 12, Soviet. Secret; No Foreign Dissem; No Dissem Abroad; Controlled Dissem; Background Use Only. Sent under a July 16 covering memorandum to Rogers in which Helms explained, "Herewith is a copy of a paper written at White House request for an analysis of Gromyko's address to the Supreme Soviet on 10 July. I think you will find it useful."

[2] See footnote 2, Document 65.

[3] Helms explained in his covering memorandum that "This 'instruction' was disseminated by CIA as CSDB–312/01562–69 of 24 June 1969. If you have not read this Soviet Circular Telegram, I would strongly suggest that you do so. Signed by Gromyko himself, it contains many interesting points on current Soviet foreign policy." On June 24, Haig sent the circular telegram to Kissinger under a cover memorandum that read:

Moscow intended to give new priority to the struggle against China, modifying other policies to achieve the isolation of Peking. This theme is of course not sounded in the speech to the Supreme Soviet, but its implications run through the entire review.

2. The secret document is explicit on the point that the USSR has no hopes of improving relations with the present Chinese leadership. Whereas Gromyko told the Supreme Soviet that Moscow stands ready to negotiate the questions disputed between the two states, the document states that "such proposals will most likely prove basically unacceptable to the present leadership of the CPR" but will be useful in their effects on the Chinese people and foreign Communists. The real task is to deny Peking friends and allies in the socialist camp, among the imperialists, and around the Chinese periphery in Asia.

3. In this regard, primary attention is given to the US. The secret document reflects the usual ambivalence about US policy: its imperialist interventions must be rebuffed, but sober elements may yet prevail in Washington. The new element is the fear that the US will find a way to use the Sino-Soviet rivalry against Moscow. While US public statements maintain an "apparently neutral line" on Sino-Soviet relations, after the Ussuri clashes "the idea of the usefulness of pressure on the USSR from two flanks—NATO and China—is ever more clearly discernible." The document draws the conclusions that, to head this off, it is necessary in current policy "to manifest restraint, moderation, and flexibility in relations with the US, to refrain from complications with her which are not dictated by our important national interests." This conclusion is worked out in a number of ways in Gromyko's subsequent formal address.

The General Line toward the US

4. In comparison to earlier set speeches of this sort, Gromyko balances professions of desire for good relations with the US with relatively little stress on the dark sides of American policy. His acknowledgment of "deep class differences" is more than offset by approving references to President Nixon's statement on an era of negotiations and

---

"I recommend that you read every page of the document . . . Quick reading confirms the extremely concerned state of mind of the Soviets with respect to the Chicom threat. It also confirms a strong suspicion on their part that we should, if we have not already started to, exploit the differences between the Soviet Union and Communist China. The report, together with others that we have picked up, simply confirms that a concerted effort on our part to at least threaten efforts at rapprochement with the Chicoms would be of the greatest concern to the Soviets. It is interesting to note that the Soviets have surmised that the best environment for their problem with the Chicoms is a détente situation." (National Archives, Nixon Presidential Materials, NSC Files, Box 710, Country Files, Europe, USSR, Vol. V) (Ellipsis in the original)

even to a "well-prepared summit meeting," the first such Soviet reference since the Inauguration. Criticism of the US role in the Middle East and Vietnam is mild; in the TASS summary,[4] designed to emphasize the points intended for foreign audiences, most of the negative remarks about Vietnam are eliminated. In both these cases, the Soviet version of linkage—that a change in US policy would contribute to the settlement of other questions—is briefly and moderately put.

Arms Control

5. The secret document is silent on this subject. To the Supreme Soviet, however, Gromyko endorses strategic arms limitations and says the USSR is preparing to negotiate this matter with the US. He rejects Chinese charges that this amounts to engaging in deception and gives several arguments which may be designed as much to win over waverers in the USSR as to affect debate in the US. One is that military superiority is unattainable because of the action-reaction phenomenon between the two military machines, and a second is the burden of spiraling costs. A third, which is much more novel in Soviet parlance, is that the requirements for quick reaction are placing the decision to go to war beyond human control and into the tubes and tapes of the computers.

6. The Foreign Minister's presentation on the NPT, a comprehensive test ban, and the seabeds treaty breaks no new ground. In the arms control discussion, however, he sweeps off the boards a number of long-standing Soviet proposals having to do with nuclear weapons, such as non-first use and liquidation of nuclear armaments. All such matters, he says, can be settled only with the participation of all nuclear powers—"and I mean all." Since he knows that the prospect of Chinese agreement is zero, this signifies the practical abandonment of such schemes.

Western Europe

7. The secret document makes two points about this region. First, the danger of Sino-West German collusion is second only to that of Sino-American cooperation against the USSR. Second, the socialist camp will have to content itself with temporary, partial solutions, to European problems, "actually putting on ice" more acute problems which cannot be agitated without upsetting NATO. These ideas are expressed, in the Supreme Soviet speech, in a rather forth-coming attitude toward West Germany and a vague proposal for four-power talks on West Berlin, unaccompanied by the usual list of pre-conditions. With respect to Bonn, the standard criticisms are condensed and put in rel-

---

[4] See footnote 4, Document 65.

atively calm tones, and the FRG is encouraged to continue its efforts to negotiate with Moscow on the renunciation of the use of force. The proposal on West Berlin seems to invite Bonn and the Western Allies to believe that, if the Federal Republic will refrain from political activities in the city, access will be undisturbed and perhaps even improved. The tone of these passages is consistent with the implication in the secret document that the USSR, for larger reasons of policy, intends no new Berlin crises for the indefinite future. Gromyko's speech is in fact being read in this manner in both Germanies; Bonn officials are anxious to investigate the negotiating possibilities, while Pankow betrays anxiety by largely ignoring these passages in its commentary on the speech. At any rate, it appears that East Germany's more far-reaching ambitions to undermine the present status of West Berlin have been decisively set aside.

Asia

8. In the light of his strictures before the Supreme Soviet about the Chinese threat, Gromyko's claim that the USSR's proposal for a collective security system in Asia is not directed against any particular country has a hollow ring. The anti-Chinese thrust of the secret document belies this assertion altogether, although it nowhere mentions the proposal. Gromyko adds no further details, even about the countries whose participation is envisaged; at one point he speaks of "all Asian states" and at another of "all interested states." It seems clear that Moscow has no expectation whatsoever of Chinese participation. It probably believes that, while the obstacles to formal action cannot be overcome, the USSR has much to gain, particularly in the post-Vietnam environment, simply from launching a concept which permits it to pose as the champion of collective security against unnamed threats. The scheme is probably also designed to preempt any US proposals for new collective organizations in the wake of a settlement in Vietnam.

Eastern Europe

9. The secret document expresses a surprising amount of concern about the role of China in the USSR's troubles in Eastern Europe. The public speech briefly refers to this and omits the conventional charges that the US and West Germany are fomenting counter-revolution in this area. The absence of even indirect attacks upon Romania reflects a Soviet decision to swallow the displeasure which Moscow finds in the US President's forthcoming visit to Bucharest. Gromyko repeats the essence of the "Brezhnev doctrine," but in a way which smacks more of defensive justification than any intent to apply it anew. He is somewhat more explicit than previous spokesmen in delimiting the sphere in which the doctrine is applicable, stating that the Warsaw Pact "will

never permit anyone to encroach on the security of its signatories and on the socialist gains in these countries." This formulation seemingly excludes Yugoslavia, a point which the USSR has never before clarified to Belgrade's satisfaction. A brief and amiable passage acknowledges the socialist character of Yugoslavia but, lest Belgrade's behavior be sanctioned as an example to other Eastern Europeans, notes that Soviet relations with that country "are not always smooth."

The Middle East

10. Gromyko's mention of the Middle East offers nothing new, and stresses again Moscow's position that Israeli occupation of Arab territory is the obstacle to a political settlement. Nevertheless, Gromyko does not indicate any extreme concern about the Arab-Israeli situation and—unlike last year—he does not threaten Israel with the consequences of failure to fulfill the Security Council resolution of November, 1967. Moreover, Gromyko notes that Israeli withdrawal must be accompanied by Arab recognition of Israel's right to exist, thus publicly recording a recent change in the Soviet position. Less authoritative spokesmen often continue to support withdrawal as a unilateral first step toward a settlement.

Conclusion

11. It would be easy to overstress the degree to which the struggle with China is affecting various aspects of Soviet policy. While this impact is evident in current Soviet documents and behavior, there is no sign of a consequent willingness to give up important Soviet interests. Indeed, many aspects of the USSR's rivalry with the US are embedded in third areas—Vietnam, the Middle East, Central Europe—where the USSR is not free to call the shots and cannot propose major compromises without risking the loss of influence. Within these limits, however, it seems clear that the China problem has now reached a degree of intensity which is moving Soviet policy onto an altered course. This course is intended to avoid unnecessary conflict with others and to make sure that states which cannot be corralled into an anti-Chinese front at least do not work parallel to or in collusion with Peking against the Soviet Union.

67.   Telegram From the Embassy in the Soviet Union to the Department of State[1]

Moscow, July 14, 1969, 2205Z.

3463. For President and Secretary from Sisco.

1. Capping a two and one half hour July 14 meeting in which assessments of present developments in the Middle East and current positions on specific elements of settlement were reviewed systematically, Gromyko asked that a message be sent to President Nixon that "Soviet intentions to make progress are very serious. We hope that we are not mistaken in believing our intentions are the same as the USG and of President Nixon personally. We trust that you will convey not only the words of our position but the sense of our policy. The Soviet government seeks common language" with the U.S. This was preceded by a general statement that if we could make progress or resolve the Middle Eastern question it would have a positive effect on other issues (unnamed) and on U.S.–USSR relations. This was the only time in the conversation that Gromyko went in any way beyond the Middle East.

2. I have been in a number of meetings with Gromyko over the last decade. There are two Gromykos: the dour and the affable. Today we saw the affable Gromyko in action. He was warm, he was relaxed, he smiled, he joked, and at no time made even a faintly threatening sound. At same time he was serious and chose his words carefully. He inquired several times regarding our specific reaction to the Soviet proposal of June 17,[2] and whether I had brought with me a counterproposal. He underscored that USSR is ready to try "to narrow the gap" in further discussions between now and mid-September when GA opens.

3. Meeting was held across the table, with four representatives present on each side. (U.S.—Sisco, Amb. Beam, Atherton, Smith; USSR—Gromyko, Vinogradov, Yakushin, Korniyenko.) Gromyko listened for most part but in opening statement, frequent responses to my presentation and concluding statement noted above, he struck three themes: (A) USSR serious about wanting settlement, and U.S. and Soviets together have opportunity bring peace to Middle East; (B) Generalities are fine as far as they go, but we need get down to specifics,

---

[1] Source: National Archives, Nixon Presidential Materials, NSC Files, Box 710, Country Files, Europe, USSR, Vol. III. Secret; Immediate; Nodis. On July 15, Saunders sent Kissinger this telegram under a covering memorandum that briefly summarized the meeting between Sisco and Gromyko. (Ibid.)

[2] See Document 58.

leaving as little unfinished business as possible for parties to deal with; and (C) USG hides too much behind Israeli "stubborness."

4. Gromyko made point of appearing flexible, several times correcting interpreter to soften formulation of a particular point. In addition, during discussion of Suez Canal and refugee aspect of settlement, while maintaining basic Soviet position, he hinted that differences could be resolved. On two fundamental issues which I stressed, however, namely need for Arab commitment to direct negotiations at some stage and to specific Arab obligations flowing from establishment of state of peace, he revealed no discernible give, but seemed more than anything else to be seeking to avoid coming to grips with issues themselves.

5. On specific points, following emerged from Gromyko:

A. He gave no explicit clue as to how serious they view violence in Middle East and risks involved; this might have been deliberate or inadvertent;

B. He adhered to Soviet notion which tends to equate end of belligerency with peace;

C. He would not be drawn out on mood and views he found in Cairo during recent trip;

D. He did not make any pitch for total withdrawal of Israeli forces from all territories;

E. Re arms limitations, he said in a seemingly apologetic tone that "unfortunately" a U.S.–USSR exchange of views on the subject is "excluded" as long as Israeli forces occupy Arab territory.

F. He defended reference in Soviet proposal to Constantinople Convention of 1888 by saying that under convention UAR would have no basis for stopping Israeli ships in absence of state of belligerency, and there would be specific agreement in package settlement ending belligerency; he also insisted there would be no threat of Israeli ships being denied passage;

G. He dodged, without closing any doors, our view on refugees that a nation of two and one half million cannot be expected to take back over million refugees. He volunteered comment that the UN resolution did not require every refugee to go to Israel and added the whole matter, including modalities, required further discussion between us.

H. On direct negotiations, he is obviously looking for a way to finesse it. He made no real defense of Arab position on this point and said somewhat lamely there are a number of different ways for the parties to negotiate.

6. I made comprehensive presentation of U.S. approach to a settlement, taking as basic theme President's statement of February 17 to

Dobrynin[3] that it would be the height of folly to let parties directly involved in the ME conflict bring about a confrontation between Moscow and Washington. Noting Gromyko's call in his July 10 speech to Supreme Soviet for USG to be more realistic,[4] I described realities of situation as we see them along following lines. I said USG neither could nor would seek Israeli relinquishment of occupied territories to conditions of insecurity. If Israel appeared stubborn, it was result of suspicion based on historical memories and experience; Arabs for 20 years had said they wanted to destroy Israel.

7. Alternatives today were limited to three: (A) status quo, which we did not like but could live with if we had to, could continue;[5] or (C) there would be negotiated settlement. We strongly favor the latter. While USG agreed that acquisition of territory by war was an anachronism and unrealistic in today's world, it was also unrealistic for UAR not to face up to need for coexistence with Israel. Israel is in occupation with Arab territory as result of military success involving what to Israelis was major national sacrifice. Israel would not give away, or permit others to give away, its victory for nothing. We disagreed with those in Israel who sought territory as price of victory; our aim was to convince Israel to settle for peace and security. If Israel was to be convinced, however, peace and security must be firm, specific, and credible.

8. Finally, I drove home that if USSR could not produce UAR on specific obligations to peace and to direct negotiations at some stage under Jarring's auspices, we could not hope to produce Tel Aviv on withdrawal. I made clear that we recognize our responsibility vis-à-vis Israel on withdrawal but said our capacity in this respect would be decisively influenced by Soviet ability to get UAR undertakings on peace and negotiations.

9. Tomorrow we meet with Deputy Foreign Minister Vinogradov. We intend: (A) to make a detailed and specific review of Soviet proposal, pointing out the advances and deficiencies; (B) present our written counterproposal with a full explanation of it; and (C) stress points

---

[3] See Document 14.

[4] Gromyko made the following statements about the Middle East in his July 10 speech to the Sixth Session of the Supreme Soviet: "The situation in the Middle East greatly affects the world situation as a whole. It would be a short-sighted policy to repose hopes, as they do in Israel, in military superiority. The surest way would be to solve the problem on the basis of withdrawal of Israeli troops from occupied areas and simultaneous recognition of the right of all Middle Eastern states, including Israel, to independent national existence, and the establishment of a lasting peace in this important area. The Soviet Union considers that all opportunities should be used for adjusting the situation in the Middle East. Any delay is dangerous and does harm to all." (*The Current Digest of the Soviet Press*, vol. 21, August 6, 1969, pp. 5–6)

[5] A handwritten "B?" appears in the margin.

which we consider fundamental. I see no reason at this point to consider fall-back language on withdrawal in absence specific movement by Soviets on peace and negotiations. Our counterproposal remains within confines of our proposal of last May. I will hint and only hint at some possible more specific formulation on withdrawal if Soviets can provide us with quid pro quo we are asking for on peace and negotiations.

10. Gromyko said he would be available for another meeting if we thought it desirable after detailed talks with Vinogradov. We have left this open for time being; a short windup session with him on Wednesday might be worthwhile. Soviets will need a good deal of time to analyze our counterproposal, and they will want to discuss it with the UAR at some stage. This could take two or three weeks; or they might wait to discuss our counterproposal with Nasser when he is in Moscow in August.

11. On basis present tentative plans, I will leave here Thursday,[6] fly to Stockholm to brief Jarring on Moscow talks, and be home Friday evening.

Beam

---

[6] July 17.

---

68.   Special National Intelligence Estimate[1]

SNIE 11–9–69   Washington, July 17, 1969.

CURRENT SOVIET ATTITUDES TOWARD THE US

This paper responds to certain specific questions concerning US-Soviet relations posed by DIA on behalf of the Commander in Chief,

---

[1] Source: Central Intelligence Agency, NIC Files, Job 79–R1012A, NIEs and SNIEs. Secret; No Foreign Dissem; Controlled Dissem. The Central Intelligence Agency and the intelligence organizations of the Departments of State and Defense and the National Security Agency participated in the preparation of this estimate, which was submitted by the Director of Central Intelligence and concurred by all members of the USIB, except the Assistant General Manager of the Atomic Energy Commission and the Assistant Director of the Federal Bureau of Investigation, who abstained because the subject was outside their jurisdiction.

Pacific. A more comprehensive survey of the principal factors which underlie the USSR's foreign policies and its international aims and intentions was issued earlier this year (NIE 11–69, "Basic Factors and Main Tendencies in Current Soviet Policy," dated 27 February 1969,[2] Secret, Controlled Dissem).

That estimate concluded that, short of major changes in the Soviet system at home, the outlook is for chronic tensions in Soviet-American relations. It also concluded that Soviet policy toward the US would probably be characterized by cautious opportunism and limited pressures, perhaps with some increased watchfulness against the development of uncontrolled risks. We retain our belief in the validity of both of these basic judgments. At the same time, we note the development of increased Soviet alarm over the future course of relations with Communist China. This alarm is likely at least for a time to have an important impact on Soviet foreign policy overall; specifically, it tends to encourage a somewhat more forthcoming Soviet attitude toward relations with the US and toward particular issues affecting the relationship.

I. The USSR's Basic Stance Toward The US

1. Soviet hostility toward the US and the West in general was born with the Bolshevik Revolution in 1917. It was nourished by US participation in the Allied military interventions which followed, and sustained through the 1920's and 1930's by the continuing struggle against "class enemies" at home and abroad. It diminished during World War II, but then reached a high point of sorts in the early 1950's, during the last few years of Stalin.

2. With Stalin's death, official attitudes were tempered somewhat. Under Khrushchev, the notion of capitalist encirclement was discarded. Limited contacts with the outside world, including the US, were permitted, and the line toward the West began to fluctuate in intensity and assume a notably ambivalent tone. The US was still evil, but "sober" elements in it were capable, in effect, of good; the US remained the hostile leader of the imperialists, but it was not necessarily seeking war; the USSR was still duty bound to defeat or convert the US, but world peace could somehow be assured if only the two countries could get together. And policies toward the US began to reflect the same kind of confusing mixture, ranging in mood and content from the urgent and provocative to the relaxed and conciliatory.

3. Khrushchev's more conservative successors have sought greater consistency and have tightened and toughened the approach. They emphasize that, as a dangerous and devious adversary, the US is

---

[2] Document 21.

to be both distrusted and despised. Nevertheless, they continue to maintain that it is desirable for the two powers to keep lines open to one another and, like Khrushchev, they still hold out the hope that mutual hostility and suspicion might some day decline.

4. The current attitudes of the Soviet leaders are, of course, conditioned by a general set of ideas, many of them ideologically predetermined. Marxist-Leninist dogma affects the way in which these men analyze the problems that confront them and, in general, influences their manner of regarding themselves, their society, and the world at large. It reinforces their feelings of distrust and hostility toward the US and severely limits their ability to approach mutual problems in a flexible mood. Moreover, the Soviet leaders now believe themselves for a variety of reasons to be on the ideological defensive; this has generated a mood of "fearful conservatism" which is likely to affect the tone of Soviet-American relations adversely for some time to come.

5. But despite the undeniable effects of doctrine, nonideological considerations are playing an increasingly important role in the formulation of Soviet foreign policies. The USSR tends to behave more as a world power than as the center of the world revolution. Thus the Soviets are inclined to establish international priorities in accordance with a more traditional view of Russian security interests and a more realistic view of the possibilities for expanding their influence. The USSR remains a thrusting and ambitious power, concerned to enlarge its world position. But it tempers its ambitions with estimates of opportunity and controls its hostility with measurements of power and risk. These opportunity/risk calculations are illustrated by the USSR's conduct in three areas which have figured prominently in Soviet-American contention in recent years: Korea, Vietnam, and the Middle East.

6. *Korea.* Moscow has for some time sought to win North Korea to a pro-Soviet stance in the Sino-Soviet dispute. This has involved fairly frequent visits to Pyongyang by top Soviet leaders and a substantial Soviet military aid program.[3] It has not, however, caught the Soviets up in any direct support of adventurous North Korean tactics against the ROK and against the US. On the contrary, we believe that the Soviets have counseled Pyongyang to proceed with caution. Provocative North Korean behavior not only raises the risk of war on the USSR's doorstep, but complicates Soviet policies toward the US, Japan, and China. In any event, Pyongyang's relations with the USSR remain somewhat strained, and Pyongyang's aspirations vis-à-vis the South are not of prime importance to the USSR.

---

[3] Soviet military aid to North Korea since 1956 has amounted to an estimated $770–$800 million. (The figures here and in footnotes to paragraphs 8 and 9 represent actual or estimated Soviet list prices.) [Footnote in the source text.]

7. There have been reports of Soviet collusion with Pyongyang in the seizure of the *Pueblo* and the shootdown of the American EC–121. We do not find these reports convincing.[4] Such behavior would be contrary to general Soviet interests, as described above. It would also seem, in view of the large scale Soviet intelligence collection effort in international waters and air space, contrary to particular Soviet interests as well. We have, in any case, reviewed the evidence specifically concerning the USSR's attitudes and policies toward these incidents and have concluded not only that Moscow was not involved in planning them but that it witnessed both affairs with some considerable discomfiture and apprehension. The text of an official classified Soviet Party report on Brezhnev's speech to the April 1968 plenum of the Central Committee, for example, does not indicate that Moscow had prior knowledge of North Korean intentions to seize the Pueblo. It clearly shows that the Soviet leaders were concerned about the possibility of a forcible US reaction and had advised the leadership in Pyongyang "to exercise restraint, not to give the Americans grounds for expanding the provocation, and to settle the incident by political means."

8. *Vietnam.* The role played by the USSR in the Vietnam war since 1965 is a more striking and more important example of Soviet opportunity/risk calculations. The opportunity was, by extensive material support to Hanoi, to help bring about a serious reverse for the US and at the same time to contest Chinese influence in Vietnam and elsewhere in Southeast Asia.[5] The risk was not only of a possible armed encounter with the US in the area but also of a radical deterioration of relations with the US generally, a development which might bring unacceptable costs and risks at other points of confrontation. Throughout the Vietnam war the Soviets have walked a careful line. They have given material and political support to Hanoi in ways which they believed would minimize the likelihood of dangerous US responses. While until the

---

[4] We have examined the statement on this subject of the Czechoslovak defector, General Jan Sejna, and find it wanting. Sejna was for a time a valuable source of information on the Czechoslovak armed forces and the Warsaw Pact, but his remarks about the Pueblo seizure—especially those which have appeared recently in the public press—are in our view highly suspect. His account, for example, of a purported meeting in Prague in May 1967 with Soviet Defense Minister Grechko—during which Grechko is said to have discussed Soviet plans for the seizure of an American intelligence collection vessel—is almost certainly inaccurate. During extended questioning, he had given no hint that any such crucial meeting with Grechko had taken place. In any case, the best available evidence is that Grechko did not visit Prague at all during April, May, or June 1967. [Footnote in the source text.]

[5] Soviet military assistance to North Vietnam began on a large scale in 1965 and since then has totaled an estimated $1.4 billion. It reached a peak level in 1967—about $500 million—but declined in 1968 (after the suspension of US bombing) to about $290 million. [Footnote in the source text.]

opening of the Paris talks they adopted a sharply hostile tone toward the US, they also refrained from provoking any crises elsewhere and were willing to pursue negotiations with the US on such issues as NPT. Since the Paris talks began, they have adopted a tone which evidences their hope of persuading the US that concessions to Hanoi would have a beneficial effect on the negotiations of other Soviet-American issues.

9. *The Middle East.* For the last dozen years or so the Soviets have regarded the Middle East as an area of confrontation with the Western Powers, in particular the US, but they also probably saw it as an area offering much more of opportunity than of risk. Their ties with and material support to the radical Arab states were aimed at using these states as instruments to undermine Western influence in the area.[6] The likelihood of any direct encounter with the US seemed slight. With the Arab-Israeli war of June 1967 and the humiliating defeat of their clients, the Soviets appear to have acquired a sharpened sense of the risks of their policy. Even now, however, they probably are less concerned about the likelihood of direct confrontation with the US than they are that their considerable investment and influence will be jeopardized either by new Arab-Israeli hostilities or by untoward political developments within the Arab states, especially Egypt. Their moves to work with the US diplomatically are an attempt to contain these risks, though they clearly do not intend to abandon the competition for influence in the area.

II. Recent Developments Affecting the Relationship

10. The USSR's calculations of opportunity and risk, its general concerns about its position as a world power, and even its apprehensions about the security of the Soviet homeland, have been greatly complicated by the leadership's growing preoccupation with the problem of China. Indeed, there is good reason to believe that the Soviet leaders now see China as their most pressing international problem and are beginning to tailor their policies on other issues accordingly. They have begun publicly to suggest the need for some form of collective security arrangement in Asia, largely, apparently, in order to contain China. And they have, in addition, taken the position that, because of

---

[6] Since 1955, the USSR has poured, or has promised to pour, into the area some $2.5 billion in economic assistance and roughly $2.9 billion in military aid. Of these amounts, the three principal radical Arab states—the UAR, Syria, and Iraq—have received or been promised over half (some $1.4 billion) of the economic aid and over 80 percent ($2.4 billion) of the military aid. Most of the balance has gone to Iran, Turkey, Yemen, the Sudan, and Algeria. All figures are as of 1 July 1969. [Footnote in the source text.]

the China problem, the USSR should generally seek to avoid provoking unnecessary difficulties with the US.

11. The Soviets do not, of course, contemplate any sacrifice of essential positions or any renunciation of traditional doctrines; they continue to view the US as basically their strongest adversary; indeed, they fear that the US might someday come to work against Soviet interests in collusion with China. But they clearly now believe that hostility toward the US and the West should be muted, at least as long as relations with the Chinese remain so tense.

12. The Soviet attitude toward the new administration in the US remains generally circumspect. Provocative acts and statements have for the most part been avoided. There have been standard denunciations of US policies and continuing attacks on "warmongers" in the US establishment, but the President has been praised as well as criticized (though not harshly by name), and it has been said that there are reasonable men in the US who seek peace. Propaganda has on the whole suggested a wait-and-see attitude, perhaps even a mildly optimistic assessment of prospects for an improvement in the relationship.

13. Indeed, despite their many reasons for sober concern about their position vis-à-vis the US, the Soviets seem now to regard this relationship in a cautiously optimistic light. Their relative military strength, especially in strategic weapons, has greatly improved over the past six or seven years. Their influence in certain important countries of the Third World has grown, and fear of Soviet aggressiveness has been declining, even—despite the invasion of Czechoslovakia—in Western Europe. During the same period, the Soviets have seen domestic stability in the US tested by disorders and severe political discord, and have observed increasing signs of public disenchantment with the scope of the US role in international affairs.

14. The USSR has also showed a relatively restrained approach to Western Europe. We do not think that the current campaign for European security signals Moscow's intention to abandon previous positions. On the contrary, the Soviets are at least as anxious as ever to gain recognition of the status quo, i.e., the division of Germany and the existence of a legitimate Soviet sphere in Eastern Europe. But they do not now seem disposed to stress the more controversial aspects of their position, nor do they appear ready to dramatize their views through provocative acts, as for example, in Berlin. At the same time, they no longer emphasize the notion that the US should stand clear of an all-European settlement.

15. The strongest and most emotional language used by the Soviets is now directed against China, not the US and the other Western powers. This shift in the intensity of feeling about foreign adversaries seems to have been reflected in the USSR's apparently increasing willingness

to discuss specific issues with the US. Thus, though the Soviet view of the US–USSR strategic relationship is overriding. Moscow's current pre-occupation with China has probably had some bearing on its attitude toward the desirability of talks on strategic arms control. Indeed, problems with China may have encouraged the Soviets to look upon arms control measures with growing interest, seeing in them a means to reduce tensions with the US and to bring additional pressures to bear on Peking.

16. In the field of strategic armaments, the Soviets now must ponder the effects of an arms control agreement in view of their improved position. None of the courses open to them can be wholly appealing. An effort to surpass, or even to keep pace with the US in the development and deployment of advanced weapons systems would require continued high expenditures, perpetuate the resource squeeze on the civilian economy, and perhaps divert funds from other military programs. And in the process, Moscow could have no assurance that it would be able to compete successfully with US technological prowess. On the other hand, a Soviet decision *not* to try to keep pace with the US seems highly unlikely; such a course would surrender many of the fruits of past investment and allow the political perils of strategic inferiority—as the Soviets conceive of them—to re-emerge. Yet a decision to seek serious arms control measures would not be easily reached. The Soviet leaders are ambitious, opportunistic, and suspicious men. They are unlikely to conclude that a strategic arms agreement is acceptable unless they are convinced that achieving and maintaining a superior position is not feasible in the future, and that the national interest could be served by a sort of strategic stabilization. On neither count does it seem likely that all the leaders would reach full agreement.

17. Nevertheless, it is still our belief that the Soviets have strong reasons—perhaps stronger than ever before—to consider carefully the whole problem of strategic arms control. In the interim since our last estimates concerning this subject, we have seen nothing which would alter this judgment.[7] On the contrary, the USSR's approach to the problem so far this year tends to confirm it. The Soviets have not concealed their suspicions of US motives. Nor have they hidden their discontent with certain US attitudes and statements, in particular US suggestions that there should be a linkage between arms control and other, broader issues. But they have also sought to appear patient about the timing of arms control talks and have tried to convince the US that they have retained a sober—though not eager—interest in the negotiation of an agreement.

---

[7] See NIE 11–68–68, "The Soviet Approach to Arms Control," dated 7 November 1968, Secret, Controlled Dissem, and NIE 11–69, "Basic Factors and Main Tendencies in Current Soviet Policy," dated 27 February 1969, Secret, Controlled Dissem. [Footnote in the source text.]

69.   **Memorandum From Harold Saunders of the National Security Council Staff to the President's Assistant for National Security Affairs (Kissinger)**[1]

Washington, July 18, 1969.

SUBJECT

Complete Wrapup on Sisco in Moscow

In a nutshell, I would characterize Joe's talks in Moscow as they appear from his reports as friendly and businesslike with a good deal more substantive discussion than was possible with Dobrynin here. Since the Soviets are holding their response to our latest formulation[2] until they have studied it further, we cannot claim to have made any important substantive headway. However, it looks to me like a useful exercise.

The principal tactical issue to come out of it is Gromyko's effort at the end to have the discussions continue in Moscow. Joe finessed that and said we will be glad to receive the Soviet response to our latest formulation anywhere and then we can arrange how to discuss it.

Attached is a full collection of his reports:

Tab A: His introductory meeting with Gromyko
Tab B: His first substantive meeting—July 15
Tab C: His second substantive meeting—July 15
Tab D: His reflections at the end of the first day
Tab E: His third substantive meeting—July 16
Tab F: His farewell call on Gromyko—July 17
Tab G: His talk with Jarring in Stockholm[3]

A résumé of the main points covered at these meetings follows:

Gromyko–Sisco—July 14 (Tab A)

Gromyko, in an affable mood, stressed the Soviet desire for peace and sent an oral message to that effect to the President. Gromyko also

---

[1] Source: National Archives, Nixon Presidential Materials, NSC Files, Box 653, Country Files, Middle East, Sisco Middle East Talks, April–June 1969. Secret; Nodis. Printed from an uninitialed copy.

[2] The text of the U.S. counterproposal to the Soviet June 17 Middle East position, delivered by Sisco to Gromyko on July 15, is in telegram 3485 from Moscow, July 15. Saunders attached a copy of it, but not as part of Tabs A–G summarized below. It is scheduled for publication in *Foreign Relations, 1969–1976*, volume XXIII, Arab-Israeli Dispute, 1969–1972.

[3] Tab A is telegram 3463 from Moscow, July 14; Tab B is telegram 3501 from Moscow, July 15; Tab C is telegram 3503 from Moscow, July 16; Tab D is telegram 3500 from Moscow, July 15; Tab E are telegrams 3546 and 3547 from Moscow, July 16; Tab F is telegram 3566 from Moscow, July 17; Tab G is telegram 2045 from Stockholm, July 18; all attached but not printed.

said it was time to get down to specifics, and that we hide too much behind Israeli stubbornness. In the course of the meeting, Gromyko hinted that differences on refugees and the Suez Canal could be resolved, but showed no give on direct negotiations and Arab obligations flowing from a state of peace. Sisco feels the Soviets are looking for a way to finesse the direct negotiations problem. Sisco sees no need to reconsider using the fall back language on withdrawal at this point.

First and Second Substantive Meetings—July 15 (Tabs B and C)

Sisco presented our revised paper with a detailed explanation in two meetings on Tuesday with Deputy Foreign Minister Vinogradov. Vinogradov confined himself mainly to questions designed to clarify our position, but which revealed little new about Soviet views.

Vinogradov did, however, say that the proposals show a considerable amount of work has been done by the US. He asked when we would be ready to show them a paper on Jordan and suggested that we might want to take the public position that the US and USSR are now working on a joint paper rather than trading counter proposals. Sisco was non-committal on both suggestions.

At the End of the First Day—Sisco's Reflections (Tab D)

1. The Soviets seem to feel the Arabs are on weak ground in trying to avoid direct negotiations, but the Soviets themselves did not give on the issue.

2. The Soviets might welcome neutral language on some key points that we turn over to Jarring because they are having problems with the Egyptians just as we are having problems with the Israelis.

3. They seem intrigued by our annual quota formulation on refugee repatriation.

4. The decision not to move the talks permanently to Moscow was very right. The Soviets are interested in giving themselves the image of peacemaker in the Middle East.

Third Substantive Meeting—July 16 (Tab E)

After lunch on Wednesday, Vinogradov made a more detailed reply to our paper and to some of our comments on their paper.

1. In listing principles and setting up procedures, the USSR has already made it clear that it is talking about peace. [Comment: Our trouble is that this is largely a negative definition, and the Israelis want a positive definition.][4]

---

[4] All brackets in the source text.

2. US procedures for achieving peace seem inadequate. [Comment: This is because we want to leave much more to the parties than the Soviets do.]

3. The Soviets want a multilateral document, not the UAR-Israel document we keep giving them, i.e., one including Jordan as well. (Even they are content to leave Syria aside.) Sisco explained again that all we are doing is attacking the UAR-Israel problem first.

4. The long section on peace-keeping was included in the Soviet document only because they feel this problem is bound to arise. They are not particularly concerned about when it is addressed.

5. They are disappointed that we won't apply the inadmissability of conquest to Gaza by agreeing that it should return to its pre-War status. Sisco explained that Gaza has never had a final status, that we have to recognize the Israelis are occupying it now, and that we want Jordan to have a voice in the final decision.

6. The Soviets don't understand why we insist on navigation guarantees from the Egyptians when a Security Council guarantee would be both easier to get and worth more to the Israelis. Sisco said we had no problems with a Security Council guarantee, but we felt an Egyptian guarantee was also necessary.

Sisco again proposed that we take the effort to find US-Soviet agreement as far as we can, and where we can't agree, use neutral language which leaves a solution to Jarring and the parties.

Vinogradov closed the meeting by saying he is pleased that we are now working on a common document instead of exchanging counter proposals. Sisco said he could not make this characterization yet.

Second Gromyko–Sisco—July 17 (Tab F)

Only three interesting new points emerged in Sisco's final meeting with Gromyko on Thursday.

1. Gromyko felt our paper shows greater flexibility.
2. The Soviets may not give us another counter-proposal, but may decide instead to go over the two latest papers with us orally.
3. Gromyko suggested continuing the talks in Moscow.

Sisco–Jarring (Tab G)

This was mainly a briefing session. Sisco feels Jarring shares his view that the Soviets are not going to push Cairo hard in the immediate future and that they will try to chip away at our position between now and the opening of the UN General Assembly.

You need not read all the attached cables. I suggest you do look at the two Gromyko conversations (Tabs A and F) and Sisco's reflections (Tab D). If you want the flavor of some of the Sisco–Vinogradov talk, I suggest Tab E, which is more Vinogradov than Sisco.

70.   Memorandum From Secretary of State Rogers to President Nixon[1]

Washington, July 21, 1969.

SUBJECT

Tripartite Initiative with the USSR on Berlin and Related Problems and Gromyko's Remarks Concerning the City

Recommendations:

I recommend that you approve instructions to our Embassy in Bonn to seek quadripartite agreement on revised talking points to be made to the Soviet Government by the three Western Ambassadors. The points in summary would be:

(a) We have noted Gromyko's remarks concerning Berlin[2] and we intend to study them together with the British, French and Germans.

(b) Meanwhile, the Federal Republic of Germany would like to remove points of friction with the GDR and discuss with it problems concerning railroad matters, inland waterways and post and telecommunications. We believe that such talks would be useful.

(c) The Federal Government might be willing to make certain compromises concerning its activities in West Berlin if this would promote a constructive Soviet and East German response.

I recommend that we instruct our Embassy in Bonn to initiate quadripartite consultations in the Bonn Group and submit agreed recommendations to governments on the response to be made to that portion of Gromyko's speech which deals with Berlin.

Discussion:

At the NATO meeting last April[3] the German Foreign Minister proposed that the Three Western Powers approach the Soviet Government and, after reaffirming Four Power responsibility for Berlin access, state that the Federal Republic was prepared to talk with the East German

---

[1] Source: National Archives, Nixon Presidential Materials, NSC Files, Box 689, Country Files, Europe, Germany, Berlin, Vol. I. Secret. A copy is also ibid., Box 341, Subject Files, Kissinger/Nixon Memoranda. There is no indication of approval or disapproval of the recommendations, but on July 22, Sonnenfeldt sent Kissinger a memorandum that recommended his approval of Rogers' proposed démarche to the Soviets. On August 5, Kissinger initialed approval for Nixon. (Ibid.) Two days later, Ambassador Beam met Soviet Deputy Foreign Minister Kozyrev in Moscow to deliver the text of Beam's oral statement; printed in *Foreign Relations,* 1969–1976, volume XL, Germany and Berlin, 1969–1972.

[2] See footnote 2, Document 65.

[3] The North Atlantic Council met in Ministerial Session in Washington April 10–11.

Government on the traffic of persons, goods, and communications between East and West Germany "including Berlin." In subsequent consultations the Three Powers and the Federal Republic agreed on the
text of talking points to be made to the Soviets. Direct reference to access to Berlin was eliminated at French insistence.

The initiative with the Soviets has not yet been taken. The French
and apparently now the British concur in it. We might be inclined to
delay an action which the Soviets could mistakenly think was connected with other current US-Soviet conversations. The German Government has, however, urged that we agree to move ahead.

Meanwhile, in his speech of July 10, Gromyko stated that if the
Three Powers are interested, the Soviet Union is willing "to exchange
views as to how complications concerning West Berlin can be prevented
now and in the future." The German Government considers that the
proposed tripartite initiative is more urgent than ever in the light of
Gromyko's remarks. If we temporize the Germans will suspect that we
are unwilling to act in their interest lest it jeopardize US-Soviet bilateral relations. We wish to prevent this and to do so before Chancellor
Kiesinger visits you on August 7 and 8.[4]

Insofar as Gromyko's remarks on Berlin are concerned, I believe
that we should study them unilaterally and in consultation with the
British, French and Germans before we decide on a response. I do not
rule out the possibility of agreeing to quadripartite talks concerning
Berlin, but I believe that we should first be sure of the objectives which
we would seek.

A telegram incorporating these proposed instructions is enclosed.[5]

WPR

---

[4] Kurt Kiesinger, Chancellor of the Federal Republic of Germany, made an official
visit to Washington August 7–9.

[5] Attached but not printed.

71.   Memorandum From the President's Assistant for National Security Affairs (Kissinger) to President Nixon[1]

Washington, July 23, 1969.

SUBJECT

The International Communist Conference

The conference which convened in Moscow on June 5 was not at all what Khrushchev had in mind when he began pressing for it in 1963–64. He clearly wanted to ostracize the Chinese and restore Soviet authority in a disintegrating international organization. While most parties at that time shared his ideological aversion to Peking's policies there was a growing apprehension over the self-proclaimed Soviet right to "excommunicate" any one. This remained the underlying issue in the intervening years.

The project lay dormant, after Khrushchev's removal, until late 1966; some of the Soviet difficulties, however, were eased by the Vietnam war and the ostensible Soviet willingness to cooperate with China in Hanoi's defense,[2] and secondly, by the excesses of the Cultural Revolution in China which dismayed most of China's communist allies, such as the Japanese party.

Brezhnev began to press for a new conference to reassess the world situation, disavowing any intention of driving the Chinese out of the international communist ranks. It took a full year, until February 1968, however, to organize even a "consultative meeting," which convened in Budapest.

The Cubans refused to attend, and at the meeting there was a major confrontation with Romania. The Soviet high priest of ideological orthodoxy, Mikhail Suslov, laid down a tough line, and launched a major attack on China. The Romanians, led by Paul Niculescu-Mizil, countered in defense of the Chinese, and when attacked by the Syrians walked out.

---

[1] Source: National Archives, Nixon Presidential Materials, NSC Files, Box 392, Subject Files, Soviet Affairs. Confidential. Sent for information. A notation on the memorandum indicates the President saw it. On June 27, Sonnenfeldt forwarded Kissinger a memorandum from the Department of State on the International Communist Conference. Three days later, Haig notified Sonnenfeldt that Kissinger wanted a memorandum on the International Communist Conference for his signature to the President. On July 18, Sonnenfeldt provided a draft of memorandum similar to the version prepared by the Department. (Ibid.)

[2] Nixon underlined this sentence up to this point.

Nevertheless, agreement was reached on a projected date of late 1968 and a single agenda item, the struggle against imperialism.

A permanent preparatory commission began sitting in Budapest. Subsequently, 88 parties were invited to participate in this work, but only 44 attended, and Romania was among the absentees.

By the time of the second preparatory meeting in June 1968, the Czech crisis was approaching a climax. There was strong opposition against proceeding with a conference until the Czech affair had been resolved. The Soviets accepted a postponement until November 1968 and had to settle for another "preparatory" meeting to discuss the final date.

The Czech invasion and the Soviet justification of "limited sovereignty"[3] created a brand new issue. At the November meeting, a number of parties insisted on a further postponement because of the Soviet invasion and the draft document was scrapped, to be replaced by a new one drawn up by a small working group. It was clear that a major issue was whether the Soviets could obtain an endorsement of their rationale for intervention in Czechoslovakia.

The last round of the preparatory meeting (May 23–June 5) witnessed a frantic struggle. About 450 amendments were presented to the main document, only about 45 were accepted. Romania sponsored about 100 amendments. By the time the meeting opened, the main document had been greatly watered down.

Victory or Defeat?

From the Soviet viewpoint the conference produced mixed results. It was by no means an unqualified victory. On the other hand, it is doubtful that the Soviet leaders regarded it as a defeat.

The fact that 75 communist parties did finally convene in Moscow after six years of wrangling, and remained for thirteen debates, with no walkouts, was a victory of sorts. To achieve this, however, meant repeated retreats and compromises, until in the end it was clearly a case of obtaining agreement to the lowest common denominator to avoid an open schism.

Moreover, 14 parties, including the Romanians and Italians, refused to accept the final document without reservation.[4] Four ruling parties were absent: China, North Korea, North Vietnam and Albania; the Yugoslavs were also absent; and the Cubans did not sign the final document, since they participated as "observers" only. India was the

---

[3] Nixon bracketed "limited sovereignty," a phrase used in the Brezhnev doctrine.

[4] Nixon underlined this sentence.

only Asian party other than Mongolia to attend.[5] Those attending and agreeing without qualification represented only one third of the Communists throughout the world.

In this sense it was a pyrrhic victory. The conference was in effect a rump session, compared to 1957 and 1960. And on the question of the legitimacy of Soviet authority as the pre-eminent party, nothing was gained. While the Soviet leaders did not expect to restore the role of "leading party," abandoned by Khrushchev, in their heart of hearts this is what they believe. They sought to demonstrate this by convening a conference that no one really wanted. An objective observer would have to conclude that the 1969 conference marked a further stage in the decline of Soviet authority over its communist colleagues abroad.

China

Even in their most optimistic moments the Soviet leaders could not have expected any formal action to outlaw the Chinese party, despite the dismay over China's radical internal policies. By prior agreement the Soviets had conceded that the Chinese issue would not be raised. Nevertheless, Brezhnev launched a major attack on the Chinese in a bitter and lengthy diatribe delivered to the second session of the conference. For the first time, he dwelt on the Chinese military threat to the USSR, and went a long way toward ultimate condemnation of the Chinese as not merely renegades but open enemies of the Soviet state.[6]

The Romanian leader, Nicolae Ceausescu, had apparently been given the text or main points of Brezhnev's speech on the preceding day and had threatened to walk out and return to Bucharest, where he would summon the Central Committee to support his action. There was a tense confrontation, but the Soviets outmaneuvered him by claiming he would look foolish if he returned home and Brezhnev did not give the speech as intended. So Ceausescu decided to wait and present a rebuttal. In fact, the China problem was first raised by Paraguay, and then elaborated on by Gomulka, before Brezhnev's major speech. Ceausescu made an appeal against further criticism, but about 55 parties spoke against China, thus giving the USSR fairly strong support.

On this issue, then, the Soviet leaders have reason for some satisfaction. They did not get approval of an edict of excommunication, but

---

[5] Nixon underlined this sentence.

[6] "China's foreign policy has, in effect, departed from proletarian internationalism and shed the socialist class content . . . these days the spearhead of Peking's foreign policy is aimed chiefly against the Soviet Union and the other socialist countries." [Footnote and ellipsis in the source text.]

did not try to. They did receive a significant degree of support, even though the limitation on their power to impose their position was clearly demonstrated.

Czechoslovakia

It is possible that had the Soviets remained silent on China, they might have escaped without a direct airing of the Czech invasion. Once the China question was broached, the dissidents were free to discuss the Czech invasion. Several delegations attacked the Soviets directly, but most remained silent and very few spoke in support. Husak had appealed to the conference before it opened to avoid the issue, but this was disregarded after the attack on China by Brezhnev.

On this issue, the final document is highly equivocal. Without mentioning Czechoslovakia, it discusses the limited sovereignty, or Brezhnev doctrine.[7] By not endorsing it as such, the conference in effect repudiated it.[8] Indeed, the document is so general and ambiguous that the Romanians are now quoting it in defense of their own independent course and the President's visit.

The Effect on Soviet Policy

It seems increasingly obvious that once the conference had been convened the Soviet leaders felt free to chart their own policy course without much regard to the actual proceedings or the final agreed documents. Indeed, Brezhnev's speech is the real Soviet position, and not the agreed statement on anti-imperialist struggle. In this regard, the Soviet position is more conservative and restrained. Brezhnev was much stronger on the themes of preventing a new war and conducting a policy of "peaceful coexistence"[9] than the conference statement, which had to be amended to conciliate militants such as the Cubans.

The follow-up speech of Gromyko suggests that what was agreed to in Moscow will have no great influence on Soviet policy, at least in the sense of forcing it into more "revolutionary" lines. Both Brezhnev and Gromyko went well beyond the conference consensus in crediting the good intentions of the US and other "sober-minded" elements in the West. Thus, one could conclude that all Moscow really wanted was a dramatic forum to attack the Chinese leaders, and once having done so, are returning to the practical business of foreign policy.

---

[7] Nixon underlined the second half of this sentence.

[8] Nixon underlined this sentence.

[9] Nixon underlined this sentence up to this point.

72.   Telegram From the Embassy in the Soviet Union to the Department of State[1]

Moscow, August 11, 1969, 1502Z.

4174. For the Secretary and Henry Kissinger.

1. At the moment the conduct of our relations with the USSR seem to have reached a marking-time stage. Despite the more positive tone of Gromyko's July 10 speech,[2] we have had no reply on SALT, the Middle East discussions are in a mechanical phase (we are receiving piecemeal the Soviet commentary on our counterproposals),[3] Soviet positions on Vietnam and Laos remain stationary, and the delay in Dobrynin's return has slowed things down, either by design or by the accident of his illness.

2. Some of the causes are understandable. The Soviets doubtless wished to study Senate testimony on the ABM and make their own evaluation of the President's world tour[4] as well as the Kiesinger visit to the US.[5] Furthermore it is vacation time with Brezhnev, Kosygin and Podgorny currently out of Moscow, although the round of official visits to and from the USSR continues apace.

3. There may be other factors which one can only surmise. From the standpoint of Soviet reaction, the US may perhaps have been too successful with its recent accomplishments which put us ahead of them. Apollo 11[6] and the favorable world response to the President's tour come to mind. With respect to the latter, it is not only the President's trip to Romania that may have caused concern but also the extension of the tour (including the Secretary's travels)[7] into areas where the Soviets are trying to stake out a position for themselves through Brezhnev's Asian security proposal.[8] Our firm support of the Thieu government has not made the Soviet's task in Vietnam any easier.

---

[1] Source: National Archives, RG 59, Central Files 1967–69, POL US–USSR. Secret; Priority; Nodis.

[2] For a summary, see Document 65.

[3] See Document 67.

[4] President Nixon's round-the-world trip from July 26–August 3 included stops in the Philippines, Indonesia, Thailand, South Vietnam, India, Pakistan, Romania, and England. For selected documentation, see Department of State *Bulletin*, August 25, 1969, pp. 141–176.

[5] See footnote 4, Document 70.

[6] On July 20, three Apollo 11 astronauts became the first men to walk on the moon.

[7] Rogers made a trip to Asia and the Pacific July 29–August 10.

[8] According to a June 27 research memorandum prepared in the Bureau of Intelligence and Research, "In his speech to the international communist conference in Moscow, Brezhnev declared that the USSR was 'putting on the agenda the task of creating

4. Added to these are Soviet preoccupations with China (with respect to which our own statements and attitudes are being carefully watched) and with Eastern Europe, expecially as the anniversary of the Czech invasion approaches. Finally there is always the German question and our relationship to it which will be examined in terms of Kissinger's talks in Washington, and may be reflected in the Soviet reply to the tripartite soundings on Berlin.

5. I have received no formal signs of Soviet displeasure with US but recent visitors and several of my colleagues have. To a greater degree than is perhaps shown in the written report, Kosygin closely questioned Hubert Humphrey[9] about the Nixon administration's intentions and sincerity, at least this is the indication Mr. Humphrey gave me when he was here. Arthur Goldberg was treated to the refrain that the USSR is looking to the US for deeds rather than words in the development of relations. As duly reported, Soviet officials have commented unfavorably to my German, Austrian and Indondesian colleagues about the President's Bucharest stay. Finally American businessmen have received expressions of dissatisfaction and disappointment that there has been no relaxation in our trade policies.

6. I hesitate to go further in characterizing the current state of our relations but mention the above to call attention to trends which may produce significant reactions. Perhaps the Soviets will charge Dobrynin on his return with presenting a clearer picture.

7. By way of exploring procedures which in themselves may be revealing, I have had in mind sounding out Kuznetsov on schedules for the conduct of pending and continuing talks. I can always adduce the Secretary's future order of business as a reason, but should this approach make us appear over-eager for negotiations, I shall desist.

Beam

---

a system of collective security in Asia.' " The memorandum went on to say that "Although Brezhnev did not elaborate further, his proposal raises the possibility of a significant shift in Soviet policy in Asia, both in terms of Soviet attitudes toward regional cooperation on a non-ideological basis, and as a response to Peking's policies in Asia aimed at isolating and containing China." (National Archives, Nixon Presidential Materials, NSC Files, Box 9, President's Daily Briefs, July 1–July 30, 1969)

[9] See Document 57.

73.   National Intelligence Estimate[1]

NIE 11/13–69   Washington, August 12, 1969.

THE USSR AND CHINA

The Problem

To estimate the general course of Sino–Soviet relations over the next three years.

Conclusions

A. Sino-Soviet relations, which have been tense and hostile for many years, have deteriorated even further since the armed clashes on the Ussuri River last March. There is little or no prospect for improvement in the relationship, and partly for this reason, no likelihood that the fragments of the world Communist movement will be pieced together.

B. For the first time, it is reasonable to ask whether a major Sino-Soviet war could break out in the near future. The potential for such a war clearly exists. Moreover, the Soviets have reasons, chiefly the emerging Chinese nuclear threat to the USSR, to argue that the most propitious time for an attack is soon, rather than several years hence. At the same time, the attendant military and political uncertainties might also weigh heavily upon the collective leadership in Moscow.

C. We do not look for a deliberate Chinese attack on the USSR. Nor do we believe the Soviets would wish to become involved in a prolonged, large-scale conflict. While we cannot say it is likely, we see some chance that Moscow might think it could launch a strike against China's nuclear and missile facilities without getting involved in such a conflict. In any case, a climate of high tension, marked by periodic clashes along the border, is likely to obtain. The scale of fighting may

---

[1] Source: Central Intelligence Agency, NIC Files, Job 79–R1012A, NIEs and SNIEs. Secret; Controlled Dissem. The Central Intelligence Agency and the intelligence organizations of the Departments of State and Defense and the National Security Agency participated in the preparation of this estimate, which was submitted by the Director of Central Intelligence and concurred by all members of the USIB, except the Assistant General Manager of the Atomic Energy Commission and the Assistant Director of the Federal Bureau of Investigation, who abstained because the subject was outside their jurisdiction. This NIE was included with materials for a meeting of the National Security Council's Review Group on November 20; see Document 101. This NIE superseded NIE 11–12–66; for text, see Foreign Relations, 1964–1968, volume XXX, China, Document 223.

occasionally be greater than heretofore, and might even involve punitive cross-border raids by the Soviets. Under such circumstances, escalation is an ever present possibility.

D. In the light of the dispute, each side appears to be reassessing
its foreign policy. The Soviets seem intent on attracting new allies, or
at least benevolent neutrals, in order to "contain" the Chinese. To that
end Moscow has signified some desire to improve the atmosphere of
its relations with the West. The Chinese, who now appear to regard the
USSR as their most immediate enemy, will face stiff competition from
the Soviets in attempting to expand their influence in Asia.

[Omitted here is the Discussion section of the estimate: Political
Background, the Military Dimension, Prospects, Impact of the Dispute
Elsewhere in the World, and Annex of Territorial Claims.]

74.   Minutes of Meeting of the National Security Council[1]

San Clemente, August 14, 1969, 9:39 a.m.–12:25 p.m.

[Omitted here is discussion of Korea and a briefing by Helms on
China.]

The President: We have always assumed that the Chinese are
hard liners and the Soviets are more reasonable. But I think this is open
to question. Look at what actually happened. Can we sustain this
judgement?

Director Helms: No. The facts don't support it.

The President: Ceaucescu[2] says that the Soviets are tougher and
more aggressive than the Chinese. We must look at China on a long
term basis. This must be very closely held. We must look at it in a bilateral context. China can't stay permanently isolated. To me, China

---

[1] Source: Library of Congress, Manuscript Division, Kissinger Papers, Box CL 312,
Meetings, National Security Council. These minutes were revised by Haig and contain
his handwritten changes. The time of the meeting is from the President's Daily Diary,
which also indicates that Nixon, Kissinger, Agnew, Rogers, Laird, Mitchell, Lincoln,
Wheeler, Richardson, Helms, Halperin, Haig, Lynn, Holdridge, and Green attended the
meeting. (National Archives, Nixon Presidential Materials, White House Central Files)
Nixon's notes on this meeting are in *Foreign Relations, 1969–1976*, volume XVII, China,
1969–1972, Document 25.

[2] Nicolae Ceausescu was the President of Romania.

uses the dispute with Russia for internal use. But to me the Soviets are more aggressive.

Director Helms: Border incidents don't prove anything, but the Soviets have moved from 15 up to 30 divisions to China's border. They now have 3 new missile sites with a range of 500 miles along the border. The Soviets fear they will soon lose their first strike capability vis-à-vis China.

The President: We must recall the Brezhnev doctrine and the invasion of Czechoslovakia. The Soviets continue to move forward and act aggressively when progress is threatened. They are a tough group. We should relook at our own estimates. They may have a "knock them off now" policy developing with respect to China.

Now, in terms of our role, I am not sure if it is in our long term interest to let the Soviets knock them off. We must think through whether it is a safer world with China down, or should we look to keeping China strong? These are rhetorical questions. The Asians fear the Soviets first, and don't want a collective security arrangement. They question this. They don't want the Soviets as their protector. We must look at China after Vietnam.

Director Helms: I think the Soviets are doing well. They are very active in Europe and also in the Middle East. They talk softer but act much tougher. The Chinese have been stalling.

Secretary Rogers: No one at State would favor a Soviet takeover of China. They also feel that the Chinese threat is greatly overemphasized. This may suggest an aggressive Soviet attitude but I am not certain.

Assistant Secretary Green: China is still feared by the Asians. It is their principal fear. They want us to remain but they might accept the Soviets as an alternative.

The President: I don't want to overdraw this, but these countries don't want the Soviets in.

Assistant Secretary Green: The Soviets are certainly probably tempted to surgically remove the Chinese nuclear threat.

(The meeting ended at 12:10 P.M.)

75.   **Memorandum From Harold Saunders of the National
       Security Council Staff to the President's Assistant for
       National Security Affairs (Kissinger)[1]**

Washington, August 18, 1969.

SUBJECT

Semyenov–Beam Meetings, July 31, August 8 and 11

The Soviets gave Ambassador Beam their comments on our counter proposals[2] in meetings on July 31 and August 8 and 11. (You have already seen a memo on the July 31 meeting.) From the three meetings the following points emerge:

1. The Soviets want to hold the bilateral talks in Moscow. Beam did what he could to discourage this, but—especially with Dobrynin "ill"—we still have the problem of how to bring the action back to Washington. The Soviets don't appear likely to give up easily and have arranged still another Middle East meeting with Beam.

2. The Soviets are doing their best to appear reasonable and forthcoming. Possible explanations for this are:

—They are genuinely interested in a settlement.

—It is useful to them with the Arabs to keep the talks going whether there is any practical result or not.

—They are trying to convince us that talks in Moscow can be more useful than talks in Washington.

3. We seem to have agreed—or nearly agreed—language on several points:

—They accept the general principles in the preamble, but they want a settlement between Israel and all the Arabs, not just the UAR. They also shy away from our language where it implies direct negotiations.

—They accept our definition of the kind of guarantees and conditions which will accompany a settlement except that they feel there is no need to include a reference to non-interference in the internal affairs of other countries. (This is not really an Arab-Israeli issue. Interference in the area is mainly in the domestic affairs of our Arab friends by the Soviets' Arab friends.)

---

[1] Source: National Archives, Nixon Presidential Materials, NSC Files, Box 650, Country Files, Middle East, Middle East Negotiations, 7/69–10/69. Secret; Nodis.

[2] See footnote 2, Document 69.

—In some instance, they agree with what we say but disagree with the emphasis. For example, they have no objection to our references to a cessation of belligerency but they feel we have unnecessarily emphasized the point. On the other hand, they feel we should be explicit about the Arabs having no obligations in a settlement if the Israelis don't fulfill their obligations. (These differences are only cosmetic as far as we and the Russians are concerned, but they are important for both of us in trying to bring along our clients.)

4. Despite all this, there are important differences remaining:

—They are still pressing for their specific plan for implementing withdrawal rather than our vaguer formulation. (The real problem here is that their plan would eliminate the direct negotiations the Israelis feel are essential.)

—They still don't like our position on borders. (Our fallback position—return to the old UAR-Israel border—would meet their needs, but presenting this depends on their being more forthcoming on Arab post-settlement obligations.)

—The Egyptians are concerned—unduly in our view—about the Suez Canal. The Soviets say Nasser thinks we are plotting to take it away from him, but he may want our language changed so that he will have some legal basis for closing the canal if the Israelis don't behave.

—The Soviets don't appear able to modify their position that DMZ's must be in Israel as well as the UAR. I suspect that this is because the Arabs are taking as stiff a line with Moscow for this position as the Israelis are with us against it.

—They still want Gaza returned to the UAR, although Semyenov said he was talking about Arab administration, not sovereignty.

—The Soviets are not willing to give Israel the kind of guarantees in the Strait of Tiran that the Israelis are demanding, although they do admit this is an international waterway. They will go as far as the great power guarantees with a UN force that Israel got in 1957 and lost in 1967. They seem to feel that gaining consent from Nasser for a UN force was a victory.

—They did not accept our refugee formula, but say they now recognize that Israel's special concerns have to be taken into account. They want the refugee solution to be left to the parties to work out through Jarring. (This is an advance over their previous position that Israel would have to abide by the UN resolutions, i.e. let all the refugees return to Israel.)

Now that we have their full reply, Joe Sisco will review and return our comments in a week or two, trying to nudge us ahead on a few points. This has been useful in getting a more precise view of the Soviet position.

Beam's reports are at Tab A.[3] Our paper is at Tab B[4] for reference.

---

[3] Attached but not printed are telegram 3946 from Moscow, July 31, in which the Embassy reported on Beam's talk with Semyenov, and telegram 3435 from Moscow, August 1, containing Semyenov's comments to Beam.

[4] Attached but not printed; see footnote 2, Document 69.

---

76. Memorandum From William Hyland of the National Security Council Staff to the President's Assistant for National Security Affairs (Kissinger)[1]

Washington, August 28, 1969.

SUBJECT

Sino-Soviet Contingencies

The two options being examined for the contingency of major Sino-Soviet hostilities should be subjected to much more rigorous examination and debate. As things now stand, the first approach—strict impartiality—seems likely to break down completely in the execution, and the second,—shading toward China—could have major consequences in our relations with the USSR.

Impartiality

This exists only in theory. In practice, the US will have to make choices which will have the net effect of a distinct sympathy for one or the other side.

Consider the following problems:

—do we continue bilateral and four-power Middle East talks with the USSR? if strict impartiality means business as usual, we should continue them; but this will be subject to the interpretation that we are condoning Soviet "aggression";

---

[1] Source: National Archives, Nixon Presidential Materials, NSC Files, Box 710, Country Files, Europe, USSR, Vol. V. Secret. Sent for information. A copy was sent to Holdridge. A covering memorandum from Hyland to Kissinger reads, "The attached memo (Tab A) represents a highly personal and apparently minority view of our choices in the event of major hostilities between Russia and China. Still, you might find it worth reading before the interagency paper is submitted next week." Kissinger's handwritten comment on the cover memorandum reads, "Note to Hyland: 1st class paper. Thanks. HK."

—would we start or continue SALT? if we did the Soviets and most of informed opinion in the world (and in China) would see it as favorable to the USSR; if we refused to talk this would be a clear retaliation, not impartiality;

—would we continue negotiations on a seabeds disarmament treaty?

—consider a UN resolution condemning the USSR (introduced by Albania); could we abstain? Moscow would be overjoyed; could we vote against the USSR and be impartial, etc.?

The point is, that in an effort to be truly impartial, we would probably wind up clearly supporting the USSR, unless we were prepared to take specific actions to indicate our disapproval, which would then amount to support to China. Indeed, trying to be even-handed and impartial or neutral once China has been attacked by major force is clearly tantamount to supporting the USSR.

Even if all of the specific problems could be miraculously sorted out, the world at large and domestic opinion is going to scrutinize our position and conclude that we favor one side.

One way out of this dilemma could be not to adopt an avowed policy of impartiality but one of enlightened self-interest, regulating our reactions, statements, and actions to the actual situation. As many have pointed out a Sino-Soviet war, for a limited period and if limited in scope, is by no means a disaster for the US. It might just be the way to an early Vietnam settlement. It might also be a "solution" to the China nuclear problem.

In any case, it is worth considering the option of being mildly pro-Soviet, trying at the same time to be mildly pro-Chinese, depending on the scope and duration of hostilities.

In other words, instead of measuring our various actions against the criteria of impartiality or neutrality, to measure each against the national objectives of the United States, which are in the process of being defined in the NSSM–63 study.[2]

Partiality Toward China

This variant does not seem to be very well thought through. Two reasons have been advanced:

—we will incline toward China to extract some Soviet concessions;

—we will incline toward China to prevent a shift in the Asian "balance" (the argument apparently being that a major defeat of China would result in Soviet predominance).

---

[2] See Document 64. The first draft of the NSSM 63 study entitled "U.S. Policy on Current Sino–Soviet Differences" was considered by an interdepartmental ad hoc group on September 3 and was discussed at a WSAG meeting on September 4, and at a NSC Review Group meeting on September 25. The final version of NSSM 63 was completed on November 10.

The notion of extracting Soviet concessions, once major hostilities have began, is extremely naive.[3] The Soviets are not going to attack China in some quixotic mood. If they take this drastic step, they will be fully and totally committed to pursue it to the end. They are already working up deep racial and political emotions in Russia. The Soviet leaders believe we should share their concern about China, and expect, at the least, sympathy and understanding of whatever actions they might take. They will almost certainly regard American gestures to China as sheer hypocrisy.

If this argument is even close to the mark, then the Soviet reaction to our slight partially toward China is likely to be massively hostile. They might not be able or want to do anything about it at the time, but it will poison Soviet-American relations for a very long time.

The notion of supporting China to some small degree because of the effect on the Asian balance is rather fatuous. Only a slight knowledge of history suggests that foreign conquest of China is not very likely (the Soviets are not so inexperienced as to believe they can conquer China). A quick "victory" simply is not in the cards. The alternative of a long, inconclusive struggle is another problem, but it need not be decided in any contingency plan at this moment.

If the Soviet blow brings down the present regime, this would not be a great disaster. A replacement would have to be anti-Soviet to come to power. The alternative of a pro-Soviet faction surfacing in Peking after an attack is too remote to be discussed; even if the Soviets could find such Chinese leaders, their tenure in China would be brief, and their authority would not extend beyond a few provinces.

The idea that we can build up political credit with the Chinese leaders by displaying our sympathies is not very convincing. If we were serious in this regard we should take actions to forestall a Soviet strike, which the Chinese could claim we have full knowledge of (cf. press reports of such a strike in all US papers on August 28).[4]

If the strike does occur, the only way to gain a real credit in Peking would be a straightforward anti-Soviet campaign. Anything short of this will probably be regarded by the Chinese as a charade. Indeed, the Chinese could already conclude that we know of Soviet intentions and are colluding with them. If and when it becomes public knowledge that the Soviets did in fact mention to us a strike against Chinese nuclear facilities, the Chinese will simply write us off as Moscow's tacit ally.

---

[3] This is not to say that the Soviets would not pay some price in advance to prevent a more accommodating US policy toward China. [Footnote in the source text.]

[4] See, for example, Chalmers M. Roberts, "Russia Reported Eyeing Strikes at China Λ Sites," *Washington Post*, August 28, 1971, p. A–1.

In sum, there is a considerable danger that by trying to be slightly sympathetic towards Peking we will court a massive over-reaction from the USSR and still accomplish very little in the eyes of this or any other Chinese leadership.

---

77.   Minutes of Washington Special Actions Group Meeting[1]

San Clemente, September 4, 1969.

SUBJECT

    Contingency Plan in the Event of Sino-Soviet Hostility

PARTICIPANTS

    Henry Kissinger, Chairman
    The Attorney General
    State—U. Alexis Johnson
    Defense—G. Warren Nutter
    CIA—Vice Admiral Nels Johnson
    NSC Staff—Helmut Sonnenfeldt; John H. Holdridge

Summary of Conclusions[2]

1. The section on Vietnam should be strengthened. A legal study of the implications of a Soviet blockade of the China Mainland was needed. Additional studies on neutrality and the potential effect on the U.S.-Soviet relationship were required.[3]

---

[1] Source: National Archives, Nixon Presidential Materials, NSC Files, NSC Institutional Files (H-Files), Box H–114, WSAG Minutes, Originals, 1969 and 1970. No classification marking.

[2] A draft of the response to NSSM 63, on "U.S. Policy on Current Sino-Soviet Differences," was the chief item on the agenda for this meeting. (National Archives, Nixon Presidential Materials, NSC Files, NSC Institutional Files (H-Files), Box H–071, WSAG Meeting, 9/4/69, Sino-Soviet)

[3] Holdridge raised this issue in talking points he prepared for Kissinger on September 3. Holdridge pointed out that, "There is a question of balance (which of course is controlled by the paper's purpose and assumptions). Two U.S. responses to a Sino-Soviet conflict are dealt with at some length—(1) a carefully studied attitude of impartiality and (2) a slight bias in favor of the Chinese. A third alternative—a policy of bias in favor of the Soviets—is suggested, but rejected. Would it be useful to consider this alternative?" (Ibid.)

2. A U.S. position of impartiality would have the practical consequences of helping the Soviets. In such circumstances we might try to
get something from the Soviets.

3. With regard to the U.S. public position in the UN or elsewhere,
we could not condone a nuclear exchange. If we wanted to quiet things
down, we must say so. For the U.S. to ask for a ceasefire without at
the same time condemning the Soviets would appear to the Chinese
as "collusion." With such a condemnation, however, it was acceptable
to ask for a ceasefire.

4. The draft should be refined to reflect two alternatives: a situation in which major hostilities were in progress, and a situation in which
the Soviets launched a surgical strike against Chinese nuclear centers.
A surgical strike would probably lead to greater hostilities, but for the
purpose of the paper this distinction should be made.

5. Section four—what to do to deter—was most pertinent and
urgent.

---

78.   Editorial Note

On September 11, 1969, from 10:17 a.m. to 12:24 p.m., the National
Security Council met in the Cabinet room to discuss the Middle East.
The day before this meeting, the President's Assistant for National Security Affairs Henry Kissinger sent Nixon a memorandum to serve as
"an analysis of the major issues which may become obscured amidst
all of the negotiating detail you will hear at the NSC meeting." After
summarizing the intricate web of Middle Eastern issues, Kissinger related them to the larger U.S.-Soviet agenda as follows:

"There are several possible ways to relate this with other issues on
the US–USSR agenda:

"1. If we were going to press Israel to accept unpalatable measures, we might expect the Soviets to press Nasser to accept some
equally unpalatable terms.

"2. If the terms are going to be harder for Israel than for the UAR
to accept, then we might look to other areas for compensating Soviet
pressure on their clients such as the North Vietnamese. Another possibility would be some sort of understanding about the limits of Soviet imperialistic ambitions in the Mid-East, Persian Gulf, Indian
Ocean.

"Whether the Soviets will respond depends heavily on how they
view their situation in the area. It is common for us to assume that time

helps them and hurts us, but there are enough disadvantages in this situation and advantages in a settlement to give us some leverage. With a settlement, they could pursue their interests without risk of war, get their fleet into the Indian Ocean and still have enough tension points like the Persian Gulf to exploit. The balance is fine enough however that they might cooperate with us in pressing a reasonable proposal on the Arabs. They apparently judge that pressing our present proposals would cost them too much in Cairo. Given this delicate a balance and our inability to press the Israelis beyond certain limits, it may be that on this issue we are negotiating in a relatively narrow field." (National Archives, Nixon Presidential Materials, NSC Files, NSC Institutional Files (H-Files), Box H–024, NSC Meetings 9/11/69)

At the beginning of the NSC meeting on September 11, Joseph Sisco, Assistant Secretary of State for Near Eastern and South Asian Affairs, who had been in Moscow July 14–17, presented his impressions of the Soviet position:

"I came away from Moscow judging: Soviets want to continue dialogue with US for both Mid-East and general reasons. Question is how Soviets view the area: If area undergoing increasing radicalization, does Moscow view this as in USSR interest?

"US–USSR ageements in talks on the following:

"—Israel and UAR would sign same agreement.
"—Recognition of Israel's right to exist.
"—Freedom of passage through Tiran. On Suez, USSR has qualified by reference to Constantinople Convention of 1888.
"—Execution of agreement would await agreement on total package—UAR, Israel and possible Jordan.
"—We have agreed on the principle of demilitarization.

"Soviet plan:

"1. Israeli withdrawal 40 miles.
"2. Opening Canal.
"3. Israeli withdrawal to June 4 lines and Gaza Strip.
"4. Demilitarization of Negev–Sinai border. Seem willing to accept only token demilitarization on Israeli side.
"5. Irrevocable UN force at Sharm al-Shaikh.

"Position US has taken:

"1. Within context of agreement, Israeli withdrawal to 'secure and recognized border' to be defined by parties. We 'do not exclude' prewar border.
"2. Demilitarization of entire Sinai.
"3. Options for Sharm al-Shaikh. Let parties negotiate. Kept open Israeli presence.
"4. Ultimately, sovereignty of Gaza would have to be determined by Jordan, UAR, Israel."

After a brief discussion of Israeli views and British and French attitudes, President Nixon asked, "What does the USSR want?" Sisco responded as follows:

"1. They want to continue talks as a deterrent in the Mid-East.

"2. As long as they talk, this is a demonstration to Arabs that they are trying to help.

"3. Be responsive to Nixon 'era of negotiations.'

"Rogers: They think they have brought Arabs farther than we have brought Israelis.

"President: Don't Soviets know Arabs will be beaten in another war. 'If they get screwed again, they won't have another Glassboro to bail them out?'

"Helms: They really want to get down to Persian Gulf.

"President: In 1967, Soviets looked unready to help Arabs. If this happened again, Soviets don't want to be in that position. Do they really believe—given that fact—that they consider this worth a US–USSR confrontation? Do they think this is about the best they can get now? They want talks to continue, but a settlement?

"Sisco: They want settlement on own terms. Soviets want Nasser as their own tool. They haven't wanted to press him.

"President: How is USSR doing in Mid-East? Not bad—some weak reeds but still not bad.

"Sisco: We have interest in stable peace. Less clear USSR sees this as its interest.

"President: USSR can have influence while situation simmers. Does anybody think US as its friend? June war a tremendous victory for Israel and USSR. From their viewpoint why change the situation. Does Moscow think they're going to have confrontation with US over Israel? 'You know damn well we're not and they know it.' Do you think they want a deal?

"Sisco: Not a deal that would cost Moscow much.

"President: We're the honest brokers here.

"Rogers: Could have a settlement that would continue exploitable tension. Meanwhile, they have isolated us from world community.

"President: 'Israel's puppet.'

"Richardson: One aspect in which USSR might want real settlement. Present situation continued strengthens fedayeen, weakens Nasser. Soviets less able to deliver if fedayeen come out on top, Soviets less able to deliver Arab demands which would then be not just return of territory but destruction of Israel.

"President: Agree but if fedayeen prevail, they too would keep situation stirred up. Soviets have to have some reason to want to settle; what is it?

"Rogers: If war broke out again, their clients would lose. Our hope is that they want to avoid a war.

"Helms: USSR wants to open Canal to get into Persian Gulf.

"Yost: On balance, USSR wants settlement but not going to jeopardize their influence. They could even shift support to fedayeen and try to ride that wave.

"What concerns me is extent to which we are in trouble with moderate Arabs. Soviets without lifting a finger are profiting.

"Formula asking Arabs at outset to come to direct negotiations is a non-starter.

"Situation is weakening moderate regimes and not increasing Israel's security. Even Moroccans and Tunisians getting worried about US position—has not gone very far yet.

"Kissinger: Soviets may have interest in Israel-UAR settlement because continued occupation of Sinai demonstrates USSR impotence. They want naval access to Persian Gulf. Plenty of tension will remain. They may see their opportunity in transitional regimens in Arabian Peninsula. I can see Soviet gains from a settlement.

"Problem of concentrating on UAR-Israel settlement is that our friend, Hussein, comes off worse than Nasser."

Before turning to the domestic implications of the administration's Middle East policy, President Nixon made the following remarks:

"I don't want to save the face of the USSR; they aren't trying to help us anywhere. I don't see why we should help them. That doesn't mean all their interests are different from ours. In developing our position, let's not give them a chance to claim credit for getting everything back for the Arabs. Mistake 'allow them to look too good.' " (Ibid.) The minutes of this meeting are in *Foreign Relations, 1969–1976*, volume XXIII, Arab-Israeli Dispute, 1969–1972.

---

79.   **Editorial Note**

On September 17, 1969, the Washington Special Actions Group met to discuss revisions to NSSM 63 on "U.S. Policy on Current Sino-Soviet Differences." Minutes of this meeting are in *Foreign Relations, 1969–1976*, volume XVII, China, 1969–1972, Document 32. The following actions were agreed: "(a) re-do section on reconnaissance capability; (b) strengthen section on Soviet blockade of China with special emphasis on U.S. military responses should the Soviets deny access to Hong Kong or interfere with U.S. shipping on the high seas; (c) take another look at the operational consequences of 'partiality' or 'impartiality,' especially in the light of U.S. actions that can be taken in NVN; (d) delete section on civil defense." (National Archives, Nixon Presidential Materials, NSC Files, NSC Institutional Files (H-Files), Box H–114, WSAG Minutes, Originals, 1969 and 1970)

Additional revisions to NSSM 63 were considered at a meeting of the National Security Council's Review Group on September 25. The paper was "to be revised to spell out the consequences of policy choices in three situations: (a) continued Sino-Soviet tension but no hostilities; (b) active U.S. effort to deter hostilities; (c) hostilities [with] one-shot strike or protracted conflict." Minutes of this Review Group meeting are in *Foreign Relations, 1969–1976,* volume XVII, China, 1969–1972, Document 36.

U.S. policy toward Sino-Soviet hostilities was also on the agenda for the Washington Special Actions Group meeting on September 29, but the conflict was discussed only briefly. According to the minutes of this meeting, "Kissinger was called out of the meeting but paused long enough to respond to a question from [William] Cargo [Director for Plan Coordination, Policy Planning Council, Department of State] pertaining to the Sino-Soviet study and its relationship to the NSSM 63 Report. Cargo said that the two efforts were distinctively different, especially in their time frames. He questioned the real utility of developing a detailed analysis, in the NSSM 63 Report, of the contingency involving an escalating crisis or rapid deterioration of the overall Sino-Soviet situation. Kissinger deferred to Cargo's judgment on how the problem should be approached but requested that neither paper neglect to examine the relationship between courses of action and their probable outcome." (National Archives, Nixon Presidential Materials, NSC Files, NSC Institutional Files (H-Files), Box H–114, Minutes, Originals, 1969 and 1970)

NSSM 63 was revised again on October 17. The summary portion on "U.S. Policy on Current Sino-Soviet Differences" reads as follows:

"This paper considers the policy options posed for the United States by the Sino-Soviet dispute on the assumption that the dispute continues to be fought out in terms of an essentially political rivalry on the present pattern; analyzes the nature of the interrelationships between the United States, China, and the Soviet Union, and examines in general terms the problems and opportunities for the United States which would result from major hostilities between the Soviet Union and China. (The immediate short-range options in the event of Sino-Soviet war are the subject of a separate contingency study.)

"*Options*

"Three broad strategies are considered.

"*Option A* would have the effect of supporting Communist China, the weaker of the two contestants, and would probably take the form of making various unreciprocated gestures towards China, such as endorsing Peking's border claims, while, at the same time, displaying reluctance to engage in negotiations with the USSR, e.g., on SALT. Pursuit of this strategy might result in some long-term improvement in the U.S.-Chinese relationship and it might also help prolong the Sino-Soviet dispute, but the Soviet reaction would be strong and adverse. The Soviets would probably pursue an intensified policy of attempting to detach Western Europe from the U.S., win over Asian countries, particularly Japan, strengthen their hold over Eastern Europe, and step up their own military program.

"*Option B* would have the effect of supporting the Soviet Union, the stronger contestant, and would take the form of maintaining our present posture towards China without change, while we adopted a generally softer line towards the USSR. It could result in a more accommodating Soviet attitude on some of the major issues between us and in the general Soviet posture, but it might have the effect of making the USSR more difficult to deal with and more ready to take pre-emptive action against the Chinese. It would damage the changes of an improvement in our relations with China.

"*Option C* would be one of overt neutrality and could be applied in one of two ways.

"*Option C. 1.* would involve our taking no action which might be construed as favoring one contestant or the other. Accordingly, we should make no effort to develop our relations with Communist China and, at the same time, avoid trying to arrive at understandings with the USSR. Such a policy would reduce to a minimum the dangers of U.S. involvement in the Sino-Soviet dispute, but would hamper pursuit of our own interests, vis-à-vis both China and the USSR.

"*Option C. 2.* would involve maintenance of a policy of neutrality, while we pursued our own long-term interests towards both China and the USSR, without undue regard to the interpretation either side might put on our actions. In implementing this policy, we should attempt to develop our relations with China, while continuing our basic support of the GRC on Taiwan, and simultaneously seek to negotiate with the USSR on the important issues between us. This option would have the advantage of leaving us free to try to work out a satisfactory relationship with each of the contestants, but it would be difficult to pursue, since it calls for constant awareness of how each of them reacted to it.

"The Interrelation: The Soviet Union, China, and the U.S.

"The Soviets almost certainly see their relationship with China as the most compelling problem in foreign affairs now confronting them.

Short of a conceivable Soviet decision to strike militarily against China, it can be anticipated that Moscow will persist in efforts to strengthen its military position along the border with China, to develop improved relations with both Communist and non-Communist countries on the Chinese periphery, to shore up its overall security position (particularly in Eastern Europe), to diminish Chinese influence in other Communist countries, to protect its political gains in the Middle East, and to establish a generally less hostile relationship with the West.

"The character of Soviet policy could change if Moscow comes to believe that the Chinese are on the way to breaking out of their largely self-inflicted isolation, and most especially if this seemed to be happening in a way that foreshadowed a real and far-reaching Chinese rapprochement with the U.S. In this event, the Soviets might well see a need to strengthen further their general military position; they might feel greater compulsion to strike militarily at China; and they might adopt a more hostile attitude toward the U.S. Alternatively, the Soviets might decide that a serious effect to improve relations with the U.S., even at the expense of concessions on specific issues, was more likely to serve their interests.

"It seems probable that the Chinese, for their part, also now regard the USSR as their most immediate and threatening adversary. They seem determined to give no ground in the quarrel, in spite of their obvious military weakness vis-à-vis the USSR. Since many of the handicaps which encumber Chinese foreign policy are of their own making, the way to greater international maneuverability is open to them—if they choose to use it. It is possible, therefore, that Peking might at some point come to see that it would be better served in the struggle with the Soviets by a more flexible posture. This could, even in the near term, lead the Chinese to seek improved relations with third countries and a somewhat less hostile relationship with the U.S. Peking recognizes its own military weakness in facing the Soviet Union and it is most unlikely that the Chinese will launch a military attack against the USSR. Nevertheless, the Chinese can be expected to react violently against any Soviet attack on Chinese territory.

"The triangular relationship between the U.S., the USSR, and China is, of course, an unequal one: U.S. and Soviet interests intersect in many parts of the world, whereas our problems with China lie mainly in Asia. For the foreseeable future, the views of Peking and Moscow as to how the world should be organized are likely to remain incompatible with ours. Thus, until a fundamental and far-reaching change takes place in China or in the USSR, the resolution of critical differences we have with either is unlikely. Nevertheless, there is today some convergence of interest between us and the USSR in the various parts of the world where our interests interact, arising mainly from our mutual desire to avoid a nuclear war. There is less convergence between U.S. and Chinese interests. Broadly, however, each of the three powers wants to avoid collusion between the other two or any dramatic expansion of the power of either adversary at the expense of that of the other.

"Growing dissidence between the USSR and China has limited both countries in the pursuit of policies basically antagonistic to U.S. interests; this is the most important benefit which assumes to the U.S. from Sino-Soviet rivalry. Beyond this, the dispute has, in a positive sense, heightened Soviet interest in developing a less abrasive relationship with the U.S. and it may at some point lead China in the same direction.

"Problems and Opportunities for the U.S. Assuming
Major Sino-Soviet Hostilities

"A change in the degree of tension between the Soviets and Chinese is a more likely prospect than a change in kind. The latter is, however, now well within the realm of the possible. There are two ways in which major hostilities might develop:

"(1) through inadvertent escalation, and
"(2) by deliberate resort to military force on a large scale.

"Given the calculus of military power only the USSR would be likely to see advantage in the second course.

"The impact of major Sino-Soviet hostilities on U.S. interests could vary significantly depending upon the nature and duration of the hostilities, the general posture of the U.S. toward the two sides, and the outcome of the war. The course and outcome of such hostilities are highly unpredictable.

"Major Sino-Soviet hostilities which did not directly involve third countries (other than Mongolia) and were fought only with conventional weapons would not necessarily be disadvantageous to us. During such a war, the U.S. could expect (1) a drastic reduction in the capability of the USSR and China to pursue policies inimical to U.S. interests elsewhere, (2) a drastic reduction in assistance to Hanoi thereby eventually enhancing the prospect for political settlement in Viet-Nam, and (3) improved relations with third countries anxious to strengthen their own security in an uncertain situation. However, if third countries in Asia or in Europe were to be drawn in on one side or the other, if wars of opportunity should break out as a result (e.g., between North and South Korea), or if nuclear weapons were used in the conflict, serious dangers and problems for the U.S. would arise.

"The general posture of the U.S. toward the Soviet Union and China at the time major hostilities broke out between them—and during the conflict—could affect U.S. ability to maximize advantages and minimize risks. If we clearly supported one side in the conflict, we would be unable to gain advantages in relations with the other and we would have difficulties with third countries not adopting the same partisan attitude. A U.S. posture of neutrality in the dispute would provide maximum flexibility in dealings with third countries and might encourage both Moscow and Peking to make concessions to ensure that the U.S. not become involved in their quarrel, since both would fear U.S. support of the other.

"The outcome of a Sino-Soviet war could have important policy implications for the U.S. If the Mao-Lin regime survived in control of China as it now exists, its prestige would be enhanced and China would probably be a more formidable opponent of U.S. interests in Asia. If the Soviets succeeded in creating puppet regimes in the Chinese border provinces, Peking might become more interested in improving relations with the U.S., but a triumphant USSR would be more difficult to deal with and Soviet influence in Asia would be enhanced to a degree and in ways inimical to our interests. If the Mao-Lin regime should be ousted as a result of the war, China might be fragmented and civil war might follow. The U.S. would then face the question of whether it should not attempt to counter Soviet efforts to gain predominant influence over more than just the border areas.

"The net balance of the advantages and disadvantages to the United States cannot be foreseen, but the possibilities that nuclear weapons might be used, that other countries might be drawn into the war, and that the outcome might shift the balance of power against us, are sufficiently great to make an escalation of hostilities something we should seek to avoid and to raise the question whether there are possible actions we could take to minimize the chances of a major Sino-Soviet military conflict.

"We have little ability to influence directly either Moscow or Peking on the question of relations with the other, since neither regards this as a question in which we have a legitimate interest. Even so, the U.S. could make it clear that it would not welcome a major Sino-Soviet conflict and believed dangerous international complications would ensue. Even if such a position did not reinforce councils of caution in Moscow and Peking, it should serve U.S. purposes in relations with third countries.

"In making contingency preparations if major Sino-Soviet hostilities seemed imminent, care should be taken to avoid creating the impression that we were preparing to take military advantage of either Peking or Moscow since this could contribute to the explosiveness of the situation." (Ibid.)

80. Memorandum From Harold Saunders of the National Security Council Staff to the President's Assistant for National Security Affairs (Kissinger)[1]

Washington, September 19, 1969.

SUBJECT

Sisco–Dobrynin Meeting, 18 September

Joe Sisco saw Dobrynin yesterday. I will attach his detailed report as soon as we get it, but in his summary cable (Tab A),[2] he reports the following:

1. The Soviets are now largely ready to buy the language on peace in point 3 of our proposal (Tab B)[3] with the exception of the commitment to control the Arab terrorists. They also want to consolidate points 3 and 12. (*Comment:* Consolidation, even without changing the substance, would lessen the overall emphasis on an Arab commitment to peace, and, of course, dropping the commitment to control the fedayeen would eliminate one crucial element and give the Israelis "proof" that the Arabs just want to get their land back and then go on with the war.)

2. On direct negotiations Dobrynin took the position that the question is difficult and should not be raised now. Sisco has the impression that the question is not closed. (*Comment:* The Soviets could, of course, be hoping to postpone the question indefinitely.)

3. The Soviets still seem flexible on refugees and asked how many Arabs would come under our annual quota proposal.

4. Dobrynin understands our desire to keep all the options on security arrangements open for the parties, but he rejected an Israeli presence at Sharm el-Shaikh.

5. Dobrynin made his usual plea for withdrawal to pre-war lines.

6. Sisco told Dobrynin that we believe that an Arab commitment to direct negotiations at some stage is the key to further movement and that the Soviets must get out in front of the Egyptians just as we are out in front of the Israelis.

They will probably meet again in New York on Monday.

---

[1] Source: National Archives, Nixon Presidential Materials, NSC Files, Box 339, Subject Files, Kissinger/Sisco. Secret; Nodis.

[2] Tab A is telegram 3084 from USUN, September 19; attached but not printed.

[3] Tab B is the June 26 U.S. statement on "Fundamental Principles"; attached but not printed.

Comment:

1. Joe Sisco feels this represents some progress—or at least flexibility for further progress. The fact remains that we are still working around the fringes of the two main issues—peace and security.

2. We are still missing the key ingredient: How much would the Russians press Nasser if we agreed to press Israel on boundaries? Joe's proposal for probing is within the context of his talks. Other less formal probes are possible.

3. In short, yesterday's talk does not really take us anywhere new.

---

81.   Memorandum of Conversation[1]

SecDel/USMC/4   New York, September 22, 1969, 10–11 p.m.

SECRETARY'S DELEGATION TO THE TWENTY-FOURTH SESSION
OF THE UNITED NATIONS GENERAL ASSEMBLY
New York, September, 1969

U.S. Participants
Secretary William P. Rogers
Ambassador Charles W. Yost
Mr. Gerard Smith
Mr. Richard F. Pedersen
Assistant Secretary Martin J. Hillenbrand
Assistant Secretary Joseph J. Sisco
Assistant Secretary Samuel DePalma
Deputy Assistant Secretary Emory C. Swank
Mr. William D. Krimer, Interpreter

U.S.S.R. Participants
Minister of Foreign Affairs Andrey A. Gromyko
Ambassador Yakov A. Malik
Ambassador Anatoliy F. Dobrynin
Ambassador Lev I. Mendelevich
Mr. Yuly M. Vorontsov, Counselor of Embassy in Washington
Mr. Valentin M. Falin, Ministry of Foreign Affairs
Mr. Yevgeniy D. Pyrlin, Ministry of Foreign Affairs
Mr. Viktor M. Sukhodrev, Interpreter

---

[1] Source: National Archives, RG 59, Central Files 1967–69, POL US–USSR. Secret; Exdis. The conversation was held at the Waldorf Towers. Drafted by Krimer and approved by Brown on September 24. On September 17, Sonnenfeldt drafted a letter for Kissinger that Nixon could send to Rogers covering talking points for his upcoming meetings with Gromyko. A covering note reads: "Ed does not have a copy of this letter in his file—nor is it in Dr. K's chron. I don't believe it was ever sent out." (Ibid., Nixon Presidential Materials, NSC Files, Box 711, Country Files, Europe, USSR, Vol. VII)

SALT

Following a private talk with Foreign Minister Gromyko Secretary Rogers stated that Mr. Gromyko had expressed the wish to be able to talk to us in confidence on this subject. The Secretary had assured Mr. Gromyko that what he had to say would be kept confidential within the limitations of our free press. The Secretary then introduced Mr. Gerard Smith as the Director of the U.S. Arms Control and Disarmament Agency and pointed out Mr. Smith's particular interest in this subject.

Foreign Minister Gromyko said that he recognized the importance of this problem; it was under thorough study in the Soviet Union and, he assumed, in the United States as well. The Soviet Union would soon reply to the last U.S. proposals concerning the time and place for preliminary discussions and would also inform us of the composition of the Soviet delegation. The reply will, of course, be positive, since the desirability of holding arms limitation talks follows logically from the position of the Soviet Government.

The Secretary took this occasion to indicate to Mr. Gromyko that our review of the situation in Helsinki had shown that it would be difficult for us to hold the talks there. We would consider Vienna or Geneva to be more suitable for the purpose; we were also receptive to the suggestion of holding the talks in two places on an alternating basis, for example three months in one place to be followed by a like period in another. We did not, however, suggest that Washington and Moscow would be suitable for this purpose.

Ambassador Dobrynin recalled that at the early stages the possibility of preliminary procedural talks in Washington and Moscow has been mentioned.

The Secretary said that in view of the delay which had occurred he did not think it advisable for the preliminary discussions to be held in Moscow or in Washington. As for a permanent site for the talks, we would be happy to consider Soviet suggestions; we were not inflexible and were willing to talk about where the meetings should be held.

Mr. Gromyko repeated once again that for the time being the problem was under study by the Soviet Government and asked not to be prodded into replying to the United States proposal, since such prodding, especially in public, would neither speed nor slow the Soviet reply.

The Secretary replied that we had not intended to prod the Soviet Government into replying, but that we had indicated to the press that we were willing to start the discussions; we were, however, quite relaxed in our position.

Berlin

Foreign Minister Gromyko said that some time ago the United States Government had proposed an exchange of views with the Soviet Government on ways of improving the situation relating to West Berlin. He also thought the present situation there was not normal as a result of certain steps taken by the Government of the Federal Republic of Germany. There was no need at this time to delve deeply into the history of this problem, since this would merely prolong discussion needlessly. In principle he agreed that it would be useful to conduct an exchange of views on this problem between the Governments of the United States and the Soviet Union, but wanted to inquire as to what the U.S. Government had in mind with respect to the results of such an exchange of views. Did the United States intend to have these results reflected in a formal document, as was customary in international practice, or did we merely want to improve the situation de facto on the basis of mutual example; in other words, what did we conceive as possible ways of reflecting the results of the future exchange of views. He suggested that if the Secretary was not ready to reply at the present moment, he might give the problem some thought and return to it at the time of their next meeting on Friday. If this was acceptable, he did want to take this opportunity to suggest Moscow as the place for holding this exchange of opinions.

The Secretary said that he understood that East Germany and West Germany had already entered into discussions on possible ways of improving relations between them, especially with respect to transportation, communications and similar matters. We would be glad if these discussions resulted in better relations between East Germany and West Germany. As for the question of Berlin, both East Berlin and West Berlin, the Secretary believed this to be of concern to the Four Powers and thought that any discussions for improving the situation there should include all four.

Mr. Gromyko emphasized that his remarks were intended to deal with the situation in West Berlin and not with the situation in Germany in general. This did indeed touch upon the interests of the other allies. Some time ago, however, the United States had raised the question of conducting an exchange of views between the Governments of the Soviet Union and the United States; today the Secretary talked about Berlin in terms of the Four Powers. Did this mean that we were withdrawing our suggestion for bilateral discussions? He was simply asking this question in an attempt to understand the Secretary's thinking on the subject and not in order to raise any objections.

The Secretary replied that he thought any discussions concerning the future of Berlin would have to include the other two powers. He would be happy to talk about how this could be brought about. In this connection, however, he was not quite sure what Mr. Gromyko had in mind as to the objectives that might be achieved in talks. The Soviet reply had not been entirely clear to us and we wondered what their ideas were.

Mr. Gromyko said that this was precisely the question he was addressing to the Secretary as representative of the Government which had proposed these discussions. It was he who was asking for clarification. What did the Secretary consider to be the best way of reflecting the results of such an exchange of views? He repeated his earlier suggestion that if the Secretary needed time to consult on this problem, they could return to it at their next meeting. If the Secretary's thinking was in terms of Four Power talks, he did not object in principle and would consider it useful to discuss ways of putting the machinery for such an exchange in motion. He thought this was something both sides should have a chance to consider and return to it later.

The Secretary agreed that this was a good suggestion and said he would be willing to discuss it further next Friday.[2]

Assistant Secretary Hillenbrand remarked that the specific form of any possible agreement, that is, whether it should be a written document or a de facto improvement, would, no doubt, depend upon the course of the discussions and could be considered as we went along.

Mr. Gromyko said that whether the talks were held on a bilateral or on a Four Power basis, inasmuch as communications to and from West Berlin passed through the territory of the German Democratic Republic, his Government would, of course, have to be in consultation with the Government of the GDR. He was just mentioning this "by the way," as it were.

The Secretary agreed to return to this question next Friday.

Middle East

The Secretary said that he and Foreign Minister Gromyko had already had some preliminary discussions on the Middle East, in which the position of each Government had been set forth, and now wanted to talk about what could be done to move the matter forward a bit. He knew that we could not resolve the matter tonight or for some time to come. He wanted to suggest that Ambassador Dobrynin and Assistant Secretary Sisco get together again starting tomorrow to examine the U.S. document submitted in July,[3] in order to identify areas of agreement and areas of disagreement. He and the Foreign Minister could discuss it further on Friday. When we came to points which we could not resolve, the points of agreement and disagreement might be passed

---

[2] September 26.

[3] See Document 67.

on to Jarring to see if negotiations between the parties could eliminate the areas of difficulty.

Mr. Gromyko replied he did not mind; the Ambassador would be ready to start working tomorrow. The Soviet Government was doing everything it could to facilitate a solution of the Middle East problem. He thought that unfortunately Israel was not doing anything to make a solution possible. He also thought the United States was underestimating its possibilities with respect to its ability to influence Israel.

The Secretary remarked that they had discussed the matter earlier. The Foreign Minister had originally said he did not think we were doing enough to influence Israel; now he had put it in a more friendly manner—that we were underestimating our possibilities in that direction. He did think it was urgent to move toward a solution of the Middle East problem and it would be good if Ambassador Dobrynin and Assistant Secretary Sisco could work out something that could be used by a four-power meeting in mid-October. He did not think there was any other way to proceed at present and was glad to see that the Foreign Minister was willing to try.

Soviet Proposals to UN General Assembly

Foreign Minister Gromyko wanted to draw the Secretary's attention to the proposals he had laid before the UN General Assembly. These consisted of two main parts. The first concerns a ban on chemical and biological weapons.[4] This was not a matter of special interest to the Soviet Union alone, but he thought it was in the interests of all powers and states. He would like to have the Secretary study the proposal and approach it objectively to see if some common language could be worked out. The second proposal concerned the maintenance of peace and international security.[5] Although the second proposal was worded in very general language, it did contain some specific provisions. In a word, he wanted to ask the Secretary to study it and he would be very glad if we could find some common language. If our

---

[4] On September 19, in an address before the UN General Assembly, Gromyko proposed an international convention that would prohibit the development, production, and stockpiling of chemical and biological weapons and of their destruction. For a full text, see *Documents on Disarmament, 1969*, pp. 457–459.

[5] In his speech at a plenary meeting of the 24th session of the UN General Assembly on September 19, Gromyko introduced a proposal for "The Strengthening of International Security." A text of Gromyko's speech in which he made this proposal is in United Nations, General Assembly, Twenty-fourth Session, *Official Records*, 1756th Plenary Meeting, September 19, 1969, pp. 7–14. Gromyko's proposal, which was placed on the agenda for the UN General Assembly, is ibid., *Annexes*, Agenda Item 103, Document A/7654 and A/7903, pp. 1–6. International reaction to Gromyko's proposal was tepid. See, for example, Richard Holloran, "Nations Show Little Interest in Pact on A-Arms," *The New York Times*, September 20, 1969, p. 10.

two powers could do anything to lessen international tensions, a great deal would have been accomplished. He thought this was indeed possible.

With respect to the first proposal the Secretary inquired of Mr. Smith if he did not think that this was a matter for the Disarmament Committee in Geneva. Mr. Smith said that would normally be the case. The Secretary went on to say that we were in accord with the objectives stated, but that he, too, was of the opinion that this was a matter normally to be taken up in Geneva. As for the second proposal, he would give it some attention.

Mr. Gromyko said that he did not know what was "normal" with respect to submitting such proposals. There was nothing in the UN Charter to direct any particular approach. He thought the "shortest" way was to lay the proposals directly before the General Assembly. He would like to speed a resolution of this problem, since the passage of time would make its solution more difficult. That was the only consideration the USSR had in putting the matter before the General Assembly.

The Secretary said maybe he had used the wrong word. He felt the CBW issue could be handled more quickly in Geneva. In the GA the proposals were likely to develop into a propaganda exercise.

Mr. Gromyko said that in fact the proposal was already before the Geneva Committee. In any case, he appreciated the Secretary's remarks.

U.S.–U.S.S.R. Maritime Agreement

Foreign Minister Gromyko inquired if the Secretary thought it would be possible to work out a maritime agreement between the United States and the Soviet Union. His country had such agreements with many other nations; in spite of the fact that both our countries were maritime powers there was no specific maritime agreement between us. Ambassador Dobrynin amplified that what they had in mind was an agreement providing for port facilities, entry of merchant vessels and similar questions. Mr. Gromyko said that it would be desirable for our two countries to work out an agreement regulating the question of receiving each other's merchant ships. He was not talking about a trade agreement at this time.

The Secretary replied that he thought we would indeed be very interested in this matter and promised to reply in detail on Friday. He thought that anything we could do in the way of such agreements would be helpful for both our countries.

NPT

The Secretary inquired as to the status of the Nuclear Non-Proliferation Treaty and asked if the Soviet Union was ready to proceed with simultaneous ratification and deposit of the Treaty.

Foreign Minister Gromyko replied that his Government had

started the process of ratification. The Foreign Affairs Commissions of the Supreme Soviet had considered the Treaty and had recommended that the Presidium of the Supreme Soviet take final action on it. The Treaty was now before the Presidium for this final act in the ratification process.

The Secretary said that we had completed all necessary steps short of actual ratification. We felt it would be useful if U.S. and Soviet ratification and deposit of the Treaty took place simultaneously. Putting these final acts on international television would send the Treaty off to a good start.

Mr. Gromyko said his Government would consider this possibility and take appropriate measures to move ratification along. In this connection he wanted to inquire as to the position of the Government of the FRG with respect to accession to the NPT. He had discussed this question with FRG Foreign Minister Brandt. Mr. Brandt had told him he thought the new Government of the FRG, to be formed after the German elections, would take action to sign and ratify the Treaty.

The Secretary said he believed that if the United States and the Soviet Union ratified the NPT, other Governments, including that of the FRG, would do so also. If, on the other hand, our two countries were to continue to hold back, there was the danger that others would lose interest.

Mr. Gromyko said that in his talk with Mr. Brandt the latter had not referred to Soviet ratification as a condition for FRG accession to the Treaty. In any case, he thought the FRG must understand that the NPT was not a matter to be played with, and suggested that the Secretary and he remain in touch to speed completion of ratification and deposit.

The Secretary agreed and remarked that it would be particularly desirable if the Treaty were ratified by both countries before the Strategic Arms Limitation Talks began, in order to spur progress in the direction of control over nuclear weapons. Mr. Gromyko said that this argument had some "reason."

82.   Memorandum From the President's Assistant for National Security Affairs (Kissinger) to President Nixon[1]

Washington, September 23, 1969.

SUBJECT

Kosygin's Mission to Peking

Very little is known of the origins or purposes of Kosygin's visit to Peking.[2] Judging from the characterization of the talks by both sides—"frank" (Chinese) and "useful" (Soviets)—there was no significant movement toward an accommodation.

The fact that the talks were held against a background of sharply-rising border tensions does suggest, however, that each side had an interest in attempting to check what seemed to be a gathering momentum toward large and more serious clashes.

The initiative apparently came from the Soviets, perhaps using the Romanians or North Vietnamese as intermediaries. The Soviets may have seen an advantage in appearing to take the lead in trying to reach an understanding, whether the Chinese agreed to the meeting or not. Should hostilities ensue, the Soviets would thus be in a position to present themselves as the aggrieved party. At the same time, the actual Soviet motive may have been to put on the record for Chinese benefit their refusal to tolerate a protracted border conflict. This is the line they took in recent letters to other Communist parties. It may not necessarily reflect a Soviet decision to escalate, but rather an effort to pressure and deter the Chinese.

The Chinese motive is a question, since so far they have been quite consistent in rejecting third party intervention or direct Soviet appeals. The Chinese willingness to receive Kosygin could reflect the more flexible Chinese diplomacy which seems to have been developing in recent months. However, the Chinese would not wish to appear to be resistant to Kosygin's visit, especially since third parties in the Communist world were apparently involved, and would want to appear at least as "reasonable" as the Soviets. In their public treatment they took

---

[1] Source: National Archives, Nixon Presidential Materials, NSC Files, Box 710, Country Files, Europe, USSR, Vol. V. Secret. The memorandum is stamped "October 6" and bears the handwritten comment "ret'd." as well as a large check mark in the upper righthand corner.

[2] According to a DIA Intelligence Summary of September 12, Kosygin met with Chou En-lai in Peking on September 11, a visit that lasted only 5 hours before the Soviet Premier returned to Moscow. (Central Intelligence Agency, Executive Registry Files, Job 93–T01468R, Box 3, Sino-Soviet Border, August–December 1969)

pains to minimize its significance by stating that Kosygin was merely "on his way home" and that Chou En-lai met him at Peking airport.

US Interests

Until we learn more of the content of the Peking discussion, it is uncertain how our own interests might be affected:

—there is nothing thus far, however, that suggests a new Sino-Soviet diplomatic offensive on Vietnam;
—there is nothing to suggest a narrowing of Sino-Soviet differences on fundamental problems;
—it is at least possible, that the failure of a personal encounter may actually worsen relations;
—sudden moves of this sort do point, however, to the caution which the US should exercise in basing its own actions solely on expected developments in the Sino-Soviet dispute; much of this relationship is still shrouded from us.

Tab A

Intelligence Analysis

Washington, undated.

CIA ANALYSIS OF THE KOSYGIN–CHOU MEETING

There are few facts about the origin of the Kosygin–Chou meeting on 11 September, and none at all about its content or results.[3]

Clearly it was arranged on short notice. When Kosygin left Hanoi, TASS announced that he had departed for Moscow. He made a brief stop at Calcutta and got as far as Dushanbe, in Soviet Central Asia, when his plane altered course and headed for Irkutsk. There it was met by a flight from Moscow which, after a brief stop, headed on for Peking.

---

[3] On September 12, FBI Director J. Edgar Hoover sent information obtained from "an extremely sensitive source" about the Kosygin–Chou En-lai meeting to Helms, Rogers, and Mitchell. According to the FBI source, "both Kosygin and Chou feel it would not be in the best interest of either country to terminate the Vietnam conflict at this time. Both feel that the Vietnam conflict is keeping the United States tied up in that area and that it is bleeding the economy of the United States to support South Vietnam." On September 17, a senior CIA analyst informed the Deputy Director of Current Intelligence of his "grave reservations about the accuracy and value of this [FBI] report." Discrediting the origin of the FBI report and its substance, the analyst concluded that "we do not think that the Sino-Soviet relationship is of the kind that would have allowed either side to discuss future plans on Vietnam as this report alleges." Apparently, the FBI information was discounted in the writing of the attached CIA analysis. An official routing slip to Helms from the Deputy DCI of September 18 reads as follows: "This came in over the weekend—as the contents are nothing really new I did not think it necessary to bother you." (Ibid., Job 80–R015080R, Box 12, Soviet)

The Soviets were the first to announce the meeting, saying the two sides "openly set forth their positions and held a conversation useful to both sides." The Chinese statement, coming a few hours later, was even more terse, saying simply that "frank talks were held" and revealing that the meeting took place at the airport.

Since the meeting, on 11 September, our monitoring has picked up no anti-Chinese polemics in the Soviet press and radio. The same is true for the Chinese radio, but two anti-Soviet press articles appeared on 11 September.

Possible Explanations:

There are several possible explanations for the unexpected and dramatic meeting. One is that the Chinese, well aware of the continuing Soviet build-up along their borders and apprehensive over the increasing speculation that Moscow intended to conduct a preemptive strike against their advanced weapons facilities, asked for the meeting in an effort to calm down their bellicose neighbor. This scenario seems highly unlikely, however. First reports indicate that Chinese propaganda against the Soviets is continuing even after the meeting. Had the Chinese proposed the talks and shown signs of apprehensiveness or fear, the Soviets would have demanded an end to such propaganda as a precondition to any easing of tension. Moreover, the Chinese communiqué on the meeting made it clear that Kosygin was treated with minimum respect during his brief visit—he never even left the airport. This is hardly the kind of treatment he would have received if the Chinese had pressed for the meeting in order to arrange some sort of accommodation with Moscow.

Another possibility is that the Soviets pressed for the meeting in order to present the Chinese with some sort of ultimatum regarding the border. Although Moscow has recently issued stern warnings to Peking through their propaganda media, this explanation for the meeting also seems unlikely. The Soviets would hardly have to send their premier to the Chinese capital to deliver such an ultimatum. Had this been their intention they could have effectively achieved their purpose by calling in the Chinese chargé in Moscow and reading the riot act to him. Furthermore, Kosygin's abrupt reversal of his flight plans in order to reach the Chinese capital seems a rather humiliating prelude to the issuance of some sort of "final warning."

Still another possibility is that the meeting was not directly related to bilateral relations between the two countries but concerned Vietnam. The Chinese may have informed the North Vietnamese that they were cutting off all Soviet arms shipments to Hanoi, for example, and the Vietnamese might have then urged Kosygin to travel to Peking to iron this problem out. Or Hanoi, pointing to Ho Chi Minh's "will," might have again urged the two parties to attempt to compose their differences. However, the North Vietnamese have been urging the two sides to do exactly this for years—with no effect. There is nothing in the present situation which would suggest that such advice would now fall on fertile soil. Moreover, when in the past the Chinese have created difficulties over Soviet arms shipments it has been the North Vietnamese themselves who have taken the initiative in straightening things out— clear indication that Hanoi recognizes that it, rather than Moscow, can apply leverage on Peking in this matter.

Yet another possibility is that a large-scale, but unannounced incident recently occurred somewhere along the Sino-Soviet border—an incident of such gravity that it required direct talks between the two premiers. This scenario would help explain the suddenness of the meeting in Peking, but it would not fit the pattern of previous major incidents occurring in the past year. Both sides have immediately publicized such incidents, and at this juncture neither side would have much motivation to conceal a new clash. Furthermore, a major clash would in all likelihood be reflected in some manner in communications intelligence, and this has not occurred.

It seems most likely that the initiative in calling for the meeting came from the Soviet Union. The Soviets probably believe:

(1) that the course of the Sino-Soviet dispute has reached a dangerous stage. It is hurting them on several fronts. The Chinese, they believe, are trying to "bleed them white" along the border. At the same time, the Soviets are being put at a disadvantage politically because their enemies and their allies as well believe them to be off-balance and on the defensive because of their preoccupation with the Chinese.

(2) Kosygin could have gone to Peking either to issue a last direct warning to the Chinese to cease and desist or face the consequences. We think it more likely that, though he may have talked in uncompromising terms to the Chinese, he was trying to discover whether there was a way to bring the conflict down from its present risky level. The hiatus in propaganda, particularly if it should continue, would point in this direction.

(3) Kosygin may also have proposed further discussions, perhaps including the issue of frontiers. He would, in this case, have made it plain that there can be talk of reducing the potential for border clashes but there can be no question of ceding territory.

(4) Whether an easing of the conflict results from the meeting, the Soviets by sending their premier to Peking will have shown the rest of the world that they were willing to go the last mile toward seeking a solution.

In view of Soviet unease over reports of a preemptive strike, it is possible that Kosygin's sole purpose was to reassure the Chinese. We think it unlikely that this was the main element in Kosygin's visit. It is more likely that he sought, at one and the same time, to indicate to the Chinese that they were not under imminent threat of devastating attack but could expect a strong reaction if there were further trouble on the border.

83.   **Memorandum From the President's Assistant for National Security Affairs (Kissinger) to President Nixon**[1]

Washington, September 26, 1969.

SUBJECT

Bill Rogers' Conversation with Gromyko

On the basis of the summary of the talk in the attached telegram (Tab A),[2] it does not appear that important new ground was broken. Most significant perhaps was Gromyko's assertion that following earlier Soviet optimism about US-Soviet relations, our subsequent decisions on ABM and MIRV[3] had raised "some doubts" in Moscow. This has come to be a standard Soviet theme, although other Soviet spokesmen have tended to cite our China policy and the Romanian trip[4] as sources of Soviet "doubts." I think Bill did well to cite the Soviets own testing of the SS–9 and of new ABMs. But I think we need to do more to make clear to the Soviets that our major problem with them is their support of Hanoi's stonewalling.

Basically, I think we need not be particularly concerned about Soviet professions of "doubts" about us because of our defense program. Moscow is well aware of the debates in this country. They realize that our strategic program has stood still while theirs has progressed rapidly. Comments like those by Gromyko are chiefly designed to provide arguments for our critics and to put us on the defensive. The major obstacle to SALT indeed may be not that we are building up our forces but that we are not. Thus the Soviets may feel they have little to gain from talks.

On specific subjects, the following points are worth noting:

1. *SALT.* Gromyko intimated that the Soviets might soon propose "preliminary" talks. This presumably refers to talks about such things as an agenda and other modalities. It is hard to say whether this cau-

---

[1] Source: National Archives, Nixon Presidential Materials, NSC Files, Box 280, Agency Files, Department of State, Vol. III. Secret; Exdis. Sent for information.

[2] Tab A is telegram 3165 from USUN, September 23, summarizing Rogers' talk with Gromyko on September 22; the memorandum of conversation is Document 81.

[3] At a news conference on March 14, Nixon announced his decision to move forward with the ABM program, which included a Safeguard system, a modified version of Lyndon B. Johnson's Sentinel system. Safeguard called for 12 separate sites for area missile defense, 19 radars, and several hundred interceptor missiles. The Nixon administration also decided to continue MIRV testing. (*Public Papers: Nixon, 1969*, pp. 208–216)

[4] See footnote 3, Document 65.

tion is due to problems of decision-making in Moscow or reflects a Soviet judgment that we are, or should be, more eager about SALT than
they. In any case, we should probably accept preliminary talks, if the
Soviets propose them and I will make sure that the Under Secretaries
Committee of the NSC, which is charged with backstopping SALT, will
prepare the necessary contingency papers for your review.

2. *Berlin.* Gromyko showed some interest in bilateral talks with us.
You had hinted at this possibility in your letter to Kosygin last April.[5]
The Soviets undoubtedly sense a good deal of Western interest in talking about Berlin, especially in the SPD and FDP in Germany which
may form the next government in Bonn. In fact, even if one could make
a case that the Soviets might be interested in a modus vivendi, there
are no signs that they will be prepared to buck the GDR's continued
interest in keeping the situation unsettled. Negotiations, whether bilateral US-Soviet or four power are therefore likely to encounter a rigid
Soviet-GDR position, while we, especially if Brandt became Chancellor, would be under pressure from our allies to come up with "constructive" proposals. And in Berlin our negotiating position is weak;
the other side holds all the cards. We thus have no interest in pushing
Berlin negotiations at this time, although we will undoubtedly come
under pressure to do so and may in the end have to go along.

3. *Middle East.* Gromyko clearly showed interest in continuing US-
Soviet contacts and these have been going forward in New York on the
basis of the documents exchanged during the summer. He stressed the
"urgency" of the subject, an attitude that is at least to some degree genuine in view of Soviet anxiety over the possibility of new full-scale hostilities in which they might again have to confront the awkward choices
of how to bail out their defeated clients. Presumably with Mrs. Meir's
visit[6] in mind, Gromyko urged the greater use of our influence in Israel. Despite Gromyko's assurance that the Soviets would do everything possible toward a settlement, it remains quite doubtful that their
definition of a settlement corresponds to ours.

4. *NPT.* Gromyko seemed not to foreclose the possibility of joint
US-Soviet ratification as we have repeatedly proposed. The Soviets will
presumably decide on their course after the German election of September 28. (Brandt told Gromyko that the FRG will sign if the SPD
wins the election. I think if the SPD leads the next coalition, this will
be the case.) I understand that people at State are thinking of a major ceremony with full TV coverage in the event the Soviets agree to
joint ratification, and Bill apparently discussed this possibility with

---

[5] See Document 28. On April 22, Beam presented Nixon's letter to Kosygin.
[6] Israeli Prime Minister Golda Meir visited Washington September 25–27.

Gromyko and UK Foreign Secretary Stewart. I think this kind of exercise would carry overtones of "condominium" and we would do well to avoid excessive atmospherics.

5. *Bilateral.* Gromyko again expressed interest in an agreement to permit Soviet merchant ships to put into US ports. This subject is under review and in principle probably should be decided favorably. But we will want to time any decision carefully so that it fits into our overall policy.

All told, I do not believe that the conversation warrants the optimistic interpretation that appeared on the front page of the *Washington Post* of September 24[7] which was based on US backgrounding in New York.[8]

---

[7] *The Washington Post* carried a cover story entitled "U.S.-Soviets Talks Buoy Americans," by Chalmers Roberts.

[8] At the bottom of the page, Nixon wrote: "K (eyes only) It may become in our interest for the Israeli to heat things up in the Mideast—The *Soviet* could be more embarrassed by this than we would be."

---

84.   Memorandum From Helmut Sonnenfeldt of the National Security Council Staff to the President's Assistant for National Security Affairs (Kissinger)[1]

Washington, September 26, 1969.

SUBJECT

Your Talk With Dobrynin

We were asked to do a talking paper. As always, one can speculate endlessly on why Dobrynin wants to see you; on the issues that amount to anything, you know better than I what you want to tell him. For what it's worth, so you might prepare your thoughts, following are some guesses about what he wants to talk about:

1. *Gromyko Coming Down to see the President.* There may be something of an Alphonse-and-Gaston game, with the Soviets waiting to be invited and we waiting to get a request. If Dobrynin fences around on this subject, I suggest you cut it short and agree to an appointment

---

[1] Source: National Archives, Nixon Presidential Materials, NSC Files, Box 489, President's Trip Files, Dobrynin/Kissinger, 1969, Part 1. Secret; Nodis.

(assuming the President is prepared to see him). Bear in mind that Gromyko is supposed to leave Wednesday, October 1, to go to Canada for a couple of days and thence directly home. One further angle: you had better settle the text of any announcement or press comment so that we don't get into the ridiculous hassle that Brandt had last year as to who requested the interview. I will spare you now any speculation as to what Gromyko may want to say to the President, but you might ask Dobrynin.

2. *Vietnam.* You know my views.

3. *SALT.* Doubtful that he would want or need to see you if the Soviets have fresh word on this. If there is a complicated or tricky procedural proposal, take note of it and promise an answer later. If he has some substantive question to raise, play it by ear.

4. *Berlin.* Very unlikely reason or topic. If it comes up, you might ask him why we should have talks at all. (Remember the President proposed talks in his Berlin speech[2] and in his letter to Kosygin in April.)[3]

5. *China.* He may have some message on this, perhaps relating to the talk of a Soviet pre-emptive strike. If he does, you could expound our declaratory policy.

6. *Soviet "Doubts" About the President's Intentions.* This involves our China policy, the Romanian trip and our defense budget.

7. *NPT ratification.* They may be ready to move. Rogers told them we would have a big ceremony. I doubt that we should.

---

[2] See footnote 7, Document 13.
[3] Document 28.

---

85.   Memorandum of Conversation[1]

Washington, September 27, 1969, 3 p.m.

SUBJECT

Meeting Between Dr. Kissinger and Ambassador Dobrynin

---

[1] Source: National Archives, Nixon Presidential Materials, NSC Files, Box 489, President's Trip Files, Dobrynin/Kissinger, 1969, Part 1. Top Secret; Sensitive. The meeting was held in Kissinger's office. Forwarded by Kissinger to the President under an October 1 covering memorandum that summarized the conversation. (Ibid.)

PARTICIPANTS

> Dr. Kissinger
> Ambassador Dobrynin

Ambassador Dobrynin came to see me at his request. I let him wait for a week but agreed to a brief appointment on Saturday afternoon.

After an exchange of pleasantries, Dobrynin remarked that his Minister regretted not having had an opportunity for a longer chat with me. Had Gromyko been able to visit Washington, Dobrynin would have given a luncheon for him and me at the Soviet Embassy. The absence of a visit to Washington made Gromyko's trip somewhat unusual. I said I regretted that his Foreign Minister did not come to Washington, as I would have enjoyed talking to him, and was sorry his schedule was so crowded. Dobrynin replied that the difficulty was the absence of a meeting with the President, which had been a standard procedure during previous visits to the General Assembly. I told him that in order to keep ourselves from being swamped we had adopted the rule that no Foreign Minister would see the President in Washington. In any event, there had never been a formal request. Dobrynin said he was not aware that there were such fine questions of protocol.

Dobrynin then remarked that his Minister had asked him to inquire whether in negotiating the Berlin issue we had any preference as to forum. Specifically, did we care whether it was discussed in a four-power or two-power forum? While the Soviet Union was willing to speak in a four-power forum, it was also prepared to have two-power discussions. I told him that four-power discussions seemed to be quite acceptable. If there was any different inclination on the part of the President, I would let him know.

Dobrynin then turned to the Middle East and said that the meeting in New York had been very constructive. Gromyko hoped that he would be able to come to a preliminary agreement with the Secretary of State before his departure on Wednesday. He asked for intercession of the White House in expediting this agreement. I replied that since matters seemed to be in train on the diplomatic level, there was no need for White House intervention. I added that Dobrynin should understand our elemental position. We had made several communications to the Soviet Union on Vietnam to which they had never replied. While this did not inhibit normal diplomatic relations, it made it very difficult for the White House to go beyond what normally occurred on the diplomatic level.

At this point, the President called.[2] When the conversation was completed, I commented that the President had called me at a provi-

---

[2] According to Kissinger's October 1 covering memorandum, he and Nixon had prearranged the telephone call.

dential moment because it enabled me to tell the President directly what was being discussed. To us Vietnam was the critical issue. We were quite prepared to discuss other subjects, but the Soviet Union should not expect any special treatment until Vietnam was solved. They should also have no illusions about the seriousness with which we took Hanoi's attempt to undermine the domestic position of the President. Dobrynin asked me whether there was any hope for a coalition government. I replied that we had covered the subject at great length previously and that I could add nothing. It was a pity that all our efforts to negotiate had failed. The President had told me in his call that the train had just left the station and was now headed down the track. Dobrynin responded that he hoped it was an airplane and not a train and would leave some maneuvering room. I said the President chooses his words very carefully and that I was sure he meant train.

Dobrynin then asked what our problem had been in the past. I said that every negotiation turned into a discussion on our readiness to accept the 10 points.[3] We could not negotiate in a forum of ultimatums. Dobrynin said that my own conversations with the Vietnamese seemed to have gone rather well. I asked him what he meant. He said Hanoi had told Moscow that they had been very impressed by my presentation and thought I understood Vietnamese conditions very well. I replied that if this were true the next move was up to them.

Dobrynin then engaged in a lengthy exposition to the effect that the Soviet Union, for its own reasons, was interested in peace in Vietnam and had in the past often been helpful. I countered that we had no illusions about Soviet help in the past. It had been considerably in the interest of Hanoi and had been largely tactical. Dobrynin said that he wanted to assure me of Moscow's continued interest in improved relations with the U.S., but it was getting very difficult to convince Moscow of our goodwill. There had been no real progress on any subject. For example, we could have been more generous on trade liberalization. I said the most important issue was Vietnam. As soon as Vietnam was out of the way and especially if the Russians took an understanding attitude, we would go further. Dobrynin smiled and said that I had an unusual ability to link things together. I told him that we had hoped to have a reply on SALT. Dobrynin said there would be a reply in due course but did not give any indication as to when.

Dobrynin returned to the subject of Soviet interest in improving relations with us. I said we reciprocated this feeling, especially after Vietnam was out of the way.

---

[3] The delegation of the National Liberation Front of South Vietnam presented a Ten-Point Peace Program at the Paris Peace Talks on May 8, 1969. The text of this program is in *Documents on American Foreign Relations, 1968–1969*, pp. 249–252.

86.   Transcript of Telephone Conversation Between President Nixon and his Assistant for National Security Affairs (Kissinger)[1]

Washington, September 27, 1969, 4:40 p.m.

Mr. Kissinger said he was just going to call the President when this call came in. He said he had an interesting conversation with Dobrynin.[2] He came in with two stupid questions: (1) whether we want to have the Berlin talks to be quadripartite or bilateral, and (2) he wanted us to use our influence to see that Gromyko and the President get together before Gromyko leaves on Wednesday[3] (K interjected here he thinks the State people have practically given away our position). K told D his call was providential—as far as the White House is concerned, we have no great incentives; D owes us an answer to the question given him in May and another in the conversation K had with him in April. As far as we are concerned, the train has left the station. The Soviets have a choice of believing the President or the *New York Times* and K, if he could advise him, would recommend that they believe the President.

D said one other thing—he knew of K's meeting in Paris.[4] K asked him what he knew. D said Hanoi told them this was the best conversation they had had and they thought something might come of it. K said if it does, they will have to make the move. We are not going to make the move, to which D didn't really respond. D said there are a lot of arguments in the Soviet Union, and they feel we are not willing to move very fast on Soviet-American relations in general. D did not mention SALT, but mentioned trade, for example. K told him that the President had told D, and K had told D, that we are going very far on trade, but we aren't going to let Communist countries supported by the Soviet Union chop us out. K said he had been very tough with D— he didn't give an inch.

K told the President he didn't think we should move very fast on the Middle East. P said the point is we can't deliver. K said that is not

---

[1] Source: National Archives, Nixon Presidential Materials, NSC Files, Box 489, President's Trip Files, Dobrynin/Kissinger, 1969, Part 1. Top Secret; Sensitive. A covering memorandum indicates that it was sent to Howe, Haig, and Lake.

[2] See Document 85.

[3] Gromyko left New York on Wednesday, October 1, where he attended the United States General Assembly and held U.S.-Soviet ministerial discussions with Rogers on September 22, 26, and 30; see Documents 81 and 87, and footnote 1, Document 85.

[4] Kissinger met secretly with North Vietnamese officials Xuan Thuy and Mai Van Bo in Paris on August 4. Kissinger's memorandum to Nixon about his conversation is in *Foreign Relations*, 1969–1976, volume VI, Vietnam, January 1969–July 1970, Document 106.

what they are asking. They want us to agree to a piece of paper for Jarring to deliver. K said they aren't anxious to get something in the Middle East—their problems with the Egyptians must be very serious. He wanted us to be very forthcoming.

P wanted to know D's attitude. K said they want major improvements in relations with us. He said they always run into trouble. He was asked in Moscow what advance has been made, and he couldn't answer. K told him he could have said "the SALT talks." D said there will be a positive answer pretty soon, but he didn't say any more about it. K said he doesn't believe the U.S. should be in a pleading position on it. He thinks we could play it the other way. If we go the hard route, and can keep them quiet, that is what we want. P said he is keenly aware that we don't want to take the hard route and make them mad. He asked K, "You have no doubt but that he is reminded of the fact we are going the hard route?" K said yes; he had been very tough on him. D has asked what K thought of the Sino-Soviet problem. K had said the Soviets have a big geopolitical problem that no death is going to solve. D had asked K whether he thought they (the Soviets) were going to attack the Chinese. K had replied that, as a historian, he thought the Soviets were considering it.

D had said something about Romania[5]—he asked who thought of it. K had replied that every fundamental decision here is made by the President, and he wasn't going to give D a checklist of who made the various proposals.

D had asked whether we had any response from the Chinese on the change in travel restrictions. K had replied that D knew as well as he that the Chinese move in very complicated ways (which didn't really give an answer to his question). K said he had been personally much more aloof with D than before.

P asked what had been said about Vietnam. K told him D had said we may not believe it, but the Soviets have a real interest in ending this war, but for different reasons than ours. K told him we have no evidence of this. K said D had said they had been helpful on the shape of the table, to which K replied that they were helpful to Hanoi on that. K gave no encouragement here, and wasn't really very pleasant. He had reminded D that we have a problem—there can be no movement until they show us.

The President said, "The summit and trade they can have, but I'll be damned if they can get the Middle East, etc." K said he doesn't see what we gain by going to a fall-back position on the Middle East. His

---

[5] See footnote 3, Document 65.

instinct for handling this, would be for Rogers to tell Gromyko we will give our answer to Dobrynin in about two weeks.

K said he thinks D came to see him to let him know they knew about K's Paris meeting, and to fix an invitation for Gromyko to see the President. D had said in all previous administrations Gromyko had been received by the President. K told D that Gromyko hadn't asked for a meeting. K told the President if Gromyko asks for a meeting, formally, the President will have to see him, but if he doesn't, K doesn't think we should invite him. K said D came back to this two or three times—(Gromyko would love to have an invitation). K further doesn't think we should encourage him to ask for an appointment.

K said to the President on the Middle East, it would help us if we didn't do anything right now—it could be done in about 10 days to 2 weeks between Sisco and Dobrynin. K said he didn't know whether Rogers will make a formal proposition—he hadn't been in touch with K. P said waiting makes sense.

P said the papers had made a big thing about Gromyko getting a warmer reception than he.[6] The reason is obvious—all the Middle East had to be silent to him; we have nothing to offer the Africans; and we didn't mention Latin America. He said he felt it was foolish to go up there. K said he didn't think the President got a cool reception; he couldn't count on the newspapers giving such a distorted picture. The President said we said things not calculated to get a warm reception.

Getting back to D and Vietnam, P asked K whether he saw much movement. K's response was that the fact that D told him about his Paris conversation, and that Hanoi considers that the most useful conversation they have had, he (K) considers positive. D had said in watching the President's news conference, it was clear the President isn't going to make any major concessions, and that it was useful to get this on the table. K thinks we will get a move within the next month.

P mentioned the demonstrations coming up on October 15. He said the Democratic National Chairman had been meeting with the doves, at the same time of his press conference, to make Vietnam a political issue. P said he didn't hit this hard with Haldeman, but he feels the real attack should be on them. K agreed, saying they got us into the war. P said our people have to start fighting harder. K said the press conference was essential and extremely helpful. He thinks events of the last two or three weeks show the long route cannot possibly work. The President agreed, especially with our 60,000-man withdrawal, reduction of the draft by 50,000 and Ho Chi Minh's death. The doves

---

[6] On September 18, Nixon addressed the 24th Session General Assembly of the United Nations. For text, see *Public Papers: Nixon, 1969*, pp. 724–731.

and the public are making it impossible to happen. He asked K, if in his planning, he could pick this up so that we make the tough move before the 15th of October. K said yes. P said he had been wondering if we shouldn't—he doesn't want to appear to be making the tough move after the 15th just because of the rioting at home. K said there is a problem, however—if Hanoi takes us seriously, and they wouldn't have told Moscow if they weren't taking it seriously, we shouldn't confuse them. If we want them to make the move, we should give them time—two weeks. His only worry is that if we went ahead with the tough move before the 15th—and there is a 10% chance Hanoi might want to move, if we hit them before they have a chance to make the move, it will look as if we tricked them. He said the President might want to consider another press conference before the 15th or a television report, saying "these people (demonstrators, etc.) are dividing the country and making it impossible to settle the problem on a reasonable basis." P said he would just as soon have them demonstrate against the plan. If we went ahead and moved, the country is going to take a dimmer view after the move than before. P would like to nip it before the first demonstration, because there will be another one on November 15. P reminded that Laird had said for three months after we do this, it will have relatively high public support. K said as an assistant, he had to give P the dark side. He suggested again the possibility of P going on television before the demonstration—possibly around Oct 10.

P said okay; they had had an interesting day; and he would see K on Monday. If Rogers calls, P will try to cool off that thing. K said Rogers can be generally positive but defer an answer for two weeks.

---

87.   Telegram From Secretary of State Rogers to the Department of State[1]

New York, September 27, 1969, 1817Z.

Secto 68/3276. Discussion of Middle East at Rogers–Gromyko meeting September 26.

---

[1] Source: National Archives, Nixon Presidential Materials, NSC Files, Box 292, Agency Files, Rogers Bilateral Talks at UN, 9/15/69–10/7/69. Secret; Priority; Nodis. Repeated to Moscow, Amman, Beirut, Cairo, and Tel Aviv. On September 29, Nixon received this telegram as part of the President's Daily Brief. (Ibid., Box 11, President's Daily Briefs)

1. Secretary met alone with Gromyko last evening for about 45 minutes before dinner and about one hour and fifteen minutes after dinner.

2. In conversation before dinner Gromyko opened conversation by asking what Mrs. Meir agreed to about the Middle East. Secretary responded that Mrs. Meir did not agree to do anything: that she was very firm in her position that Arabs must make it completely clear that they intend to seek a lasting peace with Israel and to renounce their previously stated goal of eventual destruction of Israel. Gromyko said he was certain this could be accomplished but that he thought the United States should do more to make Israel agree to responsible terms. Secretary explained that we are not in a position to force Israel to accept a settlement. Secretary then asked Gromyko if Soviet Union in a position to force Arabs to do things against their will. Gromyko replied with a smile, "well, we can bring them along some."

3. Gromyko inquired about Rhodes formula[2] and whether Mrs. Meir had shown any interest in such a procedure. Secretary stated that the United States felt that it might provide a way of getting more active negotiations underway and that Mrs. Meir did not oppose suggestion when it was discussed with her. Secretary pointed out, however, that Mrs. Meir said she would want to know more about framework for negotiations before agreeing to formula.

4. Gromyko then mentioned that Riad had told him he thought Rhodes formula might provide a way of getting negotiations started and he knew Riad had talked to Secretary about this possibility.

5. Secretary then suggested to Gromyko that Amb. Dobrynin and Sisco meet beginning Monday[3] to attempt to agree on a document dealing with the UAR-Israeli aspects of the settlement. Purpose of meeting would be to work toward a common Soviet-U.S. position paper on basis of following elements: (1) a binding commitment to a durable and permanent peace; (2) acceptance of principle of choice for refugees based on an annual quota to be repatriated and an understanding on an overall limitation; (3) freedom of passage through straits of Tehran [*Tiran*] and Suez; (4) parties would be expected to negotiate on basis all options open on following items—(a) security arrangements in Sharm El-Shaikh; (b) final disposition of Gaza, and (c) arrangements of

---

[2] Reference is to the negotiation of armistice agreements between Israel and the Arab states January–March 1949. The negotiations took place at Rhodes with Ralph Bunche serving as UN Acting Mediator. The negotiations involved separate meetings on substantive items between Bunche and each delegation until discussions reached an advanced stage, whereupon joint informal meetings were held.

[3] September 29.

demilitarized zones; (d) it would be understood that Soviet Union and United States would encourage parties to negotiate on (a), (b) and (c) on basis of Rhodes formula and under auspices of Jarring.

6. Gromyko asked Secretary how he thought the matter should proceed from that point on. Secretary said that if this procedure could be agreed upon between Soviet Union and United States it would then be forwarded to four powers for their consideration at a meeting toward end of October and that thereafter four powers would attempt to arrange for beginning of negotiations based on Rhodes formula sometime in November, Gromyko agreed that this an acceptable procedure seriously to consider.

7. Gromyko then asked questions on specific issues. He asked if proposal Secretary made suggested that border between Egypt and Israel would be pre-1967 border. Secretary said he not in a position to make that commitment but thought something along those lines might be worked out, assuming Sharm El-Shaikh issue and other aspects above could be satisfactorily resolved. Gromyko then repeated Soviet position on Sharm El-Shaikh to which Secretary replied that he thought that was a matter which should be thoroughly discussed in negotiations between the parties.

8. Gromyko also asked reasons for our opposition to reference to Constantinople convention. Secretary set forth our reasoning stating that he saw no reason to make reference to another document in agreement and, furthermore, it might be construed to be an indirect way of giving UAR unilateral right to close canal to Israel at any time it thought it might be in interest of their national defense. Gromyko said he had worked matter out very carefully with UAR and that express language in the treaty provides there could be no discrimination. He felt that it provided a stronger basis for assurance to Israel than otherwise. Secretary told Gromyko we could exchange views on legal aspects but if Soviet position was that Israel could have free passage through Suez Canal on same basis as all other nationals without any possibility of discrimination he felt sure a formulation could be worked out.

9. Gromyko raised refugee question again and a fairly extended discussion took place with a suggested ceiling of 100,000 over a ten year period. Secretary under impression that from standpoint of Soviet Union they felt some solution could be worked out along those lines although this was not explicitly stated.

10. When Gromyko raised the question, Secretary indicated that subject of West Bank also a matter that should be left open to negotiation between Israel and Jordan. Gromyko did not oppose the suggestion.

11. Secretary said that it position of United States that Jerusalem should be a united city and that question of her sovereignty should be a matter of negotiations between parties at a later date. Secretary

indicated that Israel's position was that it would be unwilling to relinquish all or any part of its claimed sovereignty over Jerusalem.

12. Secretary told Gromyko that discussion they were having was of a tentative nature and that no final agreement could be reached between Soviet Union and United States until matter reduced to writing so that there could be no possible misunderstanding between them. Secretary pointed out that in interest of our future relations it is quite important that before any agreement is reached that we clearly understand exactly what is involved. Gromyko said that he agreed with that and would be pleased to meet with Secretary again before he leaves New York with idea of discussing in specific detail the suggested course of action.

Rogers

---

88.   Memorandum From the President's Assistant for National Security Affairs (Kissinger) to President Nixon[1]

Washington, September 29, 1969.

SUBJECT

The US Role in Soviet Maneuvering Against China

In the last two months, the increase in Sino-Soviet tensions has led the Soviets to sound out numerous American contacts on their attitude toward a possible Soviet air strike against China's nuclear/missile facilities or toward other Soviet military actions. These probes have varied in character from point-blank questioning of our reaction to provocative musings by Soviets over what they might be forced to do against the Chinese, including the use of nuclear weapons. Some of these contacts have featured adamant denials that the Soviets were planning any military moves—thereby keeping the entire issue alive. (Secretary Rogers' Memorandum on this subject is at Tab A.)

---

[1] Source: National Archives, Nixon Presidential Materials, NSC Files, Box 337, Subject Files, HAK/Richardson Meetings, May 1969–December 1969. Secret. Sent for action. Drafted by Sonnenfeldt. This memorandum was sent as an enclosure to an October 23 memorandum on items to discuss with Elliot Richardson; see footnote 4 below.

Our contingency planning for major Sino-Soviet hostilities is well along, and NSC consideration of a basic policy paper on the Sino-Soviet dispute is scheduled for October 8.[2]

Meanwhile, I am concerned about our response to these probes. The Soviets may be quite uncertain over their China policy, and our reactions could figure in their calculations. Second, the Soviets may be using us to generate an impression in China and the world that we are being consulted in secret and would look with equanimity on their military actions.

A related issue is the shifting Soviet attitude on Chinese representation in the UN. We have had two indications that the Soviets, in an effort to keep the Chinese Communists out of the UN through indirection, are dangling the prospect before us of cooperation on the representation issue. Gromyko, in his UN speech, of course failed to mention Peking's admission for the first time.[3]

I believe we should make clear that we are not playing along with these tactics, in pursuance of your policy of avoiding the appearance of siding with the Soviets.

The principal gain in making our position clear would be in our stance with respect to China. The benefits would be long rather than short-term, but they may be none the less real. Behavior of Chinese Communist diplomats in recent months strongly suggests the existence of a body of opinion, presently submerged by Mao's doctrinal views, which might wish to put US/Chinese relations on a more rational and less ideological basis than has been true for the past two decades.

Recommendation:

That you authorize me to ask the Department of State to prepare instructions to the field setting forth guidance to be used with the USSR and others, deploring reports of a Soviet plan to make a preemptive military strike against Communist China.[4]

---

[2] See Document 79.

[3] Gromyko's speech before the UN General Assembly on September 19 mentioned all Socialist countries except the People's Republic of China and also avoided the issue of UN membership for the PRC. (United Nations, General Assembly, Twenty-fourth Session, *Official Records*, 1756th Plenary Meeting, September 19, 1969, pp. 7–14)

[4] Nixon initialed the approve option and added: "Base it on 'reports which have come here—etc.' " On October 23 Kissinger apparently asked Richardson to "prepare instructions to the field setting forth guidance for deploring reports on a Soviet plan to make a preemptive military strike against Communist China" based on Nixon's comments on this paper.

Tab A

Memorandum From Secretary of State Rogers to President Nixon

Washington, September 10, 1969.

SUBJECT

The Possibility of a Soviet Strike Against Chinese Nuclear Facilities

Soviet Embassy Second Secretary Davydov brought up the idea of a Soviet attack on Chinese nuclear facilities in a Washington luncheon conversation with a Department officer on August 18. I am enclosing the memorandum of conversation[5] which details the rationale for such a move which he adduced in asking what the United States reaction might be.

Davydov's conversation was unusual for the length of the argument that he presented for such a Soviet course of action. None of the other occasional references to the idea in talks with Soviets which have come to our attention have spelled out such a justification.

—In late March or early April Kosygin's son-in-law Gvishiani and Professor Artsimovich who were visiting in Boston reportedly said that the USSR would have to destroy Communist China's nuclear arsenal. They seemed to be soliciting the reaction of the American to whom they were speaking.

—Italian Communist Rossana Rossanda has claimed that, in July, the Italian Communist leadership received a message from Moscow asking how the Italians would react if, in self-defense, the Soviet Union were forced to make a preventive strike against Chinese missile and atomic installations. On the basis of past experience, Rossanda is not to be taken too literally as a reporter, and a more accurate version of her information may be contained in a Finnish Communist account of the consultations in Moscow at the World Communist Conference in June. According to this report, a Soviet leader then asserted that the USSR had a capability to deal China an immediate mortal blow (presumably more than just a strike at nuclear facilities), but did not wish to do something so "un-Leninist," except as an extreme defensive measure.

—In June the science editor of *Izvestia's* Sunday supplement asked an American Embassy officer in Moscow what the American reaction

---

[5] Attached but not printed.

to a possible Soviet attack (nature of the blow not specified) on China might be. The same Russian has avoided the subject more recently, and in response to the American's latest query two weeks ago, the editor merely said that the USSR was trying to better its relations with China. In July Sidney Liu of *Newsweek* was asked by Delyusin of the Soviet Institute of Asian and African Affairs what he thought the Chinese popular reaction would be to a major Soviet attack on China (the nature of the attack was not otherwise defined in the report).

—A Soviet communication to foreign Communist parties in early August left an impression of great concern over the future of Sino-Soviet relations, but neither of the two accounts of the message that we have indicates that it discussed such specific courses of action as a strike against Chinese nuclear facilities.

—Finally, the most recent Soviet statement on the subject was by Southeast Asia Chief Kapitsa of the Foreign Ministry who insisted to a Canadian newsman that a Soviet strike against Chinese nuclear targets was "unthinkable" and that the very idea was an invention of the Western press.

It is extremely unlikely that Davydov would be privy to top-level Soviet discussions on this matter, much less any decisions taken. Rather, it is likely that he has been given the job of getting as much information as he can on American attitudes on the China issue, and his questioning about the strike hypothesis was in the context of trying to elicit discussion of American views of Sino-Soviet relations. The idea of a strike against Chinese nuclear targets is one which has been mentioned in the United States press and talked about among diplomats and newsmen in Washington. Moreover, Davydov had been asked—at a meeting with Congressional interns a few days before the above cited luncheon—what he thought the United States attitude ought to be in the event of a Sino-Soviet war, and thus would have had occasion to have thought through some of the argumentation he used in the memorandum.

What emerges clearly from the foregoing evidence—as well as from Soviet leaders' speeches, from Moscow's propaganda, and from clandestine source reports on Soviet diplomatic anxieties—is an obvious sense of Soviet concern over troubles with China and of great interest in how others view Sino-Soviet tensions. What remains doubtful is whether the Soviets have ordered their officials systematically to canvass for reactions to a specific potential course of action—attack on Chinese nuclear targets. Nevertheless, the Department has considered the possibility that Davydov's conversation might have been the first move in such a probing operation, and, with that in view, has alerted key American posts abroad to be certain to report analogous conversations. The only response so far was from the American Embassy in

Rome. A Soviet First Secretary told Italian officials he foresaw new and more serious incidents; he was not reported to have sought reactions and there was no reference in the report to the idea of a strike against Chinese nuclear facilities.

In the absence of a cluster of such reports in a relatively short time, it would appear that Davydov's recent conversation, as well as the remarks in Boston five months ago, are curiosities rather than signals. It is certain that Moscow remains preoccupied with its Chinese problem, and the Kremlin is probably reviewing all of its options. Thus the possibility of a Soviet strike at Chinese nuclear facilities cannot be ruled out. Nevertheless, my advisers and I do not believe such a move to be probable. The Soviets would have to weigh the risk of triggering an all-out war with China, a war for which the Soviets are not likely to believe themselves yet well prepared despite their buildup since 1965. Moreover, they would not be sure of getting the entire inventory of Chinese bombs, and would in any case face the prospect that the Chinese would most likely rebuild their nuclear arsenal with renewed determination.

The National Intelligence Estimate of August 12, 1969[6] on the Sino-Soviet dispute notes that a conventional air strike aimed at destroying China's missile and nuclear facilities might be the most attractive military option available to Moscow, if the Soviets believed that they could do this without getting involved in a prolonged and full-scale war. The National Intelligence Estimate did not think it likely that the Kremlin would reach this conclusion, but felt that there was some chance that it would. Considering all of the military, political, economic, foreign policy, and ideological implications of any such Soviet attack, the Department's analysts judge that the chances of this particular course of action are still substantially less than fifty-fifty and that Sino-Soviet conflict, if it does occur, might more likely result from escalation of border clashes. That assessment seems reasonable to me.

WPR

---

[6] Document 73.

89.   Memorandum From Harold Saunders of the National
       Security Council Staff to the President's Assistant for
       National Security Affairs (Kissinger)[1]

Washington, September 30, 1969, 5 p.m.

SUBJECT

US–USSR Talks as of Mid-Day, Tuesday, September 30

Since things may move quickly in the next twenty-four hours, here is a wrapup of *where we stand just prior to Secretary Rogers' final meeting with Gromyko.* Sisco has the sense this afternoon that the Soviets may try to reach some sort of agreement in tonight's meeting and press Sisco and Dobrynin into midnight session to hammer something out. Gromyko leaves tomorrow (Wednesday) afternoon.

On the basis of this morning's meeting, Joe says Dobrynin seems to be playing with the idea of a shorter document trading Rhodes-type talks for something like Joe's new formula—subject to agreement on Gaza, Sharm al-Shaikh and demilitarization, the UAR-Israel boundary would be the pre-war line. Joe understands your instruction not to go all the way while Mrs. Meir is here—but the Secretary might ask reconsideration if he felt he had something worthwhile.

Joe's present document might thus drop suddenly into history. But as background and in case it does not, here is a *rundown on where the Sisco–Dobrynin talks stand:*

On 23 September, Dobrynin provided the clearest reading yet of the Soviet position (Tab A)[2] in the course of a point by point review of our July document (Tab B).[3] He gave the impression that the Soviets are ready to clear out some of the underbrush by reaching agreement on the wording of less important points, but there was little movement on the more difficult issues.

Summarized below is the discussion on each of the points in our July document:

1. *Direct talks.* The reference in the last preambular paragraph to the parties "convening under the auspices of Jarring" is still unac-

---

[1] Source: National Archives, Nixon Presidential Materials, NSC Files, Box 710, Country Files, Europe, USSR, Vol. V. Secret; Nodis. Sent for information. A notation on the memorandum indicates that Kissinger saw it on October 3.

[2] Tab A is telegram 3217 from USUN, September 24; attached but not printed.

[3] Tab B is the Joint U.S.–USSR Draft of Fundamental Principles, the U.S. counterproposal to the Soviet June 17 Middle East position, delivered by Sisco to Gromyko on July 15; attached but not printed.

ceptable to the Soviets. We interpret this to mean direct negotiations at some stage, leaving it to Jarring to determine how and when to get the parties together. Dobrynin said the Soviets do not bar eventual direct talks but could not commit the USSR now. [Comment: Later developments suggest they would give on Rhodes-type talks now in return for a US position on Washington to the pre-war line.][4]

2. *Phasing withdrawal.* Dobrynin is still pushing mildly for a two-stage withdrawal, which would permit clearing of the Canal to begin early. (Point 1)

3. *Canal clearing.* Dobrynin wanted nothing in the document about using of the facilities of the UN to clear the Suez Canal since this restricts the UAR's sovereignty of choice. [Comment: We can drop that.]

4. *Timing effective date of agreement.* Dobrynin continued to press the distinction between de jure and de facto peace so as to create points both at the beginning and at the end of withdrawal when positive steps toward peace could be identified. It was agreed that a further effort would be made to find language that would not get tangled up with the legal status of peace and would meet the problem of Egyptian and Israelis mutual suspicions. (Point 3)

5. *Fedayeen.* Dobrynin wanted to drop the Arab obligation to control the fedayeen. Joe resisted but agreed it might be moved elsewhere in the document. (Point 3)

6. *Boundaries.* Sisco restated and maintained our position without change, and suggested going back to it at a later stage. Our fallback was not revealed. (Point 4)

7. *Demilitarized zones.* Dobrynin said we were close to agreement. After indicating that the Soviets want some demilitarized area on the Israeli side of the boundary, he agreed to think over Sisco's proposal of merely saying that DMZ's will be established and leaving it to the parties to agree upon the area. (Point 5)

8. *Gaza.* The Soviets still want language which specifically calls for the presence of UN forces under the auspices of the Security Council with Arab sovereignty acknowledged. Sisco noted that this will be a point of major difficulty with Israel because there is a serious issue of security involved. Dobrynin said that specific reference to Israel working out the disposition of Gaza with the Jordan and the UAR under Jarring auspices was redundant and raises problems. Sisco agreed to consider taking out the reference to the three countries, but no more. (Point 6)

---

[4] All brackets in the source text.

9. *Sharm al-Shaikh.* The Soviets continued to object to our position that the parties would agree upon security arrangements. The USSR and the UAR are prepared to accept the presence of UN forces, guaranteed by the Security Council for a fixed period, but the continuing presence of Israeli troops was unacceptable. Sisco said we do not disagree with the idea of a UN guarantee, but the idea of a UN force is unacceptable to Israel. He suggested that the best solution was to come up with neutral language that will allow the parties to work something out when they begin talking. (Point 7)

10. *Canal.* Sisco made it clear to Dobrynin that any reference to the Constantinople Convention on the Suez Canal is unacceptable to us. It was agreed to refer the matter back to Secretary Rogers and Gromyko. (Point 8)

11. *Refugees.* Dobrynin said Gromyko was not very keen on our suggestion of 10,000 as an annual quota. We suggested that this be left to Jarring to work out with the parties and that the reference to refugees be limited to Israel assuming the obligations of the UN with respect to refugees. Sisco insisted that there was no way to duck the question of some sort of limitation. (Point 9)

12. *Obligations of peace.* There was no problem on points 10 (disputes to be settled peacefully); 11 (agreement to respect and recognize each other's sovereignty, territorial integrity, inviolability, political independence and the right to live in peace without acts of force); 12 (definition of agreement to terminate all claims on states of belligerency); 13 (deposition of final accord with the UN); and 14 (final agreement submitted for endorsement by the four permanent members in the Security Council).

Secretary Rogers met again with Gromyko on September 26 against the background of the Sisco–Dobrynin session and Mrs. Meir's visit. (Tab C)[5] It was agreed that, if Sisco and Dobrynin could agree on a document, an acceptable timetable might be to have it approved by the four powers toward the end of October hopefully for the beginning of Rhodes-type negotiations sometime in November, after the Israeli election.

Gromyko then probed our position on several specific issues.

—He asked if Secretary Rogers' proposal for continuing discussion suggested that the border between Israel and Egypt would be the pre-1967 border. Secretary Rogers indicated he could not make that commitment, but thought that something along those lines could be worked out, assuming that the Sharm al-Shaikh issue and other aspects could be satisfactorily resolved.

---

[5] Tab C is telegram 3276 from USUN, September 27; attached but not printed.

—A fairly extended discussion took place over the refugee issue. Secretary Rogers has the impression that some sort of ceiling can be worked out, although this was not explicitly stated.

Gromyko did not oppose the suggestion that the subject of the West Bank was a matter that should be left open to negotiations between Israel and Jordan.

90.   Letter From the Deputy Assistant Secretary of State for European Affairs (Swank) to the Ambassador to the Soviet Union (Beam)[1]

Washington, September 30, 1969.

Dear Jake:

The Secretary has not yet had an opportunity to record all the details of his private conversations with Gromyko before and after the dinner at the Soviet Mission to the United Nations on September 26; and under the pressure of business, I fear that he may not have a chance to do so. The part of the conversation which focused on the Middle East has been reported,[2] but other topics such as Berlin, China, etc., were also discussed. I want in this letter to give you something of the flavor of the conversation on these points as conveyed to a small group of us by the Secretary on September 27.

The Secretary said that Gromyko had expressed considerable concern regarding the power of the "military-industrial complex" in the United States. He questioned whether this complex is interested in arms control and disarmament, and he also reiterated the doubts he had earlier expressed as to the intentions of the Administration given the latter's policy on ABM's and MIRV. The Secretary said that he patiently explained to Gromyko that firms engaged in the manufacture of munitions and other military equipment can easily switch to production of other products needed in the civilian economy. He said he also sought to underline the genuine interest of the Administration in opening SALT without further delay. Gromyko replied that he would transmit these observations "to the Central Committee," but the Secretary

---

[1] Source: National Archives, RG 59, Central Files 1967–69, POL US–USSR. Secret; Official-Informal. Eyes Only. Copies were sent to Llewellyn Thompson and Dubs.

[2] See Document 87.

seemed uncertain whether he had succeeded in dissipating Gromyko's pat Marxist theses about monopoly capital.

The subject of China also arose, apparently at Gromyko's initiative. He said that he was gratified to know from the statements of high officials that the US Government does not wish to see an aggravation of the Sino-Soviet conflict and does not seek to exploit this conflict for its own purposes. Nonetheless, he observed that other actions and statements of the US side raise suspicions that the US Government in fact seeks advantage from the dispute. The Secretary asked Gromyko to provide specific examples of such actions and statements. Gromyko furnished no examples, perhaps because he did not wish to pursue what could easily have developed into a rather contentious conversation.

On Berlin and the possibility of quadripartite talks, the Secretary sought to elicit some clarification of the opaque Soviet response to the recent tripartite démarche.[3] As in the earlier discussion of Berlin on September 22,[4] Gromyko dealt in generalities rather than specifics and contributed nothing new. Marty had a separate conversation with Falin at the dinner which he has reported separately.[5]

The possibility of Gromyko's meeting the President during his US stay was not broached by either side.

The Secretary appeared to enjoy both of his sessions with Gromyko (a third focusing on the Middle East is scheduled for this evening), and he commented to us that they had got on a first-name basis. Marty and I believe that while the meetings were not very productive on substance (with the possible exception of the Middle East), they succeeded in permitting the two men to get to know each other. Given the apparent Soviet uncertainties concerning the policies and attitudes of the Administration, the development of this relationship is in itself useful

---

[3] For the September 12 Soviet response to the August 7 tripartite démarche, see *Foreign Relations, 1969–1976*, volume XL, Germany and Berlin, 1969–1972. In a September 26 covering memorandum to Nixon, Kissinger summarized the main points as follows: "Talks would be limited to the four powers and would concern West Berlin; the question must be approached from the standpoint of European security, and the sovereignty and legitimate interests of East Germany; it is impossible not to take into account that West Berlin's lines of communication are 'along the lines of communication of the GDR;' a normalization of relations between the GDR and Bonn proceed from the basis of 'international law,' and the principles of the Bucharest and Budapest declarations of the Warsaw Pact (i.e., recognition of East Germany, inviolability of borders, etc.)."

[4] See Document 81. For the Berlin section of that memorandum, see *Foreign Relations, 1969–76*, volume XL, Germany and Berlin, 1969–1972.

[5] Reference is to Valentin M. Falin, head of the Third European Division in the Soviet Foreign Ministry; and Martin J. Hillenbrand, Assistant Secretary of State for European Affairs. No record of their conversation has been found.

and could in the long run be most productive. The atmosphere of both dinners was relaxed and cordial.

I hope that Peggy and you had a nice leave.

Sincerely,

Emory C. Swank[6]

---

[6] Printed from a copy that bears this typed signature.

---

91.   Memorandum From Harold Saunders of the National Security Council Staff to the President's Assistant for National Security Affairs (Kissinger)[1]

Washington, October 1, 1969.

SUBJECT

US–USSR Middle East Negotiations in New York

Secretary Rogers and Gromyko failed to make progress toward coming up with a common document during their final meeting in New York. The Soviet strategy now appears to be to get a commitment to total Israeli withdrawal from Sinai and Gaza to the pre-war lines in return for their agreeing to Rhodes type negotiations (interpreted the Arab way) and peace after Israeli withdrawal has been completed and without an explicit commitment to control the fedayeen. Secretary Rogers does not believe that this is a satisfactory deal and has therefore held basically to our present position and did not put our fallback position on the table. The talks will now shift back to Washington with Joe Sisco and Dobrynin picking them up again next week.

Summarized below is where we stand with the Soviets on the major points after the negotiations in New York:

1. The Soviets will accept the *Rhodes formula* if we will be more specific on the *UAR border.* Secretary Rogers avoided being more spe-

---

[1] Source: National Archives, Nixon Presidential Materials, NSC Files, Box 650, Country Files, Middle East, Middle East Negotiations, July–October 1969. Secret; Nodis. Sent for information. A notation on the memorandum indicates Kissinger saw it. Attached but not printed are telegram 3324 from USUN, October 1, providing an account of the Rogers–Gromyko talk of September 30, and telegram 3322 from USUN, October 1, providing an account of the Sisco–Dobrynin talk of September 30.

cific on the borders because of disagreement on a number of other points in the package. On the Rhodes formula, the Secretary made clear that we are not insisting on a joint meeting of the parties at the outset and that it was advantageous not to be too precise on the details so that both parties can justify it. Gromyko had a different set of facts than ours on the Rhodes formula. While he started out by insisting that there should be an understanding between us on what it means, he seemed to be pressing this less after Secretary Rogers had explained the advantages of ambiguity.

2. We and the Soviets agree on the principle of cessation of war and the establishment of a state of peace. The Soviets, however, continue to insist that a juridical state of peace can come only after all Israeli withdrawals are completed. This is consistent with the longstanding Arab view. The Israelis, on the other hand, refuse to withdraw an inch until peace is established and all elements of the package in force.

3. The Soviets are still also insisting on a reference to the Constantinople Convention with the language concerning freedom of passage through the *Suez Canal.*

4. On *Gaza,* the Soviets want a clear-cut statement of Arab sovereignty, total withdrawal of Israeli forces, the establishment of a UN force, and reinstitution of the UAR administration that existed before the war. We stuck to our position that all options on the ultimate status of Gaza must be kept open, leaving the concerned parties to work out a solution.

5. A preliminary understanding has been reached by Joe Sisco and Dobrynin to drop any reference to *refugees.* The Soviets can not agree that the principle of choice to refugees should be balanced by an annual quota.

6. The Soviets still hold the view that the UN force should be established in *Sharm el-Sheikh.* Secretary Rogers maintained that practical security arrangements in Sharm el-Sheikh, the establishment of demilitarized zones, and the final disposition of Gaza must be negotiated with the parties on the basis of the Rhodes formula.

7. We and the Soviets have been agreed for some time on Arab recognition of Israel's right to live in peace.

Conclusion: The long and short of this is that we may move toward a much shorter document containing only the key elements. That would leave the tough issues for negotiation, which would suit Israel. Our work would be cut out for us, but we would at least be working in a negotiating context.[2]

---

[2] This portion of the paragraph is highlighted.

92.   Editorial Note

On October 7, 1969, President's Assistant for National Security Affairs Henry Kissinger sent President Nixon a paper entitled, "The Modern World, A Single 'Strategic Theater,'" dated September 29, 1969. The paper was written by Fritz Kraemer, whom Kissinger described as "an acquaintance of mine." Kissinger's covering memorandum explained that, "Although I do not agree with its every last word, it does define the problem we face—the generally deteriorating strategic position of the United States during the past decade." The paper, printed in *Foreign Relations*, 1969–1976, volume I, Foundations of Foreign Policy, 1969–1972, Document 39, was read with great interest by Nixon, who wrote numerous marginal comments. Next to the section on U.S.-Soviet relations, Nixon wrote "good analysis." The section examines the triangular relationship among the United States, the Soviet Union, and China as follows:

"You will not expect in this sketch any analysis of the complex issue of US/USSR relations. But one comment deserves to be made in the general context I have chosen: The Soviets are developing some genuine fear of Red China and its intractable leaders. They might, therefore, feel impelled by self-restraint to seek a *genuine* Kremlin/Washington détente, and even make certain concessions to the US as a conceivable future ally, semi-ally or at least friendly 'neutral' in a Soviet-Chinese confrontation. The entire Soviet assessment, however, of the weight and value of the United States as a friend or foe, will depend very largely on their considering us either strong-willed or else weak in purpose and resolve. The realists in the Kremlin may now be 'taking our measure,' and a US yielding, and reluctant to act on all fronts, will appear less interesting and important to them as a factor in the international power struggle than a super power obviously able *and* willing to use its strength." (National Archives, Nixon Presidential Materials, NSC Files, Box 397, Subject Files, A Strategic Overview)

On October 14, 1969, Special Assistant to the President Kenneth Cole returned Kissinger's memorandum and the strategic overview paper under a covering note that read: "Please note that the President wants you to send this, together with a note from the President to Secretary Laird, Secretary Rogers and Attorney General Mitchell. They should be asked to comment on it and have their comments to the President within a two-week period, due date November 6." Kissinger sent copies of the paper with the President's instruction for their comments on October 16. In addition, on October 22, Kissinger sent Director of Central Intelligence Richard Helms a copy of the Kraemer paper. (Ibid.) No record of comments from the four recipients of the strategic overview essay has been found.

93.   Memorandum of Conversation[1]

Washington, October 20, 1969, 3:30 p.m.

PARTICIPANTS

The President
Ambassador Dobrynin
Henry A. Kissinger

Ambassador Dobrynin opened the conversation by handing the President a brief announcement suggesting November 17th as the opening of the SALT talks, and suggesting Helsinki as the place. The President asked why Helsinki—he preferred Vienna. Ambassador Dobrynin replied that it did not make a great deal of difference to the Soviet Union, but since Helsinki had been proposed as one of the places by the Secretary of State in June, they decided to go along with that. The President said the Secretary of State had been under instructions to point out the difficulties of Helsinki. Ambassador Dobrynin replied that all the Secretary of State had said to Gromyko was, "to hell with 'Sinki," which is not a diplomatic suggestion. If the United States preferred some other place, this should not be too difficult.

Dr. Kissinger asked the Ambassador what they meant by preliminary discussion. He replied that this meant only the first phase of the discussions, and had no particular significance. But Ambassador Dobrynin suggested that one possible way of handling it would be by beginning in Helsinki and then moving on to Vienna. Dr. Kissinger pointed out to the Ambassador that we had to consult some Allies, but that there seemed to be no insuperable difficulties.

The President then said it would be dangerous if the talks were only a series of platitudes. Ambassador Dobrynin replied that there

---

[1] Source: National Archives, Nixon Presidential Materials, NSC Files, Box 489, President's Trip Files, Dobrynin/Kissinger, 1969, Part 1. Top Secret; Sensitive; Nodis. The conversation was held in the Oval Office of the White House. On October 17, at 4:40 p.m., Dobrynin called Kissinger to arrange a meeting to deliver to Nixon a message from Moscow regarding SALT and U.S.-Soviet relations. According to a transcript of their conversation, "K asked if Dobrynin had requested this [meeting] through the State Department. D said no, he has spoken only to K. K said then he would keep it that way." (Library of Congress, Manuscript Division, Kissinger Papers, Box 360, Telephone Records, 1969–1972, Chronological File) On October 18, Kissinger sent Nixon summary talking points in which he stressed that "*Your basic purpose* will be to keep the Soviets concerned about what we might do around November 1. You should also make clear that, whether or not they agree to SALT, unless there is real progress in Vietnam, US-Soviet relations will continue to be adversely affected." The summary talking points and longer attached briefing paper are in the National Archives, Nixon Presidential Materials, NSC Files, Box 489, President's Trip Files, Dobrynin/Kissinger, 1969, Part 1.

would be specific suggestions, depending on the range of our proposals, and they would probably be put in the form of several options.

The Ambassador then said that President Podgorny paid close attention to good relationships with the United States, and valued this private contact that had been established, but they wanted the President to hear directly their view of international relations. The Ambassador then read the attached Aide Mémoire to the President. After he was through reading the Aide Mémoire, the President pulled out a yellow pad, handed it to Dobrynin and said, "you'd better take some notes," and began to speak almost uninterruptedly for half an hour.

The President began by saying to Dobrynin, "you have been candid, and I will be equally so. I, too, am disappointed in US-Soviet relations. I am today, in office for nine months. The babies should have been born; instead, there have been several miscarriages. I recognize that the future of my country and of the world depends on the success the Soviet Union has in bringing us closer together. We have not done well. Let me point out why."

Middle East. The President pointed out that Sisco and Gromyko, and Sisco and Dobrynin, have talked, but the Soviets have been taking a hard position based on total withdrawal without asking a similar sacrifice from the UAR. The President pointed out that the Soviet client had lost the war, had lost the territory, and was in no position to be extremely aggressive. Ambassador Dobrynin asked whether the President was suggesting that total withdrawal was no longer acceptable, and why a UN force was not adequate. The President said that in light of the experience with the other UN force, one would have to understand and take account of the Israeli position. We are not intransigent, the President added, and you must not be. If you are willing to press your client, we may be able to make some suggestions to Israel. Ambassador Dobrynin began to argue and the President cut him off by saying these were technical issues which should be discussed with Sisco.

Turning to *trade, European security and Berlin,* the President said that these could be dealt with later at a very high level, if we can make a breakthrough somewhere. The Ambassador asked, "how do we make a breakthrough?"

The President ignored him and turned to *China.* He said, "Look to the future of Asia—what will Asia be 25 years from now? China will be in a position of immense power and we cannot have it without communication. Anything we have done or are doing with respect to China is in no sense designed to embarrass the Soviet Union. On the contrary, China and the United States cannot tolerate a situation to develop where we are enemies, anymore than we want to be permanent enemies of the Soviet Union. Therefore, we expect to make moves in trade and exchange of persons and eventually in diplomacy. As the Ambassador has said himself, there are enough blocs in the world without contributing to another one. He repeated this was not directed against the Soviet Union. Within 10 years, China will be a nuclear power, capable of terrorizing many other countries. The time is running out when the Soviet Union and the United States can build a different kind of world. The only beneficiary, then, of U.S.-Soviet disagreement over Vietnam is China. And, therefore, this is the last opportunity to settle these disputes.

The President then turned to Vietnam. He said that prior to the bombing halt, "which you are aware will be one year old on November 1st," Ambassadors Bohlen, Thompson and Harriman had pointed out that the Soviet Union could do nothing as long as the United States was bombing a fellow Socialist country, and that it would be very active afterwards. The bombing halt was agreed to and the Soviet Union has done nothing.

Of course, the President said, we now had an oblong table to the attainment of which the Soviet Union contributed something, but the U.S. did not consider that a great achievement. All conciliatory moves for the past year had been made by the United States. The President enumerated them.

The President said he therefore had concluded that maybe the Soviet Union did not want to end the war in Vietnam. They may think that they can break the President; they may believe that the U.S. domestic situation is unmanageable; they may think that the war in Vietnam costs the Soviet Union only a small amount of money and costs the U.S. a great many lives. The President did not propose to argue with the Soviet assessment. As a great power, it had the right to take its position. On the other hand, the Ambassador had to understand the following: the Soviet Union would be stuck with the President for the next three years and three months, and the President would keep in mind what was being done right now. If the Soviet Union would not help us to get peace, the U.S. would have to pursue its own methods for bringing the war to an end. It could not allow a talk-fight strategy without taking action.

The President said he hoped that the Ambassador would understand that such measures would not be directed against the Soviet Union, but would be in the U.S. interest of achieving peace. The U.S. recognized that a settlement must reflect the real situation. It recognized the right of all Vietnamese to participate in the political process. But up to now, there had been a complete refusal of North Vietnam to make its own proposals in order to have any serious discussion.

The President pointed out that all the Ambassador had done was to repeat the same tired old slogans that the North Vietnamese had made already six months ago, and which he knew very well could lead nowhere. It was time to get discussions started. The humiliation of a defeat was absolutely unacceptable. The President recognized that the Soviet leaders were tough and courageous, but so was he. He told Ambassador Dobrynin that he hoped that he would not mind this serious talk.

President Nixon said he did not believe much in personal diplomacy, and he recognized that the Ambassador was a strong defender of the interests of his own country. The President pointed out that if the Soviet Union found it possible to do something in Vietnam, and the Vietnam war ended, the U.S. might do something dramatic to improve Soviet-U.S. relations, indeed something more dramatic than they could now imagine. But until then, real progress would be difficult.

Ambassador Dobrynin asked whether this meant that there could be no progress. The President replied that progress was possible, but it would have to be confined essentially to what was attainable in diplomatic channels. He said that he was very happy to have Ambassador Dobrynin use the channel through Dr. Kissinger, and he would be prepared to talk to the Ambassador personally. He reiterated that the war could drag on, in which case the U.S. would find its own way to bring it to an end. There was no sense repeating the proposals of the last six months. However, he said, in the meantime, while the situation continued, we could all keep our tone down and talk correctly to each other. It would help, and would lay the basis for further progress, perhaps later on when conditions were more propitious.

The President said that the whole world wanted us to get together. He too wanted nothing so much as to have his Administration remembered as a watershed in U.S.-Soviet relations, but we would not hold still for being "diddled" to death in Vietnam.[2]

Tab A[3]

Aide-Mémoire From the Soviet Leadership to President Nixon

Moscow, undated.

While in Moscow [I] had meetings with the Soviet leaders in the course of which we discussed questions of relations between the USSR and the US.

---

[2] Nixon provides a detailed account of this conversation in his *Memoirs*, pp. 405–407. He concludes with the following description: "Kissinger came back in after he had seen Dobrynin to his car. 'I wager that no one has ever talked to him that way in his entire career!' he said. 'It was extraordinary! No President has ever laid it on the line to them like that.'"

[3] No classification marking.

The President is aware of the importance with which Soviet-American relations are viewed by our side and of the significance attached to them in Moscow. Enough time has now passed since the inauguration of the new administration in the United States to permit an evaluation of the state of Soviet-American relations in the light of the exchange of opinion that has since taken place between our Governments, as well as of the events that have occurred in the world.

I am instructed to frankly inform the President that Moscow is not satisfied with the present state of relations between the USSR and the US. One gets the impression that the American side, while declaring in general words that it is ready to pursue negotiations with the Soviet Union, evades, in fact, concrete discussion of a whole number of major questions, such as measures to be taken to ensure that allied agreements reflecting the results of World War II and outlining steps for securing peace be put into life; greater coordination of our actions aimed at settling in practice the Middle East conflict, as well as certain concrete questions of bilateral Soviet-American relations, in particular, that of trade. Moreover, in a number of cases the American side has taken steps which obviously run counter to the declarations in favor of improving relations between our countries. All this cannot but alert us and, in any case, cannot contribute to better trust which is so necessary for relations between our Governments if we are indeed to make progress in removing the abnormalities that have piled up in our relations in the past, and in settling major international issues fraught with dangerous crises.

With this in mind the Soviet Government decided to outline for the President its considerations on a number of concrete questions.

2. [sic] It is known, for example, that the Soviet Government has expressed readiness to follow the path that would facilitate doing away with the existing military blocks and groupings which, without doubt, would make a most positive impact on the world situation. Unfortunately, one has to conclude that those statements have not met a positive response from the US Government. On the contrary, it is noted in Moscow that the activity of NATO is now on the increase.

Or take, for instance, the question of drawing a line through the vestiges of the Second World War in Europe and fixating the situation that has developed there. We on our part have always expressed readiness and proposed concrete ways for a just settlement of the questions involved, with due regard to the existing realities. The American side, however, acts contrary to the obligations assumed by the United States under the Allied agreements. Why could not the US, together with the USSR as great powers and allies in the past war, make necessary efforts at last in that important field?

The Soviet side stands prepared now to start an exchange of views with the US also on the question of West Berlin. Such an exchange of views, in our opinion, can be useful if both sides are guided by the aim of contributing to a relaxation of tension in Europe and of preventing in the future frictions and complications dangerous for the maintenance of peace and stability in Europe.

3. It is also known that the US and the USSR have long been conducting an exchange of views on Middle East settlement We would like to say with all frankness, however, that, in our opinion, there has been no significant progress in this matter so far, while the situation in the Middle East in the meantime, far from getting normalized, is further deteriorating. In our deep conviction, such a course of events in no small degree is due to the failure on the part of the US to make adequate efforts to bring to an end the present arrogant behaviour of Israel which deliberately aggravates the situation and is wrecking a settlement.

Moscow would like to hope that the President will give this question all due attention and that appropriate steps will be taken from the American side to put an end to Israel's obstructionism which would pave the way toward achieving a just settlement in the Middle East.

4. In Moscow development of events around Vietnam is being watched closely as before.

The Soviet Union, as in the past, is interested in a speediest peaceful settlement of the Vietnam conflict through negotiations and on the basis of respect for the rights and aspirations of the Vietnamese people. We can responsibly state that the position of our Vietnamese friends is the same.

I would like to recall in this connection a concrete program of just and peaceful settlement, put forward by the Government of the Democratic Republic of Vietnam and the National Liberation Front of South Vietnam, and to emphasize, too, that the stubborn resistance of the American side to the creation of a coalition government in South Vietnam which would be based on the actual pattern of political forces there cannot but evoke questions as to the actual meaning of statements about the US desire to end the war in Vietnam and to achieve a political settlement of that conflict. These questions also arise in view of the fact that parallel to the Paris Peace Talks the US is conducting wide preparations for continuing the war in Vietnam.

Due note has been taken in Moscow, of course, of the hints by the American representatives about possible use by the United States of some "alternate" methods of solving the Vietnam question. Such hints cannot be regarded in any other way but as a rather open threat addressed to the DRV and the Provisional Revolutionary Government of South Vietnam.

If that is so Moscow feels that the President should be frankly told that the method of solving the Vietnam question through the use of military force is not only without perspective, but also extremely dangerous.

We hope that the United States will soberly weigh all factors connected with the continuation of the Vietnam conflict and will show a constructive approach to its solution through negotiation, on the basis of recognition of the unalienable right of the Vietnamese people to solve their matters by themselves and of withdrawal of the American troops from Vietnam.

5. Some time back due note was taken in Moscow of the assurances by American leaders to the effect that the United States was not interested in any aggravation of conflict between the Ch.P.R. and the USSR and did not have any intention to use Soviet-Chinese relations to the detriment of the Soviet Union. We, on our part, assured the President that we did not have any intention, either, to make use of difficulties in the relations between the USA and the Ch.P.R. Those American assurances were received in Moscow as a sign of sober realization by the US Government that it would be unrealistic to stake on the use of the problem of Soviet-Chinese relations for bringing pressure to bear upon the Soviet Union and for getting one-sided concessions from us.

If someone in the United States is tempted to make profit from Soviet-Chinese relations at the Soviet Union's expense, and there are some signs of that, then we would like to frankly warn in advance that such line of conduct, if pursued, can lead to a very grave miscalculation and is in no way consistent with the goal of better relations between the US and the USSR.

6. In conclusion I would like to say that the Soviet leaders who attach great significance to improving relations with the United States, would like to know the President's own opinion on the above mentioned questions, as well as on concrete steps which the American side would be ready to take in that direction.

I would also like to tell the President that the Soviet leaders continue to attach great importance not only to official but also to the existing unofficial contacts with him for a confidential exchange of opinion on questions of mutual interest.

94.   Transcript of Telephone Conversation Between President Nixon and his Assistant for National Security Affairs (Kissinger)[1]

Washington, October 20, 1969, 8:25 p.m.

P said in the meeting tomorrow with "him."[2] He would like for K to give him that message. Then if the Vietnam thing is raised (try to get it raised) the P wants K to shake his head and say "I am sorry, Mr. Ambassador, but he is out of control. Mr. Ambassador, as you know, I am very close to the President, and you don't know this man—he's been through more than any of the rest of us put together. He's made up his mind and unless there's some movement," just shake your head and walk out. He's probably right now figuring out what was said. K said he might type up everything the P said on a plain slip of paper. The P said that was fine, and K should put in whatever he wanted. Say since he gave us his notes he's entitled to my notes.[3] The P said he'll say "What does this mean? Are you threatening me?" And K should say "Please now, Mr. Ambassador, the President isn't threatening you. He just wants a little movement." K said if they ignore what you said this afternoon, they either believe that your freedom of action is so circumscribed that you can't do anything or Hanoi is out of control. The P said he thinks it's the latter; "As I said, I'm here for three years."

The P asked if K could trust Joe Alsop[4] enough to show him that. [Don't know what "that" refers to.][5] K asked what he should do with it. The P said nothing, but he's got to know. K said let me think about it. The P said, he didn't know; he probably would have to print it. K said yes, at the right moment he would have to print it. K said he had looked over Alsop's notes after he left; his notes say our Government is for the speediest conclusion of the peace negotiations. He says on the basis of giving the people free choice. In the next paragraph, he lists all the garbage they've been saying all along.

The P said the second draft (number 10) was better than the first. Said he's dictated a few little things. The P said when we get through with this we've got to lay it on the line, put that flag around us and

---

[1] Source: Library of Congress, Manuscript Division, Kissinger Papers, Box 360, Telephone Conversations, Chronological File. No classification marking.

[2] Dobrynin and Kissinger met briefly on October 21; see footnote 2, Document 95.

[3] See Document 95.

[4] Alsop was a syndicated columnist.

[5] Brackets in the source text.

let the people scream. K said well, they're going to scream anyway. The so-called moderates can't be placated. The P agreed.

The P said he would think Laird would understand this, but he guesses not. And Rogers doesn't understand it at all. K said well, you've been on the international scene most of your political life. The P interrupted, saying all of his political life. The P listed the part he played in international politics since the beginning of his political career, then said "I know those bastards—they don't know me. This is something that the world doesn't understand. They're going to find out something different." The P said he wanted K to tell the people there that the President feels it vitally important that the tone of PR be that the P comes out fighting—fighting on Haynsworth[6], on the domestic program . . . K said he would convey that Wednesday because there is no meeting tomorrow.[7] The P said there must be something. K said, well he had a meeting with Haldeman, and Ehrlichman. The P said Haldeman, Ehrlichman, and Harlow, Klein, Ziegler, Buchanan—put that line out hard and tough. Hit if for all it's worth. K said he thought everybody was looking for some lead—we need some demonstration of strength right here.

The P said on the Rogers thing, he doesn't think K ought to handle it with a phone call—he should go over there and talk to him. He should say the President has referred it to him, but with these instructions. Say the President is aware of how we don't want this going around him—we want to go right to him. And we don't want this to go out until Sunday, Sunday for the Monday papers.

---

[6] Clement F. Haynsworth of South Carolina was nominated by Nixon for the Supreme Court in August 1969. Civil rights organizations labeled Haynsworth a racist, and Democratic members of the Senate Judiciary Committee also charged him with conflict of interest in cases that had involved litigants who were customers in a company in which Haynsworth owned stock. Despite the controversies, Nixon refused to withdraw his nomination; on November 21, the Senate rejected Haynsworth's nomination.

[7] Ellipsis in the source text.

95.   Transcript of Telephone Conversation Between the
      President's Assistant for National Security Affairs (Kissinger)
      and the Soviet Ambassador (Dobrynin)[1]

Washington, October 21, 1969, 3:15 p.m.

Dobrynin wanted to check a few things on the notes K sent him.[2]
K said they were hastily done and apologized for it. D said it only
deals with the last one. K agreed and asked if D wanted him to send
the notes on the other. D said there was no hurry—at K's convenience.
K said when he looked at his notes, he forgot the reduction in military
activity. D noticed and said that the notes kept saying "they, they, they."
K said "they" refers to D's leaders. D pointed out another instance
where it said "on the other hand, the Ambassador." K said that was
also directed to D's leaders. K said he had no doubt about D's understanding—this was true all the way through—the reference to D's leaders. D said this was his impression. On page 2, line 3 it mentions the
Soviet people. K again said this should be "leaders." K said the President was talking about himself. D said he mentioned himself and gave
the name of three leaders. K said D's notes were better than his. D said
the President mentioned Bohlen, Thompson, Harriman and [omission
in the source text], not D specifically. K said that was correct, but why
didn't D put it in. K said he would correct his notes. Then in paragraph
3, D said the President mentioned that he was very happy to see the
Ambassador. D understood that he was happy rather to meet with Dobrynin, not through K. K said D misunderstood that. K had an occasion to talk with the President this morning—what he said was "that
channel should be if the problem got solved." D said—that now K and
he really have nothing to discuss unless D has something to say. K said
that was supposed to mean on important matters. D's impression was
that the President didn't specifically limit D and K unless they felt it

---

[1] Source: National Archives, Nixon Presidential Materials, NSC Files, Box 489, President's Trip Files, Dobrynin/Kissinger, 1969, Part 1. Top Secret; Sensitive.

[2] Kissinger and Dobrynin spoke briefly on the telephone at 9:15 a.m. that morning.
According to a transcript of their conversation: "The Ambassador said he just returned
from New York. K said jokingly, we turn our backs and you run off to the nightclubs of
New York. Dobrynin said he was just trying to follow the example of his good friend.
K said he would like to come to see the Ambassador for about 5 minutes. D said fine,
he would expect him in about 15 minutes." (Library of Congress, Manuscript Division,
Kissinger Papers, Box 360, Telephone Conversations, Chronological File) Kissinger apparently gave Dobrynin an unrevised version of Document 93 at this meeting. The unrevised notes with Kissinger's changes are attached to a covering memo that reads:
"Handed in a plain envelope to Ambassador Dobrynin as an aide mémoire. The copy
given to him had no classification marked on it." (National Archives, Nixon Presidential Materials, NSC Files, Box 489, President's Trip Files, Dobrynin/Kissinger, 1969, Part 1)

would be useful. It sounded like there was a limitation. K said that was not the intention. K explained that D could see the President on something very important and if the other thing were settled, quite frequently. K talked with the P after D was in. The Pres. is very agreeable to keep this channel open. D said as it is here, he may have to go the other way from now on but would like to go on with K. K said that was up to D but it should read through Dr. Kissinger and the Pres. would be prepared to talk to D if he had something specific and important.

They decided that they coincided on specifics although D said he had more details. D said he had made the call and should be hearing back tomorrow and would report the answer.

96. Memorandum From the President's Assistant for National Security Affairs (Kissinger) to President Nixon[1]

Washington, October 21, 1969.

SUBJECT

Dobrynin's Message

Taken as a whole, Dobrynin's presentation[2] was a rather standard Soviet indictment, although moderate in tone. Most of the points in the Soviet complaint against us have recently been made by other Soviet officials and in the Soviet press. It may well be that this is how the Soviet leaders in fact see our conduct; and they are partly correct: we have by and large kept aloof and held our ground on such issues as the Middle East (Golda Meir to the contrary notwithstanding) and Europe. But we have probably not done as well as we should in communicating to the Soviets that *their* behavior in Vietnam stands in the way of better relations. Your presentation may help to get this message across more clearly.

---

[1] Source: National Archives, Nixon Presidential Materials, NSC Files, Box 489, President's Trip Files, Dobrynin/Kissinger, 1969, Part 1. Secret; Nodis.

[2] See Document 93.

I suspect Dobrynin's basic mission was to test the seriousness of the threat element in our current posture and to throw out enough inducements (SALT, Berlin, direct informal contact with you) to make it politically and psychologically difficult for you to play it rough over Vietnam.

Even though some of Dobrynin's points are valid in the sense that they reflect understanding of our cool attitude, many others are pure Soviet propaganda fare. I doubt that we need to pay attention to complaints about NATO or about our failure to act in accordance with World War II "obligations." By the same token, it is curious that certain of our alleged "sins" were omitted, e.g. our supposed arms buildup as reflected in the Safeguard decision.[3] It may be that having agreed to SALT, the Soviets considered it inexpedient to get into polemics in this field.

Specific Points of Interest

1. *Vietnam.* The main point here is Soviet acknowledgement of our allusions to possible military actions. Their response was relatively mild ("shortsighted . . . extremely dangerous.")[4] But there is no doubt they are concerned and your comments might just give them ammunition to use in Hanoi in lobbying for a more flexible position. The Soviets may argue in Hanoi that only a token concession—especially when magnified by our press—would be sufficient to dissuade us from drastic action or give us a pretext to back away from our warnings. We should probably find a way to signal that token concessions would be inadequate. In any event, it will be essential to continue backing up our verbal warnings with our present military moves.

On the substantive Vietnam issues, I could find nothing new in Dobrynin's presentation. He did repeat recent Soviet references to a "speedy"—he actually used "speediest"—peaceful settlement, and asserted that their Vietnamese friends favor this too. Even if that is so—and Pham Van Dong who just completed a visit to Moscow may have given the green light for use of the phrase—it gives us nothing to go on in the absence of concrete adjustments in the Communist position.

2. *Berlin.* The Soviets again agree to talks with us but give no indication whatever that these might lead to the improvements we seek. As you know, there has also recently been an offer by ourselves, the British and French, with FRG support, to talk to the Soviets. They agreed in much the same vague terms used in Dobrynin's text. I think we should not encourage the notion of bilateral US-Soviet talks on Berlin at this stage. The Soviets would use them to stir up suspicions

---

[3] See footnote 3, Document 93.

[4] Ellipsis in source text.

among the Allies and to play us off against each other. I believe we would do best to keep this issue in the quadripartite forum for the moment and not to press too much ourselves. Since there may be a misunderstanding of our position in Moscow (you first raised the possibility of talks in your Berlin speech[5] and then in your letter to Kosygin last March),[6] we should probably tell the Soviets that we are not now interested in bilateral talks.

3. *China.* The Soviets again give vent to their underlying suspicion that we are trying to flirt with China in order to bring pressure on them. They warn us "in advance" that any such idea can lead to grave miscalculations and would interfere with the improvement of US-Soviet relations. You have already answered this point and I believe there is no advantage in giving the Soviets excessive reassurance. In any case we should not be diverted from our China policy.

4. *Middle East.* The Soviet text reflects current Soviet pessimism. We do not of course know how much trouble the Soviets have had with the Arabs over the Sisco talks. They may genuinely think we have not exerted enough pressure on Israel. It is doubtful that the impasse can be broken.

5. *Direct Contact with You.* Dobrynin's final point was obviously intended to keep a direct line open to you. I think we can take this as a signal that for all their complaints and accusations, they remain interested in normal relations.

---

[5] See footnote 2, Document 23.
[6] See Document 28.

---

97.   Minutes of Meeting of the Washington Special Actions Group[1]

Washington, October 21, 1969, 3:28–5:12 p.m.

SUBJECT

Berlin, Sino-Soviet Hostilities, and the Middle East

---

[1] Source: National Archives, Nixon Presidential Materials, NSC Files, NSC Institutional Files (H-Files), Box H–114, WSAG Minutes, Originals, 1969 and 1970. Top Secret; Sensitive. The meeting was held in the White House Situation Room.

PARTICIPANTS

Henry A. Kissinger—Chairman

State
U. Alexis Johnson
Martin Hillenbrand
William Cargo
Rodger Davies

NSC Staff
Harold H. Saunders
Helmut Sonnenfeldt
William G. Hyland
Col. Robert M. Behr

Defense
G. Warren Nutter

CIA
Thomas H. Karamessines

JCS
Vice Admiral Nels C. Johnson

SUMMARY OF DECISIONS

1. A briefing on Berlin contingency planning will be prepared for the President.

2. Unilateral and quadripartite plans for Berlin contingencies will be reviewed with special emphasis on establishing priorities among alternative courses of action.

3. A summary of recommended actions is needed for the Sino-Soviet Hostilities paper. When the summary is completed and minor revisions made within the body of the paper, it will stand approved by the WSAG. State is charged with keeping the paper current.

4. The Joint Staff will prepare a paper on rules of engagement for WSAG review.

5. The next WSAG meeting will be devoted to further review of the Middle East paper.

The Group then turned to the Sino-Soviet Hostilities paper.[2] Secretary Johnson said that, with the exception of a few minor changes which Cargo would cover with the Group, he considered the Sino-Soviet paper to be a finished product.[3]

Cargo then went over the recommended changes. (1) The paper will be modified to convey the idea that a Soviet "victory" over main-

---

[2] See Document 79.

[3] On October 20, Behr sent Kissinger a memorandum written by John Holdridge about the NSSM 63 study: "This paper has met our needs for a fast survey of what U.S. reactions should be in the event that the Sino-Soviet dispute moved into a situation involving hostilities. At the time it was begun, the prospects of a clash between Moscow and Peking seemed greater than they are today—perhaps the Soviets were actively considering taking some form of action, but now have resolved not to do so, or to defer pending the outcome of the talks in Peking." (National Archives, Nixon Presidential Materials, NSC Files, NSC Institutional Files (H-Files), Box H–114, WSAG Minutes, Originals, 1969 and 1970)

land China does not imply acquisition and absolute control over Chinese territory—but, instead, an extension of Soviet influence over a compliant CPR government. (2) With respect to U.S. actions in Vietnam (as related to Sino-Soviet hostilities), the paper will avoid the impression that a U.S. blockade of Haiphong would serve as a retaliatory measure against a Soviet blockade of Hong Kong (although that may give the U.S. a pretext). The central idea should be that we will use a blockade on the basis of what it would do for us in Vietnam, independent of its relationship to a situation of Sino-Soviet hostilities.

Kissinger asked for a summary of recommended actions to be put at the front of the paper, and then wondered if the whole paper could be incorporated in the NSSM 63 report. Cargo agreed to provide a summary but demurred in the idea of integrating the paper with the NSSM 63 report, saying that consistency between the two would suffice. Kissinger agreed on the basis that Cargo would insure consistency on a continuing basis.

[Omitted here is discussion of Berlin contingency planning.]

---

98.   Telegram From the Department of State to the Embassy in the Soviet Union[1]

Washington, October 29, 1969, 0123Z.

182821. Subject: Sisco–Dobrynin Meeting on ME October 28.

Summary: In his meeting with Ambassador Dobrynin October 28, Sisco gave Dobrynin our language on Israel-UAR boundary question, stressing that it is contingent upon Soviet agreement to equally specific language on peace and to need for Rhodes-type negotiations between parties to work out details of a settlement including (a) security arrangements at Sharm al-Shaykh, (b) demilitarized zones and (c) security arrangements for and final disposition of Gaza. Sisco also emphasized that we were not presenting elements of a new US document but rather formulations designed to reflect common US-Soviet positions for inclusion in a joint document to be transmitted to Jarring

---

[1] Source: National Archives, Nixon Presidential Materials, NSC Files, Box 650, Country Files, Middle East, Middle East Negotiations, July–October 1969. Secret; Nodis. Drafted by W.B. Smith, cleared by Swank and Atherton, and approved by Sisco. Repeated to Amman, Beirut, Belgrade, Cairo, Jidda, London, USUN, Nicosia, Paris, and Tel Aviv.

through Four Powers. In putting forth these formulations, Sisco said that we are not prepared to negotiate them further with the Soviets in any substantial way. Dobrynin undertook to obtain Moscow's reaction, stating only as personal preliminary comment that he thought too many questions had been left open and that Moscow would want document to be more specific and detailed. End Summary.

1. Assistant Secretary Sisco and Ambassador Dobrynin held third session October 28 in their ME talks since US-Soviet ministerial discussions in New York in September.[2] Responding to Sisco's inquiry if Dobrynin had comments to make, latter said he would only reiterate instruction he received earlier and imparted to Secretary and Sisco last week: There would be no Soviet reaction to US proposal re nature of common document until US position clearer on borders and withdrawal. Sisco then voiced US concern re Lebanese situation, Syrian complicity and Soviets abetting anti-US campaign in Arab world (septel).

2. Sisco pointed out that US regards process which began in New York talks last month as one of devising joint US-Soviet document. Added he wished to emphasize and hoped Dobrynin would report explicitly to Moscow that we do not consider revised formulations which we have suggested to Soviets in last few weeks as elements of any new US document. What we have tried to do is basically to reflect what we hope is concrete US-Soviet understanding reached orally on particular points.

3. US July document[3] is last US document that we intend to table, Sisco continued. Present effort is a mutual and common one of drawing up tentative joint US-Soviet document. What we are now recording are understandings or near understandings which have evolved in our discussions.

4. In New York we found common language for inclusion in Preamble on question of procedures for getting talks started between parties under Jarring's auspices. At first subsequent Washington meeting we suggested modified language to Soviets in attempt to reflect our common views on how to deal with questions of Tiran, Canal, and refugees. We also proposed a concept for dealing with what US-Soviet discussions have identified as central issues, namely: peace, withdrawal and boundaries, and practical security arrangements. As Dobrynin would recall, we said: If US and Soviets can reach agreement on specific peace language and on neutral formulations leaving to parties to work out (a) practical security arrangements in and around

---

[2] See Documents 81 and 85, and footnote 1, Document 91.

[3] Document 67.

Sharm al-Shaykh, (b) arrangements for DMZ's, and (c) security arrangements for and disposition of Gaza, then US would be prepared to consider more specific language on boundary question.

5. At last Sisco–Dobrynin meeting,[4] US proposed at Soviet suggestion a consolidated formulation of our peace point. At brief meeting last week of Secretary Rogers, Dobrynin, and Sisco it was agreed that Dobrynin and Sisco should try to approach this concept with concrete language on conditional basis. In one final effort to move things forward, we are prepared today to complete process of seeking common language for joint US–USSR document.

6. Sisco explained that we view following points which Sisco would now give Dobrynin as a package within a package. In other words, these points must stand or fall together as far as US is concerned. Sisco said that the first of the elements which the US considers to be linked is last paragraph of Preamble as it had been worked out jointly with Soviets in New York, and of which he had already given Dobrynin a copy.[5]

Begin text. Israel and the UAR, ...[6]
Agree that their representatives under the auspices of Ambassador Jarring will follow the procedures the parties utilized at Rhodes in 1949 to work out without delay, starting on the basis of the following provisions, a final and reciprocally binding accord on ways of implementing Security Council Resolution 242 of November 22, 1967 to establish a just and lasting peace. *End text.*

7. Sisco said the second element of the package within a package was the language on withdrawal which had also been worked out in New York. In giving copy of text to Dobrynin for reference, Sisco invited Dobrynin's attention to fact that all formulations being transmitted this session had following caption: "Contingent Draft for Possible Inclusion in a Joint US–USSR Working Paper."

Begin text. The parties, in reaching a final accord (contained in a final document or documents) on a package settlement on the basis of these Fundamental Principles, would determine a timetable and procedures for withdrawal of Israeli armed forces from UAR territory occupied during the conflict of 1967 to boundaries to be delineated in accordance with Point 3 as well as an agreed plan for interrelated fulfillment of all other provisions of Security Council Resolution 242. *End text.*

---

[4] See footnote 1, Document 91.

[5] U.S. formulations for a Joint US–USSR Working Paper, entitled "Fundamental Principles" was given to Dobrynin at this meeting on October 28.

[6] Ellipsis in the source text.

8. Sisco said US had reviewed this point re withdrawal as well as Point 2 which he had worked out with Dobrynin in New York (USUN 3322)[7] and which also dealt with withdrawal procedures. US was now dropping second point because we found it to be inconsistent with first point. Point 1 says parties would determine timetable and procedures for withdrawal, but old Point 2 spelled out some of timetable and some of procedure. We feel this should be left to parties, and omission of old Point 2 has additional advantage of avoiding whole problem of timing of withdrawal in relationship to other actions. Sisco added that Dobrynin would find Sisco's presentation at this session to be based on assumption that question should be avoided entirely of when peace and withdrawal are to happen in relation to each other. Sisco mentioned that he and Dobrynin could return to this subject at a later time.

9. Sisco explained that third element of package within package is consolidated US language on peace which Sisco gave Dobrynin Oct 17 (State 177075, para 14).[8]

10. Language on boundary question is fourth element. Sisco noted US July document used formula to effect that old international frontier was not excluded as secure boundary between UAR and Israel. Soviet response favored use of either of boundary language in Soviet June document[9] or of US language but with deletion of phrase "not excluded." US has now devised counter formulation to reflect possible US–USSR consensus on boundary question, Sisco continued, which does two things: (A) it reflects view that former international boundary between Egypt and Palestine should become secure and recognized boundary between Israel and UAR; and (B) it reflects view that Israel should not be asked to withdraw to that boundary except in context of peace and agreement on establishment of DMZs, security arrangements which will make boundaries secure and will assure continued free navigation through Tiran, and agreement on Gaza.

11. Sisco presented boundary formulation. *Begin text.*

The parties would agree on the location of the secure and recognized boundary between them, which would be shown on a map or maps approved by the parties which would become part of the final accord. In the context of peace, including inter alia agreement between the parties on the establishment of demilitarized zones, on practical security arrangements in the Sharm al-Shaykh area for guaranteeing freedom of navigation through the Strait of Tiran, and on practical security arrangements and final disposition of Gaza, the former international boundary between Egypt and the mandated territory of Pales-

---

[7] See footnote 1, Document 91.

[8] Not found.

[9] Document 58.

tine would become the secure and recognized boundary between Israel and the UAR. *End text.*

12. Sisco explained that fifth and last item for package within package was formulation to reflect neutral language to which Sisco had been referring since July. Sisco emphasized that new language intended not to prejudice position of either side on these points. Although Dobrynin frequently said US position is one-sided, he would see we are not trying to prejudice size or location of DMZs or specify any particular type of security arrangements or options re disposition of Gaza. US not proposing use of UN facilities to police DMZs, neither are we ruling out UN facilities. We are trying to find neutral formulations which do not prejudice either side's position. Formulation makes clear that Israel's interest in Sharm al-Shaykh area is confined to practical question of assuring free navigation through Tiran. Formulation also reflects fact that Israel has legitimate security concern in Gaza and should have voice on matter, and this in turn is inseparable in our judgment from disposition of Gaza, where sovereignty has been in abeyance for 20 years.

13. Before presenting text, Sisco stressed that if US and Soviets can agree on common document and can get parties engaged in exchange of views, and if US and Soviets continue to press parties while process under Jarring is going on, we believe that more flexibility on these three issues (DMZs, Sharm al-Shaykh and Gaza) and other subjects will develop in exchanges between parties. This will help US and USSR in trying to exercise influence on parties. Sisco added we do not envisage US and Soviet roles as ceasing with the drafting of our common document.

14. Sisco presented neutral language formulation. *Begin text.* For the purpose of ensuring the territorial inviolability of the parties and guaranteeing the security of the recognized boundary, the parties, following the procedures set forth in the last preambular paragraph of this document, would work out an agreement on:

(a) Zones to be demilitarized and procedures for ensuring their demilitarization;

(b) Practical security arrangements in the Sharm al-Shaykh area to assure freedom of navigation through the Strait of Tiran; and

(c) Practical security arrangements for and final disposition of Gaza. *End text.*

15. Sisco reiterated that items he had presented today constitute package within package and stand or fall together. US considers these formulations a fair compromise of Soviet and US positions as set forth in June Soviet document and July US document. Speaking candidly, Sisco stressed, we are not prepared to negotiate these points further in any substantial way.

16. As for rest of document, Sisco said, we gave Soviet side our proposed reflections of common positions on Tiran, Canal and refugees

on Oct 10. We have additional suggestion for dealing with the one point which both US and Soviets recognize cannot be left uncovered: interdependence of UAR and Jordan aspects. Sisco said this interdependence is particularly underscored by our discussion of refugee point. We think question of interrelationship can be taken care of by adding one simple paragraph to our non-substantive point on refugees of Oct 10. We believe that our paragraph makes clear that we are dealing with what Gromyko described well as horizontal and vertical package.

17. Sisco presented additional paragraph for refugee point. *Begin text.* It would be understood that the accord between the UAR and Israel would be paralleled by an accord between Jordan and Israel, which would include agreement on a just solution of the refugee problem. Implementation of both accords would begin only after agreement had been achieved on the entire package. *End text.*

18. Sisco observed that next point in common document as US envisages it would be language of US Point 11 in July document dealing with respect for sovereignty, on which US and Soviet sides have long been in agreement. This would be followed by old US Point 13 as amended. In NY discussions Sisco had suggested insertion of sentence on breach of final accord in language covering deposit of final accord with UN.

19. Sisco now presented text to show Dobrynin what this insertion looks like and also to reverse order of two of old sentences. *Begin text.* The final accord would be recorded in a document which is to be signed by the parties and immediately deposited with the UN. After the parties have deposited such a document, the Secretary General of the UN would be requested by the parties immediately to inform the Security Council and all UN Member States to that effect.

From the moment of deposit, the document would become binding on the parties and irrevocable, and implementation and observance by the parties of the provisions of the accord would begin. In the implementation of the final accord, it would be understood by the parties that their respective obligations would be reciprocal and interdependent. The final accord would provide that a material breach of that accord by one of the parties shall entitle the other to invoke the breach as a ground for suspending its performance in whole or in part until the breach shall be cured. *End text.*

20. Sisco said that final point in joint document remains for US side its old Point 14 re submission of final accord to UN Security Council for endorsement. We would like to suggest an amendment eliminating reference in this text to map or maps in view of new language on boundaries which Sisco had presented at this session. US does not consider reference to map as needed in final point. Moreover, since boundary language now specific, reference to map in final point could

be misleading and might even lead Arabs to wonder if we have something else in mind.

21. Sisco gave Dobrynin revised language for final point. *Begin text.* Both parties would agree that the final accord would be submitted to the Security Council for its endorsement. *End text.*

22. Sisco said this completed his presentation of language by which we had attempted to reflect joint US-Soviet views for possible inclusion in common document, based on procedures which he and Dobrynin had discussed re submission to four powers and then Jarring. Question of subsequent procedures could be discussed after we receive Soviet reaction.

23. Dobrynin referred to new US language on interrelationship between Jordan and UAR aspects. Voiced personal reaction that this provision should be placed in document as separate point at beginning or end. Sisco said he could accept this suggestion in principle. US side did not mean to infer that interrelationship is limited to refugee question.

24. Dobrynin requested clarification of Sisco's remark that US not prepared to negotiate the five elements of package within a package in a substantial way. Sisco replied that fact of the matter is US has now gone as far as it can substantively; rubber band had been stretched to fullest extent. Noted that US has engaged in no consultations with Israelis on this language.

25. Dobrynin raised issue of timing of peace in relation to withdrawal, noting it is point in which Gromyko is interested. Sisco explained that US approach is based on assumption that timing question should be set aside and worked out by parties.

26. When Dobrynin inquired re numbering of points, Sisco used occasion to strongly emphasize his earlier point that these additional US formulations do not constitute a US document. Dobrynin noted that although reference to map now deleted from penultimate point, US had retained it in new boundary language. Sisco said that reference to map in boundary provision is correct concept and should offer no substantive problem. Dobrynin recalled, as he read again through revised formulations received at this and preceding two sessions, that he had requested US clarification of term "interference" in Suez Canal provision. Sisco replied he could focus on this point at a subsequent meeting.

27. Sisco asked for Dobrynin's views on next steps in US-Soviet talks. Dobrynin remarked that joint paper which Sisco proposing seems rather different from what Soviets had in mind during New York talks. Gromyko had sought US clarifications and had said it difficult meanwhile to come to conclusion about next steps. Dobrynin added that we would now have rather short joint document which would leave

several important questions unclear, especially re peacekeeping. Question for Soviets is whether it wise to move with so many open formulations and throw entire ball back to Jarring. A basic judgment would have to be made, and Soviets might decide it wiser to try to clarify some of these open questions.

28. Sisco said again Soviets should expect no further substantive alterations. Sisco asked for Dobrynin's ideas about consultations by US and USSR with parties in area. Dobrynin said Soviets since opening of New York talks had given no texts to their Arab friends, although Gromyko gave oral briefings in New York. Sisco recalled there had been misunderstanding in this respect after his July talks in Moscow which we wanted to avoid this time. After July talks US was roundly criticized by Arab friends for holding off consultations re US document, pursuant to informal understanding between Sisco and Vinogradov. Dobrynin commented in passing that situation vis-à-vis UAR caused by this misunderstanding had made very poor impression in Moscow.

29. Newest formulations were an attempt to reflect a common US-Soviet approach, Sisco continued. As for US own position, we stand on our July document. As Sisco had already noted, we have not discussed formulations with Israelis. Before we can put proposals to Israel for consideration, we must have answer to question which Israelis will immediately ask: Does USSR accept this. We see no point in our trying to press this or that provision in Tel Aviv, Amman, or Cairo unless we know this reflects common approach. US and Soviets owe it to each other to know how other power intends to proceed with parties before other power proceeds.

30. Sisco added that US needs very specific indication from Soviets, as we have passed beyond point of fencing with each other, and as US not prepared to alter latest formulations in any substantial way. Sisco hoped Soviets would do us the courtesy of informing us ahead of time if Moscow decides to discuss formulations with Cairo. US had not decided whether to inform Arabs and Israelis about new formulations. There were three possibilities for Soviets, as for US: (a) to inform parties in general way, (b) to discuss texts with parties, and (c) to give no information at all to parties. Whatever course chosen, US and Soviets should avoid misunderstandings. No commentments [sic] made re consultation procedure either by Sisco or Dobrynin.

31. Next session tentatively scheduled for November 5.

Rogers

99.   Memorandum of Conversation[1]

Washington, November 6, 1969, noon.

PARTICIPANTS

Ambassador Dobrynin
Mr. Henry A. Kissinger

I began the conversation by saying that the President had wanted to make sure that Dobrynin understood the speech[2] properly: (1) the President wanted to point out the seriousness of the threat in case of escalation; (2) that Dobrynin should not be confused by the various arguments he had heard with respect to linkage—we considered linkage a fact and not a policy, and foreign policy was made in the White House and nowhere else; and (3) the President wanted to reiterate that we were in favor of major improvements in Soviet-US relations but not until considerable progress had been made on the Vietnam issue.

Dobrynin said with respect to the first question that they had made their point of view clear and that any escalation by us would have dangerous consequences. I told him that we had taken it into account and that anything we did would not be directed against the Soviet Union, they were the best judge of their own interests and would have to decide what to do when the time came.

With respect to the second point, he said he had no illusions about the linkage problem, and he saw not much point in repeating our well-known position. I said I just wanted to make sure that he understood and was not confused by the conflicting statements he read. I pointed to the *Izvestia* article, which had called attention to these statements. Dobrynin said *Izvestia* had only repeated what the factual situation was and had not made any editorial comments. I did not argue the point, in the belief that propaganda was one thing and their assessment of their policy was another.

---

[1] Source: National Archives, Nixon Presidential Materials, NSC Files, Box 711, Country Files, Europe, USSR, Vol. VI. Top Secret; Sensitive; Nodis. The conversation was held in Kissinger's office. Kissinger sent this memorandum of conversation to the President under a November 24 covering note. (Ibid.)

[2] On November 3, Nixon gave an address to the nation on Vietnam that was broadcast on national television. The address came to be known as the "silent majority speech," for Nixon's appeal for support for his policy from "the great silent majority of Americans" to counter the large-scale anti-Vietnam war demonstrations. For text, see *Public Papers: Nixon, 1969*, pp. 901–909. For additional background information, see *Foreign Relations, 1969–1976*, volume VI, Vietnam, January 1969–July 1970, Document 144.

With respect to the third point, Dobrynin said that his government was now beginning to understand the seriousness with which we took the position we had indicated, and had given up the illusion that they had held earlier in the year that major progress was possible even while the Vietnam war was going on. He added a little plaintively that he could not understand our attitude because the Soviet Union was not making trouble for us in Vietnam; they were not trying to embarrass us; but they could not get us out of a war into which we had gotten ourselves. I said I thought our position was clear, and there was no sense reiterating it.

Dobrynin told me that the NLF was looking at our position from the point of view that any election would be won by the government organizing it, and that we were trying to get at the conference table what we had failed to get on the battlefield. I said that we had specifically rejected such a proposition and that they knew very well that we were prepared to discuss with them how to organize the political process—they even knew how to do it.

I told Dobrynin I had been intrigued by a comment he had made the last time I had seen him; namely, that Hanoi had found the conversation with me constructive. What was it that they had considered constructive in that conversation? Dobrynin said that they found my attitude and my personality constructive—not the specific proposals which they thought repeated well-known themes.

The meeting ended with an understanding that we would meet again in about two weeks, the initiative to be left with Dobrynin.[3]

---

[3] On November 6 at 4:35 pm, Kissinger and Rogers spoke on the telephone about this meeting: "K said he [Dobrynin] didn't have very much. He came in and talked about this linkage problem and I just said to him what the President had said before. K said he would write it up and send it to R. He told D that it is a fact of life that there is some relationship but it is conditional. Rogers felt that that was the way to play it. . . . Rogers said we have never laid down any conditions on SALT. On the other hand, if we are actually having confrontation in the Middle East, it would be difficult to engage in meetings with friendly atmosphere in Helsinki. K indicated that D had come in to get clarification in his own mind since something had been mentioned in *Time* magazine 6 months ago that K had that concept. Rogers said it might be helpful if he knew when K was having these meetings. K said he would call next time." (Transcript of Telephone Conversation, Library of Congress, Manuscript Division, Kissinger Papers, Box 361, Telephone Records, 1969–1976, Telephone Conversations) (Ellipsis in source text)

100. Editorial Note

On November 10, 1969, at 3:15 p.m., the National Security Council met to discuss the upcoming preliminary round of strategic arms limitations talks, which opened in Helsinki on November 17. The minutes of the meeting are printed in *Foreign Relations*, 1969–1976, volume XXXII, SALT I, 1969–1972.

After the NSC meeting, President Nixon issued National Security Decision Memorandum 33, which spelled out the US objectives as follows:

"The United States is prepared to discuss (a) limitations on all offensive and defensive weapons systems, and (b) proposals the Soviets may advance for the work program. The Delegation should make it clear that in accepting subjects for further discussion the United States is not thereby committed to the inclusion of any given measure of limitation in a final agreement either individually or in combination with others. The President will make the judgment on what limitations are acceptable, and he will do so in light of the criteria for strategic sufficiency set forth in NSDM 16, the evaluations of the Verification Panel, and other considerations he deems pertinent." The full text of NSDM 33 is in *Foreign Relations*, 1969–1976, volume XXXII, SALT I, 1969–1972.

Issued June 24, NSDM 16 listed four criteria: "1) maintain high confidence that our second strike capability is sufficient to deter an all-out surprise attack on our strategic forces; 2) maintain forces to insure that the Soviet Union would have no incentive to strike the United States first in a crisis; 3) maintain the capability to deny to the Soviet Union the ability to cause significantly more deaths and industrial damage in the United States in a nuclear war than they themselves would suffer; and 4) deploy defenses which limit damage from small attacks or accidental launches to a low level." (National Archives, Nixon Presidential Materials, NSC Files, Box 363, Subject Files, National Security Decision Memoranda, Nos. 1–50) NSDM 16 is in *Foreign Relations*, 1969–1976, volume XXXIV, National Security Policy, 1969–1972.

101. Editorial Note

On November 10, 1969, the final version of the response to National Security Study Memorandum 63 on Sino-Soviet differences was completed. The paper was discussed in previous drafts at meetings of the Washington Special Actions Group and Senior Review Group in September and October (see Documents 77, 79, and 97). The summary of "Immediate US Policy Problems in Event of Major Sino-Soviet Hostilities," prepared by the Department of State's Policy Planning Council and printed in *Foreign Relations, 1969–1976*, volume XVII, China, 1969–1972, Document 43, includes the following:

"The U.S. would publicly emphasize its impartiality and noninvolvement, urge both sides not to use nuclear weapons, call for negotiations and the restoration of peace, and take steps to avoid any provocative actions or accidental contact by US forces with belligerent forces. If hostilities were set off by the Soviets, the US would express its strong concern, and if nuclear weapons were used, strongly condemn their employment. These points would be made privately as well to both the Soviets and Chinese. We would not take the initiative to change our bilateral negotiating posture toward the Soviets significantly in the event of the conventional conflict, but if the Soviets employed nuclear weapons, we would at least suspend arms limitation talks.

"In the event of any conventional Sino-Soviet conflict, the US military readiness and reaction posture would be strengthened by selected command and alerting actions. Scheduled overseas military exercises would be reviewed for possible provocative risks and degradation of our military posture, and force demobilization and withdrawal programs would be selectively suspended pending further analysis of the impact of Sino-Soviet hostilities on the US global force posture. In the event nuclear weapons were employed, DEFCON status would be increased, NATO consultations initiated, advanced Civil Defense plans implemented, and selected Reserve and National Guard units recalled to active duty." (Department of State, S/S Files: Lot 83 D 411, National Security Council Contingency Plans)

On November 18, Roger Morris of the National Security Staff sent Kissinger a dissenting view on the NSSM 63 study. In this memorandum, printed in full in *Foreign Relations, 1969–1976*, volume XVII, China, 1969–1972, Document 46, he argued:

"NSSM 63 seems to proceed from certain basic assumptions about the effect of the Sino-Soviet rivalry on US interests. I would argue those assumptions. In my view, the revised paper still: (a) overdraws the benefits of the dispute for the US, (b) omits significant side effects of Sino-Soviet hostility, (c) fails to probe the most likely form of a full-fledged Sino-Soviet war and (d) puts the fundamental policy choice to the President in the wrong terms." (National Archives, Nixon Presidential Materials, NSC Files, NSC Institutional Files (H-Files), Box H–040, Senior Review Group Meeting, Sino Soviet Differences, 11/20/69)

On November 20, the National Security Council's Review Group also discussed the study. Minutes of this meeting are printed in *Foreign Relations, 1969–1976*, volume XVII, China, 1969–1972, Document 47. The summary of decisions as reflected in the minutes read:

"1. The problem should be considered by the NSC even though there was no immediate operational decision to be made;

"2. For purposes of the NSC discussion, we would distinguish between neutrality on the Sino-Soviet dispute and neutrality in our relations with China and the USSR;

"3. The basic paper would be carefully reviewed by the NSC Staff and any proposed restatements would be discussed with the State representatives;

"4. Following this review, suggestions for handling the paper in the NSC would be discussed with the R[eview] G[roup] members early next week;

"5. If desired, the oral presentation for the NSC will be discussed with the State representatives;

"6. The considerations in the Defense Department supplementary paper will be brought before the NSC in some form or other." (National Archives, Nixon Presidential Materials, NSC Files, NSC Institutional Files (H-Files), Box H–111, SRG Minutes Originals 1969)

---

102.   Telegram From the Department of State to the Mission to the North Atlantic Treaty Organization[1]

Washington, November 20, 1969, 0016Z.

195006. USNATO deliver Engleberger 0830 Thursday, November 20 FYI and Noforn (except as noted in para 4 below).

Subj: Soviet Approach on European Security Conference.

Memorandum below is uncleared and subject to revision upon review.

---

[1] Source: National Archives, Nixon Presidential Materials, NSC Files, Box 711, Country Files, Europe, USSR, Vol. VI. Confidential; Immediate. Drafted by Buchanan and approved by Dubs, McGuire, Okun, Levitsky, and Springsteen. Repeated to Moscow, Bucharest, Budapest, Prague, Sofia, and Warsaw. On November 21, the Department of State included in its submission to the President's Daily Brief the statement: "Ambassador Dobrynin has presented an informal aide-mémoire to Secretary Rogers on the question of a European Security Conference." (Ibid.) This telegram was attached to a memorandum describing the Soviet démarche from Sonnenfeldt to Kissinger on December 23.

1. Ambassador Dobrynin asked for an appointment with Secretary on November 18. They met at 9 a.m. on November 19. Dobrynin then proceeded to summarize lengthy "informal oral statement," text of which he later handed to secretary. Full text of statement follows:

"(1) Soviet Government proceeds from assumption that possibilities for holding all-European conference are now increasing. During time that passed since Bucharest Declaration by socialist countries, and especially since Budapest appeal,[2] the intentions of countries which sponsored proposals for all-European conference have become more clearly understood by other European countries. A number of wrong interpretations have been dropped which did not correspond to real position of socialist countries. Discussion of proposal for an all-European conference has become businesslike and is being focused on its agenda, possible results and body of participants. The well known initiative of Finland played positive role in this respect. Thus the question of preparation and convocation of all-European conference will now arise on a more practical plane.

"Socialist countries which proposed all-European conference have carefully analyzed existing points of view, considered the opinions expressed in course of bilateral contacts and have taken into account positions of interested states. In particular, they paid due attention to opinions regarding the necessity of thorough preparation for all-European conference, its possible participants and desirability to select for the discussion at the all-European conference such questions which would allow for a broad consensus in the present conditions in Europe, and regarding which all possible participants in the all-European conference would have sufficient degree of confidence as to their productive consideration at the conference itself.

"Having taken into account all above mentioned points, countries-signatories to Budapest appeal found it useful and timely to come out with new initiative to detail further steps for convening all-European conference and to provide answers to questions, which arose in the course of discussion with various countries of the proposal to convene the conference.

"(2) The Soviet Government is convinced that convening of all-European conference in near future would serve interests of strengthening peace and security in Europe as well as interests of all European and not only European states. It stands to reason that preparatory work

---

[2] Warsaw Pact nations issued the Budapest Appeal on March 17, 1969, calling for cooperation among all European countries and a conference on European security. (*Documents on Disarmament, 1969*, pp. 106–108)

must be aimed at practical fulfillment of proposal for convening conference instead of being used as pretext for its delay or for raising various preliminary conditions. In opinion of countries-participants in Prague meeting, the all-European conference could take place in first half of 1970.

"As for place of conference, the states-signatories of the Prague statement hold the opinion that it could take place in Helsinki in view of the role played by Government of Finland in this matter.

"(3) Soviet Government fully shares view of states which believe that all-European conference must end in success—all the more so that it would be the first meeting of all European countries in the post-war years.

"In our opinion, two items suggested by Prague statement[3] for inclusion in agenda of an all-European conference 'on the assurance of European security and on the renunciation of use of force or threat of its use in mutual relations among states in Europe' and 'on expansion of trade, economic, scientific and technical ties on equal terms aimed at developing political cooperation among European states'—can become subjects on which broad agreement can be reached, given sufficient good will of the parties. (*Comment:* Dobrynin handed the Secretary the text of these draft documents.)

"Discussion of first question mentioned above could, it is believed, result in signing of final document that would proclaim principle of renunciation of use of force or threat of its use in mutual relations among states in Europe. Adoption of such document would acutally mean proclamation of principle of renunciation of war in Europe which is of special significance in view of fact that it is on the European continent that the two most powerful military-political groupings confront each other with their military forces concentrated there in immediate proximity of each other. Establishment on regional basis of principle to renounce use of force or threat of its use is in keeping with provisions of UN Charter and serves their further development. Besides it should be borne in mind that not all of states concerned—future participants in the all-European conference—are members of the UN. It goes without saying that adoption of document on non-use of force by all-European conference would by no means affect commitments assumed by states-participants in all-European conference through existing multilateral and bilateral treaties and agreements.

"Discussion of second question on agenda, which could also result in adoption of appropriate document, would allow movement

---

[3] On October 30–31, the Foreign Ministers of the Warsaw Pact countries met in Prague and adopted a declaration for an All-European Conference to be held in Helsinki in the first half of 1970.

forward toward normalization of relations among European states, prepare ground for consideration of concrete questions of trade, economic, scientific and technical cooperation among all European states and for removal of obstacles in the mentioned fields.

"An accord achieved on both mentioned questions would contribute to improvement of general political atmosphere in Europe and to growth of trust, would secure principles of peaceful coexistence and would pave way for future consideration of other problems of interest to European states, the solution of which wuld contribute to strengthening of European security and development of broad cooperation among all European states.

"We would like to make clear, that at all-European conference, as we see it, every state-participant will be given an opportunity to set forth its viewpoint on questions regarding the situation in Europe and means of strengthening peace and security on the European continent, as well as to give suggestions and considerations for development of peaceful cooperation among European countries. In other words, we have in mind that there will take place a free discussion at the conference, and that decisions will be taken on the two proposed concrete questions at the conclusion of the conference. We would like to emphasize the idea that working out agreed drafts of the possible final documents in consultations even before convocation of an all-European conference would guarantee the success of conference to a considerable extent.

"(4) As it follows from Prague statement, the Soviet Union and other Socialist countries are prepared to consider any other proposals aimed at practical preparation for and ensuring the success of all-European conference.

"Sometimes an opinion is voiced to effect that questions advanced by socialist countries are allegedly not of major scale and that cardinal problems such as German problem should be introduced at all-European conference. We do not agree with such statements at all. Suggestions to effect that German problem or other problems be included in the agenda—and such problems are understood by the West in a specific way which is clearly unacceptable to the socialist countries—would only serve to complicate if not downright torpedo convocation or, at any rate, fruitful work of the conference. One cannot but take into consideration also that as far as German problem goes there is special responsibility of victorious powers in World War II who signed the Potsdam Agreement.[4]

---

[4] Sonnenfeldt wrote "n.b., France did not sign" after this sentence.

"Nor do we agree with attempts to raise the question of West Berlin since this is a special question and it does not belong to the all-European conference.

"(5) Referring to questions which have been raised with me by U.S. officials as to attitude of Soviet Union toward U.S. participation in an all-European conference, we would like to make the following clarification.

"All-European conference is of a regional nature, open for participation by all interested European states, including, of course, the GDR on an equal footing with the FRG and on equal terms with other participants.[5] With this qualification as to the body of participants the Soviet Government believes that the United States, if there is a wish on her part, can also take part in all-European conference, since it bears definite responsibility ensuing from Potsdam and other allied agreements in force for peaceful settlement in Europe. In setting forth our position as to agenda for the conference we took into account previous contacts with U.S. representatives and, in particular, the view expressed here to the effect that acute questions, especially those within the responsibility of the participants in the Potsdam Conference, be considered outside of the framework of the all-European conference. The items we propose to include in the agenda also correspond to suggestions by the American side that such questions be taken up at the conference which could productively be discussed and acted upon. We expect that further contacts will enable us together and for the benefit of the cause (sic) to discuss problems related to preparation and holding of an all-European conference.

"(6) We would like to express hope that U.S. Government will give its due attention to proposals advanced by states which signed Prague statement, and to considerations of USSR Government on this score, and on its part will make efforts toward preparation of convening and successful holding of all-European conference. Soviet Government would appreciate considerations and suggestions which U.S. Government may think useful to express in this connection."[6]

---

[5] Sonnenfeldt wrote "quid pro quo" in the margin.

[6] Sonnenfeldt wrote "requests reply" after this sentence. In a December 23 memorandum to Kissinger about the Soviet démarche, Sonnenfeldt wrote, "In a sense, we gave our reply via the NATO Ministerial Communiqué and Declaration but, formally speaking, no reply has been made." Sonnenfeldt provided the following suggestion: "On the substance of the matter, I think we should take the line that, as the Soviets themselves recognize, the real European issues are not amenable to solution by conference diplomacy and in any case involve only a specific number of states, not all of them. If the Europeans want a conference on the type of agenda the Soviets propose, let them have one, but without us." (National Archives, Nixon Presidential Materials, NSC Files, Box 711, Country Files, Europe, USSR, Vol. VI)

2. After Dobrynin finished his summary of oral statement, the Secretary asked how long the Soviet Government would envisage duration of proposed ESC. Ambassador replied conference need not be long at all if agreement can be reached on draft documents beforehand through bilateral discussions. Obviously if conference were to discuss substance of controversial issues it could last very long time. It would be Soviet hope, however, that agreement could be reached on draft documents prepared at Prague conference before ESC convenes. The USSR assumed, Dobrynin said, that NATO countries might have two or three other issues which they would like to raise at ESC; these could also be discussed through diplomatic channels ahead of time.

3. Draft documents handed Secretary noted in para (3) above are identical with texts transmitted in London's 9176. (Text being repeated to addressees who did not received London Embtel.)

4. For USNATO—at November 20 Polads discussion of Eastern European follow-up to Prague declaration, you may inform Allies of Dobrynin call on Secretary. You may also make oral summary of principal points which Dobrynin made.

Rogers

---

103. Memorandum for the 303 Committee[1]

Washington, December 9, 1969.

SUBJECT

United States Government Support of Covert Action Directed at the Soviet Union

---

[1] Source: National Security Council, Nixon Intelligence Files, Subject Files, USSR. Secret; Eyes Only.

1. *Summary*

In accordance with NSC 5502/1,[2] as revalidated on 10 November 1960, CIA sponsors a covert action program which supports media[3] and contact activities aimed at stimulating and sustaining pressures for liberalization and evolutionary change from within the Soviet Union.

[4 *paragraphs (16 lines of source text) not declassified*]

This paper recommends that the 303 Committee approve the continuation of the covert action program directed primarily at the Soviet intelligentsia and reaffirm the approval it has given in the past to the program generally and the individual projects specifically.

The total cost of this program is $766,000. The program as a whole was discussed with and endorsed by Deputy Assistant Secretary of State Swank and Soviet Union Country Director Dubs on 21 October and 6 November 1969. The individual projects had been approved by the 303 Committee in 1967 and 1968.

2. *Proposal*

While these projects differ in their approach to the Soviet target, they share common objectives which provide the justification for continued support of their activities. The primary objective is to stimulate and sustain pressures for liberalization and change from within the Soviet Union. The neuralgic points of this disaffection—desire for personal and intellectual freedom, desire for improvement in the quality of life, and the persistence of nationalism in Eastern Europe and among the nationality groups in the Soviet Union—are the main issues exploited by these projects. A secondary objective is to enlighten important third-country elites, especially political leaders and the public-opinion shaping professions, about the repressive nature of the Soviet system and its imperialistic and self-aggrandizing foreign policy.

---

[2] Extracts from NSC 5502/1, "Statement on U.S. Policy Toward Russian Anti-Soviet Political Activities," January 31, 1955, are printed in *Foreign Relations, 1955–1957*, vol. XXIV, Soviet Union, Eastern Mediterranean, Document 3.

[3] The activities directed at the Soviet Union by Radio Liberty Committee and Free Europe, Inc., were approved by higher authority on 22 February 1969 and are, therefore, not treated in this paper. The Radio Liberty Committee, successor organization to the American Committee for Liberation from Bolshevism, is composed of three major divisions: Radio Liberty which broadcasts via short wave to the Soviet Union 24 hours a day in 18 languages; a book publication and distribution program designed to provide Soviet citizens with books not normally accessible to the Soviet public; and the [*less than 1 line of source text not declassified*] which produces research papers and publications targeted at the developing countries in Africa, the Middle East and the Far East. [*4½ lines of source text not declassified*] [Footnote in the source text.]

Anticipating the persistence of these trends in the intellectual climate of the Soviet Union in the 1970's, there is long-range merit in continuing to encourage and support the publication and distribution of dissident literature and socio-political commentary on the broad current issues and the conditions of life in the Soviet Union, even though the regime will continue to repress dissidence. Operations aimed at influencing third-country elites are based on the assumption that U.S.-Soviet competition for prestige and influence in strategic areas will continue for an indefinite period of time. It would, therefore, seem prudent to maintain a capability of influencing third-country intellectuals and elite groups through the words and voices of distinguished Soviet nationals who are disaffected.

The intellectual dissidence movement has demonstrated a vitality of its own. It is reasonable to assume that these dissidents will continue to seek outlets for literature and socio-political commentary that has thus far been suppressed. Each time the regime has silenced a group of dissidents a new group has emerged to produce a new generation of protest literature.

An American professor [2 lines of source text not declassified] reported that the dissidence is widespread among the Soviet intelligentsia and they "yearn for exposure to Western literature and cultural influence." Graphic evidence of the existence of this dissidence was provided in October 1969 by Dr. Pyotr L. Kapitsa, the "dean" of Soviet physicists, when he publicly endorsed in Washington the thesis of Dr. Andre D. Sakharov, a distinguished Soviet physicist credited with a major role in the development of the hydrogen bomb, that the United States and the Soviet Union can avoid a clash only through the convergence of their systems of government. The Sakharov thesis is set forth in a lengthy essay which has been circulating underground in the Soviet Union and which has been a staple of the CIA distribution program. Recent press dispatches from Moscow [less than 1 line of source text not declassified] indicate that the convergence ideas expounded by Dr. Sakharov are being widely circulated among the intelligentsia, including military personnel, in the form of underground mimeograph publications.

3. *Effectiveness*

[4 paragraphs (65 lines of source text) not declassified]

4. *Alternatives*

A. The United States could follow a policy of encouraging more vigorous émigré activities by more forthcoming identification by United States officials with émigré objectives, the extension of subsidies for émigré activities or organizations not presently receiving assistance from the United States Government, and adoption of a policy of open support for the independence of national minority areas such as the Ukraine. Substantial intensification of émigré propaganda activities might result in stimulating dissension inside the USSR, inducing defections and improving the collection of intelligence; identification with the independence of national minority groups could strengthen ethnic nationalist resistance to Russian domination. On the other hand, a more vigorous emigration probably would strengthen the forces of conformity and repression would retard the process of evolution in popular and leadership attitudes which the program is trying to promote.

B. It could also be argued that it would be in the national interest to divorce the United States Government entirely from the emigration and its activities. In this event the efforts of Soviet conservatives to justify repression of dissent on the basis of American "subversion" would lose some of their credibility. This argument, however, is negated by the fact that suspicions of U.S. intentions are so deeply ingrained that any change in U.S. policy toward the emigration would have minimal impact on the conservatives. Moreover, a source of support for those in the Soviet Union who are sustained by a sense of contact with the emigration would be removed and the Soviet authorities would be able more easily to foist their own version of events on the people and be under less pressure to make reforms.

5. Risks and Contingency Planning

All of the above projects have been subjected, at one time or another, to attacks by Soviet regime media, including allegations of CIA sponsorship. Each project has weathered the attacks without any apparent loss of effectiveness. It would be prudent to anticipate that the attacks will continue sporadically but without any effect on the operations.

6. Coordination

A. CIA's covert action program set forth herein was discussed with and endorsed by Deputy Assistant Secretary of State Emory C. Swank and Soviet Union Country Director Adolph Dubs on 21 October and 6 November, 1969. The individual projects[4] had been coordinated previously within the U.S. Government as follows:

[5 paragraphs (32 lines of source text) not declassified]

---

[4] Additional documentation on these projects is in the National Security Council, Special Group/303 Committee Files.

7. Costs

The allocations for the covert action program are as follows:

[*6 lines of source text not declassified*]
Total $766,000

These funds for the program are available in the FY 1970 CIA budget.

8. Recommendation

It is recommended that the 303 Committee approve the continuation of CIA's covert action program directed against the Soviet Union and reaffirm the approval it has given in the past to the individual projects, as described herein. The 303 Committee is also requested to approve the funding level for these projects as set forth in paragraph 7 above.

---

104.   Editorial Note

On December 9, 1969, in a public address before the 1969 Galaxy Conference on Adult Education in Washington, D.C., Secretary of State William Rogers outlined a proposal for an Arab-Israeli peace settlement. The position set forth in the Secretary's speech, which became known as the Rogers Plan, incorporated most of the language contained in the United States proposal handed to Soviet Ambassador Anatoly Dobrynin by Assistant Secretary of State for Near Eastern and South Asian Affairs Joseph Sisco on October 28, 1969 (see Document 98). Rogers enunciated the main elements of his plan as follows:

"Peace between the Parties

"—The Resolution of the Security Council makes clear that the goal is the establishment of a state of peace between the parties instead of the state of belligerency which has characterized relations for over 20 years. We believe the conditions and obligations of peace must be defined in specific terms. For example, navigation rights in the Suez Canal and in the Straits of Tiran should be spelled out. Respect for sovereignty and obligations of the parties to each other must be made specific.

"But peace, of course, involves much more than this. It is also a matter of the attitudes and intentions of the parties. Are they ready to coexist with one another? Can a live-and-let-live attitude replace suspicion, mistrust and hate? A peace agreement between the parties must be based on clear and stated intentions and a willingness to bring about basic changes in the attitudes and conditions which are characteristic of the Middle East today.

"Security

"—A lasting peace must be sustained by a sense of security on both sides. To this end, as envisaged in the Security Council resolution, there should be demilitarized zones and related security arrangements more reliable than those which existed in the area in the past. The parties themselves, with Ambassador Jarring's help, are in the best position to work out the nature and the details of such security arrangements. It is, after all, their interests which are at stake and their territory which is involved. They must live with the results.

"Withdrawal and Territory

"—The Security Council Resolution endorses the principle of the non-acquisition of territory by war and calls for withdrawal of Israeli armed forces from territories occupied in the 1967 war. We support this part of the Resolution, including withdrawal, just as we do its other elements.

"The boundaries from which the 1967 war began were established in the 1949 Armistice Agreements and have defined the areas of national jurisdiction in the Middle East for 20 years. Those boundaries were armistice lines, not final political borders. The rights, claims and positions of the parties in an ultimate peaceful settlement were reserved by the Armistice Agreement.

"The Security Council Resolution neither endorses nor precludes these armistice lines as the definitive political boundaries. However, it calls for withdrawal from occupied territories, the non-acquisition of territory by war, and for the establishment of secure and recognized boundaries.

"We believe that while recognized political boundaries must be established, and agreed upon by the parties, any changes in the preexisting lines should not reflect the weight of conquest and should be confined to insubstantial alterations required for mutual security. We do not support expansionism. We believe troops must be withdrawn as the Resolution provides. We support Israel's security and the security of the Arab states as well. We are for a lasting peace that requires security for both."

Rogers explained that "in our recent meetings with the Soviets, we have discussed some new formulas in an attempt to find common positions." He outlined the three principal elements as follows:

"First, there should be a binding commitment by Israel and the United Arab Republic to peace with each other, with all the specific obligations of peace spelled out, including the obligation to prevent hostile acts originating from their respective territories.

"Second, the detailed provisions of peace relating to security safeguards on the ground should be worked out between the parties, un-

der Ambassador Jarring's auspices, utilizing the procedures followed in negotiating the Armistice Agreements under Ralph Bunche in 1949 at Rhodes. This formula has been previously used with success in negotiations between the parties on Middle Eastern problems. A principal objective of the Four Power talks, we believe, should be to help Ambassador Jarring engage the parties in a negotiating process under the Rhodes formula.

"So far as a settlement between Israel and the United Arab Republic goes, these safeguards relate primarily to the area of Sharm al-Shaykh controlling access to the Gulf of Aqaba, the need for demilitarized zones as foreseen in the Security Council Resolution, and final arrangements in the Gaza Strip.

"*Third,* in the context of peace and agreement on specific security safeguards, withdrawal of Israeli forces from Egyptian territory would be required.

"Such an approach directly addresses the principal national concerns of both Israel and the UAR. It would require the UAR to agree to a binding and specific commitment to peace. It would require withdrawal of Israeli armed forces from UAR territory to the international border between Israel and Egypt which has been in existence for over a half century. It would also require the parties themselves to negotiate the practical security arrangements to safeguard the peace." (Department of State *Bulletin,* January 5, 1970, pages 7–11)

On December 10, 1969, Israel rejected Rogers' proposals. At 10 a.m., the National Security Council met to discuss the situation in the Middle East. When discussion turned to the best forum to continue negotiations, the President's Assistant for National Security Affairs Henry Kissinger made the following comments about bilateral talks between the Soviet Union and the United States:

"US–USSR talks have been confined to the UAR because the issues seemed more tractable, because a UAR settlement would facilitate a Jordan settlement and because we thought the USSR might press the UAR. Those who argued for entering those talks did so on three grounds. First, for global reasons, the US had an interest in seeing whether it could negotiate seriously on a range of important issues. Second, the USSR's persistent requests since September 1968 to talk about a Mid-East settlement suggested that Moscow might be uncomfortable in the Mid-East and might participate seriously in trying to work out a reasonable arrangement. While we maintained a proper skepticism, it made sense to probe far enough to see what was possible. Third, the USSR should pay at least as much of the price for a settlement as the U.S. in expanding its influence with its clients. Those who opposed this course argued mainly that the USSR did not want a real peace; it simply wanted to persuade us to press Israel to give back the territory of Moscow's clients. Since the USSR was not likely to act seriously, it did not make sense to formalize the USSR's role in the Mid-East by giving it a place at the peace table."

President Richard Nixon then commented:

"It has been one of our assumptions in the U.S.-Soviet talks that we could get the Soviet Union to help bring the UAR around. Mr. [John] McCloy yesterday hit hard on the following point: Nasser tells him and other American businessmen that the Egyptians don't want to be exclusively in Soviet clutches. They would like the opportunity for direct communication with the U.S. The oil people all seem to feel that we are making a mistake not to have a direct channel of communications with the Egyptians."

Rogers remarked as follows:

"We do have direct channels of communication with the Egyptians. It is interesting to note that when I sent my letter [outlining the Rogers plan] to [UAR] Foreign Minister [Mahmoud] Riad, [Soviet] Ambassador [Anatoly] Dobrynin came in and told me that [Soviet] Foreign Minister [Andrei] Gromyko had been embarrassed by what I had said in my letter. Riad had turned over a copy of my letter to Gromyko. Here was an opportunity given to the Egyptians to communicate with the U.S. and not to involve the Russians, and the first thing they did was to turn over the communication to the Russians."

After further discussion about Middle East issues not directly related to the Soviet Union, Nixon remarked:

"On the Middle East, however, it is fair to say that Soviet interests can only be served by tension. I know it is sometimes said that the Soviets are uncomfortable in the present situation. But I sometimes have trouble understanding why."

The following exchanges then took place:

"Mr. Helms: I think they want the situation to stay the way it is.

"Secretary Rogers: I am not so sure of that. I believe they are quite concerned about the consequences of the kind of explosion Israel could provoke.

"Dr. Kissinger: The longer Israel holds its conquered Arab territory, the longer the Soviets cannot deliver what the Arabs want. As that time drags on, the Arabs must begin to conclude that friendship with the Soviet Union is not very helpful—that it led to two defeats, one of which the U.S. rescued the Arabs from, and to continued impotence in regaining what they have lost.

"Secretary Rogers: The Soviets have some of the same problems with the UAR that we have with Israel. They cannot just walk in to Nasser's office and gain his acceptance of any proposition they may put to him. They must consider the fact that the more radical Arab elements like the fedayeen are going to blame the Soviets for not producing what the Arabs want.

"President: Then it is possible to argue, is it not, that if we want the Soviets to help, Israel is producing that result by scaring them. Why should it not be our policy to let Israel scare them a little bit more?

"Secretary Rogers: I think our position is pretty well spelled out now as a result of my speech last night. The position I elaborated on there is thoroughly consistent with the UN Security Council resolution." (National Archives, Nixon Presidential Materials, NSC Files, NSC Institutional Files (H-Files), Box H–109, NSC Minutes Originals 1969 [5 of 5]) The minutes of this meeting are printed in *Foreign Relations, 1969–1976*, volume XXIII, Arab-Israeli Dispute, 1969–1972.

Expansion of the Kissinger–Dobrynin Channel and Further Discussions on the Middle East, December 11, 1969–July 28, 1970

105. Memorandum From Helmut Sonnenfeldt of the National Security Council Staff to the President's Assistant for National Security Affairs (Kissinger)[1]

Washington, December 11, 1969.

SUBJECT

Informing the Soviets of our Talks with the Chinese

I notice that Gerard Smith and Ambassador Thompson proposed that Dobrynin be informed of the resumption of US-Chinese talks before it becomes public knowledge.

In the last Administration it was a standard practice for the State Department to provide Dobrynin with detailed records of the Warsaw talks. This was done at the Thompson and Bohlen level. The idea was to calm possible Soviet suspicions. It was also assumed that the Russians probably had some knowledge of the content of the talks from Polish monitoring operations and that, therefore, there was no harm in providing them with the full record.

I believe that as a matter of style, and consistent with our general approach to the Soviets and the Chinese Communists, this practice of the last Administration should not be resumed in this one.[2] I

[1] Source: National Archives, Nixon Presidential Materials, NSC Files, Box 711, Country Files, Europe, USSR, Vol. VI. Secret; Nodis. Sent for information.

[2] Attached but not printed is a December 12 memorandum from Kissinger informing Rogers that "The President agrees completely with your recommendation against advising Ambassador Dobrynin of our talks with the Chinese. He has asked that under no circumstances should we inform Dobrynin of the talks or their content. If Dobrynin questions, we should respond with nonchalance that they concern matters of mutual interest but not go beyond that."

assume that you will want to call this to the attention of the Secretary of State.[3]

---

[3] Haig's initials and the following handwritten comments appear at the end of the memorandum: "Absolutely. Hal [Sonnenfeldt]—Rogers called HAK, agreed completely with your psn [position] and on his own volunteered this psn—HAK ran by Pres—and confirmed in writing. Copy attached." At 12:22 p.m., Rogers and Kissinger spoke on the telephone about this issue. According to a transcript of their conversation, "R said Tommy [Llewellyn] Thompson recommended that we advise Dobrynin about the proposed talks with the Chinese. R said he doesn't think we should, but we wanted to give the P[resident] the chance to think about it. K said how did he know? K said I guess he got it in the traffic. R said he got it in the traffic and it's going to be in the papers. R said he thinks we should be nice in view of the SALT, but R doesn't agree. K said he agrees with R and K thinks the P will need a lot of selling to accept Tommy Thompson's view. K said he would mention it to him. K said he will say that R disagreed, but wanted to be meticulous and let K know." (Library of Congress, Manuscript Division, Kissinger Papers, Box 361, Telephone Conversations, Chronological File)

---

106.   Memorandum for the 303 Committee[1]

Washington, December 12, 1969.

SUBJECT

U.S. Policy on Support for Covert Action Involving Emigrés Directed at the Soviet Union

Summary:

The Department of State was instructed by NSDM 25[2] of September 17, 1969, to review and up-date NSC 5502/1[3] dated January 31, 1955 on the subject of "U.S. Policy Toward Russian Anti-Soviet Political Activities." That document, which was reviewed and approved again by the NSC Planning Board on November 1, 1960, has provided the authorization for CIA covert action programs directed at the Soviet Union involving émigrés from Soviet-dominated areas. In view of the essentially covert nature of these CIA programs, it has been determined

---

[1] Source: National Security Council, Nixon Intelligence Files, Subject Files, USSR. Secret; Eyes Only.

[2] NSDM 25 directed the "Disposal of Outdated NSC Policy Papers." (National Archives, Nixon Presidential Materials, NSC Files, NSC Institutional Files (H-Files), Box H–211, NSDM Files, NSDM 25)

[3] See footnote 2, Document 103.

that decisions not only on programs but also on policy should be the responsibility of the 303 Committee.

The principal policy recommendations in this paper are:

—that the present policy of selective support of émigré-related activities be continued;

—that the United States avoid policies, such as those favored by some émigrés, supporting separate nationhood for racial or language groupings within the Soviet Union; and

—that covert support activities be kept under periodic review, keeping in mind the option of withdrawing support in return for identifiable political advantages.

The CIA has distributed a related memorandum on "United States Government Support of Covert Action Directed at the Soviet Union"[4] dated December 9, 1969 which serves both as background for examination of this revised policy document and to support a request for funding for FY 1970. The CIA request does not include funds for the Radio Liberty Committee (current budget is $13,131,000) [*1½ lines of source text not declassified*] because those programs were approved by Higher Authority on February 22, 1969. The [*less than 1 line of source text not declassified*] programs for which CIA is requesting continued support involve the expenditure of $766,000 in FY 1970. These [*less than 1 line of source text not declassified*] programs have the approval of appropriate officers in the Department of State: Bureau of European Affairs (Deputy Assistant Secretary Swank and Soviet Union Country Director Dubs) and the Planning and Coordination Staff (Mr. R. Davies).

Trends in US-Emigré Relations

Anti-Soviet émigrés[5] were regarded as an important potential asset in the early post World War II years, at a time when fear of eventual if not imminent war with the USSR was very real in the West. Emigré organizations and individual Soviet refugees were in demand to help staff proliferating anti-Soviet activities and serve generally as a reserve for a possible war emergency.

After the 1950's, the United States became more selective in its support for émigré activities. It had become clear that the émigrés were hopelessly split between groups with opposing aims, philosophies and ethnic composition and that it was difficult for any government working closely with them not to be dragged into the morass of émigré politics. In the mid-1950's, efforts were, in fact, abandoned to try to unite the anti-Soviet émigrés behind a common program. The declining interest in émigrés was also related to the realization that they were aging and had grown increasingly out of touch with developments in the

---

[4] Document 103.

[5] [*3 lines of source text not declassified*] [Footnote in the source text.]

USSR. The relations between the United States Government and the émigré community also became more distant as the United States and the Soviet Union moved toward a more normal relationship.

In the early 1960's, the more responsible émigré leaders came to realize that there was no hope of returning to their homeland in the wake of a Soviet-American war or after the overthrow of the Soviet regime. They therefore shifted the emphasis of their activities toward stimulating and publicizing the growing intellectual ferment and expressions of dissidence within the Soviet Union.

United States officials had come to understand that assistance to the émigrés for the eventuality of war with or revolution within the USSR was unrealistic. The skills of the émigrés would be available in the event of war, regardless of whether or not the United States was subsidizing émigré organizations. The sort of mass unrest and revolutionary changes predicted by some émigrés were unlikely to occur within the USSR under conditions short of war. To the extent that significant changes in Soviet policy or leadership might take place, they were likely to result from the actions of a relatively narrow circle of leaders responding to changing attitudes and imperatives within Soviet soviety.

It was recognized, at the same time, that the émigrés could play an important role in overcoming the resistance to change in Soviet society by stimulating dissatisfaction with existing policy among the Soviet people, especially under the less repressive conditions which followed Stalin's death. As broadcasters, editors and scholars working for Radio Liberty and other émigré information activities, the émigrés were able to address themselves more candidly than U.S. officials could to developments within the USSR; and there was evidence that the émigrés reached an important audience in the USSR precisely because they spoke with special intimacy and concern about developments in Mother Russia. In short, the United States Government concluded that anti-Soviet émigrés had a special contribution to make to United States information programs, both overt and covert, which collectively aimed at influencing the attitudes of the Soviet people and their leaders in directions which would make the Soviet Government a more constructive and responsible member of the world community.

It was also recognized that the émigrés had a certain role to play per se. For some Soviet intellectuals and liberals, they served as in the 19th century as the "conscience-in-exile" and repository of the best cultural traditions of the Russian people and in extremis as a haven of refuge. The émigré organizations accordingly provided—and continue to provide—encouragement to intellectuals in their struggle for personal freedom against the Soviet regime.

Emigré groups have continued to seek official American recognition and support for their particular organizations and aims. In their response, American officials have been authorized to express traditional

American sympathy for all peoples struggling to preserve their cultural traditions and religious beliefs and to protect the human rights of their people. At the same time, it has long been United States Government policy to remain neutral between the Russian proponents of a unitary Russia and émigrés from national minority areas favoring separatist policies.

Nature of Present Activities

The United States Government is presently involved with the émigré community in a number of activities which are summarized below. Details regarding these activities are set forth in the CIA memorandum.

a. *Radio Liberty Committee* (RLC): (successor organization to the American Committee for Liberation from Bolshevism), RLC is composed of three major divisions: (1) a radio station (Radio Liberty) which broadcasts via shortwave to the Soviet Union 24 hours a day in 18 languages; (2) a book publication and book distribution program designed to provide Soviet citizens with books not normally accessible to the Soviet public, and; (3) the Institute for the Study of the USSR which produces research papers and publications targeted at the developing countries in Africa, Middle East, and the Far East. In all instances RLC émigré employees are picked for talent and ability without regard to private émigré political beliefs or affiliations.

[*3 paragraphs (28 lines of source text) not declassified*]

United States Policy Options

A. High Profile Support

The United States could reverse field and follow a more vigorous pro-émigré policy, which might take the form, for example, of (i) more forthcoming identification by United States officials with émigré activities and objectives, (ii) extension of subsidies for émigré activities or organizations not presently receiving U.S. Government assistance; (iii) adoption for the first time of a policy of open support for the independence of national minority areas like the Ukraine.

Pro

—Blatant support of anti-Soviet émigré activities would suggest the determination of the Administration to follow a tough policy toward the USSR, exploiting any vulnerability, in the event that the USSR does not become more cooperative on major issues in dispute.

—Any substantial intensification of émigré propaganda activities might have some feedback in terms of defections, in acquisition of information, and in stimulating dissension inside the USSR;

—United States identification with the independence of national minority areas would strike a responsive chord in an area like the Ukraine and could strengthen nationalist resistance to Russian domination.

Con

—The Soviet leaders, who are chronically suspicious of US policies, could conclude that the United States Government had embarked on a frankly subversive and hostile course of action and that it is disinterested in negotiations on outstanding issues.

—The Soviet leaders will not be induced to be more cooperative by the threat of increased American aid to the émigrés since they believe that the émigrés are feeble and that the Soviet government can control internal dissent.

—Inside the USSR, hard-line supporters of strict conformity and suppression of dissent would have their hands strengthened.

—Repression would retard the process of evolution in popular and leadership attitudes which United States policy has sought to promote.

—Support for the national independence of minority areas would alienate and unify Russian opinion everywhere so that the United States would lose with one hand what it might hope to gain with the other.

—The USSR would be encouraged to increase its own anti-American activities around the world, including support for radical and subversive movements within the United States.

—The problems of finding émigré organizations which are potentially effective and useful to the United States Government have increased with time many émigrés are now even more out-of-touch with Soviet reality, older and less active than in the early post-war years.

B. Withdrawal of All Support

The question of support for specific émigré activities is periodically reviewed. For example, a decision was taken in February 1969 to continue to finance the Radio Liberty Committee.

It can be argued that it would be in the national interest to divorce the United States Government entirely from the emigration and its activities.

Pro

—There would be a financial saving.

—A decision to withdraw American financial support from all émigré/[*activities?*]

—The existence of émigré voices speaking from abroad would continue to provide moral support and information to those Soviets who have the courage to voice their convictions openly in the USSR.

—Continuation of U.S. Government support for émigré activities on their present limited scale is not incompatible with negotiations with the Soviet Union on matters of mutual concern.

—Withdrawal of U.S. Government subsidies would eliminate, not merely the information activities which reach directly into the USSR, but also useful auxiliary activities which provide anti-communist information to target audiences in non-communist areas.

Con

—By continuing the present level of activities, the United States would not realize the advantages cited under the earlier options.

Recommended Courses of Action

On balance, the low profile policy which has evolved toward the emigration appears both realistic and well suited to United States objectives. Accordingly, it is recommended:

a. That the United States continue to work with émigrés and their organizations for the primary purpose of encouraging an evolution in attitudes within the USSR.

b. That the present general level of involvement with anti-Soviet émigrés be regarded as compatible with our limited adversary relationship with the USSR.

c. That the effectiveness of the activities presently being subsidized be reviewed periodically.

d. That the possibility of withdrawing support from émigré-related organizations, including the Radio Liberty Committee, be kept under review, on the understanding that any withdrawal should be based on concrete political advantage.

e. That any proposals to organize the émigrés for the possible eventuality of war with, or revolution in, the USSR be opposed as unrealistic and likely to damage US-Soviet relations.

f. That the United States support the aspirations of minority peoples in the USSR for preservation of their national culture, religious identity and human rights, but that it avoid identification with any émigré policy favoring separate nationhood for racial or language groupings within the Soviet Union.

g. That the United States policy of non-recognition of incorporation of the Baltic States into the USSR be maintained, subject to possible review, but that Baltic refugee organizations [*less than 1 line of source text not declassified*] be discouraged from active propaganda or other efforts to detach the Baltic States.

h. That émigré activities should continue to be monitored as appropriate even where no US subsidy is involved, since the émigrés occasionally obtain useful information on the USSR through their own channels, and are a potential source of embarrassment to the United States in its relations with the USSR.

107. Transcript of Telephone Conversation Between the President's Assistant for National Security Affairs (Kissinger) and the Soviet Ambassador (Dobrynin)[1]

Washington, December 19, 1969, 7:26 p.m.

D: Happy New Year to you.

K: I'm seeing you Monday night?[2] I'm already starving myself. We're going to solve all the problems on Monday. But I have a problem before that—that Helsinki conversation. I have been praising the Soviet Delegation for it's constructive tone and attitude. But the issue has come up—I just talked with the President—that of the site of the conference.[3]

D: I got a telegram—still in the same position.

K: When you talked to the P he understood you to say that the site is no huge problem; you said it could start in Helsinki and move someplace else. On this basis he agreed to start in Helsinki. Now Jerry Smith[4] is under the impression that your man says it has to be Helsinki.

D: You want Geneva?

K: Yes, the P prefers Vienna, with which we know you have problems. The P's basic attitude stays the same. We would consider your attitude very constructive if we could reach a compromise.

D: I will send to Moscow and see.

K: The final session is Monday (?) and we would like to end up without too many disagreements.

D: The only problem is that tomorrow is Saturday—it will be hard to [reach them—I couldn't understand exactly what would be hard, but I think that's what he meant].[5] But I'll try.

K: I'll appreciate it and I'll see you Monday.

---

[1] Source: Library of Congress, Manuscript Division, Kissinger Papers, Box 360, Telephone Conversations, Chronological File. No classification marking.

[2] See Tab A, Document 110.

[3] Kissinger spoke with the President at 7:15 p.m. The first few sentences are apparently missing from the transcript of their conversation. Kissinger then stated, "The SALT talks." Nixon asked, "[The Soviets] are going to change it?" Kissinger replied, "This is the problem. You remember our problems with Dobrynin. Bill [Rogers] was reluctant to raise the issue. You had given [Gerard] Smith the instructions and now the Russians had backed off. I thought just as a matter of discipline I ought to call Dobrynin and remind him of this conversation before." Nixon said, "Tell him we gave in on Helsinki and why not Vienna. We don't have to be anxious but the point is that it ought to be either Geneva or Vienna." (Library of Congress, Manuscript Division, Kissinger Papers, Box 360, Telephone Records, 1969–1976, Telephone Conversations, Chronological File)

[4] Reference is to Gerard Smith.

[5] Brackets in the source text.

108.   Memorandum From the President's Assistant for National Security Affairs (Kissinger) to President Nixon[1]

Washington, December 23, 1969.

SUBJECT

Recent Soviet Policy Developments: SALT, China and Germany

I thought you might be interested in a speculative piece I asked to be prepared on some aspects of Soviet policy.

The main points are: The Soviets have several balls in the air—SALT, the talks with China, and the new negotiations in Bonn; while it is tempting to see a grand design behind their diverse moves, one suspects there is a large element of improvisation.

SALT

The Soviet negotiators have been rather reserved, avoiding some key issues, and generally leaving the first moves up to us; by insisting on national means of verification, however, they have sharply narrowed the range of realistic proposals. One of their main incentives is their evident concern over Safeguard. They may hope to generate a new debate in this country by proposing a complete ban. At the same time, they have hinted at an interest in a fairly simple agreement early in the next phase.

China

Some observers see a close connection between SALT and the Sino-Soviet talks. While the Soviet position at Helsinki has been perfectly understandable in terms of the issues, they have tried to impress Peking with the possibilities of a Soviet-American rapprochement at Chinese expense. The Chinese have countered by reopening the Warsaw channel.

As for the talks in Peking, it does not appear that the interruption last week means a breakdown or new crisis. Both sides apparently see a tactical advantage to continuing the discussions. But the negotiations are stalemated, and tensions may mount again this spring when the weather makes military operations feasible. Thus the resumption of SALT may be viewed in Moscow as a kind of reinsurance against American reaction to Soviet punitive measures against China.

---

[1] Source: National Archives, Nixon Presidential Materials, NSC Files, Box 711, Country Files, Europe, USSR, Vol. VI. Secret. Sent for information. A notation on the memorandum indicates the President saw it.

Germany

The harsh line taken by Gromyko in his talks with the West German Ambassador[2] suggests that Moscow feels the China question is sufficiently under control for the time being to establish a hard bargaining position with Bonn. The Soviets would be likely to do so in any case, since they probably are calculating that the new Brandt government[3] is under pressure to demonstrate results and will be forced to make concessions. Moreover, by establishing a maximum position the Soviets are in effect laying down the terms for Bonn's other talks with the Poles, the Czechs and the East Germans.

The Outlook

By next spring the Soviets may have untangled the various lines of their Eastern and Western policies and we could look ahead to:

—a new Sino-Soviet crisis, which again would raise the ominous threat of a Soviet attack;

—renewed pressure for a European Security Conference, emanating both from Moscow and from within the Alliance;

—pressures from Bonn for us to become more active in supporting the German negotiations with the East; Brandt may want us to endorse concessions on a security conference, if his policy initiative appears to be foundering;

—the resumption of SALT, in which the Soviets might tie together SALT and European security, or present a seemingly attractive proposal intended to wipe out the Safeguard program, in return for a limitation on Soviet offensive weapons at or near parity.

The longer version elaborating on this speculation is attached at Tab A.[4]

---

[2] Gromyko met with West German Ambassador to the Soviet Union Helmut Allardt on December 8, 11, and 19. Soviet demands included FRG recognition of all postwar European borders; recognition of the FRG/GDR border; understandings on the right of both German states to represent their own interests internationally; a FRG undertaking regarding access to nuclear weapons; and FRG concession on the Munich agreement on the Oder-Niesse border. Telegrams providing accounts of their talks are ibid.

[3] Willy Brandt, who was the West German Vice Chancellor and Foreign Minister until October 21, became Chancellor of the Federal Republic of Germany on October 22.

[4] Attached but not printed.

109.   Telegram From the Department of State to Certain Posts[1]

Washington, December 24, 1969, 0034Z.

211994. Subject: Soviet Response to U.S. October 28 Proposal.

1. Ambassador Dobrynin at his request called on Secretary Rogers December 23 to convey Soviet response to October 28 formulations on Middle Eastern settlement. Sisco and Dubs also present.

2. Dobrynin said that while this reply was in form of oral statement, he was giving Secretary a Soviet language text and an informal Soviet Embassy translation of his statement.[2]

3. Secretary stressed at outset that US documents on UAR-Israeli aspect and Jordanian-Israeli part of settlement represented firm US Government positions. Secretary underscored this is as far as US is prepared to go. We believe that two documents provide framework within which parties can and should begin negotiations. Four Powers should get parties to negotiate on basis Rhodes formula, otherwise no progress can be made.

4. Dobrynin said that Secretary knew that Soviet side had no specific objection to Rhodes formula. Nevertheless in view of comments made by various parties regarding formula, Soviet side now felt Rhodes formula should not be used. Soviets feel Rhodes formula would not help very much in present state of affairs. Although Moscow is doubtful about any specific use of this formula, it is prepared to find something similar.

5. In response to Sisco's query, Dobrynin confirmed this represented a change in Soviet position. Sisco characterized this as a definite setback. Secretary had indicated in his discussions with Gromyko in New York US believes great use can be made of Rhodes formula, that it is constructively ambiguous, leaving it to each side to interpret formula in terms of its own policy.

6. Dobrynin replied that ultimately it might be possible to find some procedure involving Jarring which would be close to Rhodes formula; using this formula now would mean trouble from the start.

7. Secretary asked Dobrynin whether Soviets felt Arabs are really ready to start negotiations and whether USSR is ready for such process

---

[1] Source: National Archives, Nixon Presidential Materials, NSC Files, Box 711, Country Files, Europe, USSR, Vol. VI. Secret; Priority; Nodis. Drafted by Dubs on December 23; cleared by Brown (S/S) and Okun (S); and approved by Sisco. Sent to USUN, USINT Cairo, Amman, Beirut, Jidda, Kuwait, Tel Aviv, London, Paris, Moscow, Bucharest, Rabat, Tunis.

[2] The official translation of the Soviet text of December 23 was transmitted in telegram 212662 to Rogers in Key Biscayne, Florida, December 26. (Ibid.)

to get underway. Dobrynin did not respond directly but said USSR wishes to find more precise formulations regarding some of the issues at stake. He recalled that US had suggested possibility of finding neutral language on some questions, but reiterated that Soviet view is that more precise language should be found on such questions as DMZs, passage through waterways, and security provisions.

8. Secretary said he again wished to make clear that US has gone as far as it can go. We feel strongly that parties should begin process of negotiations. After the negotiations get underway, Four Powers could help in making suggestions and in encouraging parties directly concerned to reach agreement. We cannot overemphasize importance we attach to getting parties to negotiate.

9. Dobrynin asked what US proposes to do with respect to Jarring. Secretary said we continue to feel that best way to get Jarring started would be for Four Powers to agree on our two documents since they represent a sound framework for negotiations and are totally consistent with the Security Council Resolution. Secretary said we must get parties directly concerned negotiating and thereafter Four Powers could help prod the parties from behind the scenes while Jarring is making his efforts. He stressed that any more precise formulations would suggest that we are attempting to impose a settlement. This we cannot do.

10. Dobrynin said that Soviet statement notes that Jarring may also share view that it would not be useful to use Rhodes formula at this time because of the differences of view that have been expressed by parties regarding its interpretation.

11. Sisco said that United States feels Rhodes formula is neutral. It makes possible all sorts of diplomatic contacts, direct and indirect. It, therefore, meets main requirements of situation. Soviet change on Rhodes formula is a retrogressive step. Secretary Rogers recalled that Riad had himself raised question of the Rhodes formula during discussions in New York and had accepted it. Dobrynin suggested that Riad had accepted the formula on condition that any talks would be indirect. Secretary said let them call it indirect if they wish. We see no problem on that score. Dobrynin said that basic Soviet position is that an attempt should now be made to go beyond neutral formulations where possible in an attempt to find more precise language on elements of settlement. After this is done a formula providing for use of Jarring might be found to bring about negotiations. Dobrynin asked whether it is the United States position to give Jarring papers and to let him proceed from there in an effort to start negotiations. If this were the United States position, he doubted whether Jarring could be successful.

12. The Secretary noted that if the parties accepted Rhodes formula, they could interpret it as they desired. He reiterated that the

United States firmly believed that a settlement could not be imposed. We do not believe that documents can be given to the parties on a take it or leave it basis. Once parties agreed to negotiate with the United States papers as a framework, Four Powers could provide guidance and encouragement subsequently on specific points not covered by these documents.

13. Dobrynin asked whether the United States proposed to give Jarring all three papers, that is, the United States, French, and Soviet, that are available with respect to Jordan. Secretary Rogers said that we continue to believe US papers offer best basis for Jarring to proceed—they contain fair and equitable positions.

14. Sisco noted that United States October 28 proposal had not been formally tabled at Four Power meetings since we were awaiting a Soviet reply. He underlined that the United States October 28 proposal along with the US paper on Jordan[3] are the documents we believe should be transmitted to Jarring. Other papers that have been presented on Jordan, in our view, do not represent a real basis for negotiation.

15. Dobrynin noted that there were now two documents on the UAR and three on Jordan. He would hesitate to say that the United States paper on Jordan, for example, should be the central document. He assumed that any paper on Jordan would be of a joint nature.

16. Secretary said that we had hoped that our October 28 proposal would represent a joint US-Soviet paper since it took Soviet views into account. US does not want to consider October 28 proposal and our paper on Jordan as beginning points for negotiation among the Four Powers. We feel that we have gone as far as we can. We believe US papers provide Jarring with what he needs; they are a fair and equitable framework for negotiation.

17. Sisco said we will obviously study Soviet document carefully in an attempt to arrive at a conclusion as to whether it makes any sense to proceed any further in bilateral and Four Power talks. Principal focus in the Four Power discussions is, of course, Jordan. Depending upon the reaction to our paper on this subject, we will also wish to make a judgment regarding whether further discussions in Four Power context are useful. Soviet statement which we received today seems a reflection of its position back in June;[4] discussions of last six to seven months therefore have not carried us very far.

---

[3] On December 18, the United States presented a proposal for a Jordan-Israel settlement similar to its October 28 and December 9 plans; see Documents 98 and 104.

[4] See Document 58.

18. Secretary again asked Dobrynin whether there is a genuine interest on the part of Arab nations to negotiate a peaceful settlement. Secretary also asked whether the Arab countries are interested in a process of negotiation or whether they are simply interested in getting Israelis to withdraw and only afterward to begin negotiation process.

19. Dobrynin again refused to answer directly. He said this question was too broad and that there was no simple answer. He noted, however, that there has been some transformation in Arab thinking. For example, in past some Arab leaders had no desire to recognize existence of Israel. Subsequently, Arab leaders have indicated that they have changed their position on this score. With respect to Israelis, one difficult question was how to handle Fedayeen problem. This was difficult issue to articulate on paper. This appears to be question which could be handled satisfactorily. Soviet Union and US appear to be very close with respect to refugee problem. At same time Dobrynin said he did not understand US reluctance to mention the UN Resolution on refugees. Nevertheless, some agreement could be reached on that issue. Furthermore, Egyptians seemed willing to accept some formulation regarding the Strait of Tiran. Question of providing guarantees is a more difficult one. Soviet Union believes that guarantees could be provided by Security Council, where US and Soviet Union have veto power. UN troops under control of Security Council might, for example, be stationed at Sharm al-Shaykh. The Soviet Union cannot, however, accept the stationing of Israeli troops there as the US evidently has proposed.

20. Sisco said that US has not proposed in Moscow that Israeli forces be stationed at Sharm al-Shaykh. Soviets had conveyed this impression to Arabs, and we have spent some weeks correcting this interpretation. In Sisco's conversations with Gromyko, number of options discussed but no proposals made. Sisco recalled that it was because Israel could be expected to press an Israeli presence and Arabs a UN presence, that he came up with idea of neutral formulations prejudicing neither side's position.

21. Sisco then said he had completed a preliminary and rapid review of the text of the oral statement left by Dobrynin. His view is that it is unresponsive and not constructive. Dobrynin said lamely he would report this. Conversation concluded by reaffirmation of intention to give document thorough study and to respond in due course.[5]

---

[5] Printed from an unsigned copy.

110.   **Memorandum From the President's Assistant for National Security Affairs (Kissinger) to President Nixon**[1]

Washington, December 24, 1969.

SUBJECT

My Conversation with Ambassador Dobrynin

Attached is a memorandum of my conversation with Ambassador Dobrynin during the evening of December 22.[2] I found the following of particular interest:

—Dobrynin discussed Vietnam with a very low-key tone. His threat about what would happen if we started bombing the North again or hit Haiphong—that the Chinese would send in engineer battalions which would increase Chinese influence in Hanoi—seems almost to be an invitation for us to attack North Vietnam.

—Dobrynin said that he did not think Hanoi would have anything new to say for the next few months.

—The Russians seem eager to talk on a number of substantive issues. They are probably trying to head us towards a summit meeting. This could be a reflection of a desire for real détente, or it could mean they are getting ready to hit China in the Spring. The latter interpretation—that they are repeating their Czechoslovakia drill—is reinforced by their choosing April 16 as a date for resumption of the SALT talks.

Dobrynin suggested that he and I meet at regular intervals, discussing a particular topic at each meeting to explore what possible solutions on various issues might look like. We could decide after the discussion of each topic was completed and after it had been discussed with you whether any action was necessary—whether instructions would be given or it should be taken to another level. If you approve, I will agree to meet with him every three weeks after our return from San Clemente on an agenda to be approved by you.[3]

---

[1] Source: National Archives, Nixon Presidential Materials, NSC Files, Box 489, President's Trip Files, Dobrynin/Kissinger, 1969, Part 1. Top Secret; Sensitive; Nodis. Sent for action. A notation on the memorandum indicates the President saw it.

[2] On December 22, Kissinger sent the President a memorandum of "Points I Propose to Make to Ambassador Dobrynin at Dinner This Evening," which Nixon approved. (Library of Congress, Manuscript Division, Kissinger Papers, Box CL 215, "D" File) Before leaving for the dinner, Kissinger and Nixon spoke on the telephone. According to the transcript of their conversation, Kissinger said, "I just wanted to make sure that nothing else occurred to you." Nixon replied, "Say, the promise is great, but conditions are the same. On Vietnam, play it cool. Say well, maybe we don't need your help. If it is raised say we are really pressing across the bridge on that. Now anything we do, we don't want to take affront at it." (Ibid., Box 361, Telephone Conversations, Chronological File)

[3] Nixon initialed the approve option.

Tab A

Memorandum of Conversation Between the President's Assistant for National Security Affairs (Kissinger) and the Soviet Ambassador (Dobrynin)[4]

Washington, December 22, 1969.

SUBJECT

Conversation with Soviet Ambassador Dobrynin

After an exchange of pleasantries, Dobrynin opened the conversation by saying that he wanted to speak to me on a frank and open basis. He had missed the opportunity to talk to me for a long time, and he hoped that our meetings would be more frequent. I said that it was always a pleasure to talk to him.

Dobrynin said that when he had met with the President,[5] the President had indicated that the Middle East and other issues could be settled only on the highest level. With this, the Soviet Government agreed. On the other hand, the President had also indicated that there could be no contact on any level except the diplomatic level until Vietnam was settled. Did this mean that we did not believe that there could be any progress in our relations with the Soviet Union? I asked Dobrynin why he raised this issue now, since I thought we had explained to him at great length what our position was and that nothing had really changed. Vietnam was an important problem to us, and he knew how we related it to other issues.

U.S. Domestic Scene

Dobrynin said he wanted to be frank. He had made a careful analysis of the American domestic situation, and he had communicated it to Moscow as follows:

The President was almost certain of re-election in 1972. He had only begun to tap the right-wing votes and he could always expand his base in that direction. There was, therefore, no prospect of anyone's unseating him in 1972. If anyone wanted to wait him out, they had to be ready to wait for seven more years. This was too long for the Soviet Union, and it should also be too long for Hanoi. He therefore wanted to ask me again whether I saw any prospect for improving Soviet/American relations.

---

[4] A notation on the memorandum indicates the President saw it. Nixon wrote "K— very fascinating!" in the upper righthand corner.

[5] See Document 93.

I repeated the President's statement at the October 20th meeting that he hoped to have his Administration go down in history as one that did bring about a substantial improvement in Soviet/American relations but we wanted to proceed by concrete steps. And, of course, it was a difficult problem while the Vietnam war went on.

Vietnam

Dobrynin then turned to the war in Vietnam. He said, "You have to understand that we tried to do something last April and May, but Hanoi told us that there was no sense having a private channel unless the United States agreed in advance to negotiate about a coalition government. We cannot tell them how to fight in their own country. This is a real problem to us, and we thought it was best not to return a negative reply." I said it would have been better to return some sort of a reply, but there was no sense talking about the past.

Dobrynin then asked me how I saw the future. I said that I really had not come to discuss Vietnam, but to sum it up in a few words, we were very confident. For the first time in my experience with Vietnam, I now was certain that time was working on our side. It seemed to me that Hanoi had only two choices—to negotiate or to see its structure in South Vietnam erode. He said, "Isn't there even a slight chance that the South Vietnam Government might collapse?" I said that we were confident that we were on the right course. Maybe Hanoi would start an offensive but then, as the President had repeatedly pointed out publicly, it would have to draw the consequences. Dobrynin said, "Of course, if you start bombing the North again, or if you hit Haiphong, you realize what would happen." I expected him to say the Soviet Union would come in. But instead, he said, "What would happen is the Chinese would send in engineer battalions, and you don't want to increase Chinese influence in Hanoi." I said, "If you can live with it, we can," and in any event, our problem was to end the war in South Vietnam.

Dobrynin said that he did not think that Hanoi had anything new to say for the next few months. I told him that they knew what channels were available and that we would be glad to listen to them if they did. We would be flexible and conciliatory in negotiations. We had no intention to humiliate Hanoi, but we would not pay an additional price to enter the negotiations. Dobrynin asked me whether we were ever going to send a senior Ambassador to the negotiations. I said it depended in part on the negotiations, but I had no doubt that ultimately it would be done. He said he had to admit that nothing was going on at the negotiations now, but that he thought they were an important symbol.

I said in conclusion that if Hanoi had something to say to us it should do so explicitly, and not get us involved in detective stories in which various self-appointed or second-level emissaries were dropping oblique hints. Dobrynin laughed and said he would be sure to get this point across. He thought Hanoi had nothing to say at the moment.

The major point about the Vietnam part was the complete absence of contentiousness on Dobrynin's part. There was no challenge to my assertion that our policy was working out, and there was a conspicuous effort by Dobrynin to disassociate himself from the Vietnamese war.

Tour d'Horizon

Dobrynin asked how we looked at Southeast Asia as a whole. I referred to the Nixon Doctrine and regional groupings, etc. I asked him how the Russians saw their own interests in the area. Surprisingly, he said, "We don't have real interests there. We were drawn in in 1964 on the basis of a misunderstanding."[6]

Dobrynin then turned to other issues. He began with a familiar catalogue. He said that the Soviet Government was approaching relations with the United States with an open mind and with good will, but a number of very strange things had happened. They had made a formal proposal to Secretary Rogers about European security. They had never received a reply; instead, the Secretary had made a very anti-Soviet speech in Brussels.

On the trade bill, the Administration had not liberalized trade as[7] many in Congress had wanted.

While the SALT talks were going on, there were newspaper stories that the United States was pushing its ABM development and its MIRV development in the Defense Program Review Committee under my chairmanship.[8]

The Middle East negotiations[9] were stalled.

Deputy Foreign Minister Macovescu of Romania was received at the White House while Gromyko was not.

I had to remember that in the Soviet Union, decisions were not made by one man as in the United States, but by eleven;[10] and all these signals put together created a very bad impression. I shouldn't tell him that something had slipped in our big bureaucracy—such reports were not believed in Moscow. "Our people take orders," he said.

---

[6] Nixon underlined "basis of a misunderstanding."

[7] Nixon underlined "had not liberalized trade as."

[8] Nixon underlined most of this sentence.

[9] Nixon underlined this word.

[10] Nixon underlined most of this clause.

We managed to convey the idea that we were making everything conditional on something else.[11] For example, we were asking them to show their good intentions in Berlin before we agreed to a European Security Conference.

With respect to summits, we gave the impression that they were pleading with us where, in fact, they had not—though they were, of course, certainly willing to consider it in principle. There was one place on which one could make quick progress and that was at the summit, but we didn't seem to be interested in it. And therefore he wanted to know how I visualized the possibility of progress.[12]

I told Dobrynin that we remained interested in good relations with the Soviet Union. We were the two great powers, and we had to avoid conflict; we should speak while we were still in a position to make definitive decisions. At the same time, as the President had repeatedly pointed out, we wanted to have concrete, detailed negotiations. Until he told me just what he was aiming at, it was very hard for me to comment on his points, since I did not know what he understood by progress. For example, we had heard a great deal about the European Security Conference, but I did not know just exactly what the Soviet Union hoped to achieve there. Dobrynin said, "Well, why don't you ask us. We would be glad to tell you at any level." I said, "Well, maybe we should ask you, but why don't you tell me now." Dobrynin said, "We want existing frontiers recognized." I said, "No one is challenging the existing frontiers." Dobrynin said that he had the impression we were challenging the status quo in Germany. I told him we were not challenging the status quo in Germany, but there was a big difference between challenging it and giving juridical recognition to East Germany.

Dobrynin then asked about China. He said, "What exactly are you up to. Are you trying to annoy the Soviet Union?" He also asked how we visualized relations with China developing. I said the President had often pointed out that the 800,000,000 Chinese were a fact of international life which we had to take seriously and from which we couldn't foreclose ourselves. We were not childish, and we did not believe that we could end all the distrust immediately or have a very huge negotiation immediately. But we did want to establish some sort of relationship. Dobrynin said, "How can you do it as long as you have Taiwan?" I told him that this was essentially our problem, and that we thought we could explore possibilities. Dobrynin said, "Well, you made

---

[11] Nixon underlined most of the second half of this sentence.

[12] Nixon underlined most of this paragraph.

a rather clever move getting Japan involved in the defense of Taiwan and at the same time opening negotiations with Communist China."[13] I did not make any direct response to this. I said we had no intention of playing for small stakes with Communist China, and needling the Soviet Union was an unhistoric and not worthwhile effort. Dobrynin asked why we don't recognize Mongolia. He said that the Soviet Union would welcome it.

Dobrynin then said that he thought the Mid-Eastern negotiation could not go anywhere. Sisco was ingenious in coming up with formulae, but they always moved around in a circle and they did not take into account the power realities. He thought that the Middle East had to be settled at the highest level.

One result of the distrust between Washington and Moscow, Dobrynin said, was that a number of other countries could attempt to maneuver between us. For example, the British were always going to the Soviet Union and telling them that the United States was preventing a European Security Conference, but the Soviet Union knew the British game.[14] The British thought they had to keep the Soviet Union and the United States apart so that they could maneuver—that if the United States and the Soviet Union were together, Britain was nothing. I said that I did not know to which statements he referred, but that the British and we were in rather close accord.

Finally, I said to Dobrynin it was not very fruitful to discuss these issues in the abstract. It would be much better if we discussed them at least on a hypothetical basis, issue by issue. Dobrynin said that as a matter of fact, he was going to make exactly this proposal to me. He said that his government was aware of the fact that the President might not wish to have comprehensive solutions while the war in Vietnam was going on, but they saw no harm in exploring what such solutions might look like.[15] At least, we would both understand each other better then. He therefore wanted to suggest that after I came back from California, he and I meet at regular intervals and set aside each session for one particular topic. We could then decide after the topic was completed and after this had been discussed with the President whether any action was necessary—whether instructions would be given or it should be taken to another level. I told him that I would have to take this matter up with the President, but that, in principle, it was possible that we might proceed this way.

---

[13] Nixon underlined most of this sentence.

[14] Nixon underlined this sentence.

[15] Nixon underlined this sentence.

Dobrynin then made another effusive statement of the need for Soviet/American cooperation and of the good faith of his government and earnestness in trying to seek it. He said a good example was the rapidity with which they had agreed to the President's preference on the site for the SALT talks. He said, "You know Smith had tried for two weeks but when the President requested Geneva, we gave him Vienna even though he had not asked for it. This is what could happen in other areas if we understand each other." I told him that he could be sure I would report this fully to the President, and that I would be in touch with him after we returned from the West Coast.

---

111. Memorandum From the President's Assistant for National Security Affairs (Kissinger) to President Nixon[1]

Washington, December 27, 1969.

SUBJECT

Sino-Soviet Relations

Attached are extracts from a perceptive CIA analysis of current Sino-Soviet relations.[2] The report indicates, inter alia:

—Peking admits being forced into border talks and believes Soviet efforts to improve relations with the West are part of preparations for "dealing" with China.

—Peking's campaign of civilian "war preparations" is designed to deter a Soviet attack as well as promote national unity and unpopular domestic programs.

—Moscow will continue military pressure along the frontier and pursue diplomatic efforts to isolate China.

---

[1] Source: National Archives, Nixon Presidential Materials, NSC Files, Box 1006, Haig Files, Sino-Soviet Relations. Secret; Sensitive. The memorandum indicates the President saw it. A handwritten note in the upper-right-hand corner reads, "Take to San Clemente." Nixon arrived in San Clemente on December 30 and departed on January 5, 1970.

[2] On December 17, Director of Central Intelligence Richard Helms sent Kissinger Intelligence Memorandum No. 2625/69, entitled "Sino-Soviet Relations: The View from Moscow and Peking." Helms' covering memorandum stated, "I believe that both the President and you will find this up-dating of Sino-Soviet relations of interest." (Central Intelligence Agency, Executive Registry Files, Job 93–T01468R, Box 5, Sino-Soviet Border, Aug.–Dec. 1969) On December 27, Kissinger replied that, "The memorandum on current Sino-Soviet relations was very perceptive and most interesting. I appreciate your bringing the report to my attention and have forwarded it to the President." (Ibid.)

—Peking will remain the vulnerable and defensive party and seek to improve its international diplomatic position.

Tab A

Extracts From Central Intelligence Agency Intelligence Memorandum

Washington, December 16, 1969.

SINO-SOVIET RELATIONS: THE VIEW FROM MOSCOW
AND PEKING

Peking's Perspective: A Siege Mentality

A recent tour d'horizon [*1½ lines of source text not declassified*] has given us a good example of this conspiratorial and somewhat distorted Chinese world view. Candidly admitting that Peking had been forced into the border talks under the Soviet gun, [*less than 1 line of source text not declassified*] launched into a fascinating Chinese-eye view of Soviet foreign policy. [*less than 1 line of source text not declassified*] asserted that in seeking a European security conference and attempting to improve relations with West Germany the Soviets are trying to create a "quiet Western front" so as to be able to "deal with China in the East." The clincher [*less than 1 line of source text not declassified*] was the Soviet-US negotiations on Seabeds and SALT: he implied that before coming to final grips with the China problem, Moscow feels compelled to reach an understanding with its sometime enemy/sometime partner in counterrevolution, US imperialism.

Meanwhile, such verbal expressions of concern over Moscow's designs against China are being reinforced by a "war preparations" campaign that has been under way among the civilian population since the beginning of the present border conflict last spring. According to a series of [*less than 1 line of source text not declassified*] reports, the latest aspects of this drive are the digging of trenches and underground personnel shelters, frequent air raid drills in the cities, and the dispersal of a portion of the urban population. This does not mean that Peking is anticipating an imminent Soviet attack; fundamentally, much of what is billed as "war preparations" is designed to promote national unity and unpopular domestic programs. Nevertheless, such highly visible civil defense exercises also demonstrate to Moscow that China is prepared to resist Soviet pressure and is maintaining at least a minimum level of readiness against an attack. According to a recent [*less than 1 line of source text not declassified*] report [*less than 1 line of source text not declassified*] the Chinese leadership, has explained the "war prepara-tions" campaign [*less than 1 line of source text not declassified*] in precisely these terms. Noting that the campaign was aimed at the USSR rather than the US, [*less than 1 line of source text not declassified*] expressed a belief that Chinese "readiness" would help deter a Soviet attack and added that "if we did not prepare, the Soviets would certainly attack."

The New Sino-Soviet Equation

Whatever the course of the talks,[3] this much seems clear: they are not likely to alter significantly the present realities of the Sino-Soviet dispute or in any way diminish the ideological and political gulf sep-arating the two sides. Moscow, painfully convinced of a long-term men-ace posed by a Maoist China and encouraged by its success in intimi-dating Peking, can be expected to maintain a hard line in dealing with the Chinese. Even if the border remains calm the Soviets will almost certainly see fit to continue and perhaps increase their massive mili-tary superiority along the frontier—a very real form of military pres-sure. By the same token, Moscow appears committed to its diplomatic policy of "containment" and is not likely to back away from its efforts to isolate China within and without the Communist world.

It is difficult to overemphasize the impact of this Soviet policy on China's future domestic and international course. Peking will of ne-cessity remain the vulnerable and defensive party in the dispute and the formulation of future Chinese policy may be increasingly influ-enced by the shadow of Soviet hostility. On the domestic front, such questions as proper military tactics and planning to cope with the So-viet threat will almost certainly become contentious issues as Peking continues its efforts to construct a new domestic order out of the po-litical wreckage of the Cultural Revolution. In terms of Chinese diplo-macy the effects of this new Sino-Soviet equation have already sur-faced. The recent attempt by Peking to repair its ties with North Korea, North Vietnam and Yugoslavia were doubtless encouraged by China's growing awareness of its weak international position vis-à-vis Moscow. The future course of Chinese foreign policy will probably be increas-ingly motivated by Peking's desire to do what it can to correct this diplomatic imbalance. The fact that Chinese diplomats in Warsaw have just received the US Ambassador for exploratory talks is further evi-dence of this state of mind.

---

[3] Sino-Soviet talks took place in Moscow during the first half of December.

112.   Memorandum of Conversation[1]

Washington, December 29, 1969, 11:30 a.m.

PARTICIPANTS

  Ambassador Anatoliy Dobrynin
  Henry A. Kissinger

As you requested, I saw Anatoliy Dobrynin to tell him that you approved in principle his suggestion that we meet regularly to discuss specific topics. When I called Dobrynin to tell him that I wanted to see him, he expressed some concern that there might be some connection between my call and the delay of your vacation trip. I did not comment one way or the other except to say that my call was in connection with our dinner conversation.[2] He said he hoped that I understood that the dinner conversation was merely a frank expression of his personal views.

I saw Dobrynin at 11:30 a.m. on December 29th with the intention of spending only a very brief time with him. Instead, Dobrynin stayed for nearly an hour. I began the conversation by saying that the President had carefully reviewed the memorandum of our conversation the previous week[3] and has asked that I see the Ambassador before our trip to the West Coast[4] and to tell him that we saw some merit in the idea of private conversations between the Ambassador and me. I pointed out that the Soviet Government knew our view on Vietnam and the impact it had on other negotiations but stated that nevertheless there might be some merit in exploring what a détente might look like were the political conditions right to achieve it. Both sides had been saying for months now that they wanted to improve relations but this general formulation up to now has lacked specificity. The procedure the Ambassador had outlined seemed sensible, namely that we would set aside each meeting for one particular topic.

Dobrynin said that he had been told by Moscow that on matters of high policy he should deal primarily with me, while routine matters

---

[1] Source: National Archives, Nixon Presidential Materials, NSC Files, Box 489, President's Trip Files, Dobrynin/Kissinger, 1969, Part 1. Top Secret; Sensitive. This memorandum of conversation was attached to a January 2, 1970, memorandum from Kissinger to the President. Kissinger provided the salient points from his conversation with Dobrynin and explained that "while it produced nothing startling new, its overall tone was forthcoming, frank and reasonable."

[2] See Tab A, Document 110.

[3] Ibid.

[4] Kissinger planned to spend the New Year holiday with President Nixon at his vacation home in San Clemente on the southern California coast.

should be handled at the State Department. I replied that the President had asked me to tell him that we would assume that if matters of great importance came up they would be discussed in this channel, and that we would ignore secondary overtures. Dobrynin stated there would be no secondary overtures.

We then discussed what subjects might be included and the order in which to take them up. Dobrynin suggested European security and the Middle East. I said that there might be some merit in discussing SALT—not from the point of view of technical solutions but simply to see what sort of an arrangement was generally conceivable, whether, for example, it should be limited or comprehensive. Dobrynin thought about this for a minute and then said that perhaps we should put SALT very high on our agenda. Moscow would undoubtedly be making decisions on how to proceed with SALT during February and March and it might be helpful if we could get our general thinking in harmony. The details could then be worked out by the negotiators.

In this connection, Dobrynin said that their internal approach was entirely different from ours. We had experts strictly on disarmament, while they did not. When Dobrynin was present as Soviet SALT proposals were discussed, the Soviet group was composed of technical experts from the various ministries, including financial experts who were responsible for commenting on the budgetary implications of various proposals. But there was no single group in the Soviet Union which had a vested interest in disarmament as such. Their military men were expected to be able to handle the broad general view.

Dobrynin stressed that the President's comment that we expected to be serious and not engage in propaganda had certainly helped the Soviet's preparations.

Dobrynin then turned to the Middle East and said that in the present framework the negotiations were stalemated. He wondered how I conceived the problem. I said there were two categories of issues. One was the relation between Arabs and Israel. These, I thought, could be settled only if both great powers were willing to ask their friends to make sacrifices. There was no point in insisting on unilateral concessions. The second range of issues which had not yet even been touched upon was first, how the Soviet Union and the United States could avoid being embroiled in a war that might break out and second, how they could regulate their different interests in the Middle East apart from the Arab-Israeli conflict. Dobrynin said that the second range of questions were of very great interest in Moscow. He did not contradict my formulation of the first range of questions. He said that one remark the President had made had struck home with particular force in Moscow, namely, that "after all Israel had won the war." If that meant that we wanted to have Egypt bear the whole burden, then prospects for negotiations were dim indeed. I said the President was not stating a condition but a fact of life and that he was not saying Egypt should bear the whole burden but should keep in mind that it must bear *some* burden.

Dobrynin then said that we might not realize it but every word the President said was studied with extraordinary care in Moscow. Dobrynin asked whether I wanted to discuss Vietnam as part of our meetings and indicated that he would be prepared to do so. I showed no particular eagerness but simply pointed out that we knew what we were doing in Vietnam and that we hoped they would understand that any measures we might be forced to take would not be directed against them. Dobrynin said he was watching our policy with great interest. I also said that I hoped that the Soviets would make clear to their North Vietnamese allies that a major offensive by them would have the gravest consequences. Dobrynin made no comment.

Towards the end of the conversation, I raised the possibility of a visit by the astronauts to the Soviet Union. Dobrynin said that he wanted to be frank. The Soviet people were very emotional and if the astronauts came they would undoubtedly receive a tremendous reception. He did not know whether the Soviet leaders considered conditions ripe for the sort of demonstration that would follow.

Dobrynin said that in the next few days he would inquire at the State Department about our thinking with respect to depositing the instrument of ratification of the Non-Proliferation Treaty. Secretary Rogers had wanted to wait until enough states had ratified to put the Treaty into effect. What if this was delayed for several months? I said this was not an issue of high policy and that I was certain there would be no undue delay.

We ended the meeting with an agreement that as soon as I return from California we would arrange a schedule for our meetings.

113. Memorandum From Helmut Sonnenfeldt of the National Security Council Staff to the President's Assistant for National Security Affairs (Kissinger)[1]

Washington, undated.

Henry:

Re your Dobrynin conversation. I take it you have already sent comments to the President so this may be plugging the hole after the mouse has escaped.

You seem now to be on the foothills to the summit and yet the negotiable concrete issues seem more elusive than ever. In Vietnam, the Soviets may be genuinely concerned that we have a workable policy. If we do, there is little or nothing to talk to them about; if we don't I see no more prospect than before that talking to them is useful. On the Middle East, we can't deliver our clients and they won't deliver theirs. In Europe, they have nothing attractive to offer us except stabilizing Berlin and that is probably too good a club for them to give up. Arms issues may or may not hold promise, but anything that would really make a difference is hardly in view.

So you get down to rhetoric and atmosphere. Maybe Brezhnev wants those so he can attack China next year. Maybe he wants them because it helps him in his own power conflicts at home (it would not be the first time that tottering Soviet leaders have enlisted an American President's help to prolong their political lives). Maybe the Soviets have no clear idea at all; perhaps, as Dobrynin says, they are reconciled to the President's staying in power for seven more years anchored to a right-wing power base and they just want to keep talking because silence frightens them.

In any case, the Soviets obviously want to talk to the White House and no responsible American President can ignore that. I just hope we won't end up playing Brandt's game on a global scale.

Happy New Year.

HS

---

[1] Source: National Archives, Nixon Presidential Materials, NSC Files, Box 489, President's Trip Files, Dobrynin/Kissinger, 1969, Part 1. Secret; Nodis; Sensitive. The memorandum bears the handwritten date "Dec. 1969." It was probably written between December 29 (the date of Kissinger's last conversation with Dobrynin before the New Year) and December 31.

114.   Memorandum for the Record[1]

Washington, December 30, 1969.

SUBJECT

Minutes of the Meeting of the 303 Committee, 23 December 1969

PRESENT

Mr. Kissinger, Mr. Mitchell, Mr. Johnson, and General Cushman
Mr. Packard was out of the city
Mr. John Hart was present for Item 1
Mr. William Nelson was present for Items 2 and 3
Mr. [*name not declassified*] was present for Item 4
Mr. [*name not declassified*] and Mr. [*name not declassified*] were present for Item 5
Mr. Archibald Roosevelt was present for Item 6
Mr. Thomas Karamessines and Mr. [*name not declassified*] were present for all
items

[Omitted here is discussion of items 1–4, which are unrelated to
the Soviet Union.]

5. *United States Government Support of Covert Action Directed at the
Soviet Union*

a. The State Department memorandum for the 303 Committee
dated 12 December 1969, entitled "U.S. Policy on Support for Covert
Action Involving Emigrés Directed at the Soviet Union,"[2] was approved as a basic policy statement superceding NSC 5502/1, dated 31
January 1955, entitled "U.S. Policy Toward Russian Anti-Soviet Political Activities."

b. It was agreed that this policy statement will not be issued as a
National Security Directive Memorandum (NSDM) but will serve as
the U.S. policy authorization for the kinds of émigré activities described
in the CIA paper dated 9 December 1969,[3] titled as in the above paragraph heading.

c. [2 *names not declassified*] briefed the Committee and responded
to numerous questions on the following activities which comprise the
CIA covert action program supporting media and contact activities
aimed at stimulating and sustaining pressures for liberalization and
evolutionary change from within the Soviet Union:

[4 *paragraphs (6 lines of source text) not declassified*]

---

[1] Source: National Security Council, Intelligence Files, 303 Committee Meeting Minutes, 1969. Secret; Eyes Only. Copies were sent to Mitchell, Packard, Johnson, and Helms.

[2] Document 106.

[3] Document 103.

d. The Committee approved the continuation of the CIA covert action program including the above individual projects at the funding level contained in the CIA FY 1970 budget.

[Omitted here is discussion unrelated to the Soviet Union.]

Frank M. Chapin

---

115. Memorandum From Harold Saunders of the National Security Council Staff to the President's Assistant for National Security Affairs (Kissinger)[1]

Washington, December 31, 1969.

SUBJECT

Evolution of Positions in US–USSR Talks

On December 30, I gave you a wrapup of US and Soviet positions as stated in the US formulations of October 28 and the Soviet response of December 23.[2] Attached is a detailed study of the evolution of the US and Soviet positions through five negotiating phases since March 18. Since that study is comprehensive, following is an analytical summary of the changes on each major issue:

Negotiating Procedure

The US has insisted throughout—either in text or in gloss—on direct negotiations at some stage. In September–October, the US added the concept of Rhodes-type talks to the discussions and text.

The USSR in early phases urged us not to complicate the process by emphasizing direct contacts. In September, Gromyko told Rogers he would agree to Rhodes-type talks (though he appears to have understood that direct talks were involved only at signing) if the US were

---

[1] Source: National Archives, Nixon Presidential Materials, NSC Files, Box 711, Country Files, Europe, USSR, Vol. VI. Secret; Nodis. Sent for information. Kissinger wrote the following comments on the memorandum: "Excellent paper. Now let's get same for European Security." A large bold handwritten "P" appears in the upper right hand corner of the memorandum. Kissinger drew an arrow to the "P" and wrote, "What does this mean?"

[2] Saunder's memorandum of December 30 has not been found. The U.S. formulations of October 28 on the Middle East are in Document 98; the Soviet response of December 23 is Document 109.

more precise on boundaries. In December, the USSR returned to the position that the big powers should not commit the parties to any particular form of negotiation, but the Soviet December 23 response seemed to leave open the door to some procedure comparable to Rhodes talks.

Timing of Withdrawal and Peace

The US has insisted throughout that Israeli withdrawal would begin at the same moment the state of war is ended and a formal state of peace begins.

The USSR has persistently struggled to create a distinction that would satisfy Israel by having the peace agreement come into effect on the day Israel begins withdrawing but would permit the Arabs to say that final peace does not come into being until withdrawal is completed. They have tried to do this by distinguishing between de facto (beginning of withdrawal) and de jure (end of withdrawal) peace. The USSR has also dwelt on a two-phase Israeli withdrawal which would permit UAR troops to move into the Canal area as soon as Israeli troops have withdrawn 30–40 kilometers.

Obligations of Peace

The US has enumerated the general obligations of nations to one another as defined in Article 2 of the UN Charter.[3] In addition, the US has insisted on a stipulation that governments control all hostile acts from their territory, specifically including those of non-governmental individuals and organizations.

The USSR accepted in its June 17 document[4] the general obligations of Article 2 of the UN Charter, but has throughout resisted inclusion of any specific stipulation that would have the effect of committing the UAR to control the fedayeen. The December 23 reply neither reaffirms nor repudiates earlier acceptance of the general obligations of the Charter.

Boundaries

The US position has evolved:

—March 24: "Rectifications from pre-existing lines should be confined to those required for mutual security and should not reflect the weight of conquest."

---

[3] Article 2 of the UN Charter contains seven principles to guide the conduct of its signatory nations. The text of Article 2 is in *A Decade of American Foreign Policy: Basic Documents, 1941–1949*, p. 118.

[4] A translation of the Soviet response is in Document 58.

—October 28: Israel should withdraw to the pre-war UAR-Israel border *provided* adequate security arrangements can be negotiated in Gaza, Sharm al-Sheikh and the Sinai.

The USSR has insisted throughout on pre-war lines. As the US position has evolved, the USSR has become more precise in insisting on our affirming UAR sovereignty over Sharm al-Sheikh and Arab sovereignty over Gaza.

Demilitarized Zones

The US position has evolved from stating that the entire Sinai should be demilitarized to holding that the belligerents should negotiate their size and the procedures for enforcing them.

The USSR has consistently held that demilitarized zones should be on both sides of the borders, not giving advantage to either side. The UN Security Council should work out procedures for enforcing them.

Waterways

The US has insisted throughout on freedom of passage for Israel through the Straits of Tiran and the Suez Canal. In its latest formulations, it has linked security arrangements at Sharm al-Sheikh to securing free passage through the Straits.

The USSR has accepted the principle of free passage but linked passage through the Canal to the Constantinople Convention of 1888 which permits governments sovereign over canals to close them to states with whom they are at war. This has provided the UAR's justification for closing the Canal to Israeli in the past. [The US has resisted this.][5]

Refugees

The US has accepted the principle of free choice for the refugees between repatriation to Israel and resettlement with compensation. But the US has balanced this with progressively more specific provisions to give Israel control over the individuals and the total number of refugees allowed repatriation. The latest formulation includes an annual quota.

The USSR simply calls on Israel to carry out past UN resolutions which call for repatriation or resettlement with compensation. The USSR has resisted any restrictions, although in mid-summer they were willing to discuss it as a possible side understanding.

---

[5] Brackets in the source text.

Nature of Agreement

The US, while experimenting with language, has from the start insisted that the final accord should be an agreement or contract between the parties, should be reciprocally binding, should be signed by the parties and should be deposited with the UN for endorsement by the four permanent members of the Security Council.

The USSR in earlier stages clearly accepted the idea of a binding document—a final accord *between* the parties—signed by the parties and deposited at the UN. However, the December 23 reply ignored this point entirely.

Conclusion

What most strikes me after completing this review of the documents is the cavalier nature of the December 23 Soviet reply. After actively discussing a joint document between June 17—when they produced a draft of their own—and September 30, they simply turned aside our October 28 formulation—containing the position they wanted from us on boundaries—as providing no basis for a joint document.

This has taken place when—as a review of the above positions shows—we might well reach agreement if they would take as much distance from the UAR's position as we have from Israel's.

There seem theoretically to be two possible explanations:

—They are testing whether a flat rejection will cause us to make a few last concessions.

—They are sufficiently content with the present situation not to be willing to press until after the Arab summit,[6] which they may have calculated would turn out worse for the US than it did.

It may be that Nasser's failure at the summit to win the political, financial or military backing he wanted slightly increases our advantage. In any case, the December 23 response is such a step backward that it warrants a sharp rebuff and even telling Dobrynin that we have nothing more to say.

---

[6] An Arab summit, which included the Defense and Foreign Ministers of 13 Arab countries, met in Rabat, Morocco December 21–23 to discuss a common military and political strategy against Israel. The summit ended without issuing a communiqué.

116.   Telegram From the Department of State to the Embassy in the Soviet Union[1]

Washington, January 6, 1970, 2326Z.

Todel 3727/1975. Subj: Your January 7 Meeting with Gromyko—Viet-Nam. Ref: Moscow 46 (Notal).[2]

Deliver at Opening of Business.

1. We do not believe that you should raise Viet-Nam with Gromyko. The Soviets have recently shown some concern at our alleged downgrading of Paris talks and some interest in probing further our intentions with regard to negotiations. Should Gromyko raise this question, you should suggest to him that Soviets discuss these matters with our Delegation in Paris which is fully empowered to discuss any serious proposals with other side.

2. If Gromyko persists and launches into usual Soviet presentation about unrepresentative nature of Thieu Government and desirability of coalition, you should respond along following lines:

A. The basic fact about political situation in South Viet-Nam is that the Communists represent only small minority of population. Non-Communists may be divided among themselves to some extent but the people are basically united in not wishing to be taken over by the Communist minority.

B. This is why neither United States nor GVN is afraid of truly free elections in South Viet-Nam. There are many ways of assuring that elections would be completely free and we are willing to talk about any of them. We would prefer that neither American troops nor North Vietnamese troops remain in South Viet-Nam during elections but even on this point we are flexible: both US/free world and DRV forces might be withdrawn to base areas within South Viet-Nam while elections are taking place.

C. Communists are doing badly in South Viet-Nam and would be well advised to negotiate while they can. Soviets should not be misled by false reports of Communist military successes. VC/NVA are consistently losing many times the numbers killed on our side even though there are now relatively fewer Americans engaged than before. These losses plus high number of Southerners defecting from other side dur-

---

[1] Source: National Archives, RG 59, Central Files 1967–69, POL US–USSR. Secret; Immediate. Drafted by Kirk; cleared by Dubs, Matthews, Sullivan, Swank, and Eliot; and approved by Rogers. Repeated to Paris, Saigon, London, and New Delhi.

[2] Telegram 46 from Moscow, January 6, confirmed Beam's appointment with Gromyko for January 7. No record of this meeting has been found.

ing the past year have led to constantly increasing proportion of North Vietnamese in enemy ranks. This in turn leads population increasingly to regard North Vietnamese as a foreign occupying force driving more and more people into the arms of GVN. GVN control over countryside is steadily expanding and increasing in depth.

D. We can understand Communist fear that as a minority they might suffer persecution or discrimination during an election period and a non-Communist electoral victory. We believe there should be binding guarantees against such persecution or discrimination. These could be worked out in negotiations.

E. We are entirely willing to see NLF play a legitimate role in the political process of South Viet-Nam but only in proportion to the support they enjoy among the people. Idea of imposed coalition government is not acceptable. If Communists want guarantees against persecution and discrimination, there are other ways in which these can be secured.

F. Communists will find it far more difficult to negotiate a settlement after it has been demonstrated that GVN can hold its own without help of American combat forces. At such a time our own influence in favor of a compromise settlement would be less than it is today. Therefore, it appears to us that it would be in enlightened self-interest of any true friend of North Viet-Nam and Viet Cong to urge them to negotiate seriously and to seek political compromise while there is still time.

3. Material in paragraph 2 could also be used by U.S. representatives in other conversations with Soviets.

Rogers

---

117. Memorandum From Helmut Sonnenfeldt of the National Security Council Staff to the President's Assistant for National Security Affairs (Kissinger)[1]

Washington, January 8, 1970.

SUBJECT

US-Soviet Diplomacy on European Security

---

[1] Source: National Archives, Nixon Presidential Materials, NSC Files, Box 667, Country Files, Europe, European Security Issues, U.S. and Soviet Diplomacy. Secret; Nodis. Sent for information. Sent under a January 9 covering memorandum from Haig to Kissinger.

Our dealings with the USSR on European issues, at least in recent years, are not strictly speaking analogous to our talks with them on the Middle East or arms control questions. On these latter matters we have had sustained negotiations either culminating in an agreed document (arms control) or revolving around such a document (Middle East). Since 1959, we have not really had this type of negotiation on European matters.

Rather there have been a series of long-range artillery duels via public declarations (usually, though not exclusively, issued by our respective alliance groupings), interspersed with occasional, random and disjointed bilateral conversations at various levels.

We have, by and large, been scrupulous in not making ourselves the Western negotiating agent on Europe; even if we had wanted it otherwise, it is not now likely that our allies would let us. If, on the other hand, we wanted to begin dealing with the Soviets on European questions, without the blessing of the allies, the effect on NATO would almost certainly be chaotic. In this connection, it is of interest that Gromyko has now come forward with the suggestion to Ambassador Beam that there should be bilateral US-Soviet talks on a European security conference. Dobrynin's strongly reiterated insistence on a direct US reply to the Soviet démarche of November 19[2] is undoubtedly also related to this.

Diplomacy in this area has also been complicated by numerous side-shows—not unnaturally, since the interests of a great number of states, East and West, are involved. A review of US and Soviet exchanges therefore does not provide a complete picture—although it does provide the essence. The present paper does not attempt to include the mass of exchanges, public and private, among individual European states, nor our own occasional exchanges, notably with the Poles and Romanians who, while supporting Soviet and Warsaw Pact positions, do so for reasons and with accents of their own.

It should also be noted that some US-Soviet negotiations while ostensibly or mainly on matters other than regional European ones, have profound impact on Europe. This was true of the test ban negotiations[3] in several different ways, profoundly true of the NPT negotiations and will be even more true of SALT. We have not tried in the present paper to analyze these interrelationships.

Finally, European security, broadly construed, includes economic and technical matters, in addition to political and military ones. While

---

[2] See Document 102.

[3] Reference to the negotiations that culminated in the Limited Test Ban Treaty of 1963.

these have not recently figured in US-Soviet exchanges, they have done so at various times in the past and they remain very prominent in intra-European contacts on East-West issues. (Eastern Europe's relationship to the European Communities is a problem complex of increasing weight if and as the Communities develop and may in the middle run outweigh most if not all the other East-West issues in Europe.) In any case, we do not get into this entire area in the present paper.

Basically, despite the huge volume of documents and the smaller, though considerable volume of private talk, the fact is that European issues have not been ripe for concrete negotiation between ourselves and the Soviets. Even today, with the volume of private talk picking up, the issues have been largely procedural: do we or do we not have a conference; how should it be prepared, etc. (For the Soviets, admittedly, this has substantive interest since the mere convening of a conference is of advantage to them.)

The one real substantive subject, that of our and Soviet troops, has not been talked about seriously since Khrushchev and LBJ exchanged pen-pal letters in 1964[4] (Note: this is not generally known), when we rejected the idea of mutual cuts. While Dobrynin has now responded to Elliot Richardson's prodding by indicating that the Soviets would give serious consideration to a NATO proposal, it is far from clear that serious *US-Soviet* negotiations on this matter will (or should) be undertaken.

Other potential negotiating issues relate to Germany. You will recall that the President in his letter to Kosygin last April[5] offered bilateral soundings on Berlin, and the Soviets have shown some interest. But we are probably well out of the bilateral channel on this one since (a) the subject hardly promises to be productive for us and (b) we should do nothing to undermine allied cohesion on this subject.

In sum, when all is said and done, direct US-Soviet negotiations on Europe which would in any sense be directed at changing the status quo would at present be either (a) artificial and contrived, or (b) not in our interest, or (c) not in the Soviet interest. At the same time, while the status quo is not all that bad right now for us, at least when compared to other status quos, it is not desirable, or feasible, to seek US-Soviet negotiations which would sanctify it. Of all the Western powers we should be the last one to underwrite Moscow's free hand in Eastern Europe (especially since we are in process of developing a special relationship with Romania); and we certainly have no interest in negotiating the disruption of the Western alliance with Moscow.

---

[4] Khrushchev's message is printed in *Foreign Relations*, 1964–1968, volume XIV, Soviet Union, Document 36.

[5] See Document 40.

This would not rule out conversations with the Soviets to see what if anything of substance they want to talk to us about on Europe; but we should do so with the utmost caution and take meticulous care that the Allies are kept informed.

This paper includes the following parts:[6]

Part I—A resume of the issues that have figured in US-Soviet exchanges, public and private (Tab I)
Part II—A chronology of major statements by both sides (Tab II)
Part III—A comprehensive selection of documents (Tab III)

---

[6] All three attachments were attached but are not printed. A handwritten comment next to the last one reads "held in Washington." The first two were dated January 8.

---

118. Memorandum of Conversation[1]

Washington, January 20, 1970.

PARTICIPANTS

Ambassador Anatoliy Dobrynin
Henry A. Kissinger

Dobrynin called in the morning, saying he had an urgent set of matters to discuss. We set the appointment for 4:30 in the afternoon.

Dobrynin began the conversation by asking what had happened in Warsaw.[2] I said I had not seen any reports yet. He asked whether I was going to tell him what had happened in Warsaw. I replied that I didn't think he would believe it if I told him and, in any event, we were not in the habit of conveying our diplomatic conversations. Dobrynin then said that China was a neuralgic point with them. Of course, he recognized that China could not represent a military threat to the Soviet Union until 1979, but people were not very rational on that issue and we should keep this in mind. In particular, we should not try

---

[1] Source: National Archives, Nixon Presidential Materials, NSC Files, Box 711, Country Files, Europe, USSR, Vol. VI. Top Secret; Sensitive; Eyes Only. The conversation was held in Kissinger's office. Kissinger sent this memorandum to Nixon under a January 27 covering memorandum that summarized the "most interesting points" of his meeting with Dobrynin.

[2] From January 12–16, Chinese and U.S. representatives resumed talks in Warsaw to explore an improvement in bilateral relations.

to use China as a military threat. I said that this seemed to me vastly exaggerated. There was no possibility of China's representing a military threat, and even less possibility of China's being "used," whatever that meant, by the United States. Our relations were so far from normalcy that there was no sense even discussing such ideas. Dobrynin said he personally agreed, but he just wanted to convey the intensity of feeling in Moscow. I said we, too, had our neuralgic point: for example, broadcasts on the Moscow radio in which American prisoners held in North Vietnam were broadcasting to America. This was an unfriendly act. Dobrynin said he had already been informed to that effect by the State Department and he frankly did not know enough about the situation to comment.

Dobrynin then asked whether he could request a personal favor of me. A group of Soviet editors were coming to the United States and would visit Washington on February 2nd or 3rd. Would I be willing to see them? I said, yes, if it were done on a strictly off-the-record basis. Dobrynin said he had never leaked to the press, and their press was very disciplined. I said that I would be glad to see them and that I would be delighted if he joined them. I would set aside an hour on either February 2nd or 3rd.

Dobrynin changed the conversation and said a curious thing had happened. The First Secretary of the Japanese Embassy had called on the First Secretary of the Soviet Embassy to inquire about a remark I allegedly made to the Japanese Ambassador to the effect that we were planning a summit meeting with the Soviet Union in late summer or early fall. Was there anything to this remark? I said that I had never talked to the Japanese Ambassador alone on any subject and that Dobrynin could be assured that if the subject of summits ever were raised by us, it would be done strictly between Dobrynin and me, and no foreign ambassador—indeed, no other member in our bureaucracy would be involved.

Dobrynin then said that Moscow wanted to reiterate how much it welcomed our readiness to engage in direct talks between him and me on a variety of subjects. He recommended that we take two subjects first—Europe and SALT. We would discuss these subjects thoroughly, one subject at a time. I said that he had to understand that our discussions would have to be entirely hypothetical, a position the President had often explained. The final resolution would depend on a number of factors, including the overall political climate. Dobrynin said he understood. Nevertheless, in a few days he would take the initiative to propose a meeting on Europe. He suggested that I then take the initiative in proposing a meeting on SALT, but that the second meeting should take place no later than the first week in March, and the first meeting proportionately earlier. I told him that I would be interested to hear some concrete proposals on Europe, though, so far, the topics had not seemed too promising. He said he would be concrete.

Dobrynin then turned the conversation to West Berlin and handed me some talking points about the situation in West Berlin which he considered extremely grave and provocative. The note itself was very tough (it is attached to a separate memorandum).[3] I told Dobrynin that any unilateral action in or around Berlin would have the gravest consequences. I would study the talking points and if I had any reply to give, I would make it. However, I saw no sense in our discussing Europe if there were even the prospect of a unilateral Soviet action on Berlin. Dobrynin said that the Soviet Union did not make much fuss last year when the German President was elected in Berlin, but now, in effect, the whole German Parliament was meeting in Berlin again in the guise of various committees, and this could not continue.

Dobrynin parted with the understanding that he would call me when he was ready to discuss European matters.

Attachment

Démarche Delivered by the Soviet Ambassador (Dobrynin) to the President's Assistant for National Security Affairs (Kissinger)[4]

January 20, 1970.

The authorities of the FRG have officially announced their intention to hold sessions of the Bundestag committees as well as meetings of the factions and other parliamentary organs of the Federal Republic in West Berlin in the next few weeks. Moreover provocative nature of such a venture not only is unconcealed but rather is openly displayed—an attempt again to use West Berlin to aggravate international situation.

The Soviet Government has drawn the attention of the Government of the FRG to serious consequences which this course of action

---

[3] Printed as attachment below. The démarche was also sent as an attachment to a January 22 memorandum from Kissinger to Nixon. In his memorandum, Kissinger made four recommendations which the President approved: "1) you have noted the Soviet statement on Berlin; 2) you cannot agree that the German actions referred to contradict past U.S.-Soviet exchanges regarding Berlin; 3) we have no desire to have any tension over Berlin and hope this is also true for the Soviets since any crisis in that area would have an adverse effect on our relations; 4) we continue to be prepared to seek genuine improvements in the situation in Berlin and for this reason have joined with our Allies in proposing talks on the subject." (National Archives, Nixon Presidential Materials, NSC Files, Box 711, Country Files, Europe, USSR, Vol. VI) On January 22, Kissinger also informed Rogers about Dobrynin's démarche on Berlin and reported, "I made no comment." (Ibid.)

[4] No classification marking.

by Bonn in West Berlin affairs may have. The question of West Berlin has also been touched upon in the recent conversations of the USSR Ambassador in the GDR with the US Ambassador in the FRG and, therefore, the American side must be aware of our views on this matter.

The state of West Berlin affairs was already discussed in my conversations with you, Mr. Kissinger, in February and March last year.[5] At that time it was noted on the American side that it was necessary to avoid repeating what had occurred around West Berlin in connection with holding presidential elections there.[6] It was also noted that events there should not make Soviet-American relations feverish and that third countries should not be allowed to make crises in West Berlin from time to time. This viewpoint has been taken into account by us in our final consideration of practical steps to be taken with regard to West German provocations.

On the basis of the known facts we cannot come to the conclusion that the American side has reciprocated. Without getting now into the matter of Soviet-American exchange of views on the West Berlin question which for reasons, better known to you, Mr. Kissinger, did not materialize, we cannot but point out, however, the obvious discrepancy between the political evaluations and practical measures by the US Administration, in the question of West Berlin as well.

The line of the FRG in West Berlin matters has been and continues to be incompatible with the status of West Berlin. The special status of West Berlin as an entity existing separately from the Federal Republic and not subject to its jurisdiction is an objective fact which has found its reflection in US official documents as well. This is the only ground for mutual understanding between our powers in this matter.

The Soviet Government does not accept arguments to the effect that this sort of demonstration on the part of the FRG took place in West Berlin in the past. Violation of law does not make new law. Repetition of violations may only have as its consequence taking of more serious measures which will show that West Berlin is not the right place at all for stirring up tension in Europe notwithstanding the attitude of other countries towards the FRG actions in West Berlin.

You, Mr. Kissinger, have suggested to openly exchange considerations on questions where the interests of the US and the USSR closely adjoin. We would like to express today a wish that the US Government give anew a thorough thought to the situation developing around West Berlin.

---

[5] See Documents 14 and 27.

[6] See Document 3.

Clearly, there can be no two views about the fact that the actions by the FRG authorities are far from contributing to a better climate for exchange of opinion on West Berlin. The motives of actions by certain circles in Bonn are obvious. But what is the guiding criteria of the Governments of the Western powers who bear their share of responsibility for West Berlin and who show indulgence towards the unlawful policy of the FRG? In any case the Soviet Government cannot but take into consideration all those circumstances and draw from them appropriate conclusions about the positions of the parties.

I have instructions to convey these considerations to the attention of the President and to express our hope that the American leadership share the concern of the Soviet Government over the continuing attempts by some circles to make Soviet-American interests clash, in such an acute point as West Berlin as well. Failure to take measures to cut short such attempts would amount to contradicting the special obligations for maintaining peace and security which rest on the USSR and the US.

119.   Telegram From the Department of State to the Embassy in the Soviet Union[1]

Washington, January 23, 1970, 0117Z.

010865. Subject: US Reply to Soviet statement of December 23 on Middle East.[2]

1. Text of oral statement made on Jan 22 by Assistant Secretary Sisco to Soviet Ambassador Dobrynin follows. British, French, and Israeli Embassies provided with Sisco's oral statement January 22 (septels). Jordanian Amb will be briefed Monday PM.

2. *Begin text.*

Oral Reply to Soviet Oral Comment of December 23, 1969.

The US Government has studied carefully the oral statement delivered by Ambassador Dobrynin to the Secretary of State on December 23, 1969.

---

[1] Source: National Archives, Nixon Presidential Materials, NSC Files, Box 711, Country Files, Europe, USSR, Vol. VI. Secret; Exdis. Drafted by W.B. Smith (NEA/IAI) and approved by Sisco and in substance by Anderson. Repeated to Amman, USINT Cairo, Beirut, London, Paris, Tel Aviv, USUN, Kuwait, Jidda, Nicosia, Belgrade, Algiers, USINT Khartoum, Rabat, Tripoli, and Tunis.

[2] See Document 109.

As the Soviet Government is aware, the proposals we developed and suggested to Soviet representatives over a period of many weeks, most recently on October 28, 1969,[3] were designed to provide a framework for Ambassador Jarring's guidance with respect to the UAR-Israeli aspect of a settlement, to be paralleled by proposals for the Jordanian-Israeli aspect which we subsequently submitted in the Four Power talks in New York on December 18, 1969. The formulations of October 28, in the form of a proposed joint US–USSR working paper, drew upon elements of both the Soviet document of June 17, 1969[4] and the US document of July 15, 1969[5] and were intended to reflect common positions. As such, they represented a serious attempt on our part to meet both Soviet and US views on certain fundamental issues. We reject the Soviet allegation that our position as reflected in the proposed October 28 joint US–USSR working paper is one-sided. It is a fair and balanced document which meets the legitimate concerns of both sides.

There is need for negotiations between the parties to begin promptly under Jarring's auspices. The October 28 and December 18 documents deal with the key issues of pace, withdrawal and negotiations to reach the agreement called for in the UN Security Council Resolution of November 1967. These two documents provide an equitable framework which would enable Ambassador Jarring to convene the parties immediately and get on with his task of promoting the just and lasting peace called for by the Security Council resolution. In this connection, the Soviet contention that the US has now proposed to limit itself to "neutral formulas alone" is without foundation.

The Soviet oral response of December 23 and the position being taken by the Soviet representative in the Four Power talks on the Jordanian-Israeli aspect are not constructive, are delaying the prompt resumption of the Jarring mission and have raised doubt in this government as to the Soviet desire for a stable and durable peace in the Middle East. We see no significant difference between the present Soviet position and the position stated in the Soviet proposals of December 1968 and June 1969.

We do not believe it is useful to comment on every point in the Soviet response of December 23 since the US position and the reasons for it have been fully explained to Soviet representatives on many occasions in the past. We do wish, however, to draw to the attention of the Soviet Government the following:

We note that the Soviet Government no longer supports the provision for negotiations between the parties under Ambassador Jarring's

---

[3] See Document 98.
[4] See Document 58.
[5] See Document 67.

auspices according to the procedures the parties utilized at Rhodes in 1949.[6] This retrogression in the Soviet position is particularly regrettable, since the formulation on this point contained in the October 28 working was worked out jointly by Asst. Secy. Sisco and Ambassador Dobrynin following the understanding reached by Secretary of State Rogers and Foreign Minister Gromyko during their talks at the UN. Resolution 242 calls upon Ambassador Jarring to promote agreement. In the context of the resolution, this clearly means agreement between the parties concerned, which can only be achieved through a process of negotiations—A view which the Soviet Government indicated it shared in accepting on a contingent basis the Rhodes negotiating procedure in the proposed October 28 joint document.

The Soviet response of December 23 misrepresents the US position on the question of withdrawal of Israeli armed forces from UAR occupied territory, implying that our position does not envisage such withdrawal when in fact our proposal makes clear that withdrawal should be to the former international boundary once the parties have agreed upon their commitments to a contractual peace and have negotiated between them under Jarring's auspices the practical arrangements to make that peace secure.

The Soviet reply is completely unresponsive to our suggestions, on which we have placed particular stress from the start, for language to give specific content to the parties' commitments to the just and lasting peace. We note, in particular, that the Soviets have linked withdrawal not with the establishment of peace between the parties but with "cessation of the state of war." The USSR will recall that the Security Council resolution is very specific: its principal objective is the establishment of a just and lasting peace between the parties. Does the Soviet Union agree with the specific formulations on peace contained in the suggested October 28 joint paper? A clear, and not evasive, response is required.

The US Government believes the Soviet Union should reconsider its views in light of these observations.

End text.

Rogers

---

[6] See footnote 2, Document 87.

120. Memorandum for the Record[1]

Washington, January 23, 1970.

SUBJECT

    Decisions and Actions as a Result of the President's Talk with Ambassador Beam, January 23, 1970[2]

1. The President wishes the Ambassador to get reciprocity with respect to access to Soviet leaders comparable to that afforded Ambassador Dobrynin here.

2. The President approved the idea of arranging reciprocal visits by high officials. Specifically, he is in favor of a visit to the United States by Soviet Minister Kirillin.[3]

3. The President believes that more of our diplomatic contacts with the Soviets should be handled by Ambassador Beam. Mr. Kissinger and Under Secretary Richardson are to canvass matters on which this can be done. Further US moves in the Middle East negotiations might be made in parallel in Washington and Moscow.

4. The Ambassador is to do periodic think-pieces for the President about the Soviet situation. The President is interested in the economy and in the Soviet leaders and their motivations.

5. The President wishes no initiatives taken on Vietnam with the Soviets for at least the next 60–90 days. If the matter should come up, the Ambassador should play it cool and talk confidently about our policy. He is to indicate that the President has given up on the Soviets so far as getting any useful help from them is concerned. He is very disappointed with the Soviet performance. We will now end the war our way, taking whatever measures may be needed. Such matters would not of course be directed against the USSR. We should not be in a position of begging the Soviets for anything. Perhaps later, a different approach toward the Soviets may be in order.

---

[1] Source: National Archives, Nixon Presidential Materials, NSC Files, Box 711, Country Files, Europe, USSR, Vol. VI. Secret; Nodis. Sent for information.

[2] Nixon met with Beam from 1:09 to 1:40 p.m. on January 23. (Ibid., White House Central Files, Daily Diary) On January 23, Kissinger provided talking points, prepared by Sonnenfeldt, for the President. Kissinger met with Beam on January 22 at 5 p.m. No record of that meeting has been found. On January 21, Sonnenfeldt sent Kissinger a memorandum that included talking points which could serve for both meetings with Beam. Sonnenfeldt added, "You may want to ask more specifically for [Beam's] recommendations as to what he could usefully do in Moscow that might give him more opportunity to see top Soviet leaders. One idea is the proposal that we should invite more second-level Soviet leaders to visit." (Ibid.)

[3] Soviet Deputy Chairman Vladimir Alekseyevich Kirillin.

6. The President wants the Ambassador to take up anti-US propaganda. He should point out that the Administration has engaged in no cold war rhetoric but, while Soviet leaders have observed circumspection, the current propaganda output may make it hard to hold the line here.

7. The President approved the idea of Under Secretary Richardson visiting the USSR some time this year.

8. The Ambassador should let us know when he thinks a cabinet level visit to the USSR is useful for us.

Henry A. Kissinger

---

121. Letter From Chairman of the Council of Ministers of the Soviet Union Kosygin to President Nixon[1]

Moscow, January 31, 1970.

Dear Mr. President:

According to information now available the Israeli leaders, ignoring the decisions of the Security Council have in fact resumed anew military actions against the Arab states, including bombings of population centers of the UAR in the immediate vicinity of Cairo. Not only military installations of the UAR and Jordan are being attacked but also civil population, destruction is being brought to towns, villages, industrial and other installations. The aims of these adventurist actions are clear—to force the neighbouring Arab countries into accepting the demands which are put forward by Israel. All this takes place at a time when the UAR and other Arab countries, honoring decisions of the Security Council, are not so far[2] striking back at Israel.

In this instance as in determining their position in Middle Eastern affairs in general the Israeli leaders are evidently proceeding from the assumption that the US will go on supporting Israel and that under these circumstances the four great powers will fail to come to a common view on the implementation of the decisions of the Security Council.

---

[1] Source: National Archives, Nixon Presidential Materials, NSC Files, Box 340, Subject Files, Dobrynin/Kissinger. No classification marking. The letter was an unofficial translation from Russian.

[2] Nixon underlined "not so far."

There is danger that in the immediate future the military actions may become widescale while the decisions of the Security Council and the UN General Assembly will be loosing weight in the eyes of world public.[3]

We are now studying the question to what extent the Israeli counting on political and other support from outside has ground and has been coordinated with the diplomatic actions by certain powers. We consider it our duty however to draw your attention, Mr. President, to the highly risky consequences the course chosen by the Israeli leaders may have both from the point of view of the situation in the Middle East and international relations as a whole.[4]

We proceed from the conviction that stable peace can and should be established in the Middle East. The Soviet Union has persistently strived for this and has influenced its friends accordingly. If on the other hand the US Government supported its pronouncements in favor of peace in the Middle East by practical steps, and in the first place— vis-à-vis the Israeli leaders, then there would not have been such a situation in which for two years and a half the occupier continues to hold the occupied lands, hundreds of thousands of Arabs are forced to abandon their homes and people continue to perish.

Adherence by Israel to its present course may only widen and deepen the conflict,[5] perpetuate tension in one of the most important areas of the world since it is impossible to force the Arab countries to reconcile themselves to the aggression, to the seizure of their territory.

It is in the interests of universal peace and international security to warn the Government of Israel against adventurism, to undertake urgent and firm actions, which will help in stopping the growth of military tension and will make Israel listen to the voice of reason. We believe that this would also correspond to the national interests of the United States.[6]

We would like to tell you in all frankness that if Israel continues its adventurism, to bomb the territory of UAR and of other Arab states, the Soviet Union will be forced to see to it that the Arab states have means at their disposal, with the help of which a due rebuff to the arrogant aggressor could be made.[7]

---

[3] Nixon underlined most of this sentence.

[4] Nixon underlined most of this paragraph.

[5] Nixon underlined most of this phrase.

[6] Nixon underlined "to warn the Government of Israel against adventurism" and highlighted this paragraph.

[7] Nixon underlined most of this phrase.

The situation in the Middle East urgently dictates the necessity of immediate cessation by Israel of its dangerous armed attacks and sorties against the UAR and other Arab states.

The four powers are capable and must compel Israel to abandon its policy of military provocations and to see to it that a lasting peace be established in the Middle East.

We believe that now it is necessary also to effectively use the mechanism of bilateral and four-power consultations in order: 1) to ensure speediest withdrawal of Israeli forces from all the occupied Arab territories, 2) to ensure establishment of peace in the Middle East.[8]

Withdrawal of forces is the key question for establishing peace. If it is solved then there would hardly be any particular difficulties on the way to agreement on other questions.

We would like you, Mr. President, to appraise the situation from the viewpoint of special responsibility for the maintenance of peace which lies on our countries. As for the Soviet Government, there is no lack of goodwill on our part as well as resolution to act in the interests of peace in the Middle East.[9]

Appropriate communications have been sent by us to Prime Minister Wilson and President Pompidou.

Sincerely,

A. Kosygin

---

[8] Nixon underlined these points.
[9] Nixon underlined most of this phrase.

---

122.   Transcript of Telephone Conversation Between Secretary of State Rogers and the President's Assistant for National Security Affairs (Kissinger)[1]

Washington, January 31, 1970, 9:20 p.m.

K: I'm sorry to take you away from your dinner (Rogers was at a post-wedding dinner at the Jockey Club). We had a call from Dobrynin

---

[1] Source: Library of Congress, Manuscript Division, Kissinger Papers, Box 361, Telephone Conversations, Chronological File. No classification marking.

1½ hours ago who said he had a personal message from Kosygin.[2] He asked if he could see the President. I told him he was at David.[3] He asked if he could bring it by to me—which has been done. It is a message about the Middle East; its major points are: the Israelis have resumed in effect military action against the Arab states.[4] If it continues, consequences will be risked. The USSR will be forced to see to it that the Arabs have the means at their disposal to rebuff the Israelis. If the Israelis withdraw, other things will fall into place. The message is somewhat moderate, but it has that threat in it. The President has given me some of his thoughts. Would you agree if I gave them to Sisco and he could work out an answer with you?

R: Does it call for an answer soon?

K: When Dobrynin called, he asked if he could have an answer by Monday.[5] I said "no." He said, "Tuesday?" I told him I couldn't accept a deadline. There may be some urgency in our getting to Sisco. The message said that similar letters have gone to Wilson and Pompidou.

R: I feel we should downplay its importance—we can't let them give us these ultimatums.

K: The President thinks so too. It would be unfortunate if outside powers got themselves involved directly or indirectly. I think we should say we have put our proposal down, and we have stated what we think of withdrawal.

R: I took a hard line with [omission in the source text] yesterday.

K: I will call Sisco now.[6]

R: I will get it from Sisco then.

---

[2] Document 121.

[3] Nixon left for Camp David at 4:46 p.m. on January 31, and returned on February 1 at 10:37 p.m. (National Archives, Nixon Presidential Materials, White House Central Files, Daily Diary)

[4] In early January, Israel began a bombing campaign in Egypt's heartland in an attempt to force Nasser to shift military forces away from the canal area.

[5] February 2.

[6] At 9:30 p.m., Kissinger called Sisco. According to a transcript of their conversation, "K told Sisco about Dobrynin's call and the message from Kosygin and said he would like to tell him what the President thinks. It has to be handled very confidentially. Sisco said he would come in immediately." (Library of Congress, Manuscript Division, Kissinger Papers, Box 361, Telephone Conversations, Chronological File)

123. Memorandum From the President's Assistant for National Security Affairs (Kissinger) to President Nixon[1]

Washington, February 1, 1970.

SUBJECT

Message from Kosygin

The *key points in the message* from Kosygin which Ambassador Dobrynin gave me last night (Tab A)[2] are:

1. The Israelis have in effect resumed military action against the Arab states.

2. The USSR is studying to what extent Israeli action has been coordinated with [U.S.][3] diplomatic action.

3. If Israel continues, this will widen the conflict with highly risky consequences for the situation in the Mid-East and international relations as a whole. If Israel continues, "the USSR will be forced to see to it that the Arab states have means at their disposal" to rebuff Israel.

4. The Four Powers must compel Israel to stop and to see that a lasting peace is established. Withdrawal of Israeli forces is key; if this is solved, there would hardly be any difficulty on other questions.

My *thoughts about this message* are as follows:

1. The tone is relatively moderate, but nevertheless this is the first Soviet threat to your Administration, so the tone of your reply will be important. The Soviets avoid directly threatening action of their own. So far, it would seem that they are loath to make this a U.S.–USSR confrontation.

2. There is evidence that the combination of our firmness and the Israeli raids are hurting Nasser.

—There is a strong likelihood that Nasser made a secret visit to Moscow January 22–27. That may be the background for this note.

—Nasser told the Jordanian Foreign Minister that he cannot accept our position

(a) because the USSR won't let him, and
(b) because he would appear to be capitulating if he negotiated while the Israeli bombing continues.

3. The Soviets seem to have become increasingly concerned about a peace plan with a U.S. label on it.

---

[1] Source: National Archives, Nixon Presidential Materials, NSC Files, Box 489, President's Trip Files, Dobrynin/Kissinger, 1970, Part 2. Secret; Nodis. Sent for information. There is no indication on the memorandum that the President saw it.

[2] Printed as Document 121.

[3] Brackets in the source text.

—This document suggests action by the Four Powers, and Kosygin has sent it to Wilson and Pompidou.

—It implies that we can compel the Israelis to settle.

4. The letter holds out the bait that if the cease-fire could be restored and withdrawal achieved, other issues would fall into place. It does not spell out a view on the other issues and therefore leaves the Soviet view vague. What is worse, the position that Israel must withdraw before other issues are settled is a return to the Soviet position of 1967, which seems to negate much of the progress made in the U.S.–USSR talks last summer.

5. The overall conclusion from the message and the circumstances surrounding it is that they are not in the stronger position vis-à-vis us. Our policy of holding firm creates the following dilemma for them: If they *do not* agree to our proposals, they get nothing, the onus for escalation falls on them and their client will lose if the escalation leads to a major clash. If they *do* agree, they would have to deliver their client on our terms.

The *strategy of our reply* that I propose is:

—to come down very hard on the Soviet threat;
—to relate Israeli observance of the cease-fire to corresponding observance by the other side, including irregular forces;
—to press the Soviets to spell out their views on what the Arabs would commit themselves to if Israel withdrew.

Because this message is going to both Prime Minister Wilson and President Pompidou, I believe State must be brought in. I have talked to Secretary Rogers and given him the memorandum at Tab B[4] suggesting the elements of a reply based on our conversation from New York. I have also talked to Joe Sisco who agrees with this general approach.

I have also told Ambassador Freeman[5] that we have a message and will talk to him before replying. I will reach Ambassador Lucet[6] tonight. These small gestures of consultation are worth the effort since they will have the letter anyway. After we have a draft reply, we should seriously consider telling the Israelis.

We will have a draft reply for your consideration on Monday.[7] My recommendation is that we should hold it, however, until at least Wednesday and preferably Thursday.

---

[4] Not attached.
[5] John Freeman, British Ambassador.
[6] Charles Lucet, French Ambassador.
[7] February 2.

124. Memorandum From the President's Assistant for National Security Affairs (Kissinger) to President Nixon[1]

Washington, February 2, 1970.

SUBJECT

Soviet Internal Troubles

Several recent events have led the Kremlin watchers to conclude that there may be trouble in the top Soviet leadership. Few observers are yet predicting a major purge or the downfall of Brezhnev, Podgorny or Kosygin, but the economic problems are serious enough for some casualties to occur. Moreover, further economic reorganization seems inevitable, which, in turn, would aggravate political tensions.

Background

What has been happening in the Soviet Union in the past several years is that the rate of economic growth has been declining. Last year industrial growth hit rock bottom, the lowest rate since 1946, and the prospects are not much better for 1970. The overall economic growth was only 2½ percent, the lowest since 1963.

Bad weather last year played a role, but the basic problems are a decrease in industrial investment, and more important, a failure to maintain increases in productivity—sometimes called the technological gap.

After the fall of Khrushchev the new leaders set out to increase the supply of consumer goods, and at the same time raise spending for defense, including the large buildup in the Far East. Though they recognized that the Soviet economy was stretched thin, they hoped that an industrial reform involving use of the "profit system," would provide a new stimulus to investment and growth.

Last December, when Soviet party and government meetings were held to review the state of the economy and approve the economic plan for this year, matters came to a head. Brezhnev apparently made a long speech (never released) in which he lambasted nearly everyone—planners, management, as well as the average worker, for lack of discipline, poor performance by ministries, etc. He was also highly critical of agriculture, primarily failures in stockbreeding, and the decrease in the production of meat, milk and eggs (a chronic Russian complaint).

---

[1] Source: National Archives, Nixon Presidential Materials, NSC Files, Box 711, Country Files, Europe, USSR, Vol. VII. Secret. Sent for information. Drafted by Sonnenfeldt on January 31.

No remedies are in sight, and what Brezhnev offered was mainly exhortation to "improve organization and management, strengthen discipline," i.e., formulas which date back to Khrushchev's days.

The reason, of course, is that the Soviet leaders are reluctant to face up to the failure of their own industrial reforms. None of the leaders can suggest a new program of reform which would spur economic progress and at the same time preserve central political control. This is a central Soviet dilemma.[2]

Other Evidence of Dissension

Added to these underlying problems have been a number of those signals that the experts usually associate with political troubles in the Kremlin.

Last November, the Soviet party, after numerous postponements, held a huge conference on collective farming to create a Cooperative Farm Union, empowered to direct regional agriculture. Instead a rather meaningless advisory council was created and the meeting ended in great disarray.

In the last several months there have been more than the usual number of removals of middle to upper level echelon officials, including a party secretary in the regional republics.

Conclusions

In examining the stability of the political leadership, CIA, in the attached report (Tab A)[3] concludes that despite some evidence of political troubles, tensions are not climbing sharply. The nearness of the Lenin 100th anniversary (April 1970)[4] is an incentive for the leadership to keep affairs on an even keel.

If and when the unity breaks down, however, CIA sees a possible generational split developing between the older politburo members (Brezhnev, Kosygin and Podgorny) and a younger group. This latter group, chiefly First Deputy Premiers Mazurov and Polyansky and the aggressive trade union leader Shelepin may be more and more impatient with the temporizing policies of the older leaders.

The Party Congress, which is expected this year, might bring problems to a head. All of the top leaders will want to ensure their supporters retain key positions. The older group under Brezhnev may try to expand its mandate at the Congress, while the younger group would be inclined to block this prospect.

---

[2] Nixon highlighted the last two sentences of this paragraph and wrote, "The critical point."

[3] Attached but not printed.

[4] Nixon circled "100th anniversary (April 1970)" and wrote, "K—let us now plan to treat this with 'intelligent neglect.'"

Implications for the US

Foreign policy issues do not seem to play a major role in current problems, but differences over China, and over relations with the West, quite possibly related to SALT and the defense budget, may contribute to frictions and differences over internal matters.

Perhaps the more basic aspect for us is that the present leadership may simply be running out of gas, and that a change is likely to come sooner rather than later. If so, we might be wary of committing ourselves to the present leadership,[5] or relying on their stability as a longer term element in our calculations.

---

[5] Nixon underlined this phrase and wrote, "K—note (they may need *us* for a price.)"

---

125.   Memorandum From Secretary of State Rogers to President Nixon[1]

Washington, February 2, 1970.

SUBJECT

Soviet Message of January 31 on the Middle East

Attached is a suggested reply to the Kosygin message of January 31 on the Middle East.[2] We will discuss our proposed reply, after your approval, with the UK, France and with the Israelis, whose cooperation is essential in restoring cease fire conditions in the area. Your reply would then be handed to Dobrynin.

A prompt reply would have the advantage of informing Kosygin of the current efforts we started on our own several days ago to help bring about restoration of the UAR-Israeli cease fire. We agree with the argument that we should not appear to be excessively hurried and in fact we would not be ready to respond before Tuesday.

---

[1] Source: National Archives, Nixon Presidential Materials, NSC Files, Box 340, Subject Files, Dobrynin/Kissinger. Secret; Nodis. Kissinger forwarded Rogers' memorandum on February 3 with the recommendation that the President approve the draft reply. Nixon initialed his approval that same day. (Ibid.) On February 2, Rogers informed Beam of Kosygin's letter and summarized the main points of the U.S. response. (Ibid., Box 711, Country Files, Europe, USSR, Vol. VI)

[2] Attached but not printed. The draft reply was used almost verbatim for the message that was sent to Kosygin; see Document 126.

On the other hand, undue delay in informing the Soviets of our efforts would play into their strategy to place the onus for the current situation on the United States and to garner credit in the Arab world for applying pressure on the United States and Israel.

There are several observations regarding the Kosygin letter which are worth mentioning.

First, its principal thrust seems to be to get us to get the Israelis to lift the military pressure on Nasser. It could possibly signal that Nasser may be about ready to give up for the time being his war of attrition tactics and he may be looking for a way out. The Rabat Conference[3] has helped free Nasser's hands in this regard, since he can always say his attempt to mobilize Arab resources fell far short of what he needs. He is also freer after Rabat to pursue a political solution if he so decides. This is why I feel it is so important to continue to stand firm on our two United States peace proposals and to maintain our efforts to convince Cairo and Moscow to adopt a positive stance toward them, as has Hussein.

Second, the inability of Cairo to respond effectively to the Israeli deep penetration raids is no doubt embarrassing to Moscow. We surmise, though we are not sure, that Kosygin's letter stems from Nasser's reported trip to Moscow which must also have involved further UAR arms requests. As a minimum, we are reasonably certain that Nasser encouraged Moscow to come forward with a concrete arms proposition to Jordan. The reference in the message that the Soviets would be "forced to see to it that the Arab states have means at their disposal" could signal that the Soviets have taken a decision to give more arms to Nasser, though there is nothing to indicate any change in their policy of providing measured amounts, or that they have decided provide more sophisticated weapons. It may also be intended to discourage us from providing Israel with additional arms. Moreover, short of nuclear weapons, the Soviets know as we do, that more matériel to the UAR cannot have an immediate effect on the arms balance or result in a sharp increase in UAR effectiveness, since the problem is not hardware but Egyptian lack of training and overall qualitative capacity. In short, the Soviets are in somewhat of a squeeze at the moment, and it should not be precluded that in time a more responsive reply to our two peace proposals will come forth.

Third, while it might be tempting to make only pro-forma efforts to achieve restoration of the cease fire and let pressure mount on the Soviet Union and Nasser, this carries with it elements of risk. Since Soviet

---

[3] Reference is to the Arab summit that included the defense and foreign ministers of 13 Arab countries, which met in Rabat, Morocco, December 21–23 to discuss a common military and political strategy against Israel.

prestige is involved, they might see themselves under increasing pressure to do something visible and concrete to reverse the present trend. The Israeli attacks have made their point psychologically and have achieved the military objective of reducing their casualties on the Suez front. Much of the UAR military capacity in the Suez area has been destroyed. If Nasser as a quid pro quo is ready to abide by the UN cease fire resolutions and let up for the time being on his declared war of attrition, it is in the Israeli and United States interests to restore observance of the cease fire. Moreover, as long as the deep penetration raids go on, it is unlikely that Nasser can take any positive moves toward a peace settlement. This is not to say that the converse is true; even if Israel relaxed its military pressure, there is no assurance Nasser would move toward a settlement.

Fourth, there are some important tactical considerations on how to handle the Kosygin letter.

The letter has propagandistic overtones seeking to pin responsibility exclusively on Israel and the United States. Our reply must be framed on the assumption we may find it necessary and desirable to make it public if the Soviets play their message that way.

The Soviet letter is firm, one sided, and is confined exclusively to the Middle East; but it has an element of threat to us in that it first implies we are in collusion with Israel and then warns of giving the Arabs more means to rebuff the Israelis. Our response on this point in particular should be firm.

It is important to note that Kosygin does not propose that the United States and the Union of the Soviet Socialist Republics bring joint influence to bear on both sides to restore the cease fire; his focus is primarily on Israeli responsibility for the situation, American collusion, and the need for total Israeli withdrawal. For this reason, I suggest that your reply inform Kosygin of the steps we have taken and are taking through diplomatic channels to ensure compliance with the UN cease fire resolutions. We believe that joint action by the Four Powers is undesirable since it would offer more opportunity for the Soviets to exploit this as responsive to their pressure. We therefore should tell the UK and France that we agree that the UN cease fire should be restored, that our own efforts have been in train for some time, and that each should do what he can through diplomatic channels to help bring about a mutually respected cease fire.

Finally, we believe your reply should place considerable emphasis on the need for a positive reaction by the Soviets to the two United States peace proposals.

WPR

126.   Letter From President Nixon to Chairman of the Council of Ministers of the Soviet Union Kosygin[1]

Washington, February 4, 1970.

Dear Mr. Chairman:

Your message of January 31 has been studied carefully.[2] For its part, the United States intends to continue its efforts to promote a stable peace between the parties in accordance with the UN Security Council Resolution of November 22, 1967[3] and to encourage the scrupulous adherence by all concerned, not just one side, to the cease-fire resolutions of the United Nations. I can assure you, Mr. Chairman, this is the steadfast policy of the United States.

We do not accept the views expressed by the Soviet Government in explanation of the current situation in the Middle East. We have been using our influence with both sides urging strict observance of the cease-fire. Thus any implication that the United States has been a party to or has encouraged violations of the cease-fire is without foundation.

Moreover, your attempt to place responsibility on one side is not supported by the facts; there have been repeated violations of the UN cease-fire resolutions by both sides. Full compliance with these resolutions on all fronts, including the prevention of fedayeen attacks against Israel, would help establish a more favorable atmosphere for progress towards a settlement.

As I have pointed out, the United States, just shortly before the receipt of your letter, discussed this matter with both Israel and the UAR and urged both sides to adhere strictly to the UN cease-fire resolutions. We intend to continue these discussions in order to bring about early restoration of the cease-fire between Israel and the UAR. It will be recalled that in early 1969 the UAR announced and initiated a policy of non-observance of the cease-fire. An early indication by the UAR that it will abide by the UN cease-fire resolutions if Israel will do the same

---

[1] Source: National Archives, Nixon Presidential Materials, NSC Files, Box 765, Presidential Correspondence, Kosygin. Secret; Nodis. According to a February 3 memorandum from Kissinger to Rogers, President Nixon approved Sisco's delivering the letter to Dobrynin on February 4. Additional copies were to be delivered to the Ambassadors of France and Great Britain following delivery of the original. (Ibid.) According to telegram 17418 to Moscow, February 4, "Sisco handed President's reply to Kosygin letter to Ambassador Dobrynin at 3 p.m. today." (Ibid., Box 711, Country Files, Europe, USSR, Vol. VI)

[2] Document 121.

[3] See footnote 4, Document 2.

would contribute to a reduction of tension and violence and facilitate a political solution. We are prepared to continue our efforts in that direction. We are not aware of any recent Soviet efforts to this end.

We have noted the reference in your message to the effect that "the Soviet Union will be forced to see to it that the Arab states have means at their disposal . . . ".[4] The United States has always opposed steps which could have the effect of drawing the major powers more deeply into the Middle East conflict. This could only complicate matters further.

For this reason, the United States: (1) supports the prompt restoration of the cease-fire; and (2) favors an understanding on limitations of arms shipments into the area. The question of arms limitations was raised directly with Mr. Gromyko in July of last year, our willingness to discuss this important subject was reaffirmed in my speech before the General Assembly[5] this last fall and subsequently was again taken up with Mr. Gromyko by Secretary Rogers,[6] and our strong preference for limitations was reiterated as recently as January 25.[7] Our proposals for discussion of this matter were rejected by the Soviet Union.

While preferring restraint, as I indicated on January 25, the United States is watching carefully the relative balance in the Middle East and we will not hesitate to provide arms to friendly states as the need arises.

On the broader question of a peace settlement, the United States remains committed to help achieve a peace agreement between the parties as called for by the UN Resolution of November, 1967. We have noted your point to the effect that if the question of withdrawal were resolved, there would be no serious obstacles to agreement on other questions. As you know, there can be no withdrawal unless there is full agreement between the parties on all of the elements of a peace settlement. In this connection, the proposals of October 28 and December 18, 1969,[8] meet the legitimate concerns of both sides on all key questions, including withdrawal. We believe these proposals constitute reasonable guidelines which would provide Ambassador Jarring the means to start the indispensable process of negotiations between the parties under his auspices. It is a matter of regret that Soviet unre-

---

[4] Ellipsis is in the source text.

[5] The text of Nixon's address before the 24th session of the General Assembly of the United Nations on September 18, 1969, is in *Public Papers: Nixon, 1969*, pp. 724–731.

[6] Reference is to U.S.-Soviet ministerial discussions between Rogers and Gromyko on September 22, 26, and 30 in New York; see Documents 81 and 87 and footnote 1 to Document 91.

[7] For Nixon's remarks on January 26 about supplying military equipment to the Middle East, see "Message to the National Emergency Conference on Peace in the Middle East," in *Public Papers: Nixon, 1970*, p. 18.

[8] See Document 98 and footnote 3 to Document 109.

sponsiveness to these proposals is holding up this process; a more constructive Soviet reply is required if progress towards a settlement is to be made.

We note your desire to work with us in bringing peace to this area. We do not believe peace can come if either side seeks unilateral advantage. We are willing to continue our efforts to achieve a stable peace in the Middle East in a spirit of good will.

We are providing copies of this communication to Prime Minister Wilson and President Pompidou.

Sincerely,

Richard Nixon

---

127. Memorandum From the President's Assistant for National Security Affairs (Kissinger) to President Nixon[1]

Washington, February 4, 1970.

SUBJECT

Further Thoughts on Kosygin Middle East Message: An Inept Performance

The more I reflect on the Kosygin letter, the more inept, and for that reason, disturbing[2] a performance I find it.

Regardless of whether it was intended as a serious diplomatic move or as a pressure play—and the simultaneous and ostentatious transmittal of the letter by Soviet Ambassadors suggests that it was intended to become public—the purpose of the operation presumably was to get the Israelis to desist. In addition, the Soviets no doubt would have wanted to keep the three Western powers off balance and arguing with each other and to maintain the gulf that has been opening between us and the Israelis. Beyond this, they must be anxious to keep their reputation as an effective protecting power of the Arabs alive.[3]

---

[1] Source: National Archives, Nixon Presidential Materials, NSC Files, Box 653, Country Files, Middle East, Sisco Middle East Talks, Vol. III. Secret; Nodis. According to another copy of this memorandum, it was drafted by Sonnenfeldt. (Ibid., Box 340, Subject Files, Dobrynin/Kissinger) Sent for information. A handwritten note on the first page indicates that a copy with Nixon's comments was sent to Sonnenfeldt on February 23.

[2] Nixon circled this word and wrote: "I agree—Confused men do the unexpected *and* wrong things."

[3] Nixon underlined most of this sentence and wrote: "(most important for them)."

It is doubtful whether any of these purposes will in fact be accomplished, at least with any degree of permanence; meanwhile certain other effects of the letters would appear to be distinctly to Soviet disadvantage.

It should not have taken much intelligence to expect at least the US (if not France and the UK) to reply that it favors restoration of the cease-fire on a reciprocal basis. Moreover, the Soviets must have known by January 31 that we were already busy diplomatically in both Cairo and Jerusalem to this end; and that the Israelis have already said that they will abide by a reciprocally observed cease-fire.

Thus the upshot of the Soviet move will be to place the onus for getting the cease-fire restored on Nasser and the Arabs, and through them on the Soviets themselves, rather than on us and the Israelis. But this produces a situation for which Nasser can hardly be grateful: if he gives any kind of positive response, he will be seen as doing so under pressure of Israeli military action. In addition, it would also point up Nasser's, and Soviet, impotence since they seem unwilling or unable to control the Fedayeen whose activities will presumably wreck any cease-fire after a period of time.

If the cease-fire is not restored, as seems likely in view of Soviet inability to deliver their clients, the Soviets are stuck with their threat to provide means for a rebuff. But merely sending more equipment, even if it is more advanced, is unlikely to accomplish anything, at least if the past is any guide. So the onus of escalation is on the Soviets and the Kosygin letter has added to its weight.

If one of the letter's purposes was to keep the Western powers at odds with each other, or at least not to drive them more closely together, its tone and content will tend to have the opposite effect. True, there will be continuing differences about the utility of the four-power forum, and to that extent the Soviets did not calculate incorrectly. But the threat element has also produced a quickening of Western consultation and efforts to attune the responses.

Another effect, which cannot be in Moscow's interest, is to dissipate what had threatened to become a US-French confrontation on arms shipments. The new, explicit Soviet threat to increase arms deliveries has now, inevitably, drawn a response from us which explicitly ties the arms issue back into the US-Soviet context (even though the French angle remains as well).

Some have argued that whatever else the Soviets were attempting to do, their main political purpose was to re-emphasize US identification with Israel by (1) implying actual US-Israeli collusion, and (2) drawing from the US a new statement of support for and defense of Israel which will offset the impression of the last few weeks that we were drifting apart. Even if it is granted that when the exchange is complete we will again look to be somewhat more firmly on Israel's side, the ultimate effect of this may well not be in Moscow's interest: if Nasser is prepared to promise reciprocal observance of the cease-fire he will, as noted above, be doing so in response to Israeli military pressure for which we will also get some of the credit; if the fighting goes on despite the Soviet threats, we will be credited with having faced down the Soviets. Moreover, if there turns out to be some Soviet or Arab flexibility with respect to our[4] October proposals, we will get the credit both for having made those proposals and for having induced Soviet/Arab flexibility by standing firm in the face of Soviet threats. While the ensuing situation would involve us in problems with the Israelis, the net effect would be to make us appear as the most influential outside power in the region.

But if for some or all the above reasons the Soviet move is inept, it is also disturbing. Since it is unlikely to produce a cease-fire, except under conditions little short of humiliating for Nasser, the pressure on the Soviets to make good on their threat will rise. This basic danger is not a new one; but the Soviets have engaged more of their prestige and thus stand to lose more of it if the Israeli attacks continue, and if our answer is widely interpreted as a rejection of their threats. The Middle Eastern problem has frequently lurked beneath the surface of Soviet leadership politics and in 1967 was used by a rebellious faction in an indictment against the present leaders. This could happen again under present internal conditions in Moscow and lead the leaders to do something brave to recoup.

---

[4] Nixon highlighted this part of the paragraph and wrote the following comments: "I completely disagree with this conclusion—The Soviets know that Arabs are long on talk. We have been gloating over Soviet 'defeats' in the Mideast since '67—State et al said the June war was a 'defeat' for Soviet. It was *not*. They became the Arabs' friend and the U.S. their enemy. [unintelligible] this is what moves their intent."

128.   Memorandum From the President's Assistant for National Security Affairs (Kissinger) to President Nixon[1]

Washington, February 6, 1970.

SUBJECT

Further Background on the Kosygin Letter

In an earlier memorandum[2] I speculated on the inept position adopted by the Soviets in the Kosygin letter. At the time I thought that perhaps the Soviet reaction reflected internal strains and frustrations in the wake of an exasperating visit with Nasser. [2 *lines of source text not declassified*]

Brezhnev was obviously bitter about the Israeli raids, and especially the accuracy of the strike on the house of the Soviet advisers, which he implied was deliberate. His concern, however, was mainly on how to keep the incident quiet and out of the public eye. [*less than 1 line of source text not declassified*] also indicates that top Soviet military leaders had been meeting on the Middle East and that Brezhnev had a personal hand in the drafting of the letter to you. Thus, the raid of January 28 may have triggered a Soviet decision to send the letters to you, Pompidou and Wilson to justify a new shipment of Soviet arms.

Brezhnev refers to sending "a system" after first sending "means of defense." [*less than 1 line of source text not declassified*] sheds no further light on what kind of weapons might be involved. One interpretation could be that the new system will be offensive weapons (more advanced aircraft or even tactical missiles) but that new radars or surface-to-air missiles will have to be installed first. It could be that both systems are defensive, however. We will watch this closely and prepare a more extensive review of the possibilities in the next few days.

As I noted, the ill-timed demand for a cease-fire played into our hands quite nicely, in view of our efforts in Jerusalem and Cairo. This may be explained by the fact that Brezhnev expected the letters to go forward on that same day (January 29), when in fact they were not delivered until January 31, that is, after we had initiated our soundings on a cease-fire. The desire of the top leaders to fire off an immediate démarche may also explain the little thought given to whether a call for a cease-fire would put Nasser in an untenable position either to agree under pressure or turn down Israeli agreement to mutual cessation.

---

[1] Source: National Archives, Nixon Presidential Materials, NSC Files, Box 711, Country Files, Europe, USSR, Vol. VII. Secret; Sensitive. Sent for information.

[2] Document 127.

In short, the Soviets seem to be responding emotionally to the killing of Soviet advisers and out of frustration over their inability to do much about the entire state of affairs. This, of course, could have some ominous implications for future moves, since as I noted in my earlier memorandum, the Middle East was a source of internal tensions within the Soviet leadership at the time of the June war. Brezhnev may be worried that his own position is vulnerable to charges of softness, and the letter could have been for the record to protect himself against any new Kremlin debate over Middle East policy. On the other hand, a failure of his initiative may make him even more vulnerable. In this connection, Brezhnev referred to the "nervous strain" of his job, and some trouble with his throat. This is the second time in the last two months that we have noted Brezhnev having health problems.[3]

---

[3] Nixon underlined most of these two sentences. He added an exclamation point and wrote, "K—and Jefferson complained of 'headaches' every afternoon in his last 3 years as President!"

---

129.   Memorandum From the President's Assistant for National Security Affairs (Kissinger) to President Nixon[1]

Washington, February 6, 1970.

SUBJECT

Thoughts on Soviet Response to Nasser's Arms Requests

[5 lines of source text not declassified] This raises the question of what specifically the Soviets might have in mind. To answer this question it is necessary to look at both the current state of the Egyptian military forces vis-à-vis Israel and the realistic options open to the Soviets.

The Egyptian Military Situation

The most basic fact about the Egyptian forces is that, despite all the equipment the Soviets have provided since the 1967 war, they are still no match for the Israelis. This is particularly true of the Egyptian air force and air defense system. The Israelis have systematically knocked out the Soviet-provided air defense positions along the Suez

---

[1] Source: Library of Congress, Manuscript Division, Kissinger Papers, Box SCI 17, Memoranda to the President, January–April 1970. Top Secret; Codeword. Sent for information.

Canal almost as fast as they have been set up and have proved that they can now fly their aircraft against targets almost anywhere in the Nile Valley, including around Cairo. Moreover, the Egyptian air force, with a severe shortage of trained and qualified combat pilots, is unable to either challenge the Israelis effectively in the skies over Egypt or to launch significant retaliatory attacks against Israeli targets. The situation is so bad in fact that Nasser even admits it in public. Nasser must have pressed the Soviets very hard for the means to combat Israel's air supremacy during his secret trip to Moscow January 22–26.

What Can the Soviets Do?

Assuming that the Soviets wish to avoid a major escalation of the hostilities that would risk a confrontation with us, they do not seem to have many options.

Their easiest choice would be simply to replace Egyptian losses by rebuilding radar and SA–2 installations. This would carry the least risk of further Soviet involvement, but would not significantly improve Nasser's position either, since the Israelis have the capacity to keep knocking them out.

More and better planes—there has been speculation on an improved MIG–21 or so-called MIG–23—will not alone help Nasser, although there may be pressure to provide them. The Egyptians are unable to employ effectively what they already have. Nasser admitted this at the Rabat Summit [*less than 1 line of source text not declassified*] in an interview reported earlier this week. Moreover, it would take too long to train the necessary Egyptian pilots and technicians to operate the aircraft, related ground-control facilities and air defense systems necessary to make an appreciable impact on the present situation.

If the Soviets were to provide Nasser with effective means to offset Israeli supremacy, it would seem that they would have to begin inserting their own people into more exposed combat positions, perhaps billed as "volunteers." The consensus developing at CIA is that they would begin to do this in defensive areas, perhaps providing more sophisticated radar and air defense systems run by Soviet operators. The low altitude SA–3 system, currently deployed outside the Soviet Union only in Eastern Europe and even there only operated by Soviet personnel, would seem to be the most likely candidate.

The Soviets could also begin to supplement Egyptian pilots with their "volunteers." This would also probably require the use of Soviet ground controllers, since the Egyptians are not very effective in this area either, the language problem would seem to necessitate this and Soviet pilots have never been known to fly missions without using their own people for ground support.

The Soviet aircraft-pilot-ground control option, however, while real, runs a greater risk of significant escalation than providing and operating more and new air defense facilities. The Israelis, among the best and most experienced combat pilots, would surely be tough game for the Soviet "volunteers" especially if they were inadequately supported from the ground. The thought of Soviet pilots and planes being shot down in Egypt and Israel must certainly give the Soviet pause for thought. CIA thinks that if Soviet pilots were employed, they would be used for defensive missions only. This would cut the risks some.

Another possibility is that the Soviets could help the Egyptians to develop an air defense system similar to that employed by North Vietnam. This would involve saturating areas to be defended with SA–2 missile sites and more conventional anti-aircraft defenses for the lower altitudes.[2] The present Egyptian MIGs could also be used to backstop this arrangement or improved versions could be employed if necessary. While this would involve equipment such as that the Israelis have already destroyed, this approach would involve quantities and concentrations not tried before in Egypt which might increase the cost to Israel as they did to us in Vietnam. There are, of course, differences in terrain which might make this harder to do in the UAR. Soviet personnel would have to be used but in less directly exposed positions on the ground.

There are other actions which the Soviets could take to buttress Nasser militarily, but for now they seem less real. Short range missiles for example are a possibility. Such a move would run the strong risk of serious Israeli retaliation and do nothing about Israeli freedom to strike any and all Egyptian targets, military as well as industrial. Unless preceded by an improved air defense ring of some kind, even short range missiles with conventional warheads would be vulnerable to Israel preemptive attacks. They would, of course, also raise the possibility of escalation of the hostilities beyond a point where the Soviets might be able to maintain some control over events.

Conclusion

Therefore, the situation is difficult for Moscow because the Soviets seem to have little middle ground between involving their own pilots to make Egyptian defense really effective and resigning themselves to what would probably be a less than effective effort by ground technicians manning anti-aircraft defenses. It is true that they did a creditable job in North Vietnam and might try that approach. But if they

---

[2] Nixon highlighted this part of the paragraph and wrote "Most likely. It worked in Vietnam against us!" in the margin.

once involve their pilots, their prestige would be directly engaged, and someone would have to lose—either the Soviets or the Israelis.

I have called a meeting of the Washington Special Action Group for Monday[3] to examine these possibilities and to refine our contingency plans in response to them.

It seems clear that the Soviets feel compelled to make some move in Nasser's support. The first question is whether they will confine that move to a token gesture or attempt to do something effective against Israeli attacks. If the latter, this would almost certainly seem to involve Soviet personnel. The second question, therefore, is whether they insert Soviet personnel into direct combat situations or leave them, as they are now, in defensive ground positions where they do not bring Soviet prestige into face-to-face confrontation with Israel.[4]

---

[3] See Document 130.

[4] Nixon wrote the following comments at the bottom of the page: "K—I think it is time to talk directly with the Soviet on this—Acheson's idea—'let the dust settle' won't work—states 'Negotiate in any form' won't work. We must make a try at a bilateral talk to see if a deal in our interests is possible."

---

130. Minutes of Washington Special Actions Group Meeting[1]

Washington, February 9, 1970, 10:21–11:02 a.m.

SUBJECT

    Possible Soviet Moves in Egypt

PARTICIPATION

    Chairman—Henry A. Kissinger

State	CIA
Mr. Rodger Davies	Mr. Thomas H. Karamessines
Defense	NSC Staff
Mr. Richard Ware	Mr. Harold Saunders
Mr. Robert Pranger	Col. Robert Behr
JCS	Mr. Keith Guthrie
Lt. Gen. John W. Vogt	

---

[1] Source: National Archives, Nixon Presidential Materials, NSC Files, NSC Institutional Files (H-Files), Box H–114, WSAG Minutes, Originals, 1969 and 1970. Secret; Nodis. The meeting was held in the White House Situation Room.

SUMMARY OF CONCLUSIONS

1. A US position for dealing with possible Soviet moves in Egypt must be ready within one week. The WSAG will meet on the afternoon of Wednesday, February 11 to draw up an initial position and will meet again Monday, February 16 to give the problem further consideration.

2. In connection with preparation of the US position the following papers should be prepared:

a. Assistant Secretary Sisco should submit on February 9 proposals for intensifying our diplomatic efforts to bring about a cease fire and, in this context, to warn the Soviets against further intervention in Egypt. These proposals should take into account the possible usefulness of a renewed cease-fire effort in dealing with public opinion pressures, staving off a further Israeli request for aid, and placing the onus on the Soviets for escalating the Arab-Israeli conflict.

b. For WSAG consideration at its February 11 and 16 meetings the military situation in the Middle East and the options open to the United States should be reviewed. This review should be related to the existing contingency plans, particularly Tab H (action by Soviet naval forces) and Tab D (responses to Soviet overt intervention in renewed Arab-Israeli hostilities) of the WSAG contingency plan of October 1969.

The analysis should take into account the overall power situation in the Middle East and not just the Arab-Israeli dispute. State and CIA should coordinate in preparing this aspect of the study.

c. The ad hoc Under Secretaries group is to meet Monday, February 16 to consider the paper that has been prepared on aid to Israel. This paper must be coordinated with current contingency planning and should discuss what aid levels to Israel are appropriate in the light of foreseeable Soviet moves. It should also consider tacit US Government facilitation of Israeli military purchases in the US.

Mr. Kissinger summarized the circumstances requiring the WSAG to meet. There were hints that the Soviets might take some action, as yet unspecified, in the Middle East. It was essential we make sure our plans were in order and, that all possible contingencies had been examined. The study prepared by CIA suggested the following possible Soviet actions: (1) improvement of UAR ground-to-air defense, with some Soviet personnel made available for this purpose; (2) introduction of Soviet pilots, probably with associated ground-control installations; and (3) introduction of offensive weapons such as bombers and missiles. Mr. Kissinger asked if there were any new possibilities.

Mr. Karamessines said there was nothing further to add at this time. However, we might get some more information as a result of the Cairo meeting, since Nasser might tell his Arab colleagues what he expected or had requested from the Soviets.

Mr. Kissinger said he was concerned about one further possibility—that the Soviet fleet in the Mediterranean might take retaliatory action against Israel. Mr. Karamessines commented that while anything was possible, naval action did not seem consistent with the thrust [*less than 1 line of source text not declassified*] by Soviet officials regarding the Near Eastern situation. Mr. Saunders pointed out that naval action was considered in the October 1969 WSAG contingency plan at Tab H, where it was suggested that we might respond by taking action against the Alexandria port facilities.

After noting that consideration should also be given to the more remote possibility of Nasser's loss of power, Mr. Kissinger suggested that the military situation in the Middle East and the options open to the US be reviewed and considered by the WSAG on Wednesday, February 11.[2]

Mr. Kissinger asked about the timing of possible Soviet action. Mr. Davies suggested that the Soviets would move quickly for psychological purposes. Mr. Saunders observed that they might wait to see what decision we made on aid to Israel in the wake of Kosygin's letter[3] to the President. Mr. Kissinger said he had noted the same theory in the press and asked who was putting out this idea. Mr. Saunders said that it appeared to be a complete fabrication, perhaps disseminated by the Soviet Embassy.

Mr. Pranger noted that [*less than 1 line of source text not declassified*] the Soviets would be increasing their freighter traffic through the Bosporus in the next few days. Mr. Davies suggested that the Soviets might just announce that they were going to provide air cover to Cairo; and Mr. Saunders noted that, [*less than 1 line of source text not declassified*] they could take the steps necessary to provide such an air defense within one week.

Mr. Kissinger said that the preceding discussion confirmed the need for a WSAG meeting as early as February 11 to give preliminary consideration to what the US should do. Discussion of the Middle East situation could be completed at a subsequent WSAG meeting on February 16. It was agreed that the February 11 meeting should be scheduled late in the afternoon to provide the maximum possible time for completing the necessary staff work.

Mr. Kissinger asked General Vogt to have a look at the existing military contingency plans. He noted that increased Soviet involvement would at the very least probably result in some attrition of the Israeli Air Force, and that this would generate pressure for US aid to Israel. General Vogt said the Israelis will probably move to take out any new defensive system installed in Egypt by the Soviets. He thought the Israelis had the capability to do so, even if the defenses were manned by the Soviets.

---

[2] See Document 134.
[3] Document 121.

Mr. Kissinger observed that the implications of Soviet action would be different, depending on whether or not the Soviets acknowledged that they were assuming responsibility for the air defense of Cairo. If the Soviets maintained that an improved defense system was Egyptian, even though run by the Soviets, Brezhnev would probably be under less immediate internal pressures to retaliate in the event Soviet personnel were injured by Israeli attacks. In either case, however, we are likely to face a difficult situation. If Soviet help on air defense results in losses for the Israeli Air Force, we will probably get requests from Israel for aid. On the other hand, if the Israelis challenge the new defenses, the Soviets will eventually feel compelled to respond. They may act immediately if they have publicly acknowledged responsibility for Egyptian air defense; the time fuse may be a few months longer if the presence of their personnel is unacknowledged.

General Vogt pointed out that Soviet interest in defensive armaments for the UAR suggested that they were anticipating Israeli attacks. Thus, the Soviets might seek to keep their involvement covert. He observed that the Israelis had taken out all of the earlier Soviet SA–2 installations that threatened Israeli operations in the Cairo area. [2 *lines of source text not declassified*] General Vogt added that if the Soviets were to install the more sophisticated SA–3's in Egypt, they would be taking a major new step, since these weapons had never heretofore been deployed outside the USSR. One result might be an Israeli request to us for more sophisticated counter-measures.

Mr. Saunders noted that the existing WSAG plan did not cover the contingency of Soviet intervention solely for the purpose of defending the UAR, with Soviet units and aircraft operating only within Egypt. Mr. Kissinger replied that it seemed hard to see how Soviet action to install a major new defensive system would not sooner or later escalate the conflict and lead to one of the contingencies discussed in the existing plan. The Israelis would feel compelled to challenge the new defenses, and this could lead to a Soviet-Israeli confrontation.

In response to Mr. Kissinger's questions, General Vogt said that Israeli pilots in F–4's or Mirage III's would probably be more than a match for Soviet pilots in Mig 21's. He doubted that the Israelis would lose one plane for every two lost by the Soviets.

The discussion then turned to possible Soviet supply of offensive missiles to the Egyptians. Mr. Davies emphasized the concern which would be generated in Israel if the Soviets were to announce the installation of missiles with a 200-mile range. In response to Mr. Kissinger's questions, General Vogt said that the Soviets could provide a missile such as the Frog which has a two-mile CEP (circular error, probable) at a range of 200 miles. This would permit bombardment of the Tel Aviv suburbs. With high explosive warheads, this would be primarily a terroristic weapon and would cause little damage. General Vogt added that the Israelis soon will also have an offensive capability in the form of the Jericho missile.

Mr. Kissinger asked if the Soviet decision to aid the Egyptians was irrevocable. Mr. Davies and Mr. Karamessines agreed that it was. Mr. Kissinger asked if anything was to be achieved by our trying to warn the Soviets against such a step. Mr. Davies suggested that it would be desirable to intensify our diplomatic effort toward a cease fire, and Mr. Karamessines added that this would help us in dealing with public opinion. Mr. Kissinger then asked that Assistant Secretary Sisco send over a paper dealing with this "today" (February 9).

Mr. Kissinger observed that one explanation for the spate of Soviet Embassy-inspired stories linking a US decision on aid to Israel with the Kosygin letter was that the Soviets had made the decision to step up assistance to Nasser and were attempting to shift to us the blame for escalating the dispute. He suggested that if we moved fast on the diplomatic front, we could appear to be making a response to the Soviets and might thus stave off another Israeli request for aid. He added that it was important that the ad hoc Under Secretaries group on aid to Israel meet on February 16. The staff paper prepared for the Under Secretaries must be coordinated with our other planning, so that we would be able to decide what aid levels to Israel would be appropriate in the light of foreseeable Soviet moves in Egypt.

Mr. Kissinger asked about the possibility of avoiding US Government decisions on aid to Israel while allowing the Israelis to purchase military equipment in this country. We would, of course, want to know what the Israelis were buying, but we would make no announcements. Mr. Davies agreed that the less that was said on the record, the easier it would be for us to aid Israel. It was agreed that our ability to do this would depend to some extent on the type of equipment the Israelis were seeking.

General Vogt suggested that arrangements could be worked out with the Israeli Air Force to keep Israeli purchases as quiet as possible. He added that it would be useful to see how our equipment fares against that which the Soviets might supply.

Mr. Kissinger directed that the possibility of tacit US facilitation of Israeli purchases be covered in the study being prepared for the Under Secretaries group. He added that if a decision were made to offset Soviet equipment supplied to Nasser, we needed to consider what we should do. We also needed to decide whether the introduction of Soviet combat personnel into Egypt would trigger one of the contingencies covered in existing plans.

Mr. Kissinger asked that in connection with the current review State and CIA prepare an analysis of Soviet moves in the light of the overall power balance in the Middle East and Africa. Possible establishment of a Soviet power base in this area was a matter of serious concern.

Mr. Kissinger suggested that the best means of warning the Soviets might be a Sisco–Dobrynin meeting on achieving a cease-fire. Mr. Karamessines and Mr. Davies agreed. Mr. Kissinger asked that Assistant Secretary Sisco address this matter in the memorandum to be submitted "this afternoon" (February 9). At the suggestion of Mr. Karamessines, Mr. Kissinger also suggested that Mr. Sisco consider in his memorandum the possible advantages of publicizing promptly any measures which the Soviets might take to step up their aid to Egypt.

Mr. Ware said that in considering this we ought to think about where it leads in terms of US involvement in the Middle East. Mr. Pranger suggested we might try to warn the Israelis about the increased dangers of attacking Egyptian defenses in the event the Soviets openly acknowledged their own involvement. Mr. Kissinger doubted that we could ask the Israelis not to attack or tell them that we would not provide them aid.

Mr. Kissinger then directed that Tab D (response to Soviet overt intervention in renewed Arab-Israeli hostilities) and Tab H (action by Soviet naval forces) of the October 1969 WSAG contingency plan be reviewed in the context of the current possibilities for Soviet action in Egypt which might result in attrition to the Israeli Air Force and damage to Israeli territory. A judgement was needed on the circumstances under which we would prefer each of the options discussed in the October 1969 plan: military aid to Israel, interdiction of Soviet supplies, and US military intervention. Mr. Kissinger again emphasized the importance of considering the problem in the context not just of the Arab-Israeli dispute but of the overall power situation in the Middle East.

In answer to General Vogt's question, Mr. Kissinger said that JCS should submit its review of military plans directly to the NSC.

131.   Memorandum of Conversation[1]

Washington, February 10, 1970, noon.

PARTICIPANTS

    Ambassador Anatoliy Dobrynin
    Henry A. Kissinger

The meeting took place in the Library in order to avoid newspaper speculation.

After some preliminary pleasantries, I told Dobrynin that I had asked him to come to make a few points to him on behalf of the President. I then made the following seven points from my memorandum to the President of February 10:[2]

(1) It had come to my attention that one of the junior officers of the Soviet Embassy had complained to one of our journalists that we did not take the Kosygin letter sufficiently seriously.

(2) We are assuming that serious communications will be made directly by Dobrynin to me and therefore we will not comment officially.

(3) We want Dobrynin to know that the Kosygin letter received the highest level attention. Given the fact that the Soviet side had distributed it in regular channels in London and Paris, we had no choice but to deal with it in a similar fashion here.

(4) The President is prepared to have bilateral discussions on the Middle East in the Dobrynin–Kissinger channel with a view to finding a solution fair to everybody.

(5) We want the Soviet leaders to know that the introduction of Soviet combat personnel in the Middle East would be viewed with the gravest concern. We are choosing this method of communication because we do not want to make a formal démarche. At the same time, we want to make sure that the Soviet leaders are under no misapprehension about the possibility of grave consequences.

(6) The President remains committed to his policy of seeking a resolution of outstanding disputes with the Soviet Union on the widest possible front.

(7) In this spirit, I propose a meeting to discuss SALT on February 17.

When I was finished, Dobrynin was extremely affable. He said he understood perfectly. He wanted to assure me that the Soviet leaders

---

[1] Source: Library of Congress, Manuscript Division, Kissinger Papers, Box CL 215, "D File". Secret; Sensitive.

[2] Earlier that day, Kissinger sent Nixon a memorandum providing the seven points he planned to make to Dobrynin. The President initialed his approval. (National Archives, Nixon Presidential Materials, NSC Files, Box 711, Country Files, Europe, USSR, Vol. VI)

had no intention of exacerbating tensions. They had, however, wanted to indicate that the situation was getting serious. The primary concern of the Soviet leaders was another round of the arms race in the Middle East, just as we had indicated.

On the other hand, the Soviets were displeased by the tactics that were being used; for example, at the precise moment that the President's reply was handed to Dobrynin by Sisco, Secretary Rogers was handing the text of the reply to Ambassador Lucet. Considering that the letter was written by the Soviet Prime Minister to the American President, Dobrynin thought that the reply might well have been handed back by the Secretary of State. At any rate, it would have been more polite to let the Soviet Ambassador have it an hour or two before the allies of the United States. Secondly, it did not make a very good impression on the Soviet Union that the essence of the reply was leaked to the press before it could even have been received in Moscow. This was a beef with the general tactics used by the State Department. For example, Sisco's reply to the Soviet answer to our memorandum of October 28th[3] was leaked to the press five hours before it was transmitted to Dobrynin. As a result, Dobrynin had the essence of the reply in his pocket before Sisco even started speaking. Dobrynin said, moreover, that the State Department had misrepresented the Soviet note of December.[4] It was not intended as a rejection of our proposals of October 28. On the contrary, it represented a direct invitation for further talks, and it was deliberately presented as being negotiable.

Dobrynin said that Kosygin was a very mild man, and he was astonished to read in the American press that his letter was intended to convey a threat. The letter had intended to state the dilemmas of the Soviet Union in the Middle East and the problems that were being raised. I said I was glad to hear that because I could only underline what I had said earlier—that the introduction of Soviet combat forces would have the most serious consequences. Dobrynin said he understood perfectly, and he only hoped that we took into account Soviet problems when we made any decisions about future weapons deliveries to Israel.

Dobrynin then asked me whether he had understood me correctly that the Middle East could be the subject of conversations in the Kissinger–Dobrynin channel. I said, yes—not in the detail that had been characteristic of his talks with Sisco, but rather in terms of general principles. If we could come to some understanding of general principles, Sisco could handle the details. Dobrynin said he would report this to

---

[3] The Soviet oral reply is in Document 98.

[4] Document 109.

Moscow, and he was sure that they would be glad to hear it. Moscow wanted to know whether we were engaged in a propaganda battle or in a serious effort to settle, and he repeated that the Soviet note of December did not represent the last Soviet word on the subject.

132.   Memorandum From the President's Assistant for National Security Affairs (Kissinger) to Nixon[1]

Washington, February 10, 1970.

SUBJECT

Cautioning the USSR against Escalating the Mid-East Arms Race

The intelligence of the last few days suggests that the USSR may have decided to give the Egyptians some sort of "system" designed to counter Israeli air operations. As noted in the memo sent you last week-end,[2] the Soviet action could fall into three broad categories:

—improvement of ground-to-air defenses using substantial numbers of new Soviet technicians and perhaps more advanced surface-to-air missiles; or
—open Soviet involvement in the air defense of Egypt, perhaps including Soviet pilots flying interceptors;
—introduction of an offensive weapons system such as surface-to-surface missiles or Soviet pilots flying attack missions.

If the Soviets involve themselves openly, this will raise serious questions for us: Can we afford to let the Soviets openly assume responsibility for the defense of a Mid-Eastern nation without responding? On the other hand, is it in the U.S. interest to move toward a confrontation with the USSR over Israel's strategy of bombing the UAR?

These larger questions are being dealt with urgently this week in the Special Actions Group.[3] However, since it is patently preferable—if possible—to prevent this kind of situation from developing, the tactical question today is whether we should follow up your letter to

---

[1] Source: National Archives, Nixon Presidential Materials, NSC Files, Box 711, Country Files, Europe, USSR, Vol. VI. Secret; Nodis. Sent for action. Drafted by Saunders based on a February 9 memorandum from Sisco and Richardson to Kissinger entitled "Cautioning USSR Against Qualitative Escalation of Armaments in the Near East." (Ibid.)

[2] Document 128.

[3] See Documents 130 and 134.

Kosygin[4] with approaches to Dobrynin and perhaps Gromyko (Ambassador Beam sees him Wednesday for a broad discussion) to caution against dangerous escalation.

This would have to be done delicately since the obvious Soviet counters will be that we should first halt Israel's bombing and agree not to ship more arms to Israel. We would also have to avoid giving the impression that recent Soviet moves have us excessively worried.

Our answer on each of the first substantive points could be that (1) we are prepared to work with Israel for return to observance of the cease-fire provided both sides agree and (2) we are prepared to discuss arms limitation to both sides.

The most delicate question is how we show our own resolve. So far we have indicated our determination not to let the local arms balance shift against Israel. Since Israel's superiority over the Arabs is substantial, that would not be difficult to achieve even with small shipments. But if the Soviets enter the picture, more may be required and our response would assume a direct anti-Soviet character.

For the moment, it is probably best to stick to language expressing strong concern over escalation, (1) repeating our intention not to permit a change in the military balance and (2) leaving to the imagination what "escalation" means as far as we are concerned.

I believe some such approach is desirable. Your letter to Kosygin set the stage but some follow-up would give us a better feel for what it is possible to achieve with the Soviets in the way of restoring the cease-fire and achieving some slowing of the arms race.

In my next talk with Dobrynin I could make the points that (1) The introduction of Soviet combat personnel would be an act of the gravest sort and (2) we are willing to continue talks with them to find a peaceful solution. But in diplomatic channels, there are two ways of making such an approach:

1. Assistant Secretary Sisco could make the approach to Dobrynin. This would have the disadvantage of being pointed only at the Mid-East and perhaps displaying excessive concern and running across direct approaches we might make to Dobrynin.
2. Ambassador Beam could be instructed to include this on his broad agenda with Gromyko tomorrow. As you know, he has asked for more of this sort of thing to do.

Recommendation: That you approve having Ambassador Beam raise this with Gromyko.[5]

---

[4] Document 126.

[5] Nixon initialed his approval on February 11, and Beam met with Gromyko the same day; see Document 136.

133.   Telegram From the Embassy in the Soviet Union to the Department of State[1]

Moscow, February 11, 1970, 1530Z.

738. Subject: Call on Gromyko—Middle East. Ref: State 020685.[2]

1. Discussion of ME took up approximately ⅔ of my 90 minute review Feb. 11 with Gromyko. Other subjects in septels.[3]

2. I led off, closely following points in reftel, and stressing positive points of President's reply[4] to Kosygin. Discussing need for ceasefire and reports of additional military assistance to UAR, I wished to caution against such assistance as could increase the level of violence on both sides. For this reason, the USG favors scrupulous adherence by both sides of UN ceasefire resolutions and I mentioned US approaches being made respectively in Cairo and Feb. 12 Four-Power meeting. At same time I was obliged to state that if USSR introduced more sophisticated weaponry or took other steps of extraordinary nature, we would have no alternative but to consider setps to restore the balance.

3. Gromyko took up ceasefire first. He said USSR could not consider ceasefire outside the context of actions which Israel is taking. These actions are flagrant military provocations, and are expression of Israel's complete ignoring of UN decisions. Soviets must draw conclusion that US statements that it will take steps toward Israel and will cool off extremist statements have not been justified. Ceasefire and ME situation cannot be discussed without considering concrete actions being taken by Israel, which is carrying out systematic, provocative attacks on Arab states. Neither USSR nor USA has received reports that UAR actions are not consistent with UN decisions. It is not UAR, Syria, Jordanian, or other Arab troops which are on Israeli territory, but the reverse. Gromyko then asserted it would be hard to find one honest objective world statesman who would say that the Arab states are to blame for tense ME siuation. The fault lies with Israel.

4. On arms deliveries, Gromyko wished to remind the US of Sov. Govt. position, which has been expressed in messages to the USG and by Kosygin to the President. Moscow is not against discussing question of limiting arms deliveries to the ME. However, USSR proceeds from idea that for all practical purposes such discussion is not possible while

[1] Source: National Archives, Nixon Presidential Materials, NSC Files, Box 711, Country Files, Europe, USSR, Vol. VI. Secret; Priority; Nodis.

[2] Telegram 20685 to Moscow, February 9, contained Rogers' instructions for Beam. (Ibid.)

[3] Not further identified.

[4] Document 126.

Israel occupies Arab territories. To discuss matter while Israeli troops are on Arab territories creates false, distorted situation. If USG wishes to find just solution to this question, it cannot object to the Soviet Government's position. When the question of the withdrawal of Israeli troops is resolved, as well as other problems relating to Middle Eastern settlement, our two sides could begin to discuss question of limiting arms deliveries to ME. Once Israeli troops withdraw, Gromyko did not think US and USSR would face tremendous difficulties on limiting arms deliveries. Any possible agreement would depend, however, on concrete positions of parties.

5. Gromyko said Soviet Government had paid attention to statement expressed in President's message to Kosygin regarding US interest in restoring relative balance in the event anything is done for benefit of the Arabs. He said USSR regrets that USG poses the question way it has. Israel, which ignores UN decisions, occupies Arab territories and by its policies, is source of tension and acute situation in ME. In Soviet view, USG would occupy more just position if it used all its possibilities and influence to bring about reduction of tension in area exert influence on Israel, instead of taking position it did in President's message. While USG says USSR should exert influence on Arabs, the victims of Israeli aggression, and hints that in interest of maintaining the balance US will take certain steps, the US is making statements regarding new deliveries of phantoms. Mention is made of dozens of plans, but perhaps it may be more. US actions can only complicate the situation. USG proposals are one-sided, pro-Israel and not objective. They are not designed to help reach agreement.

6. Gromyko went on to assert the USSR had made many efforts to find an agreement. At times it seemed to Moscow that our two sides had achieved some rapproachment of positions. However, under the influence of facts not known to the Soviet side, the US would then begin to retreat from its previous positions, would reorient its stand. Such an approach undermines all positive movement in negotiations.

7. Gromyko said the development he was talking about has found expression in the positions taken by the US representative in the Four-Power talks. In effect, the US adopting a take-it or leave-it approach, which the USSR rejects. The USSR wishes to find an agreement acceptable to all parties. However, if in the future the USG continues to use this approach, it promises little in the way of achieving agreement.

8. Gromyko then said that the USSR is ready, just as before, to continue Two-Power ME talks. He wanted me to inform my government of this. At the same time, he said he would like to have the USG occupy a more constructive position than heretofore.

9. Gromyko said he would like to make an observation not directly connected with my remarks, but related to the general problem

of finding a ME settlement. In essence, he said there seemed to be no divergences of views between the USSR and the USA when the USG asserts that it is not enough to solve just the question of the withdrawal of troops, but that other questions need to be settled. We both agree that what is needed is the cessation of war and the establishment of a durable peace. We both seem to attach great importance to the idea of a durable peace, yet nothing comes of this and it puzzles the USSR. Perhaps misunderstandings have or are taking place. Gromyko said USSR was ready to do whatever is necessary henceforward so situation can be normalized and not worsened but this does not all depend on USSR.

10. I responded by saying my remarks were intended to follow up on the President's reply to Premier Kosygin and to draw attention to the 3 special suggestions which might help the situation in the ME. I did not wish to recapitulate the President's letter, which I was certain would receive due consideration by the Soviet side. I noted the President had said the ceasefire had been violated by both sides, and that the UAR in early 1969 had announced a policy of not observing the ceasefire. I wished to stress, however, that a ceasefire was a means and not an end in itself, but intended to moderate the current situation and to facilitate negotiations for a settlement. Under such circumstances why would anyone want to oppose a ceasefire. I added that, should the USG decide to provide planes to Israel, this would be done in light of the balance existing in the ME, a balance which might be disturbed by Soviet deliveries to the Arabs. The US has been frank in its position, for example President Nixon made this point in his Jan. 26 message[5] to the American Jewish community meeting in Washington.

11. Referring to Gromyko's assertion that US seemed to be backing off from various positions on ME, I pointed out that any changes we had made were for the purpose of finding a fair-handed solution. Actually, the evolution in our position had sometimes been made for this purpose in the direction of Arab and not solely Israeli interest and had been in response to Soviet urging, as for instance in the the matter of outlining our ideas on frontiers. We certainly could not be accused of pointing our position toward a more adamant, rigid line. In conclusion I stressed we fully appreciate the importance the Arab states attach to withdrawal, which is a key feature to our proposals. The Arabs, however, should not underestimate what the establishment of peace means, not only to the Israeli Govt., but also to world opinion at large.

---

[5] See footnote 6, Document 126.

12. Gromyko reiterated his assertion about the US tending to back off from previous positions. I responded briefly by saying I did not want to renegotiate everything that had been done in New York and Washington, but wished only to concentrate on certain points which the USG felt would bring about an early normalization in the area. I closed this part of the discussion noting I was pleased that the Soviets apparently also wish an early normalization of the situation.

13. *Comment:* Despite his sophistry, Gromyko was even-tempered in his presentation and seemed to be impressed by the steps we are taking to urge a ceasefire and by our warnings concerning an arms escalation in the ME.

Beam

---

134.   Minutes of Washington Special Actions Group Meeting[1]

Washington, February 11, 1970, 4:25–5:27 p.m.

SUBJECT

   Possible Soviet Moves in Egypt

PARTICIPATION

   Chairman—Henry A. Kissinger

   State
   Mr. U. Alexis Johnson
   Mr. Rodger Davies

   Defense
   Mr. Richard Ware
   Mr. Robert Pranger

   JCS
   Lt. Gen. John W. Vogt

SUMMARY OF CONCLUSIONS

1. The WSAG working group paper[2] should be refined to categorize possible Soviet actions to strengthen Egyptian defenses and iden-

---

[1] Source: National Archives, Nixon Presidential Materials, NSC Files, NSC Institutional Files (H-Files), Box H–114, WSAG Minutes, Originals, 1969 and 1970. Top Secret; Nodis. The meeting was held in the White House Situation Room.

[2] A paper entitled "Increased Soviet Involvement in UAR Military Effort—Contingencies and Options," was drafted by Saunders and Rodger P. Davies for consideration by the WSAG working group. (Ibid.)

tify US options in response. The paper should discuss the issues raised by these options, make clear relative US and Soviet military capabilities in the Middle East, and consider the impact which Soviet actions could have on the overall balance in the Middle East.

2. An analysis should be prepared of what would be involved if the Soviets were to install an effective air defense for Egypt. This should include information on likely types of equipment, numbers of personnel, lead time, and means of transporting to the UAR.

3. Existing Middle East contingency plans should be reviewed to determine their applicability to the present situation.

4. CIA should prepare an analysis of possible Soviet intent in diverting an intelligence collection ship to a location south of Cyprus.

5. The WSAG will meet on February 16 for further consideration of Middle East contingency planning.[3]

6. The results of the WSAG studies will be made available to the Ad Hoc Group on aid to Israel. The Ad Hoc Group will meet February 17 or 18 to consider pending proposals on supplying military equipment to Israel. It will meet later to consider overall US strategy in dealing with the Middle East situation.

7. Proposals on all available intelligence capabilities covering possible Soviet moves in Egypt should be prepared for discussion by the 303 Committee on February 17. These proposals should take into account possible means of improving Israeli reconnaissance.

Mr. Kissinger said that at this meeting the WSAG should review existing contingency plans to consider whether they fitted the situations that might arise as a result of Soviet moves in Egypt. It would be up to the principals to decide the timing and nature of any action that might be taken. WSAG approval of a plan did not constitute a recommendation to go forward with the actions specified in the plan.

Mr. Karamessines reviewed new intelligence. [*less than 1 line of source text not declassified*] Nasser in his address to the chiefs of state meeting in Cairo said the Soviets had promised him support by all necessary means. [*less than 1 line of source text not declassified*] officials confirmed that Nasser had visited Moscow and claimed that the Soviets had committed themselves to supply all arms needed to regain the occupied territories. Specifically, [*less than 1 line of source text not declassified*] officials spoke of Soviet willingness to offer Mig 23's and other sophisticated air defense systems if the US provided Phantoms to Israel.

---

[3] A February 16 covering memorandum for these minutes from Jeanne Davis to U. Alexis Johnson, Warren Nutter, Nels Johnson, and Thomas Karamessines informed them that the February 16 meeting was postponed until further notice. (Ibid.)

General Vogt commented that the Mig 23 seemed an unlikely choice, since it was in short supply, was too sophisticated for the Egyptians, and was not suited to prevailing air combat conditions in the UAR-Israel conflict.

Mr. Karamessines mentioned reports that the Soviets might supply surface-to-surface missiles with a range of up to 800 miles and that Soviet pilots might be made available for purely defensive purposes. Nasser had spoken of Soviet irritation at Israeli intransigence and particularly at injuries to Soviet personnel from Israeli air attacks which had resulted in one dead and several wounded, including a general. Nasser, emphasizing the need to improve his air defenses, had admitted that SAM's and radars had been taken from the front lines to assist against low-level Israeli attacks against Cairo.

Mr. Karamessines also noted [*less than 1 line of source text not declassified*] estimates that in Moscow Nasser had requested both offensive and defensive weapons and had found the Soviets generally receptive. However, [*less than 1 line of source text not declassified*] thought the Soviets might hesitate to supply offensive weapons and would be more likely to strengthen Egyptian air defenses with improved SA–2's, SA–3's, or anti-aircraft artillery. [*less than 1 line of source text not declassified*] believe that these improvements would require substantial Soviet manning. General Vogt agreed that Soviet personnel would be needed.

Mr. Karamessines said that a Soviet signal intelligence ship returning from the Mediterranean to the Black Sea had interrupted its voyage and was now operating south of Cyrpus.

General Vogt suggested that the Soviets might be expecting the Israelis to introduce new electronic systems as a response to new armaments to be given by the Soviets to the Egyptians. The Israelis might need new equipment if the Soviets brought in SA–3's. Nevertheless, the intelligence ship could not be required for this purpose in the near future since installation of SA–3's would take a long time. Answering a question from Mr. Karamessines, General Vogt said that the ship would probably not greatly improve Egyptian ability to anticipate Israeli attacks.

Mr. Kissinger said the explanations offered for the activities of the intelligence ship were not very persuasive and asked that an analysis be prepared of Soviet intentions in placing the ship off the Israeli coast.

Mr. Ware asked how many personnel might be involved in operating SA–3's. General Vogt replied that there was little information available but estimated that the total might be about the same size as an SA–2 battalion, which had 700.

General Vogt added that the JCS thought we ought to consider improving our capability to detect possible Soviet moves. The group then discussed at some length various ways to increase reconnaissance, including improvement of Israeli capabilities. General Vogt believed we could do little in this line for the Israelis in the immediate future but might be able to help increase their capabilities over the longer run. He emphasized that in considering the need for better reconnaissance we should think about a program to be conducted over a considerable period of time. The consensus was that a decision on reconnaissance would not be required prior to Tuesday, February 17. Mr. Kissinger directed that proposals covering all available intelligence capabilities be prepared for discussion by the 303 Committee on February 17.[4] These proposals should take into account the possibility of improving Israeli reconnaissance. It would then be possible to have recommendations available for the President by February 18.

Mr. Johnson said that everything points to the Soviets using our decision on aid to Israel as the peg for action on their part to support Nasser. Mr. Kissinger observed that Soviet inaction could very quickly affect their standing in the Middle East.

Mr. Kissinger said that there were three contingencies that needed to be considered: (1) an unacknowledged Soviet move to strengthen UAR air defense by providing equipment and technicians; (2) open Soviet acknowledgement of some Soviet responsibility for UAR air defense; and (3) Soviet threat of offensive action against Israel. The WSAG should list possible US responses to Soviet actions; these could be categorized as diplomatic action, providing aid to Israel, and military measures. It was agreed that the working group paper prepared as a result of the February 9 WSAG meeting could serve as a basis for this analysis. Once the WSAG had assembled its findings, it could place them before the NSC or the Ad Hoc Group on aid to Israel.

The group then considered whether there was any sort of assistance the Soviets could provide that would be effective in stopping the Israeli penetration attacks. Mr. Kissinger pointed out that to stop the attacks would imply that the Israelis would suffer substantial losses. This would create additional problems for us. Mr. Karamessines said that intelligence reports indicated the Soviets might try to give the Egyptians an anti-aircraft capability similar to that they had provided the North Vietnamese. The consensus was that because of Egyptian ineffectiveness, providing them such a capability would probably mean the introduction of Soviet crews.

Mr. Kissinger asked that estimates be prepared of what would be required for an effective Egyptian air defense, including how much

---

[4] Minutes of this 303 meeting are in *Foreign Relations,* 1969–1976, volume XXIII, Arab-Israeli Dispute, 1969–1972.

equipment and personnel would be needed and how transportation to Egypt could be arranged. General Vogt suggested that the Egyptians were concerned primarily about the Cairo area, and that this could probably be covered with 10 battalions of ground-to-air missiles.

Mr. Kissinger suggested that Soviet bombers and pilots might be the cheapest way of creating an effective deterrent against Israeli attacks. General Vogt said that Soviet bombers operating against Israeli defenses could well suffer substantial losses. The Soviets would probably be reluctant to put their prestige on the line in this way. Answering a question from Mr. Pranger, General Vogt said that the intelligence ship would not be useful to feed information to bombers.

General Vogt said that one other possible defensive measure would be for the Soviets to provide an SA–4 mobile system, with associated radar facilities. This would not stop the Israeli penetrations but would make them more costly. Responding to Mr. Johnson's question, General Vogt said that this equipment could be transported by air but would involve tonnages far greater than the Soviets have heretofore flown into Egypt. He noted that the Soviets had obtained overflight permission from Turkey for previous airlifts to Egypt.

Mr. Kissinger again pointed out that we would be faced with a problem if improved Egyptian defenses inflicted losses which the Israeli Air Force could not withstand. General Vogt said that even if the Egyptians had a system equivalent to the North Vietnamese, losses would still not be great—perhaps one per 1000 sorties.

Mr. Karamessines asked about the status of diplomatic efforts. Mr. Kissinger said the approach to the Soviets discussed at the February 9 WSAG meeting had been approved and was being made. Mr. Karamessines then asked about the old proposal for withdrawal of forces from the Suez Canal. The consensus was that there was no possibility that such an approach would be effective at this time and that the basic problem remained the Israeli penetration attacks.

Mr. Kissinger pointed out that diplomatic and supply pressures on Israel were an important part of the inventory of measures which the US might take. Mr. Johnson said that the detailed planning should be reviewed to ensure it is consistent with what we are now working on. Mr. Kissinger agreed and noted that the existing plans for the most part assumed a situation in which the Israeli forces were being driven back in a Soviet-backed effort to oust them from occupied territory. Mr. Davies added that we should look closely at those provisions of the contingency plan covering (1) interdiction of Soviet supplies to Egypt and (2) a one-time retaliatory strike responding to a Soviet attack on Israel. Mr. Kissinger cautioned that we would not wish to rush into military action. Mr. Ware asked if we had the assets to consider a retaliatory strike. General Vogt said that we could mount a strike; but if the Soviets responded, they could rapidly outbid us. Mr. Johnson added that all the analysis done so far had shown that the Soviets would be in a superior military position in the event of a crisis in the Middle East. Mr. Kissinger stressed that it was important that this point be made clear to the President.

Mr. Kissinger asked that the working group established after the February 9 WSAG meeting[5] refine their paper to categorize possible Soviet moves, identify US options in response, discuss the issues these options raise and consider the impact on the overall strategic situation in the Middle East. The WSAG would meet again on the morning of February 16. The papers prepared by the WSAG should be made available to the Ad Hoc Group on aid to Israel. This Group should meet February 17 or 18 to consider pending proposals on providing military equipment to Israel. Later the Ad Hoc Group could meet again to consider the overall US strategy in dealing with Middle East problem.

---

[5] See Document 130.

---

135.   Memorandum of Conversation[1]

Washington, February 18, 1970.

PARTICIPANTS

Ambassador Anatoliy Dobrynin
Mr. Henry A. Kissinger

I had lunch served in the downstairs Library at the White House Mansion in order both to avoid the press' seeing Dobrynin coming in and to avoid staff members' asking questions. Another reason was to show Dobrynin that we were paying some special attention.

Dobrynin began the conversation by giving me a picture that I had seen at the Soviet photo show the evening before. It is of a dog looking at a syringe with great apprehension, and had amused me very much. He had written a little inscription on the back.

---

[1] Source: National Archives, Nixon Presidential Materials, NSC Files, Box 489, President's Trip Files, Dobrynin/Kissinger, 1970, [Part 2] Vol. I. Top Secret; Sensitive; Eyes Only. The meeting was held in the Residence Library.

We then turned immediately to the President's annual report,[2] which had been published the night before. Dobrynin said that he had read the report with the greatest care and that he had found it on the whole a well-balanced document. In fact, he thought that it would be well received in the Soviet Union, except for a number of items. First, he had noticed that there were only two foreign leaders mentioned in the report—President Thieu and President Ceausescu. This, Dobrynin said, would rub people the wrong way. The second thing, to which there would be great exception taken in the Soviet Union, was the list in the Introduction of countries where the Red Army had been used since 1945. I told him that, of course, he had to understand the report was not written primarily for Moscow audiences and that as far as the mention of Ceausescu was concerned, there was no particular intention attached to it. He said he just wanted to be sure that it was one of these drafting problems which might indicate a certain priority in the President's attitude, but which was not directed at the Soviet Union.

Dobrynin then asked a number of questions about the organizational part of the report. Specifically, he wanted to know the difference between the group dealing with crisis management and the groups dealing with programs—e.g., the differences between the Verification Panel and the Washington Special Actions Group. I gave him a rather general description. Dobrynin said that in the Soviet Union, of course, decisions were taken in a different manner; that is to say, there was no coordination between departments at a lower level. Each department worked independently, and all issues were resolved at the higher level.

Dobrynin then asked about a phrase in the report which said that the only status quo in the world today is the fact of change. Did that mean that we no longer recognized the existing dividing lines in Europe? I said it was odd for a Marxist to argue that such a phrase produced any difficulties, since after all, all of Marxist theory was based on the theory of history. Dobrynin smiled and said that in Europe we are fomenting the maintenance of the status quo. I said the distinction had to be made between existing dividing lines in Europe and existing frontiers. We certainly recognized all existing national frontiers, but we did not recognize the East German boundary as a national frontier. This did not, of course, mean that we would support the use or the threat of force with respect to it.

---

[2] The text of Nixon's "First Annual Report to the Congress on United States Foreign Policy for the 1970s" is in *Public Papers: Nixon, 1970*, pp. 116–190. On February 25, Kissinger sent Nixon a memorandum that provided excerpts of foreign media reaction. The Soviet reaction was given as follows: "A Soviet writer commented in *Izvestiya* that 'President Nixon is trying to pacify the American people and make them favor the present Government course.'" (Ibid., Box 326, Subject Files, Foreign Reaction to President's Annual Review of U.S. Foreign Policy)

Dobrynin replied that this explanation was perfectly agreeable to the Soviet Union. Could he communicate it to his government? I told him that existing national boundaries would not be challenged by this Administration, and I said as far as I knew, I had never heard anyone express any different view. Dobrynin said he had been puzzled because the previous Administration had given him formal assurance to that effect, and we had not yet done that.

Dobrynin then turned to the issue of sufficiency and said this was, of course, a very vague term on which further discussion might be useful. He wondered in what respect the ABM fitted into the sufficiency concept. He said that it was unfortunate that Helsinki was immediately followed by the ABM announcement. I told him that the ABM announcement came up, as he knew very well, as part of our regular budgetary cycle. It would have come up in January regardless of Helsinki, and nothing had happened in Helsinki that could affect our budgetary decisions. As he knew very well, we were engaged in a purely exploratory conversation.

Dobrynin then asked about the difference between area defense and point defense. I gave him a very crude explanation because I did not want to go into missile characteristics. With the President's authority, I gave him a brief account of what the request would be like for next year, and I told him it was a minimum request which would keep the program going but which would retain all options for SALT.

Dobrynin said that he simply did not understand how the Minuteman defense could also be useful for area defense and how, if it was useful for area defense, it could make any difference to the Soviets what our intentions were. I told him that the best thing would be if I would let one of my technical experts explain the system to him, and we arranged a meeting for some weeks ahead.

Dobrynin then read a little note to me (attached)[3] which did not, he said, represent a formal communication but some tentative instructions. The note reads as follows:

"At the time of the Helsinki meetings the American delegation emphasized that it displays business-like attitude toward discussing the problem of curbing strategic offensive and defensive armaments race. We would like to say frankly that further development raises questions on our side in this respect.

"We do not understand, in particular, what was that that guided the American side when despite agreement about the confidential nature of the talks it in fact released to the press through its various spokesmen many elements of the contents of the Helsinki negotiations.

---

[3] Not attached.

Such an approach can hardly make a favorable impact on the atmosphere of the talks in the future.

"We would also like to stress that in the light of the exchange of views in Helsinki we are puzzled by the position on issues of strategic armaments taken by certain members of the U.S. Government, in particular, by the U.S. Secretary of Defense Laird. Mr. Laird has recently come out demanding substantial speed-up in the deployment of the ABM 'Safeguard' system, as well as declared the intention to speed up the development of a new type of strategic bomber and underwater long-range missile system. The Pentagon also advocates development of a new ground-based intercontinental ballistic missile.

"The demands by members of the U.S. Government that the U.S. should expedite nuclear missile arms race make for some thought as to the intentions here with respect to achieving agreement on curbing strategic offensive and defensive arms race.

"It is known that earlier, when the U.S. Government was taking its decision on deployment of the 'Safeguard' system President Nixon connected its deployment with the course of Soviet-American talks."

A question arises as to whether it should be understood that the Laird statement about speeding up the ABM deployment in the U.S. is connected with the position that the American side is going to take at the Soviet-American negotiations in Vienna?

"The Soviet Union in preparing for the Vienna talks proceeds from the assumption that statements by the American delegation at the Helsinki talks reflected the position of the Nixon Administration, and that that position has not changed during the time passed since the end of Helsinki negotiations. However, in connection with the Secretary of Defense Laird statement a question arises whether or not the American delegation is going to change its position?"

I told Dobrynin that the best way to proceed would be for us to schedule another conversation devoted primarily to SALT. I told him that we were serious, and that it was difficult to talk in the abstract. Dobrynin wanted to know whether we were interested in a comprehensive or a limited agreement, whether we were going to change our position in Vienna, and what approach we were going to take. I told Dobrynin that we should have a full discussion, and that we might set up two channels—one for the formal negotiations, and one between him and me to deal with general principles.

136. Memorandum From the President's Assistant for National Security Affairs (Kissinger) to President Nixon[1]

Washington, February 18, 1970.

SUBJECT

Ambassador Beam's Talk with Gromyko on the Middle East

Ambassador Beam met with Gromyko on February 11[2] to follow up on your response to the message to Kosygin.[3] He was under instructions to stress (1) the need for a cease-fire in which both sides would stop shooting, (2) our continuing interest in talks on arms limitation, and (3) our desire for a more positive response to our proposals for a peaceful settlement between the Arabs and the Israelis.

Gromyko's Response

Cease-Fire: Gromyko said that the USSR could consider neither a cease-fire nor the whole Mid-East situation outside of the context of the actions which Israel is taking. Israel is carrying out systematic, provocative attacks on the Arab states. "Neither the USSR nor USA has received reports that UAR actions are not consistent with UN decisions." [Beam later rebutted this allegation.][4] The fault lies with Israel.

Arms deliveries: Gromyko reminded us of the position Kosygin took in his recent message to you.[5] Moscow is not against discussing limitations on the delivery of arms to the Middle East but for all practical purposes such discussion "is not possible" as long as Israel occupies Arab territories. When the question of the withdrawal of Israeli troops is resolved, as well as other problems relating to a Middle East settlement, arms limitation talks on the Middle East could "begin." Though he did not think there would be any tremendous difficulties, any possible agreement would depend, however, on the concrete positions of the parties.

---

[1] Source: National Archives, Nixon Presidential Materials, NSC Files, Box 711, Country Files, Europe, USSR, Vol. VI. Secret; Nodis. Sent for information. Drafted by Sonnenfeldt and Saunders on February 12. The draft contained the following concluding sentence that Kissinger deleted: "I believe we must continue to confront the Soviets with the risks of intervention while leaving open the possibility for genuine diplomatic negotiation."

[2] See Document 133.

[3] Document 126.

[4] Brackets in the source text.

[5] Document 121.

Gromyko also said that the Soviets had "paid attention" to the part of your message to Kosygin on the U.S. restoring the balance if anything is done to benefit the Arabs. The USSR, according to Gromyko, regrets the way we have posed this question. Israel is the source of the tension in the Middle East and the U.S. would be in a "more just position" if it exerted maximum pressure on the Israelis.

Instead the U.S. says that the USSR should exert pressure on the victims of Israeli aggression and hints that in the interest of maintaining the balance we will take certain steps (like new deliveries of Phantoms).

U.S. Proposals: The U.S. proposals for a peace settlement are one-sided, pro-Israeli and not objective. The USSR had made many efforts to reach an agreement, but every time there was "some rapprochement" of positions the U.S. would retreat to previous positions and undermine positive movement in the negotiations. This is reflected in the Four Power talks where the U.S. is taking a take-it-or-leave-it approach and which promises little in the way of achieving agreement.

Nevertheless, Gromyko later in the conversation said that the USSR remains ready to continue the Two Power talks, though he would like us to take a "more constructive position." The USSR is puzzled by the lack of progress since we seem to agree on the fundamentals. Perhaps misunderstandings here or there are taking place. The USSR is ready to do whatever is necessary to normalize the situation and not worsen it, but this does not all depend on the USSR.

Comment: The general thrust of Gromyko's response seems to be a firm reiteration of the positions the Soviets have been taking for some time. They continue to place the entire blame for the escalation of the fighting on the Israelis and picture the Arabs as the innocent victims of U.S.-Israeli collusion. They show no inclination to press Nasser on the restoration of the cease-fire or a peace settlement. Similarly, the Soviets continue to reject serious consideration of limiting arms shipments to the Middle East on the grounds that nothing constructive can be accomplished until there is a peace settlement. At the same time, they leave the door slightly open to continuing bilateral talks with us or multilateral talks including the British and French as a means of constructing a diplomatic alternative. Their basic problem is that to be really helpful to the Arabs they would have to provide effective military support. But this, they fear, could lead to confrontation with us.

Gromyko's response points up the Soviet dilemma but does not provide new evidence of their intentions. They are not anxious for a confrontation with us over the Middle East even though Kosygin's letter itself injected strong elements of confrontation. But they are under increasing pressure to do something for Nasser and may already have made some new commitment to him, at least to increase the pressures on the U.S. and Israel. Their immediate aim may be to force the Israelis, through us, to cease the air attacks on the Egyptian heartland. Failing that, they seem to be preserving the option of offering some new movement in the Four Power or even the Two Power talks which might persuade us to hold off on arms deliveries to Israel, or—if that doesn't seem feasible or attractive—involving themselves more directly in the defense of the UAR. We cannot be sure that the Soviets have irrevocably decided to come to Nasser's aid with more and improved weapons and/or direct involvement of their own people in the hostilities. On the other hand, the present diplomatic exchange could be mainly for the record and to justify such a move.

In short, the Soviets continue to walk on a dangerous tightrope and seem not yet to have decided on a definite course. All that seems clear is that at least on the surface they have left the most important options open, while trying to force the Israelis to call off their attacks and prevent us from sending more Phantoms. The tough and dangerous decisions—whether and how to bail out the Egyptians or whether and how to make a genuine diplomatic move that would persuade the Israelis to stop their attacks—are still ahead for the Soviets.

---

137.   Special National Intelligence Estimate[1]

SNIE 11–16–70   Washington, February 19, 1970.

SOVIET ATTITUDES TOWARD SALT

Discussion

How the Soviets Saw Helsinki

1. It was plainly the view of the Soviet delegation at Helsinki that the first round of talks was to be no more than preliminary and

---

[1] Source: Central Intelligence Agency, NIC Files, Job 79–R1012A, NIEs and SNIEs. Top Secret; Sensitive; Limited Distribution. According to a prefatory note, the Central Intelligence Agency and the intelligence organizations of the Department of State, Defense, Atomic Energy Commission, and the National Security Agency participated in the preparation of this estimate, which was submitted by the Director of Central Intelligence and concurred by all members of the USIB. This SNIE superseded SNIE 11–16–68, November 7, 1968, "The Soviet Approach to Arms Control," which "dealt with the attitudes the Soviets might be expected to bring to talks on limiting strategic weapons (SALT). It discussed how such factors as the USSR's economic position and its view of the strategic relationship with the US might be thought to bear on the Soviet approach to SALT." It is printed in *Foreign Relations, 1964–1968*, volume XI, Arms Control and Disarmament, Document 291.

exploratory. But the Soviets were also intent on demonstrating by their demeanor—the avoidance of propagandistic or tendentious debating tactics—that Moscow was ready for a serious exploration of the prospects for strategic arms control. They wanted, in return, renewed evidence of American "seriousness."

2. The essential test of this seriousness, in the Russian view, is whether the US is ready to acknowledge that it does not think of itself as bargaining from a position of strategic superiority and will treat with the USSR as an equal. Thus, at Helsinki, the Soviets tried to satisfy themselves that the US did not aim to use the talks as a lever to obtain concessions from the USSR on other international issues; among other reasons, because they did not want the impression to be left that the USSR needed arms control more than the US did. So too, the Soviets insisted that an arms control agreement must assure "equal security" for both sides and not give a military advantage to either.

3. Other than to carry out this kind of broad reconnaissance of US intentions, the instructions of the Soviet delegation at Helsinki seemed to call generally for letting the US take the lead in opening substantive issues. The Soviets were quick, however, to endorse certain broad propositions which the US put forward as essential premises for an agreement. Thus, they affirmed that they understood mutual deterrence to be the governing principle of the US-Soviet strategic relationship. And they recognized officially for the first time the interrelationship between offensive and defensive strategic systems and acknowledged that defensive, as well as offensive, systems can pose a threat to stability.

4. Generally, on broad concepts underlying the problems at issue the Soviets demonstrated sophistication; this was apparently intended to show their seriousness as well as to assert their claim to equality. Insofar as the Soviet statements approached more concrete issues, they reflected primarily a concern to lay the groundwork, at least for bargaining purposes, for definitions which would include or exclude weapon systems to the Soviet advantage. But it did not appear that the Soviets had even in their own minds a fully coherent view of the various elements which might go into an eventual agreement, and some of their points were made as a response to an illustrative negotiating outline offered by the US.

5. Moscow's willingness to move on to a second round of talks indicates that it found US motives in SALT to be sufficiently "serious." No doubt some in the Soviet leadership were already persuaded of this, but others probably argued that the results of Helsinki should be awaited. In any case, it appears that Moscow was uncertain until the discussions were nearly ended whether they had gone well enough to warrant the conclusion that a second phase would have reasonable chances of success from the Soviet point of view. The decision to go ahead only

after a four-month interval may have been due to foot-dragging by some elements in Moscow, though it could equally have resulted from recognition that much more elaborate preparation would be needed than had been thought.

6. Probably the Soviets left Helsinki without a clear understanding of the shape and content of an agreement at which the US might be aiming. That the US presented categories and definitions which the Soviets took to be self-serving presumably did not disturb them greatly, though they probably came away uncertain as to how flexible the US would be in this regard. Some features of the US presentation may have genuinely puzzled them, notably the tentative approach to the ABM problem and the mention of MIRV only in passing, as part of a list of component parts of missile systems. They may still be uncertain concerning the degree to which the "illustrative elements" outlined to them actually represented an initial US negotiating position. They are also probably confused concerning the extent to which the US intends to press for qualitative as well as quantitative limitations.

7. In particular, the Soviets are probably uncertain as to how comprehensive and complex an agreement the US will eventually seek. Even in a fairly simple agreement, the standards of equivalence will be difficult to establish, due to asymmetries in the structure of strategic forces—a fact that both sides acknowledged at Helsinki. And the Soviets are probably not sure whether the US will be satisfied to rely for verification on national means only. Nevertheless, they have probably concluded tentatively that the US approach did not disclose any insuperable obstacles to an eventual agreement and that the chances of working out an agreement satisfactory to the USSR were good enough to be worth pursuing further.

Factors Bearing on Soviet Negotiating Tactics

8. The Helsinki round was altogether too preliminary and tentative to have clarified Soviet motives in entering SALT. Nevertheless, it strongly suggests that Moscow is seriously interested in discovering whether the intensity of the strategic arms competition can be contained, through SALT, on terms which do not prejudice Soviet security. The USSR's interest in exploring this avenue seems to rest, in the first place, on its perception of the present state of the strategic relationship with the US. Economic considerations also bear on the Soviet attitude toward SALT, as do certain Soviet foreign policy concerns, e.g., Western Europe, NATO, and China. But, at the same time, there are a number of factors which set limits to how far and how fast Moscow will go in SALT.

9. *The Strategic Relationship with the US.* We have no way of knowing with certainty whether the Soviet leaders believe that the present

strategic relationship is the best they can now hope for and, if they do, whether they also think that long-term stabilization of this relationship is desirable or even possible. It may be that the decision-making apparatus in Moscow has not come to a firm consensus on such questions. There is agreement in Moscow, of course, that the USSR must have rough parity at least. It is possible that some Soviet leaders believe that a useful margin of advantage in strategic weaponry is attainable. We do think, however, that as the Soviet leaders now see the future they believe that it will not be feasible to attain superiority of a clear and decisive nature.[2] They may fear, in fact, that the technical and economic capabilities of the US will enable it to reduce the USSR's relative position once again.

10. If these are the views the Soviets entertain about the present situation, they may see value in an agreement which would stabilize the present situation. They might want such an agreement in a form which would not foreclose their options if and when they came to a different view of what the strategic relationship might be. They would be realistic enough to recognize, however, that an agreement loose enough to permit them some future freedom of choice would also give the same to the US.

11. *Economic Considerations.* At a time when the rate of industrial growth is declining, when the agricultural sector remains in parlous condition, and when it is openly acknowledged that the Soviet economy is lagging behind technologically, the Soviet leadership must be reluctant to face the prospect of additional heavy arms expenditures.

---

[2] Maj. Gen. Rockly Triantafellu, the Assistant Chief of Staff, Intelligence, USAF, disagrees with the assessment in this sentence. He believes as follows:

While the Soviets are sensitive to the possibility of the US embarking on an expanded strategic military program (including MIRVs, hardening, mobility, and ABMs), they are also sensitive to the mood of the US toward decreasing military expenditures. A judgment as to whether the Soviets would consider feasible the attainment of clear and decisive superiority must be addressed in the context of past Soviet decisions. The Soviets mounted an enormous effort to develop and deploy strategic military nuclear systems (ICBMs, SLBMs, aircraft, and ABMs) to overtake the US in numbers and weapon yield and to achieve an initial advantage in ABM capability. While the decision to catch up posed a severe technological and economic challenge to the Soviets, they accepted the challenge and have now achieved at least parity. At the same time, they have continued to greatly expand their military research programs, have continued to develop new systems—such as fractional orbit and depressed trajectory missiles—and have continued the pace of their deployment of strategic systems. Therefore, in reviewing past Soviet achievements and weighing their present and future actions, there is no evidence to support a view that the Soviets will ignore an opportunity to forge ahead. The goal may now seem to them closer at hand than it was 10 years ago. The resources in terms of technical and scientific personnel, production capacity, and internal political control are available to motivate and facilitate a Soviet decision to achieve clear and decisive strategic superiority. [Footnote in the source text.]

Any easing of the strategic arms burden would make possible the redistribution of scarce investment funds and high-quality human resources. On those grounds, some Soviet leaders probably wish SALT well. Others would probably welcome the opportunity to shift resources within the military establishment itself. Nevertheless, given its present size, nature, and rate of growth, the Soviet economy could, if need be, support even higher levels of arms spending than at present. Though probably an important consideration, the state of the Soviet economy will not be the decisive factor in the Soviet approach to SALT. It does not oblige the USSR to seek agreement.

12. *SALT and Current Soviet Foreign Policies.* While its assessment of SALT's impact on the US-Soviet strategic relationship is paramount in Soviet thinking, Moscow must also realize that SALT is now involved in the total context of its foreign policy, and particularly its relations with the US. If a failure in SALT were to be added to differences over Vietnam and the Middle East, relations between the two great powers would tend to deteriorate. Such a trend at present would probably cause the USSR considerable concern. The USSR's current European diplomacy, which aims at generating an atmosphere of détente, would suffer a setback. Moreover, the Russians could expect the Chinese, seeing the failure of the US-Soviet enterprise and foreseeing the possibility of further overtures toward themselves from the US, to adopt a more uncompromising line toward Moscow. On the other hand, the Soviets could calculate that, if SALT were to show signs of progress, certain issues in US–USSR relations might become more manageable from their point of view.

13. Taken together, considerations of this kind do give Moscow incentives for taking a positive approach to SALT, at least initially. On the other hand, the Soviets will not wish the US to believe that it has leverage in SALT because of the USSR's broader policy concerns, and they will not, in fact, make important concessions because of such concerns. Actually, they will hope that as SALT develops they will have opportunities to exploit weaknesses and divisions in the US and between the US and its allies. They are likely to exercise restraint in this respect, however, so long as they think they have a good chance of getting a satisfactory agreement.

14. *Domestic Politics.* The deliberations which led up to Moscow's acceptance of the US proposal for SALT were long and probably hard. There is no reason to suppose that the decision to go ahead, so deliberately reached, is likely to be easily reversed. Most signs indicate, however, that the prevailing instinct in Moscow is to move into SALT slowly and carefully. The momentousness of the negotiations for the national security of the USSR, as for that of the US, inevitably impresses itself on the minds of the Soviet leadership. The intrinsic complexity of the

issues involved and the lack of experience of negotiation in this sensitive area also make for a cautious approach. Decisions which might not come easily in any circumstances will, moreover, in this case be affected by the ungainliness of the Soviet decision-making process and the conservative reflexes of the collective leadership.

15. A Soviet official at Helsinki confirmed that control over the delegation's activities came, as might have been surmised, from the Politburo itself, through the foreign ministry machinery. This procedure will presumably be maintained through the Vienna phase. The Politburo's watchfulness is not surprising, given not only the inherent significance of the issues but also the possible domestic effects of the decisions to be made and their implications for relations among the top leaders. None of the decisions faced by the present governing committee have cut across so many bureaucratic interests. Though some of these interests will have a positive attitude toward SALT, many of them will have misgivings. Among the latter will be that part of the economic bureaucracy which has a vested interest in defense industry and its many allies in the party apparatus. And, of course, the Politburo will need to give weight to military views, toward which it has been generally attentive in recent years.

16. *Military Attitudes.* A large part of the Soviet military establishment—probably the bulk of it—undoubtedly has serious reservations about strategic arms limitations. But some of the military leaders have long resisted the high priority given to strategic weapons at the expense of the traditional arms of service. In recent years, the militarization of the Sino-Soviet dispute has greatly enlarged requirements for general purpose forces. Moreover, some military writers see in the nuclear stalemate a need to improve capabilities for conventional warfare, especially in view of NATO's adoption of a strategy of "flexible response." An arms limitation agreement which freed resources to meet these requirements would surely be welcome in some military quarters. Thus, the political leadership will probably not receive uniform advice from the military establishment as the negotiations develop.

[Omitted here is discussion on possible Soviet positions at Vienna printed in *Foreign Relations, 1969–1976*, volume XXXII, SALT I, 1969–1972.]

33. *Concluding Observations.* Given the distances that will separate the two sides on most of the above key issues and the complexities that will need to be overcome, the Soviets have almost certainly not yet decided whether, in the end, an agreement acceptable to them can be achieved. Nor is there a single view in Moscow at present as to whether Soviet long-term interests would be better served by stabilizing the strategic relationship under an agreement rather than by continuing a competitive situation. The play of group interest and personal ambition which will surround this choice is bound to be intense.

34. Clearly there is much in the traditional Soviet outlook which would generate negative attitudes toward the idea of agreed stabilization. Long-held premises about the inevitability of conflict, mistrust of American motives, fear of being duped, even ignorance of the relevant technical facts would help to sustain such attitudes. And it is true that conservative instincts seem to be dominant in the present leadership.

35. On the other hand, there are obviously a number of people, including some military men, who have the ear of the leadership and will be able to make a strong case for a serious try at stabilization by agreement. The argument for easing economic pressures is a strong one, particularly for those who want more margin to experiment with economic reform. It will be said that as the arms race enters a new technological phase Soviet chances of lagging seriously behind are high. Some will argue that at present levels of strength strategic weapons are no longer as critical to the power competition, that, in fact, if the strategic arms race can be contained by agreement, other factors, including conventional military power, could be enhanced and would better serve the security and ambitions of the USSR.

36. We see no way of forecasting how such arguments will net out. Obviously the concrete choices presented by the interaction of the two sides in negotiations will be more determining than arguments made in the abstract. We would judge, however, that at present the Soviet leaders have a consensus, perhaps a shaky one, that the option of strategic stabilization by agreement should be given a long, hard look through SALT.

138.   National Intelligence Estimate[1]

NIE 11–6–70   Washington, March 5, 1970.

SOVIET POLICIES IN THE MIDDLE EAST AND MEDITERRANEAN AREA

Summary

A. Over the last 15 years, the USSR has established itself as a major power factor in the Mediterranean world. By exploiting postcolonial resentments and especially the Arab-Israeli conflict, the Soviets have sought to deny the area to Western interests and influence. Their calculation has been that the displacement of Western with Soviet influence would constitute a broad strategic reversal for the West and a considerable gain for themselves. Nevertheless, they have not seen the area as one which engaged their most vital national interests; these remain focused on their relations with the US in general, on Eastern and Central Europe, and on their conflict with Communist China.

B. The Arab-Israeli conflict provides the Soviets with their greatest means of leverage in the Middle East, but it also faces them with the most severe complications. They have extended enough military aid to the radical Arabs to become thoroughly involved in the latter's cause, but their efforts have not created an effective Arab defense. Israeli military attacks, particularly against Egypt, intensify this Soviet dilemma. They wish to provide Egypt with effective defense, but seek also to minimize the risks of direct involvement; yet if they sought to defuse the situation by pressing the Arabs to make concessions to Israel, they would jeopardize their influence in the Arab world. Barring a de-escalation of the Arab-Israeli conflict, the Soviets will probably step up their aid to the Egyptians, and they may provide new weapons systems and additional personnel to improve Egyptian air defenses.

C. Despite the Soviet support for the Arab cause in the Arab-Israeli conflict, Moscow's relations with the radical Arab states are subject to occasionally serious strains; none of these countries is entirely

---

[1] Source: Central Intelligence Agency, NIC Files, Job 79–R1012A, NIEs and SNIEs. Secret; Controlled Dissem. According to a prefatory note, the Central Intelligence Agency and the intelligence organizations of the Department of State, Defense, and the National Security Agency participated in the preparation of this estimate, which was submitted by the Director of Central Intelligence and concurred by all members of the USIB, except the Assistant General Manager of the Atomic Energy Commission and the Assistant Director of the Federal Bureau of Investigation, who abstained because the subject was outside their jurisdiction. This NIE superseded NIE 11–6–67.

responsive to Soviet pressures, and each is jealous and suspicious of the others. The still more uncontrollable fedayeen movement is a problem for Moscow, chiefly because any direct Soviet support for it involves embarrassment in Moscow's relations with established governments; nevertheless, we think the Soviets will continue to develop relations with the fedayeen discreetly.

D. The Soviets have aspirations to establish themselves in the western Mediterranean as well, but Tunisia and Morocco remain generally wary of the USSR and retain strong ties with the West. Algeria has accepted Soviet assistance, but more recently it has been drawing nearer to its immediate neighbors and to France. Although the new regime in Libya has close ties with Egypt, it shows no signs of welcoming a Soviet presence, and Nasser is probably not anxious to encourage Soviet influence there. Among European states with interests in the area, Moscow must be concerned to avoid provoking alarm by its activities in the Mediterranean lest this compromise its policies in Western Europe; France, in particular, has ambitions to enlarge its role in the Mediterranean.

E. Since the June War in 1967, the Soviet military presence has grown in the area: roughly 5,000 Soviet military advisers are now stationed in several area countries; the Soviet naval squadron in the Mediterranean has been strengthened, and is supported by air and port facilities in Egypt. How the USSR might use its military strength in the Mediterranean area in times of crisis and war is examined in this paper in four major contingencies: (1) Arab-Israeli hostilities short of all-out war (paragraphs 41–48); (2) full-scale Arab-Israeli war (paragraphs 49–51); (3) other disputes in the area in which Soviet interests were involved (paragraphs 52–53); and (4) East-West hostilities involving both the US and the USSR (paragraphs 54–55).

F. The Soviet presence in the Mediterranean region is likely to prove durable. Radical nationalist forces will continue to work against Western interests and will continue to receive Soviet support. Thus the rivalry between the US and USSR in the area is likely to persist at least so long as it continues in the world at large.

Discussion

I. The Strategic Setting: Broad Soviet Considerations and Objectives

1. Soviet power first moved into the Mediterranean in the mid-1950s. Seizing on the opportunities for influence offered by Arab-Israeli antagonisms and by increasingly militant and anti-Western forms of Arab nationalism, and leap-frogging over the Middle Eastern members of the newly formed Baghdad Pact (Turkey, Iran, and Iraq), the USSR eased its way into both Cairo and Damascus with offers of arms, economic aid, and political support. During the 1960s, through

the use of these and other conventional instruments of influence and power, the USSR became the primary backer of the radical Arab states. Today the Soviet Union is a major factor in the Middle East, with a number of client states in varying degrees of dependency and with elements of its own armed forces now present in the area. The Soviet leadership almost certainly sees its gains here as the most extensive and successful of all its efforts to expand Soviet influence in areas of the world once dominated by the West.

2. Clearly, the Soviets have in this period looked upon the Middle East as an area of strategic importance. A part of this attitude no doubt was inherited from their predecessors; Czarist planners traditionally viewed this part of the world as a special Russian sphere of interest and periodically sought to expand Russian power southwards. In modern times, especially since the death of Stalin, this geopolitical emphasis has been accompanied by an ideologically inspired hope that the anticolonialist attitudes of the Third World could be made to work for social change and for the emergence of local power elites sympathetic to communism. And this has been joined with the view that the Middle East has become one of the main arenas of the Soviet struggle with the West and the US. The Soviets may see the area as more complicated and the opportunities less immediate than they did in 1955 when they first undertook a military supply program for Egypt. But they evidently still hope to bring the states of the region into an anti-Western alignment and ultimately to establish their own hegemony there. Finally, the area is seen in Moscow as a strategic military zone: in hostile hands, it could pose a threat to the USSR and block Soviet access to the Mediterranean; in friendly hands, it protects the USSR's southwestern border and permits Moscow to move its influence into the Mediterranean world and beyond. The Middle East and much of the non-European Mediterranean world are thus, in the Soviet world view, proximate, important, and vulnerable.

3. This is not to say that the Soviets attach the same weight to their problems and objectives in the Middle East and Mediterranean basin as they do to their prime concerns elsewhere. Their stake there is less critical to their interests than their relations with the US in general, their concerns in Eastern and Central Europe, and their conflict with Communist China. It is in these areas and with these countries that the most vital of Soviet national interests are directly engaged. There are in addition certain self-imposed limitations on Soviet policies in the Mediterranean area and the Middle East. The preservation of the USSR's position in the Middle East would not be worth the serious risk of nuclear war with the US, whereas its presence in, say, East Germany, might be. But at least until recently Moscow has been able to base its approach in the Mediterranean area on calculations of opportunity and risk within the area concerned without serious conflicts with its objectives elsewhere.

4. Inevitably, as the degree of its involvement in the area has grown and the level of its commitment risen, the USSR has found itself faced with mounting costs and risks. It has exhibited some anxiety to control these risks and to curb the excessive enthusiasms of some of its clients. But it has also chosen to live with danger, and its position is now potentially vulnerable to the pressures and perils of events over which it may have little or no control—the actions of the Arab states, of Israel, and even of the US. Broadly speaking, Moscow has behaved as if it wishes the Middle East to remain an area of at least some tension. It apparently believes that the risks attending this are manageable, and that continued polarization in the area will make it increasingly difficult for the conservative Arab states to maintain their ties with the US, thus decreasing US influence throughout the area. But the Soviets clearly recognize that in the event of another explosion in the Middle East they would be faced with some very hard choices.

II. Instruments of Soviet Power in the Area

5. In moving into the Mediterranean, the Soviets have used the conventional instruments of power available, short of the actual use of force, to exploit the opportunities open to them. They have used military and economic assistance as a means of penetration and as a way of promoting Arab dependence on the USSR; they have maneuvered politically to pressure and seduce and support; and they have introduced their own naval power into the area as a means of adding to their influence and diminishing that of their antagonists.

6. *Military Aid.* The first and still most important Soviet instrument of influence is military assistance.[2] Since the mid-1950s, the USSR has extended $2.8 billion of such aid to four Arab states—Egypt, Iraq, Syria, and Algeria; this represents roughly half of all Soviet military aid to non-Communist countries. Egypt, with over $1.4 billion in aid, is by far the largest beneficiary. Iraq and Syria have also become almost wholly dependent on the USSR for weapons, equipment, and spare parts. It was Moscow's prompt and extensive resupply operation in the wake of the June War which quickly restored the leverage it had momentarily lost in the Arab world.

7. *Economic Assistance.* The USSR has also engaged in substantial economic aid programs in the Middle East and the Mediterranean area.[3] Since 1957, the Soviets have committed at least $2.6 billion of economic aid to Egypt, Iran, Turkey, Iraq, Algeria, and Syria (in that

---

[2] See Appendix, Table I. [Footnote in the source text. The appendix is not printed.]

[3] See Appendix, Table I. [Footnote in the source text. The appendix is not printed.]

order)—about 40 percent of their total economic aid commitments to all non-Communist countries. These programs serve different policy aims in different countries. In the case of Egypt, for example, the aim is to assist the development of the leading Arab nation as a Soviet client, and to reinforce the overall pattern of dependency on the USSR; with Iran, there is a solid economic basis for expanded relations as well as the political purpose of helping to loosen Iranian ties with the West. Though in other areas of the world Moscow is becoming more selective and tough-minded, the policy of economic assistance in the Middle East and the Mediterranean area is likely to continue on a substantial scale for the foreseeable future.

8. *Other Economic Interests.* Economic interests play a role in Soviet policy, but not a decisive one. The Soviets want to maintain access to the waterways of the area; over half the Soviet merchant marine tonnage is based in Black Sea ports. Continued closure of the Suez Canal increases the cost of Soviet shipping east of Africa, but Moscow has learned to live with this situation, however unhappily. The USSR also has some interest in Middle Eastern oil and gas, both for itself and for the countries of Eastern Europe. Although Soviet supplies of petroleum appear adequate for domestic consumption and substantial exports for many years to come, East European and Soviet imports from the Middle East would release corresponding quantities of Soviet oil and gas for additional sales in hard currency markets. But Communist imports are likely to remain a small proportion of Middle East oil sales, and such imports would be further limited by the desire of the producing states to sell elsewhere for hard currencies.

9. *The Soviet Military Presence.* The Soviets have substantially increased their military presence in the eastern Mediterranean since the June War. The number of military advisers attached to Arab forces has been greatly increased and the Soviet naval squadron has been strengthened. The squadron's political objectives apparently are to show the flag, to demonstrate support of the USSR's allies in the area, and to reveal to the world that the Mediterranean Sea is no longer an exclusive preserve of the US Sixth Fleet. Its primary military roles are to monitor the Sixth Fleet, to complicate and inhibit its operations even in peace time, to develop capabilities against Polaris submarines and, in the event of hostilities, to attempt to deny Western naval forces the use of Mediterranean waters. Currently, the Soviet naval units also seem to have some effect in deterring Israeli attacks on Egyptian ports.

10. From the few surface ships and submarines deployed in 1964, the Soviet Mediterranean squadron has since grown to become the largest Soviet naval force outside home fleet operating areas. Except for occasional peaks, the Soviet squadron usually consists of about

12 surface combatants, 2 or 3 landing ships, and 8 to 10 diesel and nuclear-powered submarines. Normally, between 12 and 15 auxiliary ships provide logistic support and 1 to 3 are intelligence ships. Normally, 2 to 4 of the surface combatants are equipped with surface-to-air or surface-to-surface missiles, and 1 or 2 of the submarines are nuclear-powered. In addition, 6 Soviet naval reconnaissance aircraft (TU–16s), and 3 antisubmarine warfare (ASW) amphibian aircraft operate from Egyptian air bases in support of the squadron.

11. We estimate that the Soviets have roughly 5,000 military advisers stationed in the area—about 3,000 in Egypt, 1,200 in Algeria, 500 in Syria, a few hundred in Iraq, and lesser numbers in the Sudan, Yemen, and South Yemen. Although these advisers are not known to have command authority, in Egypt and Syria they occupy important advisory positions at or near command levels, and are present with units down to battalion/squadron level.

12. Since the June War the Soviets have concluded a number of "facilities arrangements" with Egypt which permit the Soviet naval squadron to make regular use of repair facilities in Alexandria and of storage facilities there and in Port Said. We have no evidence of any such approach to Syria. The Soviets would probably like to have similar facilities in the western Mediterranean. They apparently sought such arrangements with Algeria, but have been rebuffed. In fact, the Algerians have recently called for the withdrawal from the Mediterranean of the fleets of all non-riparian powers.

13. Soviet naval units, both surface and submarine, use the Egyptian facilities throughout the year; both surface vessels and submarines are at times supplied and repaired by Soviet tenders which remain on station in Alexandria. While not bases in the conventional sense—the Egyptians evidently retain formal control—these facilities do provide support services in much the same way. But in case of a major East-West crisis the availability of these facilities to the Soviets might be uncertain and would depend to an important degree on the circumstances of the crises.

14. For purposes of refueling and resupply, the Soviet Mediterranean squadron relies primarily on 12 naval anchorages (most in international waters). It uses Egyptian shore facilities more on a basis of convenience than actual need, though these do enable it to extend the length of time its diesel submarines remain in the Mediterranean from two months to six. We believe that the Soviets would be reluctant to undercut their anti-imperialist propaganda by seeking to establish bases of their own in Arab lands. And even the radical Arab governments would want to avoid the stigma of such bases (though Egypt no doubt derives some comfort from the presence of Soviet naval vessels as deterrents to Israeli action).

III. Policies in the Middle East

The Arab-Israeli Conflict

15. The evident damage done to Soviet standing in Arab eyes during the June War has since been repaired and the Soviet position strengthened. Moscow has established itself even more firmly as the champion of the radical Arabs, thus gaining an enlarged presence, a degree of Arab support for Soviet policies elsewhere, and a major voice in international negotiations concerning the area. The USSR has achieved this position at a price, not only in terms of the hardware involved in resupplying the Arabs but also in terms of the strains created by the increasingly critical Arab-Israeli conflict and the USSR's inability to produce either an acceptable solution or adequate protection for its clients. But these strains are not likely to undermine Soviet influence seriously so long as the Arabs have no alternative sources of great power support against Israel and continue to regard the US as committed to Israel's cause. In any case, the patron-client relationship involves a degree of Arab leverage over the Soviets as well as vice versa. For, in the Arab-Israeli conflict, the Soviets are more a prisoner of Arab emotions than the architect of Arab policies.

16. The Soviets have not, however, harnessed themselves to the more extreme aims of the Arabs toward Israel, and it is unlikely they will do so. Moscow continues to accept the legitimacy of Israel's statehood and Soviet diplomatic activity proceeds from the premise that a negotiated settlement should give Israel security. Yet the Russians recognize that in order to maintain their position with the Arabs they must maintain a generally hostile posture vis-à-vis Israel and broadcast their firm opposition to Israel's policies.

17. There has clearly been a large element of temporizing in the USSR's approach to international negotiations on the Arab-Israeli question. It has sought through talks with the US and others to influence US policy in the area and to demonstrate to the world at large that the Soviet interest is in peace. The Soviets place a high value on their brokerage function; they would be extremely displeased if, for example, Egypt sought to by-pass them in any serious negotiations on the future of the area. But it seems certain that the Soviets are not ready at this time to urge on their Arab clients the kind of concessions which might open up the possibility of a genuine settlement.

18. This does not rule out the possibility of Soviet support at some point for steps toward a modus vivendi to defuse the situation. In certain circumstances, the Soviets might actively seek an arrangement which would diminish the dangers of renewed hostilities while still allowing them to enjoy the fruits of continued Arab-Israeli tension. Even here, however, Moscow must be concerned not only with the terms of the arrangement but with the Arab reactions to them. In any case,

Moscow is not likely to put very heavy pressure on the Arabs—such as a threat to suspend all arms aid—in order to bring about a modus vivendi.

19. The Soviets probably will be inclined to stay with a policy which will bend with events, hoping by it to avoid being drawn into conflict, while reinforcing their political and military presence in the area. It may be, however, that events—with an assist from the Israelis—will not permit the Soviets to maintain so comfortable and rewarding a course. Indeed, aggressive Israeli policies against Egypt point up a sharpening Soviet dilemma: whether to seek to preserve the Nasser regime by giving it a new level of support—thus increasing the risk of direct Soviet involvement—or alternatively, to press the Arabs toward a distasteful accommodation—thus risking a loss of influence in the Arab world.[4]

20. Soviet calculations have certainly taken into account that Israel has the capability to develop and produce, and might soon be in a position to deploy, nuclear weapons. The Soviets probably believe that such weapons would be chiefly useful to Israel as a deterrent against Arab invasion—something not likely to be attempted at any early date. Hence, while the USSR would take advantage of any Israeli nuclear weapons to mount a political campaign against Israel and to emphasize Arab dependence on the Soviets, it would probably not take seriously the possibility of their actual use unless Israel faced a desperate situation. Even in such circumstances, although Soviets have the capability to deploy nuclear weapons under their control on Egyptian territory, we think it highly unlikely that they would do so even under heavy Arab pressure. They would be more likely to threaten Israel from their own territory or from their ships in the Mediterranean.

The Arab States

21. The degree of Soviet influence over individual Arab states varies—and will continue to vary—considerably; it is probably highest in Egypt and nil in Saudi Arabia. Among the revolutionary states, Syria, Iraq, and South Yemen would be more susceptible to Soviet urging or advice than Algeria and Yemen. Kuwait, Lebanon, and Jordan are not anxious to cooperate with the Soviets but try to maintain good relations.

22. In Egypt, Moscow can influence the government's attitudes on a variety of external questions and can expect to play some role in the formulation of Egyptian economic and military policies. There is a great

---

[4] Possible additional forms of military support that the Soviets might consider are discussed in paragraphs 41–51. [Footnote in the source text.]

deal, however, that the Soviets almost certainly *cannot* do in Egypt. They cannot guarantee that Nasser will remain in power; his fate will depend on his health and on his own political skills. They cannot dictate the choice of his successor since they lack either a strong political organization within Egypt or a candidate for the succession whom they could cultivate without alienating Nasser himself. And, in the last analysis, they cannot control Cairo's behavior on questions the Egyptians consider vital.

23. If Soviet influence over Egypt has its limitations, these are even more marked elsewhere in the Arab world. Ideologically, the regime in Syria has a good deal in common with Moscow, and it is almost wholly dependent on the USSR for military equipment. Offsetting this, however, are several negative factors. Syrian nationalism is xenophobic. Of the Arab states bordering Israel, Syria is the most intransigent, rejecting all efforts toward a political settlement and encouraging a "war of national liberation." Moreover, Syria is dominated by a frequently changing coterie of military men; close Soviet relations with today's leaders carry the risk of offending those of tomorrow. The latter consideration also applies to Iraq. In Jordan, the Soviets have had little success in expanding their influence since Hussein has so far chosen to deal with the Western powers which have long supported his regime and supplied his army. Soviet prospects would presumably improve if Jordan accepted Soviet arms or if the fedayeen came to dominate the regime.

24. Despite the USSR's extensive influence in some Arab capitals, the fortunes of individual governments in the Arab world are largely beyond Moscow's ability to control. The Soviets cannot guarantee a regime's survival, nor can they be assured of success should they seek to bring one down. The Soviets will thus probably stand aside in the event of important disruptions, moving in to attempt to capitalize on events as the dust settles. Though surely concerned about the uncertainties which would flow from Nasser's removal, and though they would seek to forestall such an eventuality, active Soviet intervention on behalf of Nasser would be unlikely. Revolutions in Saudi Arabia, Jordan, or Kuwait might be cheered by the Soviets, but could not now be inspired by them.

25. There are still further complications in Soviet dealings with the Arab world. The trade of most of the states of the area is still heavily oriented toward the West.[5] Moreover, while the radical Arabs are united in their hostility to Israel, the governments of Egypt, Syria, and Iraq profoundly dislike and distrust one another. They are actively competitive in inter-Arab affairs, and Soviet policies concerning one may seriously complicate policies toward another.

---

[5] See Appendix, Table II. [Footnote in the source text. The appendix is not printed.]

26. The Soviets have for the most part limited their dealings and their material support to existing governments, but there have been exceptions. Thus, the USSR provided arms and diplomatic support to the FLN during the Algerian revolution; it has consistently championed a special status for the Kurds in Iraq; it has also tried (though modestly) to promote the fortunes of Communist parties in such countries as Iraq, Syria, and Lebanon.

27. With the fedayeen, the Soviets have dealt cautiously, mostly through intermediaries. This is partly because of the fedayeen's penchant for free-wheeling militancy, which Moscow cannot hope to control, and partly because of its reluctance to get involved in rivalries between them and governments of the area. Yet the Soviets now appear to believe that dealing with the fedayeen exclusively through the medium of Arab governments will no longer suffice in the face of an emerging sense of a Palestinian identity. Peking's vocal support of fedayeen extremism adds to Soviet inducements to keep lines out to these movements. Although a Fatah delegation has been in Moscow recently, the visit was unofficial, and arms to the fedayeen probably will continue to be channeled through area governments. Soviet support for the fedayeen will continue to be discreet, in an effort to avoid antagonizing Arab governments.

Non-Arab States

28. Concerning Israel itself, Moscow does not have full mastery over its own policies. It is obliged by its relations with the radical Arabs, in fact, to maintain a hostile attitude. This is made easier by the USSR's unremitting opposition to "Zionism," which the Soviet leaders see as an internal security problem in the USSR and Eastern Europe. As noted, Soviet policy does not seek the destruction of Israel. Not only would this remove the Soviets' principal leverage on the Arabs; Moscow also recognizes that Western military and political support makes Israel a factor with which the Soviets must contend.

29. The USSR enjoys no special relationship with Greece, Turkey,[6] or Iran and, in fact, suffers from the legacy of the period when it posed an active threat to all three. Soviet ambitions in these states are curbed by the membership of all three in US-supported alliance systems and, in general, by the anti-Communist convictions of all three governments. Nonetheless, Soviet relations with these states have improved as a consequence of a major Soviet effort—begun almost a decade ago—to recast its image into that of a peace-loving and benevolent neighbor.

---

[6] See NIE 29.2–70, "Turkey Over the Next Five Years," dated 3 February 1970, Secret. [Footnote in the source text; for text see *Foreign Relations, 1969–1976*, volume XXIX, Eastern Europe; Eastern Mediterranean, 1969 1972.]

Economic aid to both Turkey and Iran, sales of military equipment to Iran, and promises of a profitable trade with Greece are intended to add substance to the new image.

30. Economically, at least, Iran has gone the furthest in response; it has contracted for at least $115 million worth of Soviet arms, and a Soviet sponsored 650 mile pipeline—now nearing completion—will bring over $60 million worth of natural gas annually from the Persian Gulf to the Soviet Caucasus. Turkey has accepted some Soviet economic aid and seeks to avoid antagonism in the relationship, but the climate between the two countries is certainly not warm. Greece under the junta is vigorously anti-Communist, and trade will probably remain the most significant contact with the USSR. Moscow probably expects at least Turkey and Iran to draw farther away from the US and hopes to benefit from such movement. But the chances for a significant increase in Soviet influence in these three countries will be limited for some time to come.

IV. Policies in the Western Mediterranean

North Africa

31. Though the western Mediterranean is not without its attractions and its opportunities for the makers of Soviet policy, the USSR's presence is far less conspicuous and its prospects are much less promising than in the Middle East. Two circumstances shape the politics of the area in ways not wholly congenial to Soviet interests. First, Algeria, Morocco, and Tunisia have had long associations with France which have shaped their cultures, their economic associations, and their political outlooks. Second, though there is wide popular support for the Palestinian cause within the west Arab states, their government leaders are less willing than the eastern Arabs to accept Nasser's leadership, less dependent on Soviet support, and more suspicious of the policies and motives of both Nasser and the USSR.

32. Recent developments in North Africa pose further obstacles to the growth of Soviet influence there. Tunisia, Algeria, and Morocco are patching up old quarrels which for a time contributed to Algeria's desire for Soviet support. These states are, in addition, moving somewhat closer to France as a result of French efforts to improve relations. Moreover, in the wake of the Libyan coup, concern over the westward extension of Nasser's influence has grown in all three countries. Their tendency to draw together may in time produce a sense of community divergent from that of the eastern Arab nations.[7]

---

[7] NIE 60–70, "The Outlook for North Africa," is scheduled for publication in March 1970. [Footnote in the source text. NIE 60–70 is in the Central Intelligence Agency, NIC Files, Job 79–R1012A, NIEs and SNIEs.]

33. Algeria is more revolutionary, more anticolonialist, and more anti-US than Morocco and Tunisia. It is thus easier for the Algerians to find a common cause with both the Egyptians and the Soviets. The Algerians have received substantial amounts of Soviet arms and military training assistance as well as Soviet support in a variety of economic development projects. But they have not allowed the Soviets to influence their domestic affairs, to interfere with their relationship with France, to reorient the great bulk of their trade away from Western Europe, or to guide the course of Algerian foreign policy in general. There has also been recent evidence of frictions in Soviet-Algerian relations. Algeria has views on some international issues which coincide with those of the USSR; yet it is not a client state, nor is it likely to become one.

34. Libya's military junta is unsure of its internal position and uncertain about both domestic and foreign policies. The junta, or at least its head, Colonel Qaddafi, has sought and received support—1,500 troops and several hundred technicians and advisers, as well as public backing—from Nasser. The latter no doubt welcomes the chance to extend his own direct influence into Libya, and he would be disinclined to see this eroded by the USSR's playing a major role there. The Libyan regime, perhaps at Cairo's urging, has several times rebuffed Soviet diplomatic overtures and Soviet offers of arms; it apparently prefers to buy from France and other Western suppliers. At least as long as the present junta stays in power, we think it unlikely that the Soviets will gain significant influence in Libya.

35. This is not to say that Libya lacks attraction for the Soviets. The USSR's Egyptian-marked reconnaissance aircraft flying from Egypt can cover the Mediterranean as far west as Sardinia. The use of Wheelus airfield in Libya would extend the range of TU–16 reconnaissance aircraft beyond Gibraltar. Moscow might thus seek to pressure Nasser into exerting his influence on the Libyan junta to provide these facilities for Soviet use. Nasser would be reluctant to do so, but he is deeply beholden to the Soviets, and it is possible that he might agree to some such arrangement—and the Libyans reluctantly acquiesce in it—if Soviet pressures were severe. Even in these circumstances, Soviet use of Libyan facilities would probably be limited and covert. Only a very small Soviet presence would be required, especially if Soviet activities were confined to refueling.

36. Malta is also attractive to Soviet planners inasmuch as its location is strategic and its economy faltering. If Malta is unable to strengthen its economy through assistance from the West, it may turn to the Soviets for aid. Overtures have been made by the Soviets, but thus far Soviet fleet visits have been denied and Soviet offers to provide economic assistance have been declined. Elections must be held by March 1971; a change in government could pave the way for closer

association with the Soviets. Although the Soviets may seek limited facilities in Algeria, Libya, and Malta through which to stage their reconnaissance aircraft, none of these countries is likely to extend such facilities at this time.

European States

37. In Western Europe, Soviet policy aims currently at promoting an atmosphere of détente and ultimately at reducing the US presence on the continent. Moscow will not wish to jeopardize these objectives by initiatives in the Mediterranean which would alarm the countries of Western Europe. It probably calculates that moves which seemed to threaten to cut off Western Europe from the Arab countries and their oil would stiffen the Western posture toward the Soviets—both in the Mediterranean and in Europe itself—and help consolidate ties between Western Europe and the US.

38. In fact, there are now signs of some change in European attitudes—a gradual increase in concern over the growing Soviet presence in the Mediterranean. No general alarms have yet been sounded, nor does there appear to have been any significant political pressure for changes in overall policies toward the USSR. But concern is increasing in West European military circles and this has been reflected in specific countermeasures under NATO auspices, such as the establishment of NATO machinery to monitor the activities of the Soviet naval squadron in the Mediterranean.

39. France, which has strong interests in certain Arab states, has been the most active of the West European states in the Mediterranean. In recent months Pompidou has sought to enhance France's position as a Mediterranean power by improving relations and influence with countries on both shores of the Mediterranean from Gibraltar to Greece. The Soviets have sought to take advantage of this policy, specifically of French support of the Arabs in their contest with Israel. But while Moscow has tried to use France to divide the Western powers—as in the Four Power talks on a Middle East settlement—the Soviets must also be concerned that the French are their rivals. The sale of French arms to Libya, for example, may have deprived the USSR of an opportunity to sell its own weapons to that country and prevented it from extending its influence over the Libyan junta. Similarly, France's efforts in North Africa will help to counter Soviet influence in Algeria and to block it in Morocco and Tunisia.

V. Soviet Capabilities and Intentions in Certain Contingencies

40. The enlarged Soviet military presence in the Mediterranean area has substantially increased Soviet influence and required all interested states, including the US, to take account of Soviet attitudes and possible actions. How and in what circumstances the Soviets might

make *actual* use of their military power is considerably less clear. The paragraphs which follow examine possible Soviet actions and capabilities in four major contingencies: (a) Arab-Israeli hostilities short of a full-scale conflict, i.e., the present situation; (b) all-out Arab-Israeli war; (c) other area disputes in which Soviet interests were involved; and (d) East-West hostilities.

Arab-Israeli Hostilities Short of All-Out War

41. The current success of Israeli military activities against the Arab states has no doubt added to Soviet disillusionment with the Arabs' ability to use modern equipment effectively. At the same time, Israeli activities increase Arab pressures on the Soviets for more advanced types of equipment. The Soviets have turned down a number of Arab requests in the past and have to date carefully limited both the quantity and quality of arms shipments, partly because of the Arabs' limited ability to absorb such matériel. They are in the awkward position of having provided enough to be thoroughly involved, but of not having supplied support of a kind or nature to do a successful job of defending Egypt. Appeals from Cairo for additional help have become more urgent as Israeli raids have intensified.

42. Moscow is clearly aware that greater direct involvement entails heightened risks. It must be concerned that substantially greater assistance to the Arabs would not satisfy them but only stimulate demands for even greater Soviet support in the future. Not only would large-scale effort be very costly to the Soviets, but it would involve such an enlarged Soviet presence as to change the character of the Soviet-Egyptian relationship in ways that would raise problems for both parties. Yet these hazards have to be weighed against alternatives which may seem to the Soviets to be at least equally unpalatable. Certainly Moscow does not like to see Cairo helpless in the face of Israeli air assaults. Certainly it does not wish this sort of circumstance to weaken Nasser's position and jeopardize domestic stability in the UAR. And certainly it would be fearful that a refusal to aid the UAR in its hour of need would threaten to disrupt relations with Egypt and damage Soviet prestige throughout the Arab world.

43. We believe that the Soviets will decide, if they have not already done so, that some sort of favorable response to Egyptian requests is necessary unless Israeli attacks near Cairo are soon stopped. A decision by the US to provide additional modern aircraft to Israel would make such a Soviet response even more likely. But it will not suffice to increase the flow of air defense equipment the Egyptians already have, as the Soviets have recently done. The principal Egyptian problem is the lack of certain more advanced weapons systems and above all of qualified personnel to operate an integrated air defense system effectively. Hence any significant improvement in Egyptian

defenses, at least in the short run, would almost certainly require Soviet personnel to man the network.

44. Additional Soviet support for Egypt's air defense could be at various levels. An integrated defense designed to protect the Cairo area might involve providing advanced interceptors, several battalions of advanced SA missiles, and additional antiaircraft artillery (AAA). Major elements of such a system would have to be directed, operated, and maintained by Soviet personnel, including pilots, for a considerable period, perhaps indefinitely. The Soviets might hope that this system would deter attacks on Cairo or subject the Israeli Air Force to unacceptable losses. While this system would leave other prime areas open to attack, the Soviets might calculate that it would suffice to serve Nasser's political needs.

45. If the Soviets felt that they had to provide protection for the bulk of Egypt's population, industry, and military installations, they would have to turn to more sophisticated equipment and establish air defense coverage of the lower Nile valley and the Suez Canal area. Such a system would require expanded early warning ground control intercept (EW/GCI) radars, many more advanced interceptors, greater numbers of improved SA missiles and additional AAA for key point defenses. To make the system operational within a few months would require the introduction of entire Soviet units involving many thousands of men.

46. The foregoing discussion of possible Soviet levels of support for Egyptian air defense is only illustrative; a number of variations are conceivable. The Soviets would of course strongly prefer to keep their support at the lowest possible levels of risk and cost. In deciding what levels of support would prove sufficient to their objectives, their risk/advantage calculus would have to weigh possible Israeli responses as well as Nasser's requirements. In view of the stake the Soviets have in Nasser's survival, and in the preservation of their relations with the radical Arabs, the Soviets may feel obliged to enlarge their risks.

47. To deter Israeli raids the Soviets might consider deploying in Egypt missiles with HE warheads capable of striking Israel proper. The Soviets, however, would have to weigh the chances that such a deployment would simply provoke the Israelis into larger attacks, perhaps on these missile installations themselves. Moreover, the threat of indiscriminate missile attacks on Israeli cities, let alone the actual delivery of such attacks, would involve the Soviets in an undertaking repugnant to much of world opinion, and one they would necessarily estimate would greatly increase the chances of direct US involvement. For these reasons, we think it highly unlikely that the Soviets would deploy such weapons. Similarly, we think it virtually inconceivable that they would consider deploying CW weapons there.

48. It might be that, coincident with moves for some form of greater support in Egypt's defense, the USSR would put pressure on the Egyptians to agree to military or diplomatic steps to defuse the present tension. Once Egypt's defenses seemed more formidable, the Soviets might feel more free to encourage a cease-fire, whether formal or tacit. They will probably continue to be unresponsive to US appeals for a formal agreement to limit arms shipments to the Middle East, but if the crisis continues to intensify, they might tacitly consent to curb additional arms shipments to Egypt if the US makes no additional aircraft sales to Israel.

Full-Scale Arab-Israeli War

49. Full-scale Arab-Israeli war could not be simply a replay of the 1967 war, if only because the Israelis now occupy extensive Arab territories. Whatever the course of the military action, the Soviets would surely not want to show themselves to be as helpless as they were in 1967. The presence of numbers of Soviet advisers with Egyptian and Syrian troops and of naval units in the area would make for a degree of involvement in any case Whether the Soviets would consider intervening in a larger and more overt way would presumably depend on the course and duration of the war, and above all on their estimate of the US response.

50. Present Soviet capabilities to intervene in such a war with quick and decisive effect are significant but not appreciably greater than they were in June 1967. Although Egypt has made facilities available to the Soviet squadron and to naval reconnaissance aircraft, there are no Soviet ground or tactical air units ashore in the Mediterranean area. The Soviets could bring in such forces from the USSR, but they would have difficulty in making them operationally effective in a short-lived war. The USSR could also provide some covert military support— pilots in Egyptian-marked planes flying against Israel or, more likely, in defense of Arab cities; ground support crews; and perhaps some naval personnel.

51. But given the probability of Israeli victory in fairly short order, the odds would be high that the Soviets would fear involving themselves militarily in a losing cause, with all the political damage within and outside the area that this would entail. Since the Soviets would have an effect only if they intervened quickly, and on a scale which they would estimate would risk involving the US, we doubt that they would embark on such an adventure.

Intervention in Other Area Disputes

52. The instability of certain client states of the USSR and various disputes between Arab states could produce situations which threatened the USSR's friends or interests. In such circumstances, the Soviets might

be tempted to use military force—as they have done in a limited way in the Yemen civil war. Such possibilities could arise in the course of the chronic factional struggles in Syria or Iraq, or if there were a request for direct Soviet military help from Nasser in a domestic crisis. In a situation involving struggle between rival Arab groups, Moscow might think it could pre-empt a Western move by moving in troops itself. At present the Soviets have a limited capability for rapid intervention. There may be as many as 500 naval infantry troops with the Mediterranean squadron—sufficient for a token landing. A substantial force could be moved in relatively quickly from the USSR, but this would entail overflight problems with Iran, Turkey, or Yugoslavia.

53. The Soviets would almost certainly be reluctant to commit their own armed forces in the Middle East for such purposes. For one thing, coups in the Middle East usually occur too quickly for intervention by outside powers to be decisive. More basically, the Soviets have no wish to find themselves embroiled in Arab domestic strife, particularly if there is a risk of finding themselves on the losing side. And they are likely to avoid any actions—such as moving troops into Syria—which might bring about all-out Arab-Israeli warfare or threaten to involve the US. In general, the rule that the Soviets prefer to avoid risks in unpredictable and uncontrolled situations would apply in such cases.

East-West Hostilities

54. In nuclear war, the Soviets' primary concern in the Mediterranean would be to limit damage from Western strategic forces, particularly ballistic missile submarines. At this time, Soviet ASW capabilities against the latter are extremely poor, despite the deployment of more modern ASW surface ships, including the helicopter ship, Moskva. Newer classes of Soviet ships, including nuclear-powered attack submarines, may soon be deployed to the Mediterranean. By 1975 Soviet capabilities to detect Polaris-type submarines may be somewhat improved, especially in restricted areas such as the Mediterranean. But the Soviets would still be unable to impair gravely the value of Polaris as a strategic weapon in the Mediterranean.[8]

55. At present, Soviet military capabilities for non-nuclear war with Western powers in the Mediterranean are limited by the lack of tactical air support and an inadequate and vulnerable logistics system. A significant effort to ameliorate these shortcomings would be

---

[8] For a fuller discussion of the ASW problem, see paragraphs 144 through 149 of NIE 11–14–69, "Soviet And East European General Purpose Forces," dated 4 December 1969, All Source. [Footnote in the source text. The text of NIE 11–14–69 is ibid.]

extremely expensive and would draw down from more pressing general purpose force needs elsewhere. Efforts to acquire military bases for use in such conflicts would be a difficult and politically risky course. In the event of a major crisis in this area, the Soviets would be able to augment their Mediterranean naval squadron. If conflict were to break out, they would seek to attack Western naval forces, particularly aircraft carriers. In addition, the Soviet threat to Western naval forces and lines of communication would be enhanced by the difficulties of detecting Soviet submarines, and by the USSR's capability of bringing more submarines into the Mediterranean from the Atlantic.

VI. Long Term Prospects

56. Some aspects of the Soviet position in the Mediterranean area are of course susceptible to direct Soviet control. The strength of the USSR's naval squadron, the size of its military and economic assistance programs, and the degree of its political support for radical Arab objectives all are dependent on decisions made in Moscow. But many of the basic circumstances which shape Soviet policy in the area are determined in the main by decisions made elsewhere—in Tel Aviv, in Cairo, in Washington. In the totality, then, the USSR is only one of several principal actors in the area and it is always possible that—as during the June War of 1967—it will find itself playing a part not entirely of its own devising.

57. It is true nonetheless that Moscow's assumption of a leading role in the area is a significant and probably durable accomplishment. It does not now appear that the USSR will again be content to play a minor role in the Middle East and the Mediterranean. Even in the event of another Arab-Israeli war and another defeat for major Soviet clients, the Soviets would almost certainly retain some sort of position in the area—though it would probably for a time be reduced—and would continue to have a voice in the shaping of postwar configurations. With or without such a war, the political climate of the region is likely to remain generally turbulent. Radical nationalist forces will continue to work against Western interests in the area and in their endeavors will no doubt continue to find Soviet support.

58. It seems entirely plausible that Soviet estimates of the USSR's prospects in the Mediterranean basin do not depart substantially from the general picture sketched above. In any case the Soviets must be optimistic about their ability to remain among the major movers of the area. Still, over a decade of close involvement with their mercurial clients has probably persuaded them to be fairly cautious in their assessments. Certainly they can have few illusions about the military capabilities of the Arab states. And just as certainly they cannot believe that the problems of the more immediate future will always resolve themselves to the benefit of Soviet interests. By the same token, however, occasional setbacks

and miscalculations will probably not seriously discourage them or deflect them from their course. In any case, the rivalry between the US and the USSR in the Mediterranean is likely to persist at least so long as the contest between them continues in the world at large.

[Omitted here is the appendix comprised of two tables entitled "Soviet Military and Economic Aid to Area Nations, 1954–1969" and "Total Exports and Imports of Area Nations With Communist (USSR and East Europe) and Industrial Free World Countries, 1966–1968."]

139. Letter From President Nixon to Chairman of the Council of Ministers of the Soviet Union Kosygin[1]

Washington, March 6, 1970.

Dear Mr. Chairman:

I am writing you to ask your government's assistance in achieving full compliance with the 1962 Geneva Agreements on Laos.[2] These Agreements were intended to protect the independence and neutrality of Laos and to prevent the use of Lao territory for interference in the internal affairs of other countries.

The presence of over 65,000 North Vietnamese troops in Laos and their recent offensives represent a major violation of these Agreements. I believe that this situation calls for prompt action by your government and the other signatories of the Agreements.

The Democratic Republic of Viet-Nam has disregarded the Geneva Agreements from the very beginning. In 1962, only 40 North Vietnamese "advisers" and "technicians" were withdrawn from Laos through the inspection machinery set up for the purpose, while thousands of North Vietnamese troops remained in the country. Since then, in persistent, flagrant violation of the Agreements, the Democratic Republic of Viet-Nam has continued to send thousands of soldiers into Laos to fight there and through Laos to fight in South Viet-Nam.

---

[1] Source: National Archives, Nixon Presidential Materials, NSC Files, Box 101, Vietnam Subject Files, Laos Statement, Vol. 2. No classification marking.

[2] On March 6, Nixon released a statement entitled, "About the Situation in Laos," which announced that he was writing British Prime Minister Harold Wilson and Kosygin as co-chairmen of the 1962 Geneva Conference to help in restoring the 1962 agreements. (*Public Papers: Nixon, 1970*, pp. 244–249)

The record of North Vietnamese aggression against Laos has been documented in official papers published by the Royal Government of Laos, including messages to the Co-Chairmen of the Geneva Conference, and in reports by the International Commission for Supervision and Control pursuant to its responsibility under the 1962 Agreements.

Under Article 8 of the Protocol to the Declaration of the Neutrality of Laos, your Foreign Minister is jointly charged with the Foreign Minister of the United Kingdom with supervision over the observance of the Declaration and Protocol. I assure you that my Government would welcome any reasonable steps which the Co-Chairmen might take to assure that the Geneva Agreements are complied with, that the sovereignty, independence, neutrality, unity and territorial integrity of Laos are preserved, and that Lao territory is not used for the purpose of interference in the internal affairs of other countries.

Specifically, I understand that the Prime Minister of the Royal Government of Laos has recently addressed an appeal to the Co-Chairmen to bring about consultations among the signatories of the Geneva Agreements on Laos under the provision of Article 4 of the Declaration. My Government would welcome such action on the part of the Co-Chairmen and is prepared to cooperate fully.

Sincerely,

Richard Nixon

---

140.   Memorandum of Conversation[1]

Washington, March 10, 1970.

PARTICIPANTS

Ambassador Anatoliy Dobrynin
Dr. Henry A. Kissinger
Dr. Lawrence E. Lynn

I met Dobrynin in the Military Aide's Office at the White House at 3:00 p.m. The meeting had come about because during our last conversation Dobrynin had indicated some doubt about the relationship

---

[1] Source: Library of Congress, Manuscript Division, Kissinger Papers, Box CL 215, "D" File. Secret; Sensitive; Eyes Only. The conversation was held in the East Wing of the White House. Kissinger forwarded this memorandum to President Nixon under cover of a March 11 note.

between the Safeguard components for area defense and the Safeguard components of point defense, and I told him that I would give him a briefing explaining the difference.

I took Larry Lynn of my staff along. We talked briefly about the problem of area defense and of point defense, the various types of missiles that were necessary for both, and why the area defense we were planning was not a threat to the Soviet Union. It was clear, however, that Dobrynin was not interested in that. He asked a few perfunctory questions which, incidentally, showed that he had studied the subject very carefully. He then said that he wanted to talk to me alone.

He made the following points:

I. *SALT.* Dobrynin said he had been asked by the Soviet Government to make three points with respect to SALT:

a. The Soviet Government agrees with our proposition that he and I might have an exchange of views both before and during the SALT talks with a view to coming to a conclusion between us on some of the principal outstanding issues.

b. The Soviet Government wanted the President to know that the Soviets were approaching the Vienna discussions[2] very seriously and would try to find an area of agreement.

c. The Soviets were prepared to discuss either comprehensive or separate agreement. They believed that a comprehensive agreement would be better because it would lead also to a solution of other political problems. But they were prepared to make separate agreements, provided it was understood that the limited agreements would not preclude coming eventually to a comprehensive agreement.

Dobrynin said that the Soviet Government had some doubts about the seriousness with which we approached the negotiations and that it had some genuine worries whether we really meant to have a negotiation. I told him that we were extremely serious about the negotiations and that we were hoping to come to an agreement. I said that they should know the President well enough by now to realize that our approach was always concrete and detailed and that the way to find out whether we were serious would be for them to engage in serious discussions. I was sure they would not be disappointed.

Dobrynin then turned the conversation to the Middle East.

---

[2] The second round of SALT negotiations began in Vienna on April 16.

II. *Middle East.* Dobrynin said he had been asked by the Soviet Government to give me an answer to some representations I had made to him on February 10.[3] These representations were as follows:

a. It had come to my attention that one of the junior officers of the Soviet Embassy had complained to one of our journalists that we did not take the Kosygin letter[4] sufficiently seriously.

b. We are assuming that serious communications will be made directly by Dobrynin to me and therefore we will not comment officially.

c. We want Dobrynin to know that the Kosygin letter received the highest level attention. Given the fact that the Soviet side had distributed it in regular channels in London and Paris, we had no choice but to deal with it in a similar fashion here.

d. The President is prepared to have bilateral discussions on the Middle East in the Dobrynin–Kissinger channel with a view to finding a solution fair to everybody.

e. We want the Soviet leaders to know that the introduction of Soviet combat personnel in the Middle East would be viewed with the gravest concern. We are choosing this method of communication because we do not want to make any formal démarche. At the same time, we want to make sure that the Soviet leaders are under no misapprehension about the possibility of grave consequences.

Dobrynin said in reply to these propositions the Soviet Government wanted to make the following comments in strictest confidence:

"Under instructions from Moscow I would like in confidence to express some considerations in connection with the aggravation of the military situation in the Middle East.

"Guided by special responsibility of our countries for the maintenance of peace A.N. Kosygin has already drawn the attention of President Nixon to the dangerous escalation of Israel of military actions against the UAR and other Arab countries and called upon the U.S. Government to use its influence so that Israel stop its armed attacks, dangerous for the cause of peace. The head of the Soviet Government stated at the same time that on its part the Soviet Union would show good will and determination to act in the interests of peace in the Middle East.

"It has been noted in Moscow that the American side, persistently putting forward the proposal on the cessation of fire on both sides, gives as its reasons the need to create a favorable situation for the search of political settlement. At the same time the United States ignores the fact that Israel not only occupied by means of aggression substantial Arab territories for the liberation of which the Arab peoples are now

---

[3] See Document 131.

[4] Document 121.

fighting but continues barbaric air raids against areas deep in the UAR and other Arab countries.

"We would like to draw the attention of the American side to the need for a realistic approach towards this question with due regard to the political situation in the Arab countries caused by the people's indignation at the Israeli aggression. In order to have the escalation of military operations in the Middle East discontinued it is necessary first of all that Israel take practical steps in this direction. We have reason to count that if the Israelis stop their bombings of the UAR, the UAR on its part will display restraint in its actions, without, of course, any official statements to that effect.

"I would like to ask you, Mr. Kissinger, to bring the context of this conversation to the attention of President Nixon. I would like to receive a reply to this communication."

Dobrynin asked me what I thought of these propositions. I said it was very interesting; I would take it up with the President and let him know.

Dobrynin then said that he had to tell me in confidence that he had been instructed to call on Secretary Rogers[5] and would offer the continuation of bilateral discussions. I said I had wondered when they would get tired of the quadripartite meetings. Dobrynin smiled and said, "We'll let the quadripartite meetings go on, but we prefer to talk in the bilateral forum." He said that, as he remembered it, there were two outstanding issues: one having to do with the state of peace, and the second having to do with the obligations of the two sides. He could tell me in strictest confidence that the hang-up on the first point would be met by the Soviet formulation.

Up to now, the Soviets had only offered a cessation of the state of war; they were now ready to talk about establishing a state of peace. As for the obligations of the two sides, the Soviet Union also was prepared to make a concession. Until now the Soviet Union had insisted that control of irregular forces would not be possible or would be solved automatically. They were now ready to offer a formulation which would make it the responsibility of the Arab governments.

He said there were a number of other issues with which he did not wish to bother me. For example, he said the Soviet Union wanted the UAR to have full sovereignty over the Sinai, but also that it recognized that Sharm al Sheikh and surrounding territories would be put under a UN force which could be removed only by the unanimous vote of the Security Council's permanent members. In other words, we could have a veto over the international presence in Sharm al Sheikh.

---

[5] See Document 141.

He asked me what I thought our reaction to these proposals would be. I said I would have to study them but he could be sure that if there were a positive possibility of making progress, we would be very receptive. I would be in touch with him next week about it. Dobrynin asked whether he could come to me if he reached some impasse with Sisco or the Secretary. I said I was always willing to see him.

Dobrynin then pointed out that it would be possible to arrange some formula for direct negotiations as long as we did not use the "Rhodes Formula."[6] And, of course, both sides would have to join the document.

(All these things seem to me major steps forward.)

III. *Vietnam.* At the end of the conversation, Dobrynin asked how the trip to Paris[7] had gone. I said that it had been all right. I asked him what he had heard about it. He said the Vietnamese had told him that no real progress had been made and that I had had nothing new to say. He asked me whether I had been encouraged. I said I have been in this position too long to be either encouraged or discouraged. Dobrynin said, "Well, if there was any more than what they have told us, it would be the first time that they haven't told us the truth." I said I wouldn't want to shake his confidence in his allies.

Comments:

Dobrynin made a number of significant concessions:

(1) He offered a ceasefire along the Suez Canal, thus enabling us to show the Israelis that we have achieved something for them with our policy on the Kosygin letter.

(2) In the negotiations on Egypt our policy of relative firmness has paid off on all contested issues. The Soviet Union has made a first move and, while it may not be enough, at least it showed that holding firm and offering no concessions was the right course.

---

[6] See footnote 2, Document 87.

[7] On February 21, Kissinger met secretly with Le Duc Tho at one of the residences of the Democratic Republic of Vietnam in Paris. On February 22, Kissinger sent Nixon memoranda of his conversations with Le Duc Tho. (National Archives, Nixon Presidential Materials, NSC Files, Box 852, For the President's File—China Trip, Vietnam Negotiations, Camp David, Vol. II) The memoranda are in *Foreign Relations, 1969–1976,* volume VI, Vietnam, January 1969–July 1970, Documents 189, 190, and 191.

141. Telegram From the Department of State to the Embassy in the Soviet Union[1]

Washington, March 12, 1970, 1805Z.

36337. 1. Ambassador Dobrynin called at his request on Secretary morning March 11 and made detailed presentation, main thrust of which was that Soviets would like to resume US-Soviet Middle East talks and are prepared meet US wishes for more detailed formulation on question of peace providing US will be more forthcoming on question of withdrawal, particularly re Sharm al-Shaykh, Gaza and Syria.

2. Soviet Minister Counselor Vorontsov subsequently called on NEA/IAI Country Director Atherton with copy of Dobrynin's talking points. Vorontsov declined leave text but let Atherton read it and take full notes, on which following paragraphs are based.

3. *Begin Talking Points.* Further aggravation of Middle East situation makes it urgent that energetic steps be taken to arrest increasing tensions in area. Soviet Government believes that, in addition to ending barbaric Israeli bombings of UAR civilian centers, there is need for new effort by major powers to achieve political settlement.

4. Soviet Government continues to believe that Middle East settlement should result in just and lasting peace, not just unstable and temporary armistice. Given tense Arab-Israeli relations, there is need for cautious, protracted and serious work to bring positions of parties closer.

5. Soviet Government intends to continue seeking settlement through exchange of views with USG, although US January reply was far from constructive. Just and lasting peace is possible on basis of earlier Soviet proposals but, to facilitate agreement, Soviet Government has additional considerations to offer.

6. Taking into account questions raised by USG, Soviets are prepared to discuss those questions, including establishment of peace, in bilateral talks. Preamble of Soviet plan recognizes need for just and stable peace in Middle East. USG has stressed that this question is of prime importance and has said that if Arabs show readiness to establish peace this would remove serious barriers to agreement. Soviet plan is sufficiently clear on this point. Nevertheless, with view to achieving understanding, Soviet Government would be ready to supplement provisions in its plan on cessation of state of war by provision on establishing, as result of settlement, a state of peace.

---

[1] Source: National Archives, Nixon Presidential Materials, NSC Files, Box 340, Subject Files, Dobrynin/Kissinger. Secret; Nodis; Noforn; No Distribution Outside Department. Drafted by Atherton on March 11, cleared by Eliot, and approved by Sisco. Repeated to USUN.

7. Soviet plan has sufficient concrete provisions about obligations of parties resulting from cessation of state of war and establishment of peace. USG, however, seeks more detail on these points as is clear from its October 28 and December 18 papers.[2]

8. Soviet Government is prepared to meet US wishes on this question if US side shows due understanding of questions whose solution is of interest to Soviet side, first and foremost those questions concerning the unequivocal recording of provisions for the withdrawal of troops.

9. USG has still not indicated that it shares Soviet view that sovereignty over Sharm al-Shaykh belongs to UAR. USG has also given no assurances that Israeli troops are to withdraw from Gaza sector and that this Arab territory is to be restored to its pre-June 1967 borders with the previous situation there re-established. Soviet Government raised these questions in its December 23, 1969 document[3] and USG has still not replied.

10. Replies on these points are important since Soviet Government is convinced that principal issue of settlement is withdrawal of troops and establishment of secure and recognized boundaries. Without exact formulations on these questions, there can be no possibility of moving on whole question of settlement.

11. In addition to agreement on withdrawal of troops from all occupied territories and status of peace, it would be useful to consider and agree on other unresolved provisions of UAR-Israeli settlement. Soviet Government proceeds from assumption that both our sides will strive to broaden area of agreement between them.

12. Question of Jordan-Israel settlement being considered by Four Powers in New York, but problem of Syria remains untouched in both Two and Four Power talks. Soviet Government notes that USG has avoided taking position on this question, citing as reason Syrian rejection of SC Resolution 242. In Soviet view, position of Syrian Government does not relieve us of task of working out concrete aspects of Syrian-Israeli settlement. If just solution found, Soviet Government is convinced difficulties stemming from Syrian position would disappear. Principal aspects of Soviet June 17, 1969, plan[4] relate to all countries directly involved in conflict. Soviet Government expects USG to express concrete views on questions touching directly on problem of Syrian-Israeli settlement.

---

[2] See Document 98 and footnote 3 to Document 109.

[3] See Document 109.

[4] See Document 58.

13. Soviet Government wishes to raise another matter which it does not consider unimportant. Soviet Government expects USG to take measures to prevent leaks of information about confidential US-Soviet discussions, which adversely affect course of our consultations. Examples have been publication of text of Kosygin letter and Estabrook report in *Washington Post* of February 19 Four Power meeting.[5]

14. Soviet Government wishes to stress that it assumes USG will be guided by broad interests of international security and of development of relations between our two states. US and Soviet interests will be served by Middle East not becoming arena of unwanted confrontation. Soviet Government believes this can be achieved and will continue its efforts in this direction in hope USG will do the same. *End Talking Points.*

15. Secretary responded that we would study both the suggestion to resume bilateral discussions and the substantive Soviet proposals. He made clear that if we should agree to resume bilateral talks, there would have to be an understanding of what the resumption of those talks signifies. Our willingness to resume talks could not be interpreted to mean an acceptance of the Soviet proposals or that we were willing to make concessions going beyond our present position as reflected in the October 28 and December 18 documents.

Rogers

---

[5] Reference is to a March 10 story in *The Washington Post* by Robert H. Estabrook entitled "France's Mideast Optimism Challenged." According to Estabrook "U.S. and British spokesmen took issue today with the statement by French Foreign Minister Maurice Schumann that the Big Four's Middle East discussions have moved into a thaw." (p. A–14)

142. Letter From Chairman of the Council of Ministers of the Soviet Union Kosygin to President Nixon[1]

Moscow, March 13, 1970.

Dear Mr. President,

We have carefully studied your letter of March 6, 1970.[2] We have also received an appeal from Prince Souvanna Phouma with a proposal on conducting consultations between the States which signed the 1962 Geneva Agreements on Laos.

My colleagues and I are perturbed by the situation in Laos, which has lately become aggravated. And we, for our part, have pondered over the causes of this aggravation and over what measures could be undertaken to restore peace and tranquility to the territory of Laos.

I should not like, at this time, to go into the background of the present events in Laos, since this would hardly erase the differences that exist in the way our two sides appraise what is happening in that country.

The situation in Laos, as is quite obvious, is directly connected with the general situation on the Indo-Chinese peninsula. The cessation of the war in Viet-Nam and a political settlement would facilitate the restoration of peace in Laos as well.

To speak, in the present situation, about consultations between the States Parties to the 1962 Convention on Laos is, in our view, completely unrealistic. Do you think it possible to consider the situation appropriate for such consultations when the United States continues the war in Viet-Nam and expands armed intervention in Laos? Moreover, the coalition government created in Viet-Nam in accordance with the 1962 Geneva Agreements, in view of the actions of the right-wing forces, has been paralyzed.

It is precisely those right-wing forces which, supported by the American Airforce and actively using special troops under American command, carried out in September of last year attacks in the Kuvshinov [?][3] Valley area, which for a long period of time was under the control of the Pathet-Lao and left-wing neutralists. Patriotic forces took measures to return to their previous positions.

---

[1] Source: National Archives, Nixon Presidential Materials, NSC Files, Box 765, Presidential Correspondence, USSR, Kosygin. Confidential. Translated by the Department's Division of Language Services.

[2] Document 139.

[3] Brackets in the source text.

The matter of restoring peace in Laos should, obviously, begin with consultations between the political forces of Laos. The other day the Central Committee of the Patriotic Front of Laos proposed a concrete and, it seems to us, a highly realistic five-point program for a settlement. As a result of this program, peace would be restored in Laos if all countries respect the sovereignty, independence, neutrality, unity and territorial integrity of the Kingdom of Laos, in accordance with the provisions of the 1962 Geneva Agreements on Laos, the cessation of U.S. intervention in Laotian affairs, including the bombing of Laotian territory, the non-participation of Laos in military alliances with other countries and the banning of foreign troops and bases in Laos, respect for the throne, the holding of general, free and democratic elections to the National Assembly and the formation of a democratic government of national unity, the holding during the period from the restoration of peace to the general elections of a political consultative conference with the participation of representatives of the interested parties of Laos for settling all the affairs of the country and forming a temporary coalition government, the uniting of Laos through consultation between the Laotian parties on the basis of the principal of equality and national consent. But, first of all, as set forth in the above-mentioned statement of the Central Committee of the Patriotic Front of Laos, it is essential that the U.S.A. put an end, in the near future, to the escalation of the war and completely and unconditionally cease the bombing of the territory of Laos—only thus can conditions be created which will permit the interested Laotian parties to meet with each other.

Thus, it is a question of the necessity, first of all, of the cessation of American intervention in the affairs of Laos, and of Vientiane maintaining a position of neutrality, as stipulated by the Geneva Agreements.

We welcome the planned contacts between Prince Souvanna Phouma and Prince Souphanouvong and consider that this is exactly the path which, in the event of the cessation of American intervention, will permit ensuring a détente in Laos and create the necessary conditions for a political settlement in that country.

As for the Soviet Government, it will, for its part, henceforth undertake efforts directed toward the cessation of military activities in Laos and toward the creation of conditions that will enable that country to develop along the path of peace, independence and neutrality.

Sincerely,

A. Kosygin[4]

---

[4] Printed from a copy that indicates Kosygin signed the original.

143. Memorandum From the President's Assistant for National Security Affairs (Kissinger) to President Nixon[1]

Washington, March 13, 1970.

SUBJECT

The New Soviet Tactic on Middle East Talks

Secretary Rogers has sent you the attached account of his March 11 meeting with Ambassador Dobrynin on the Middle East.[2]

The Meeting. Ambassador Dobrynin proposed resumption of bilateral talks on a Middle East settlement. He indicated Soviet willingness to consider a more precise formulation on the obligations each side would undertake in a peace settlement provided the U.S. would indicate a willingness to consider the Soviet position that Sharm al-Shaikh would return to Egyptian sovereignty, that an irrevocable UN presence would be stationed there to assure freedom of passage through the Gulf of Aqaba and that Israeli troops should withdraw from Gaza with the pre-war situation there re-established. He also said that the Soviets would expect us to express "concrete views" on a Syria-Israel settlement.

Secretary Rogers responded that we would study these proposals. He made it clear, however, that if we should agree to resume bilateral talks there would have to be an understanding that this did not mean we accepted the substantive Soviet proposals or that we would be willing to make concessions beyond our present position.

What Does It Mean? It is not yet clear exactly what the Soviets are up to with this apparent switch from a propagandistic and unconstructive approach to more flexible tactics. As you know, an earlier signal came in the March 5 Four Power session where the Soviets rather suddenly began to indicate their willingness to resume a constructive dialogue after weeks of attacking us in that forum. This bid to resume the bilateral exchange—which was broken off in December when the Soviets responded to our proposals on the UAR-Israel aspect in a

---

[1] Source: National Archives, Nixon Presidential Materials, NSC Files, Box 711, Country Files, Europe, USSR, Vol. VII. Secret; Nodis. Sent for information. Drafted by Saunders and sent to Kissinger on March 13. On March 19, Haig returned this memorandum to Saunders under a covering memorandum with the following note: "Hal, please note HAK had some strong views to make concerning several paragraphs of the attached." The memorandum was not initialed by Kissinger and apparently did not go to Nixon.

[2] Attached but not printed is a March 12 memorandum from Rogers to Nixon reporting on the March 11 meeting with Dobrynin much as it is summarized in this memorandum. See Document 141 for an account of a subsequent discussion by Vorontsov and Atherton on the same issue.

strongly negative and retrogressive manner—apparently is a follow-on to that move. In neither case, however, have they indicated that they are prepared to yield substantially on the issue most important to us and the Israelis—a specific Arab obligation to control the fedayeen and on how the parties will actually negotiate a settlement. Instead, they continue to press for concessions that Nasser demands and that the Israelis would not accept.

It could be that the Soviets came to feel increasingly isolated in the Four Power talks as we persistently stuck to our proposals, the British backed us up and the French search for the middle ground floundered. They may have feared that we were growing tired of their abuse in the Four Power talks and were prepared, if necessary, to end the talks and leave the onus for the deadlock with them. It may also have become increasingly apparent to them that we were not ready to make any more concessions, at least without substantial quid pro quo.[3]

It may be that the Soviets are concerned to defuse the growing appearance of confrontation, which they themselves launched with the Kosygin letter. This course left them with the ultimate option of having to escalate their involvement. An additional tactical motive may relate to the Soviet sense of timing on the decision of supplying Phantoms to Israel. The Soviets may have thought a show of flexibility at this time would tip the outcome against a new supply.

I note that Dobrynin's presentation seemed to pick up the thought in your foreign policy report that our approach to the Middle East will be guided by broad interests of international security and development of relations between our two states—another suggestion the Soviets may be backing away from the confrontation track.[4]

Whatever the cause, there are indications that the Soviets and Egyptians want to keep the negotiating option open. These recent moves were immediately preceded by a visit of Deputy Foreign Minister Vinogradov to Cairo. Egyptian Foreign Minister Riad recently agreed to keep up "political activity" without making a concession on basic issues.

Conclusion: There may be some merit in letting the Soviets sweat it out a bit longer in hopes that they may change in substance as well as approach. They have come to us with a bid to resume the bilateral talks, but have not yet indicated any real give in substance. If we intend to stick with our proposals in their present form, there would

---

[3] Kissinger wrote "Since when do the Soviets give a damn about being isolated" in the left margin, and "Maybe to hold [?] us quiet while they introduce SA–3" in the right margin.

[4] Kissinger wrote "Adding Syria guarantees future [unintelligible] exacerbation with Israel" in the margin beside this paragraph.

seem to be little point in reopening the bilateral dialogue and ease the apparent pressure on the Soviets without any promise of substantive progress.

There is also the problem of what to do with the Four Power talks. The British and especially the French see this forum as being the most productive and might be dismayed to see us abandon it again for private talks with the Soviets. The French, of course, have been difficult and the British are showing signs of becoming somewhat of a problem, but both are still manageable. We may even be able to buy more time in the Four Power talks if our current gambit to shift them away from drawing up guidelines for Jarring to developing an interim progress report for U Thant works out. This could also serve to keep the heat on the Soviets.[5]

These are just preliminary considerations for your thought.[6]

---

[5] Kissinger wrote "All this is trivial. Talks aren't ends in themselves. Question is what do we get out of 4-power or 2-power talks. Which forum is best? If we want 2-power talks, who cares about 4-powers" at the bottom of the page.

[6] Kissinger crossed out this sentence.

---

144. Memorandum From the President's Assistant for National Security Affairs (Kissinger) to President Nixon[1]

Washington, March 13, 1970.

SUBJECT

Trouble in the Soviet Leadership

In the last week we have received several diverse reports that could point to trouble within the top Soviet leadership.[2]

---

[1] Source: Library of Congress, Manuscript Division, Kissinger Papers, Box SCI 17, Memos to the President, January–April 1970. Top Secret; Codeword. Sent for information. A notation on the memorandum indicates it was returned on March 17.

[2] On March 11, Sonnenfeldt forwarded a letter to Kissinger that alluded to reports carried by the Reuters news service, to the effect that Kosygin may retire and a major fight among the Kremlin leaders may ensue. Sonnenfeldt added, "the Kremlinologists at CIA and State are taking it all with a grain of salt so far. Stories of this kind are inherently hard to assess. However, there is probably enough meat here to warrant a brief report to the president, as a follow-up to the earlier more extensive memo of last month." (Ibid.)

—[1 *paragraph (4 lines of source text) not declassified*]

—Gus Hall, the American Communist leader, received information recently (reported by the FBI) that while Brezhnev had emerged as "head man" in recent months, there was maneuvering in the Kremlin leadership and that there would be a purge of "scapegoats" for failures in the economy.

—A Reuters report from Vienna, quoting sources in Yugoslavia and Prague, claims that Brezhnev and Kosygin have been attacked by other party leaders for major failures, and that these accusations were in the form of signed document; the challengers are supposed to be Shelepin, Maxurov and Suslov.

—[1½ *lines of source text not declassified*] suggested considerable nervousness on the part of the Deputy Premier Polyansky over his public "image."

While the Reuters report seems dramatic and too detailed for plausibility, recent signs taken together seem to point to increasing problems within the leadership. As noted in an earlier memorandum to you, the heart of the problem seems to be the dissatisfaction over economic matters.

An "honorable" retirement for Kosygin might be a logical way to break a deadlock at the top. At the same time, there have been recurring reports of his failing health. Recently, a Soviet guide at the Soviet photographic exhibit here was overheard to say that Kosygin was due for an operation.

If there is major trouble of the kind reported by Reuters, however, this would be a different matter and could have more far-reaching policy implications. Unfortunately, there is never any sure way to confirm these events, until after they have already taken place, and we are faced with the results.

This bears watching, of course, and I will forward any reports that seem plausible, especially if there seems to be a relation to major policy issues.

145.   Memorandum of Conversation[1]

Washington, March 20, 1970, 2:15 p.m.

PARTICIPANTS

Ambassador Anatoliy Dobrynin
Dr. Henry A. Kissinger

Dobrynin opened the conversation by asking whether there had been some response to his démarche of 10 days ago.[2] I said, "Yes, as a matter of fact that is why I asked you to come to see me." I said we had taken the communication from the Soviet Government with extreme seriousness, as we do every other communication from Moscow. We had, in fact, begun discussions with the Israelis about a ceasefire and had obtained Israeli approval. But within 24 hours of calling them in to make it final and to establish definite time limits, we learned about the introduction of Soviet SA–3 missiles and Soviet combat personnel. I had warned Dobrynin about the serious consequences of such a step. The move was reminiscent of some tactics employed several years previously on the occasion of the Cuban crisis. The Soviet Government had to learn that the President could not be dealt with on this basis.

As a result, the President had canceled his request to the Israelis for a ceasefire, and the matter was now off. If the Soviet Union wanted to make a more equitable proposal some other time, we would be willing to consider it.

Dobrynin made some half-hearted comments to the effect that he didn't know anything about these missiles. But if they were defensive, why did we object? I said, "Because it might be that the ceasefire was just being used to improve the Egyptian military position—to improve Egypt's defenses. Once they were fully installed, Egypt could break the ceasefire and Israel would be at a great disadvantage." If the Soviet Union wanted to make a more equitable proposal, we would be willing to consider it.

Dobrynin said he would have to go to his government and come back with new instructions. He underlined Moscow's great eagerness to dampen down the Middle East situation, and he said he hoped that Secretary Rogers would reply soon to his overture of some weeks ago to restart the bilateral negotiations.

---

[1] Source: Library of Congress, Manuscript Division, Kissinger Papers, Box TS 36, Geopolitical File, 1964–1977, Soviet Union, Chronological File, 3/69–6/70. Top Secret; Sensitive; Eyes Only. The conversation was held in the library of the White House residence. Kissinger forwarded this memorandum to President Nixon on March 26.

[2] See Document 140.

I then made a general comment. I said that we were at an important turning point. We were prepared to deal with the Soviet Union precisely, correctly, unemotionally, and thoroughly in the direction of détente, if the Soviet Union would forgo its policy of attempting to squeeze us at every opportunity. For example, when we recommended the ceasefire to Israel, we did so even though we knew the military situation favored our friends. The introduction of Soviet military personnel could only lead to a Vietnam for the Soviet Union, since all we had to do was send in equipment which they could only match by personnel. Nevertheless, we were not trying to take advantage of the situation.[3]

I could not say the same for the Soviet behavior in Laos, I continued. We were very disappointed by the Prime Minister's reply. Dobrynin said we completely misunderstood their role in Laos; they were only being kept informed. They were not making any suggestions and they thought, in any event, that the figures we gave for North Vietnamese troops in Laos were much too high.

Dobrynin then said that he had had a report from Paris that my conversations there were leading towards a positive direction. I said he had to check with his friends—that I would not give him any comment.[4]

Dobrynin then said the Soviet Union was eager to get the bilateral talks on the Middle East[5] started. I mentioned that we were prepared to talk seriously on all issues and that we were ready to move to higher levels of conversations if there were progress, but that the Soviet Union could not continue to press in other areas without the most serious consequences.

---

[3] Nixon highlighted this paragraph.
[4] Nixon highlighted this paragraph.
[5] Nixon underlined "Middle East."

146.   Memorandum From the President's Assistant for National Security Affairs (Kissinger) to President Nixon[1]

Washington, March 21, 1970.

SUBJECT

Letter From You to Premier Kosygin

At the WSAG meeting on the afternoon of March 19,[2] it was agreed that one of the political moves which we might carry out in response to the situation in Laos would be to go back to the Soviets with a tough letter from you telling them that it was their duty to support the Geneva Agreements. In this letter we would make plain that we would not accept their contention that they had no responsibility and add that such a reaction might have an adverse effect on US–USSR relationships.

A letter to this effect from you to Premier Kosygin is at Tab A. I consider that this letter, which was drafted by State, appropriately conveys the message which we want the Soviets to receive, and also lets them know the gravity with which we view developments in Laos. I believe that your sending the letter to Kosygin would be a useful move. State proposes that we follow it up by sending letters from you to each of the other Geneva signatories calling attention to the threat to Laotian neutrality which now exists, and observing that the signatory powers accordingly have the responsibility of supporting Prime Minister Souvanna's appeal for consultations under Article IV of the Geneva Agreements on maintaining the neutrality of Laos.

Recommendation:

That you sign the letter to Premier Kosygin at Tab A.

---

[1] Source: Library of Congress, Manuscript Division, Kissinger Papers, Box CL 215, "D" File. Secret. Sent for action. Drafted by Holdridge on March 20.

[2] On March 19, from 1–2:20 p.m., the WSAG met to discuss the situation in Laos. Minutes of the meeting are in *Foreign Relations*, 1969–1976, volume VI, Vietnam, January 1969–July 1970, Document 204.

Tab A[3]

Letter From President Nixon to Chairman of the Council of Ministers of the Soviet Union Kosygin

Washington, March 21, 1970.

Dear Mr. Chairman:

I wish to thank you for your assurance that you and your government are concerned about the situation in Laos and have considered steps that might be taken to permit peace to return to that country. While I agree with you on the importance of internal consultations among the Lao themselves, I am unable to share your view that consultations among the signatories of the 1962 Geneva Agreements on Laos are unrealistic and would not be helpful.

Indeed, I find the position of your government illogical and unconvincing. In your letter[4] you connect the problem of Laos with the general situation on the Indo-China peninsula and refer to American interference in the affairs of Laos. Therefore, even though you do not refer to the Democratic Republic of Vietnam's flagrant violations of the independence, neutrality and territorial integrity of Laos or its use of Lao and Cambodian territory for aggression against the Republic of Vietnam, you clearly recognize the international character of the problem of Laos, including violations of the Geneva Agreements of 1962 on Laos. A solution to the international aspects of the Lao problem is the proper responsibility of the mechanisms established by the 1962 Conference. I would be less than frank if I did not point out that the opposition of your government to the holding of consultations under Article IV of the Declaration on the Neutrality of Laos is totally indefensible given your admission that you consider there have been violations of the neutrality of Laos. It is not a question whether the present situation is "good" for such consultations; it is precisely because the situation is not good that such consultations must be held. I call upon you, Mr. Chairman, as the head of one of the two governments most specifically charged by the Geneva Agreements with the supervision over their observance to fulfill your responsibility and, together with the United Kingdom, to call for consultations to consider measures which might prove to be necessary to insure the observance of the sovereignty, independence, neutrality and territorial integrity of the Kingdom of Laos.

---

[3] No classification marking.

[4] Document 142.

As I noted in my previous letter,[5] the principal cause of the present hostilities in Laos is the presence there of over 65,000 North Vietnamese troops. The restoration of peace in Laos cannot, therefore, be accomplished solely through consultations among the political forces there as you suggest. Such internal talks can serve a useful purpose, as they did in 1961 and 1962, as an adjunct to international actions dealing with the basic cause of the Lao problem, North Vietnamese aggression in Laos and use of Lao territory for interference in the internal affairs of other countries. I need hardly remind you that the United States air activities in Laos are in response to these antecedent North Vietnamese actions.

I assure you that the United States Government will spare no effort to bring peace to Laos through full implementation of the 1962 Agreements. I welcome your assurances that the Soviet Government will continue to make efforts aimed at the cessation of military actions in Laos and the creation of conditions for the re-establishment of peace and neutrality. For there can be little doubt that failure to bring peace to Laos will have repercussions beyond the confines of that region of the world and adversely affect our relations. I confirm my Administration's desire to base our relations on the principle of negotiation rather than confrontation and I therefore call upon you to reconsider your position concerning consultations under Article IV of the Declaration on the Neutrality of Laos. I again urge that your government join with mine and the governments of the other signatories in fulfilling the responsibilities we assumed in 1962.

Sincerely,

RN[6]

---

[5] Document 139.

[6] Printed from a copy that indicates Nixon signed the original.

---

147. Memorandum for the Record[1]

Washington, March 25, 1970.

SUBJECT

Talk with President Nixon

---

[1] Source: Central Intelligence Agency, DCI Helms Chronological File, Job 80–B01285A, Box 11, Folder 9, Secret. Drafted by Helms.

1. The President called Henry Kissinger and me into the Oval Office after the NSC meeting today for what turned out to be a 25-minute discussion of a variety of subjects, including SALT, Laos, Cambodia, Cuba, and black operations.

[Omitted here is discussion of Cuba and Laos.]

4. With respect to black operations, the President enjoined me to hit the Soviets, and hit them hard, any place we can in the world. He said to "just go ahead," to keep Henry Kissinger informed, and to be as imaginative as we could. He was as emphatic on this as I have ever heard him on anything. He indicated that he had had a change of mind and thought that Radio Free Europe should be continued. I took this moment to hit hard on the point that I felt strongly the United States should give up nothing which constituted a pressure on the Soviet Union or an irritation to them without exacting a specific price in return. The President agreed with this and pointed out that we had had nothing from the Russians—in the recent past "except assistance on the shape of the table at the Paris talks." I indicated that we were coming up with a paper on covert actions aimed at the Soviet Union.

RH
Director

148. Telegram From the Department of State to the Embassy in the Soviet Union[1]

Washington, March 28, 1970, 0302Z.

44154. 1. Following is the oral statement made by the Secretary in response to Dobrynin's oral statement of March 11.[2] Secretary and Dobrynin met on March 25 with Sisco and Vorontsov also present. Vorontsov took careful notes on the following. No paper was given. Separate cable being sent which reports additional comments.[3]

---

[1] Source: National Archives, Nixon Presidential Materials, NSC Files, Box 653, Country Files, Middle East, Sisco Middle East Talks. Secret; Nodis; Noforn. Drafted and approved by Sisco on March 25, and cleared by Hawley (S/S). Also sent to USUN. This telegram was attached to an April 8 memorandum from Saunders to Kissinger which is printed as Document 151.

[2] See Document 141.

[3] Not further identified.

"We have studied carefully the oral statement conveyed by Ambassador Dobrynin March 11 and would like to comment on it point-by-point.

"We agree that there is need for steps to arrest the increasing tensions in the Middle East. This was the purpose of our proposals for restoration of the ceasefire and for arms limitation talks, which the Soviet Government has not accepted. We do not share the Soviet Government's one-sided view that an end to Israeli bombing would in itself be productive. The Soviet Government knows that it was the UAR which initiated a policy of nonobservance of the ceasefire. There can only be a decrease in the level of violence if observance of the ceasefire is reciprocal. We urge the Soviet Government to reassess its position both with respect to the ceasefire and arms limitation talks.

"We agree with the Soviet Government on the need for new efforts to achieve a political settlement. This is why we have urged the Soviet Union to take a more constructive approach to the proposals of October 28, in which we sought to reflect joint US-Soviet views, and to the December 18 proposals.

"We note with satisfaction that the Soviet Government has reaffirmed the need for a just and lasting peace which is, of course, the stated purpose of Security Council Resolution 242. We are also pleased that the Soviet Government has referred to the need to bring the positions of the parties closer. This has been repeatedly emphasized by us as an essential element of both the Two Power and Four Power talks.

"We also note that the Soviet Government wishes to continue exchanging views on a bilateral basis. We have no objection in principle to resuming the Two Power talks at an early date. The probability that such talks would prove fruitful would be enhanced if the Soviet Union could provide beforehand certain clarifications of its position. In saying that it is prepared to meet the wish of the United States for greater detail on the question of peace, does the Soviet Government mean that it would accept Point 2 of our proposals? The Soviet answer to this question will contribute to a clearer understanding between us about the basis for resuming our bilateral exchanges. In saying this, we clearly understand that Soviet acceptance of the language of Point 2 would be contingent upon agreement on all other points of difference between us. Major power agreement on guidelines for Jarring must be a package just as the final agreement between the parties themselves.

"We note that the Soviet Government wants us to show understanding on questions of interest to it including above all the question of withdrawal. This question is also of interest to the United States, and we have said many times there can be no peace without withdrawal. We have made our position on withdrawal quite clear. As concerns the UAR, to which the Ambassador's oral statement referred, we have said

Israel should withdraw to the old international boundary. We have also said that in our view there must be agreement between the parties on practical security arrangements in the Sharm al-Shaykh area. Such arrangements would have to provide an absolute guarantee of free navigation through the Strait of Tiran as called for in Resolution 242; it is not our intention that they should call into question UAR sovereignty over Sharm al-Shaykh.

"With respect to Gaza, our view is that it is a special case since the question of sovereignty there has never been resolved. The Soviet Government calls for the re-establishment in Gaza of the pre-June 1967 situation. That situation, however, was based on the Armistice Agreement of 1949, whereas we are now seeking a final peace. Re-establishment of the pre-June 1967 situation would be inconsistent with the view, expressed elsewhere in the Ambassador's statement, that a settlement 'should result in just and lasting peace, not just unstable and temporary armistice.' In light of this consideration and of the unresolved question of sovereignty, we believe the disposition of Gaza is an appropriate subject of negotiations between the parties.

"We agree with the Soviet Government that it would be useful to consider other unresolved provisions of a UAR-Israeli settlement and that both our governments should strive to broaden areas of agreement between us. Among these unresolved provisions is the question of the method of reaching agreement, to which we attach importance and which must be considered in light of operative paragraph 3 of Resolution 242.[4] The Ambassador's statement did not refer to this question. Does the Soviet Government still accept the language on the Rhodes formula agreed between us in September? If not, does the Soviet Government have alternative language to propose which would make equally clear that the negotiating process under Ambassador Jarring's auspices would include both indirect and direct negotiations at various stages as was the case when Dr. Bunche dealt with the parties in 1949.

"On the problem of Syria to which the Ambassador's statement referred, our position is clear. Syria has rejected Resolution 242 and has not cooperated with Ambassador Jarring. In these circumstances, Jarring cannot carry out his mandate of promoting agreement on the Syrian aspect of a settlement since the process of reaching agreement requires the cooperation of both sides. There is thus no basis for developing guidelines for Jarring on the Syrian aspect. There is no other

---

[4] Paragraph 3 reads as follows: "*Requests* the Secretary-General to designate a Special Representative to proceed to the Middle East to establish and maintain contacts with the States concerned in order to promote agreement and assist effort to achieve a peaceful and accepted settlement in accordance with the provisions and principles in this resolution." (UN doc. S/RES/242 1967)

route to a settlement than Resolution 242 and the Jarring Mission. Once agreement has been reached and carried out between Israel and the UAR, and between Israel and Jordan, there should be no difficulties in the way of Syria's taking the necessary steps which would make possible consideration of a settlement also between Israel and Syria.

"With respect to the question of press leaks, we assure the Soviet Government that we share its desire to avoid such leaks. Both of us must recognize, however, that in view of the deep interest in Middle Eastern developments, press contact cannot be completely avoided. As for the leak of the exchange of letters between Chairman Kosygin and President Nixon, we reconfirm our previous assurance to the Soviet Government that it is not our policy to publish such confidential correspondence with other heads of government, that we did not do so in this case, and that we regret these letters were made available to the press by others to whom they were entrusted.

"Finally, the Soviet Government is correct in assuming that the United States is guided by a desire to strengthen international security and to develop the relations between our two nations. We are pleased that the Soviet Government feels, as we do, that it would serve neither of our interests for the Middle East to become an area of confrontation between us."

149.   Memorandum From the President's Assistant for National Security Affairs (Kissinger) to President Nixon[1]

Washington, undated.

SUBJECT

Exploitation of Tensions in the Soviet Union and Eastern Europe

Attached is an excellent CIA paper describing covert action programs being undertaken to exploit tensions in the Soviet Union and

---

[1] Source: National Archives, Nixon Presidential Materials, NSC Files, Box 711, Country Files, Europe, USSR, Vol. VI. Secret; Sensitive. Drafted by Kissinger and Haig on April 6. Haig sent it to Kissinger on April 6 under a covering memorandum that reads: "Attached is a memorandum for the President forwarding the excellent CIA paper on Tensions in the Soviet Union and Eastern Europe. I have informed Director Helms that you believe this is a first-rate paper and appreciate his forwarding it to you." The memorandum is an unsigned copy.

Eastern Europe and identifying activities which may be emphasized in the future. In assessing Soviet vulnerabilities the report notes that:

—Although the internal dissident is not likely to significantly influence Soviet society in the short term, existing trends toward more active dissidence could be affected by external developments. The discrediting of the regime by a serious economic crisis or another Czech-type crisis might promote radical changes in the internal political climate.

—Suppression of the growing intellectual dissent by Soviet authorities has disillusioned many foreign Communists and Soviet sympathizers.

—Among the non-Russian minorities in the Soviet Union dissent is vocal and widespread.

—There is also increasing criticism of the Soviet economy.

—In Eastern Europe where the tensions are greater and the Western orientation much stronger the Soviets will have to rely on force to maintain hegemony.

There are numerous indications of the effectiveness of the program CIA conducts to capitalize on Soviet vulnerabilities:

—Radio Free Europe, which broadcasts to an Eastern European audience of over 30 million that swells dramatically during crises, is frequently denounced by Communist leaders. Czech Party Secretary Husak, for example, has blamed RFE for his party's inability to win over the Czech population.

—Radio Liberty which broadcasts to the Soviet Union has had a significant role in increasing manifestations of dissent and opposition among the Soviet intelligentsia. Defectors have often commented on the significant impact of the broadcast of documents written by protesters.

—The $150 million spent annually by the Russians for jamming operations which are only marginally successful is indicative of the value of Radio Free Europe and Radio Liberty which cost less than $35 million to operate.

—Publication of smuggled manuscripts and magazines geared to the Eastern European audience and distribution of books not available in Communist countries have also made an impact.

Emphasis on the following activities is being considered in planning for future operations:

—greater exploitation of dissent through modernized radio transmitting facilities, wider dissemination of criticism by the intellectuals, and stimulation of nationality aspirations among Soviet minorities;

—attacks on Soviet activities outside the bloc and intensified exploitation of anti-Communist themes abroad;

—developing leaders capable of providing a democratic alternative to Soviet-supported front organizations;

—selective use [*less than 1 line of source text not declassified*] to increase distrust of Russians in developing countries and exploiting Soviet sensitivity to local hostility and exposure of their activities;

—preparations for covert programs to offset the threat of Communist election victories in the Free World. Past examples of successful operations include Guyana in 1963 and Chile in 1964.

Tab A

Paper Prepared by the Central Intelligence Agency[2]

Washington, undated.

TENSIONS IN THE SOVIET UNION AND EASTERN EUROPE
CHALLENGE AND OPPORTUNITY

Introduction

At no time in the history of the Soviet Union to date have political forces outside the Communist Party leadership played a significant role in influencing events. The Party apparatus, the KGB and the deeply vested interests of the Soviet State hierarchy are experienced in coping with dissidence of all types, and have an impressive record of asserting their will at any cost to the rest of society. The KGB in particular has an almost perfect record of successful penetration, manipulation and suppression of opposition elements. In addition there is an historic tradition of public apathy, largely unchanged even today among the workers and peasants of Russia, and dissident elements find little encouragement at the grass roots. The authorities have often exploited the antipathy of the working class toward the intelligentsia in suppressing incipient demonstrations.

Thus the experience of Russian history strongly argues against the proposition that the internal dissident will significantly influence Soviet society in the short term. The conditions, nevertheless, which abet existing trends toward more active and articulate dissidence could be

---

[2] Secret; Nodis. Helms sent this paper to Kissinger under a March 30 covering memorandum that reads: "Pursuant to the interest expressed by the President [see Document 147] in a review of our covert action activities with respect to the Soviet Union and, more particularly, what we might additionally do, we have prepared the attached paper." (Ibid., Box 433, Backchannel Files, Backchannel Messages, Black Operations)

affected by external developments. A discrediting of the regime by, say, another Czechoslovak crisis or a serious economic crisis, might well promote radical changes in the internal political climate. The paragraphs that follow should be considered in this light.

Intellectual Dissent

To describe the nature and scope of dissidence in the Soviet Union today poses the risk of over-emphasis. The Soviet regime is by no means on the brink of collapse. On the other hand, something new has indeed emerged in Soviet society since Stalin's death. The growing demand for freedom of expression has been widely reported in the Western press, and its suppression by Soviet authorities has in turn contributed to disillusionment among foreign Communists and Soviet sympathizers.

The top rank of dissenters in the Soviet Union includes leading scientists, some of whom share the views of Andrey Sakharov, an eminent scientist. In 1968, Sakharov in a long pamphlet advocated radical changes in human society the world over. Speaking of his own country, he called for tolerance of political opposition, elimination of censorship, and frank discussion of Stalin's use of terror. Later in 1968, other prominent scientists including Peter Kapitsa, the Soviet Union's leading theoretical physicist, told Western colleagues that they agreed with Sakharov. The Sakharov pamphlet has never been published in the Soviet Union, but through Western radio broadcasts and publications Sakharov's words have been carried back to his countrymen.

After the scientists, next in prestige come the writers, whose tradition of social concern goes back to Turgenev, Tolstoy and even earlier. Their involvement in politics and protest has almost always been reluctant. Alexander Solzhenitsyn tried for years to remain aloof, but his determination to write what he believed and his refusal to conform to the requirements of the Party put him squarely against the censors and the Soviet Writers' Union. Last fall the Writers' Union expelled Solzhenitsyn for his recalcitrance. Learning that he had been expelled without an opportunity to defend his position, Solzhenitsyn wrote a letter to the leaders of the Union that epitomizes the attitude of the creative intelligentsia toward the Party hacks who control the institutions of Soviet society. "The face of your clock has been rubbed out: Your clock is far behind the times. Open your heavy curtains. You do not even know that outside it is already day . . . .[3] In this time of crisis in our dangerously sick society you are not able to suggest anything constructive, anything good, only your own hatred and your spying on others and your determination to coerce and never to let go."

---

[3] All ellipses are in the source text.

Beyond the circle of leading scientists and writers there are the active dissidents themselves. Most of them are younger members of the intelligentsia, but their ranks also include workers, teachers, and other professionals. A leading physicist in this group runs the only "underground press" known to exist in the Soviet Union. In May 1969 fifteen of the most active dissidents organized a Committee for the Defense of Human Rights, and petitioned the United Nations to protest against violations of human rights in the USSR. They were joined by some fifty other persons who publicly announced their support of the Committee. When the first petition received no answer, they sent a second. Now, ten months afterward, ten of the fifteen of the organizers of the Committee have been imprisoned or placed in mental hospitals, a favorite device of the regime for handling awkward cases.

In April 1968 the group began a bi-monthly *Chronicle of Current Events,* reporting in detail on arrests, threats and other coercive acts the Soviet regime uses to suppress opposition, plus the latest news concerning underground literature and petitions. Ten issues of the *Chronicle* were subsequently circulated in hundreds of typewritten copies inside the USSR. A few copies of each reached the West, where they have been republished and broadcast back into the Soviet Union.

The writing and circulation of protest documents of many varieties, typed in carbon copies or handwritten, continues in the face of regime repression. In early 1968 the trial of Ginsburg and Galanskov inspired hundreds of Soviet citizens to risk censure, job loss or imprisonment by appealing to the authorities on behalf of the defendants. The petitioners and protestors have since supported other causes, and have proposed their own political programs as alternatives to the Communist Party's dictatorship. As one leader of the dissident movement, Lydia Chukovskaya, wrote: "The conspiracy of silence is at an end."

In reaction to the increasing repression of creative freedom in the USSR, outstanding representatives of the Soviet intelligentsia have forsaken their homeland for life in the West. In addition to Stalin's daughter, Svetlana, they include three distinguished writers, a prominent philosopher and editor, a young nuclear physicist, two outstanding musicians, a magazine editor, two leading experts on cybernetics, a movie director, a film critic and three students from Moscow University's Institute of Eastern Languages.

The picture of the Soviet Union that these defectors paint is one of increasing cynicism and alienation on the part of the intelligentsia, and apathy and bitterness in the working class. The philosopher mentioned above had this to say on the subject: "People are still afraid to trust one another entirely. I shared my real views only with three other men. Yet one knows how everybody feels—disillusioned, contemptuous of the bosses and frustrated by the Party careerists who know nothing but how to win and keep power. Now these careerists sense their isolation from the rest of the population. They no longer believe in anything. There are no idealists like my father left among them. They only know that to keep their power they must stick together, like cattle surrounded by wolves."

Minority Repression

Among many of the non-Russian minorities in the Soviet Union, dissent is vocal and widespread. It is also vigorously repressed. In the Ukraine, the arrests of hundreds of Ukrainian dissidents in 1965 and 1966, and subsequent repressions, have been vigorously protested by leading Ukrainian scientists, artists, and writers, including Oleg Antonov, one of the Soviet Union's leading aircraft designers.

The contempt of the Baltic people for Soviet rule remains as strong as ever. It is no longer expressed in hopeless armed resistance, as it was twenty years ago. Instead, these small nations manifest a vigorous determination to preserve their national cultures. Even the local Communist Party apparatus has sought to assert a degree of autonomy. In Estonia many works of Western literature that have never been published in Russian are printed in the native language. Two of the major underground documents recently proposing alternatives to the Communist dictatorship originated in Estonia.

Economic Unrest

Since the December 1969 Central Committee Plenum, the Soviet press has given increasing attention to the lethargy of the economy. The best informed defectors and even Soviet economists depict the economy as suffering from overcentralization, rigid control, and a system of falsification and misrepresentation that prevents anyone from knowing what the true conditions are. A recent letter to Brezhnev circulated through underground channels in Moscow described the problems of the economy in the following terms: "It is obvious to everyone that in our system nobody is involved in real work. They only throw dust in the eyes of the bosses. Phony events, such as jubilees and special days, have become for us more important than the real events of economic and social life. . . . Other states in which the economy is not ruled from the heavens, but from earth . . . are outdistancing us more and more . . . Freedom to discuss problems openly, only such freedom, can put diseased Russia on the road to recovery."

Eastern Europe

In addition to its domestic problems, the Soviet Union has had chronic difficulty in managing its satellites in Eastern Europe. In Eastern Europe the tensions in society are much greater than in the Soviet Union, the Western orientation much stronger, and the possibility exists that at some future time one or more of these countries may successfully make the transition that Czechoslovakia essayed in 1968. It seems inevitable that, as long as the Soviet Union maintains its current system, it will be impossible for the peoples of Eastern Europe to live in real harmony with the Soviet Union and that, to maintain hegemony in the area, the Soviets will have to continue to rely upon force.

Dissident elements in the USSR and Eastern Europe display remarkable sympathy and understanding for their fellows throughout the whole Soviet dominated region. Pavel Litvinov, Larissa Daniel and others were exiled from Moscow for trying to stage a peaceful demonstration against the Soviet invasion of Czechoslovakia. Others protested the biased reporting in the Soviet press and Soviet threats before the troops moved in. Intellectuals in all Eastern European countries have actively collaborated with the Soviet dissidents, and have expressed their sympathy for those arrested and imprisoned.

With its easier access to the West, Eastern Europe acts as a conduit for books, letters, manuscripts and ideas. The flow back and forth across the Soviet borders is relatively easy and constant. The fact that Eastern European standards of tolerance and freedom of expression, although restrictive, are well above the levels permitted in the Soviet Union makes the region's ability to influence the Soviet Union a consideration of major importance to the United States.

II

Covert Action Programs Targeted at Eastern Europe and the USSR

Current CIA operations targeted at Eastern Europe and the USSR are designed to foster the tensions and cleavages outlined above. Their aim is not to promote armed rebellion, but rather to encourage the movement for greater personal freedom within the Soviet Union and to weaken the ties between the nations of Eastern Europe and Soviet Russia.

Radio Broadcasts

Free Europe, Inc., and Radio Liberty Committee, Inc., were organized in 1949 and 1951 respectively by the CIA. The major activity of each operation is radio broadcasting. Radio Free Europe and Radio Liberty programming centers are located in Munich, Germany. Their staffs, composed largely of Soviet and Eastern Europe expatriates with Americans in key policy positions, represent a unique concentration of expertise and professional talent.

Radio Free Europe (RFE)

RFE currently broadcasts 19 hours daily into Poland, Czechoslovakia and Hungary, 12 hours to Romania, and 8 hours to Bulgaria. It also conducts an extensive and respected research program on Eastern

Europe. The radio has achieved a high degree of Eastern European listener acceptance as a station which identifies with their needs, thoughts and aspirations. It is estimated that over 30 million people listen to RFE broadcasts. This percentage rises dramatically during periods of international crisis. RFE is denounced almost daily by Communist media, and on occasion by key figures of the Eastern European governments. Czechoslovak Party Secretary Husak has publicly placed a large share of the blame on RFE for his Party's inability to win over the Czechoslovak population.

The station is a political force with which the Eastern European regimes must reckon. The reason for this lies partly in RFE's pattern of cross-reporting—i.e., reporting in detail to all the Eastern European countries on domestic developments in the individual countries. This is in effect the principal way the peoples of the area learn of significant developments in their own and neighboring countries. It can be demonstrated that RFE's repeated exposure of domestic policies and methods has forced modification of censorship and similar restrictions in several of the Eastern European countries.

RFE's role in the 1968 Czechoslovak crisis is a striking example of the radio's effectiveness. Prior to the ousting of Party First Secretary Novotny in January 1968, RFE was the chief source of factual information and research analysis on domestic affairs for much of the Czechoslovak population. After the Soviet invasion and the loss of their new-found freedom, the Czechoslovak people again became dependent on the round-the-clock reporting of RFE. Audience research indicates that RFE's listenership rose to 70 percent of the population. The station received thousands of letters extolling its programs, while the Communist news media unleashed an unprecedented series of attacks on RFE. The Soviet journal *Red Star* described the radio as the "most strategic weapon in the global psychological war being carried on by the United States against the world socialist system."

Radio Liberty (RL)

Radio Liberty broadcasts round-the-clock in the Russian language, 14 hours a day in Ukrainian, and at varying lengths in 15 other national languages. In contrast to RFE, RL is targeted against the more restrictive Soviet system. Effectiveness is more difficult to measure. However, letters from listeners, defector reports and legal travelers indicate that there is a sizeable audience. It is generally agreed that RL merits a significant share of the credit for the increasing manifestations of dissent and opposition among the Soviet intelligentsia. In this respect the Sinyavskiy–Daniel trial of 1966 was a landmark. RL played a unique role in conveying the facts, the significance, and Western reactions to the trial to the Soviet people. RL has also broadcast back into the Soviet Union detailed information on every important letter, protest document, and piece of underground literature which has reached the West through underground channels. Recent Soviet defectors, among them the author Anatole Kuznetsov, have specifically cited RL's vital function in providing such information and thereby expanding the scope and depth of dissident attitudes.

Communist Attacks on the Radios

Soviet and Eastern European attempts to discredit RFE and RL are intensive and coordinated. The Communist regimes are particularly discomfited by the two radios' detailed news coverage and highly effective cross-reporting of internal developments, and by their exploitation of intellectual ferment, nationalist tendencies and general dissent within the Soviet Union.

A measure of the Soviet concern over Western broadcasts is the extent of the Soviet jamming effort. At this time, Czechoslovakia and Bulgaria also extensively jam RFE broadcasts. According to a VOA study, the Soviets use 2,000–2,500 jammers at an estimated annual cost of $150,000,000. As indicated above, however, the jamming is marginally effective inasmuch as the target audiences hear the radios on one or more frequencies. The cost of the Soviet jamming effort can be put into perspective by comparing it with the annual operating costs of FE, Inc., and RLC, Inc., $21,723,000 and $12,770,000 respectively. The radios represent a 20-year investment of over $400,000,000.

Non-Radio Programs of Free Europe, Inc., and Radio Liberty Committee, Inc.

In addition to the radios, FE, Inc., and RLC, Inc., sponsor book distribution programs. FE, Inc., also administers a program of support for exiles who fled Eastern Europe during the early post-war period. RLC, Inc., sponsors the Institute for the Study of the USSR in Munich, Germany.

FE, Inc., and RLC, Inc., have distributed a total of two and one-half million books and periodicals in the Soviet Union and Eastern Europe since the late 1950's. The titles comprise works which are not available in those countries because their content is considered ideologically objectionable.

The book programs are, for the most part, demonstrably effective in reaching directly significant segments of the professional and technical elite, and through them their colleagues in the Soviet Union and Eastern Europe, with material that can inferentially be said to influence attitudes and reinforce predispositions toward intellectual and cultural freedom, and dissatisfaction with its absence.

The [*less than 1 line of source text not declassified*] is a research organization supported by Radio Liberty Committee, Inc. It is also heavily engaged in a publications program designed to counter Soviet propaganda in underdeveloped nations. In 1969 over 135,000 copies of its publications were distributed to the Arab countries of the Middle East. The [less than 1 line of source text not declassified] also publishes the prestigious "Prominent Personalities in the USSR" and sponsors symposia which bring together the foremost Western experts on the USSR to consider new approaches to dealing with the Communists. A recent budget reduction levied on Radio Liberty Committee, Inc., has led to a decision to terminate the [less than 1 line of source text not declassified], although efforts are being made to find ways to carry on certain of its activities independently.

[6½ pages of source text not declassified]

Election Operations

There have been numerous instances when, facing the threat of a Communist Party or popular front election victory in the Free World, we have met the threat and turned it successfully. Guyana in 1963 and Chile in 1964 are good examples of what can be accomplished under difficult circumstances. Similar situations may soon face us in various parts of the world, and we are prepared for action with carefully planned covert election programs when U.S. policy calls for them.

150.   Memorandum of Conversation[1]

Washington, April 7, 1970, 8 p.m.

PARTICIPANTS

> Ambassador Dobrynin
> Mr. Kissinger

The conversation took place at Dobrynin's initiative prior to his departure for the Soviet Union for consultations.

Vietnam

After an exchange of pleasantries, Dobrynin turned the conversation to Vietnam. He said that he wanted to understand our position: were we committed to maintaining an anti-Communist Government in Saigon or were we willing to settle for true neutrality?

---

[1] Source: Library of Congress, Manuscript Division, Kissinger Papers, Box TS 36, Geopolitical File, Soviet Union, Chronological, 3/69–6/70. Top Secret; Sensitive. The conversation was held at Dobrynin's residence. Sent to Nixon by Kissinger under an April 13 covering memorandum that summarized the conversation.

I asked why he wanted to know. Dobrynin said that if we were interested in maintaining an anti-Communist Government, the war would inevitably go on. If we were interested in a neutral government, then the Soviet Union might be able to be of some help. He knew we could sustain the war for another seven years if we wanted an anti-Communist Government, but this wouldn't lead to any conclusion.

When I probed his comment that the Soviet Union could be of some help, he said it might be possible to find some formula for neutrality. I replied that it depended on what they understood by neutrality. If they meant that neutrality entitled them to select the participants in a government and that the process had to begin with our eliminating our allies and the people we had been supporting, then this was absolutely out of the question. If their definition of neutrality matched what was commonly understood by that term, then there existed a real possibility for progress.

Dobrynin then asked me about our views of a political settlement. I said that the sharing of political power was not an easy matter to define and that I did not want to be doctrinaire about it. It seemed to me, however, that:

—first, one had to accept the Saigon Government as an objective reality;
—secondly, some process had to be developed to consult the will of the people;
—thirdly, there would have to be guarantees that would enable the participants in the political process to survive defeat.

Dobrynin said that he would think about this and report fully to his government.

Middle East

Dobrynin next turned the conversation to the Middle East. He said that we might not believe it, but the Soviet Union was genuinely interested in a compromise. However, he had come to the conclusion that talking to Sisco was getting to be a waste of time. Sisco was trying to be a great diplomat and operator. He was dealing with Dobrynin as if Dobrynin did not have any experience in diplomacy himself. For example, Sisco was asking him to write down the conditions of peace or Arab peace obligations without in advance committing himself to the withdrawal of Israeli forces from Egyptian territory. This was an amateurish maneuver. Sisco could choose those elements of the Soviet proposal he liked while the Soviets were compromising themselves with the Egyptians, who were not in any event enthusiastic about the whole negotiating process.

Dobrynin said that it would be good if I intervened. I replied that we had made one effort to intervene and had been tricked by the Soviet introduction of SA–3s.

Dobrynin said that he had been instructed to tell me that the offer of a cease-fire still stood. He did not understand why we should be bothered by the SA–3s which were purely defensive weapons.

I told him that one of the most difficult issues in the history of disarmament negotiations has been how to define "defensive." If the Israelis were deprived of air retaliation, they lost their most effective counter to Egyptian guerrilla raids. Thus, SA–3 missiles could, in fact, enhance the Egyptian offensive capability. Dobrynin said that this was not true as long as the Israelis maintain air superiority on their side of the Suez Canal.

He then asked tentatively what we would say if the Soviets promised to keep their deployment confined to Alexandria, Cairo and the Aswan Dam. I replied this might be worth considering. Dobrynin said he would come back to this proposition.

Dobrynin repeated that the Soviets were interested in a real compromise. He said they were prepared to agree to establishing a state of peace and to spell out the conditions and obligations of peace with great precision once they knew what we were prepared to do. He thought that all we were doing was sending Sisco on a fishing expedition.

I said it was true that the President did not take the same active interest in the Middle East negotiations that he did, for example, on Vietnam and SALT. However, this could change if we saw some degree of Soviet cooperation on the Middle East issues that concerned us most.

SALT

Dobrynin said that he couldn't recall our beginning a negotiation in which the two sides knew so little about one another. He said perhaps we should have made some concrete proposal to him informally on which he could have sounded out his government. In the previous Administration, Foster always let him know the Administration's thinking.

I told Dobrynin that I had offered to talk to him but he had never picked this up. After some inconclusive fencing about who had been responsible for the offer not being taken up, Dobrynin said that his government was serious about these negotiations. However, my suggestion that he and I settle the matter in our channel presented a difficulty. Semenov was a Deputy Foreign Minister and it was hard for a mere Ambassador to interject himself. It would help their deliberations in Moscow if I gave him some feel for what our position was likely to be. They would consider that as a sign of our good faith.[2]

---

[2] Nixon highlighted this paragraph.

I told Dobrynin that before he left I would indicate whether our position involved a comprehensive or a more limited option, but I would not give him the substance. I reaffirmed my willingness to settle a more limited agreement in this channel with him.[3]

Possible Summit

Dobrynin then asked whether we would be prepared to expand trade. I said that this depended on the general state of our relationship.

This caused Dobrynin to say that he had noticed that at the beginning of each Administration there was great reluctance to make progress. Towards the end of an Administration the willingness for progress increased, but by then time had run out. For example, Johnson tried to have a summit in the last six months of his Administration when it no longer made sense. It would have been very easy to arrange one several years earlier.

I said that for us summits were instruments; everything depended on what we wanted to achieve there. In principle, though, we were willing to have a summit with the Soviet leaders if it would lead to some practical result.

Dobrynin became visibly attentive. He had thought we were not interested and had told his leaders that a summit was not possible before 1971–1972. They had been very interested last year but had been put off by us. He asked if I was sure we were willing to have a summit. I replied that we were, under certain circumstances, for example, if there were the prospect of a major breakthrough on Vietnam. I was willing to discuss the general framework of the summit with him in any event.

Dobrynin said that one good way to have a summit would be for Kosygin to head the delegation to the U.N. and then meet the President in this context. I told him I would want to consult the President on that and would let him know before he left.

Dobrynin said that the two most fruitful subjects for a summit were SALT and the Middle East. I said we, of course, were interested in Vietnam. He replied that Vietnam could not be put on the agenda for a summit, but it could certainly be discussed once the parties got there. I suggested that he discuss the matter in Moscow and we could then pursue the conversation after he returned. Dobrynin insisted that there was great interest in a summit in the Soviet Union, and he was certain that our talk would be well received by his superiors.

Dobrynin then showed me some films of Siberia and of the Bolshoi Ballet. I left the Embassy about midnight.

---

[3] Nixon highlighted this paragraph.

151.   Memorandum From Harold Saunders of the National Security Council Staff to the President's Assistant for National Security Affairs (Kissinger)[1]

Washington, April 8, 1970.

SUBJECT

Renewed Dobrynin Talks on Mid-East—Recapitulation

Following is a recapitulation of the four recent meetings with Dobrynin on the Mid-East. The Rogers–Dobrynin meetings of March 11 and 25 set the stage for two Sisco–Dobrynin meetings on April 1 and 6.

Rogers–Sisco–Dobrynin, March 11 [Tab A][2]

In brief, Dobrynin indicated Soviet willingness to resume bilateral talks and to meet U.S. wishes for a more detailed formulation on the obligations of peace provided U.S. will be more forthcoming on the question of withdrawal, particularly re Sharm al-Shaykh, Gaza and Syria.

The key to reading the specific points Dobrynin made is to note that he is talking about modifications in the USSR's June 1969 proposals[3]— not the U.S. October 28 document.[4] In other words, the Soviets seemed to be wiping the slate clean of Sisco's Moscow talks last July[5] and Secretary Rogers' New York talks in September[6] which provided the basis for our October 28 document.

Against that implicit backdrop—later made explicit by Dobrynin— Dobrynin made these specific points:

—The USSR would be ready to supplement provisions in its plan on cessation of state of war by a provision on establishing, as a result of settlement, a state of peace.

—The USSR is prepared to meet U.S. wishes for greater detail on the obligations of the parties resulting from a state of peace "if the U.S. side shows due understanding of . . . those questions concerning the unequivocal recording of provisions for the withdrawal of troops."

—The U.S. still has not indicated that it shares the Soviet view that sovereignty over Sharm al-Shaykh belongs to the UAR.

---

[1] Source: National Archives, Nixon Presidential Materials, NSC Files, Box 653, Country Files, Mideast, Sisco Mideast Talks, Vol. III. Secret; Nodis. Sent for information. A notation on the memorandum indicates Kissinger saw it. Copies were sent to Haig and Lord.

[2] Ellipsis and all brackets are in the source text. See Document 141.

[3] See Document 58.

[4] See Document 98.

[5] See Document 69.

[6] See Documents 81 and 87.

—The U.S. has given no assurances that Israeli troops are to withdraw from the Gaza sector and that this Arab territory is to be restored to its pre-June 1967 borders with the previous situation there re-established.

—The position of the Syrian government does not relieve us of the task of working out concrete aspects of a Syrian-Israeli settlement.

Secretary Rogers made clear that if we agreed to resume bilateral talks this would not signify acceptance of the Soviet proposals or willingness to go beyond our October 28 or December 18 documents.

Rogers–Sisco–Dobrynin, March 25 [Tab B][7]

This was the meeting right after announcement of the U.S. decision on Israel's arms requests. Secretary Rogers expressed concern over introduction of SAM–3's into Egypt and stressed several times our concern over involvement of additional Soviet personnel there. Dobrynin was "not in a position to comment." He maintained that U.S. expression of intent to maintain Israel's superiority was not helpful to U.S.-Soviet efforts to achieve a peaceful settlement; it would be better if the two sides were equal militarily. The Secretary reminded Dobrynin that Moscow had not responded to U.S. proposals for arms limitation talks.

In replying to Dobrynin's presentation of March 11, the Secretary made these points on the effort to achieve a settlement:

—We have no objection in principle to resuming talks soon. Chances would be improved if the Soviet Union could provide beforehand certain clarifications of its position.

—In saying that it is prepared to meet the U.S. wish for greater detail on the question of peace, does the Soviet Government mean that it would accept Point 2 of our documents [where the obligations of peace are spelled out]?

—We have made our position on withdrawal clear. As concerns the UAR, we have said Israel should withdraw to the old international boundary. There must also be agreement between the parties on practical security arrangements in the Sharm al-Shaykh area. These arrangements would have to provide an absolute guarantee of free navigation through the Straits of Tiran. It is not our intention that they should call into question UAR sovereignty over Sharm al-Shaykh.

—Gaza is a special case since the question of sovereignty there has never been resolved. The pre-June 1967 situation, which the Soviet Union wants restored, was based on the Armistice of 1949, whereas we are now seeking peace.

—Does the USSR still accept the language on the Rhodes formula agreed between the U.S. and USSR last September? If not, does the USSR have alternative language that would include both indirect and direct contacts?

---

[7] See Document 148.

—The U.S. position on Syria remains clear. Syria has rejected the UN resolution. There is no basis for developing guidelines for Jarring on the Syrian aspect.

Sisco–Dobrynin, April 1 [Tab C][8]

Sisco and Dobrynin reviewed where the talks stand. While Sisco noted the appearance of greater oral flexibility, his inclination was to press for written counter language from the USSR. Ambassador Beam concurred and added his doubt that Moscow would move quickly to contribute new language. When Sisco suggested that Dobrynin offer changes in the U.S. October 28 paper, Dobrynin said he had instructions to talk only from the Soviet June 1969 paper.

The specific results of the meeting were:

—The Soviets continued unwilling to join in an appeal to the parties to restore the cease-fire but proposed working quietly in Tel Aviv and Cairo for a de facto cease-fire.

—The Soviets continued adamant against arms limitation talks.

—The Soviets are willing to consider a formulation on peace along lines proposed by the U.S. provided the U.S. is willing to commit itself to total withdrawal, specifically including withdrawal from Gaza and Sharm al-Shaykh. Dobrynin refused to agree to point 2 of our October 28 document but said the Soviet formulation is close to ours.

—Dobrynin proposed a slight variant of the past Soviet proposal on the relationship between the timing of withdrawal and the entry into effect of peace obligations. This has the effect of advancing Arab de jure acceptance of peace.

—Dobrynin refused to accept U.S. language on controlling the fedayeen but maintained the Soviets had language in mind that might approximate this.

—The Soviets no longer accept the present formulation on the Rhodes formula. Dobrynin's informal alternative went something like this: The parties will have contact between themselves through Jarring with the understanding that he could use various forms.

—Dobrynin insisted that there be specific reference to a UN force at Sharm al-Shaykh, its removal being subject to major power veto. He categorically precluded any Soviet troops being involved in such a force.

Sisco–Dobrynin, April 6 [Tab D][9]

Sisco suggested that the Soviets submit in writing any formulation they have in mind on peace and negotiations if they find U.S. formulations of October 28 unsatisfactory. Dobrynin reluctantly agreed to put this request to Moscow.

---

[8] Tab C, attached but not printed, is telegram 47932 to Moscow, April 2.
[9] Tab D, attached but not printed, is telegram 51251 to Moscow, April 8.

Dobrynin submitted a text calling for Israeli withdrawal from Sinai, Sharm al-Shaykh, Golan Heights, Gaza and West Bank. The slight difference from the June 1969 Soviet proposal is that it calls for a UN buffer to be established by stages as Israeli forces withdraw.

Sisco pressed for Moscow's reaction to Secretary Rogers' expression of concern over introduction of SA–3's into the UAR. Dobrynin refused to make any commitment.

Conclusion

The Soviets have reopened the dialogue by going back to June 1969. Sisco is pressing them to submit their views as emendations of our October 28 document which incorporated the results of the most constructive part of the U.S.–USSR dialogue last July–September. So far it is a stand-off. The ball is in the Soviet court to decide whether to submit views in writing.

---

152.   Memorandum of Conversation[1]

Washington, April 9, 1970.

PARTICIPANTS

Ambassador Anatoliy Dobrynin
Mr. Henry A. Kissinger

Ambassador Dobrynin came in as we had agreed at the dinner on April 7th, to get answers to two questions: (1) whether we wanted the summit talks handled through a visit by Kosygin to the United Nations as Head of the Soviet Delegation, and (2) how we proposed to handle the SALT talks. In the latter connection, Dobrynin had told me that it would help him if he could get some advance information so that he could show that he is in direct and close contact on SALT matters with the White House.

I told Dobrynin with respect to the first question that if a summit meeting were to take place this year, we would prefer to handle it out-

---

[1] Source: Library of Congress, Manuscript Division, Kissinger Papers, Box TS 36, Geopolitical File, Soviet Union, Chronological File, 3/69–6/70. Top Secret; Sensitive; Eyes Only. The meeting was held in Kissinger's office at the White House. Kissinger forwarded this to Nixon under an April 18 covering memorandum that summarized the conversation. The covering memorandum bears the handwritten comment, "This should have sensitive handling."

side the United Nations and as a separate initiative. Of course, we would not preclude the Soviet Prime Minister coming here but, on the whole, we would like to take it as a separate initiative.

With respect to the SALT talks, I told Dobrynin that we would present a very comprehensive proposal at Vienna, including qualitative as well as quantitative restrictions. On the other hand, we did not exclude a simple agreement this year. The best way to handle it would be for the Vienna talks to concentrate on comprehensive measures, while he and I would try to work out a limited agreement in the interval. One way might be for a recess to be taken after a few months in Vienna, during which time the President and the Soviet Prime Minister could break a deadlock and then meet to ratify it at a summit. Dobrynin said he understood and he would let me have an answer when he returned.

Dobrynin then reverted to our discussion of two days previously and asked me much the same question about Vietnam that he had already asked. How did we propose to share political power? Were we really willing to have a neutral government? How did we visualize the political evolution? I told him that the situation in Vietnam could only increase the complexity for all countries, and that it would affect our attitude on many subjects, including the Middle East.

Dobrynin then asked me about the Middle East, again making the argument that we were not really pushing as hard on the negotiations as we could. I said, "No, we, not the Soviet Union, made the last proposals." We were standing by our October 28th position. Dobrynin said the October 28th position is an old story, and we need a new position. I told him that there was no sense debating the problem because the situation was as follows: The President did not really require the Jewish world since he had been elected largely without it and, in this respect, he was freer than any other President. On the other hand, as long as the war in Vietnam continued, he did not want to alienate people with so much influence in the mass media. Therefore, the key to our attitude on the Middle East would be found in the Soviet attitude toward Vietnam. Dobrynin said that he understood this, and he had in fact reported this to Moscow.

I then asked Dobrynin about possible changes in the Soviet leadership. He said he did not think any were likely before the Party Congress, but that it was very probable afterwards. He also reaffirmed that there had been no improvement in Sino-Soviet relations.

153. Memorandum From the President's Assistant for National Security Affairs (Kissinger) to President Nixon[1]

Washington, undated.

SUBJECT

TASS Issues Statement on Cambodia

The Soviet news agency TASS has issued a formal statement (Tab A)[2] on Cambodia. The statement is generally cautious in tone, not committing the Soviets to any course of action but demonstrating their continued interest in and concern about developments in Southeast Asia. The statement does not explicitly repudiate the Lon Nol Government; it makes no reference to Sihanouk. It makes no mention of possible U.S. aid to Cambodia. It stands in marked contrast to the tough statements emanating from Hanoi and Peking. Moreover, although it expresses concern about the overall peaceful settlement of the problems of Indo-China, it makes no references to the recent formation of the "Indo-China Peoples' Front." In fact its references to a peaceful settlement "of the problems of Indo-China" might be a hint that the Soviet Indo-China conference proposal is not entirely dead. The difference in this Soviet statement and the Hanoi approach is particularly striking because there have been recent conferences between Hanoi Party First Secretary Le Duan and top Soviet officials in Moscow.

The TASS statement leads (and ends) with the following sentence: "It is believed in the Soviet Union that attempts to undermine Cambodia's neutrality and widen imperialist aggression in the Indo-China peninsula may have the most serious consequences for the cause of peace and security in Southeast Asia." The statement then condemns at length the reported massacres in Cambodia; it relates them to our policy of Vietnamization (allegedly setting Asians against Asians) and claims that this "cannot but cause concern among those who are interested in the earliest resolution of the dangerous conflict and a peaceful settlement of the problems of Indo-China."

---

[1] Source: National Archives, Nixon Presidential Materials, NSC Files, Box 711, Country Files, Europe, USSR, Vol. VII. Confidential. Sent for information. Drafted by Holdridge and Richard Smyser on April 24. The memorandum is an uninitialed copy.

[2] Attached but not printed.

154. Telegram From the Embassy in the Soviet Union to the Department of State[1]

Moscow, April 27, 1970, 1545Z.

2114. Subject: Middle East: April 27 Meeting with Vinogradov. Ref: Moscow 2099.[2]

1. I opened meeting with DepFonMin Vinogradov by pointing out that we wished to clarify that in our view next step in Sisco–Dobrynin talks following Dobrynin's return to Washington must be written Soviet indication of what they will accept of our Oct 28 formulations,[3] particularly on peace and negotiations.

2. Vinogradov said Soviet impression was that Dobrynin had offered constructive new approaches to finding common ground on ME settlement, but Sisco had been vague in his responses and then left "abruptly" for tour of ME and meeting in Tehran. Vinogradov "did not think" question of receiving formulations in writing had come up, but if common ground was found it could be expressed in writing. Main question now is how USG envisages continuation of bilateral talks.

3. I pointed out that we had been extremely explicit on question of main concern to Soviets—withdrawal—in our Oct 28 paper and now it was Soviet turn to be explicit on peace, which was subject of major concern to US and Israelis.

4. Vinogradov said Sov Gvt had frequently heard that USG had gone as far as it could in Oct 28 proposal. Such language frequently used in negotiations but if US really means that its proposal is non-negotiable there is no point in further bilateral talks. He asked specifically if US plan subject to modification, adding that answer to this question was very important and would "help solve many problems, including organizational problems of further work."

5. I replied that I was obviously not prepared to discuss any modification to our Oct 28 paper, especially since it was drafted to take account of Soviet propositions on a number of issues and was extremely explicit on withdrawal. US position is that we have been very forthcoming and now it is Soviet turn to be specific on peace. After studying

---

[1] Source: National Archives, Nixon Presidential Materials, NSC Files, Box 711, Country Files, Europe, USSR, Vol. VII. Secret; Nodis.

[2] Telegram 2099 from Moscow, April 27, provides the initial summary of Beam's meeting with Vinogradov. (Ibid.)

[3] See Document 98.

Soviet language on peace and negotiations, we could then decide how far we could go together in pursuit of goals of UNSC resolution.[4]

6. Vinogradov agreed that Soviets should be more specific at some time on peace, but said that as US has tried to produce balanced peace plan from its point of view, Soviet plan also balanced from its vantage point. "Frankly," he said, "Sov Gvt ready to negotiate, to continue bilateral talks, to find workable solution which would satisfy all countries of region as quickly as possible. Situation on ground getting worse from point of view of both sides, and action necessary." He expressed hope that both sides can reach stage where something can be submitted in writing (to four) but issue now was how to proceed in bilaterals since Dobrynin, who in hospital for medical check to be followed by rest, will not return to Washington before end of May. (Vinogradov returned to this point later to stress that end of May is earliest return could be expected).

7. As to procedure for next round of negotiations, I said that key element would be Soviet readiness to produce written language amplifying its unclear and inadequate position on peace.

8. Vinogradov said that the procedures to be adopted for talks would depend on who was conducting them. He said that if he were participating he would prefer to first identify all points of agreement and disagreement orally, then would try to bridge existing gaps in further oral discussions. After this, he would try to jointly formulate agreed language on points at issue. He objected to the idea of exchanging "artillery barrages of paper" which might prove unnecessary and have the further effect of binding the participants to new positions, at least for a time.

9. Speaking "off the record" Vinogradov criticized US Oct 28 position as a "good step forward" on borders combined with "several steps backward" on vital issues such as Sharm, Gaza and security arrangements which were left aside for "direct negotiations." He claimed that although USG "sold" its proposal nicely it came as big surprise to Sov Gvt which hoped bilateral talks would be marked by continuing progress forward rather than retrogression. Before I could nail him on this he went on to say that counter-accusations that the Soviets had reneged on Rhodes formula were incorrect, since Soviets have not stepped back from it in substance. Although Israelis destroyed viability of Rhodes formula, Soviets still for flexible formula providing for negotiations through Jarring.

10. Vinogradov said Soviet Gvt ready to talk to USG and talk extensively, basically to avoid confrontation in area but also to find means

---

[4] Reference is to UN Resolution 242; see footnote 5, Document 2.

of working together to achieve peace. He agreed with my observation that there was great similarity in US and Soviet positions, though from different points of view.

11. I denied that our Oct 28 proposal represented a step backward in any sense in the US position, pointing out that the idea of neutral formulations to cover points where no agreement possible was a concept Soviets accepted. Accusations of Soviet bad faith following presentation of our Oct 28 paper were natural result of procedures followed, where Soviets advanced many informal ideas orally which evaporated later. In contrast, we produced our ideas in writing and then married them to Soviet ideas in our Oct 28 paper. Later this became "the American position" while the Soviet position on peace and negotiations remains vague.

12. I also argued that process of committing ideas to paper during negotiations binds neither party since negotiations ad referendum pending agreement on whole package. Neither side need commit themselves on paper but it is essential that each understand other's position precisely.

13. Vinogradov agreed, saying "this should be done," but added that the main question was where and by whom. He said Sovs would prefer round in Moscow, although if USG wishes it would be possible to continue with Vorontsov in Washington.

14. If talks to be held in Moscow, Vinogradov indicated he would head Soviet team and would prefer starting with brief session to review positions of both sides and identify issues where agreement exists. He said Soviet Govt and he personally would of course welcome Sisco as US negotiator.

15. Throughout discussion Vinogradov was amiable and nonpolemic and attempted to give the impression of potential flexibility.

Beam

155. Memorandum From the President's Assistant for National Security Affairs (Kissinger) to President Nixon[1]

Washington, April 29, 1970.

SUBJECT

Memorandum of Conversation with Soviet Chargé Vorontsov

The Soviet Chargé, Vorontsov, called on me at his request at 3:30. He handed me the attached note. I pointed out that it said nothing about foreign troops in Cambodia. Vorontsov said the only foreign troops in Cambodia that were confirmed were South Vietnamese. I said that in view of his inadequate knowledge of Cambodia, there was no point in continuing the conversation and that I hoped that if there were another occasion to discuss Cambodia he would be better briefed.

He asked me if the President's speech[2] was firm. I said yes and I would call him in if I had anything further to say on the subject.

Tab A

Note Delivered by the Soviet Chargé (Vorontsov)[3]

I have informed Moscow of what you told me concerning Cambodia and I am instructed to forward through you to President Nixon the following.

Moscow would like President Nixon to be clear about our definitely negative attitude towards the United States interference into internal affairs of Cambodia. The enlargement of this interference in any form could not but further complicate the situation in Indochina area—which is dangerous enough even without that—and consequently the international situation in general, for what the United States would be fully responsible.

Therefore Moscow hopes that President Nixon will weigh once more all the consequences of such his step and will take a decision not to make it.

---

[1] Source: National Archives, Nixon Presidential Materials, NSC Files, Box 711, Country Files, Europe, USSR, Vol. VII. Secret; Eyes Only.

[2] On April 30, Nixon delivered an address to the nation on radio and television about his intention to send U.S. forces into Cambodia. (*Public Papers: Nixon, 1970,* pp. 405–410)

[3] No classification marking.

This position of ours is defined by a consistent course of the Soviet Government which has come out in favour of respect of Cambodia's neutrality and of insurance of its territorial integrity and sovereignty.

---

156.   Memorandum From the President's Assistant for National Security Affairs (Kissinger) to President Nixon[1]

Washington, May 5, 1970.

SUBJECT

The Kremlin Scene

For the last several weeks there has been unusual interest and speculation about the situation within the top Soviet leadership. You are probably aware of many of the rumors and the more sensational reports.[2]

The consensus inside the government, and concurred in by some leading scholars, seems to be that there has, in fact, been trouble in the leadership, but that the resolution, if only temporary, has been in Brezhnev's favor.

His image is sharper—as the result of intensive nation-wide television exposure; his confidence is apparently reflected in his wide-ranging speeches covering all important internal and external topics. And several second level personnel changes, [1 line of source text not declassified] suggest he is on top.

What is not clear, however, is the source of the trouble. One view is that it has been Brezhnev's doing: the result of the pointed attacks he launched last December against the government's management of the economy. This theory is documented mainly from material drawn from open sources.

---

[1] Source: Library of Congress, Manuscript Division, Kissinger Papers, Classified Files, Box CL 211, Geopolitical Files, Soviet Union, Chronological Files. Confidential. Drafted by Hyland on April 28. The memorandum was a copy with an indication that Kissinger signed the original. Sent for information. The memorandum indicates the President saw it on May 20.

[2] Telegram 424 from Moscow, January 26, reported press rumors about Brezhnev's absence from public view since December 19, 1969. (National Archives, RG 59, Central Files 1967–69, POL 15–1 USSR)

An alternative explanation is that Brezhnev was challenged for his many failures in economic policy (a CIA report[3] to this effect from good sources [*less than 1 line of source text not declassified*] is the main evidence). He may have been on the defensive until fortuitous illnesses in the politburo, plus a possible opportunistic switch by Shelepin, shifted the balance in Brezhnev's favor and actually enabled him to score some temporary gains. Others feel Shelepin was beaten in a straightforward power struggle.

Whatever the dispute over scenarios, there is hard evidence of three politburo meetings between 24–27 March. About this time the violent press campaign on the economic failures abated, and Brezhnev emerged from his shell with his television speeches. Some observers believe that Brezhnev was only able to win the day by considerable compromise on his economic campaign—that is, by softening the harsh, purge-like atmosphere he was generating.

The question remains whether Brezhnev's gain has been at the expense of collective leadership in general, or only because of the weakening of some of the stronger, more senior members of the politburo (Kosygin and Suslov). Many observers believe that Kosygin will retire—honorably—and that this is part of the political play in Moscow.

Signs of Disarray

Though there is agreement that the "crisis" has been resolved for now, there are still some strange anomalies in Soviet behavior.

—For example, Malik's contradictory statements on a Geneva conference are still puzzling.

—A similar incident occurred in the Middle East. The Soviet press attaché in Amman was quoted (accurately, it is claimed) making outrageous new pronouncements on Soviet support for the liquidation of Israel. The next day he repudiated his remarks. Another Soviet diplomat, in Baghdad, made a somewhat similar comment recently.

A monumental mistake was uncovered in the 50,000 word Lenin Theses; it turned out that a long quotation of "social factors of force" attributed to Lenin was actually from the Austrian Social Democrat Otto Bauer, whom Lenin had roundly attacked as a "renegade." This was discovered by the East Germans, and then widely publicized by the Chinese.

—Finally, there was an amusing lapse by Andrei Kirilenko, a senior politburo member and a long-time associate of Brezhnev, dating back to the Ukraine and presumably one of the more powerful leaders. He made a speech in Yerevan on April 14, two days before the opening of SALT, which contained the following blooper:

"Preliminary talks were held in *Helsinki* on reducing strategic nuclear weapons. These talks (SALT) will continue in Vienna *in May*."

---

[3] Not found.

Apparently Kirilenko's speech writers dusted off an old text from last fall and central censorship either didn't see it, or know the facts, or bother to correct a senior leader.

All of these suggest that there has been an unusual air of uncertainty and preoccupation in Moscow in recent months.

---

157. Memorandum From the President's Assistant for National Security Affairs (Kissinger) to President Nixon[1]

Washington, May 6, 1970.

SUBJECT

Kosygin's Press Conference on Cambodia

Premier Kosygin employed some harsh, denunciatory language in his press conference (May 4) *but* he made no new commitments, nor did he foreshadow any major diplomatic action by the USSR to support Hanoi.

His main theme was that our actions in Cambodia would reverberate on both US-Soviet relations and the "entire international situation." He sought to imply that other political issues would thus be affected: "What is the worth of international agreements in which the United States is taking part *or is going to take part* if it violates so unceremoniously the commitments it has assumed?" When asked, however, if he meant to imply if the Soviet position in the SALT talks would be broken off, he dodged a direct reply and said they would be "on guard."

In dealing with the immediate situation in Indo China, Kosygin's language was virulent, but he stopped short on a number of key points. He did not commit the USSR to a new level of material aid, but said that this would be "re-examined." He referred to Sihanouk as the "lawful head of state," but only in the past tense. He termed the fighting in Cambodia a "civil war," but did not disavow the Lon Nol government, or pledge Soviet support to Sihanouk, or the Indo China People's Front.

He did appear, however, to rule out any international conference, though this was in the context of the Indonesian effort.

---

[1] Source: National Archives, Nixon Presidential Materials, NSC Files, Box 712, Country Files, Europe, USSR, Vol. VIII. Secret. Sent for information. The memorandum indicates the President saw it. Drafted by Hyland on May 4. On May 5, Rogers drafted a memorandum for Nixon about Kosygin's press conference, which bears the handwritten comment, "OBE'd per S'[onnen]feldt's office." Rogers's memorandum is ibid.

Similarly, he evaded a direct reply on whether the ICC should be reconstituted.

On one point, Kosygin seems to have gone further than other Communist statements: he claimed that the bombing at North Vietnam "actually nullifies the decision of . . . President Johnson on the termination of all air bombings . . . "[2] He did not spell out what actions, if any, this meant for the Communist side.

There is little doubt that the Soviets have deliberately escalated their rhetoric, in a rather dramatic way by Kosygin's unique participation. One motive presumably was not to be out-planked [flanked] on the left by the statements simultaneously coming out of Hanoi, Peking, and Pyongyang.

But the content, stripped of its expected propaganda stridency, leaves the Soviet position much the same as it was on the immediate issues in Southeast Asia, with the possible exception of another backward step away from an international conference.

Nevertheless, the Premier has set the stage for retaliatory political action by linking our action in Cambodia with the general international situation and implying an effect on the Soviet delegation position in the SALT talks.

I suspect that the Soviets are very uncertain what the effect of our Cambodia action will be on the situation on the ground in Southeast Asia. The Soviets may also be uneasy about our general posture toward them, in light of the publicity for their increasingly dangerous involvement in the Middle East. In these circumstances, the Soviet leaders apparently are not about to underwrite a vast new Indo China strategy, particularly if Chinese influence over Sihanouk and the new Indo China Front is going to grow.

The Soviet aim seems to be to give a general warning without trying themselves to any given course. They recognize, of course, that by implying a wider effect of Cambodia on other international issues, they can exploit concern in this country.

It appears uncertain whether the Soviets intend to withdraw from the SALT talks. It might seem an attractive way to exploit US domestic reaction but their interests in these talks go beyond the immediate problems of Southeast Asia. It seems more likely that the Soviets will downgrade the talks, and try to use the events in Southeast Asia as a means to make new overtures to the Europeans, trying to split our Allies (e.g., France) from the United States. Indeed, Kosygin noted in this press conference that the events in Cambodia made a European Security conference all the more necessary.

---

[2] Ellipses in the source text.

158. Memorandum From Director of Central Intelligence Helms to the President's Assistant for National Security Affairs (Kissinger)[1]

Washington, May 13, 1970.

SUBJECT

Action Program to Exploit "Tensions in the Soviet Union and Eastern Europe—Challenge and Opportunity"

REFERENCE

Memorandum to the Director from Henry A. Kissinger, dated 14 April 1970,[2] Subject: Exploitation of "Tensions in the Soviet Union and Eastern Europe—Challenge and Opportunity"

1. This will be the first in a series of monthly progress reports[3] that I propose to make on our program of action designed to put pressure on the Soviets. It will be keyed to my conversations with you on this subject, and will tie in with our *Tensions* paper. It will also respond to your 14 April memorandum, which asked for specific plans for operations that we consider feasible and for additional steps we recommend to exploit tensions in the Soviet Union and Eastern Europe.

2. I have instructed my staff to pursue this program as a high priority undertaking. Many of our on-going operations fit precisely into the pattern we have discussed, and while calling on our stations for an intensification of current effort in this specific direction, I propose at the same time to give you a more detailed picture of what is actually being done. Thus, Attachment No. 1[4] presents a breakdown by region of a number of active operations, many of which are already causing the Soviets considerable discomfiture.

3. I have alerted [*less than 1 line of source text not declassified*] virtually all—of our stations and bases to the urgency I attach to rapid

---

[1] Source: Central Intelligence Agency, Executive Registry Files, Job 80–R01284, Box 5, S–17.10, Tensions in USSR, 1970. Secret; Sensitive; Eyes Only. On June 16, Peter Jessup, staff member for the 303 Committee, informed Helms of the following: "General Haig requests that this office do the summary of the exploitation of tensions in the USSR and the bloc from now on. The first memorandum from Kissinger to higher authority was drafted by Commander [Jonathan] Howe. It seems perfectly reasonable that this should be done by the Chapin/Jessup/DePue axis, thereby reducing outside access to this material." (National Security Council, Intelligence Files, Box 7, CIA/Exploitation of Tensions, 4/7/70–12/4/72)

[2] Not printed. (Ibid.)

[3] Monthly progress reports, using a similar format to this first report, were issued through 1972. Helms' covering memoranda and the reports are ibid.

[4] Attached but not printed.

development of new initiatives in this field. I have made it clear that the objective is not only harassment of the Soviets, but sustained pressure through covert means to induce on their part a more cooperative posture on international issues of vital importance to the U.S. Government. This is to be done by exacerbating their sensitivities both within the USSR and East European countries, and abroad in areas where the Soviet presence or interests are significant political factors. The over-all program, however, is not to be limited to short-term impact operations. We will also give careful thought to corresponding action efforts of a long-term and positive nature, aimed at neutralizing Soviet covert political operations in important "third countries." In addition to stepping up the pace of their current operations, I have asked our stations to give us their best thinking and ideas for new programs. To date, we have received detailed and thoughtful responses [*less than 1 line of source text not declassified*], and the outlook is encouraging.

4. To give you further perspective on this effort, I would like to say that we have refined our analysis of Soviet vulnerabilities somewhat since completing the *Tensions* paper, and it seems to me that the majority of our operational approaches will be concentrated in a number of sensitive zones where we believe the Soviets are particularly susceptible to covert action exploitation. These include the following:

a. Sino-Soviet tensions. The Sino-Soviet border conflict and the world-wide struggle for control of Communist parties make the Soviets highly susceptible [*1 line of source text not declassified*].

b. Soviet involvement in the Middle East. Because the Soviet presence in the Middle East entails many volatile factors, there will be opportunities for inducing strain between the Arabs and the Soviets.

c. Soviet relations with East Europe. The steady growth of nationalism in East Europe in the face of Soviet military intervention and economic exploitation makes this area a fertile ground for [*less than 1 line of source text not declassified*] operations to heighten tensions between the USSR and its vassal states.

d. Soviet/Cuban relations. Castro's well-founded suspicion regarding Soviet maneuvers to dominate political and economic life in Cuba, possibly affecting Castro's own future leadership, creates a situation that invites [*less than 1 line of source text not declassified*] manipulation.

e. Soviet domestic dissidence and economic stagnation. By fostering unrest among the Soviet intelligentsia it may be possible to create pressures inducing the Kremlin to curtail its foreign involvements in order to concentrate on critical domestic situations.

5. As we move ahead, I naturally expect to draw more heavily on proposals coming in from the field, supplementing what we have under way and what we can generate at the Headquarters end. Attachment No. 2[5] will give you a cross-section of plans now in the mill, many

---

[5] Attached but not printed.

of which I hope to go ahead with as soon as possible. Attachment No. 3[6] offers ideas for possible action in the future. Most of these are still in the process of scrutiny and appraisal, but they give you a picture of our trend of thought.

6. I will look forward to your initial reaction to this material and I will be happy to discuss any aspect of it at your convenience.[7]

Richard Helms[8]

---

[6] Attached but not printed.

[7] At the bottom of the page is the handwritten comment, "P.S. Please return these papers for safe keeping. R.H."

[8] Printed from a copy that indicates Helms signed the original.

---

159.   Memorandum of Conversation[1]

Washington, June 2, 1970, 3 p.m.

Part I

SUBJECT

Middle East

PARTICIPANTS

The Secretary	Ambassador Dobrynin
Assistant Secretary Sisco	Yuli Vorontsov, Minister-Counselor,
Mr. Dubs, EUR/SOV	Soviet Embassy

At the outset of the meeting, the Secretary asked about Dobrynin's health. The Ambassador said he felt good.

Dobrynin said he understood that the meeting this afternoon would focus on the Middle East. Nevertheless, he was prepared to discuss other matters, such as European affairs and SALT, in the future at the Secretary's convenience.

Dobrynin said that he had been authorized during his recent consultation in Moscow to inform the U.S. Government that he was prepared to continue discussions on the Middle East with Mr. Sisco. He hoped that mutual efforts would lead to a solution. The Soviet

---

[1] Source: National Archives, Nixon Presidential Materials, NSC Files, Box 712, Country Files, Europe, USSR, Vol. VIII. Secret; Nodis. Parts I–III, were drafted by Dubs on June 3. The meeting was held in Rogers' office.

Government was also interested in finding guidelines which Ambassador Jarring could use in the search for a settlement on the Middle East.

Dobrynin then referred to his conversations with Mr. Sisco prior to the latter's trip to the Middle East. Dobrynin noted that the U.S. side had expressed an interest during those talks in obtaining more detailed formulations on the nature of peace and the obligations which the sides would undertake. At the same time, the Soviet side had indicated an interest in more precise language from the U.S. on the question of withdrawal and other matters. Dobrynin said he was instructed to present formulations on the two points mentioned and that he hoped these points would meet the wishes of the U.S. Dobrynin then handed the Secretary two papers with the following formulations (*Note:* these actually are extensions or modifications of points 3 and 11 of Section II of the Soviet paper of June 17, 1969):

"Point 3, Section II

From the moment of deposit with the UN of the concluding document or documents the parties shall refrain from acts contradicting the cessation of the state of war and the establishment of the state of peace, in accordance with paragraphs 10 and 11, with the understanding that, juridically, cessation of the state of war and establishment of the state of peace will begin at the same time of the completion of the first stage of the withdrawal of Israeli troops from the territories occupied during the conflict of 1967."

"*Point 11, Section II*

The Arab countries, parties to the settlement, and Israel mutually agree
—to respect and recognize the sovereignty, territorial integrity, inviolability and political independence of each other and their mutual right to live in peace in secure and recognized borders without being subjected to threats or use of force;
—to undertake everything that is necessary so that any military or hostile acts, with the threat or use of force against the other side will not originate from and are not committed from within their respective territories;
—refrain from intervening directly or indirectly in each other's domestic affairs for any political, economic or other reasons."

Dobrynin commented that these two formulations along with others they had presented to Sisco previously would stand or fall together. In any event, he expressed the hope that they would remain confidential. The Soviet side looks forward toward movement from the U.S.

Commenting that we would look at the two formulations carefully, the Secretary then recalled his conversation with Dobrynin of March 25,[2]

---

[2] See Document 148.

at which time he had noted that the U.S. found the operational involvement of Soviet military personnel in the UAR defenses to be serious and potentially dangerous. The Secretary noted that in reply Dobrynin had expressed the view that Soviet actions were of a defensive nature and that Dobrynin had expressed the hope that the U.S. would be of some assistance in getting the Israelis to desist from deep-penetration raids. Since that conversation, the Secretary noted Israel has halted the deep-penetration raids and Israeli representatives have publicly stated that Israel would observe a cease-fire. In addition, Prime Minister Meir has publicly accepted, during a speech in the Knesset, Security Council Resolution 242. The Secretary said that Israel's position on deep-penetration raids was announced by Israeli Defense Minister Dayan on May 4. Subsequently, on May 26, Dayan went further by indicating that Israeli air activity was being limited to an area 30 kilometers west of the Canal. These moves on the part of Israel represented real progress, and we feel that we have been helpful in this context by urging Israel to cease its deep-penetration raids. Furthermore, in our view, Prime Minister Meir's acceptance of Security Council Resolution 242 provides a basis for negotiations.

The Secretary then said that the U.S. remained deeply concerned over the increased military involvement of the Soviet Union in the UAR. In view of this concern he wished to convey a statement,[3] the text of which would be provided to the Ambassador after the meeting. The statement, which he wished to convey to the Soviet Government, reads as follows:

"The USSR has indicated that Soviet military activities in the UAR will remain defensive. We want to make clear that we would not view the introduction of Soviet personnel, by air or on the ground, in the Canal combat zone as defensive since such action could only be in support of the announced UAR policy of violating the cease-fire resolutions of the Security Council. We believe that introduction of Soviet military personnel into the delicate Suez Canal combat zone could lead to serious escalation with unpredictable consequences to which the U.S. could not remain indifferent. In this connection, we believe, and I am sure you do, it is neither in the interest of the Soviet Union nor the United States for the Middle East to become an area of confrontation between us."

The Secretary then noted that the Soviet Union had at one point indicated an interest in a cease-fire in the area. The U.S. side would like to renew discussions on this subject with Dobrynin as well as on the general matter of a Middle East settlement. With respect to the

---

[3] According to Kissinger's memoirs, *White House Years*, p. 574, "Rogers called in Dobrynin to read him the following extraordinary statement, without informing me or (so far as I know) Nixon."

continuation of the talks between the Ambassador and Mr. Sisco, we believe this very desirable. We welcome the written formulations provided by the Ambassador and are willing to resume bilateral discussions very soon.

Mr. Sisco noted that the U.S. side would wish a bit of time to review the new formulations and to consider them in the light of papers that had been exchanged previously.

Dobrynin emphasized that the formula on mutual obligations should be kept very confidential. He had no particular problem regarding publicity surrounding meetings but did hope that the substance of the proposals advanced during conversations would not be revealed publicly. Dobrynin noted further that he had no objections to having the fact revealed that new proposals were advanced, so long as the substance was not disclosed. He warned that if the proposals were leaked, the Soviets would not feel bound by them. Mr. Sisco suggested that any public disclosure that new formulations had been advanced would only arouse curiosity and could lead to unwarranted speculation. Mr. Sisco, therefore, suggested that nothing be said publicly on this score. Dobrynin agreed.

The Secretary then asked Dobrynin whether he could provide any clarification regarding the Soviet Union's intentions with respect to Soviet personnel and military equipment in the UAR. Dobrynin replied that he was not qualified to discuss "military details." He referred to the Dayan statements regarding penetration raids and wondered whether these represented personal comments or whether they were sanctioned by the Government of Israel.

Alluding to the Secretary's remarks, Dobrynin said that the only thing that has happened in the Middle East is that deep-penetration into UAR air space and bombardment of heavily populated Egyptian areas by Israel have ceased. This is the only thing which has really changed in the Middle East. He added that the outlook for the Middle East was not very hopeful if U.S. policy was aimed at maintaining Israel's military superiority and Israel's policy of dealing from a position of strength. If, on the other hand, the U.S. wants to find a solution that would be fair to both Israel and the Arab countries, the Soviet Union would be willing to cooperate. Frankly, Dobrynin said, maybe the situation now is a little more equal in the military sense. Perhaps this provides a good opportunity to advance toward a settlement. The Soviet Union feels that the time may be ripe. Dobrynin stressed that the Soviet Union does not feel that anything has happened in the way of a developing confrontation between the Soviet Union and the U.S. He wanted to assure the Secretary that the Soviet Union does not want such a confrontation, even though he claimed that some forces in the world and pro-Zionist forces in the U.S. would like this to happen. Dobrynin proceeded to repeat that nothing has changed drastically in the situation, looking at it coolly and realistically. A possibility for a peaceful settlement still exists, and there is no doubt from the Soviet side with respect to not wanting a confrontation.

In reply to Dobrynin, the Secretary said there should be no doubt that the U.S. wanted a fair and equitable solution. Our formulations of December 9[4] indicated that. These proposals were unacceptable to Israel, and the UAR had not accepted the proposals either. With respect to other comments by Dobrynin, the Secretary said that we felt strongly that a shift in the military situation had taken place. It is conceivable that the Arabs, having felt deeply humiliated in the past, may be in a better frame of mind now. The basic question, however, is whether the Soviet Union and the Arabs really want a peaceful settlement. We feel that we should actively pursue a political solution. The Secretary underlined that any additional actions by the Soviet Union, especially toward the Suez Canal, could be highly explosive and that is why we felt it necessary to make the statement that we did. We believe that the time is ripe to work toward a peaceful settlement and we will work actively toward this end. The Secretary said that he could not think of anything that would be more helpful in improving the world atmosphere at the moment than a peaceful settlement in the Middle East. He reminded Dobrynin that Israel's actions and statements over the past weeks were not totally apart from what we have done in urging Israel to be more flexible in its positions. In addition to the statements and actions he had already referred to, the Secretary cited Foreign Minister Eban's comment that the world would be surprised at the concessions that Israel would make once genuine negotiations got underway. We have not seen anything similarly forthcoming from Nasser's side, however. The Secretary said that he hoped the Soviet Union would impress upon the Arabs the importance of a settlement. Otherwise, it can be seen that the fedayeen would become more and more a factor in the situation and unlikely to be subject to the influence of others.

In response to Dobrynin's request, Mr. Sisco said his office would provide Mr. Vorontsov with the text of the statement made by the Secretary as well as information bearing on the statements of Defense Minister Dayan and Prime Minister Meir to which the Secretary had referred.

Part II[5]

SUBJECT

NATO Communiqué and Declaration

---

[4] See Document 104.

[5] Confidential.

[Omitted here is the same list of participants as in Part I.]

During a meeting which focused on other matters, the Secretary noted that he had just returned from a NATO meeting in Rome.[6] He wished to provide the Ambassador with copies of the NATO Communiqué and Declaration on Mutual and Balanced Force Reductions.[7] The Secretary commented that the Italian Government was asked by NATO to transmit these documents to European governments, including the Soviet Government. Nevertheless, he wished to provide a copy to the Ambassador as a courtesy, noting at the same time that we view these documents seriously and that we hoped the Soviet Union would give serious consideration to them and respond constructively.

Dobrynin suggested that he and the Secretary might talk about the document and other European matters in the near future. The Secretary suggested that they might get together next week.

Part III[8]

SUBJECT

SALT

[Omitted here is the same list of participants as in Part I.]

The Secretary took advantage of Dobrynin's call to indicate that Ambassador Smith had sent a cable to Washington suggesting that we impress upon the Soviets that it would be helpful if they would be more specific with respect to their SALT proposals and answers to our questions.

Dobrynin said that the Soviets were at a point of trying to sort out the proposals that had been advanced by the U.S. The Soviets were attempting to ascertain whether it would be useful to concentrate on a broad approach or to focus on items which might be the subject of an initial, limited agreement. Dobrynin indicated that he would convey the Secretary's comments to Moscow.

---

[6] Rogers headed the U.S. delegation to the ministerial meeting of NATO, which was held in Rome, May 26–27. A text of his arrival remarks is in Department of State *Bulletin*, June 22, 1970, p. 776.

[7] A text of the NATO communiqué is ibid., p. 775.

[8] Secret; Nodis.

160.   Memorandum for the Record[1]

Washington, June 5, 1970.

SUBJECT

>   Conversation with Yuly Vorontsov, Counselor at the Soviet Embassy, at the Motion Picture Association of America, June 4

The only substantive conversation was as follows:

Joe Sisco came up and, in the course of some banter about whether or not this would be a busy summer, said that the Soviets should recognize that large Congressional majorities could still be mustered for anti-Soviet positions. Specifically, he said, that the 76 [73] Senators[2] who are urging the President to sell Phantoms to Israel did so out of a deep concern over Soviet actions. It did not take much to arouse this country against the Soviets if a threat to our interests was sensed. Sisco said that this ready reservoir of popular US anti-Soviet sentiment could well make life more difficult for both our governments.

Vorontsov said the Israelis were trying to get the US and the Soviets embroiled with each other and were responsible for the Congressional actions. In Soviet judgment, most Americans understood the policies of confrontation could not accomplish anything vis-à-vis the Soviets, who could not be intimidated. Most US people wanted the US to keep its hands off in the Middle East and elsewhere. Only the Israelis and a few Americans were picturing the Middle East conflict as one between the Soviet Goliath and the Israeli David.

I said that Vorontsov should not underrate the suspicion of the USSR that remains among many Americans, even if it seems now to be largely beneath the surface. Americans were still capable of being aroused by Soviet efforts to damage our interests. It was a mistake to think that the Israelis alone were responsible for pressures on the Phantoms or for our concern about Soviet conduct in the Middle East.

Helmut Sonnenfeldt[3]

---

[1] Source: Library of Congress, Manuscript Division, Kissinger Papers, Box CL 284, Memcons of Staff, January–September 1970. Confidential. Sent for information. Copies were sent to Kissinger and Ash.

[2] In reaction to the President's decision to postpone delivery of F–4 Phantom jet fighter–bombers to Israel, 73 Senators sent a letter to the President urging him to reconsider.

[3] Printed from a copy that bears this typed signature.

161. Memorandum of Meeting[1]

Washington, June 5, 1970.

President's Meeting with his Foreign Intelligence Advisory Board

PARTICIPANTS

The President	Dr. William Baker
Admiral George Anderson	Mr. Franklin Murphy
Mr. Gordon Gray	Governor Nelson Rockefeller
Mr. Robert Murphy	Mr. Henry A. Kissinger
Mr. J. Patrick Coyne	
Brigadier General A.M. Haig, Jr.	

The President convened the meeting at 12:05. He introduced the meeting by pointing out that he was to have a National Security Council meeting sometime in the following week.[2] He made the following points to the Foreign Intelligence Advisory Board:

—Escalation by the Soviets has put the heat on the United States and the recent action by 73 Senators[3] outlining support for the President in this crisis underlines the importance of the event.

—The President pointed out that the Board should be aware that Arab moderates could be inclined to lean in the direction of the United States due to the Soviet aggressiveness.

—The Arab moderates obviously do not want the balance of power to shift them.

—It is difficult to maintain a balance in the Middle East with the introduction of Soviet combat personnel into Egypt. The President pointed out that some maintained position that we should do nothing. But if we do nothing the Israelis may be forced to act. Also, it is apparent that there will be no settlement without U.S. and Soviet agreement. This may be possible sooner or later. If we wait for later, then the President visualizes some flash point with great dangers which might then ultimately result in agreement. The Soviets on the other hand probably are delighted with a status quo since they are exploiting it with greatly increased influence.

The President also pointed out that the Soviets fear the fedayeen just as does Nasser. However, on balance, to the degree that we line up solidly with Israel, the Soviets acquire support from the other elements by default. Finally, the President emphasized that the main danger today is that Israel may move militarily and that we will be looking

---

[1] Source: National Archives, Nixon Presidential Materials, NSC Files, Box 275, Agency Files, PFIAB, Vol. IV. Top Secret; Sensitive. The meeting was held in the Cabinet Room.

[2] See Document 166.

[3] See footnote 2, Document 160.

down the barrels with the Soviet Union again. On balance, the President believes that if there is to be a settlement, it must be imposed. It would be a settlement which would be not to the liking of either Israel or the Arabs. It is really a question of the degree of dissatisfaction shared by both. For this reason, the U.S. and the Soviets must talk, but at a time and under circumstances in which the Soviets feel it is in their interest to do so. They do not feel this way at present. So we must keep them worried about the Middle East. The President emphasized that he had no domestic political problem on this issue and it would be influenced only by the national interests. At present, he feels that it is necessary that we put Israel in a position that they can be a serious worry to the Soviets. The President added that the U.S. has no illusions about Four Power or Israeli/Nasser talks. The only solution would be one imposed by both the United States and the Soviet Union.

Franklin Murphy stated that the Arabs feel that the loss of oil is a deterrent to the United States and its actions with respect to Israel. He wondered whether or not we were studying the implications of what it would mean to lose Middle East oil. The President replied that this would be a serious turn of events, especially from Europe's point. On the other hand, the President pointed out the Arab oil producers cannot drink their oil and must have a market. This was the issue in Iran some years ago.

Franklin Murphy then added: Isn't there a wheel within a wheel. Without the benefits and revenues from the oil in Kuwait and Saudi Arabia, Egypt and the fedayeen movement would collapse. Dr. Kissinger added that the fedayeen movement was fundamentally subsidized by the moderate Arabs, as well as some Soviet support.

Robert Murphy stated if we examine the Middle East issue in depth, I feel that what you have said will be largely verified. The President replied: Yes, this indicates that the oil problem is not quite so bad as frequently depicted, and that in any event the Arabs must sell their oil.

Admiral Anderson stated that it is also important that we, the United States, do not get isolated on this issue and that we keep our moderate Arab friends with us. The President agreed that this is necessary on the surface at any rate.

Governor Rockefeller stated that as we look down the road, we can see the Soviets behind all the problems in the Middle East and he wondered whether or not they could absorb all of the Middle East's oil.

Franklin Murphy stated that while these are the realities of the Middle East situation, the evidence is that the Soviet's role in the Middle East is not understood in the Moslem world and they view it as strictly an anti-Israeli problem. Dr. Kissinger stated that the Moslems worry about the Soviet Union on entirely different grounds. Robert Murphy stated that he believed that on balance the Soviets do not enjoy that much prestige in the Middle East among the Arab nations. The President interrupted, nevertheless the wheels continue to turn. He wants to consider this issue on the 16th of June with the view of deciding where we go from here.

[Omitted here is discussion of Southeast Asia.]

162. Memorandum From Harold Saunders of the National Security Council Staff to the President's Assistant for National Security Affairs (Kissinger)[1]

Washington, June 8, 1970.

SUBJECT

Secretary Rogers' Conversation with Dobrynin

Attached is a copy of the memorandum of conversation between Secretary Rogers and Ambassador Dobrynin on June 2 (Tab A).[2] You are already familiar with the general outline of their discussion and the memcon adds little of importance to that. It does, however, give the text of the new Soviet formulations on the nature of peace and the obligations which the Arabs and Israelis would undertake in a peace settlement. You will recall that Assistant Secretary Sisco feels that these formulations represent a "slight advance." The following is a more detailed assessment.

The Formulations

Dobrynin informed Secretary Rogers that he was authorized to continue discussions on the Middle East with Assistant Secretary Sisco. He then referred to his discussion with Sisco earlier this year during which Sisco had asked for more detailed Soviet formulations on the nature of peace and the obligations which the Arabs and Israelis would undertake. At the same time, Dobrynin noted he had indicated the Soviet interest in more precise U.S. language on withdrawal and other matters. Dobrynin then handed the Secretary two papers with the following formulations (actually extensions or modifications of two points

---

[1] Source: National Archives, Nixon Presidential Materials, NSC Files, Box 712, Country Files, Europe, USSR, Vol. VIII. Secret; Nodis. Sent for information. A notation on the memorandum indicates Kissinger saw it.
[2] Document 159.

made in the original Soviet paper of June 17, 1969, with our underlining added):[3]

"Point 3, Section II

From the moment of deposit with the UN of the concluding document or documents the parties shall refrain from acts contradicting the cessation of the state of war and the establishment of the state of peace, in accordance with paragraphs 10 and 11, with the understanding that, *juridically, cessation of the state of war and establishment of the state of peace will begin at the same time of the completion of the first stage of the withdrawal of Israeli troops* from the territories occupied during the conflict of 1967."

"Point 11, Section II

The Arab countries, parties to the settlement, and Israel mutually agree

—to respect and recognize the sovereignty, territorial integrity, inviolability and political independence of each other and their mutual right to live in peace in secure and recognized borders without being subjected to threats or use of force;
—*to undertake everything that is necessary so that any military or hostile acts, with the threat or use of force against the other side will not originate from and are not committed from within their respective territories;*
—refrain from intervening directly or indirectly in each other's domestic affairs for any political, economic or other reasons."

In conclusion, Dobrynin commented that these two formulations along with the others that had been presented to Sisco previously—that is the June 1969 Soviet document and presumably Soviet commentary since early March—would stand or fall together.

Background

The new formulations must be viewed against the background of the recent history of our dialogue with the Soviets on a Middle East settlement (see Tab B[4] for a more detailed recapitulation). You will recall that in early March Dobrynin indicated to Secretary Rogers the Soviet willingness to resume bilateral talks and to meet U.S. wishes for more detailed formulations on the obligations of peace *provided* we would be more forthcoming on the issue of withdrawal, particularly regarding Sharm al-Shaikh, Gaza and Syria. He also said the USSR would be ready to supplement provisions in its plan on the cessation of the state of war by a provision on establishing, as a result of settlement, a state of peace. Dobrynin was not, however, addressing himself

---

[3] Printed here as italics. See Document 58.
[4] Tab B is printed as Document 151.

directly to our October 28 document[5] but rather was talking about modifications in the USSR's June 1969 proposals.

Before Dobrynin returned to Moscow, he had three other meetings at State on the Middle East—another session in late March with Secretary Rogers which completed setting the stage for two Sisco–Dobrynin meetings on April 1 and 6. Secretary Rogers made it clear that we were unwilling to go beyond our earlier proposals (the October 28 document on the UAR and the December 18 proposals on the Jordan aspect), although we had no objection to resuming the bilateral talks. Assistant Secretary Sisco's talks with Dobrynin were not very fruitful, although the door was left open to further discussions. Essentially, they reviewed the state of play, and Dobrynin made clear he had instructions to talk only from the Soviet June 1969 paper.

Analysis

It is possible to see, as Sisco does, a "slight advance" over their earlier positions. The caveat should be quickly added, however, that this may be highly illusionary. The Soviets have made an apparent concession on one key issue—Arab control of the fedayeen—but seem to have retrogressed in other important areas since last March. On balance, therefore, it may be that there is really no net movement in our favor.

On the positive side, the Soviets, after many months of pressure from us, have finally agreed in effect to the principle of the Arab governments assuming the obligation to control the fedayeen after a settlement. This has been a key issue for us because there is virtually no chance of bringing the Israelis along without such an Arab commitment. They have also given us half a loaf on the juridical timing of peace by saying now that a formal state of peace can come into effect after completion of the first stage of withdrawal.

On the negative side, the Soviets, by talking about modifications in their June document, seem to be wiping the slate clean of Sisco's Moscow talks last July and Secretary Rogers' New York talks in September which provided the basis for our October 28 document. In effect, they are still rejecting our total package in favor of building on their initial, and to us unacceptable, approach of a year ago. In fact, Dobrynin's comment that the two new formulations on peace would stand or fall together with "others" that had been presented to Sisco has a somewhat negative ring.

The Soviets seem to have raised other new barriers to progress. Their continuing insistence on obtaining more precise language from us on the question of withdrawal is probably the best example. In the Four Power talks they have made total withdrawal without any border

---

[5] See Document 98.

rectifications the condition for any further movement and they seem to be implying the same in our bilateral dialogue. At a minimum they want us to fill in the gaps such as Gaza, Jerusalem, Sharm al-Sheikh that we have so far left to the parties to negotiate. There is yet to be a satisfactory response from the Soviets on how the parties will negotiate, since they apparently wrote off the Rhodes formula last March.

Conclusion

On the whole it is difficult to hold out much hope for progress in the bilateral talks with the Soviets. They seem to be following a game plan that gives us just enough bait to remain interested while they try to sell us a position based on maximum Arab demands. For instance, the Arab commitment to control the fedayeen is important to us and the Israelis, but it hardly matches with our agreeing to spell out more on the withdrawal issue. Acceptance of control over the fedayeen is an important concession from the Soviets and Arabs but withdrawal is the foundation of the entire Israeli position.

The interesting question to ask, however, is: Does Moscow want these talks more than we do? It would seem to me that the USSR has a greater interest than we do in talking just for the sake of talking. They want to preserve the image of reasonableness while they help the Egyptians militarily and benefit from the deteriorating situation on the ground. Also, Nasser seems to want to keep the negotiating option open and it would be difficult for the Soviets to cut him off. Our main interest is in real progress toward a settlement. We have some interest in looking reasonable too, but in present circumstances we are billed as the obstacle to progress, so the talks do not provide much in that regard. They could be broken off *if* we chose some other move that would cast the U.S. as the peacemaker and the USSR as the obstructionist.

I will be sending you shortly a more comprehensive analysis of our talks with the Soviets on the Middle East.

163.   **Memorandum From William Hyland of the National Security Council Staff to the President's Assistant for National Security Affairs (Kissinger)[1]**

Washington, June 8, 1970.

SUBJECT

Soviet Intentions in the Middle East and Our Options

Any decision made on the Middle East necessarily involves some basic assumptions about the character of the Soviet position.

The point is correctly made that had it not been for the deep penetration raids the Soviets would not have involved themselves directly. This is probably right. The Soviets had no master plan. We have the hardest possible intelligence that the decisions leading to the present situation were approved by Brezhnev on January 28–29, in the wake of Nasser's secret visit to Moscow. The Soviets had no choice but to support Nasser, and strong moves were obviously called for.

Nevertheless, it is highly irrelevant to our present policy choices whether the Israelis are at fault. The character of the Soviet move into the UAR should not be underrated simply because Israeli action precipitated it.

It is a unique turn of Soviet policy—never before have the Soviets put their own forces in combat jeopardy for the sake of a non-communist government. They have only done so now because of the enormous stakes involved for their power position. One of the dangerous consequences of their forward policy in the Middle East is that having accumulated a large vested interest, they have had to devise new ways to protect their gains. It is not only a question of Soviet willingness to accept a much higher level of risk, it is their willingness to do so in a situation over which their control is limited, and in which no one, including the Kremlin, can foresee the outcome. This is why it is a dangerous path the Soviets have embarked on, and why we must treat it with the utmost seriousness.

It is argued that now [that] the Soviets have rescued Nasser both of them may suddenly change their spots, and be prepared to negotiate seriously. This is to say the least, doubtful. Having scored an immense psychological gain, with apparent impunity, it has generally

---

[1] Source: National Archives, Nixon Presidential Materials, NSC Files, Box 712, Country Files, Europe, USSR, Vol. VIII. Secret. Sent for information. A notation on the memorandum indicates Kissinger saw it.

been the Russians tactic first of all to consolidate their gains, and then press forward, testing the ground as they move. Clearly, there is no evidence from the Soviets that their bargaining position has softened. To seize on minor changes in old Soviet formulas as "movement" is a delusion. If anything, the Soviet position is tougher now than only a few weeks ago.

The toughening can only spring from their estimate of what their moves have cost thus far and what the future risks and gains are. Looking at our position and the Israeli standdown from deep raids, the Soviets must conclude that we have acquiesced in their direct intervention. Indeed, they could well read our latest statement (Rogers to Dobrynin)[2] as confirmation that we accept the Soviet claim of "defensive" involvement, and are only concerned that a movement toward the canal would not be "defensive."

Thus, the question of whether the Soviets will in fact, begin to inch forward becomes a crucial determinant. The policy issue is: are the Soviets more likely to extend their protective umbrella if we proceed with the sale of aircraft to Israel, or if we withhold them?

The conventional wisdom is that the Soviets will probably not move, mainly because of the risk of combat with the Israelis. There is, however, some evidence that they are indeed already "inching" forward (the construction sites along the canal). Moreover, it would seem a logical extension of Soviet strategy to do so. The near term Soviet objective in the Middle East is to destroy Western influence. The main enemy is not Israel but the West in general and the United States in particular. The road to the displacement of the West, however, now lies through Soviet demonstration that they cannot only protect their clients, but reverse the losses they suffered in 1967.

One means of doing so is to negotiate a settlement. But this presumes that the Soviets prefer a stabilized situation to one of controlled tensions. The history of Soviet involvement demonstrates that their major gains have come during periods of tension and crises, and that during periods of relative quiet on the Arab-Israeli front, Soviet influence suffers. Thus, there is every reason to doubt that the Soviets want a settlement on any terms but Israeli capitulation, unless the Arabs themselves are prepared to make the concessions.

The means to humiliate Israel and force their withdrawal is first of all to demonstrate that Israel has waning international support and, of utmost importance, waning support from the US. Second, the Soviets and the Arabs must demonstrate in practice that Israel's options are gradually but steadily narrowing.

---

[2] See Document 159.

The Soviets could conclude that the present situation represents a sufficient gain to test the possibilities of discussion with us. Their opening moves in New York and in the conversation with Secretary Rogers do not support such a conclusion. Indeed, the two and four power talks seem a dismal failure. Thus, one suspects that the key to the next phase is our reaction on the ground. If we do nothing or very little to support Israel, the Soviets will then be tempted to cut a further slice of the salami and inch forward to the canal. If, however, we support Israel the Soviets will be forced to pause and consider the consequences of their increasing involvement.

As for the argument that this is exactly what the Soviets want us to do because it will demolish our position in the Arab world, this also is debatable if not altogether wrong. (It is made exclusively by Arabs and not Sovietologists.) The Soviets respect power and strength. They understand military strength best of all. This does not mean, of course, that they are eager to fight, or that they believe in the indiscriminate use of force. But they do not understand restraint; it confuses them, and in the end leads them to conclude that there is room for their own forward movement.

If the United States does not support Israel demonstratively with military assistance, the Soviets will ponder why we refuse to do so. Ultimately, they will conclude that we are deterred because of either domestic, political and economic concerns or because of the consequences of military escalation. Soviet denials, talk of confrontation and their attempts to blame Israel for such notions suggest sensitivity (and vulnerability) to strong US moves. No one can *guarantee* what the Soviets will do if we do reinforce Israel but one can be fairly confident that a display of weakness will not be met with conciliation and compromise.

Our Options

The two strategies presented in the first Review Group paper in effect reject this analysis. The essential judgment as presented in that paper is that it is preferable to exploit the present situation to put Israel under pressure, than to "confront" the Soviet Union. And that if this fails we can always confront Moscow.

The way in which the Options and argumentation are constructed, one cannot but agree.

No one should want to confront the USSR deliberately in the way it is described in the State paper. It would be insane. For example, having decided on some undefined posture of "confrontation" we close off all escape hatches for the USSR by breaking off the diplomatic contact.

There are a number of aimless military "moves" described. The only principle seems to be that to move pieces on a chess board is a policy. What would the Soviets conclude? That we were about to fight? Not likely. More likely that we were engaging in some bluff. What would be the objective of military posturing? What would our demands be? They are nowhere spelled out. Are we seeking Soviet withdrawal? A settlement? Or, as is seen from this scenario, a whopping open-ended crisis.

One can only conclude that this course was described in such a way as to increase the attractiveness of the second strategy—the "path of accommodation."

Presumably, no one opposes the "path of accommodation" but how to embark on such a course is the real issue. The paper presumes that putting Israel under pressure is the best way. Suppose, by some wild stretch of the imagination, that Israel buckled under our pressures. Would a compromise settlement then be likely? If the Arabs and the Russians sense this trend why should they make concessions. Better to wait, they would reason.

Our aim should not be an imposed settlement, which could not possibly be durable, but one that emerges from the common interests of both sides. This is a cliché, but still valid. The course described in the State paper, however, could only feed Arab ambitions and frustrate the Israeli to the point of desperation.

The immediate task is to create a political-military environment that provides an incentive to both sides to either stabilize the present situation or make mutual concessions.

This leads to the main point. It is mandatory to the creation of such an environment that we counter the Soviet intervention with a credible demonstration of our own—a demonstration that we are not cowed by the prospect of escalation or by the costs to our political and economic interests in the Arab countries.

Warnings alone are not enough. Indeed, since we have presented several serious warnings, the more we present the less credible. Breaking off contacts serves no end, and moving military forces is at least premature (the Pueblo fiasco should demonstrate the futility of moving aircraft carriers and airplanes that we do not intend to use).

Because the dispatch of aircraft to Israel has become the symbol for measuring our policy, it has, perhaps unfortunately, become the only immediate issue.

Only *after* demonstrating our willingness to take up this option can we expect to convince Israel of the need to make some political concession and convince the Soviets and Arabs that we are not deterred by their recent actions.

How many planes [and] in what sequence are secondary issues which should not obscure the primary challenge of the Soviets. The announced basis for such a move should be that the Soviets by their direct involvement have threatened the military balance, that we have failed to receive a satisfactory explanation of their aims or reassurance of their intention. Accordingly, we are committed to maintain the position of Israel.

164. Memorandum From the President's Assistant for National Security Affairs (Kissinger) to President Nixon[1]

Washington, June 8, 1970.

SUBJECT

Soviet Moves on Southeast Asia

We have learned that a Soviet Deputy Foreign Minister, N.P. Firyubin, is coming to New York next week to "visit" the Soviet UN Mission and confer with Ambassador Malik. The interesting aspect is that Firyubin's area of substantive responsibility includes Southeast Asia. Moreover, visits by Soviet deputy foreign ministers to the UN (when little is happening there currently) are not usual, although Firyubin may be filling in for First Deputy Minister Kuznetsov who normally supervises Soviet UN activities but is currently tied up in negotiations with the Chinese. With the next UN General Assembly being a special one in view of the 25th anniversary, Soviet planning for it may be more than routine and might include a trip here by Kosygin. Other heads of government are planning to attend. It is quite likely, however, that Firyubin's purpose may not only be to talk with Malik on UN matters, but to make himself available for contacts with us. Any such contacts, in view of his responsibilities, would logically focus on Cambodia, Laos or Vietnam.

He could simply be on a fishing expedition to gain first hand a better insight into our policies and future moves. If Firyubin has some special message he will undoubtedly take the initiative to let us know.

---

[1] Source: National Archives, Nixon Presidential Materials, NSC Files, Box 712, Country Files, Europe, USSR, Vol. VIII. Secret. Sent for information. Drafted on June 4 by Sonnenfeldt who forwarded it to Kissinger under a covering memorandum that reads: "As you requested, I have done a memorandum for the President (Tab A) speculating on some of the reasons behind the unusual visit of Soviet Deputy Foreign Minister Firyubin to New York." A notation on the memorandum indicates the President saw it.

Whether this trip could involve an important political break in the Communist position on Indochina is simply not predictable. On the record, it seems unlikely that the Soviets are in a position to take any major initiative at this time because of their more complicated relations with Hanoi and Peking. It seems likely that the Soviets, therefore, are acting on their own.

They may have in mind, however, testing our reaction to some future moves on the negotiating front, including the possibility of a new international conference or the re-establishment of the ICC in Cambodia.

Our Embassy in Moscow speculates that Firyubin will sound out U Thant and interested states on Cambodia, in anticipation of U Thant's trip to Moscow in mid-June.

It is also worth recalling that Malik has played a key role in breaking two crises (in 1949 and 1953). This was remembered at the time of his trial balloon on an Indochina conference in April. Perhaps Firyubin wishes to discuss some new scenario with Malik and insure a better coordination with Moscow.

In short, we cannot be at all sure what is up. It does seem that this is no routine visit and the Soviets may be probing for some new contacts or testing the ground for future moves on the Southeast Asia front. Some light might be shed on the Soviet position when we learn the details of Gromyko's discussion on Indochina during his current Paris visit.[2]

---

[2] Gromyko visited Paris June 1–5. In a memorandum from Rogers to Nixon drafted in EUR but apparently never sent, the Secretary described Gromyko's visit as follows: "Although Gromyko's visit was useful to the French in calling attention to their role as an independent major power, it yielded nothing new on the substantive side and disappointed them in some respects. The problem was the Soviets' unwillingness to make concessions these days, even to please friends like the French. Additionally, if some reports can be credited, Gromyko was not very adept at sugar-coating the unpalatable pills he dispensed to his French hosts." (Ibid., RG 59, Central Files 1970–73, POL 1)

165. **Memorandum From Harold Saunders of the National
      Security Council Staff to the President's Assistant for
      National Security Affairs (Kissinger)**[1]

Washington, June 9, 1970.

SUBJECT

Evolution of Positions in US–USSR Talks on the Middle East

Attached is a detailed study of the evolution of the U.S. and Soviet positions on a Middle East settlement through six negotiating phases over the last 15 months.[2] Since that study is comprehensive, the following is an analytical summary of the changes on each major issue.

Negotiating Procedure

The US has insisted throughout—either in text or in gloss—on direct negotiations at some stage. In September–October of last year, the U.S. added the concept of Rhodes-type talks to the discussions and text.

The USSR in early phases urged us not to complicate the process by emphasizing direct contacts. In September, Gromyko told Rogers he would agree to Rhodes-type talks[3] (though he appears to have understood that direct talks were involved only at signing) if the U.S. were more precise on boundaries. In December, the USSR returned to the position that the big powers should not commit the parties to any particular form of negotiation, but the Soviet December 23 response[4] seemed to leave open the door to some procedure comparable to Rhodes talks. In April, Dobrynin told Sisco that the Soviets could no longer accept the Rhodes formula. Dobrynin's informal alternative was that the parties would have contact between themselves through Jarring with the understanding he could use "various forms."

Timing of Withdrawal and Peace

The US has insisted throughout that Israeli withdrawal would begin at the same moment the state of war is ended and a formal state of peace begins.

The USSR has persistently struggled to create a distinction that would satisfy Israel by having the peace agreement come into effect on

---

[1] Source: National Archives, Nixon Presidential Materials, NSC Files, Box 646, Country Files, Middle East, General, Vol. VI, August 1970. Secret; Nodis. Sent for information. The memorandum was not initialed by Saunders.

[2] Attached but not printed.

[3] See footnote 2, Document 87.

[4] See Document 109.

the day Israel begins withdrawing but would permit the Arabs to say that final peace does not come into being until withdrawal is completed. Until recently, they have tried to do this by distinguishing between de facto (beginning of withdrawal) and de jure (end of withdrawal) peace. In their most recent formulation, however, the Soviets have compromised by saying that juridically cessation of the state of war and establishment of the state of peace will begin when the "first stage" of Israeli withdrawal is completed. The USSR has also dwelt on a two-phase Israeli withdrawal which would permit UAR troops to move into the Canal area as soon as Israeli troops have withdrawn 30–40 kilometers.

Obligations of Peace

The US has enumerated the general obligations of nations to one another as defined in Article 2 of the UN Charter. In addition, the US has insisted on a stipulation that governments control all hostile acts from their territory, specifically including those of non-governmental individuals and organizations.

The USSR accepted in its June 17 document[5] the general obligations of Article 2 of the UN Charter, but until recently resisted inclusion of any specific stipulation that would have the effect of committing the Arabs to control the fedayeen. They have recently (June 2), however, given in to us on this point.

Boundaries

The US position has evolved:

—March 24: "Rectifications from pre-existing lines should be confined to those required for mutual security and should not reflect the weight of conquest."
—October 28: Israel should withdraw to the pre-war UAR-Israel border provided adequate security arrangements can be negotiated in Gaza, Sharm al-Shaykh and the Sinai.

The USSR has insisted throughout on total withdrawal to pre-war lines. Since we went to our fallback position on October 28,[6] the Soviets have increasingly pressed us to be more detailed and specific especially on Gaza, Sharm al-Shaykh and the Golan Heights. They appear to be in the process of making any further progress contingent on this issue as they have already done in the Four Power Talks.

Demilitarized Zones

The US position has evolved from stating that the entire Sinai should be demilitarized to holding that the belligerents should negotiate their size and the procedures for enforcing them.

---

[5] See Document 58.
[6] See Document 98.

The USSR has consistently held that demilitarized zones should be on both sides of the borders, not giving advantage to either side. The UN Security Council should work out procedures for enforcing them.

Waterways

The US has insisted throughout on freedom of passage for Israel through the Straits of Tiran and the Suez Canal. In our October formulations, we have linked security arrangements at Sharm al-Shaykh to securing free passage through the Straits.

The USSR has accepted the principle of free passage but linked passage through the Canal to the Constantinople Convention of 1888 which permits governments sovereign over canals to close them to states with whom they are at war. This has provided the UAR's justification for closing the Canal to Israelis in the past. [The US has resisted this.][7]

Refugees

The US has accepted the principle of free choice for the refugees between repatriation to Israel and resettlement with compensation. But the US has balanced this with progressively more specific provisions to give Israel control over the individuals and the total number of refugees allowed repatriation. The latest formulation includes an annual quota.

The USSR simply calls on Israel to carry out past UN resolutions which call for repatriation or resettlement with compensation. The USSR has resisted any restrictions, although at one point they were willing to discuss it as a possible side understanding.

Nature of Agreement

The US, while experimenting with language, has from the start insisted that the final accord should be an agreement or contract between the parties, should be reciprocally binding, should be signed by the parties, and should be deposited with the UN for endorsement by the four permanent members of the Security Council.

The USSR in earlier stages clearly accepted the idea of a binding document—a final accord *between* the parties—signed by the parties and deposited at the UN. However, the December 23 reply ignored this point entirely and the Soviets have not clarified it since then.

Conclusions

What most strikes me after completing this review is how little real progress we have made after 15 months of talking with the Sovi-

---

[7] Brackets in the source text.

ets on the Middle East. For all practical purposes, we are now effectively back to where we began when the Soviets presented their working document to us in June 1969. After actively discussing a joint document between June 17—when they produced their draft—and September 30, the Soviets in December simply turned aside our October 28 formulations—containing a major concession from us on boundaries—as providing no basis for a joint document.

Now they have reopened the dialogue with a concession to us—Arab control of the fedayeen—but have linked it to our being even more forthcoming on the withdrawal issue (in effect asking us to bargain away all of Israel's position). Moreover, by continuing to insist on talking only about modifications in their June documents, the Soviets seem to be wiping the slate clean of Sisco's Moscow talks last July[8] and Secretary Roger's talks in September[9] which provided the basis for our October 28 document.

Beyond this there are a number of important issues on which the Soviets have either retrogressed (negotiating procedures, withdrawal, nature of agreement), held firm (waterways, refugees, demilitarized zones) or not moved enough on to make any real difference (timing of withdrawal, juridical state of peace).

It is hard to escape the conclusion that the Soviets are not negotiating in good faith with us. They seem to be too content with the present situation on the ground and our difficulties in the area to back down much from the maximum Arab demands. This has taken place when—as a review of the above positions shows—we might well reach agreement if they would take as much distance from the Arab position as we have taken from Israel's. Yet we have no evidence that the Soviets intend to do this.

If this is a valid interpretation, the logical question then arises as to why the Soviets seem intent on keeping up a dialogue on the Middle East. It may be that they view the bilateral talks as a potential escape hatch if the situation on the ground begins to get out of hand and their commitments to the Arabs start them down the road to a confrontation with us and Israel. They are after all playing a dangerous game with their SA–3s and pilots. It may also be that the Soviets view their talks with us as a way of keeping us a bit off guard as their military presence increases in the area and as a potential safeguard against some precipitate act by us to reverse the situation. Finally, there is the apparent fact that Nasser still wants to keep the political settlement option open and the Soviets would rather do his bidding than let him alone with us.

---

[8] See Document 69.
[9] See Documents 81 and 87.

166.   Editorial Note

On June 10, 1970, the National Security Council met from 9:36–11:24 a.m. to discuss the Middle East. In an unsigned and undated memorandum for President Nixon about issues for the meeting, Henry Kissinger, the President's Assistant for National Security Affairs, described the "implications of the Soviet presence in Egypt":

"The character of the Soviet move in the UAR should not be underrated.

"You may hear the argument made (by Defense) that this move was precipitated by Israeli action or that it is purely defensive and does not threaten Israel. These arguments do not meet the main point: This is a unique turn of Soviet policy—never before have the Soviets put their own forces in combat jeopardy for the sake of a non-Communist government.

"It is argued that now the Soviets have rescued Nasser both of them may suddenly change character and be prepared to negotiate seriously. This seems doubtful. Having scored a psychological gain with apparent impunity, it has generally been the Soviet tactic first to consolidate their gains and then to press forward, testing the ground as they move.

"The problem, therefore, is not simply that the Soviet military presence may have, at a minimum, limited Israeli military options. The problem is that the USSR has established a new kind of foothold in the UAR and the U.S. has a strong interest in preventing its consolidation and expansion.

"Some Common Perceptions—A Critique

"You will hear argument over what the U.S. interest requires and how far the U.S. should go in trying to check the USSR. Some of this argument rests on assumptions that should be carefully examined.

"1. The Israeli view is that if Israel and the U.S. will only stand fast, the USSR and the Arabs will decide to negotiate. This means that the U.S. must give Israel all the equipment it needs and make no concessions to the USSR.

"The problem with this is that the Israelis have not really offered the Arabs a negotiating position the Arabs could even consider accepting. So the Arabs feel they have no choice but to fight. Thus the U.S. is left backing Israel in a war of attrition that seems likely to lead only to another war—probably involving the USSR—without any negotiating escape to offer Moscow.

"2. The Defense Department view is that all we have to do is to get the Israelis off the Suez Canal to begin the process of reaching a settlement and that will prevent further erosion of U.S. influence. Their argument is that the U.S. has no interest in the Mid-East great enough to warrant a nuclear showdown with the USSR. The U.S. is militarily over-extended and has every interest in avoiding involvement in the Mid-East. Besides, the Arab-Israeli problem is not susceptible of military solution.

"The problems with this view are that: (a) If the U.S. shows that it does not have enough interest in the Mid-East to warrant a showdown, then the USSR will never back off. (b) If Israel does not believe the U.S. will defend its existence against the USSR, Israel will have no incentive whatsoever to agree to a settlement based on withdrawal from present lines.

"3. It is also commonly said that the Soviets are acting in the UAR purely in a defensive capacity and that the U.S., therefore, need not be concerned because the Soviets will not threaten Israel.

"Yet it would be logical for the USSR to extend its influence as far as possible. The near term Soviet objective in the Middle East is to destroy Western influence. The main enemy is not Israel but the West in general and the U.S. in particular. Therefore, it must be assumed that the USSR will do all it can to that end—over and above defending their client." (National Archives, Nixon Presidential Materials, NSC Files, Box 1155, Harold Saunders Files, US Peace Initiative for Mid-East, 6/10– 7/23/70)

At the NSC meeting on June 10, President Nixon opened by asking Director of Central Intelligence Richard Helms for a briefing on the Middle East:

"Mr. Helms began by noting that the new Soviet presence required careful evaluation. Israel retained military superiority, but the elements of the Soviet presence are under careful study.

"The Soviets have 4–5 regiments of SA–3 missiles in the UAR and 3–5 squadrons of Soviet-piloted MIG 21 aircraft.

"The President interjected: 'Are you stating that as a fact? Are we now convinced?'

"Mr. Helms replied that we feel no doubt that these forces are there. The debate within the intelligence community is over how they have been used. We have intelligence on the forces themselves [2 lines of source text not declassified] On the basis of intelligence from all these sources, the presence of the missiles and the pilots is unquestioned. The big issue is how the Soviets intend to use them.

"The President asked what the number of Russians in Egypt other than diplomats is. Mr. Helms replied that it is in the neighborhood of 10,000. It has doubled in the last six months.

"Mr. Helms continued, saying that the Soviet forces are located mainly in the Nile valley. The Israelis have confined their recent attack to the area ajacent to the Suez Canal. The question now is whether the Soviets will refrain from moving their missiles and pilots into that area near the Canal and whether the Israelis will refrain from challenging the Soviet pilots.

"Intelligence confirms 13 sites of SA–3 missiles. These are manned by 2600–3700 Soviet personnel. There are probably 6–7 other sites under construction. These are located in the Nile Delta north of Cairo, west of Cairo, south of Cairo in connection with a Soviet-manned airfield and at Aswan. The Israelis have unconfirmed reports of SA–3 sites—but not equipment—along the Canal.

"This equipment arrived in March and April. Three squadrons of Soviet-piloted aircraft are flying from three bases—15 aircraft in each squadron with about 90 pilots by present count. The pilots arrived in February and March. [2 *lines of source text not declassified*]

"As a rule, the Soviets stay clear of the Suez Canal. The one major exception [4 *lines of source text not declassified*]

"Israel has publicly stated that it would avoid the Nile valley but would maintain supremacy over the Canal. Israel has said it would bomb anything along the Canal. They have been bombing heavily bunkers they maintain are being built to house equipment related to the SA–3 missile. U.S. intelligence analysts are inclined to think that these sites are for the SA–2 missile, but they have been so heavily bombed that we may never know what they were intended for.

"On the ground, the Israelis only have some 5–700 men along the Bar Lev line on their side of the Canal. There are some 93,000 Egyptians on the other side of the Canal altogether. Dayan says that the main Israeli objective is to keep these Egyptians from massing for a cross-Canal attack.

"As far as the Arab-Israeli military balance is concerned, the UAR has some 210–250 aircraft in 20 squadrons. But it does not have enough qualified pilots. Israel has 81 supersonic aircraft and 121 subsonic aircraft and 500 jet pilots. Israel's superiority rests on pilot quality. We assume that Israeli pilots are the equal of ours. Israel keeps 85% of its aircraft flying, while the Egyptians keep only about 75% in the air. The Israelis are able to mount 5 sorties per aircraft per day, while the Arabs can only manage 2. Israeli aircraft have superior performance characteristics. The addition of some Soviet pilots will improve the UAR ability to intercept Israeli attackers if the Soviets engage. Soviet pilots are probably more capable than the Egyptian pilots. But they lack combat experience.

"The new factor in the situation is the potential for attrition of Israeli aircraft in a prolonged contest with the Soviets. They could exhaust the Israelis in both aircraft and pilots. Israel could at some point come to consider losses intolerable. The present Israeli losses are somewhat less than the annual traffic toll. In terms of economic or demography Israel could stand such levels of losses. But Israel takes losses hard and any level of losses creates a psychological factor on which the Israeli level of tolerance is relatively low.

"This is why Israeli strategy is based on the pre-emptive strike to keep the enemy from bringing its numbers to bear against Israel. This strategy now seems unworkable. It has for some time because of the dispersal of Arab aircraft and the hardening of protective hangars on Arab airfields. Now there is the additional factor that the presence of Soviet pilots could bring on a U.S.-Soviet clash. With the strategy of pre-emption perhaps lost to Israel, the Israelis have more reason than ever to try to control the area along the Suez Canal. The Israelis believe that unless they sustain their present level of attacks or increase it, the Arabs will be so emboldened as to step up the war of attrition.

"Israel's ability to maintain air superiority seems to depend on what the Soviets do. The indicators of Soviet intention are the fact that one Soviet pilot on May 14 did pursue an Israeli aircraft and the [*less than 1 line of source text not declassified*] which indicate the possibility that the Soviets are moving SA–3 missile sites up to the Canal. On the other hand, since May 14, there has been no identified incidents of Soviet pilot pursuit. If the Soviet pilots are ordered to keep their present pattern this situation could go on for some time. If they move up to the Canal, Israel could be quickly worn down. Even at that, the impact of such a Soviet move might be more important psychologically than militarily.

"At the least, the Soviet presence has probably already emboldened the Arabs. At most, a situation has been created in which the balance could be altered to Israel's disadvantage. Again, the real effect on the balance will depend on what the Soviets decide to do.

"U.S. assistance to date is as follows: 40 Phantoms have been delivered and 3 have been lost; 10 remain to be delivered. Eighty-eight Skyhawks have been delivered with 12 remaining."

After a brief discussion of [other subjects] Nixon returned to the Soviet Union:

"The President said that he wanted to be sure he understood one point: Is it true that, since World War II, the Soviets have not lost any men in non-Communist countries in combat situations? Mr. Helms replied that Soviet officers have been lost in Egypt in the last year. They may also have lost a few in Korea which we never identified—some Soviet pilots.

"The President said this fact underscored for him the enormous significance of this recent Soviet step. It involves Soviet personnel in becoming casualties in a combat situation outside a Communist country. To them, this poses a very serious problem. [*2 lines of source text not declassified*]

"Mr. Helms replied that [2 *lines of source text not declassified*]. The judgment which he had described was not just a casual one.

"The President asked what the Soviets say about the fact that they have generally had a free ride for the last 25 years, using proxies to do their work for them.

"Secretary Rogers said the Soviets do not talk about numbers of combat personnel. They do not deny or admit that they have combat personnel or pilots in the UAR. They say that the reason the Soviets are training Egyptian forces is that the Israeli deep penetration raids in January made this necessary. Whatever the Soviets are doing, the Soviets say has a purely defensive role. They say that they have to back up Nasser. The Secretary concluded that, as long as the deep penetration raids do not continue, the present posture will probably be maintained.

"Secretary Rogers continued that this is a good time to try to get negotiations started. The parties have never really negotiated with each other. This is a good time. Israel is concerned about its future. Nasser is concerned about the Soviet presence. The Soviets are possibly willing to help with a political settlement, though maybe this possibility is remote. But for the first time the Soviets seem to be talking in more serious terms.

"The Secretary proposed that the U.S. use the next three months to try to get negotiations started. He felt that we should continue to sell planes to Israel at about the same rate as in the recent past. At the same time we should make a major effort in New York under Ambassador Jarring to get negotiations started. 'We think there is a good chance Israel will go along now.' The Secretary said his plan is to have a low-key announcement in about a week. He thought there was a possibility to get negotiations started. Until we do, there is no possibility of a settlement. He repeated that he felt the Israelis and the Soviets are interested.

"The President turned to Dr. Kissinger to brief on the issues involved.

"Dr. Kissinger said he had intended to draw together some of the issues which had been raised in the Special Review Group meetings on this subject, but he would like to go back a half a step to start with.

"The immediate issue is aircraft for Israel. The State Department view has been as Secretary Rogers outlined it—that we should continue some shipments of aircraft to Israel while we launch a diplomatic initiative. The Defense Department view has been that we should provide no planes now because deliveries would inflame the Arab world.

"Dr. Kissinger continued that discussion of some of the issues underlies any decision we may make on aircraft. For instance, although the facts of Soviet intervention in the UAR are pretty agreed, there are different views of Soviet purpose and of the significance of the Soviet move:

"—One view is that the Soviet move is entirely defensive, that the Soviets had no choice but to make this move in response to Israel's deep penetration raids and that the significance of the move is therefore limited.

"—Another view is that, whatever Soviet intentions are, we are confronted with certain results. The Soviet move does free the UAR to be more belligerent. Even if there is an Arab-Israeli settlement, if the Soviet forces remain in Egypt, the UAR will feel stronger in whatever adventures it decides to pursue. Britain did not want an empire; it simply acquired one in the course of seeking coaling stations on the commercial route to the Far East. The practical consequence of a Soviet presence in the UAR is that it is a major geopolitical fact with which we have to deal. The consequences cannot be judged by Soviet intent.

"Secretary Rogers asked what difference it makes which view one takes. Dr. Kissinger replied that the view one takes makes some difference on whether the USSR is confronted now or not. The President said there was a question of whether the USSR should be confronted on a broader front. Dr. Kissinger pointed out that even if the Arab-Israeli dispute is settled, that still leaves a problem for the U.S. in that the Soviet Union can work behind the radical Arabs in further eroding U.S. influence in the area.

"The President asked whether it is in the Soviet interest to see an Arab-Israeli settlement. The USSR may not want to see Israel 'go down the tube.' It may well be that the Soviets have an interest in having Israel there as a 'burr under the U.S. saddle.' The President said he questioned whether the Soviets have an interest in a real settlement; he could understand their interest in a truce or a cooling of the situation but had more question about a full settlement. He felt that Dr. Kissinger's point is relevant and that it is not right for the US to look at what the Soviets are doing in the UAR as an isolated problem.

"Secretary Rogers said he thought everyone could agree to that.

"Mr. Packard noted one Soviet interest that had not been mentioned: The Soviets want the Suez Canal open."

After discussion of other Middle East issues, Kissinger raised additional points about the Soviet Union. According to minutes of the meeting:

"Dr. Kissinger returned to the thread of his briefing, noting that the third element that must be dealt with in any strategy is the USSR. The normal pattern of Soviet activity is to begin with a relatively modest step and then to inch forward testing the ground as they go.

"The President interjected by asking how the Soviets proceeded in Cuba. The replies were vague, and Dr. Kissinger continued briefing.

"Dr. Kissinger said that the problem with the USSR is to convince them that their present course has incalculable risks. But at the same time we do not want to engage Soviet prestige and leave the Soviets no escape. The choice for the U.S. is not whether to try for a settlement or to confront the USSR. The choice is how to do both in order to achieve a settlement."

After a brief discussion of other factors affecting a Middle Eastern peace settlement, discussion returned to the Soviet position:

"The President said he still came back to a basic point that militates against a settlement: What is in it for the Soviets? The present situation is costing them some money. They may be concerned about a possible confrontation with the U.S. But if they look at that proposition coldly, they know as well as we know around the NSC table that the likelihood of U.S. action directly against them is 'in doubt.' It did not use to be in doubt. That was what the Lebanon invasion of 1958 was about.

"Again looking at the Soviets: they have made noises that they would like to see a settlement. They have a muscle-bound bureaucracy and have trouble seeing things in gradations. It may be that as far as the Soviets are concerned our job is to get them to play a role in imposing a settlement. The ingredient that is missing and has to be supplied in some way is the incentive to them to play that role.

"Secretary Rogers noted that the Soviets are concerned about the Chinese and about the Fedayeen. Soviet officials often allude to those problems. Nasser is concerned about what has happened in Jordan and that he may be in some danger.

"Ambassador Yost said that the Soviets do not call the tune in Cairo. If a settlement in Arab interests emerges, he did not believe that the Soviets could prevent it.

"Mr. Sisco said that, while he agreed about the Fedayeen and the Chinese, he put greater weight on what the Soviets think of American will. The real leverage on the USSR is fear of a confrontation with the U.S. We ought to be looking at the 6th Fleet to see whether it is projecting American power to the maximum extent. His conclusion, he said, is that the Soviets feel now that they can broaden the conflict. We are essentially up against a Soviet political strategy, but at the end of the line they must feel that they could run into a confrontation with the U.S.

"Mr. Richardson indicated his agreement. He felt that we need to find a way to use the only lever that we really have—the Soviet fear of confrontation.

"Mr. Packard said that this is a matter of timing. He said we have to move ahead soon. We should avoid moving planes. He liked the idea of having a pool of aircraft perhaps in Texas as a reserve for Israel which would not be moved to Israel unless the situation required.

"The President concluded the meeting by saying that he would look at all of this."

(National Archives, Nixon Presidential Materials, NSC Files, NSC Institutional Files (H-Files), Box H–109, NSC Minutes, Originals, 1970)

---

167.   Memorandum of Conversation[1]

Washington, June 10, 1970, 7:05–7:34 p.m.

PARTICIPANTS

> The President
> Ambassador Dobrynin
> Henry A. Kissinger

Prior to our departure for the *Sequoia*,[2] the President asked me to take Dobrynin to the Map Room in the Residence where the President joined us for a few minutes.

The President said that he was delighted that we were going to the *Sequoia* for a talk and he hoped that we would enjoy the breeze and talk fully. He wanted Dobrynin to know that I had his full confidence and that this was the channel in which he wished things to be settled. He also stressed to Dobrynin that things that were in the public arena might be put in other channels but, if serious business was to be done, it was to be done in our channel.

He reminded Dobrynin that at their last meeting, he had told Dobrynin that he had been in office nine months and it was about time that the baby was born; therefore, there was a certain disappointment that there had been no progress. He wanted him to know that he was prepared to let bygones be bygones and start afresh if the Soviet Union was prepared to take a similar approach. He wanted it clearly understood that the course on Vietnam was set and there was no sense in trying to press us to change our policies. Similarly, he understood certain Soviet security requirements that we were not disposed to challenge. He wanted Dobrynin and me to speak in this spirit.

---

[1] Source: National Archives, Nixon Presidential Materials, NSC Files, Box 489, President's Trip Files, Dobrynin/Kissinger, 1970, Part 2, Vol. I. Top Secret; Sensitive; Nodis. The conversation was held in the Map Room at the White House. The time and place of the meeting are from the President's Daily Diary. (Ibid., White House Central Files)

[2] The Presidential yacht.

Dobrynin asked whether he could make a few comments. He said that he appreciated that spirit and he felt the same way. It was time to let bygones be bygones and concentrate on the future. There was no sense in arguing about how we got into Cambodia and other areas of the world. The future would determine how able we were to solve the problems of peace. He did want to say, however, that the Soviet Union was very eager to come to an agreement on the Middle East, but was being constantly thwarted by the petty legalism of Sisco's approach. He would like to urge the President to take a personal interest in the negotiations, because only a willingness to deal with the problems at the highest levels would make it possible to come to a conclusion.

The President emphasized that we had an NSC meeting on the Middle East[3] and that this was one area in which matters could get out of control because of the pressures of public opinion. He said, "The Fedayeen are not in your control, and our public opinion is not in our control." Dobrynin said, "The Fedayeen are not in our control but we don't let them control our actions, and we make very sure that we keep tight control of our military forces." The President said that he just wanted Dobrynin to understand that we were serious in our efforts, but that we were pragmatic and precise. He hoped that he and I would speak in that spirit.

---

[3] See Document 166.

---

168.   Memorandum of Conversation[1]

Washington, June 10, 1970, 7:30 p.m.–1 a.m.

PARTICIPANTS

Ambassador Dobrynin
Henry A. Kissinger

After a brief meeting with the President, which is the subject of a separate memorandum of conversation,[2] Dobrynin and I left for the

---

[1] Source: National Archives, Nixon Presidential Materials, NSC Files, Box 489, President's Trip Files, Dobrynin/Kissinger, 1970, Part 2, Vol. I. Top Secret; Sensitive; Nodis. The conversation was held on the *Sequoia*.

[2] Document 167.

Sequoia.[3] Dobrynin began the conversation by saying that he hoped for very complete results and complete discussions. The difficulty with some of our present negotiators was that they didn't seem to be well briefed, like the Secretary of State; or if they were well briefed, like Sisco, they were too petty and never saw the wood for the trees.

He said that Cambodia had had at first a very severe impact on the Soviet leadership. When he had come to Moscow with my suggestion for a summit meeting,[4] Podgorny, Brezhnev, and Kosygin had been extremely interested. However, as time went on after the Cambodian events, opinion shifted and they believed I had mentioned a summit meeting merely to hold them quiet while we were preparing the Cambodian invasion. I said it was probably futile to argue this point but I could assure him that the Cambodian invasion was not planned before April 20, and as he remembered, I warned Vorontsov immediately that if North Vietnamese attacks on Cambodia did not stop we might have to take drastic measures.

Dobrynin asked what North Vietnamese operations we objected to. I said that as long as they stayed in the base areas we could live with the situation, though we didn't like it. Once they left the sanctuaries, however, they represented an intolerable threat to the security of our forces by turning the whole country into one base area. Dobrynin said that he was prepared to speak about Cambodia a little later, but he first wanted to pick up the President's points which were that we should forget about the past and concentrate on the future, and in the future it was necessary to come to some very concrete understandings between the United States and the Soviet Union. He suggested that we take up the subjects in the order mentioned by the President: SALT, first; the Middle East, second; Europe, third; and, Vietnam last. I said I could agree except that I wanted to put Europe in the last spot and put Vietnam and Southeast Asia before it.

---

[3] Earlier that day, Kissinger sent Nixon talking points for his meeting on the *Sequoia*. Kissinger explained that this was his first private meeting with Dobrynin since April 9. Nixon initialed his approval of Kissinger's positions. (National Archives, Nixon Presidential Materials, NSC Files, Box 489, President's Trip Files, Dobrynin/Kissinger, 1970, Part 2, Vol. I)

[4] Kissinger's talking point on a summit reads: "At our last meeting I had indicated the possibility of you and Premier Kosygin breaking a Vienna SALT deadlock and ratifying the agreement at a summit meeting. Dobrynin said he would explore this in Moscow and have an answer upon his return. I plan to let him take any initiative on the question of a summit meeting. I would say that I will take this up with you, while repeating that we would be interested in a summit that was assured of a significant agreement on at least one issue." (Ibid.)

SALT

We then turned to SALT.[5] Dobrynin said that he wanted to find out whether our understanding of April was still adequate, i.e., whether we were still prepared to have a limited agreement, and if so, how we should handle business in Vienna. Should we tell our negotiators in Vienna that they had gone far enough or that we wanted them to explore a little further; or did we want to charge them with making specific agreements?

I told him that it seemed to me that the negotiators in Vienna could go on for another three weeks, during which time he and I might discuss the specific principles of a settlement and agree on a general outline. We could then decide whether to have that taken up at Vienna or whether we should have it discussed in some other forum. Dobrynin said this was agreeable to him and that their delegation would be instructed accordingly.

He then asked me what I understood by a limited agreement. I said that to us a limited agreement meant a ceiling on offensive weapons and a limitation on defensive weapons to what we call national command authority levels. Dobrynin said this was not a very limited agreement because it encompassed the whole range of strategic forces.

I asked him whether the Soviets had another definition. He said that to the Soviets limited agreement meant that the Soviets probably would prefer a limitation on ABM deployment with some general agreement about protection against provocative attacks, which he explained meant third country attacks. I told him that this was almost certainly unacceptable to us. It would be more useful to explore some package that involved ceilings on all strategic forces.

Dobrynin then said that this raised a number of issues. Our package had been weighted against the Soviet Union. For example, we had established a ceiling of 1,710 missiles and a separate ceiling of the existing forces of bombers, giving us 500 and giving them 250. This established an inequality which was unfortunate, of course. There were some Soviet scientists who said both sides already possessed overkill and therefore it didn't make any difference. He did not want to argue that point, but he did wish to point out that the symbolic effect of the Soviet Union accepting inferiority in any category would be very bad and very hard to sell.

Another aspect of the bomber package was that the Soviet Union had no equivalent for our aircraft carriers and, therefore, there should be

---

[5] The second phase of the strategic arms limitation talks between the United States and the Soviet Union began in Vienna, Austria, on April 16, 1970.

some limitation on their deployment. I pointed out that aircraft carriers did not play a significant role in our strategy against the Soviet Union, but that any limitation on their deployment would affect their utility against other countries. Dobrynin said that if we were concerned about aircraft carriers we had to agree to the principle of some form of compensation for the Soviets, either in the form of giving them additional units of missiles or in some other way. He also pointed out that we were counting their tanker planes as bombers while we did not count ours.

I told him that the way to advance this problem would be for him to give me some idea of what they meant by compensation. If it was a symbolic compensation, we might consider it. If it was a major one, it would be difficult. I also pointed out to him that NCA levels involved limitations on radars and not just on missiles. He asked me to explain this, and I gave him a brief explanation of the differential lead time between missiles and radars. Dobrynin replied that radars useful for missile tracking were clearly distinguishable from others. He thought this was a proposition that could be entertained as long as it did not involve the destruction of existing radars and only limitations on building new ones. We summed up the results of this part of the discussion as follows:

1. The Vienna Conference would go on for another three weeks exploring the packages.
2. In the meantime, Dobrynin and I would work on the general principles.
3. He would give me some idea of what the Soviet Union understood by compensation.
4. I would explore whether there were other limitations available on the bombers. (I was thinking of the fact that budgetary reasons might force us to reduce our bomber force and that we might throw that into the equation.)

Middle East

Dobrynin then launched into an impassioned discussion on the Middle East. He said that we completely misunderstood Soviet motivations and intentions, and that we had to look at the problem from the Soviet point of view. We might not believe it, but the Soviets had not taken advantage of a tenth of the opportunities they had had to place military forces into several of the Arab countries. In 1967 the Egyptians had offered them naval bases and free use of all of the air bases if they only came in. Since then they've had repeated offers from Egypt and from Syria to put military forces into their countries, but they had always refused.

However, the deep penetration raids of the Israelis had left them no choice. They could not permit one of their friends in the Middle East to be totally humiliated and destroyed and there were no other means available to protect them. The Soviet Union desired no military presence in Egypt and it thought that the time was ripe to make a comprehensive settlement.

On the other hand, a comprehensive settlement in the Middle East was out of the question along the lines of the Sisco–Dobrynin conversations. Sisco constantly was raising pettifogging objections and was trying to draw him into drafting specific clauses of an agreement. Dobrynin said, for example, that the two offers he had brought back with him from Moscow matched almost verbatim the formulations that Sisco had demanded of him. Nevertheless, it was treated as only a minor concession because he had referred him to the Soviet June 9 document rather than to our October 28 document. He said we had to understand the fact that the Soviet Union could not accept the United States document as a basis for a settlement. On the other hand, it would not insist on its own and in its final formulation would come up with something that would not be ascribable to either side.

The major decision that had to be made was whether both sides were willing to make significant progress now. This required filling in the gaps of the agreement: specifically, on withdrawals, on Sharm-el-Sheik, on demilitarized zones and similar matters. This would then be put as a recommendation to Jarring who would take it up with the parties.

I asked whether he was talking of an imposed settlement. Dobrynin said, "No, not imposed. But of course our recommendations would carry a great deal of weight." And he added, "Believe me, that if we make a proposition to the Arabs, we will also see to it that it is accepted." However, he said it was essential that we make a prior decision that there would be a concrete agreement. He said that the time was short and that there were only a few months left before events could take an unpredictable turn.

I told him that for us the presence of Soviet combat personnel in Egypt was a matter of the very gravest consequence which sooner or later would produce a major difficulty with the United States and could perhaps even lead to a confrontation. We have no incentive at all in a settlement which would leave combat personnel in Egypt.

I, therefore, wanted to know whether, assuming that there were a peace settlement, the Soviet Union would be prepared to withdraw its combat personnel. Dobrynin asked what would happen if the Israelis started deep penetration raids in this period. I said I was talking about what would happen after, not before, there was an agreement between the Israelis and the Arabs.

Dobrynin said that under those conditions it was conceivable to him that the Soviet Union might agree to withdraw its personnel. He said he would query Moscow and get me an answer at our next meeting on whether the Soviet Union would withdraw its combat personnel as part of a general Middle East settlement.

Dobrynin then asked me if I had anything specific to propose on the Middle East. I said that under the right circumstances it was not inconceivable to me that we would be prepared to discuss a general settlement of the Middle East issues with the Soviet Union as long as it was understood that the Soviet Union would ask for some sacrifices from the Arabs commensurate to the sacrifices we would have to ask from the Israelis.

This led Dobrynin into a long exposition of the Soviet position and an explanation of the many sacrifices they had already made, specifically with respect to Sharm-el-Sheik, demilitarized zones, conditions of peace, and control of the Fedayeen. Dobrynin then asked me what was new in my proposal. I said the newness in our proposal was the willingness to discuss the specific terms of the settlement and not just the general outline. Dobrynin said frankly there was nothing new in that because Rogers had already made that proposition to him when they were having drinks on Monday, but he was happy to see that it was backed by the President.

Dobrynin then read to me a long statement which he allegedly got from the newspaper and which paralleled the State Department recommendation to the President. He asked me what I thought of it. (I later learned from Sisco that the Secretary gave most of this to Dobrynin at their meeting on June 8.)[6] I told Dobrynin that this was one of the proposals that was before the President. Many elements of it might have interesting aspects, but I did not want to comment prior to a Presidential decision.

Dobrynin again made an impassioned plea for a settlement of the Mid-Eastern issue which could only drag us all into incalculable results. He said that the Soviet Union was willing to guarantee access through the Straits of Tiran and the Suez Canal. When I raised the objection that the Soviet Union had gone no further than to guarantee the 1888 Convention, he said this was only because it represented the only usable legal document to guarantee free access. They were prepared to define access in any way that would meet Israeli objections.

We left it that I would talk to the President and inform him before we made a major move and that he would find out from Moscow whether the Soviet Union would be prepared to withdraw combat personnel as part of a general settlement.

---

[6] Kissinger is in error; the meeting was on June 2. However, Kissinger received a memorandum from Saunders on June 8 summarizing the conversation. See Document 159.

Southeast Asia

The conversation then turned to Southeast Asia. Dobrynin said that he found it very difficult to understand how we thought a peaceful settlement was now possible. He did not doubt the military gains that we had made in Cambodia, but on the other hand, we had given the Chinese a tremendous shot in the arm. The Chinese were now using Cambodia as a campaign against the Soviet Union, and had tried to induce the Soviet Union to cancel all meetings with the United States. Also, China was clearly in the ascendance in Hanoi. The result would be that it would be very difficult to make a settlement. The Chinese would never accept a pro-American government in Cambodia and neither would Hanoi.

I said that we did not expect them to accept a pro-American government in Cambodia. We were perfectly willing to live with a Sihanouk-type government provided it did not give Communist supplies access into the sanctuaries. Dobrynin wanted to know whether we had been prepared to accept the sanctuaries if the North Vietnamese had not moved out of them. I told him that, of course, we had accepted them for many years and that we had never made any plans for attacking them until after their threat to Cambodia had become evident.

Dobrynin said that I might not believe it, but they had no particular interest in a Communist government in Cambodia because such a government was certain to be dominated from Peking. He hoped that we had noticed that they had maintained a Chargé in Phnom Penh and had not recognized Sihanouk, even though Kosygin had written him some letters. He also called my attention to the article in the *New York Times*. He added, "Well, whatever has happened in Cambodia has happened, and there's no sense in talking about past history." He wanted to know what sort of political settlement for Cambodia we had in mind. I replied that we would certainly be willing to accept a government that had the general composition of the Sihanouk government. In fact, the government in Phnom Penh was the Sihanouk government minus Sihanouk.

Dobrynin then wanted to know whether we were prepared to partition Laos. He said he had heard this as a suggestion from the State Department. I said that there were many ideas floating around but we were certainly prepared to discuss any reasonable plan that would assure the neutrality and security of Southeast Asia.

With respect to South Vietnam, Dobrynin said that for the North Vietnamese, the only interesting point was the political settlement. They did not much care about the rate of American troop withdrawals. They did not believe in a process of free elections, and as long as we insisted on them, there was no hope of a political solution. I pointed out to him the passage in the President's April 20th speech[7] that indicated that we were flexible with respect to the determination of the popular will. Dobrynin wondered whether this proposal was still open. I told him all proposals had been reiterated in the April 30 and June 3 speeches.[8]

Dobrynin asked me about my assessment of my talks with the North Vietnamese. I said that the North Vietnamese had missed a great opportunity, and that if they had told Moscow that we had been rigid, they were severely mistaken. After all, the President need not send his personal advisor to negotiate if he wanted merely to have the stalemate that already existed in Paris. There was no sense in repeating standard positions. Dobrynin obviously had not read a very full account of the meetings because he kept saying that the impression that Hanoi had left with them was that we had been very rigid. Dobrynin said he didn't see any possibilities for great movement at this moment, but that the situation might change after the end of our Cambodian operation.

Europe

We then turned to Europe. Dobrynin said that we were the chief obstacle to the European Security Conference idea that they had put forward. I said that they had never explained satisfactorily why it was necessary to have a big conference simply to settle cultural and trade matters. Dobrynin said that it was impossible to please the United States. When they had proposed to Johnson to have a European Security Conference, they had been accused of wanting to settle too much. In this Administration, they were accused of trying to settle too little. He said we were oscillating between being too specific and being too vague.

For example, he simply did not know what we meant by mutual balanced force reductions and, frankly, he had the impression that we didn't know ourselves what we meant by the term. As an example of how impossible it was to deal with us, he mentioned the luncheon conversation he had had with Elliot Richardson.[9] He said Richardson had handed him a State Department working paper on mutual balanced

---

[7] The relevant passage reads: "A fair political solution should reflect the existing relationship of political forces within South Vietnam. We recognize the complexity of shaping machinery that would fairly apportion political power in South Vietnam. We are flexible; we have offered nothing on a take-it-or-leave-it basis." For a full text of Nixon's "Address to the Nation on Progress Toward Peace in Vietnam," see *Public Papers: Nixon, 1970*, pp. 373–377.

[8] On April 30, Nixon gave an "Address to the Nation on the Situation in Southeast Asia." (Ibid., pp. 405–410) On June 3, Nixon delivered an "Address to the Nation on the Cambodian Sanctuary Operation." (Ibid., pp. 476–480)

[9] A memorandum of Richardson's conversation with Dobrynin is in the National Archives, Nixon Presidential Materials, NSC Files, Box 712, Country Files, Europe, USSR, Vol. VIII.

force reductions and had asked him to comment on it. Dobrynin replied it was very unusual for a foreign diplomat to comment on a working paper of another foreign office. When he had called this to the attention of Richardson, the latter replied that he needed Dobrynin's comments in order to bring the military around in our country. I told Dobrynin that I would be ready to talk in concrete details about mutual balanced force reductions later this summer, after we had worked out our own thinking a little more fully.

Soviet-American Relations

We then turned to the general subject of Soviet-American relations. Dobrynin said that when the Administration had come into office, the leadership in Moscow was very concerned, given the past reputation of the President. Then, there was a period of relative hopefulness. This was dashed by the visit to Romania and there was a period of stagnation. Then, just when things began to pick up again, we had invaded Cambodia. Nevertheless, the Soviet leadership was willing to let bygones be bygones, as long as we understood that their desire for an agreement did not reflect weakness and that their domestic difficulties were figments of the American press.

I told him that we recognized the Soviet Union as a major country. We, of course, assumed that any agreement they made would reflect mutual interests and could not be imposed by either side. Our view was that either we could proceed along tactical lines as we had for most of our relationship in the post-war period, or we could make an effort at a fundamental improvement in relations. If we did the latter, the United States would be prepared to make a serious effort in the channels that the President had indicated, with the purpose of marking this Administration as the one in which the basic turning point towards peace had been made. Such an agreement would, of course, have to include that neither side would take advantage of any difficulties that the other might face in other parts of the world.

This led Dobrynin to ask me how we were getting on in our relationship with China. I said that it was very interesting that China was vitriolic in its public attacks but very polite in its private conversations. Dobrynin said that he suspected as much. He said, "Are you going to try to get on better terms with Communist China?" I responded that we would continue talking but their own experience must teach them that progress would not be very rapid. Dobrynin believed China would try to lead a crusade against us. I said that we were relaxed about this and would probably try to stay in contact with them.

Conclusion

We then summed up the conversation by listing the things that were going to be done. Dobrynin would try to get an idea from Moscow of what was meant by compensations in SALT and a position on the withdrawal of Soviet forces from the Middle East in case of a settlement. I would give him some idea of the range of limited agreements that we could discuss and some procedure for approaching the Middle East problem.

There was some extended conversation about the various personalities with whom Dobrynin had worked here, and his own estimate of them which was extraordinarily shrewd. For example, he said that he had never been much for Robert Kennedy because he thought that underneath his liberal facade, he was an extremely tough man. After about a year, he would have been the most intransigent cold warrior that had ever been in the Presidency. Of the Secretaries of State that he had met he thought Dulles was the most impressive and Rusk was the most reliable. I did not ask him to speak about any members of the present Administration.[10]

---

[10] On June 15, Kissinger sent Nixon a memorandum, drafted by Winston Lord, summarizing his June 10 conversation. Kissinger's memorandum bears Nixon's handwritten comment "K—good job—now we shall see." In the summary of Kissinger's discussion with Dobrynin about SALT, Nixon wrote "very significant! (China) (phase II)" next to Kissinger's statement: "The Soviet definition consists of limiting ABMs to defense against third country attacks." In the section about Dobrynin's comments on Southeast Asia, Nixon underlined and wrote "interesting" next to Kissinger's statement: "While we had made some military gains, Chinese influence in the region had been bolstered and prospects for a settlement set back." (Ibid., Box 489, President's Trip Files, Dobrynin/Kissinger, 1970, Part 2, Vol. I)

---

169. Memorandum of Conversation[1]

Washington, June 19, 1970.

SUBJECT

    Ambassador Jacob D. Beam's Meeting with President Nixon,
June 18, 1970, 3:30 p.m.

---

[1] Source: National Archives, Nixon Presidential Materials, NSC Files, Box 712, Country Files, Europe, USSR, Vol. VIII. Secret; Nodis. Drafted by Beam. A June 22 covering memorandum from Sonnenfeldt to Kissinger explained that "the conversation actually occurred in reverse order to that indicated in the notes, with the President asking Beam a series of questions for about 15 minutes and then giving Beam guidance toward the end of the meeting." A copy was also sent to Rogers.

The President gave me his views as follows on a number of basic issues between the US and the USSR. He strongly favored an increase in American commercial sales to the USSR (including Gleason gear) under conditions of a hoped-for and an anticipated improvement in the atmosphere later this summer. He did not want to attach explicit conditions since this would provoke a bad reaction, but economic moves could "kick along" the process of working out a live-and-let-live arrangement.

Within this context the President wished me to get the idea across that he was resolved to lay the basis for realistic negotiations with the Soviet Union. We had a policy and plan for Vietnam, which would take on further substance at the end of our Cambodian operation and he was determined to stop the war.

As regards the Middle East, we envisaged initiatives which would open up possibilities for negotiations in this area as well. The Soviets should, of course, display restraint.

The President said we were also intensely serious about SALT and it was clear both sides would profit from an understanding which would lighten the financial burden for us and would spare the Soviet Union a costly competition in keeping up with our technology and military production.

The President hoped that the range of subjects he was offering as suitable for negotiation would prove attractive to the Soviets. Although the establishment of true friendship between the two countries was probably illusory because of Soviet attitudes, the basis could be laid by which the two competing great powers could order their affairs for the furtherance of world stability. The President wished it to be made clear that our intentions and plans were to move forward. He thought there were signs recently of Soviet movement, too.

The President mentioned some personal ideas about pursuing the relationship further.

The President asked me for my views on the Middle East and Indochina. I gave reasons why I thought the Soviets neither wanted the total elimination of Israel nor chaos in the Middle East, especially because of their involvement with Communist China. As regards Indochina, I felt North Vietnam was the apple of their eye in Asia and in fact the main base for Soviet influence, present and future, in Asia. As a result of Sihanouk's defection in the direction of Communist China, the Soviets were extremely concerned about losing the North Vietnamese to Chinese domination. The Soviets were waiting to see how they could best protect their interests in a sorting out of developments in Indochina. Possibly they had considered multilateral discussions, as indicated by Jacob Malik's suggestion in New York, but they had apparently been unable to obtain Hanoi's consent.

The President asked me about leadership problems in the Soviet Union. I referred to changes which might take place either in the wake of the Supreme Soviet elections which have just been held, or in connection with the Party Congress mooted for late October or early November. The President thought the regime might well wish to have some kind of an agreement in SALT before or at about the time of the Party Congress.

In reply to the President's question, I expressed the view that chances of change in the Politburo could be about 50–50 during the course of the current year, resulting from the aftermath of the Supreme Soviet elections and the Party Congress. I felt Brezhnev would probably profit and stressed the point that he was a man not to be underestimated. Although he was held to be unimaginative, he is forceful, a good administrator and a formidable personality in debate. (I had in mind information from Czech sources about his handling of Dubcek at the critical meetings before the Soviet invasion in August 1968.)

The President said he was considering sending out Secretaries Hardin and Stans to Moscow, perhaps in August. The President will make his decision in July. He said he would like to receive some Soviet political personalities in return, but I pointed out this might be difficult before the end of the year because of a possible Soviet Party Congress session in the fall.

---

170.   Editorial Note

On June 20, 1970, Secretary of State William Rogers and Assistant Secretary of State for Near Eastern and South Asian Affairs Joseph Sisco met with Soviet Ambassador Anatoliy Dobrynin to present United States proposals on securing a Middle East peace settlement. Rogers stated the following U.S. position:

"a) We are proposing that the UAR, Israel, and Jordan promptly begin discussions under Ambassador Jarring's auspices, according to whatever procedures are recommended by him, for the purpose of the agreed implementation of the November 1967 Security Council Resolution.

"b) We are proposing, as a basis for the commencement of Jarring's efforts, that the UAR, Israel, and Jordan make identical statements that they (a) accept Resolution 242 and (b) agree that the purpose of the discussions to be conducted by Ambassador Jarring is to reach agreement on the establishment of a just and lasting peace between them based on (i) mutual acknowledgment by the UAR, Jordan and Israel of each other's sovereignty, territorial integrity, and political independence; and (ii) withdrawal of Israeli forces, both in accordance with Resolution 242.

"c) To facilitate Ambassador Jarring's mission we are further proposing that the UAR, Israel, and Jordan subscribe to a full restoration of the ceasefire, effective July 1 until at least October 1.

"d) To be effective, the ceasefire would have to include an understanding that (a) both sides would stop all incursions and all firing, on the ground and in the air, across the ceasefire lines, (b) the UAR would refrain from changing the military status quo (by emplacing SAMs or other new installations in an agreed zone west of the Suez Canal ceasefire line), and (c) Israel would observe a similar standstill on new installations in a similar zone east of the Canal.

"e) We are suggesting that this proposal be incorporated in a report from Ambassador Jarring to Secretary General Thant, which the parties would accept as a basis for talks under Ambassador Jarring's auspices.

"f) The U.S. Government is making every effort to secure Israel's acceptance, and our hope is that the USSR, jointly or in parallel with us will seek the acceptance and cooperation of the UAR."

After hearing Rogers's points, Dobrynin expressed two concerns. First, would the procedures in the new formula for bringing parties together overcome the traditional practice of one side insisting on direct negotiations while the other side insisted on indirect discussions? Second, was the United States not, in effect, "throwing away" the results of the Two-Power and Four-Power negotiations? To the first concern, Rogers replied that the "wording of formula in effect gave Jarring discretionary power with respect to procedural arrangements." Sisco added that "each side would have to justify entering negotiations with other side within framework of its own policy and its preferred procedure of negotiations." On Dobrynin's second concern, Rogers "took considerable pains to assure Dobrynin that Two-Power and Four-Power negotiations would continue in parallel with negotiations between parties directly concerned and that once latter under way the Four Powers would be in a position to influence their course and make a real contribution to a settlement." (Telegram 97773 to Moscow, June 20; National Archives, Nixon Presidential Materials, NSC Files, Box 1155, Saunders Files, US Peace Initiative for Middle East, 6/10–7/23/70, Vol. 1, 3 of 5)

At a press conference on June 25, 1970, Rogers made the following statement about the Middle East that incorporated the points made 5 days before to Dobrynin:

"Recent and disquieting events in the Middle East led President Nixon, on April 29 to order a thorough review of all political and military aspects of the problem. That review has now been concluded. As a consequence of the review, the United States has undertaken a political initiative, the objective of which is to encourage the parties to stop shooting and start talking under the auspices of Ambassador Jarring in accordance with the resolutions of the Security Council. Our objective in launching this initiative has been to encourage the parties to move towards a just and lasting peace which takes fully into account the legitimate aspirations and concerns of all governments and peoples of the area. In light of that objective, we believe it would not be useful to disclose at this time details of the political initiative or to discuss publicly military assistance for Israel. We believe that this is the time for such an initiative which we have launched directly with the parties and with other interested powers." (Department of State *Bulletin,* July 13, 1970, page 26)

---

171.   Memorandum of Conversation[1]

Washington, June 23, 1970, 6:45 p.m.

PARTICIPANTS

Ambassador Anatoliy Dobrynin
Mr. Henry A. Kissinger

The conversation came about in the following way. First, there were indications that the Soviet delegation wanted to wind up the SALT talks in Vienna. Secondly, Gerry Smith was pressing for new instructions authorizing him to offer a more limited option. Third, the President did not want the settlement to be arrived at in Vienna but, if possible, at a summit meeting. He asked me to find out from Dobrynin what the Soviet real intentions were, especially with respect to the conversations we had had in April[2] prior to Dobrynin's departure for Moscow where it was agreed that, if possible, if there should be a deadlock in Vienna, we would break it at a summit.

I saw Dobrynin in the Map Room of the White House and said to him that we were at a point where some decisions had to be made with respect to instructions for the Vienna delegation and that it would help us to understand Soviet intentions properly. I said Semyonov's suggestion of an early end of the Vienna phase could lead to three interpretations: (1) the Soviet Union did not want an agreement on SALT this year at all; (2) the Soviet Union wanted an agreement at Vienna and was using this device in order to elicit a different American proposal; and (3) the Soviet Union wanted an agreement but not at Vienna

---

[1] Source: National Archives, Nixon Presidential Materials, NSC Files, Box 489, President's Trip Files, Dobrynin/Kissinger, 1970, Part 2, Vol. I. Top Secret; Sensitive. The conversation was held in the Map Room at the White House.

[2] See Documents 150 and 152.

and was stalemating the talks there in order to permit the other leaders to settle the issue. I would appreciate Dobrynin's guidance.

Dobrynin, who was noticeably more businesslike and less cordial than at previous meetings, said the first interpretation was clearly out of the question. The Soviet Union did want an agreement on SALT even though our two positions were not yet close enough to set a definite date. As for Vienna, it was the Soviet Union's judgment that an agreement, including offensive and defensive weapons, could not be negotiated in the time available at Vienna. As for the third interpretation, he was without instructions and he would have to inquire in Moscow.

Dobrynin asked what I thought of an agreement confined to ABM. I said I saw no reason to change our position since the last time we met. I also mentioned to Dobrynin that I had been waiting for him to give me some answers to questions I had put to him on the *Sequoia*.[3] Dobrynin said that I have so many questions that it was hard for him to know to which I was referring. I said that this was the first time that I had seen Dobrynin miss a point, and I was particularly concerned about the Middle East. Dobrynin did not take the bait about the suggestion of Soviet troop withdrawal in case of a settlement. Instead, he said, "We offered you bilateral talks. We made a major proposal. We considered it a significant concession. In return, we have had no reply for three weeks, and then you make a unilateral overture. It is your problem now, and we are out of it. We suspect that you may have to come back to us later, but whether our concessions will still be open then remains to be seen."

I said that the American initiatives should be seen as a corollary to the two-power discussions, not as a substitute for them. Dobrynin replied that I well knew his attitude towards Sisco's conduct of the negotiations and until we started getting serious, there wasn't really too much hope for progress. At any rate, it was no longer the Soviet Union's problem and was ours. Dobrynin promised me an answer by the time we returned from San Clemente.[4]

---

[3] See Document 168.

[4] Nixon and Kissinger were in San Clemente June 26–July 6. (National Archives, Nixon Presidential Materials, White House Central Files, President's Daily Diary)

172.   Memorandum From the President's Assistant for National Security Affairs (Kissinger) to President Nixon[1]

Washington, June 25, 1970.

SUBJECT

The Soviet Leaders Speak Out

Last week the three top Soviet leaders—Brezhnev, Podgorny and Kosygin—all gave their "election" speeches. Taken together they represent a rather comprehensive report on current Soviet policies.

No major shift is foreshadowed in the three speeches on foreign policy. All of the leaders seemed to take a somewhat softer line than might have been anticipated in light of tensions in the Middle East and Asia. We came in for what appears to be a standard share of criticism, some of it sharp and pointed, especially for our policies in Southeast Asia. Yet there seemed to be an effort to insulate Soviet-American relations in general, from specific crisis areas.

Kosygin was the most forthright in calling for establishment of good relations; Podgorny was the more pessimistic in describing our relations as "frozen." Brezhnev, who was in the middle, rhetorically asked if good relations were possible, and answered positively. In particular, he took pains to stress that it would be possible to solve major international problems with the U.S.

There was no mention whatsoever of SALT, in marked contrast to Kosygin's press conference[2] of May 4 in which he warned that our Cambodian operations generated distrust that could affect SALT.

The Soviet position on Vietnam and Cambodia, stripped of some of the propaganda hyperbole, was rather guarded. Brezhnev spoke of Soviet support for the "just principles and demands of the patriotic forces of the peoples of Vietnam, Cambodia and Laos as the basis for a political settlement,"—thus slighting the military aspects.

On the Middle East, however, the Soviet position remained tough. Brezhnev boasted that the "defense capacity" of the Arab states had been "restored," and that the "liberation" of the captured Arab territories was the "key prerequisite" for a settlement.

---

[1] Source: National Archives, Nixon Presidential Materials, NSC Files, Box 712, Country Files, Europe, USSR, Vol. VIII. Confidential. Sent for information. A notation on the memorandum indicates the President saw it. A copy was also sent to Sonnenfeldt, who drafted the memorandum to the President based on a June 10 memorandum from Hyland to Kissinger summarizing Kosygin's foreign policy address, and another on June 12, summarizing Brezhnev's election speech. (Both ibid.)

[2] See Document 157.

The most optimistic note in all three reports concerned European affairs. Relations with Germany was singled out for a positive evaluation, and Brezhnev generally anticipated a favorable conclusion to the current negotiations with Bonn on a renunciation of force treaty. (He spoke before the recent German elections which may have the effect of inhibiting Brandt's policy.)

In contrast to the favorable impression of their Western prospects, all of the Soviet leaders were critical of Peking and pessimistic over their border talks. Kosygin was more restrained, Podgorny the sharpest, and Brezhnev, again, in the middle.

Most of the speeches of the leaders were taken up with internal matters, with all making the usual pledge of a better lot for the Soviet people. Sharp differences were apparent, however, over the question of continuing the economic reform. Brezhnev mentioned it only in passing, Podgorny added a critical note, and only Kosygin made a spirited defense of the reform. All this suggests that drafting of the next five year plan, which is now underway, may be causing divisions within the leadership. This may be part of the growing speculation, confirmed by several sources, that Kosygin will go into voluntary retirement this year, which probably would strengthen Brezhnev's predominance.

---

173. Memorandum From the President's Assistant for National Security Affairs (Kissinger) to President Nixon[1]

Washington, June 26, 1970.

SUBJECT

Kosygin Reply to Your Letter on Laos

After a three-month interval Premier Kosygin has replied to your March 21 letter,[2] appealing to interested states to renew international

---

[1] Source: National Archives, Nixon Presidential Materials, NSC Files, Box 765, Presidential Correspondence, Kosygin. Confidential; Exdis. A note from Rosemary Woods to the NSC Secretariat indicates that Kosygin's letter was sent directly to Kissinger, who had Saunders work on a response to it. Holdridge and Sonnenfeldt forwarded this memorandum on June 22 to Kissinger with the following comments: "We note that the [Kosygin] reply is very hard, and characteristically blames the U.S. for all the problems of the Indo-China region. It makes no reference to the presence of North Vietnamese troops anywhere in Indo-China. We recommend that no further action be taken by the President, but that you call in Dobrynin or Vorontsov to set the record straight on the North Vietnamese responsibility for the tensions in Indo-China."

[2] Tab A, Document 146.

consultations concerning Laos (Tab A). The reply, as anticipated, rejects your appeal. The tone, however, is polemical and tough.[3]

Kosygin emphasizes that your appeal "sounds unconvincing" because of our "armed intervention" in Laos, and our failure to make a similar appeal at the time when operations intensified last autumn and led to the capture of a series of areas long under the control of the "patriotic forces."

As for convening the Geneva conference (1962) in "one form or another", this is rejected by Kosygin as "unreal in present conditions . . ."[4] when there is going on a war unleashed by the USA against the Vietnamese people as well as armed intervention in the affairs of Laos and now also Cambodia."

He adopts a much tougher position than heretofore on the Souvanna Phouma Government, claiming that there is "no such government (of national union)" as created by the Geneva accords. It must be created by the "political forces" of Laos, he asserts. And he cites as the basis for internal consultations among the Laotians, the proposals of the Pathet Lao. He adds, however, that even these consultations cannot lead to the restoration of peace: "the war cannot be brought to a close" or consultations "moved off dead center" as long as the U.S. continues bombing and "generally interferes in Laotian internal affairs."

Substantively, this reply represents some hardening of the Soviet position, which is consistent with the tougher line reflected in the recent letter from Souphanavoung to Souvanna Phouma and the increased military action of the Communist side. It comes close to saying the Geneva agreements are a dead letter, and that even those parts pertaining to the coalition government are no longer valid. This is probably intended to increase the pressures on Souvanna, who is always concerned with signs that the Soviet might formally withdraw recognition of his government. The letter stops short of this, however. One possible sign of flexibility is the failure to make cessation of the bombing a precondition to talks among the Laotians.

The hard line taken by Kosygin in his reply can be considered pro forma, in that the Soviet position on Laos has consistently been to support Hanoi and the Pathet Lao, and to blame the U.S. for all the problems of Vietnam, Laos, and now Cambodia. The tone of the reply may also reflect Soviet frustrations over the way that Soviet influence in Hanoi has declined recently as Chinese influence has grown. Koysgin

---

[3] Nixon circled "polemical and tough" and wrote: "K—perhaps our statements and ltrs have been too soft and thus misunderstood? Toughen them up."

[4] Ellipsis in the source text.

may in effect be saying that the Soviets simply do not want to be involved in Indo-Chinese affairs under present circumstances.

I do not believe that the reply merits any further action on your part. We do not wish to become engaged in an unproductive exchange with the Soviets. However, for the purpose of setting the record straight on the causes of the tensions in Indo-China and denying the Soviets the last word on this, I believe it would be useful for me to set the record straight with Dobrynin when I next see him and lay it on the line as to the presence of North Vietnamese troops in Vietnam, Laos, and Cambodia as the source of all the trouble.

Tab A

Letter From Chairman of the Council of Ministers of the Soviet Union Kosygin to President Nixon

Moscow, undated.

Dear Mr. President:

We would like to make several observations concerning your letter regarding Laos.

It was pointed out in your letter that the Government of the United States does not spare any efforts to secure peace in Laos by means of the full implementation of the 1962 Geneva agreements. One could only welcome such a statement, if it indicated the intention to end the American intervention in Laos, which would conform to the obligation of the USA under these agreements. Unfortunately, the situation has been and is entirely otherwise; the American Air Force continues the bombardment of the territory of Laos; American "Advisers" are in the ranks of the armed forces of one of the Laotian sides and frequently participate directly in military operations.

In these conditions the appeal to other states by the U.S. Government to fulfill the 1962 Geneva agreements and to maintain the independence, neutrality and territorial integrity of Laos sounds unconvincing at the very least. You, Mr. President, directly admit the presence of "American Military—air activities in Laos." But instead of the cessation of these actions your letter only poses the question of international consultations. More to the point, for some reason the U.S. Government did not raise the question of international consultations when, last autumn, as a result of American armed intervention, military operations in the Plain of Jars and the central part of the country sharply intensified which led to the seizure of a series of areas that for a long time were under the control of the patriotic forces of Laos.

We cannot share also your appraisal of our position on the question of holding consultations among the countries participating in the 1962 Geneva conference on Laos. Bilateral consultations and exchange of opinions between governments on the question of the situation in Laos take place almost continually. In particular our attitude toward the February 28, 1970 message of Souvanna Phouma was communicated to the Laotian representatives in Moscow and Vientiane. A reasoned (motivirovanny) answer was given by us to the government of England concerning the inappropriateness of sending message on this question on behalf of the two Cochairmen. The Soviet Government maintains contacts with appropriate socialist countries. As far as we know, the British Cochairman also has exchanged opinions on this question with a number of countries in addition to the Soviet Union.

If the U.S. Government has in mind not this type of consultation but the convening in one or another form of a conference of participating states of the 1962 Geneva conference, then it is completely obvious that the convening of such a conference is unreal in present conditions, when there is going on a war unleashed by the U.S.A. against the Vietnamese people as well as armed intervention in the affairs of Laos and now also Cambodia. It is hardly possible to deny this.

Let us take only the question of the representation of Laos at such a conference. The Government of National Unity of Laos, established in conformity with the 1962 Geneva agreements, would have to be represented at it. But after all it is well known that at the present time there is no such government. It is necessary to recreate it, and only the political forces of Laos themselves can do this. The patriotic front of Laos, in its March 6 statement, proposed concrete measures aimed at the re-establishment of the Government of National Unity and the restoration of peace in Laos. Precisely in connection with this we expressed the opinion in our March 13 letter that the matter of the normalization of the situation in Laos should begin with consultation among the political forces of Laos, and that a good foundation for these consultations is the proposals advanced in the above-mentioned statement of the patriotic front.

I would like to point out that our letter of 13 March in no way contends that consultations among Laotian political forces can by themselves, if left to their own, lead to the restoration of peace there. As was justly pointed out in the March 6th statement of the patriotic front, the war in Laos cannot be brought to a close and the matter of a settlement will not get off dead center while the U.S.A. continues bombing Laotian territory and generally interferes in Laotian internal affairs.

The Soviet Government has already stated its opinion concerning how much American armed invasion in Cambodia has complicated the situation in Indo-China as a whole. I do not intend now specially to dwell on this question. In this instance it is necessary only to note that this invasion makes even more unreal raising the question of some kind of "international consultations" on Laos.

In conclusion I would like to express great regret, which is shared by my colleagues in our leadership, that the U.S. Government, instead of taking realistic measures for the cessation of the war against the Peoples of Indo-China and the establishment of peace in Southeast Asia, has taken the the path of spreading this war. This complicates the situation not only in Southeast Asia but in the whole world and naturally cannot but affect also the relations between our countries. I would like to express the hope that the Government of the U.S.A. and you personally will arrive at the only correct conclusion the cessation of interference in the internal affairs of the People of Indo-China and the withdrawal of American forces from this region. We are convinced that such a decision would radically change the situation in this region in favor of peace and would meet the interests of the whole world.

Respectfully,

A. Kosygin[5]

---

[5] Printed from a copy that bears this typed signature.

---

174. Memorandum From Harold Saunders of the National Security Council Staff to the President's Assistant for National Security Affairs (Kissinger)[1]

Washington, June 26, 1970.

SUBJECT

Middle East Dialogue with the Soviets

The Soviets have now tabled their new formulations[2] in the Four Power talks. Since this step brings into the open the debate over their significance, I thought you might want to look at this issue in detail.

---

[1] Source: National Archives, Nixon Presidential Materials, NSC Files, Box 646, Country Files, Middle East, General, Vol. VI, August 1970. Secret; Nodis. Sent for information. Not initialed by Saunders. The memorandum indicates Kissinger saw it.

[2] See Document 159.

You will recall that those formulations (a) concede Arab control of the fedayeen and (b) advance the time when peace would become effective.

At Tab A[3] is a memo produced by the Bureau of Intelligence and Research at State on the new Soviet formulations. I call it to your attention because it presents a much more hopeful interpretation than either Bill Hyland or I have provided you in recent memos and because it will have a lot to do with conditioning State's interpretation.

Following are a brief summary of the major points in the INR memo and a short critique of it.

INR Memo

The INR memo argues: "The fact that Moscow is now willing to advance beyond dead center on two questions which the UAR has in the past been unwilling to confront and which involve a long-resisted Egyptian surrender, in principle, of the strongest Egyptian bargaining ploys against Israel, implies that the USSR has strong policy reasons for moving to this position." Since presumably the Soviets were willing to use their new leverage with Cairo to extract these concessions, "the resultant impression is that the USSR means to convey a signal of its desire to bargain seriously."

Moscow's move is seen as having two immediate tactical advantages:

—First and foremost, it appears designed to force the U.S. to face up to the problem of its relationship with Israel. Moscow expected its move would complicate the U.S. decision on jets for Israel. But more important, Moscow may see this as the ultimate inducement to press Israel to withdraw.
—Second, it may have been calculated to remind us that no direct U.S. approach to Nasser attempting an end run around Moscow can succeed.

The memo then moves on to discuss Soviet motivations:

—It is assumed that the Soviets would not have made their move if they had not been prepared for a positive U.S. response that could eventually lead to a settlement on favorable terms. Moscow's postulated readiness to settle the Arab-Israeli problem rests on indications that they are still considerably worried about an Israeli attack against the Arabs and a possible American military involvement in future hostilities as well as the effect of heightened tension in the Middle East on important ongoing Soviet-American relationships in other fields.

---

[3] Attached but not printed is a June 9 intelligence brief, "USSR-Israel-Arab States: Moscow's Push Toward a Middle East Settlement," prepared by the Bureau of Intelligence and Research for the Secretary.

—The Soviets would like to open up the Suez Canal.

—It is asserted that the USSR no longer believes that its leverage with the UAR and other Arab states depends on opposing a settlement. Even with a settlement it is thought that Moscow would have many things going in its favor in the Middle East.

The INR memo concludes that, even though Soviet interest in dampening the Arab-Israeli dispute now seems substantial, it is unlikely that it is strong enough for them to willingly undercut the position they have so painstakingly and expensively built up in the area. The new positions communicated by Dobrynin imply that Moscow means business *but* that the deal will have to meet Arab sensibilities on regaining their territories and on the refugee problem. Finally, the Soviets will be anxious to keep the diplomatic action in our bilateral channel in order to emphasize their co-equal role with us in the region and as the best way to overcome both Cairo's possible faint-heartedness and Tel Aviv's probable obstructionism.

Critique

While many of INR's points seem valid, it seems to have been written out of the context of the record of the past year's negotiations. A review of that negotiating history clearly reveals that after 15 months of effort there has been little, if any, net progress toward coming up with a joint document. It is true that the Soviets have suddenly re-opened the bilateral dialogue, which for all practical purposes was suspended since late last October, but they have done so in a way that attempts to wipe the slate clean of all we have discussed over the last year.

The simple fact is that their new formulations are changes in *their* June 1969 document, which we felt we passed in our drafts of last July and October. One of their two opening concessions on the peace issue—Arab control of the fedayeen—is important but it simply does not stack up to what they want us to do in return. They want us to give away Israel's entire position on withdrawal before the peace negotiations—which their document ignores—even begin.

It is correct, as the INR memo says, that the Soviets have again signalled a desire to bargain. However, the terms are such that I question whether we are yet within range of serious negotiation unless the U.S. is prepared to press now for Israeli acceptance of certain borders before negotiations begin. Moreover, while I can find several strong incentives for the Soviets to keep the talks open, I still see none that are compelling enough for them to back down very far from the maximum Arab positions. I can see why they might want to re-open the negotiating door as a safety exit because the potential for their military involvement. But my guess is that they would like to draw the present situation out just as long as they can—see the U.S. position eroded just as much as possible—before they turn to political settlement.

Attached at Tab B[4] is a copy of a memo I recently sent to you spelling out in more detail my analysis of our bilateral talks with the Soviets.

---

[4] Attached but not printed.

---

175.   Telegram From the Embassy in the Soviet Union to the Department of State[1]

Moscow, June 30, 1970, 1608Z.

3592. Subj: Meeting with Gromyko on Middle East. Ref: A. State 102700;[2] B. Moscow 3589.[3]

1. I spent ninety minutes June 29 discussing our ME initiatives with Gromyko. He was accompanied by MEA USADiv Chief Korniyenko. Although Gromyko seemed somewhat tired, he listened carefully through my presentation. He put his remarks and questions to me in a direct, serious, and non-polemical manner.

2. Following my presentation, based on para 2(a) through (j) of reftel a, and subparas 6(a) through (g) of State 102616, Gromyko said he wished answers or clarifications to several questions. First, the US says it would not be good if the Arabs and USSR put forward as a preliminary condition for negotiations the demand that Israeli forces must withdraw from all, he said, occupied territories. Is the US against this demand as a general thesis or only as a preliminary condition? It was, Gromyko added, very essential to have an answer to this question.

3. I said we would oppose the demand if it were a preliminary condition for negotiations, simply on practical grounds. In any event, it would not be attainable before negotiations could take place since boundaries and the modalities of withdrawal were to be the subject of

---

[1] Source: National Archives, RG 59, Central Files 1970–73, POL US–USSR. Secret; Priority; Nodis.

[2] Telegram 102700 to Moscow, June 28, provides instructions for Beam's talk. (Ibid.)

[3] Telegram 3589 from Moscow, June 29, provides a brief summary of Beam's talk. (Ibid.)

negotiations themselves. If the Arabs insisted on their demand as a preliminary condition, there would be little prospect of a political settlement either through Jarring's mission or through major-power talks. I pointed out that the principle of withdrawal and non-acquisition of territory is set forth in UNSC Res 242, which we support. That res, however, does not specifically stipulate withdrawal to the June 5, 1967, line.

4. To seek a formula which goes beyond the wording of the Res, I said, would delay the start of talks under Jarring and slow down progress in the major-power talks. Meanwhile, there would exist the danger of military escalation and further reduction of our ability to be helpful as a result of this delay. I added as final comment that the US is already on record in its Oct and Dec documents as envisaging no substantial changes in June 1967 lines, and that we endorsed total Israeli withdrawal from UAR territory.

5. Gromyko asked if we intended to submit our proposals to the four-power talks in NY. I replied that since all the appropriate parties had been apprised of our proposals, I assumed they would be discussed at NY although I was not certain as to how this would be done.

6. Gromyko then asked if the USSR could expect a clear answer to the latest Soviet proposals put forward in our bilaterals and tabled in the four-power talks.

7. I said I was certain the Soviets would receive a reply. I went on to say that what we were now proposing was an emergency procedure to get talks started between the Israelis and Arabs. If they are started, the two- and four-power talks would continue, aimed at working out detailed instructions and bringing pressure and influence to bear for the purpose of narrowing the gap.

8. Gromyko said the USSR was pursuing its study of our new proposals, and could give no final answer now, particularly since Moscow had not yet received detailed analyses of the US proposals from appropriate Arab govts. He added that in general Moscow knew their viewpoints.

9. Gromyko then asserted that the US proposals lack clarity on certain major questions. For example, on the question of withdrawal of Israeli troops from all occupied territories, he repeated his question, does the US oppose this demand as a preliminary condition or as a general thesis? The question of withdrawal of forces and the establishment of peace are major questions to which clear US explanations are required, he said.

10. Furthermore, Gromyko continued, the US advocates continuation of the Jarring mission—as does the USSR. The question arises of what will Jarring be guided by in carrying out his contacts with both sides. He needs detailed guidelines. However, apart from the general provisions of UNSC Res 242 and a temporary ceasefire, the US pro-

posals contain nothing concrete, no detailed instructions. Gromyko went on to suggest that if the USG did not wish to work out guidelines for Jarring in our bilateral channel, the USSR still felt guidelines were necessary and that they could be worked out in the four-power talks. Moscow would accept any form for working out instructions so long as they lead to positive results.

11. Finally, Gromyko said, Moscow still has not received reactions from Washington on some other Soviet ideas, which perhaps were under study by the US. He then reiterated that his preceding remarks were aimed at eliciting clarification on a number of unclear points in the US proposals and that his remarks had been of a preliminary nature. He would return to a final assessment of the US proposals.

12. I said we would take note of his questions and in the meantime I would reply on the basis of information available to me. I went on to say that the purpose of our proposals was to start the two parties negotiating under Jarring's auspices. No one could dictate. Jarring was there to launch the negotiations, to mediate to the best of his abilities. If both sides could, without qualification, accept UNSC Res 242, they could meet indirectly under Jarring's mission. Meanwhile, if Jarring needed assistance and guidance, this could be provided by the two- and four-power channels.

13. The essential thing, I stressed, was that the two sides be brought together in a negotiating stance even if it is impossible at the outset to give Jarring instructions. It was also our view that the problem will become clearer more quickly once talks begin. The danger is that while we wait for agreement on instructions in the two- and four-power talks, the situation on the ground is likely to get worse and military pressures on both the US and USSR will increase.

14. Gromyko asked if Israel had given its reply to our proposals, to which I answered I knew of no such reply to date.

15. He then remarked that the US takes the position that the sooner the talks start the better. However, he went on, experience shows that if there is no agreement on guidance for Jarring, there is no progress. The Soviet Union does not want to put the damper on Jarring, whom it supports. However, while Moscow wants the start of negotiations, it sees no point in starting just for the sake of starting. Is it our goal, he continued, to have Jarring go to the area and return without anything? Gromyko emphasized that among the govts which share major responsibility there must be understanding and agreement regarding the major tasks and questions. Otherwise there can be no positive results.

16. I replied that if the USG could get Israel to accept UNSC Res 242, indirect negotiations, and the principle of withdrawal, this would be a great step forward in contributing to the start of negotiations. As regards the Arabs, I referred to my initial presentation which pointed

out that under the US proposals we are asking them to do no more than they themselves have earlier they were prepared to do. Our proposals ask more of the Israelis than of the Arabs. What we are proposing, I said, was an important procedural step to break an impasse; an urgent initiative of this type was called for. I added that the the two- and four-power talks could at the same time deal with substantive questions.

17. After asking us again to reflect on the questions he had posed, Gromyko returned to suggesting that we should give Jarring clear instructions regarding withdrawal and the establishment of peace. I replied that the first thing was to get the parties together in negotiations which would clarify the substance of the issues.

18. At the end of the meeting I commended to Gromyko's attention the very carefully drafted presentation the Dept had given me to put before him. (At Fonoff request the text is now being checked by Polansky with the Soviet interpreter.)

19. At reception last night for visiting Mayor Washington Korniyenko made it clear that the two major points the Soviets will hammer away at are (1) absence of instructions for Jarring, and (2) failure to deal with "the Arab demand for total Israeli withdrawal." Since the Soviets frequently offer lack of response as an excuse for doing nothing, I suggest we again try to tie these questions down as best we can.

Beam

---

176.   Memorandum From Harold Saunders of the National Security Council Staff to the President's Assistant for National Security Affairs (Kissinger)[1]

Washington, July 2, 1970.

SUBJECT

Soviet Response to Middle East Initiative

---

[1] Source: National Archives, Nixon Presidential Materials, NSC Files, Box 646, Country Files, Middle East, General, Vol. VI, August 1970. Secret; Nodis. Originally sent for information, but Saunders changed it to action. Copies were sent to Haig and Lord.

Assistant Secretary Sisco met again July 1[2] with Ambassador Dobrynin concerning our new Middle East initiative. This account is as interesting in revealing the emerging nature of our diplomatic initiative as it is in confirming emerging outlines of the Soviet response.

Summary of Conversation

Sisco began by explaining, in answer to a question Gromyko had asked Ambassador Beam,[3] that we oppose the Arab demand for an Israeli commitment to total withdrawal as a pre-condition to negotiations or to Four Power agreement on guidelines for Jarring. He said we feel that the final borders must be agreed between the parties, not imposed, but should exclude other than insubstantial changes. Sisco also said that we wanted positive reaction from the parties before submitting our proposals in the Four Power forum and that delaying tactics in hope of getting the initiative changed through the major power talks would simply not work. Finally, Sisco noted that the new Soviet formulations (presented last March directly to us and more recently in the Four Power talks) are a "step forward" and our reply would be influenced by (1) whether the negotiating process under Jarring begins and (2) by the degree of Soviet military aid to the Egyptians.[4]

Dobrynin took the line that our proposals were too thin and that in his opinion it would be best to table our initiative in the Four Power talks where they could be strengthened with the suggestions of other powers. Why, he wondered, had the U.S. taken a unilateral initiative instead of discussing it first in the major power forum, particularly when the Soviets had just made a forthcoming move on the issue of peace that we had stressed so much. Dobrynin stressed the continuing Soviet interest in the U.S.–USSR talks and Moscow's disappointment over the delay in the U.S. answer to the new Soviet peace formulations.

Comment

In our official contacts with the Soviets on the new initiative, they have at all levels indicated their suspicion of our strategy. A certain measure of mutual suspicion is probably inevitable in dealing with the Soviets, but in this case, it is probably increased by the timing of our initiative which did come on the heels of what they regard as the first real concession they have made in over a year of talks on the Middle East. That concession (Arab control of the fedayeen) is only one aspect

---

[2] In telegram 105385 to Manila, Beirut, Cairo, and additional posts, July 2, the Department reported on their discussion. (Ibid., Box 1155, Saunders Files, U.S. Peace Initiative for Middle East, 6/10–7/23/70, Vol. 1, 4 of 5)

[3] See Document 175.

[4] Kissinger wrote "What proposals are new initiatives?" in the margin.

of the larger problem and came with unacceptable strings attached (acceptance of the rest of the Soviet proposals and especially a prior Israeli commitment to total withdrawal) but it presumably was carefully weighed and probably intended to draw us out from behind our inflexible position. Now, in the Soviet eyes, we have responded, for all practical purposes, by sidetracking the Two Power and Four Power channels in favor of a unilateral and direct approach to the parties with essence of our earlier proposals.

More important, however, than this Soviet suspicion, is their concentration on the issue of total Israeli withdrawal. Dobrynin did not get directly into this but from all indications, including Ambassador Beam's recent talk with Gromyko, this is why the Soviets keep harping on fleshing out our initiative in the Four Power forum. Of course, it might be natural to expect positions on both sides to harden on this issue just before a possible negotiation.

The most important question for the Soviets, and for that matter for Nasser, is whether the U.S. is prepared to press the Israelis to withdraw totally from the occupied territories if the Arabs make the concession of agreeing to negotiations. All of the Soviet talk about the need to give Jarring more detailed guidelines really boils down to the Soviets pressuring us to settle the boundary issue before Jarring resumes in contrast to our insistence on having negotiations start before boundary issues as Gaza, Sharm al-Shaikh and Jerusalem are worked out. This has been the essence of the Soviet strategy in the Four Power talks for some time and they apparently intend to pursue it in response to our new initiative.

The most important insight that comes to me out of the first week's maneuvering over our initiative is this: It is, at the moment, little more than an energetic effort to rush the Soviets and Egyptians to agree to begin negotiation in hope that the U.S. will make the key concessions on boundaries in return. We have hinted; but we have not decided. We may not want to make that decision. But Dobrynin sees the effort for what it is, and I will be surprised if the Egyptians and Soviets let us get away with it. We are asking them to play their key card with no more than a hint that we might play ours in return.

177.   Memorandum of Conversation[1]

Washington, July 7, 1970, 2:30 p.m.

PARTICIPANTS

> Ambassador Anatoliy Dobrynin
> Henry A. Kissinger

SALT

The conversation came about because Dobrynin had sent me an Aide Mémoire[2] while I was in San Clemente in reply to the conversation I had had with him on June 23, 1970.[3] In this reply, the Soviet Government indicated that they would be prepared to make an agreement at Vienna on ABMs and on the issue of accidental and provocative attacks, but that they did not think it likely that an agreement could be reached on the limitations of offensive weapons at Vienna. I wanted to get clarification on that point.

I deliberately conducted the meeting in a somewhat cool and aloof manner. I asked Dobrynin how he explained the first section of his Aide Mémoire. Did it mean that agreement on offensive weapons was impossible or that agreement would be very difficult? Dobrynin said that in view of all the important obligations that they had raised, the offensive limitations would have to be dealt with in two stages—an agreement in principle to be followed by detailed negotiations. He did not believe that this could be accomplished in the three weeks that were remaining in Vienna. He did want me to know, however, that the Soviet leaders had shown their good faith by instructing Semyonov first, to stay in Vienna at least until August 1st, and secondly, to concentrate for a while on the provocative and accidental attack aspect in order to give us a chance to develop our position.

I said to Dobrynin that we were going to have a meeting the next day to consider various aspects of the matter, particularly whether we could agree to a separate ABM ban. I also told him that I noticed that the last two paragraphs of his Aide Mémoire explicitly established the concept of linkage which they had strenuously rejected the year before. Dobrynin replied that they had become convinced by the persuasiveness of my argument that this was a correct course. We left this part of

---

[1] Source: Library of Congress, Manuscript Division, Kissinger Papers, Geopolitical File, Box TS 36, Soviet Union, Chronological File, 7/70–1/71. Top Secret; Sensitive. The conversation was held in the Map Room at the White House.

[2] Attached. Sent to Kissinger from Dobrynin, through Colonel Kennedy, while Kissinger was in San Clemente.

[3] See Document 171.

the conversation with my saying that I would let Dobrynin know after the meeting of our advisers whether we would agree to a separate ABM ban. Dobrynin added that, if that were done, the agreement could be signed later on this summer by the Foreign Ministers, perhaps at the United Nations. I said that this was a matter we could discuss after there had been an agreement in principle.

Middle East

Dobrynin then raised the subject of the Middle East in a much more conciliatory way than in the previous conversation where he said that the Soviets were practically out of it. He said he couldn't understand why we made the statements we did in San Clemente.[4] He thought that at such a delicate moment, it would have been best for us to keep quiet, but he wanted me to know that the Soviet Union sought no confrontation and that the Soviet leaders were eager to have a political settlement. I responded that somehow or other I had gained the impression from our last conversation that he thought that now that the US was negotiating with the Middle Eastern parties directly, the Soviet Union was absolved of any direct responsibility. Dobrynin replied that if he gave that impression, he regretted it. He wanted me to know that he was fully authorized to talk to me at any moment and to come to an agreement with me. I said that I did not have enough time to discuss the Middle East at this particular moment, but that when I gave him our answer on the ABM proposal, I would let him also know about our thinking on the Middle East. Dobrynin again effusively reiterated his desire to have an understanding with us, and we let the matter drop there.

Comment

It would be difficult to exaggerate the change in tone between the conversation on June 23rd and this conversation on July 7th. Dobrynin was conciliatory, effusive, and obviously taken aback by the various comments that had been made about the Middle East.

---

[4] On July 1, while in San Clemente, Nixon was interviewed by the American Broadcasting Company and talked about a variety of foreign policy issues, including the Middle East. A text of these comments is in *Public Papers: Nixon, 1970*, pp. 543–559.

Attachment[5]

Aidé-Mémoire From the Soviet Union

Moscow, undated.

President Nixon's and Dr. Kissinger's considerations regarding the course of strategic arms limitation talks in Vienna have been carefully studied in Moscow, and I am instructed to outline the following considerations of the Soviet side in this connection.

1. Soviet-American strategic arms limitation talks have been underway for over two months now, and we agree with the opinion of the American side that the time has come to sum up certain results of the exchange that has taken place and to try to determine how these negotiations could be most productively continued.

The Soviet Union views with importance the problem of strategic arms limitation and is prepared to conduct fruitful talks in this field. At the Vienna negotiations we have advanced a broad program of measures which is a comprehensive one and embraces all strategic arms systems capable of delivering nuclear strikes against targets on the territories of the sides. We have chosen this approach proceeding from the necessity of ensuring equal security for both sides which constitutes an indispensable condition for agreement.

The proposals outlined by the US delegation have been carefully considered in Moscow. While those proposals have been presented to us as based on a broad approach to the problem of strategic arms limitation, we have noted that the American side proposes to include into the framework of agreement not all types of strategic arms leaving aside the question of US aircraft-carriers, aircraft and forward based missiles carrying nuclear charges, as well as of other systems the geographic location of which makes it possible to strike targets on the territory of the other side. Such a proposal, clearly, cannot be taken as a basis for solving the problem of strategic arms limitation because it would give advantages to one of the sides.

A number of other proposals by the US side has also been aimed at attaining one-sided advantages. These include proposals to the effect that Soviet heavy missiles be singled out as one separate category and a special ceiling be placed on them, that a quantitative level for strategic bombers be secured to the advantage of the US, as well as proposals regarding a ban on mobile launch missiles, limiting wing missiles, Diesel submarines, etc.

---

[5] Top Secret; Eyes Only.

With the view of surmounting the existing differences we have come out for, in case the US retains forward-based nuclear means, the Soviet Union's receiving an adequate compensation. Such compensation could take the form, for example, of quantitative reduction of corresponding armaments from the other side. However, before citing any specific figures in this connection it is necessary to come to terms in principle on all these questions.

In analysing the situation at the talks one has to state that there exist differences between the sides which could be overcome only in the process of further thorough and all-round consideration. It is hardly possible to envisage that this could be accomplished at the present Vienna stage of the talks.

We would like to hope that the US Government will again give thought to our considerations and arguments, outlined in Vienna, in favor of such comprehensive solution of the problem of strategic arms limitation that would ensure equal security for both sides.

2. It has been noted in Moscow that certain points in common have emerged in the questions of limiting ABM development and of measures for reducing the danger of missile-nuclear war between the USSR and the US resulting from accidental or unsanctioned use of nuclear weapons.

Considerations have been advanced from the American side concerning the possibility of reaching agreement on limiting the ABM systems to two points/Moscow and Washington/. We are prepared to consider this proposal as a basis for obtaining agreement on the question of limiting deployment of the ABM systems.

As regards specific questions which arise in this connection/number of launch installations, their location and the like/, these, in our view, could be agreed on without difficulties.

The same applies also to the problem of reducing the danger of missile-nuclear war between our countries. The Soviet delegation in Vienna has necessary instructions for a concrete discussion on this question.

In conclusion we would like to say that, in our profound conviction, one of the most important conditions for a successful development of the strategic arms talks which have such a paramount significance for the destinies of world peace, is the state of the international situation as a whole.

It is believed in Moscow that for speedy achievement of agreement it is necessary in every way to avoid complications in the international situation and to apply all efforts to make healthier the world atmosphere. It should be emphasized that the Soviet side attaches great importance to this.

178. Transcript of Telephone Conversation Between President Nixon and his Assistant for National Security Affairs (Kissinger)[1]

Washington, July 7, 1970, 7:30 p.m.

K: Mr. President

P: Hi Henry

K: I just wanted to tell you I talked to Dobrynin today.[2]

P: Yeah, yeah. (Wanted to know about the outcome)

K: I don't know what you did with the Arabs . . .[3]

P: Pleasant talk

K: Want an agreement on SALT, we can sign at any level. He said about the Middle East—why did you raise it now? I told you I wanted to talk to you. (Didn't raise it the last time I saw him.) He said come to dinner, come to lunch. I told him I just may.

P: Do you think he really is frightened?

K: Frightened, we are getting their attention. After this thing, he said we will offer you these (proposals?), he was drooling all over the place.

P: Nothing about Vietnam. Push him off, we will handle it ourselves. The press and newspapers are getting very [omission in the source text]. About the Russian SAMs, want to know how you can let them get away with it.

(Three new SS–9s were mentioned)

P: I hope he is disturbed.

K: Yes, he is disturbed I think on the Middle East. If we don't pull away too much . . . Sisco . . . (the only contribution I have, it isn't enough we may have to do more).

P: I am for Israel, for reasons. Want to let a little country survive—can't let the Russians come in and control the crossroads of the world. I think the fact our perils [sic] work so closely, the big stakes is Soviet/American confrontation.

[Omitted here is discussion of topics unrelated to the Soviet Union.]

---

[1] Source: Library of Congress, Manuscript Division, Kissinger Papers, Box 364, Telephone Conversations, Chronological File. No classification marking.

[2] See Document 177.

[3] All ellipses in the source text.

179.   Memorandum of Conversation[1]

Washington, July 9, 1970, 5:30 p.m.

Ambassador Anatoliy Dobrynin
Mr. Henry A. Kissinger

SALT

After some desultory talk about my new office, I opened the conversation by telling Dobrynin that I had followed the reporting from Vienna with great interest. As a specialist in the Congress of Vienna,[2] I could only congratulate Semyonov on having learned some of the tactics. I referred specifically to the note he handed over to Smith at a concert which seemed almost to suggest a form of alliance between the United States and the Soviet Union against countries that had engaged in provocative acts. Dobrynin said he did not know how the note was handed over, but of course, he was familiar with the formulation.

I said that I looked at the accidental war problem on two levels: (1) the technical means of notification which we were studying and which I did not think would present any undue problem; and (2) the political implications of some of the cooperative arrangements that they were suggesting which represented a significant change in the international environment as it had developed since the war. I wanted to talk to him about that second aspect a little later, but I wanted first to turn to the overall issue of SALT. Dobrynin interjected to point out that the formulation handed by Semyonov to Smith had been prepared by the Delegation in Vienna. He could tell me frankly that he, Dobrynin, had had his doubts about it because he was afraid that too great significance was going to be read into it. If we wanted an agreement without that particular clause, this would not become a sticking point. Dobrynin indicated that the major political fact for the Soviet Union was an agreement on provocative attack, not individual clauses, and there would not be any undue haggling. I told Dobrynin that we should defer discussion of this until I gave him our general view.

I said that the President had decided after careful study that it was not possible to separate the components of a SALT agreement—that it was necessary to have a limitation on offensive weapons together with a limitation on ABM's. We were prepared in principle to discuss accidental war limitations. I added that recent missile starts of SS–9 and

---

[1] Source: National Archives, Nixon Presidential Materials, NSC Files, Box 489, President's Trip Files, Dobrynin/Kissinger, 1970, Part 1, Vol. 2. Top Secret; Sensitive. The meeting was held in Kissinger's White House office.

[2] In 1957, Kissinger published *A World Restored: Metternich, Castlereagh, and the Problems of Peace, 1812–1822,* which analyzed the Congress of Vienna that established a post-Napoleonic European settlement.

SS–11 groups underlined for us the danger of an ABM limitation which would leave our Minutemen exposed to a Soviet first-strike. Dobrynin said that I knew they didn't intend to make a first strike. I replied that I knew no such thing, looking at their weapons deployment; in any event, it didn't make any difference what I knew but what reasonable people could deduce from the weapons situation.

Dobrynin said that he didn't think it would be possible to come to an agreement under these conditions. I replied that perhaps the delegations could be instructed to emphasize the ABM part to get that out of the way. Dobrynin asked, "Well, why not then agree on the partial accord after all?" I said this was not possible for the reasons I had given to him. I added, however, that I would be prepared to continue discussions with him during the summer and that I was certain we could narrow the differences to a manageable form. Dobrynin said that he would be prepared to do this but he thought that SALT was in essentially good shape and that we could come to an agreement, if not this year, then in the early months of next year. He emphasized again that they would be prepared to drop any offending clauses in the accidental war part of the agreement, that these were not matters of principle with them. I said that this was not the issue—the issue to us was not to break out the defensive from the offensive parts of the agreement.

Dobrynin then raised the question of how long the recess should be, saying that the Soviet Government would prefer November 1st. I said we would prefer something like September 15th. When Dobrynin asked where that would leave us, I replied that it seemed self-evident to me that it takes two to start a negotiation. He said he wanted us to understand that the November 1st deadline was unconnected with any deliberate attempt to slow down the talks, but had rather to do with the internal operating methods of the Soviet government. Many of their key people would be on vacation in August, and they would not be able to do a systematic review until September.

Dobrynin also asked me what would be new in our package. I said it was hard to go into precise detail, but there would be a limit on offensive units and a sub-limit on heavy missiles. He asked me how we would handle the problem of compensation, i.e. the issue of the relationship between IRBM's on their side and forward deployed tactical aircraft on our side. I said it seemed to me the best way to handle it was through exclusion—that they would not be counted on either side. Dobrynin indicated that this would not present an insuperable difficulty. He again called my attention to the part of the Soviet Aide Mémoire[3] which said that an ABM agreement could, in their view, be agreed on "without difficulty." He said this was a very significant statement. I

---

[3] See the attachment to Document 177.

replied that I understood, and that we should, however, now proceed to work as expeditiously as possible on a comprehensive statement.

The conversation then turned to general subjects. I said that I wanted him to know that the President had read the article that Semyonov had handed to Smith at a concert with the greatest care. He had come to the conclusion that the most significant aspect of it would be the political one; however, such a politically important matter should not be handled within the context of SALT, but should be handled at a higher level. I therefore wanted to return to my conversation of April 12th[4] in which I had suggested a specific procedure for coming to an understanding of fundamental issues so that major progress could be made. Dobrynin evaded the issue and said that he had thought that Cambodia had ended this concern and, in any event, he was prepared to discuss the Middle East with me.

Middle East and Summit Meeting

He then launched into a long discussion of the Middle East. He said, "Talking to Sisco is like throwing beans against a wall," which is allegedly a Russian proverb. On the other hand, he said, Beam was always totally uninstructed and only listened politely to what Gromyko had to say, whereupon he would then insist that he had to go for new instructions. He thought it was essential that we come to a political agreement and he said he was fully authorized to deal with me.

I stated that he still owed me an answer to the questions which I had put to him three weeks ago. In contrast to his meeting with me just before San Clemente,[5] he now remembered the question very well. He said, "Look at it, Henry; you have never stated a proposition to me of a political settlement in the Middle East. All we have from you is one question, namely, whether we will withdraw our troops in case of a settlement. On the other hand, we don't know what you mean by a political settlement." I asked, "Do I understand then that if I tell you what we understand by a political settlement, you will tell me that you are prepared to withdraw your troops?" Dobrynin indicated that this might be a fair conclusion, but he was not totally unambiguous about it. He said he thought that he and I could settle the matter of the Middle East between ourselves. I responded that I doubted that this would be possible because it was a matter of extraordinary delicacy for us and we had to do it in the right framework.

I then returned to the formulation at Vienna, but Dobrynin turned the conversation by saying that this was not the most crucial aspect. I fi-

---

[4] No record of a meeting on that date has been found. Kissinger was apparently referring to his April 14 meeting with Dobrynin.

[5] See Document 171.

nally got straight to the point and said as follows: "Anatoliy, when I spoke to you on April 12th, you know very well that I was not talking about how to handle the Middle East. We had made a specific proposal to you about a meeting at the highest level. We are proposing this because it is early enough in our Administration to have a fundamental departure in our relationships with the Soviet Union. However, if too much more time is spent, we are going to make whatever agreements we do at a point in the Administration when they can no longer be effectively implemented. Therefore, the decision is up to you, but there's no sense beating around the bush." Dobrynin became very serious and dropped his jocular manner. He said, "You recognize, of course, that Cambodia and the approaching Party Congress make this a difficult matter for us." I said, frankly, I was looking at problems from our point of view, and it was up to him to take care of his problems.

Dobrynin then stated that this was a matter, of course, of the greatest importance which had to be reported directly to Moscow, and he would want to sum up his understanding: (1) the President was proposing a summit meeting; (2) the summit meeting should consider a fundamental reappraisal of American-Soviet relations. I said that was correct. Dobrynin asked when the meeting should take place—were we thinking of 1971 or 1972? I replied, no; we were thinking of this year. In response to his query, "before or after the elections?", I said that this was to be settled after we knew how it was going to be discussed.

Dobrynin then asked what the agenda of a summit might be. I said, "SALT, the Middle East, European security, and any other issue that either party wanted to place on the agenda." Dobrynin replied that if it is to be on the Middle East, he and I had to make some agreement ahead of time to see whether there was some progress. I said I was prepared to talk to him. Dobrynin asked whether he understood correctly that I would not be prepared to talk to him unless there were to be a summit. I responded that I had no instructions on that point, but that obviously the President's attitude would be affected by how the Middle East would fit into the general picture. Dobrynin said, "It is clear, and I will report back to you."

He then launched into a long discussion along familiar lines of Soviet good faith in the Mid-East negotiations. He repeated that they had made two significant concessions, both of which had been ignored. He said they had always wanted to settle it with us. He insisted that the two alleged concessions still stood, and that he had waited for us to give him a response. In contrast to his previous meeting with me before we went to San Clemente, he reiterated the urgent desire to settle the Mid-East problem. He said, "I am authorized by the Soviet Government to tell you that we seek no confrontation." I replied, "I am authorized by the American Government to tell you that we seek no confrontation. We were not threatening you; we were stating an objective fact of the trend." He said he wished we hadn't used the word "expel," for this had a tendency to make people feel that their national pride was involved and issues of backing down would be raised. I said that it was not a question of backing down but a question of the objective reality in which, despite what the great powers might want, events might force them on a collision course. Dobrynin asked me whether I thought we were on a collision course now. I said that reluctantly I had to conclude that we were.

Dobrynin reiterated that the Soviet Union sought no confrontation and was prepared for a political settlement. He said that while he did not know the details of Soviet deployment in Egypt, he thought it had been blown up out of all proportion, and the Soviet Union was not advancing forward. There were shifts within a well-understood plan. On the other hand, he said, the Soviet Union could not accept the proposition that air supremacy over both sides of the Suez Canal was an Israeli right that could never be challenged. I said, "Well, this is a point of disagreement between us, but it is not one that we can settle now. The main point you have to understand is that the introduction of Soviet combat personnel into Egypt represents serious problems for us, and the more permanent it appears, the more serious the problem grows." I told Dobrynin also to remember that the President moved circuitously, but that he eventually always did what he said he would do. Dobrynin said, "It is clear, and we ought to try to work on a political settlement and time is getting very short." I said I agreed with him.

He then asked me whether we would be prepared to discuss a European Security Conference at a summit. I replied that we probably would be. Dobrynin then said that as far as he could understand it, the agenda would be SALT, European security, and the Middle East; he told me that he would be back to me.

Comment

The meeting took place in an extremely cordial atmosphere. Dobrynin's affability was much more pronounced than at the meeting before we went to San Clemente, and his eagerness to prove Soviet good faith was sometimes almost overpowering.[6]

---

[6] On July 16, Kissinger sent Nixon a summary of the highlights of his conversations with Dobrynin on June 23, July 7, and July 9 and attached copies of the memoranda of conversation. The President saw the summary. (National Archives, Nixon Presidential Materials, NSC Files, Box 489, President's Trip Files, Dobrynin/Kissinger, 1970, Part 1, Vol. 1)

180.   Telegram From the Embassy in the Soviet Union to the Department of State[1]

Moscow, July 11, 1970, 1158Z.

3835. Subj: Call on Gromyko on ME. Ref: Moscow 3825.[2]

1. At seventy-five-minute meeting July 10 Gromyko was attentive but seemed to be stalling for time. He was non-belligerent and avoided giving offense. Following is full account of discussion.

2. I noted that Sisco had seen Dobrynin July 1[3] to answer some of the questions Gromyko had raised with me June 29.[4] I then told Gromyko we would like his reactions to our answers in due course but now wished to raise the problem of the ME military situation which was causing us great concern and worry. I told him I had been asked to recall Secy Rogers' June 2 conversation with Dobrynin[5] and went on to read him the following, with particular reference to the Secy's June 2 statement.

3. "Asst Secy Sisco in his talk July 1 with Amb Dobrynin replied to the questions you asked regarding the Arab demand for total withdrawal and the relation between the US initiative and Four-Power talks. Sisco also described our views regarding consideration of the Syrian aspect. We would be interested in having in due course your reactions.

4. "In the meantime an especially serious development has come to the fore. I have been asked to recall Secy Rogers' conversation with Amb Dobrynin June 2 and to refer particularly to Secy Rogers' statement about Soviet military involvement and to Amb Dobrynin's comments that the SovGov wished to avoid a US-Soviet confrontation. Amb Dobrynin remarked then that maybe the situation now is a little more equal in the military sense and perhaps this provides a good opportunity to advance toward a settlement. He said the possibility for peaceful settlement still exists and said there should be no doubt that the Soviet side does not want a confrontation.

---

[1] Source: National Archives, Nixon Presidential Materials, NSC Files, Box 1155, Saunders Files, U.S. Peace Initiative for Middle East, 6/10–7/23/70, Vol. 1, 5 of 5. Secret; Priority; Nodis. On July 8, Sonnenfeldt and Saunders sent Kissinger a memorandum seeking his approval of instructions for Beam's talk with Gromyko on the Middle East. Kissinger initialed his approval on July 8. (Ibid., NSC Files, Box 712, Country Files, Europe, USSR, Vol. VIII)

[2] In telegram 3825 from Moscow, the Embassy provided Beam's highlights of his meeting with Gromyko on July 10. (Ibid., Box 1155, Saunders Files, U.S. Peace Initiative for Middle East, 6/10–7/23/70, Vol. 1, 5 of 5)

[3] See Document 176.

[4] See Document 175.

[5] See Document 159.

5. "We would like to know whether these views are still valid as of today. We ask this question because indications have been increasing during the past that Soviet military personnel have in fact moved into close proximity to the Suez Canal. New deployments of Soviet surface-to-air missiles make this conclusion inescapable.

6. "I have been asked to re-read to you the text of Secy Rogers' statement to Amb Dobrynin of June 2, which is as follows (Ref para 3 State 085691).

7. "I have been asked to say that in our view the latest Soviet actions in support of UAR military activity in proximity to the Canal cannot be characterized as defensive, since their net effect is to bolster UAR policy of violating the ceasefire. There is a serious question whether new Soviet support of the UAR in the Canal combat zone has not now led to a major qualitative change in the military balance. Given the UAR policy of attacking along the ceasefire line, we view Soviet activity as contributing to a serious escalation of the conflict.

8. "To understand our own position it is useful to go back to Premier Kosygin's Jan 30 [31] message[6] to the US, France, and the UK. The US replied to Premier Kosygin in a flexible, constructive manner.[7] Then on March 23 Pres Nixon announced deferral on arms delivery for Israel. However, the result has been no ceasefire, no arms limitation talks, but indeed the introduction of new modern arms into the UAR. Another pressure developed on the USG when 79 [73] senators declared that the US should accede to Israel's request for more aircraft. This has not been done. We came forward with a procedural initiative to get the parties themselves to begin discussion. Furthermore, we have continued our restraint on arms deliveries.

9. "We have previously on numerous occasions requested an authoritative statement of the Soviet Union's intentions with respect to Soviet personnel and military involvement in the UAR but have received no satisfactory reply. A clear understanding on our part of Soviet intentions might help us avoid a serious miscalculation. We would still welcome such a statement. We will in any case interpret concrete Soviet actions in their own right and will be required to consider appropriate steps in the light of such Soviet actions.

10. "The final question is the opportunity which the present moment offers for a movement toward a settlement. We hope we may soon receive your reaction to our proposal for getting the parties negotiating under Jarring. This in turn would provide a favorable opportunity for greater activity in the major-power talks. As Sisco said to

---

[6] Document 121.

[7] Document 126.

Amb Dobrynin, the US initiative offers the Soviet Union and the UAR an excellent and rapid way to test the seriousness of the US about peace.

11. "The escalating situation along the Canal again underlines the need for more speedy and effective efforts toward political settlement and validates the relevance of the US initiative. We again strongly urge that the Soviet Union not allow the opportunity presented by our initiative to slip by."

12. After hearing my statement, Gromyko said the question arises as to how one should explain this appeal to the SovGov. Is it not, he asked, explained by the fact that the USG is preparing the soil for giving arms to Israel? In other words, the question arises because, on the one hand the USG has stated its readiness to renew the Jarring mission; on the other hand, we have statements such as the one you have made today. If the USG really would like to renew the Jarring mission, moreover with the aim of having it succeed, the USSR has been and is for its resumption. Why then are hints being made regarding possible developments of events such as are contained in your statement, Gromyko went on.

13. The USSR has always proceeded from the position that we must find a political settlement to the ME situation and remove the dangers inherent in that situation. The USSR has repeatedly stated this, for example in the Soviet PriMin's letters to Pres Nixon, in statements by Soviet leaders at the time of the Supreme Soviet elections, and in his discussions with ME. The USSR has repeatedly stressed it wants a political settlement of the ME situation, to eliminate an aggravation of the situation and to bring about a radical change in the interests of peace.

14. Gromyko went on to say that if one looks objectively at the situation, one cannot find differences between the words and concrete deeds of the USSR in the ME. He asserted that the USSR does not wish to see contradictions within the positions of the govts with which it is exchanging views on the ME. He said there should not be contradictions in the positions of the USG and would like the USG to occupy the same position in words and deeds.

15. He said my statement contained the assertion that Soviet personnel in the UAR represented a danger and that their presence in certain areas of the UAR can or may lead to an escalation or an increase in tension in this area. Gromyko said the USSR categorically rejects this assertion.

16. He went on to say that the USSR has a certain number of advisers in the UAR. They had said so in statements made by the head of the SovGov, for example at a recent press conference. These personnel are in the capacity of advisers. Their number represents a threat

to no one and their presence in the UAR cannot lead to an exacerbation of the situation. They have a purely defensive character and operate in this capacity.

17. Gromyko then said he did not wish to touch on purely military aspects of the question. He did not wish to refer to types of arms and their locations mentioned by ME and about which he presumed I had information from Washington. He then went on to say that even if something along the lines of what I said had taken place, one could not but draw the conclusion that the question relates to purely defensive actions on UAR territory. He said Israel was occupying foreign territory, that the area across the Canal belongs not to Israel but to the UAR, and represents territory captured by the Israelis. He said he wished to repeat that even if such things had taken place, they would be purely defensive actions. He went on to stress that he had not used the conditional tense accidentally.

18. Israel, he said, is spreading tendentious information and conjecture which the USG should not believe. The Israelis have a definite purpose in doing so, and if one should believe them, then one would think that Israeli and Soviet pilots are clashing. This is totally absurd. Perhaps, he went on, the Israelis wished to cause provocations, but we should not let them get away with this. As far as the Soviet Union is concerned, it thinks the USG should proceed coolly toward the problem and be guided by the lofty considerations of a political settlement of the ME situation.

19. In various discussions the Soviet Union has held, it has tried to convince everyone of the need to strive for political settlement of the ME problem, to establish a firm peace in the ME with guarantees for a peaceful, independent existence for all states in the region, including Israel. This settlement should include the withdrawal of Israeli troops from all occupied territory.

20. Gromyko said the Soviet Union follows this policy, and its latest proposals were guided by it. At the same time, he alleged the USSR begins to notice a lessening of interest on the part of the US in seeking ways for a political settlement. Even on questions in which the USG has expressed views similar to those of the USSR, he alleged that Moscow sees a diminution of US interest. He said he thought we would have welcomed the latest Soviet proposals, but instead Moscow has been puzzled by a lowered US interest, for example on the question of withdrawal and the establishment of peace.

21. Regarding a Soviet response to the US proposals, Gromyko said the Soviet proposals had been made earlier and Moscow had not heard from the USG. Therefore, the USSR has a more convincing reason to expect an answer from the USG first. Moscow would like to know the US position on the withdrawal of troops and the establishment of peace

which the USG has until now considered to be the crucial issue, and probably still considers as such.

22. With respect to the US proposal about the resumption of the Jarring Mission, Gromyko said this was no great problem. The USSR has always advocated its renewal if it could lead to successful results. The question is not one of the resumption of the Jarring Mission. It is a matter of solving the basic question, the solution to which will not come of itself. He then asserted the USG always seems to dodge away from the main issues when there is need to move forward on questions of substance.

23. He then said his remarks were not a final, formal reply and that the Soviets would give an answer to the US proposals. In doing so they would take into account the statements I had made today as well as other statements.

24. I told Gromyko I had several remarks to make about his comments. We were addressing our appeal to the USSR because the indications we had were that Soviet military support and activity in the UAR has increased. The available evidence has impressed the USG, which would not have raised the issue if there were not a substantial increase, which creates a more dangerous situation in the area. It is important that the USG is convinced of the validity of the information and may have to act on it. The USG has not, as far as I know, been preparing new deliveries to Israel. We have suspended action on the Israeli request for more planes. We have done so in the interest of not escalating the situations, of not making it more tense.

25. I said it was well known the UAR had repudiated the ceasefire and was acting in violation of the ceasefire. Its actions are not purely defensive in this sense. Soviet support and increased military aid has changed and is changing the military situation between the Arabs and the Israelis. This increases the possibility of undesirable and unforeseen actions. Furthermore, it is forcing the USG to review its own position with respect to Israel where we have, until now, shown restraint by not escalating our military deliveries.

26. We do not have precise, accurate information from the Soviet side regarding its military activity in the UAR. This situation may engender exaggeration and speculation, but the evidence available to us is impressive and very disturbing. I went on to say that I was sure he would believe that the US is taking it seriously and that is why we have spoken on sober terms in Moscow and Washington.

27. I then went on to point out that we were happy to note that the Soviet Union, like the USG, believes in the necessity for political settlement of the situation in the ME. Regarding withdrawal and a peace settlement, the USG was certainly no less interested in these points than the USSR. We were glad to note that there was some

advance in the latest Soviet proposals. Far from ignoring these pro-posals, we thought they offered something to build on in the proper setting and at the proper time.

28. I went on to stress that our initiative was not intended to set aside the Two- or Four-Power talks or the Soviet proposals. It was suggested as an emergency measure to bring the parties into discus-sion on the basis of firm acceptance of UNSC Res 242. We were not asking anything of the USSR or the Arabs to which they had not already agreed. On the other hand, we were asking the Israelis to en-gage in indirect negotiations and to commit themselves to with-drawal. The purpose was to revive the Jarring mission and to get talks started.

29. Discussions have taken place in NY and Washington for over a year on the matter of giving guidance to Jarring. We still think it will take time to reach agreement on precise instructions and guidance to Jarring. In the meantime, the opportunity would be lost to bring to-gether the parties and to reduce tensions and ease the exceedingly dan-gerous situation which is building up. It is our view that once talks start under Jarring, the Two- and Four-Power talks will have much more meaning.

30. The USSR and the USG will have the duty and the opportu-nity to narrow the gap between the two sides. I said that up until now the talks in NY and Washington had been operating in a vacuum, and Gromyko broke in to ask in what respect. I answered they had not brought the two parties together, and our aim was to launch Jarring and to bring the parties into discussion. We hoped our procedural sug-gestion would appeal to all concerned as an emergency measure, as a way of escaping from a dangerous situation. I stressed again that we wanted the Soviet govt to consider seriously the advantages.

31. Gromyko responded by saying that if any undesirable devel-opments take place in the ME, this would be due to actions undertaken by the Israelis or by the wishes of the USG. Otherwise, there can be no undesirable developments in the area. He went on to say that the USSR was not only against an exacerbation of the situation but for finding a solution to the problems of a political settlement. He then reiterated this assertion that any undesirable developments in the ME would be due to actions taken by the Israelis and USG toleration of such actions. He said that if there are hotheads in Tel Aviv who want to exacerbate the situation and to provoke a major incident, he hoped the USG would finds ways to cool these hotheads. The USG should proceed from the fact that it has interest in preserving peace. He went on to say that he understood the Arabs plan to answer the USG proposals.

33. [sic] I told Gromyko I thought it was unfair of him to accuse us of doing undesirable things. We were trying to get Israel to accept

UNSC Res 242 and firmly to accept the principle of withdrawal and to engage in negotiations.

34. Gromyko broke in to say he understood this. He said the USG thinks it would be achieving a great deal to get Israel to accept the principle of withdrawal. However, what the USSR wants is total Israeli withdrawal from all territories. What troops and what territories, these are the main questions. The UAR does not want to discuss the issue if it is only a question of withdrawal of Israeli troops from Sinai. In the Soviet view, it would not be a very great advance if the USG were able to get the Israelis to agree only in principle to withdrawal.

35. I told Gromyko our concern was to get the two parties together so that they could negotiate this issue along with the question of frontiers which must be established by agreement. I went on to stress that our concern was about the developing military situation. I said that if the Soviet Union could provide clarification about the actual state of affairs and its intentions, it might help to reduce our anxiety.

36. Gromyko said he had nothing to add. He wished to say only that the USG should approach the situation coolly and not make any judgments based on the views of certain govts or hotheads.

38. [sic] In conclusion I expressed the hope he would treat seriously our concern about the developing military situation in the ME.

Beam

---

181. Memorandum From the Assistant Secretary of State for Near Eastern and South Asian Affairs (Sisco) to the President's Assistant for National Security Affairs (Kissinger)[1]

Washington, July 13, 1970.

SUBJECT

Meeting with Ambassador Dobrynin

---

[1] Source: National Archives, Nixon Presidential Materials, NSC Files, Box 340, Subject Files, Dobrynin/Kissinger. Secret; Nodis; Personal; Eyes Only. On July 17, Kissinger forwarded this to Nixon under a covering memorandum that reads: "You will see that Sisco made some extremely useful points concerning recent Soviet moves in the region, their unwillingness to explain their actions, and the nature of your personal approach and policy. I think Sisco's presentation should prove helpful and is another reason for you to compliment him when you see him." Nixon wrote the following note on the covering memorandum: "K—Tell Sisco an *excellent* follow-up to my recent instructions to him."

I wrote a very brief telegram[2] covering my last conversation with Dobrynin. What is not contained in the telegram is that I gave the Ambassador some personal impressions—strictly personal—of the atmosphere which the continuing increased Soviet military involvement in the UAR is creating which increases the risks of possible confrontation with us. I said that it would be well for Dobrynin to reflect that the President at the outset of his Administration had declared an era of negotiations. For seventeen months we had negotiated in good faith, and we feel that the Soviets have not come half the way; and that our restraint on the military side has not been met by restraint but rather by a fundamental decision on the part of the Soviet Union to involve its personnel in an operational capacity. This is a most serious decision for the Soviets to have taken, and our concern has increased not only because of the creeping process in recent weeks, but also because of Soviet unwillingness to tell us quietly and confidentially what their intentions are and what the outer limits of their involvement may be as they see it.

I said I had watched our President for months and felt that he had offered political proposal after political proposal, and political option after political option in the context of the United States exercising great restraint in the face of pressures for providing Israel with substantial numbers of additional aircraft. I hoped that Dobrynin was not reporting to Moscow that our involvement in Vietnam reflected any lack of resolve in the Middle East. The President was a man of peace, a man who wanted a negotiated settlement, but also a man of firmness and toughness, which it would be well for the Soviet Union to take fully into account as it develops Middle East policy. He would not be pushed around in the Middle East or anywhere else. These were only personal judgments I was expressing; but I would advise Dobrynin to take very, very seriously the words expressed by the President some months ago that the United States would view with deep concern any attempt by the Soviet Union to dominate the Middle East.

Dobrynin responded critically of the recent "tough talk" which he said would not force the Soviet Union to make decisions of the kind it would not wish to make. He remonstrated several times that the emphasis on the Soviet role was creating a crisis atmosphere, and that it was not making it easier for Moscow to take constructive initiatives during the current discussions with Cairo. At the same time, he was quick to say, these were personal remarks and we would be receiving the replies to our political initiative at an early date.

---

[2] Telegram 111425 to Moscow, July 13. (Ibid., Box 490, President's Trip Files, Dobrynin/Kissinger, 1970, Vol. 3)

I concluded this portion of the conversation by saying that I just wanted personally to get this off of my chest, and that I had no authority to say any of this. I wanted to say what I said because the Soviets in the past have miscalculated regarding United States intentions and it was important he reflected to Moscow the resolve and the fiber and the determination of the President, as I read the situation.

I have brought this memorandum to the attention of Secretary Rogers.[3]

J.J. Sisco

---

[3] At 5:40 p.m., Kissinger and Sisco spoke on the telephone about Rogers' reaction to Sisco's meeting with Dobrynin. According to a transcript of the telephone conversation, Kissinger told Sisco that the President was behind him. Sisco replied, "Well, between you and me the only flack I got was from the Secretary of State." Kissinger responded, "Really? The President is a terribly perceptive man. He told me he would bet me a thousand to one that you got hell from the Secretary and he wanted me to call you and reassure you. I didn't pick that up. What did he give you hell about?" Sisco replied, "It's a long story. Let's just say that I took it and it's over. I just don't want this thing to go on." (Library of Congress, Manuscript Division, Kissinger Papers, Box 364, Telephone Conversations, Chronological File)

---

182. Memorandum From the President's Assistant for National Security Affairs (Kissinger) to President Nixon[1]

Washington, undated.

SUBJECT

The Moscow Communiqué on Nasser's Visit

The joint communiqué issued at the conclusion of Nasser's 19–day visit to the Soviet Union (attached)[2] concentrates most heavily on the Middle East situation, although there are references to other major world problems. Typical of such pronouncements, the communiqué is a carefully worded document reaffirming mutual support and friendship and shedding very little light on what actually transpired during Nasser's extended talks with the Soviet leaders. One of its more

---

[1] Source: National Archives, Nixon Presidential Materials, NSC Files, Box 712, Country Files, Europe, USSR, Vol. VIII. Secret. Sent for information.

[2] Attached but not printed. Nasser returned from the Soviet Union on July 17.

significant aspects is the fact that the communiqué appears to align the UAR with the USSR on a global basis although not in every detail nor in every way.

The Middle East

There is almost no hint of conclusions reached and the U.S. initiative is not even mentioned.

On the terms of a settlement, it is a standard reiteration of the Egyptian position which the Soviets have long supported. The line is the usual insistence that the establishment of a just and durable peace in the Middle East can only be realized by the adoption of measures insuring the cessation of Israeli "aggression" and the withdrawal of Israeli forces from all occupied territory as well as the full implementation of the November 1967 Security Council resolution and the application of UN resolutions pertaining to the Palestinian refugees.

On further Soviet aid to the UAR, there are no details. Continuation of assistance is affirmed in general terms, and there is one reference to the need for "urgent measures" to compel the Israelis to withdraw.

For the most part, however, the general tone is relatively calm, unemotional and non-belligerent. There are, of course, some of the usual references to "aggressive imperialistic forces" and their plots and Israelis "aggressive and expansionist policy" supported by the U.S., but this is not overdone. More notable is the recurrent stress on peaceful settlement.

It may be notable that, in addition to omitting any mention of the U.S. initiative, there is no effort to respond to our statements from San Clemente.[3]

If anything, this statement seems to support the conclusion that we will get at least a qualified reply to our initiative rather than a flat rejection.

Other Topics

One of the more interesting aspects of the communiqué is its breadth in mentioning a wide range of international issues.

On these other issues, it is substantively a rather routine document, broadly alining Nasser with the Soviets but still preserving a good deal of distance between the UAR and the USSR. In particular, on European questions, while the UAR joins the Soviets in applauding those who have recognized the "sovereignty and independence" of both the FRG and the GDR as well as approving post-war European

---

[3] See footnote 4, Document 177.

borders (not mentioned by name, incidentally), Nasser is specifically *not* cited as endorsing Soviet proposals for a European security conference. Nor is there in the communiqué an overall attack on NATO, as would be normal between the USSR and a Communist satellite. On the other hand, on subjects of long-standing Soviet-UAR agreement—anti-colonialism, Rhodesia, South Africa—the communiqué records the usual congruence of views. The U.S. is attacked only once—for supporting Israel. SALT is not mentioned, but the disarmament negotiations in Geneva in which the UAR has generally supported the Soviets—and in which our differences with the Soviets are not as great as in the past—are referred to favorably.

Indochina

The portion of the statement dealing with Indochina appears to be merely pro forma and even somewhat moderate in some of its formulations. While it reiterates the customary attacks on U.S. "interference" and "aggression" it does not support the more extreme Hanoi position. It merely describes Hanoi's ten points as a "a good basis" for a political settlement. This could be attributed to a Soviet desire at this point to distance itself somewhat from Hanoi's diplomatic moves, or might be designed to conform to the general tone and content of the Soviet-UAR communiqué itself.

---

183.   Memorandum of Conversation[1]

Washington, July 20, 1970, 10:30 a.m.

PARTICIPANTS

Ambassador Anatoliy Dobrynin
Mr. Henry A. Kissinger

The meeting was requested by Ambassador Dobrynin. He was extremely jovial and friendly, and opened the conversation by asking me whether I could recommend any good movies. I said no, I very rarely went. He said he had read reports that "Patton" was very popular in

---

[1] Source: National Archives, Nixon Presidential Materials, NSC Files, Box 489, President's Trip Files, Dobrynin/Kissinger, 1970, Part 1, Vol. 1. Top Secret; Sensitive; Eyes Only. The conversation was held in the Map Room at the White House. Under cover of a July 21 memorandum, Kissinger sent Nixon this memorandum of conversation and a summary of his conversation with Dobrynin. (Ibid.)

the White House. I replied that I had seen these reports also. He asked how I compared "Patton" with the "Battle of Kursk" which he had shown at the Motion Picture Association. I told him they were not easy to compare. "Patton" was about a romantic hero and stressed the role of the individual while the "Battle of Kursk" stressed the role of matériel, not of the individual.

Dobrynin said the only individual who really counted in World War II in the Soviet Union was Stalin, and his great attribute was that he had absolutely iron nerves. He was the one senior leader who refused to leave Moscow even though the Germans were only 10 miles away and, by this act of defiance, he rallied a lot of doubters. Also, Stalin had unbelievable powers of concentration. He, Dobrynin, was a young aide in the Foreign Office and he remembers that on the way to the Tehran conference, Stalin gave orders to be left alone in his compartment. He was not shown any documents and he sat there for three days, as far as anyone knew just staring out of the window, thinking and concentrating. Then, from the Soviet point of view, he gave an absolutely masterly performance at Tehran.

Dobrynin also told me that Stalin personally picked the Soviet Chief of Protocol in 1943 at the Tehran Conference because there was a young Soviet diplomat who knew a Churchillian idiosyncrasy which was always to ask for three Scottish tunes from visiting bands that no one had ever heard of in order to embarrass them. The young diplomat found out and when Churchill requested these tunes, the Soviet honor guard was ready to play it. Stalin asked who had thought this up and immediately appointed him Chief of Protocol in the Foreign Office even though he was only 30 years old at the time. Dobrynin said that he turned out to be the best Chief of Protocol the Soviet Foreign Office had ever had. He added that being Chief of Protocol in the Soviet Union was even more difficult than here because we had only one man in charge, while after Stalin, placing the Soviet leaders in their proper order was an act of political significance.

European Security

Dobrynin then turned to the subject at hand. He read me a Note Verbale which his government had asked him to transmit to us. The text is as follows:

"In continuation of our exchange of views on the questions touched upon at our meeting of June 10[2] I would like to say the following to be transmitted to President Nixon.

---

[2] See Document 168.

"The affirmations made in the course of the above meeting by President Nixon and, on his instructions, by you, Dr. Kissinger, concerning the interest of the US in maintaining the territorial status quo in Europe and the absence of intentions on the part of the US to act counter to this or in general to take any steps in the direction of aggravation of the situation in Europe, have been noted in Moscow. Likewise noted in Moscow was President Nixon's statement to the effect that the US Government recognizes special interests of the Soviet Union in Eastern Europe and has no intention to ignore or undermine them due to the unrealistic nature of such a course. Those are, without doubt, realistic judgments.

"Likewise, the Soviet Union is convinced that recognition of the realities that have come into being in Europe, constitute that necessary foundation upon which a stable peace on the continent as well as in the world at large can and must be built.

"An important step on the way to strengthening peace in Europe would be speedy preparation and convocation of an all-European conference on problems of security and cooperation in Europe as proposed by the Soviet Union and other European Socialist countries.

"It should be emphasized that the Memorandum adopted by the Governments of European Socialist countries in Budapest on June 22[3] takes into account also the wishes of other possible participants in such a conference expressed in the course of bilateral and multilateral consultations. Taken into account, too, are the wishes expressed by the American side both with regard to participation of the US in the all-European conference and regarding questions to be discussed at the conference or in connection with it.

"Taking into consideration, in particular, the wishes of the US Government the Soviet Government together with the other Governments which adopted the said Memorandum, have come to the conclusion that consideration of the question of reducing foreign armed forces on the territory of European states would serve the interests of détente and security in Europe.

"In our view, this question could be discussed in a body on questions of security and cooperation in Europe which is proposed to be established at the all-European conference. At the same time we are prepared to discuss this question also in another manner acceptable to interested states, outside of the framework of the conference. Such an approach opens wide possibilities in selecting appropriate methods of

---

[3] The Foreign Ministers of the Warsaw Pact nations met in Budapest June 21–22 and approved a memorandum on the holding of an all-European conference to deal with security and cooperation.

discussing this question and takes into account the experience that has already been accumulated in considering outstanding problems of such kind, in particular between the USSR and the US.

"The questions of man's environment, which the American side is interested in, could be, in our opinion, discussed within item 2 of the proposed agenda for the all-European conference.

"We proceed from the assumption that in view of these clarifications the United States should have no reason for delaying further convocation of the all-European conference by way of presenting various preconditions. We hope that the US Government will adopt a more constructive position and will thereby contribute to making the preparation of the all-European conference a more practical business."

I asked what the phrase meant that in connection with a mutual balanced force reduction, an approach "opens wide possibilities in selecting appropriate methods of discussing this question" on a bilateral basis. He responded that the choice of appropriate forums could be determined after we had agreed in principle. He said he recognized that he owed me some answers to other questions, and they would be forthcoming within the next few weeks. I told him, of course, that I had to check my answer with the President, and I wanted to remind him that I had listed European Security as one of the three topics at our last conversation. I thought the tone of his note was constructive, and we would try to handle our reply in a constructive manner. I would let him know what the response would be.

SALT

Dobrynin then turned the conversation to SALT. He said that we had not yet presented our formal proposals and he wondered when they could expect them. I replied that they would have them certainly the next day, but they would be along the lines foreshadowed in my recent conversation. He said he recognized that we would not split off ABMs as a separate agreement and asked about the accidental war question. I told him that Smith was under instructions not to split off anything, but that I would be willing to explore with him separating out of the accidental war question those issues which concerned only our two countries, such as unauthorized launches of missiles or mass flights of bombers, from issues that affected third countries, such as the note Semyonov had handed to Smith at a concert. I stated that there might be a possibility of a limited technical agreement along these lines, but that Smith was not authorized to negotiate it. This would have to be done between Dobrynin and me. Dobrynin said he would come back to me on that.

Southeast Asia

Dobrynin then raised the question of Laos. He said he had read press reports that we were planning a Cambodian-type operation there.

What was there to such reports? I replied, "Anatoliy, you wouldn't believe me if you suspect us of planning a military operation. Nothing I say will convince you. If we are not planning one, it would be stupid for me to say anything, so I will not talk about military operations."

He said he didn't think we would launch one, but that there was a chance that the South Vietnamese would launch one. I asked him why he raised the question. He replied that he wanted me to understand that the Soviet Government attached the greatest importance to the neutrality of Laos. He thought we could work cooperatively for a solution of that problem and he wanted us to know that this was the spirit of the Soviet Government. I stated we were in favor of both Laos and Cambodia being neutral. Dobrynin said Cambodia was a much tougher problem and perhaps the way to get at it was first to assure the neutrality of Laos. I said I'd always be willing to listen to specific proposals.

He then asked about Thieu's readiness to have a coalition government. I replied our position on that subject was well known, but that I would hardly have talked to Le Duc Tho if we were not prepared to have serious discussions. It was up to Hanoi to meet us with equal seriousness.

German-Soviet Talks

Dobrynin then asked about the conversation with Scheel.[4] I replied that we had done nothing to discourage Scheel and we were in general in favor of a relaxation of tensions. He asked me for my personal views of the document. I said that I thought that Gromyko was a very good negotiator, but I repeated that we would do nothing to discourage the Germans and that we in general favored a relaxation of tensions.

Dobrynin said that he would be in touch with me when he had other things to communicate and he hoped I would do the same.

The meeting concluded after about an hour.

---

[4] Foreign Minister Walter Scheel of the Federal Republic of Germany visited Washington July 17–18. During his visit, Scheel discussed the talks that would begin at the end of July between the FRG and the Soviet Union on the mutual renunciation of force.

184. Memorandum of Conversation[1]

Washington, July 23, 1970, noon.

SUBJECT

Middle East

PARTICIPANTS

The Secretary
Anatoliy F. Dobrynin, Soviet Ambassador
Joseph J. Sisco, Assistant Secretary for Near Eastern and South Asian Affairs
Adolph Dubs, Country Director, Soviet Union Affairs

Ambassador Dobrynin, at his initiative, called on the Secretary to present an oral statement on the Middle East.

The oral statement, a text of which in both the English and Russian languages was handed to the Secretary after Dobrynin's presentation, reads as follows:

Begin text

"The Soviet Union, as the Government of the United States is well aware, from the very start of the Arab-Israeli conflict in the Middle East has consistently sought a settlement of this conflict through political means on the basis of the UN Security Council Resolution of November 22, 1967. With this aim in mind the Soviet Union repeatedly introduced proposals directed towards practical implementation of this Resolution.

"The U.S. Government declares now that it agrees to a resumption of the mission of Ambassador Jarring, Special Representative of the UN Secretary General in the Middle East. It is well known that the Soviet Government has always insisted on the necessity of carrying out the mission entrusted with Ambassador Jarring, that it put forward appropriate proposals to this end and made efforts so that his mission be effective enough.

"That is why the Soviet side not only holds no objections to this effect but, on the contrary, it reiterates its position with regard to the necessity of resumption by Ambassador Jarring of his mission. Positively evaluating the possibilities in Ambassador Jarring's mission, we are ready to go on making contribution in the future as well so that

---

[1] Source: National Archives, Nixon Presidential Materials, NSC Files, Box 1155, Saunders File, U.S. Peace Initiative for Middle East, 6/10/70–7/23/70, Vol. 1, 5 of 5. Secret; Nodis. Drafted by Dubs and cleared by Sisco in draft. The conversation was held in the Secretary's office. The memorandum is part I of III.

contacts between the sides through Jarring which could be resumed in the nearest future could produce positive results.

"As we know, the Governments of the UAR and Jordan have expressed their readiness to cease fire for a definite period of time if Israel also takes upon herself the same obligation. The Soviet Government's attitude to this is positive.

"Undoubtedly, the success of Ambassador Jarring's activities requires that both sides unequivocally declare their readiness to implement the above mentioned Resolution of the Security Council in all its parts. The Soviet side hopes that the American side is being guided by the same motivations. The Governments of the UAR and Jordan have repeatedly stated and are confirming now that they are ready to implement the Resolution in all its parts. Therefore it is necessary that Israel should also clearly state her readiness to implement this Resolution. Otherwise the sides would find themselves in an unequal position: one of them does recognize the November Resolution of the Security Council and expresses its readiness to implement it while the other side ignores it.

"At the same time in the interests of success of Jarring's mission it is important that he should have a definite enough understanding as to the basis upon which contacts should take place between the sides in search of ways to implement the Resolution of the Security Council. For the success of Jarring's mission first of all a direction is required on the main questions of settlement—the withdrawal by Israel from the Arab territories occupied during the conflict of 1967, including the question of secure and recognized boundaries along the lines which existed prior to the conflict in June 1967, and the simultaneous establishment of a just and stable peace in the Middle East. The U.S. Government, on its part, has also repeatedly emphasized the utmost importance of the above mentioned questions. Both of these questions are organically connected with each other and should be considered jointly. Appropriate proposals to this effect have been put forward by the Soviet Government in the course of Soviet-American exchange of opinion on June 2[2] and also at the four-sided consultants in New York. The American side has not given so far its reply to the above mentioned proposals—neither in the course of bilateral exchange of opinion nor at the four-sided consultations. Yet these proposals are in complete conformity with the Security Council Resolution and the Soviet Government is expecting a reply from the U.S. Government.

"Parallel to the resumption of activities by Jarring and the initiation through him of contacts between the parties the four-sided consultations

---

[2] See Document 159.

in New York should be made more active to work out agreed guide-lines for Jarring. The Soviet Government on its part will be doing its best to facilitate it." *End text*

After making his oral statement, Dobrynin commented as follows, presumably on instructions from his Government:

"Our statement has been made in the expectation that the American Government will, indeed, make necessary efforts towards achieving a just political settlement of the Middle East problem and will exert due influence upon Israel.

"Besides, we are taking into consideration the clarifications by the American side that—with Jarring's activities resumed—the bilateral consultations will continue and that the American side will show an active and constructive approach to the discussion of matters of settlement in the Middle East both in the course of the four-sided and of the bilateral consultations."

After thanking Dobrynin, the Secretary recalled that one of the important considerations in our proposal regarding a ceasefire was that each side would commit itself not to improve its military position. The Secretary said we assume that a military standstill as part of the ceasefire is also acceptable to the Soviet Union. Dobrynin responded affirmatively adding, "Yes, of course." It was his understanding that Foreign Minister Riad's statement to the Secretary covered this point.

The Secretary asked whether the Soviet side saw any objections to releasing the Arab response to our initiative. Dobrynin replied that it was his understanding that the UAR did not intend to publicize its response. In any event, he suggested that this matter be raised with the Egyptians. The Secretary said it would be helpful from our standpoint to make public the simple UAR statement accepting our proposal. He understood Dobrynin's remarks to mean that publicizing the response would be acceptable to the USSR if this matter could be worked out with the UAR. Dobrynin said that he did not anticipate any objections from the Soviet side.

The Secretary added that the U.S. would do its part in support of Jarring to bring about a settlement, and he indicated our willingness to continue the Two and Four-Power talks. The Secretary said that he viewed the Soviet's response as an indication that the USSR was interested in a peaceful settlement. Such a settlement would be in the mutual US–USSR interest and in the interest of the world community.

Dobrynin stressed that the USSR has no objections whatsoever to having Jarring resume his mission in a few days. He wanted to be sure that the U.S. understood that the comment in the oral statement referring to the absence of a U.S. reply to the Soviet June 2nd proposals was not meant to be a Soviet precondition for resumption of Jarring's mission.

Dobrynin asked whether the U.S. Government had had any reply from Israel. The Secretary indicated that we would inform Dobrynin as soon as we could regarding his query.

(An official translation of the text of the Soviet oral statement[3] is attached. The official translation does not vary in any substantive respect from the English translation made by the Soviet Embassy.)

---

[3] Attached but not printed.

---

185.   Memorandum Prepared by the President's Assistant for National Security Affairs (Kissinger)[1]

Washington, July 23, 1970.

Conversation with Dobrynin—July 23, 1970

Dobrynin was at the White House in his capacity as Acting Dean of the Diplomatic Corps for the reception of President Kekkonen.[2] He had called me earlier to tell me that he had been instructed to deliver the Soviet reply to our Middle East peace overture at noon at the State Department. But, as a matter of courtesy, he wanted to leave a copy with me two hours before then. I therefore suggested to him that he join me in the Map Room after the ceremony.

In the Map Room, Dobrynin was extremely cordial and asked me whether I was now optimistic about the Middle East. I said, "I'm always realistic—neither optimistic nor pessimistic." He asked me what I thought would be a logical place for the conference to occur. I said it might be Cyprus or New York. Dobrynin replied that he felt the Soviet Union would prefer New York, but it was not a key issue.

He then handed me the Soviet note[3] which is attached. After I had read it, Dobrynin asked me whether I thought it was in a constructive spirit which I affirmed. Dobrynin then asked who I thought would win the Nobel Prize for having brought about this peace settlement— Rogers or the White House. I said that we were not in competition and,

---

[1] Source: National Archives, Nixon Presidential Materials, NSC Files, Box 489, President's Trip Files, Dobrynin/Kissinger, 1970, Part 1, Vol. 1. No classification marking.

[2] President Urho Kekkonen of Finland visited the United States July 23–27.

[3] The note is identical to the text presented to Rogers the same day; see Document 184.

in any event, he was such an acute observer of the American scene that I had no doubt that he had formed his own conclusion. Dobrynin said that in his whole experience he had never seen foreign policy decisions so centralized and he knew where the real power lay. I said that we had collective leadership, and on this note, we parted.

186. Memorandum From the President's Assistant for National Security Affairs (Kissinger) to President Nixon[1]

Washington, July 23, 1970.

SUBJECT

Ambassador Dobrynin's Reply to the U.S. Mid-East Initiative

At Tab A is the text of Ambassador Dobrynin's statement.[2] At Tab B is a detailed commentary on it.

Perhaps the most important element in the Ambassador's exchange with the Secretary was Dobrynin's categorical assurance that the cease-fire will also include a military standstill. As we defined "standstill" in describing our initiative last month, that would mean no major troop movements and no new installations in the combat zone. This will be a key element in our approach to the Israelis.

The Soviet response is:

—mild and non-polemical in tone;
—substantively complementary to the UAR response;
—tantamount to a Soviet endorsement of the UAR acceptance with no unexpected hookers.

While they do not refer explicitly to our formula for beginning of talks under Jarring, they say that they favor both a cease-fire and resumption of Jarring's mission.

The Soviets have emphasized—as did the UAR—that it is essential for the Four Powers to provide Jarring with detailed guidelines. The next major issue then—if the details of the cease-fire were confirmed and the Israelis accepted—would be debate over how detailed the U.S.-Soviet agreement should be before Jarring begins talks. The

---

[1] Source: National Archives, Nixon Presidential Materials, NSC Files, Box 489, President's Trip Files, Dobrynin/Kissinger, 1970, Part 1, Vol. 1. Top Secret; Nodis. Sent for information.

[2] See Document 184.

U.S. would have a case for resumption on the basis of its formula alone, but the Soviets could slow the beginning of a substantive exchange pending more detailed U.S.-Soviet agreement.

To put the Soviet reply in perspective, it must be kept in mind what the Soviets are gaining and what they are conceding.

They would be getting *indirect* talks started—if the Israelis accepted—and would be getting Israelis acceptance of at least the principle of withdrawal. Whatever that may mean in precise terms, it is more restrictive rather than less. The USSR also seems to see greater promise than in the past that the U.S. is prepared to press Israel. If it is genuinely concerned about further military escalation, it is also getting an opportunity to stop the shooting while the Soviet involvement appears on a rising trend of effectiveness.

They would be conceding a commitment to talk without a precise U.S. or Israeli commitment to total withdrawal. If they honored the military standstill, they would be stopping short of depriving Israel of air supremacy over the Suez combat zone. They would also be accepting the success of a unilateral U.S. initiative to get talks started. While they have their own image of increasing military effectiveness along the Suez Canal to rest on, they could also appear to have been influenced by the firm stand taken in San Clemente. They would also appear to be acknowledging tacitly their own desire to limit their military involvement.

Above all, of course, it must be remembered that the Soviets will be in an advantageous position if Israel does not accept. If Israel accepts, the U.S. will have brought the situation over the first major political hurdle but there will still be the cease-fire to be defined in credible terms and hard bargaining ahead on both sides, perhaps even before a serious substantive exchange can begin.

Tab B

Paper Prepared by the National Security Council Staff

Washington, July 23, 1970.

COMMENTARY

1. The USSR reaffirms that it continues to seek "a settlement of this conflict through political means on the basis of the UN Security Council resolution."

Comment: The USSR has been consistent on this general point. The issue has always been the price to be paid for a political settlement.

2. The USSR agrees to "the necessity of resumption by Ambassador Jarring of his mission."

Comment: The USSR nowhere specifically mentions the U.S. formula for getting Jarring started. It seems implicit that the UAR response, in Soviet eyes, takes care of that. Therefore, the Soviets seem to be saying that they are willing to facilitate resumption of talks on the terms the U.S. has proposed, although that is not explicit.

3. The USSR's "attitude is positive" toward Egypt's and Jordan's expressed "readiness to cease fire for a definite period of time if Israel also takes upon herself the same obligation."

Comment: We have had no response from Jordan ourselves, so it is interesting that the USSR is speaking for Jordan. This may partly result from a slip in Egyptian coordination. The main point is Soviet endorsement of the cease-fire. What remains imprecise is whether both Egyptians and Soviets accept the U.S. definition of cease-fire to include military standstill—no major troop movements and no new installations.

4. Jarring's success "requires that both sides unequivocally declare their readiness to implement" the UN resolution in all its parts. The UAR and Jordan have declared their readiness. It is "necessary that Israel should also clearly state her readiness . . . "[3]

Comment: This introduces an element of uncertainty. There has been a theological argument for more than two years over the word "implement." Because the UAR claims that the Security Council resolution intends total Israeli withdrawal, it contends that agreement to "implement" the resolution is agreement to total withdrawal and that all that is needed is a timetable for withdrawal. Because the Israelis claim that the resolution only intends negotiation of an agreement on final boundaries, it has refused to use the word "implement." We have supported the Israeli argument that negotiation must precede implementation. The element of uncertainty grows from the fact that the U.S. formula for beginning talks—which the UAR has now accepted—avoids this argument. It does not seem that the USSR is setting a new condition for beginning talks—it does not suggest a modification of the U.S. formula to include this and seems tacitly to leave that to the UAR. On the other hand, it does say that Jarring's success "requires" such a declaration by Israel.

5. " . . . in the interests of success of Jarring's mission it is important that he should have a definite enough understanding as to the basis upon which contacts should take place between the sides in search of ways to implement 'the UN resolution'. . . . first of all a direction is required on the main questions of settlement—the withdrawal by Israel from the Arab territories occupied during the conflict of 1967—in-

---

[3] All ellipses are in the source text.

cluding the question of secure and recognized boundaries along the lines which existed prior to the conflict in June 1967—and the simultaneous establishment of a just and stable peace in the Middle East."

Comment: The UAR in its written response also made the point that Jarring must have detailed guidance. What this means is that the Arabs and the Soviets would like the U.S. and the USSR to do the preliminary negotiating and drafting while Jarring tries out various drafts on the parties. The U.S. preference is for the big powers to do less of this formally and turn over the bulk of the drafting job to Jarring with help from us in the wings.

6. The USSR is expecting a U.S. reply to its June 2 proposals.

Comment: Pressure for U.S. response is consistent with the above point. The Soviets want the U.S. to re-engage in the big-power talks.

7. Parallel to resumption of Jarring's activities, the Four Power talks should be "made more active to work out agreed guidelines for Jarring."

Comment: It is difficult to know what to make of Soviet emphasis on the Four Power forum in their formal document, except that the Soviets have had some success in establishing better cooperation with the French in the last couple of months. We prefer the two-power forum. In the supplementary note on top of the basic Soviet paper, Dobrynin did make it clear that Moscow wants the two-power talks to continue active.

---

187.   Telegram From the Embassy in the Soviet Union to the Department of State[1]

Moscow, July 25, 1970, 0915Z.

4134. Subject: Soviet Reply re Soviet Arms to UAR and Gromyko Comments on Procedures for Jarring Mission. Ref: Moscow 4131.[2]

1. Following is informal Embassy translation of statement on Soviet arms to ME handed to me late afternoon July 24 by Gromyko (Reftel). He said this was not identical to the one handed by Dobrynin to Secy July 23,[3] which related to Jarring mission. July 24 statement was

---

[1] Source: National Archives, Nixon Presidential Materials, NSC Files, Box 1155, Saunders File, U.S. Peace Initiative for the Middle East, June Initiative, 6/10/70–7/23/70, Vol. 2, 2 of 5. Secret; Immediate; Nodis.

[2] Telegram 4131, July 24, briefly reported Gromyko's call on Beam about procedures for the Jarring mission. (Ibid.)

[3] See Document 184.

of more general nature, and was Soviet reply to our request for information about their military intentions in ME.

2. *Begin text:* A. In connection with your July 10 statement[4] concerning the ME situation, and similar statements made by the American side to the USSR Amb in Washington, it is requested that the following answer of the SovGov be brought to the attention of your Govt.

B. The Soviet Union has always proceeded and proceeds from the conviction that a way can and must be found toward a political settlement of the ME conflict and thereby the elimination of the danger which has been created in this region. This is our firm position. One would wish that the USG would also adhere to such an approach.

C. As we have already repeatedly stated to the American side, we consider that the establishment of a firm peace in the ME by means of a political settlement of the conflict corresponds to the interests both of the countries which are direct participants in the conflict, as well as the interests of the USA and USSR. Only in this way can the existence and independence of all states of this region, including Israel, be guaranteed. It goes without saying that such a political settlement implies (Podrazumevayet) the withdrawal of Israeli troops from all the territories which they are occupying. It would not be realistic to count on firm peace in the ME without this.

D. All Soviet proposals during the exchange of views with the American side, including also our most recent proposals on the key questions of a settlement, to which the American side until recently has attached—in its words—great importance, have been aimed at achieving the goals of a just political settlement in the ME. And if now the bilateral Soviet-American exchange of views has been halted, then this is not at all our fault. It is then turn of the US to answer our most recent proposals, during the formulation of which the desires of the American side also were taken into account.

E. In the statements made by you, as well as in certain other statements recently by American officials, assertions are contained about allegedly existing discrepancies between the SovGov's line for a political settlement of the ME conflict and its steps toward rendering assistance to the UAR in the matter of strengthening its defense capability. However, without contradicting facts and common sense, it is impossible to prove that the actions aimed at halting Israel's continuing aggression against neighboring Arab states—whatever parts of the territories of these states such action touch upon—do not have a defensive but some other kind of character. In that connection, the assertions that measures for strengthening the UAR's air defense signify allegedly a change in the military balance between the sides are also

---

[4] See Document 180.

totally without foundation. If one follows this logic, then it turns out that when the Israeli air forces were able to bomb with impunity the UAR's territory, this was considered by the US as evidence of some sort of "balance," but when they are deprived of such a possibility, this is declared to be a "dangerous violation of the balance."

F. Such a logic, of course, suits Israel, which is not squeamish about disseminating various sorts of concoctions for its provocative purposes. But when statements, which obviously do not correspond to the real state of affairs, emanate from the American side, then, naturally, the question arises: what purposes are being pursued by this. If this is being done in the hope of somehow "justifying" further steps for rendering military support to Israel, the consequences of such a course of action and the responsibility which would lay on it in this instance should be clear to the USG.

G. Thus, in confirming its firm policy of searching—together with the USA, given its readiness for this—for ways for a peaceful political settlement in the ME, the SovGov deems it necessary to state that an undesirable development of events in the ME can take place only in the event that it will be caused by corresponding actions of Israel and in the event the USG desires this. We do not see other reasons for an unforeseen development of events in the way of exacerbating the situation in this region. One would hope that the USG will act, carefully weighing all circumstances, and will be able to cool the ardor of those hotheads in Tel Aviv who would like to undertake new, dangerous provocations.

H. As regards the question of activation of the Jarring mission, we do not see great difficulties in this question. We have always advocated the maximum use of the possibilities of this mission and we are for its success, about which the SovGov once again informed the USG on July 23. But the main thing is the essence of the questions of a settlement, which is the goal also of Jarring's mission, and the essence of the positions of the states on these questions. *End text.*

3. I told Gromyko I would send this statement to Washington. I then said that, regarding the suspension of bilateral talks, no blame or accusations had been made. The reason related to the presentation of our initiative, to which we now have UAR and Soviet responses.

4. Regarding the two statements I had made, their aim was to seek clarification of Soviet military programs in the UAR. We had no ulterior motives, or intentions to cover up further US deliveries to Israel. In this respect, in fact, we have shown restraint regarding new deliveries. We were seeking information and clarification from the Soviets in order to be reassured that the military situation in the ME would not escalate. I said we would carefully study Gromyko's statement and Washington would have to determine its significance and whether it provided us with more information.

5. Gromyko said if USG wished to contribute to a lessening of tension, the first step would be to influence Israel to give a positive reply, to state in clear terms that it accepts and will fulfill UNSC 242. Israel should do what the UAR has done. Gromyko said he did not know if Jordan had replied yet. Then, Gromyko continued, Jarring presumably should go somewhere and meet with some persons to begin the exchange of views.

6. Gromyko said the important thing was the substance of the matter. The Arabs will be asking Jarring what is the nature of the Israeli and US positions. If Jarring says they have no position, Gromyko said he did not know how long negotiations would continue. Therefore, agreement should be reached—and the sooner the better—on the platform by which Jarring should be guided.

7. I told Gromyko we believed the first step was to gain acceptance by both sides of UNSC 242. If we could bring this about, Jarring would have a useful basis to begin his talks.

8. Gromyko then indicated that the Soviets would be interested in having our reply to their proposals. (He obviously had in mind their new formulations on peace, State 102698; and Dobrynin's June 2 meeting with the Secy, State 85691.) I said Washington was continuing to give them careful study. He then said that Amb Dobrynin would be leaving for vacation "in a few days."

9. I asked Gromyko if he thought the Four-Power talks would now go more slowly, with the action shifting to Jarring. Gromyko pressed the point that the Four-Power talks must continue, in order to provide the basis for the beginning of Jarring's negotiations. Without such guidance, there was the danger that the contacts would not result in anything. Gromyko expressed the view that mere acceptance by the parties of UNSC 242 would not be enough for success. Jarring would have to have in his possession recommendations worked out in the Four-Power talks. At the same time, Gromyko indicated Moscow would not object to bilateral talks in this matter.

10. I again pointed out the importance as a basis for Jarring's mission of having both sides accept UNSC 242. By way of example, I drew his attention to the fact that Bunche had undertaken his earlier ME mission without detailed guidance. Gromyko responded by saying the situation was much more complicated now.

11. Rather than continue this aspect of the discussion to the point where Gromyko might feel compelled to say that the Four-Power talks would have to provide Jarring with instructions before he could begin his negotiations, I said that we would carefully consider his remarks and that we would doubtless have ideas of our own about future procedures.

Beam

188. Transcript of Telephone Conversation Between the President's Assistant for National Security Affairs (Kissinger) and the Soviet Ambassador (Dobrynin)[1]

Washington, July 27, 1970, 8:45 a.m.

D: Two things I would like to mention to you. First, I am going home for consultations on Wednesday.[2] Before I go I have something I would like to tell you about the question you raised.

K: Would you like to come out here?

D: No, I will probably write to you. I will put it in a paper then and give it to your man. The essence is that we are prepared to do this one but it should be on a mutual basis and take into consideration the political settlement.

K: What does mutual mean?

D: I mean only one side . . . obligation.[3]

K: But we don't have any.

D: Then it is better for you.

K: I understand and that is the right way to put it.

D: Same as on the question of arms limitations. Same as before and in the same context we are prepared to discuss the second question you raised. I will put it as briefly as possible and give it to your man.

K: I will send Colonel Kennedy again.

D: My government considers it very important our contacts on the Middle East.

K: Between our governments or you and me?

D: It is the same thing. I mean our contacts, you and me and then general. But first our contacts.

K: I appreciate all of this—how long will you be gone?

D: I don't know—maybe two to three weeks. After the consultations I will spend some time with my family. Maybe to the end of August. You don't have anything to say about the European thing I discussed with you?

K: No, except we are going to try to apply them in a constructive spirit.

---

[1] Source: Library of Congress, Manuscript Division, Kissinger Papers, Box 364, Telephone Conversations, Chronological File. No classification marking.

[2] July 29.

[3] Ellipsis in the source text.

D: If you have anything to tell me I will be here till Wednesday.

K: Let me talk to the President today. I will call you in any event before you leave. And don't be gone too long—you don't want me to get into mischief.

D: No, I am sure there will be no problem.

K: It seems to be going along well.

D: I will tell you what—not a unilateral approach and second is the political settlement and third—there are really three things—the importance of the contacts and we can work out a settlement on the Middle East.

K: I will talk to the President, but should I send Colonel Kennedy over immediately?

D: Yes.

K: I will send him over in the next hour.

189.   Transcript of Telephone Conversation Between the President's Assistant for National Security Affairs (Kissinger) and the Soviet Ambassador (Dobrynin)[1]

Washington, July 28, 1970, 3:25 p.m.

K: I am sitting on back patio thinking about peaceful coexistence.

D: Good for you, Henry. I am living with the same thought. I will be in Moscow thinking in the same way.

K: When you talk to your leaders I hope you convey that thought to them. I gave your message[2] to the President. This is not the way to give you an answer but we thought it was a constructive reply and we will be taking a personal interest, as you have also recommended to us on this problem from now on. We will also know some of the details from now on, but not as well as our friend Sisco.

D: I understand.

K: On the other matter which you brought up with me, we also looked at this and we also find elements of discussion on it when you return.

---

[1] Source: Library of Congress, Manuscript Division, Kissinger Papers, Box 364, Telephone Conversations, Chronological File. No classification marking.

[2] See footnote 3, Document 185.

D: Elements for discussion?

K: What we need, Anatol, on that is some program of how to get from here to there which I have often suggested to you. We need to work out some procedure for getting things going on the European thing.

D: On the European?

K: On the European. We will talk to you when you return. We are looking at it in a constructive attitude.

D: From here to there? On the main question.

K: Well, that too but I am assuming that you will reply when you are ready. We have never really had any discussions on European matters, you and I, and it would be useful to clarify some of that. The President has asked me to let you know of our constructive spirit.

D: This is No. 2.

K: Yes.

K: When are you leaving?

D: Tomorrow night.

K: When are you coming back?

D: I hope by four weeks—just enough to gain strength to conduct discussions.

K: That will give you an unfair advantage.

D: What about you?

K: I am working on the budget. You are building so many SS–9's. You are upsetting the balance.

D: Do you expect reply only on what I said to you—but on when we begin to move.

K: Well, I would think fairly soon after that but it would be helpful to have you where we can talk to you, particularly on the issue which you brought back in your message to me. I think that would be easier to discuss on a restricted basis.

D: Yes. This is out of question. I was thinking on the more diplomatic side.

K: What way? Do it in Moscow?

D: On your proposal on how we will move.

K: We would then try to get the ceasefire agreed to.

D: I think you already discussed this with the Egyptians in my impression.

K: Yes. If I may make suggestion, it would be extremely helpful if you would exercise restraint.

D: I think meeting productive.

K: I think shortly afterwards one can start activating the [omission in the source text].

D: It could begin in New York.

K: That would be one possibility. I have heard Cyprus as another.

D: We will say nothing. New York is a good place.

K: We have no objection to that. It is a natural place.

D: I think it can be worked out.

K: Whom do I deal with when you are gone?

D: I hope you won't spoil my vacation. I hope that there will be no surprise like last time when I went home to Moscow on major issues. There will definitely be no answer to No. 1 question.

K: Watch your language. I don't anticipate anything. You know our basic position. If your friends in Hanoi do something, we would have to react. But you should expect nothing from us.

D: I am talking about our conversation.

K: I understand very well.

D: I also.

K: Come back reasonably rested but not so much that you have the advantage over us. I will be dealing with Vorontsov.

D: I will be here.

K: I don't anticipate any bilateral business but if we want to get urgent message to you—

D: I will be the man.

K: We look forward to seeing you when you come back.

D: I got letter today thanking me for very good reception at White House when your assistants were there. They gave your personal greetings.

K: Thank you very much.

190. Transcript of Telephone Conversation Between President Nixon and his Assistant for National Security Affairs (Kissinger)[1]

Washington, July 28, 1970, 4 p.m.

K: Just wanted to tell you I have talked to Dobrynin[2] and I just told him we considered his reply.[3] I said be absolutely sure it stays in channel. I said we would get answer to big question when he returns. He said he hoped we would not surprise him as the last time. I said unless our friends in Hanoi do something, we anticipated nothing. He was slobbering all over me. He said he and I would have a lot of business when he returns.

P: You figure about three weeks.

K: About the middle of August.

P: What we mainly want to do is keep all of this in strictest of confidence. On the Middle East thing, it may break. If we could just keep the situation confused for a while—keep it from breaking down.

K: On the one hand, keep it confused but also keep the Israelis from starting something and also from telling so much that the Israelis would bring their troops out. That would be a tremendous coup.

P: A reduction of arms too. That would put the Israelis in a pretty good position.

K: I talked with Bill [Rogers] several times about his conversation with Rabin. I am going to stay out of it. We have given Rabin assurances on the first two points. Bill is working the rest out. We will get answer today or tomorrow.

P: It will be interesting. You gave him exactly the right line. We are not going to be quiet if other side does something.

K: I think they want meeting as much as we do. They didn't have to give us these two answers.

P: I have the feeling that they want a meeting to solidify their framework. More and more they have historical perspective. They cannot look without concern on the enormous colossus of China. Also they feel that the Chinese may not give a damn. They could not only wipe out 20 or 30 Russian cities. What do they care.

K: They could march into Siberia. That is pretty unpopulated.

[1] Source: Library of Congress, Manuscript Division, Kissinger Papers, Box 364, Telephone Conversations, Chronological File. No classification marking.
[2] Documents 188 and 189.
[3] See footnote 3, Document 185.

P: It is desolate there.

K: Things are certainly travelling much more than we thought they would.

P: We must be quite firm but not give them anything to bitch about. I know that their position is not changed.

Soviet Military Buildup in Cuba and Crisis in Jordan, August 4–October 9, 1970

191. Memorandum From the President's Assistant for National Security Affairs (Kissinger) to President Nixon[1]

Washington, August 4, 1970.

SUBJECT

Soviet Note on the Middle East

You will recall that I mentioned to you earlier this week that the Soviets had given us a forthcoming note concerning their "military presence" in Egypt. I think you will be interested in seeing the exact text of the message, which was delivered in Washington and is attached at Tab A.

In a telephone conversation with Ambassador Dobrynin he stressed, as the note does, the cosmetic importance to Moscow of making the removal of military presence a mutual obligation. When I pointed out that we do not have such a military presence, Dobrynin replied, "Then it is better for you." He also reiterated the willingness of the Soviets to discuss regional arms limitations and the great importance his government places on contacts with us on the Middle East, both in our channel and generally.

I told Dobrynin that I had informed you of his message, that we thought it was a constructive reply, and that we will be using my contacts with him more often on the Middle East issues.

---

[1] Source: Library of Congress, Manuscript Division, Kissinger Papers, Geopolitical File, Box TS 36, Soviet Union, Chronological File, 7/70–1/71. Top Secret; Sensitive; Eyes Only. Another copy in the file indicates it was drafted by Lord on July 31 and the President saw it.

586

Tab A

Message From Chairman of the Council of Ministers of the Soviet Union Kosygin to President Nixon

Moscow, July 27, 1970.

Referring to our previous conversations the following is authorized by Moscow to be transmitted to the President.

Since President Nixon expressed his wish to know the intentions of the Soviet Government regarding the prospects of the Soviet "military presence" in the UAR we would like the President to recall that it was not the Soviet Union who initiated the arms race in the Middle East. We have always believed and believe now that appropriate steps towards limiting this arms race would not contradict the interests of countries of that area. At the same time, for obvious reasons, we can not discuss the question of unilateral assurances from the Soviet side in terms of our accepting any preliminary conditions.

As we already stated to the US Government earlier, the Soviet side would be ready to discuss the question of limiting the shipments of arms to the countries of the Middle East after a political settlement has been achieved. At that time the question of "military presence" in that area of the world by non-Mideastern countries could probably also be considered. Naturally, in this case it would be a matter not only for the Soviet Union but also for other states involved to assume appropriate obligations.

The Soviet side regards its contacts with the American side on the Middle East question as very important ones and sincerely wants these contacts to bring about concrete results in terms of a speediest achievement of a lasting and just peace in the Middle East.

192.   Memorandum of Conversation[1]

Washington, August 4, 1970.

Conversation with Vorontsov—Map Room

I saw Vorontsov at his request. He had called in San Clemente to say that he wanted to have an appointment as soon as I got back. When I saw him, he was extremely cordial and read me the attached communication from the Soviet Government. I asked him on what this was based. He replied that there had been many news stories about the American determination to defend Guantanamo and many incorrect allegations about Soviet buildups in Cuba.

I asked in what way he thought we should confirm the understanding and what he thought the understanding was. He said an oral statement from me would be enough and he took the understanding to be that we would not invade Cuba by military force. I said I would have to discuss the matter with the President and let him know.

There was then some desultory conversation about Dobrynin. Vorontsov said he knew the Kremlin was taking my recent communications extremely seriously, and that he thought matters were now on a good turn. Vorontsov is, of course, without any authority to negotiate and therefore he sticks strictly to his instructions.

HAK

Tab A

Note From the Soviet Government

Moscow, August 4, 1970.

The increase lately in the United States of activity hostile towards Cuba could not but attract attention in Moscow. Certain anxiety has been caused, in particular, by attempts to unite various groups and organizations of Cuban counterrevolutionary emigration in the United States and by resuming of sabotage and subversive activity of these organizations against Cuba, directed from American territory among other places. There has been an increase in number of provocative

---

[1] Source: Library of Congress, Manuscript Division, Kissinger Papers, Geopolitical File, Box CL 215, Soviet Union, Chronological File, "D" File. No classification marking.

appeals in the American press and of ambiguous statements on the part of certain officials of the United States.

We would like to stress that in the Cuban question we proceed as before from the understanding on this question reached in the past, and we expect that the American side will also strictly adhere to this understanding.

---

193.   Editorial Note

In *White House Years,* Henry Kissinger, the President's Assistant for National Security Affairs, describes his and President Richard Nixon's reactions to the Soviet note on Cuba delivered by Yuli Vorontsov on August 4, 1970 (Tab A, Document 192):

"Nixon and I even speculated that the message delivered by Vorontsov might be a token of Soviet goodwill to improve the atmosphere for a summit in the fall. Our complacency was reflected in our reaction to an FBI report which, as chance would have it, reached us on August 5; it claimed that two boats hired by exiles in Miami would try to sink a Soviet tanker headed for Cuba." (page 634)

Concerned that the Cuban exile operation might provoke a crisis between the United States and the Soviet Union, the National Security Council staff immediately began monitoring the situation. On August 5, at 9:35 p.m., General Alexander Haig, Deputy Assistant to the President for National Security Affairs, and Arnold Nachmanoff, NSC Operations Staff officer for Latin America, spoke on the telephone. Haig informed Nachmanoff of the following:

"I spoke to Henry [Kissinger]. He thinks the best bet is to call the Coast Guard and get the Coast Guard duty officer. Henry wants you to get some war game contingency plans. I mentioned the possibility of notifying the Soviets and Henry said he didn't think we should now and if we do, we should go to the President. We don't want this to happen at this point in time. I will now tell [Captain] Dan[iel] Murphy to check with NMCC for more feedback from CINCLANT [Commander in Chief, Atlantic]. They can not engage in anything like this—if they can get a fix on it and buzz it, they might frighten it away. Check the Coast Guard." (National Archives, Nixon Presidential Materials, NSC Files, Box 998, Haig Chronological File, Haig Telecons, 1970)

In an August 6 memorandum to Nixon, Kissinger summarized the administration's follow-up actions concerning the Cuban exile operation:

"A Coast Guard cutter was dispatched to intercept and escort a Soviet tanker, the only known Soviet vessel scheduled to traverse the

Straits, to prevent possible attack. An extensive air and sea search during the night has failed to locate the Cuban-manned vessel. Although our intelligence agencies are still attempting to corroborate the report, the search is continuing today." (Ibid., Box 25, President's Daily Briefs)

By August 10, the possibility of a crisis over the Cuban exile operation subsided. In an August 10 memorandum to the President, Kissinger explained: "The search for possible Cuban exile vessels allegedly involved in attempting to attack a Soviet ship was concluded Saturday morning. In view of the time elapsed, the probability of the raid occurring had become very low. The Coast Guard has returned to normal operations and U.S. Navy P–3 aircraft have been released from surveillance/patrol flights." (Ibid.)

---

194.   Memorandum From the President's Assistant for National Security Affairs (Kissinger) to President Nixon[1]

Washington, undated.

SUBJECT

"Understandings" with Soviet Union at the Time of the Cuban Missile Crisis

You asked me for the precise language relating to our "understandings" with the Soviet Union at the time of the missile crisis. Attached at Tab A are excerpts from the letters and messages exchanged between President Kennedy and Chairman Khrushchev in October, 1962 and December, 1962. Copies of the full texts of those letters and messages are attached at Tab B.[2]

The Khrushchev–Kennedy exchanges indicate clearly that there was an implicit understanding that we would agree to give assurances against an invasion of Cuba if the Soviet Union would remove its offensive missiles from Cuba under UN observation and would undertake, with suitable safeguards, to halt the re-introduction of such

---

[1] Source: National Archives, Nixon Presidential Materials, NSC Files, Box 783, Country Files, Latin America, Cuba, Understanding with USSR at Time of Cuban Missile Crisis. Confidential with Nodis Attachment. Sent for information. Another copy of this memorandum indicates it was drafted by Nachmanoff on August 4. A handwritten note, stamped August 14 and initialed by Haig, reads, "Nachmanoff. Via Davis—for file where easily available. Excellent job, Arnie!" Below this comment in an unknown handwriting is the note, "Not going to Pres." (Ibid.)

[2] Attached but not printed.

weapons systems into Cuba. However, the agreement was never explicitly completed because the Soviets did not agree to an acceptable verification system (because of Castro's opposition) and we never made a formal non-invasion pledge. The negotiations between McCloy and Kuznetzov, which were designed to work out a satisfactory means of formalizing the Kennedy–Khrushchev "understanding" eventually just fizzled out.

The "understanding" we have with the Soviets, therefore, is an implicit one, which was never formally buttoned down. In fact, the Soviets removed their missiles and there is no evidence that they have re-introduced them; and we, of course, have not invaded Cuba.

Tab A

Excerpts From Letters and Messages Between President Kennedy and Soviet Chairman Khrushchev

Washington, undated.

Letter from Khrushchev to Kennedy—October 26, 1962[3]

"If assurances were given by the President and the government of the United States that the USA itself would not participate in an attack on Cuba and would restrain others from actions of this sort, if you would recall your fleet, this would immediately change everything. I am not speaking for Fidel Castro, but I think that he and the government of Cuba, evidently, would declare demobilization and would appeal to the people to get down to peaceful labor. Then, too, the question of armaments would disappear, since, if there is no threat, then armaments are a burden for every people. Then, too, the question of the destruction, not only of the armaments which you call offensive, but of all other armaments as well, would look different."

. . . "I propose: We for our part will declare that our ships, bound for Cuba, will not carry any kind of armaments. You would declare that the United States will not invade Cuba with its forces and will not support any sort of forces which might intend to carry out an invasion of Cuba. Then the necessity for the presence of our military specialists in Cuba would disappear." (Nodis)

---

[3] For text, see *Foreign Relations, 1961–1963,* vol. VI, Kennedy–Khrushchev Exchanges, Document 65. All ellipses are in the source text.

Text of Khrushchev Message to Kennedy Broadcast October 27, 1962[4]

"I therefore make this proposal: We agree to remove from Cuba those means which you regard as offensive means. We agree to carry this out and declare this pledge in the United Nations. Your representatives will make a declaration to the effect that the United States on its part, considering the uneasiness and anxiety of the Soviet state, will remove its analogous means from Turkey.

"Let us reach agreement as to the span of time needed for you and us to achieve this. After this, persons enjoying the confidence of the U.S. Security Council might check on-the-spot fulfillment of the pledges assumed. Of course, the authorization of the Governments of Cuba and Turkey are necessary for entry into those countries of these plenipotentiaries and for inspection of fulfillment of the pledge assumed by either side."

. . . "we will make a statement within the framework of the Security Council to the effect that the Soviet Government makes a solemn promise to respect the inviolability of the frontiers and sovereignty of Turkey, not to interfere in its internal affairs, not to invade Turkey, not to make its territory available as a bridgehead for such an invasion, and will also restrain those who contemplate perpetrating aggression against Turkey both from the territory of the Soviet Union and from the territory of other neighbor states of Turkey.

"The U.S. Government will make a similar statement within the framework of the Security Council in respect to Cuba. It will declare that the United States will respect the inviolability of the frontiers of Cuba and its sovereignty, undertakes not to interfere in its internal affairs, not to invade, and not to make its territory available as a bridgehead for such an invasion of Cuba, and will also restrain those who might contemplate perpetrating aggression against Cuba, both from the territory of the United States and from the territory of other neighboring states of Cuba.

"Of course, for this we would have to agree to some kind of time limit. Let us agree to some period of time, but not to delay—two or three weeks; not more than a month.

"The means situated in Cuba which you have stated are perturbing you are in the hands of Soviet officers, therefore, any accidental use of them to the detriment of the United States is excluded. . . . if there is no invasion of Cuba or attack on the Soviet Union or any other of our allies, then of course these means are not and will not be a threat to anyone, for they are not there for the purpose of attack."

---

[4] For text, see ibid., Document 66.

Letter from Kennedy to Khrushchev—October 27, 1962[5]

. . . "The first thing that needs to be done, however, is for work to cease on offensive missile bases in Cuba and for all weapons systems in Cuba capable of offensive use to be rendered inoperable, under effective United Nations arrangements.

"Assuming this is done promptly, I have given my representatives in New York instructions that will permit them to work out this week end—in cooperation with the Acting Secretary General and your representative—an arrangement for a permanent solution to the Cuban problem along the lines suggested in your letter of October 26th. As I read your letter, the key elements of your proposals—which seem generally acceptable as I understand them—are as follows:

"1. You would agree to remove these weapons systems from Cuba under appropriate United Nations observation and supervision; and undertake, with suitable safeguards, to halt the further introduction of such weapons systems into Cuba.

"2. We, on our part, would agree—upon the establishment of adequate arrangements through the United Nations to ensure the carrying out and continuation of these commitments—(a) to remove promptly the quarantine measures now in effect and (b) to give assurances against an invasion of Cuba and I am confident that other nations of the Western Hemisphere would be prepared to do likewise.

"If you will give your representative similar instructions there is no reason why we should not be able to complete these arrangements and announce them to the world within a couple of days."

Message from Khrushchev to Kennedy—October 28, 1962[6]

"In order to eliminate as rapidly as possible the conflict which endangers the cause of peace, . . . the Soviet Government, in addition to earlier instructions on the discontinuation of further work on weapons constructions sites, has given a new order to dismantle the arms which described as offensive, and to crate and return them to the Soviet Union."

"I regard with respect and trust the statement you made in your message of October 27, 1962, that there would be no attack, no invasion of Cuba, and not only on the part of the United States, but also on the part of other nations of the Western Hemisphere, as you said in your same message. Then the motives which induced us to render assistance of such a kind to Cuba disappear.

---

[5] For text, see ibid., Document 67.

[6] For text, see ibid., Document 68.

"It is for this reason that we instructed our officers—these means as I had already informed you earlier are in the hands of the Soviet officers—to take appropriate measures to discontinue construction of the aforementioned facilities, to dismantle them, and to return them to the Soviet Union. As I had informed you in the letter of October 27, we are prepared to reach agreement to enable the United Nations Representatives to verify the dismantling of these means."

"Thus in view of the assurances you have given and our instructions on dismantling, there is every condition for eliminating the present conflict."

. . . "If we do take practical steps and proclaim the dismantling and evacuation of the means in question from Cuba, in so doing we, at the same time, want the Cuban people to be certain that we are with them and are not absolving ourselves of responsibility for rendering assistance to the Cuban people."

Letter from Khrushchev to Kennedy—December 11, 1962[7]

"More resolute steps should be taken now to move towards finalizing the elimination of this tension, i.e. you on your part should clearly confirm at the U.N. as you did at your press conference and in your messages to me the pledge of non-invasion of Cuba by the United States and your allies having removed reservations which are being introduced now into the U.S. draft declaration in the Security Council and our representatives in New York should come to terms with regard to an agreed wording in the declarations of both powers of the commitments undertaken by them."

. . . "I will tell you frankly that we have removed our means from Cuba relying on your assurance that the United States and its allies will not invade Cuba. . . . We hope and we would like to believe—I spoke of that publicly too, as you know—that you will adhere to the commitments which you have taken, as strictly as we do with regard to our commitments. We, Mr. President, have already fulfilled our commitments concerning the removal of our missiles and IL–28 planes from Cuba and we did it even ahead of time. It is obvious that fulfillment by you of your commitments cannot be as clearly demonstrated as it was done by us since your commitments are of a long-term nature. But it is important to fulfill them and to do everything so that no doubts are sown from the very start that they will not be fulfilled."

"Therefore, Mr. President, everything—the stability in this area and not only in this area but in the entire world—depends on how you will now fulfill the commitments taken by you. Furthermore, it will be

---

[7] For text, see ibid., Document 83.

now a sort of litmus paper, an indicator whether it is possible to trust if similar difficulties arise in other geographical areas."

"We believe that the guarantees for non-invasion of Cuba given by you will be maintained and not only in the period of your stay in the White House."

... "But the confidential nature of our personal relations will depend on whether you fulfill—as we did—the commitments taken by you and give instructions to your representatives in New York to formalize these commitments in appropriate documents. ... it is necessary to fix the assumed commitments in the documents of both sides and register them with the United Nations."

Letter from Kennedy to Khrushchev—December 14, 1962[8]

"You refer to the importance of my statements on an invasion of Cuba and of our intention to fulfill them, so that no doubts are sown from the very start ... The other side of the coin, however, is that we do need to have adequate assurances that all offensive weapons are removed from Cuba and are not reintroduced, and that Cuba itself commits no aggressive acts against any of the nations of the Western Hemisphere. As I understand you, you feel confident that Cuba will not in fact engage in such aggressive acts, and of course I already have your own assurance about the offensive weapons. So I myself should suppose that you could accept our position—but it is probably better to leave final discussion of these matters to our representatives in New York."

---

[8] For text, see ibid., Document 84.

---

195.   Memorandum of Conversation[1]

Washington, August 7, 1970.

Conversation with Vorontsov

I saw Vorontsov at the request of the President to give him the following communication.

---

[1] Source: Library of Congress, Manuscript Division, Kissinger Papers, Geopolitical File, Box CL 215, Soviet Union, Chronological File, "D" File. No classification marking.

We have noticed with satisfaction the assurance of the Soviet Government that the understandings of 1962 are still in full force. We take this to mean that the Soviet Union will not emplace any offensive weapons of any kind or any nuclear weapons on Cuban soil.

For our part, the President wishes to point out that although we have heard repeated reports of increased Soviet activity in Cuba, he was exercising the utmost restraint in not increasing reconnaissance activities. He was maintaining the understandings of 1962 which I was hereby authorized to reaffirm. Specifically, the United States would not use military force to bring about a change in the governmental structure of Cuba.

I then said I wanted to add a personal observation to the formal communication. It had come to our attention that Soviet long-range airplanes of a type that were suitable to nuclear bombing missions were flying with increasing regularity to Cuba. While we believed that these planes were on reconnaissance missions, we thought, nevertheless, that this might provide a basis for approaching the limit of our understandings. It would certainly be noticed if the Soviet Union kept such operations to an absolute minimum. The same went for Soviet fleet activity in the Caribbean. I pointed out that these were not conditional but rather atmospheric.

I then added that we were showing our good faith by having assigned two Coast Guard cutters in recent days to shadow a Soviet ship which we believed was in imminent danger of being attacked by some Cuban exile groups.[2]

Vorontsov said he appreciated the good spirit in which I had made these observations and he was certain that the Kremlin would be very happy to receive them. It was in sharp contrast, he added, to our last conversation on April 30[3] when he had been in a position (correctly) to point out to me that a Soviet reaction to our Cambodian venture would be extremely unfortunate. I told Vorontsov that the major problem now was to see what concrete progress could be made in the area of negotiations.

HAK

---

[2] See Document 193.

[3] The last conversation between Kissinger and Vorontsov actually took place on April 29; see Document 155.

196.   Memorandum of Conversation[1]

Washington, August 13, 1970, 2:30 p.m.

PARTICIPANTS

Chargé Vorontsov
Henry A. Kissinger

The meeting lasted about a half hour. I asked Vorontsov to see me on the basis of a report by a New York photographic manufacturer called Mr. Hament,[2] who alleged that he had been asked to visit the Soviet Embassy and had been told there of the Soviet interest that President Nixon visit the Soviet Union before the end of October. (Attached is a memorandum[3] for the President by Bill Casey, a business associate of Hament's.)

I opened the meeting by telling Vorontsov that we had had a rather strange communication from a New York photographic manufacturer and wondered whether he knew him. I mentioned Mr. Hament's name and Mr. Vorontsov said yes he had met him at some social function at the Soviet Embassy. I then told him the substance of Casey's memorandum and said that it was difficult to know how to respond. If it was a serious communication, we would of course want to make our comments. On the other hand, if it was a general communication which Hament overplayed then we could drop it. The major point was that if it was a serious communication there was some time problem and we could therefore not play it the usual way.

I said that I understood that Vorontsov himself had attended the meetings. Vorontsov said this could not be true since on July 28 he was not in the Embassy. He said that he had only come back from the Soviet Union on July 29 and had only seen Dobrynin at the airport for

---

[1] Source: Library of Congress, Manuscript Division, Kissinger Papers, Geopolitical File, Box TS 36, Soviet Union, Chronological File, 7/70–1/71. Top Secret; Sensitive. The conversation was held in the Map Room at the White House. The memorandum was sent under an August 22 covering memorandum from Kissinger to Nixon that summarized this meeting with Vorontsov.

[2] Harvey Hament was a New York distributor of films and photographic items who was trying to conclude a contract with the Soviets that would provide him exclusive rights for the marketing of Soviet cultural films and television shows within the United States. For several years, the KGB had been cultivating him unsuccessfully as a channel to the White House. Memoranda from Helms to Haig, November 19 and December 10, suggesting that the Soviets were attempting to use Hament as an "important unofficial channel to the White House" are in the Central Intelligence Agency, Executive Registry Files, Job 80–R01580R, Box 10, S–17.3, Soviet, 1/1/70–12/31/70 and ibid., Box 12, Soviet, respectively.

[3] Attached but not printed.

a farewell exchange of views. He said that it sounded to him as if this was not a serious communication but that Hament had played up a general expression of interest into a very specific proposal. However, he would check it and let me know.

I then told Vorontsov that regardless of whether this particular thing was a serious communication, I wanted to use this occasion to discuss the general subject of a higher level meeting. Vorontsov said that he was, of course, familiar with the subject having read the record of my previous conversations with Dobrynin. (Note: Dobrynin had told me that Vorontsov was the only person in the Embassy who was informed of them. This was done in order to prevent a situation from developing while Dobrynin was out of town and no one present at the Soviet Embassy would have any information.)

Vorontsov said he knew for a fact that the subject was under very active discussion in Moscow at the moment. Indeed, one of the reasons for Dobrynin's return to the Soviet Union was so that he could participate in these high level meetings with the top leadership. They were probably now at the Crimea for a leisurely discussion and we would no doubt receive an official reply.

I said the difficulty was that we had to make our plans for the fall and winter and that we had kept a number of them in abeyance in order to be able to respond to the possibilities. For example, we had been told that Kosygin would come to the United Nations General Assembly but we had never had any official word. Vorontsov said that he did not have any word on this either, and he doubted that Kosygin knew.

I said, of course, that we had discussed various levels for meetings and various possible occasions but that the matter was in abeyance until we got some further word. I told Vorontsov that it would be highly desirable for us to have some preliminary indication fairly soon. Vorontsov said he would get word to us. He said he certainly felt that his leadership believed now that there were many advantages in high level meetings as was proved by the recent high level visitors to Moscow, particularly Brandt.

After an exchange of pleasantries the meeting ended.

Henry A. Kissinger

197. Memorandum From the President's Assistant for National Security Affairs (Kissinger) to President Nixon[1]

Washington, August 19, 1970.

SUBJECT

My Meeting Today with Vorontsov on Possible Summit Meeting

Soviet Minister Vorontsov came in today to give us an answer to our query about their interest in a summit meeting, prompted by recent Soviet approaches to Mr. Harvey Hament.[2]

Vorontsov handed me a rather vague note, attached at Tab A, which indicates that Moscow has decided to play the subject of a possible summit meeting coolly, at least for the time being. The note states that Dobrynin brought to the attention of the Soviet leadership your idea of a summit meeting, and declares the Soviets' "positive approach" to a summit, "provided that such meetings are duly prepared allowing thus to count on getting results." It then invites your concrete suggestions about moving toward a summit, saying that Moscow will be ready to study them attentively.

In our brief conversation Vorontsov said that Mr. Hament had exaggerated the importance of his conversations with Soviet officials and that these encounters were not serious. He denied that a large meeting had taken place as described by Hament.

Our response to the Soviets, I believe, should be played coolly like their note itself. I propose that I go back to Vorontsov and merely tell him that we are prepared to move toward a summit meeting within the framework that Ambassador Dobrynin and I have been discussing, recalling that we had set a tentative agenda featuring European security, SALT, and the Middle East. I would add that the next step will have to be to set a date and that November or December are impossible.

Recommendation:

That you approve my responding to Vorontsov in this fashion.[3]

---

[1] Source: Library of Congress, Manuscript Division, Kissinger Papers, Geopolitical File, Box TS 36, Soviet Union, Chronological File, 7/70–1/71. Top Secret; Sensitive; Eyes Only. Sent for action.

[2] See footnote 2, Document 196.

[3] Nixon initialed the "approve" option.

Tab A

Note From the Soviet Government

Moscow, August 19, 1970.

The Soviet Ambassador has brought to the knowledge of the Soviet leadership the idea of President Nixon, which was forwarded through Dr. Kissinger, about arranging of a Soviet-American meeting on the highest level.

The American side is aware of our positive approach to the contacts on the highest level, including the form of personal meetings of the leaders of the two powers—the USSR and the US, provided that such meetings are duly prepared allowing thus to count on getting results.

With such an understanding of this question Moscow will be ready to study attentively concrete suggestions which President Nixon may wish to put forward in development of the general idea expressed by Dr. Kissinger on instructions from the President in the conversations with the Soviet Ambassador.

It would be desirable to know what problems and in what light does the American side intend to suggest for the consideration.

---

198.   Memorandum for the Record[1]

Washington, August 24, 1970.

SUBJECT

Meeting between Soviet Chargé d'Affaires Vorontsov and General Haig, August 24, 1970

General Haig met with the Soviet Chargé d'Affaires Vorontsov at 10:00 a.m. on Monday, August 24, 1970 in Dr. Kissinger's Washington White House Office.

After a formal exchange of greetings, General Haig handed Mr. Vorontsov the written communication (copy of which is attached at Tab

---

[1] Source: Library of Congress, Manuscript Division, Kissinger Papers, Geopolitical File, Box TS 36, Soviet Union, Chronological File, 7/70–1/71. Top Secret; Sensitive.

A). The message was typewritten on plain paper with neither heading nor signature, in conformance with instructions received in the message of August 22d from Dr. Kissinger to General Haig at Tab B.[2]

Mr. Vorontsov read the communication carefully. He then stated to General Haig that he understood it completely. General Haig then stated to him that he, General Haig, had also been instructed to deliver the following oral message from Dr. Kissinger: The U.S. Government believes that pending progress between Dr. Kissinger and the Soviet Ambassador on the agenda items contained in the U.S. communication that it might be of value to fix a date for a meeting between President Nixon and Chairman Kosygin or General Secretary Brezhnev, or both, on the occasion of the Anniversary of the United Nations General Assembly during the week of October 18 in New York. General Haig reiterated that the months of November and December would pose insurmountable problems for the U.S. side for such a meeting since the President would be involved in a heavy work schedule associated with the preparation of the President's Annual Message to the Congress. Finally, General Haig stated that Dr. Kissinger would be most grateful for an early response from the Soviet side as to the feasibility and timing of the suggested venue. Mr. Vorontsov stated that he would be in immediate touch with Moscow and anticipated an early response.

The meeting adjourned at 10:07 a.m.

Tab A

Message Handed to the Soviet Chargé d'Affaires (Vorontsov) by the Deputy Assistant to the President for National Security Affairs (Haig)[3]

Washington, August 24, 1970.

The President has studied with great care the communication forwarded to him through Dr. Kissinger by the Soviet Chargé D'Affaires.

For a meeting at the highest level the President wishes to repeat the agenda items already outlined to the Soviet Ambassador by Dr. Kissinger. These topics and their possible outcomes are:

European Security—Agreement in principle on the calling of a conference.

---

[2] Attached but not printed is a backchannel message from Kissinger through Winston Lord to Haig outlining Nixon's message and instructions for delivery.

[3] No classification marking.

Middle East—Discussions of a comprehensive political-military solution.

SALT—Agreement on the general outline of an accord.

Provocative Attacks—Initiation of discussions at the highest level only.

Principles of Co-existence—With special reference to Southeast Asia.

Trade—Measures to expand trade.

Other topics either side may wish to raise.

Dr. Kissinger is prepared to conduct preliminary discussions on these topics with the Soviet Ambassador.

The President wishes to point out that preparations for the new session of Congress make November and December unfeasible for a meeting.

The President will study attentively proposals the Soviet side may put forward in reaction to this communication.

---

199. Memorandum From the President's Assistant for National Security Affairs (Kissinger) to President Nixon[1]

Washington, undated.

SUBJECT

Possible Meeting with Kosygin

As we await Soviet reaction to our latest exchange, I thought you might want to have some reflections on the subject of summits. This memorandum discusses the background of U.S.-Soviet summits; Kosygin's role in the Soviet leadership and his personal traits; and the role a trip of his would play in current Soviet policy generally.

---

[1] Source: National Archives, Nixon Presidential Materials, NSC Files, Box 713, Country Files, Europe, USSR, Vol. IX, August 1–October 31, 1970. Secret; Sensitive; Nodis; Eyes Only. Sent for information. The memorandum was not initialed by Kissinger, and there is no indication it was sent to the President. According to a handwritten note on the August 25 covering memorandum from Lord to Kissinger, this memorandum was drafted on August 26. Lord's memorandum explains: "Hal Sonnenfeldt sent out some revisions in the last couple of pages in the memorandum. He knows nothing about your exchanges with Dobrynin and Vorontsov, so I had to delete some of his material toward the end of the memo which suggests that we should send a positive signal to the Soviets and ways in which to do this."

Over the years, summit meetings with American Presidents have held as much, albeit rather different, fascination for Soviet leaders as vice versa. It has always been one of the paradoxes of Bolshevik behavior that their leaders have yearned to be treated as equals by the people they consider doomed. For Khrushchev, consorting with the high and mighty of the capitalist world roused some of the impulses of the parvenue. But the totality factors that have gone into Soviet thinking and feeling (as into American) have been complex and ambivalent and defy precise definition.

Certainly, in the last 15 years or so—since the Geneva summit—there has been the element of coresponsibility for the survival of mankind that is so uniquely part of the American-Soviet relationship by virtue of our size and power. In many ways, the psychological adjustment to this special relationship has been harder for the Soviets who were raised in a value system of victors and vanquished, of historically-ordained and objectively determined class hostility which temporary, subjective factors could not really change.

In any event, there is now a history of Soviet leadership interest in communication with American Presidents; and the same impulse, whatever its wellsprings, has existed among American Presidents since Roosevelt. This has been true despite the fact that summits, since World War II, have produced few if any specific results, except procedural ones: i.e., agreements to have more meetings, at lower levels. It might be argued that the 1959 Eisenhower–Khrushchev summit, by producing agreement on a four-power summit six months hence gave Berlin that much of a lease on life. But in the end that four-power summit, in 1960, aborted and Berlin lived on, anyway.

Many hold the view that a summit is useful for atmospheric reasons, to make it easier for countries to reach subsequent understandings; from this perspective, agreement all too often becomes an end in itself. However unimportant or irrelevant the settlement may be, it is said to contribute to a climate of confidence which will "improve" the situation.

The usual consequence of such an approach is that more ingenuity and effort are put into finding things to agree on than in coming to grips with the issues that have caused the tensions. As a result the difficulties which are "ironed out" are often soluble only because they are inconsequential. This distortion is forgotten and the mere fact that something is settled, no matter how trivial, is said to be "progress." Such agreements, therefore, become a means of postponing instead of solving the real issues. They do not lessen the tensions but rather perpetuate them.

The topics which were slated for discussion at the Paris summit conference in 1960 are evidence of this point: exchange of persons, nuclear testing, arms control, and Berlin. They are either so unimportant that they can be solved fairly easily and without the attention of heads of state, or they are so complicated that a summit conference can at best serve as a means for deferring decision.

The intangible results of meetings between American and Soviet leaders are harder to define and more controversial; many observers think that these results far outweigh the absence of concrete ones: e.g., the supposedly tacit agreement in 1955 that nuclear war was unthinkable; or the impact on Sino-Soviet relations of the mere fact of the Camp David meeting in 1959; or the ultimate effect on Soviet strategic doctrine and on their view of the ABM of McNamara's Glassboro lectures to Kosygin in 1967. These things are hard to judge; but that American-Soviet summits involve or produce some special chemical mixtures that American-Mexican ones don't is undoubtedly true. The only question is whether the mixture is for good or ill.

Nor have domestic political considerations always been absent—on either side. Khrushchev saw his cavortings with the Capitalist great as enhancing his stature at home. In Kosygin's case, foreign trips and summit meetings are not so much part of a personal "election campaign" (although, in fact, the current pre-Party Congress period is something not unlike an American election campaign). Rather, as the representative of the aging Soviet Troika, a Kosygin trip to New York and meeting with the American President—especially if they could be depicted as successful—would be used on arguments against Young Turk elements in the Party who are critical of the moribund approaches of the now top ruling group which has now been at the top for six years. Arguments like "we know how to handle the American ruling group" undoubtedly figure in internal debates.

It may be that in this particular year a Kosygin foray into the West is connected with a general Soviet effort to delineate certain more orderly relations with the West. This could be because of the uncertainties of the Chinese challenge, the instabilities in Eastern Europe which the Czech invasion submerged but did not remove and the need for greater certainty in economic planning at a time when the USSR faces tough and expensive economic and technological choices.

Perhaps we need not take quite so epochal a view of a possible Nixon–Kosygin meeting. After all, Kosygin is *not* the Soviet summit. (In fact, one of President Johnson's unending frustrations was that he could never quite find his Soviet equivalent: sometimes it was Brezhnev, sometimes Kosygin and sometimes—usually only for purposes of writing messages beginning with "Your Excellency"—it was Podgorny.) Kosygin quite evidently is number 2 in the USSR in many important ways; yet some would argue that someone like Kirilenko, who might some day be General Secretary, is more like the real number 2 than Kosygin. Kosygin has never challenged Brezhnev for the top spot, though we know that he has sometimes done things in ways that made Brezhnev feel he was showing insufficient deference to number 1. Kosygin obviously is a manager who likes to manage, sometimes he cuts corners, even around the Party. (Yet, as a Marxist, on many issues we know him to be almost a Puritan.)

If Kosygin comes to New York, it will not be because *he* decided to come but because the Collective, whatever precisely that is, decided he should go. He may or may not have plenipotentiary power on some issue or other. In 1967, we know he frequently checked with the home office for instructions; though in London in 1966, our intelligence caught him slipping a couple of things past the lethargic Brezhnev in the interest of speed. (Speed, cutting corners, getting things done, indeed, is where Kosygin's main troubles with Brezhnev have been. His strength has been that he has not reached for the top job and, in fact, does not have the constituency in the Party for doing so.)

An intriguing question, if Kosygin comes toward the end of October is whether by that time November 2 will be so close that he would be able to give President Nixon the Soviet counterproposal on SALT (assuming the Soviet leadership can agree on one). Then again, if Bahr's analysis of Soviet interests has any merit, would Kosygin come in October to offer some interesting proposition on Berlin? SALT (including the fascinating and ramified third country problem) and Berlin are the two issues on which Soviets could make really interesting offers on their own initiative. On the Middle East, they are not free agents. However, even if Kosygin made such moves, it is unlikely that he would be here long enough or that his terms would be so close to ours that anything remotely close to conclusive negotiations could be expected.

As in the past, Kosygin would come not only in the expectation of seeing our President. The Soviets have in recent years acquired a certain interest in the UN and in the potential it provides for a Soviet role as the defender of small, formerly colonial countries. Depending on where the Middle East situation stood, the Soviets could also, under his leadership, seek to start an anti-Israel/US bandwagon as they abortively tried in 1967. They could try a push for admission of divided countries, with Germany in the vanguard. In sum, the strand in Soviet policy that gropes for co-responsibility, condominium, duopoly with the US remains vigorously accompanied by other strands more directly and more obviously prejudicial to our interests. Kosygin would be here to exemplify this multiplicity of tendencies. (The more hopeful strand, incidentally, would continue whether Kosygin came or not, though it might perhaps be set back a little if the Soviets felt they had been deliberately snubbed or insulted.)

Kosygin has on occasion in the past demonstrated keen negotiating skill. Even if undoubtedly acting on Politburo orders, and closely flanked by the diplomatic and military expertise of Foreign Minister Gromyko and Defensive Minister Grechko, Kosygin deserves much credit personally for bringing off the Tashkent-compromise between India and Pakistan. (It should be added that the establishment of peace, or at least the prevention of war on the Subcontinent was genuinely in the Soviet national interest—as it was in ours—since war might have faced the Soviets with the dilemma of openly supporting India against a China-supported Pakistan.)

The sudden fatal heart attack of Indian Prime Minister Shastri at Tashkent has never been traced, by any one, to the effect of his personal encounters with Kosygin. Indeed none has ever attributed to the Soviet Premier the capacity for personal brutality and crudeness that, according to the most reliable reports, were displayed by Brezhnev, for example, just two years ago when the kidnapped, Liberal Czechoslovak leaders were Kremlin "guests."

We know that Kosygin is tough and unyielding, if need be. We know, too that while foreign policy is not his first love, he briefs himself meticulously and masters the subject matter at hand and the Soviet position on it.

Kosygin has sometimes been identified with the "liberal" wing of the Soviet leadership, mostly because of his interest in economic advancement and efficient management. His son-in-law, Gvishiani has been responsible for expediting certain kinds of technical US-Soviet exchanges. Yet none could, like Kosygin, survive near the very top of Soviet leadership for over thirty years without at least having acquiesced in the brutalities of the regime. His origins are in the Leningrad Party organization which was almost completely purged by Stalin. Like the rest of the sixty-odd year-olds in the Politburo, Kosygin has had to walk over corpses to be where he is.

Kosygin has also showed considerable shrewdness in dealing with Americans, even if, as one must assume, his general conduct was on orders from the Politburo. There have been several instances when he has impressed Americans, and others, as the equivalent of the manager of a large Western corporation. But in 1965—to cite just one example—he displayed unusual psychological adroitness when dealing with Averell Harriman. On the first day of the Governor's visit, Kosygin was tough, dour and almost brutal in depicting the deleterious effects of the American aggression against the DRV. The Americans were depressed and their telegrams showed it. On the second day, Kosygin painted vistas of US-Soviet cooperation once we had only screwed up enough courage to get out of Vietnam. He reminded Harriman how he had successfully negotiated the test ban treaty and subtly suggested that there might well be other treaties (at that time the NPT was the great US dream) that the Governor might bring to fruition.

Without attempting psychological judgments, the Governor's firm conviction that somehow, sometime the Soviets would "help" us in Vietnam seems to have stemmed from that second day's encounter in 1965.

---

200. Memorandum From the President's Deputy Assistant for National Security Affairs (Haig) to the President's Assistant for National Security Affairs (Kissinger)[1]

Washington, September 1, 1970.

SUBJECT

PFIAB Recommendation on Sino-Soviet Intelligence Affairs

The attached package[2] is a followup of the FIAB's concern on the Sino-Soviet issue registered to you at last month's luncheon. While it goes somewhat beyond the pale of their areas of responsibility, I do think that we should handle it seriously, given the responsible attitude of the FIAB. I do not think the draft reply prepared by Hyland[3] fits the bill in any sense in that it passes the buck back to Burke to deal with Helms on something that the FIAB has quite rightly brought to your attention as a followup of their luncheon meeting with you.

I am also not so sure that an NIE of the kind requested would not better be put into a NSSM prepared by us which would reconvene a special Ad Hoc group of experts to review the entire issue and to have at its disposal the earlier work done by the NSC staff on this issue.

If you agree, I will send this back to Sonnenfeldt for the preparation of a comprehensive NSSM and for the development of

---

[1] Source: National Archives, Nixon Presidential Materials, NSC Files, Box 276, Agency Files, PFIAB, Vol. V. Secret. Sent for action.

[2] Attached but not printed at Tab B is an August 10 memorandum from Gerard Burke, Acting Executive Secretary of PFIAB, to Kissinger summarizing the PFIAB meetings of August 6–7.

[3] Attached but not printed.

recommendations for the composition of an Ad Hoc group of the caliber that offers some hope for a decent product.[4]

Tab A

Memorandum From William Hyland of the National Security Council Staff to the President's Assistant for National Security Affairs (Kissinger)[5]

Washington, August 28, 1970.

SUBJECT

PFIAB Recommendation on Sino-Soviet Intelligence Affairs

In its early August meeting PFIAB considered the problem of current intelligence estimates of possible developments in the Sino-Soviet confrontation (Tab B). They apparently conclude that, as a "matter of high priority," a national intelligence estimate should be prepared on the timing, nature, scope, duration and probable outcome of military operations that might be initiated by the USSR against China. Second, they recommend a similar estimate on implications as to the effect on US interests of such hostilities. Finally, they suggest a study of courses of action available to the US (1) to avoid becoming involved, and (2) to improve US relative positions vis-à-vis the two contestants in areas of US interests.

Comment:

I do not understand why you, rather than Dick Helms, are the addressee of this memo; presumably PFIAB recommendations were also passed to CIA.

The projected studies would do no harm, though probably not much good either. We have been through this exercise twice. It is doubtful that we will produce a better paper than the one shepherded by Roger Morris last year (which still must exist somewhere). Moreover,

---

[4] Kissinger initialed the "disapprove" option and added: "I would request an NIE minus C." On September 3, Haig sent Sonnenfeldt a memorandum instructing him to follow-up on items "A" and "B" of Burke's August 10 memorandum. Those items read as follows: "a) the timing, nature, scope, duration, and probable outcome of military operations that might be initiated by the USSR; b) implications as to the effect on U.S. interests of such hostilities; c) courses of action available to the U.S.: to avoid becoming involved; to improve U.S. relative positions vis-à-vis the two contestants in areas of U.S. interests such as Berlin, the Middle East and Southeast Asia."

[5] Sent for action.

the National Intelligence Estimate is not the form for the kind of study that might provide a helpful background. A CIA, or CIA–DIA study without the need for careful coordination, and containing considerable factual data on troop dispositions, capabilities, and possible attack scenarios, would be best. As for the implications of US interests, this is not an intelligence matter and should not be.[6]

If PFIAB and the intelligence community want to perform a service, they might consider a different aspect entirely. No amount of intelligence guessing on a Sino-Soviet war is of any value unless hostilities seem imminent; when they did last year, the most we got was a waffle. Intelligence might perform a service, however, by considering what factors might lead to a Sino-Soviet accommodation. This is usually ignored, but would be as important for our interests as a war. Moreover, we in the West have comfortably come to regard Sino-Soviet hostility as a permanent feature of the landscape, much as we did monolithic communism. Yet many Sinologists believe much of the hostility is due to Mao and Maoism. Indeed, there is ample evidence that the early phase of the cultural revolution was sparked by a dispute over relations with the USSR—with an important part of the Chinese establishment, including some of the military, disposed to patch up the dispute. The Soviet-German treaty ought to be a reminder that patterns of international politics can shift rapidly.

I have done a memo from you to the PFIAB (Tab A) indicating that you have no objections to the first study, ignoring the policy aspects which are not in the PFIAB bailiwick.

Recommendation

That you sign the memorandum to the PFIAB at Tab A.
Mr. Holdridge concurs in this memo.

---

[6] A handwritten note from Winston Lord at this point reads, "Burke memo does not suggest that it is—WL."

201.   Telegram From the Embassy in the Soviet Union to the Department of State[1]

Moscow, September 3, 1970, 2000Z.

5076. Dept please pass Immediate info to London, Paris, Beirut, Jidda, and Kuwait. Ref: State 144257.[2]

1. I made oral statement per paras 26–29 Reftel[3] to Soviet Dep FonMin Vinogradov late afternoon September 3, mentioning previous talk on same subject with Kuznetsov August 22.[4]

2. Vinogradov then launched into lengthy, repetitive, and largely unyielding reply. Although he said his remarks were preliminary in nature, and that my oral statement would be studied, the manner in which he made his comments suggested he may well have been expecting my approach. Following is account of discussion.

3. First, he could not accept wording in oral statement that USSR along with UAR would bear responsibility for possible resumption of fighting. The USSR could never accept such an accusation. The USSR was not engaged in hostilities in ME, and therefore could not be held responsible for things with which it is not connected.

4. Second, he said he could see very clearly our idea was to cover up for recent Israeli actions. The well-known facts were that Israel had disrupted the NY talks. It was unwilling to accept resumption of Jarring mission, had done so only in "funny way," and then Tekoah ran off to Israel and is still there. The Arabs are still in NY. Why then blame USSR/UAR for disrupting the talks?

5. Third, the US was accusing the UAR of a "kind of violation" of ceasefire agreement. However, one does not know if there were violations. For its part, the UAR accuses Israel of violating the agreement. Since US planes are flying over Eastern side of Suez Canal and can see over both sides, USG should be able to determine accuracy of UAR charges. Therefore, my statement looked "strange."

---

[1] Source: Library of Congress, Manuscript Division, Kissinger Papers, Geopolitical File, CL 172, Jordan Crisis, September 1970, Selected Exchanges, Soviet Union. Secret; Immediate; Nodis. Repeated to USINT Cairo, Tel Aviv, USUN, and Amman.

[2] Telegram 144257 to Moscow, September 3, reported on the administration's evaluation of the apparent violation of the cease-fire agreement between Israel and the UAR by the latter, which was supported by the Soviet Union. (National Archives, RG 59, Central Files 1970–73, POL 27–14 ARAB–ISR)

[3] Paragraphs 26–29 contained instructions for Moscow to transmit the oral statement described below to the highest possible level at the Soviet Foreign Ministry.

[4] No record of this meeting has been found.

6. I told Vinogradov that, while we were taking up matter with UAR, we regarded the USSR as involved since Soviet weapons and personnel were there and that their people on the ground must have knowledge of developments which were contrary to the ceasefire agreement. He asserted that any talk of ceasefire violations should be established by "both sides." In proposing the ceasefire agreement, the US said that verification of observance should be done by national means. The US may be right in charging that violations have occurred, but neither "you nor we," he asserted, know whether they have actually taken place. We both know clearly only that Israel has raised a hue and cry about violations.

7. He then said "there were no Soviet weapons in the UAR," although the UAR had bought Soviet weapons. There were no Soviet troops there; only advisers and technicians. Therefore, the situation was different than represented, and he said the USSR was in no way involved in the ME crisis. I told Vinogradov my government would take note of his statement, and added that it was our belief that Soviet personnel were involved with complicated weapons in the UAR.

8. I stressed our concern over the situation, noting that we had approached the GUAR regarding the violations I was speaking to him about. I said both the USG and the GOI were convinced that ceasefire violations had taken place, and handed him list of coordinates contained in paras 16–18 of Reftel. These violations were reason, I said, why the Israelis were staying away from NY. Although we were pressing them to return to NY to resume the talks, the GOI was confronted with a serious domestic situation as a result of the violations. This simply was a factor which we should both realize. In response to Vinogradov's question, I said we had raised with the GOI Egyptian charges of Israeli violations and were pressing Tel Aviv for more precise information.

9. Vinogradov then returned to his assertion that we were trying to put the blame on the USSR rather than where it belonged. I responded that we shared a joint responsibility. The USG was convinced that the ceasefire has been violated, and that the situation is extremely serious. The ceasefire and talks may be in jeopardy. Therefore, both of us should approach the situation in the spirit of taking steps to maintain the ceasefire.

10. Vinogradov then said that our accusations were wrong. He could see, he asserted, that the US wished to prepare the ground for the disruption of the talks and the resumption of hostilities. I immediately interrupted, saying this was not true. There was not the slightest such intention on our part, and I repudiated his suggestion. The situation was serious. The UAR had violated the ceasefire. We should both be concerned about such a development inasmuch as it could lead to a breakdown in the talks.

11. Vinogradov then backed off somewhat, especially when I asked him whether the Soviet Government should not be concerned, assuming our charges were true. He replied the USSR did not want the talks to break down. He said Moscow had supported the US initiative, whereas Israel had been reluctant to do so. Now Israel was accusing Cairo of violating the ceasefire as a pretext for trying to disrupt the talks. The situation, according to Vinogradov, was serious because of all the "shouting" Israel was doing; if the talks were resumed the situation would not be serious.

12. He then asked if I did not think that the ceasefire agreement provided for maintenance and the repair and restoration of facilities, to which I replied that our information clearly indicated that the violations I was talking about went far beyond repair and restoration.

13. Vinogradov then charged that we were making our accusations and drawing conclusions before waiting for the results of our approach to Cairo. He wondered how we could put ourselves in the role of being the only judge in such a complicated situation and why we wished to take on such a role.

14. I reiterated that, because of the seriousness of the situation, we were approaching both the UAR and Moscow. I then said that, as a personal suggestion, it seemed to me that if something could be done, quietly and without publicity, it might improve the situation. If the UAR would withdraw some—maybe not all—of its missiles as a gesture, this would be a small step toward restoring confidence and returning Israel to the conference table.

15. The discussion then turned to Jordan, with Vinogradov saying that their information indicated the situation was "no worse—no better." It was his assessment, Vinogradov said, that it would not be useful for Iraq to do something "serious." He did not, however, know how Jordan had behaved. The Soviet concern, he asserted, was to have good conditions for the Jarring mission. I closed by stating both our governments were faced by a situation of extreme seriousness.

16. State 144297[5] received after FonOff meeting. Gromyko understood to be on leave so that Vinogradov and Kuznetsov highest officials available.

Beam

---

[5] Telegram 144297 to Moscow, September 3, reads, "Re State 144257, we strongly urge you to make the démarche to Gromyko." (National Archives, RG 59, Central Files 1970–73, POL US–USSR)

202. Telegram From the Embassy in the Soviet Union to the Department of State[1]

Moscow, September 5, 1970, 1531Z.

5122. 1. EmbOff summoned to Soviet Foreign Office urgently 5 PM Saturday September 5 to receive following statement which read orally by Zinchuk, Deputy Head of American Section. Informal Embassy translation follows.

A. Begin text. According to information received by the Soviet Government, the Israeli Air Force intends to carry out on Sunday, September 6, bombings of a number of regions of the UAR in the zone of the Suez Canal beyond the ceasefire line. Thus, the Israeli ruling circles, encouraged by the constant declarations from Washington about an increase in military deliveries to Israel, in addition to the sabotage they are conducting of the talks in New York, are now preparing to set out on a course of direct military provocations against the UAR with the aim of disrupting the efforts toward a peaceful settlement of the middle-east conflict.

B. The Soviet Government expects that the Government of the USA will urgently undertake the necessary steps to restrain Israel from the dangerous actions it is planning, the entire responsibility for the consequences of which, under whatever pretexts they might be carried, would fully fall on Israel and the United States. End of text.

2. Zinchuk commented that they had asked us to come urgently to receive above declaration in view of shortness of time before actions referred to in note were supposed to be undertaken. Emboff said we would transmit context of declaration to department with greatest speed.

Beam

---

[1] Source: Library of Congress, Manuscript Division, Kissinger Papers, Geopolitical File, CL 172, Jordan Crisis, September 1970, Selected Exchanges, Soviet Union. Secret; Flash; Nodis. Repeated to Cairo and Tel Aviv.

203.   Telegram From the Department of State to the Embassy in the Soviet Union[1]

Washington, September 5, 1970, 2101Z.

White House please pass San Clemente for Secretary Rogers and Kissinger from Sisco.

146306. Subj: Soviet Démarche on Middle East and U.S. reply.

1. Soviet Chargé Vorontsov called urgently afternoon September 5 on Assistant Secretary Sisco to present démarche re alleged Israeli intention to mount air attack on UAR regions beyond ceasefire zone on September 6 which is identical to démarche received in Moscow (Moscow 5122).[2]

2. Sisco said we had just received the Soviet message which was passed to our Embassy by Soviet Foreign Ministry official Zinchuk in Moscow. Suggesting Vorontsov note his following remarks, Sisco stated Soviet message will be studied. In U.S. view, if cause is removed, then danger would be removed. This situation has been brought about by violations of ceasefire/standstill agreement which were brought to attention of Soviet Government in specific detail over past days, most recently on September 3.

3. Sisco continued that way to remove danger is for situation to be rectified immediately. We have provided specific locations of violations to Soviet Government. There have been serious violations in our view of at least three kinds: (A) construction which has increased total number of sites, (B) number of SA–2 and SA–3 missiles have been installed where there were none before ceasefire, and (C) missile sites have been occupied which previously were unoccupied.

4. Sisco pointed out Soviet and USG agreed to ceasefire/standstill. It is clear this agreement does not sanction aforementioned activity, or moving around missiles from position to position, installing missiles, new construction, or increasing operational readiness. All this is contrary to para C of ceasefire/standstill agreement, text of which Sisco then read to Vorontsov.

5. Sisco said we feel that USSR cannot take position expressed to US by Deputy Foreign Minister Vinogradov that it has no responsibility for this matter. There no need to outline how heavily involved USSR is in UAR with its own personnel and equipment. USSR and US agreed

---

[1] Source: National Archives, Nixon Presidential Materials, NSC Files, Box 713, Country Files, Europe, USSR, Vol. IX. Secret; Immediate; Nodis. Repeated to Tel Aviv, USINT Cairo, Amman, London, Paris, and USUN.

[2] Document 202.

on ceasefire/standstill in hope that it would lead to serious talks and political solution. Violations are serious, and both USSR and UAR would be taking on heavy responsibility if they should lead to breakdown in peace efforts.

6. Sisco observed that Soviet démarche contains allegation which also was stated to US by Vinogradov. Sisco stated US rejects categorically Soviet charge that US is attempting to establish grounds for resumption of military activities and break-off of talks. Sisco asked Vorontsov what possible incentive US could have to torpedo its own initiative after weeks of work with parties to bring about its acceptance.

7. Sisco continued what US wants is what Mr. Brezhnev said USSR wants in recent public statement: honest observance of agreement. This is important agreement between US and USSR. For agreement to work confidence between us is needed. If there cannot be confidence on this agreement, a question is raised as to what kind of confidence there can be between us in other areas.

8. Sisco pointed out that whenever nations take risks for peace— and US proposal was accepted on all sides—danger exists that any breakdown will bring about even more difficult situation than existed before acceptance of proposal. Sisco urged that Soviet Government examine very carefully information we provided in Moscow and take every feasible measure to rectify situation and bring about end of violations. This would remove danger and risks to which Soviet message refers.

9. Vorontsov said he would relay US comments and that Moscow and Washington understand each other's positions. He returned to Soviet note; he said most pressing matter is information in Soviet message about impending Israeli actions and asked that he should tell Moscow as to what US will do. Sisco replied US will study Soviet message; Sisco refused to be drawn out further. Vorontsov added Soviets expect US will take action because time is running out. Sisco replied he had nothing further to add.

10. *For Moscow:* you should follow up immediately with highest available MEA official, responding to Zinchuk statement[3] along preceding lines.

Johnson

---

[3] This statement was transmitted in Document 202.

204.   Transcript of Telephone Conversation Between the President's Assistant for National Security Affairs (Kissinger) and the Assistant Secretary of State for Near Eastern and South Asian Affairs (Sisco)[1]

Washington, September 6, 1970, 10:30 a.m.

S: Henry, we have just received a telegram from Moscow[2] which you probably will have received in San Clemente by now. I am having a check run. Let me read it to you because it is a note—an oral type thing. (Sisco read the message.)

S: The Soviet Government expects that the Government of USA will undertake the steps to prevent Israel from taking the steps they are planning. Our man in Moscow believes we should come back urgently with action he recommends.

K: Thing is not true, of course.

S: We have talked about this here and think it affords us an opportunity to do the following. Vorontsov just asked to see me urgently and he is meeting with me at 2:30 pm today. At the meeting I will just say thank you very much and receive the message. I will take two steps. We ought to tell the Israelis that this note has been received and, of course, we wish to repeat to them what we really said the other day that we assume that there is not going to be any unilateral action on their part and how serious this would be. The second phase would be to go back to the Russians and say we have taken action in this regard but we want to say to you that you have a responsibility and we have then put them in a position of getting these things out of here and then to conclude by saying once these missiles have been removed, you, the Russians will no longer have any worry about this. I would like to proceed this way. This raises the question of the letter you have.

K: The Secretary does not wish to send it. And I am not prepared to overrule him.

S: Then we can proceed in this way which will achieve the same thing but it gives us the opportunity to (K interrupted here).

K: Let me tell you my reaction. I would not give color to the fact that we have taken appropriate measures. That gives them a shot at the Arabs. All we need to do is tell Rabin that we have had this communication and I would not make any new views. I would not go back

---

[1] Source: Library of Congress, Manuscript Division, Kissinger Papers, Box 364, Telephone Conversations, Chronological File. No classification marking.

[2] Document 202.

to the Russians today and then today I would go back with essentially what you have done here.

S: Without claiming the credit.

K: That would be my recommendation.

S: Okay, that makes sense. I will proceed with that.

K: Good.

---

205. Memorandum From Helmut Sonnenfeldt of the National Security Council Staff to the President's Assistant for National Security Affairs (Kissinger)[1]

Washington, September 16, 1970.

SUBJECT

Soviet Reply to our Mid-East Démarches

Deputy Foreign Minister Vinogradov's omnibus reply to our three démarches[2] offers nothing concrete that would indicate that the Soviets or UAR intend to restrain their missile build-up, let alone tear it down. *Yet,* both the tone of the oral statement and Vinogradov's comments suggest that the Soviets may have blinked, if only slightly.

There is very little truculence in the formal statement and, rather plaintively, Vinogradov asked "rhetorically," how could rectification be accomplished? This last question is perhaps the operative part of the Soviet presentation, and may be the diplomatic opening that we need, especially if coupled with that part of the formal statement—which Vinogradov called attention to—that offered bilateral talks or a multilateral effort to move toward a settlement.

This could be pure evasion, particularly in light of the continuing missile build-up and direct Soviet involvement in it. (This last aspect incidentally seems to be getting lost in the shuffle. We will ultimately have to face up to the question of how to deal with the issue of Soviet presence.) On the other hand, having sliced several large chunks off the salami both the Soviets and the UAR may feel that they can resume

---

[1] Source: National Archives, Nixon Presidential Materials, NSC Files, Box 713, Country Files, Europe, USSR, Vol. VIII. Secret; Nodis. Sent for urgent information. Initialed by Kissinger.

[2] See Document 201.

political maneuvering to bring the Israelis back to the conference table, or at least to retrieve what they may have lost politically by the violation through isolating Israel (and us) as the opponents of talks.

The fact that Vinogradov displayed responsiveness to the concept of "rectification," even if rhetorically, could be a key opportunity. Read one way, this could be a cautious invitation for us to respond and could be a signal that the Soviets do not reject the idea privately broached by Beam to Vinogradov on September 3,[3] that removal of some missiles would be a necessary sign of good faith. Under this interruption, the Soviets could be inviting us to follow up and give them our ideas of what would constitute rectification, but in the secrecy of bilateral channels.

If so, it would be a great mistake to become involved in the morass of detailed numbers games over this or that missile site, or as currently proposed by Sisco, to put to the Soviets a list of actions they should take.

What we need is a concept that matches our general position that neither side should gain a military advantage and that a balance should be maintained. Under this approach what we should concentrate on is the *number of operational missile sites* as of August 10 and tell the Soviets that what we expect is that they will, in whatever manner they choose, restore this situation. If the Soviets do not accept our estimate of number of operational missile sites and claim there were less, so much the better. If they claim there were more, within limits we could go along and say this becomes the new ceiling. This approach focuses on the critical military item (missile launchers) and avoids the ambiguity of "related" equipment, occupied vs unoccupied, mobile vs stationary, SA–2 vs SA–3.

This approach could be linked to the other Sisco idea of cancelling out violations in return for dropping further investigation of Israeli violations.

In any case, it is worth exploring whether Vinogradov has in fact given a signal, or is merely throwing sand in our eyes. It does not appear to warrant, however, the proposed Sisco approach of elevating the rhetoric but rather a fast, but quiet Beam–Vinogradov negotiations. That this had already started would, presumably, have some effect on the meetings with Mrs. Meir.

Hal Saunders points out that it is difficult from intelligence to determine the number of operational sites. Using "occupied" sites might bring us close enough to the general concept to establish a reasonable

---

[3] See Document 201.

base. The intelligence people would have to go back over the photos and do a best guess list of occupied sites which represent military capability. He feels that this approach might be a better one than the more elaborate Sisco proposals now that there may be some opening to explore, but wonders whether the Soviets are really prepared to make that kind of concession given the fact that they and the Egyptians have not even broken stride in their build-up since our approach of September 3.

I do not know of course whether, in fact, the Soviets will make any concessions. The point is that we probably should exhaust this possibility, particularly in view of what may have been some very mixed signals to the Soviets during August. If it proves fruitless, we will have to haul out the heavy artillery.

206. Memorandum From Helmut Sonnenfeldt of the National Security Council Staff to the President's Assistant for National Security Affairs (Kissinger)[1]

Washington, September 16, 1970.

SUBJECT

Our Signals to the Soviet Union and Their Possible Misconstruction as a Source of Crises in US-Soviet Relations

I should like very briefly to convey to you my deep concern that in the present Middle Eastern situation we may have (unwittingly) misled the Soviets to believe that cheating on the cease-fire was a matter of indifference to us and that we may have thereby contributed to a potentially much deeper crisis.

Interpretation of Soviet conduct is a tricky and quite inexact exercise and I am very conscious of all the pitfalls and evidential gaps and ambiguities in this sort of analysis. I also do not claim to know or to have followed in detail all that we may have said and done with respect to the present state of affairs.

I am disturbed by the present train of events because of a history of US-Soviet crisis situations which lends itself to the respectable

---

[1] Source: National Archives, Nixon Presidential Materials, NSC Files, Box 713, Country Files, Europe, USSR, Vol. IX, August 1, 1970–October 31, 1970. Secret; Nodis; Eyes Only; Outside System. Sent for urgent information.

hypothesis that, especially in election years, we may be prone to give the Soviets the impression that they are relatively free to do certain things inimical to our interests; that they then do them; that we then react and find ourselves propelled into potentially dangerous and damaging confrontations. Some work has been done on this hypothesis as it relates to Suez (1956), various phases of the Berlin crisis, and, most especially, the Cuban missile crisis (1962). I have not done the research myself, do not have the required mass of findings or data available and would question some of the conclusions that have been advanced.

But, to take Cuba 1962, there is a tenable theory that runs somewhat as follows:

—that with the minimal camouflage accompanying the heavy Soviet military movements into Cuba during the spring and summer, including at first SAMS and then M/IRBM-associated gear, the Soviets must at least have suspected that we had an idea of what they were doing;

—that what was said (especially, at that time, by a phalanx of White House assistants and hangers-on) and done by us during the summer could well have appeared to the Soviets as US acquiescence in what they were doing, including in the Soviet depiction of it as solely "defensive";

—that Khrushchev may have concluded that as long as he did not flaunt his action in our face before the fall election we would remain passive and that, indeed, it was politically more important to us that nothing leaked out before November than that the Soviets would acquire some 40-odd additional first-strike strategic launchers;

—that even or especially the President's public warnings against offensive deployments as late as September 11, when they were well underway (plus further ongoing negotiations, e.g. on NPT), were interpreted in Moscow as further signs of toleration, if not collusion;

—that our blowing the issue wide open on October 22[2] thus came as a complete surprise and could well have led to so irrational a Soviet reaction as to produce disaster.

I am drawing no *precise* analogies. One can't. I do suggest, however, that the nature, timing and speed of our cease-fire initiative, the relative looseness of its terms, the informality of its consummation, our reluctance to concede violations and our other statements and actions *after* violations began could have led the Soviets to conclude that all that really mattered to us was a cease-fire in a pre-election period in which we preferred not to confront the awkward choices of continued open warfare. They could, therefore, have concluded that what they know are violations certainly of the spirit and also of the terms of the

---

[2] On October 22, 1962, President Kennedy delivered a radio and television report to the American people on the Soviet arms buildup in Cuba. (*Public Papers: Kennedy, 1962*, pp. 806–809)

agreement were not of vital interest to us. They could thus have been surprised by our subsequent apparently real indignation at what was happening (having meanwhile given the UAR, and themselves, the green light to proceed with violations and thus put their prestige on the line). Or they may even yet believe that we are merely play-acting.

I have sent you another memo, on the latest Beam–Vinogradov exchange,[3] to suggest that the Soviets may just possibly now be sufficiently worried about our further reaction that they are willing to consider some form of "rectification"; or that at least they are trying to maneuver politically to inhibit us from acting. On the other hand, this is far from clear. And there is no telling what may happen to the cease-fire and what the Soviets may do in the face of some unilateral Israeli act of "rectification" (or some new US act of support for Israel) when they may well have thought of themselves (and their clients) as acting on the Suez west bank with our toleration. (Even more than in Cuba, the Soviets this time *knew* for certain that *we* knew the standstill was being violated.)

I do not claim to know the right way to communicate our intentions and conceptions of interests (assuming we ourselves know and agree what they are) to the Soviets in a way that minimizes the danger of misconstruction and subsequent deep confrontation. Nor, emphatically, do I exonerate the Soviets, who after all are the perpetrators of or accessories to the inimical acts in question.

I merely note from past involvement in these matters that our propensity to give the wrong signal has been considerable and that a theory is intellectually quite tenable that holds that some major US-Soviet crises of the past, especially in months before US elections, can be correlated to what we ourselves say and do, including at highest (presumed or actual) levels. Admitting that I have not been very close to Middle Eastern developments and to our explicit and implicit communications to the Soviets about them, I nevertheless wish to register my deep concern that this theory has acquired additional weight by recent events.

---

[3] See Document 205.

207.   Memorandum From the President's Assistant for National Security Affairs (Kissinger) to President Nixon[1]

Washington, September 18, 1970.

SUBJECT

> Recent Soviet Naval Activity in Cuba

Analysis of reconnaissance flight photography over Cuba has this morning confirmed the construction of a probable submarine deployment base in Cien Fuegos Bay. Specifically:

—A Soviet submarine tender is anchored next to four buoys which the Soviets have placed in the Bay.

—[less than 1 line of source text not declassified] submarine nets have been emplaced across the approach to the deep water basin in which the mooring buoys and the tender are located.

—A Soviet LST is anchored at a fuel pier and a Soviet tanker is anchored in the northern bay.

—Two special purpose barges are also located in the area.

—Special construction on Alcatraz Island, an island in the Bay, appears to have been completed. This includes an administrative area, two single-story barracks, a soccer field, basketball court and probably handball, volleyball or tennis courts. An offshore wharf and swimming area are on the east side of the island and a platform tower has been constructed just south of the administrative area.

The foregoing situation acquires special significance in the light of the conversations I had with Chargé Vorontsov on August 4[2] in the White House Map Room. You will recall that I saw Vorontsov at his request on that occasion. He called me in San Clemente to say he wanted to have an appointment as soon as I got back. When I saw him he was extremely cordial and read a communication which he handed to me.

The text of the note which is at Tab A[3]:

—Expressed Soviet anxiety over alleged attempts by Cuban revolutionary groups in the United States to resume sabotage and subversive activity against Cuba from the U.S. soil.

—Complained about provocative articles in the American press and ambivalent statements on the part of the U.S. officials concerning Cuba.

---

[1] Source: National Archives, Nixon Presidential Materials, NSC Files, Box 782, Country Files, Latin America, Cuba, Soviet Naval Activity in Cuban Waters (Cienfuegos), Vol. I. Top Secret; Sensitive; Eyes Only. In the upper right hand corner is the handwritten remark, "Late AM Report." Attached but not printed is a map of the Caribbean Sea with Cienfuegos circled.

[2] See Document 192.

[3] Attached but printed as Tab A of Document 192.

—Stressed that the Soviets were proceeding on the Cuban question from the understanding with regard to Cuba that existed in the past and confirmed that the Soviets expected us to adhere to this understanding.

Note: The so called understanding to which Vorontsov was apparently referring was arrived at during the Cuban missile crisis. In essence, during the exchanges between the U.S. and the Soviets in 1962 at the time of the Cuban missile crisis we were given assurances that the Soviets would not locate nuclear weapons on Cuban territory in return for assurances from the U.S. government that we would not undertake military action to change the government of Cuba.

On August 7[4] I stated to Vorontsov that at your request I had been instructed to give him the following reply:

—The U.S. notes with satisfaction the assurance of the Soviet government that the understandings of 1962[5] are still in force, adding "We take this to mean that the Soviet Union will not place any offensive weapons of any kind or any nuclear weapons on Cuban soil."
—I stated further that you wish to point out that although we have heard repeated reports of increased Soviet activity in Cuba that you were exercising the utmost restraint in not increasing reconnaissance activity.
—You were maintaining the understandings of 1962 which I was hereby authorized to reaffirm.
—Specifically the U.S. would not use military force to bring about a change in the governmental structure of Cuba.
—I then added that it had come to our attention that Soviet long range airplanes of the type suitable for nuclear bombing missions were flying with increasing regularity to Cuba. While we believe these planes were on reconnaissance missions we thought nevertheless that this might constitute a basis for approaching the limit of our understanding. It would certainly be noticed if the Soviet Union kept such operations to a minimum. *The same applied to Soviet naval activity in the Caribbean.*
—I called Vorontsov's attention to the fact that we had taken protective measures in recent days with respect to a Soviet ship which reportedly was in danger of attack from Cuban exile groups.
—Vorontsov indicated he appreciated the good spirit in which the observations were made and was certain that the Kremlin would be very happy to receive them.
—I concluded by telling Vorontsov that the major problem now was to see what concrete progress could be made in the area of negotiations.

Today's photography readout confirms that despite the exchange between Vorontsov and myself the Soviets have moved precipitously to establish an installation in Cien Fuegos Bay which is probably designed to serve as a submarine staging base in the Caribbean. Because

---

[4] See Document 195.
[5] See Document 194.

of the seriousness of this situation I have asked CIA to provide me with a briefing at 12:30 today at which time we will carefully evaluate the full range of photographic evidence now held in an effort to determine more precisely the full scope of Soviet activity in Cuba. I am also initiating, on an urgent basis, a detailed analysis of the strategic implications of this development.[6]

---

[6] At the bottom of the page, Nixon handwrote the following comments: "I want a report on a crash basis on 1) what C.I.A. can do to support *any* kind of action which will irritate Castro; 2) what actions we can take which we have not yet taken to boycott nations dealing with Castro; 3) most important what actions we can take covert or overt to put missiles [unintelligible] the Black Sea [unintelligible] some trading stock."

---

208.   Minutes of Senior Review Group Meeting[1]

Washington, September 19, 1970, 10–10:45 a.m.

SUBJECT

Cuba/USSR—Military Activity in Cienfuegos

PARTICIPANTS

Chairman—Henry A. Kissinger   JCS—Adm. Thomas H. Moorer
State—U. Alexis Johnson   NSC Staff—Viron P. Vaky
Defense—David Packard
CIA—Richard Helms

SUMMARY OF DECISIONS

1. There would be a restricted NSC meeting on the subject on Wednesday, September 23 immediately following the regularly scheduled one.[2]

2. There would be a pre-NSC meeting Tuesday afternoon[3] (time to be announced). Johnson and Kissinger would check to see if Llewellyn Thompson could not be present to discuss the Soviet perception of the situation.

---

[1] Source: National Archives, Nixon Presidential Materials, NSC Files, NSC Institutional Files (H-Files), Box H–111, SRG Minutes, Originals, 1970. Top Secret; Sensitive. The meeting was held in the White House Situation Room.

[2] See Document 214.

[3] The President's Daily Diary does not indicate that a meeting was held before the NSC meeting scheduled for 12:07 p.m. on September 22. (National Archives, Nixon Presidential Materials, White House Central Files)

3. Admiral Moorer is to prepare a paper on the strategic significance of the Soviet activity in Cienfuegos.[4]

4. Discussion of possible US responses will be deferred to give the principals time to consider the matter.

5. If there are press leaks, everyone will "stone-wall," simply saying we constantly receive such reports and we constantly and carefully evaluate them; no further comment.[5]

Dr. Kissinger stated that the Cuban/Soviet Base problem was to be discussed only in this very restricted group. The President and Secretary Rogers want to keep it very restricted. They want to avoid a crisis mood until we know what we are going to do. Therefore, each principle is to keep the circle that knows about this very small and paperwork very restricted.

Dr. Kissinger then asked if there were any new facts to add to the intelligence we now have on the Cienfuegos area.

Mr. Helms said there was nothing to add to the report[6] circulated yesterday.

In response to Dr. Kissinger's question as to military significance, Admiral Moorer said that there was no question but that the Soviets were building an advance submarine base. This kind of installation would enable the Soviets either to have submarines come into the port or have the tender rendezvous anywhere in international waters. It greatly increases the on-station time of the subs.

Dr. Kissinger observed that there was some evidence this is also an R&R area. Thus he assumed they could fly in reserve crews and rotate crews via the tender. All the servicing of the subs could take place in international waters; in short, it was possible for the Soviets to operate in a "legal" way that would make it very difficult for us to meet.

Admiral Moorer suggested, however, that this might be a violation of the 1962 Kennedy–Khrushchev agreement.[7]

Mr. Johnson pointed out that strictly speaking there was never an "agreement" in 1962. There was an exchange of letters some of which crossed each other. In essence, the discussion then concentrated on UN inspection. The only thing we focussed on were land-based missiles and IL 28's. There was really nothing else, and no "agreement" in the conventional sense.

---

[4] Document 211.

[5] See footnote 2, Document 221.

[6] Not found. A September 18 memorandum from Nachmanoff to Kissinger summarizes the report. Kissinger included the information in his memorandum to the President on that day; see Document 207.

[7] See Tab A, Document 194.

Dr. Kissinger agreed with this interpretation based on his review of the record and talks with McCloy and McNamara.

Dr. Kissinger pointed out that what the Russians did in 1962 was "legal." What President Kennedy did was to react on the basis of a challenge to our security. There were two questions—Do the Russians violate an international understanding with this activity? Probably not. Secondly, what do we do from the security aspect?

Mr. Johnson cited President Kennedy's press conference of November 20, 1962, in which the President said that peace in the Caribbean would depend upon strategic weapons being removed from Cuba and "kept out in the future" under adequate measures of inspection. This was the only specific thing we had, although everyone agreed that this was only a unilateral declaration of our own position. (A copy of the text of the November statement was given to Dr. Kissinger.)[8]

Mr. Johnson asked if there was any evidence as to whether the base accommodated Y-Class subs or attack subs or both.

It was generally agreed it could accommodate both.

Admiral Moorer pointed out that the base extends the operation of either Y or E class subs. The Soviets can now do with 1 what it now takes 5 to do. The net effect is to permit them to maintain a greater number of subs on station with the same force level.

Mr. Packard pointed out that the Soviets put up this installation in a hurry, something they do not usually do. They apparently want to have it quickly as a fait accompli. He believed the Soviets may want it in existence before the November 1 SALT talks.[9]

Mr. Johnson added that this was his theory.

Dr. Kissinger asked Admiral Moorer to do a paper on military implications. He asked if the Russians would store missiles at the base, and inquired as to what we did.

Admiral Moorer replied that we keep weapons on the tender, and that is what they will undoubtedly do.

Mr. Johnson and Mr. Packard both pointed out that the Russians were doing just what we are doing in advanced areas.

Mr. Helms said he was surprised they had not done it sooner.

Mr. Packard also pointed out that apart from the SALT angle, the number of Y class subs becoming operational now made the establishment of this kind of advanced base installation more sensible from the Russians' viewpoint.

---

[8] For text, see *Public Papers: Kennedy, 1962*, pp. 830–838.

[9] The third phase of SALT was to begin on November 2 in Helsinki.

Dr. Kissinger then asked if it was agreed that any decision we make in this regard must be on the assumption that the base can be used for Y Class, not just attack subs; in short, there was no point in trying to distinguish—the base is to be assumed to be for both. All agreed.

Secondly, Dr. Kissinger suggested that the strategic situation is different from 1962.

Mr. Packard agreed, saying this does not change the balance very much.

Mr. Johnson agreed, pointing out that the 1962 situation did constitute a major change of the strategic balance.

Mr. Packard said we must nevertheless assess the matter carefully, and that one danger was to the US bomber bases. The subs would have to get in close to our shore and they would need about 4 to 5 Y Class subs to have a credible threat against the bases.

All agreed with Dr. Kissinger's observation that what the Russians are doing is comparable to our building a sub base on the Black Sea.

Dr. Kissinger said that the President wanted an NSC discussion of this subject on Wednesday (Sept. 23) with just the major principals concerned—Rogers, Helms, Laird, Moorer. This would be done after the regular NSC meeting. We will operate on the assumption that the base is designed for Y Class subs and the question is whether a base of that kind requires a US response and if so what it should be.

Dr. Kissinger again asked Admiral Moorer to prepare a paper on what the base does for Y Class subs, for attack subs, to the strategic balance. The worldwide USSR naval picture should be included.

Dr. Kissinger asked how we can get a sense of Soviet perception of the situation.

Mr. Packard expressed the view that it is a long-range naval plan; he did not think it was a nuclear strike move, just a long-range build-up of power.

Mr. Helms observed that the Russians are doing the same thing in the Indian Ocean—they have built an airfield on the "God-forsaken is-land" of Scotoa, which belongs to South Yemen.

Admiral Moorer stated it may be just the beginning, and they might want to put up facilities in Chile.

Mr. Johnson said he would like to talk to "Tommy" Thompson on the Soviet angle.

Dr. Kissinger said that maybe Thompson should talk to the whole group. They agreed that Dr. Kissinger would check with the President and Johnson would check with Secretary Rogers, and they would be in touch with each other.

It was further agreed that there would be a pre-NSC meeting on Tuesday afternoon.

Mr. Helms pointed out that the jumpiest people in the world about Cuba are in the Congress.

Mr. Packard pointed out that the only reason for some speed is that the story is likely to leak, and may leak by Wednesday. Everyone agreed that they would just stone-wall it.

In response to Dr. Kissinger's question, everyone said they would prefer to think about the matter before proceeding to discuss possible US responses. It was agreed that consideration should proceed through the spectrum from doing nothing on up, but at the moment the meeting had gone as far as it could.

---

209. Memorandum From the President's Assistant for National Security Affairs (Kissinger) to Secretary of Defense Laird[1]

Washington, September 21, 1970.

SUBJECT

Sino-Soviet Border Dispute

As you know, the President is most interested in developments relating to the Sino-Soviet border dispute. It would be helpful to have a memorandum[2] which assesses the significance of the continuing buildup of military forces on the Soviet side of the border.

In particular, the memorandum should address the question of what the present level of Soviet forces along the border tells us of their intentions. It should address in particular the question of whether the current Soviet strength in the border area is sufficient only for defense against a possible Chinese attack or whether it is enough to allow the Soviets to invade China and if so, how far into China. The memorandum should also examine the question of what more, if anything, we

---

[1] Source: National Archives, Nixon Presidential Materials, NSC Files, Box 225, Agency Files, Department of Defense, Vol. VIII, July 21, 1970–September 1970. Secret; Sensitive. Drafted by Latimer on September 15.

[2] On October 22, Laird sent Kissinger a paper entitled "Soviet Force Level on Sino-Soviet Border," under a covering memorandum that read: "While [the enclosed report] cannot tell us definitively what Soviet intentions are, it does indicate the extent and general significance of the Soviet buildup. The buildup of Soviet forces has been steady and methodical but is inadequate for a major and prolonged offensive against the Chinese. The further buildup required for a major offensive would amost certainly be detected by intelligence." The CIA response is Document 227.

might expect to see on the Soviet side before an invasion, more trucks, armor, logistics buildup, etc.

If you agree, a due date of 7 October 1970, would be good.

Henry A. Kissinger[3]

---

[3] Printed from a copy that indicates Kissinger signed the original.

---

210.   Memorandum From Viron Vaky of the National Security Council Staff to the President's Assistant for National Security Affairs (Kissinger)[1]

Washington, September 22, 1970.

SUBJECT

The Cuban Side of the Soviet Military Activity in Cuba

In concentrating on the Soviet intention and plans regarding Cienfuegos, we should not ignore the other side of the equation—what does Cuba get out of lending its territory for this purpose? The answer would be illuminating as to what Cienfuegos is all about.

Cienfuegos may be the key to a number of puzzling and otherwise unexplainable things that have happened in the past two or three years:

(a) Evidence that the Soviets are increasing their control over the Cuban regime, and some reports that Castro is unhappy at this and somewhat impotent. The attached memo which I sent to you on September 8 describes some of these; note Castro's alleged comment on Soviet "coldbloodedness and ruthlessness."

(b) In several speeches last Spring, castigating exile activity, Castro made curious references that they (exiles) would not stage out of Central America or the Bahamas if Cuba had long range military aircraft. He would add "but of course we don't." However, the references were almost in the sense of "just wait."

---

[1] Source: National Archives, Nixon Presidential Materials, NSC Files, Box 782, Country Files, Latin America, Cuba, Soviet Naval Activity in Cuban Waters (Cienfuegos), Vol. I. Secret; Sensitive; Eyes Only. Sent for information. Vaky's memorandum is Tab A of a September 22 memorandum from Haig to Kissinger for the NSC meeting on Cuba held September 23. Sent for information; designated "non-log."

(c) Cubanologists have long puzzled about why Castro made such a point of a ten million ton sugar harvest when it was such an improbable thing to achieve. The most interesting theory is one Rand researchers have developed linking back to Cuba's support of the USSR in the Czechoslovakia crisis:

—At that time Castro delayed for about a month before speaking out, and it seemed fairly clear that he was struggling with himself. He finally came out for the Soviets. If, the theory goes, the Soviets put the economic squeeze on him at that time because they needed his support in international socialist terms, Castro is the type to chafe at this dependence and seek to build his base to contest this kind of control.

—The ten million ton harvest was a typical Castroist mission— the subjective willing of a goal—which if he succeeded would have refurbished his leadership and his charisma—and his control over the society.

—To have failed and to have had to admit it decreases this control and leadership. He is now weaker; he gambled and lost. The Soviets can work their will with less sensitivity for Castro's wishes.

With reference to Cienfuegos, there are several possibilities; moreover, they are not mutually exclusive:

1. The Russians forced Cuba's consent with economic blackmail.
2. They bribed Castro with promises of additional economic and military aid, and perhaps a promise of protection against overthrow.
3. They bribed Castro's cooperation with promises to underwrite the export of revolution—Soviet naval units in the Caribbean could provide cover for clandestine guerrilla expeditions.

The last seems the least likely; to stimulate Castro's revolutionary exploits again goes counter to every other stance they are taking as to the via pacifica. On the other hand, the Russians could possibly have made a conscious decision to press the erosion of US influence in the continent by a variety of means.

There is no evidence of increased aid, either military or economic, but that of course could be in the future. An intelligence effort to check on weapons flow would be particularly interesting.

I am most intrigued, however, by the possibility that the Russians made a cold decision and then proceeded to ram it down Castro's throat. It is a tactical decision which may well have sprung out of their success in forcing Castro to bow to their wishes on Czechoslovakia— if we accept that theory for the moment. This may have made them realize—after clashes with Castro's maverick ideology—that Cuba could be theirs in absolute terms.

Tab A

Memorandum From Viron Vaky of the National Security Council Staff to the President's Assistant for National Security Affairs (Kissinger)[2]

Washington, September 8, 1970.

SUBJECT

Soviet Activity in Cuba

Attached is an interesting CIA report[3] indicating increased Soviet control over the Cuban Communist Party. According to this report, the machinery of the Communist Party of Cuba (PCC) is increasingly controlled by young Soviet-trained officials whose primary loyalty is more to international Communism than to Castro or Cuban revolution. Castro only recently became aware of the extent of Soviet control when it was proposed that the position of Prime Minister be occupied by some one other than the Secretary General of the PCC. Since Castro holds both positions, the proposal in effect was that he give up the Secretary Generalship.

The report also cites Castro as commenting on Soviet "cold-bloodedness and ruthlessness" and that Latin American revolutionaries would have to face opposition from both the U.S. and the Soviet Union. Castro is also reported to have said he believes part of Cuba's economic problems are due to the rigidity of the Soviet style of Soviet-trained officials.

Comment: Note that CIA suggests that the Cubans may have deliberately surfaced this line to provoke a pro-Castro reaction among the revolutionists abroad. While that is a possibility, there have been several other reports indicating that there is some dissention between the old 26th of July veterans of the revolution and the younger technocrats who are largely Soviet-trained. There have also been fairly firm reports of Soviet domination of the Cuban intelligence apparatus, the DGI, and of increasing control of the Foreign Ministery by "Soviet-phyles." A key figure in all this is Carlos Raphael Rodriquez, the only old-time Communist party leader to have survived the ten years of Castro's revolution. He is smart, tough, and without any question the Soviets' man in Havana.

---

[2] Secret. Sent for information. The memorandum is initialed by Kissinger.

[3] CIA Intelligence Information Cable TDCS DB–315/04525–70, September 2, on "Indications of Increased Soviet Control Over Communist Party of Cuba and Reaction of Fidel Castro" is attached but not printed.

211. Paper Prepared by the Chairman of the Joint Chiefs of Staff (Moorer)[1]

Washington, undated.

SUBJECT

Assessment of Soviet Military Activities

1. Our latest intelligence indicates that the Soviet Union may be developing the port of Cienfuegos, Cuba, into a base capable of supporting nuclear submarines. This is but the latest in a series of moves that appear to fit into a pattern which indicates increasing Soviet hostility toward the United States and a willingness to take greater risks in pursuing objectives inimical to the security of the United States. Several Soviet actions which illustrate this pattern are listed below:

—Soviets continue to construct strategic missiles, SSBNs, and a new strategic bomber during SALT.

—Soviets have increased the threat to NATO Europe by deployment of ICBMs with improved accuracy replacing older MRBM/IRBMs.

—Soviet conventional forces in Europe have been strengthened. General Goodpaster has pointed out that the land, sea, air and missile forces of the Warsaw Pact represent a concentration of military power far in excess of defensive needs.

—Soviet actions in Czechoslovakia indicated that they will not hesitate to employ military force when their vital interests—as they define them—are at stake. The continuing occupation force has served to strengthen Soviet forces in Eastern Europe by five divisions.

—Soviet Navy deployments are increasing in scope and frequency, and in April 1970, the Soviet Navy conducted the most extensive exercise ever attempted by any navy, operating simultaneously in three oceans.

—Soviet merchant fleet has increased from 432 to 1,717 ships in the post-World War II period.

—Soviet influence in the Arab world, Soviet military presence in the Middle East and Soviet naval operations in the Mediterranean have increased dramatically in the past three years.

—Soviets have virtual control of UAR air defense and have challenged US peace initiative by violation of standstill provision with massive buildup of missile defenses along Suez Canal.

---

[1] Source: National Archives, Nixon Presidential Materials, NSC Files, Box 782, Country Files, Latin America, Cuba, Soviet Naval Activity in Cuban Waters (Cienfuegos), Vol. I. Top Secret; Sensitive. On September 22, Haig forwarded this paper to Kissinger for the NSC meeting on Cuba held on September 23.

—Soviet airfield construction activity has been reported on Socotra Island in the Gulf of Aden.

—A Soviet naval task force has been operating in the Indian Ocean on a semi-permanent basis since November 1968, and aircraft landing rights have been acquired in Mauritius. Somalia recently has become pro-Soviet in its orientation.

—Election of a Marxist President in Chile may present the Soviet Union with an opportunity to expand military as well as political influence into the southern cone of the Western Hemisphere.

—Three Soviet fleet visits have been made to Cuba (July/August 1969, May/June 1970 and September 1970), and TU–95/BEAR D reconnaissance aircraft made three flights to Cuba in April and May of this year.

2. Military implications of the Soviet pattern of increasing military capabilities are clear. In the strategic field, they have attained a position of relative strength that makes the US nuclear deterrent credible only in extremis. They are developing the airlift, sealift, and submarine forces to project and support military power throughout the world. The establishment of Soviet bases in the Western Hemisphere or Indian Ocean would spread our ASW forces thinner, make our sea LOCS even more difficult to protect, and enhance Soviet efforts to penetrate the areas economically and politically. It would appear that the Soviet Union is boldly pursuing more aggressive policies in the Middle East, Indian Ocean, and Western Hemisphere.

3. Offsetting, in part, this steady buildup in Soviet capabilities has been some ostensible cooperation in diplomatic moves. They have agreed to SALT—even though they continue to build while talking. They have signed a non-aggression pact with the FRG and have raised the possibility of a Conference on European Security and force reductions in Europe. The Soviets urged the Arabs to accept a Middle East ceasefire, but have assisted in violating the standstill aspects of the ceasefire. (This makes one wonder how reliable Soviet adherence to a SALT agreement would be.) However, while professing peaceful intentions, military capabilities have been improved across the board.

4. The latest and perhaps the most serious challenge to US security interests is occurring in Cuba. Recent port improvements and construction activity at Cienfuegos indicate that the Soviets are establishing a facility that will support naval units, including nuclear submarines, in the Caribbean and the Atlantic. A detailed assessment of the military significance of a Soviet naval base or naval support facility at Cienfuegos is contained in enclosure 1.[2]

---

[2] Attached but not printed. Also attached but not printed are enclosures on "Actions to Signal Resolve and to Prepare for Military Action to Eliminate or Neutralize Soviet Base at Cienfuegos" and "Actions Designed to Eliminate or Neutralize Soviet Base at Cienfuegos."

5. Soviet use of Cienfuegos to directly support Y-class submarine operations, or indirectly by basing support ships there for at sea rendezvous, would represent a significant increase in the strategic threat to the United States due to the additional on-station time and extra stations that could be covered, for example, in the Gulf of Mexico. A sharp reduction in transit time would have the effect of increasing the size of the Soviet submarine fleet and decreasing the time available to detect submarine movements. Early model SSB/SSBNs could be employed without a long, noisy transit. Sustained operations in the Caribbean or Gulf of Mexico would threaten additional areas of the US and increase the vulnerability of SAC to SLBM attack.

6. Attack submarines utilizing Cienfuegos would have additional time on station for operations against our SSBNs and other naval forces based at Charleston, Mayport, Key West, Guantanamo, and Roosevelt Roads. The vulnerability of our naval forces, merchant ships and sea LOCS would be increased. As with SSBNs, supporting attack submarines at Cienfuegos would have the effect of giving the Soviets a net increase in available force levels.

7. If the foregoing assessment is valid, then appropriate countermeasures appear necessary. They fall into two categories: those dealing with the overall trend in Soviet capabilities, and those focusing on the specific activity at Cienfuegos. The countermeasures are, of course, related to our national objectives which remain sound and should not be changed. In connection with the overall expansion of Soviet capabilities, the following broad politico-military countermeasures seem appropriate:

a. Intensified intelligence effort to deepen our knowledge of Soviet capabilities and trends in ballistic missile submarines, ICBMs and MRBMs.

b. Tough negotiating line with the Soviets in such areas as Berlin, SALT, MBFR. We should not pass up opportunities to point out the stark inconsistency between the Soviet's professed intentions to ease tensions, and their growing world-wide capabilities and actions.

c. Shore up NATO. Actions include initiatives to bring France into closer cooperation, efforts to prevent any unravelling effect on NATO by the FRG's Eastern policy, and revalidation of our military posture in Western Europe.

d. Provide sufficient economic and military aid to counter growing Soviet influence in less developed nations.

e. Increased world-wide US naval presence. This would counter demonstratively the increased Soviet naval presence in areas such as the Indian Ocean, the Mediterranean, the Caribbean, and possibly off Chile if that situation develops to Soviet advantage.

f. Enhance the capabilities of our Strategic Forces and General Purpose Forces.

8. Turning to specific countermeasures for Cienfuegos, we must first determine the extent of the capability to support SSBNs and the

pattern of operations. This will involve a cautious increase in aerial and off-shore surveillance to detect levels of sea and shore activity, types and numbers of vessels, types and quantities of equipment and supplies, and personnel. If Cienfuegos does develop into an SSBN base, the countermeasures listed below should be considered:

a. Protest the existence of the submarine support base and demand its removal, claiming violation of the 1962 understandings. This could involve a direct confrontation over such measures as quarantining Cienfuegos, boarding and search of enroute Soviet ships, surface and sub-surface surveillance of Soviet vessels, clandestine sabotage efforts, or placement of negotiation hazards. Additional illustrative actions both to signal our resolve and to remove the base are listed in enclosures 2 and 3.

b. Negotiate removal. This would involve determining some suitable US quid pro quo in exchange for Soviet withdrawal from the base. While these actions would avoid a direct confrontation, they would clearly erode our military capabilities and freedom of action.

c. Obtain assurances on the non-offensive nature of the base. However, the long history of Soviet deviousness makes this a high-risk action for the United States.

9. In conclusion, if Cienfuegos emerges as an active submarine base, it would increase significantly Soviet capabilities in the Western Hemisphere. The missile crisis in 1962 drew a line against Soviet military expansion in this Hemisphere and we should toe that line now even though our relative strategic posture has deteriorated since October 1962. If we do not, the Soviets might mistake acquiescence for weakness and be encouraged to develop other bases in this Hemisphere. Accordingly, the following actions should be undertaken:

a. Increase intelligence operations to determine conclusively whether Cienfuegos is an active submarine base. If it is, then appropriate countermeasures should be employed to force removal. We could not rationalize the continuing presence of such a base, nor should we negotiate its removal by sacrificing some of our freedom of action or capabilities.

b. Continue the urgent, detailed assessment of Soviet military capabilities in relation to our capabilities in order to determine appropriate countermeasures.

c. Maintain tight security over disclosure of all aspects of Soviet activities in Cienfuegos to avoid a premature disclosure which could foreclose options available to the United States.

212. Memorandum From the President's Assistant for National Security Affairs (Kissinger) to President Nixon[1]

Washington, September 22, 1970.

SUBJECT

Soviet Naval Facility in Cuba

I. The Current Situation

A. The Soviet Facilities

Photographic intelligence indicates the USSR is constructing a naval support base, apparently for submarines, in Cienfuegos Bay, Cuba. Definite identification of this activity was first made from U–2 photography [*less than 1 line of source text not declassified*].[2]

The facilities at present consist of a Soviet submarine tender moored to four heavy buoys in the bay. Two Soviet submarine support barges, a landing ship, a heavy salvage vessel, and a rescue vessel are in the harbor. Other ships that had been there—a tanker and two missile anti-submarine warfare (ASW) ships—have departed. Construction on Cayo Alcatraz, an island in the bay, consists of two single story barracks, sports area (soccer field, basketball and tennis courts), an offshore wharf and a swimming area. Three AAA sites and a communications antenna array are also in the harbor area.

None of this construction or naval activity was in the area on [*less than 1 line of source text not declassified*] the last prior date on which U–2 photography of the bay was available. All of this was thus accomplished in the intervening four-week period, suggesting that it was done on a crash basis.

The installation is similar to what we have in Holy Loch, and is of semi-permanent nature. It would appear at this point to have the capability of servicing submarines, including nuclear subs, and of providing rest and recreation facilities for naval crews as well as permanent support personnel. No other naval support capabilities are evident at this point.

---

[1] Source: National Archives, Nixon Presidential Materials, NSC Files, Box 782, Country Files, Latin America, Cuba, Soviet Naval Activity in Cuban Waters (Cienfuegos), Vol. I. Top Secret; Sensitive; Eyes Only. Designated "non log." Not initialed by Kissinger. There is no indication it was sent to the President.

[2] The Soviet naval activity was summarized in a CIA intelligence memorandum, which Helms sent to Kissinger on September 21 with the note, "Henry, the essential points here will be included in my NSC briefing Wednesday [September 23] morning." (Ibid.) See Document 215.

B. The Background

Circumstantially, this construction appears to be part of a series of events involving Soviet-Cuban military relations which have stretched over the last year:

—In July 1969 a Soviet naval group, including a nuclear submarine, visited Cuba for two weeks.

—The Soviet Minister of Defense visited Cuba for eight days from November 12–19, 1969, the first visit by a Soviet Defense Minister to the Western Hemisphere.

—Raul Castro, the Cuban Minister of the Armed Forces, visited the USSR for one month from April 4 to approximately May 13.

—On April 22 and again on August 23 Castro made public remarks welcoming close military ties with the Soviets.

—Three flights of Two TU–95 Bear surveillance/reconnaissance aircraft were made to Cuba on April 18, April 25 and May 13.

—A Soviet naval task force paid a two-week visit May 14 to Cienfuegos. Two units called at Havana subsequently for a ceremonial visit.

—On August 4, in a note for you, the Soviets complained of new exile activities and asked if the 1962 understanding was valid; we replied that it was.

—The current ships now in Cienfuegos were first noticed moving to that area on August 28.

II. Military Significance

There is a wide spectrum of views regarding the military significance of this development. The JCS believe that the military impact would be significant equating, in the case of submarines, because of increased on-station time, to approximately one-third of the size of the Soviet Ballistic Missile Submarine (SLBM) force. Additional advantages they cite include:

—The establishment of SLBM patrol stations in the Gulf of Mexico;

—The option of keeping all missile submarines (SSBN) in port at Cienfuegos and either launch from port or deploy rapidly as the situation dictates;

—The lessening of personnel hardship and the concommitant increase of SSBN crew effectiveness by significantly decreasing at-sea time.

The JCS further believe that this action fits into an overall Soviet pattern which indicates increasing Soviet hostility toward the U.S. and a willingness to take greater risks in pursuing their objectives. In support of this contention they note, among other Soviet actions, the following:

—the continued construction of strategic missiles and SSBNs during SALT;

—dramatic increases in Soviet naval forces and operations in the Mediterranean and Indian Ocean;

—virtual Soviet control of UAR on defense and the challenge to the U.S. peace initiative by violation of the standstill provision with a massive buildup of missiles along the Suez Canal;

—the Soviet fleet visits and flights of TU–95/Bear D reconnaissance aircraft to Cuba; and

—improvements in Soviet military capabilities across-the-board while ostensibly cooperating in a number of diplomatic moves.

I share the JCS's concern with Soviet intentions. I also share their concern over the increasing Soviet military capabilities vis-à-vis the U.S. and this is a matter which we are carefully analyzing. However, I believe the development of the port of Cienfuegos into a base capable of supporting nuclear submarines would add only marginally to the total Soviet capability for attacking the U.S. with nuclear weapons. The fact of the matter is that there are always some Soviet subs off our East Coast with the capability to launch missiles against most targets in the U.S. If they want, the Soviets can increase this number at any time by simply increasing their force levels. Having a base at Cienfuegos makes it easier to achieve such an objective but at considerably higher risks considering past U.S. reactions to Soviet military activities in Cuba. Unlike 1962, the Soviets have a massive land base missile capability which continues to grow.

If my view that the increase in military capabilities of the Cienfuegos base would be only marginal is correct, then the Soviet action becomes even more puzzling. *Why run such high risks for such low returns in increased military capability?* This strongly suggests that this Soviet move is perhaps more politically-motivated than militarily.

III. Soviet Intentions

There are several basic questions:

—Why, at this time, have the Soviets embarked on a venture that they should know has a low flashpoint in terms of American sensitivity?

—Why, beforehand, did the Soviets seek to reaffirm the 1962 post missile crisis understanding on the flimsy pretext of the threat to Cuba?

—Having reaffirmed the essentials of the 1962 understanding, why did the Soviets almost immediately proceed to violate the spirit if not the precise letter of that understanding?

—Finally, how does the move into Cuba relate, if at all, to the larger posture of Soviet behavior, especially in the Middle East?

There are several possible explanations:

1. It could be that this move in Cuba is simply *to show the flag*, perhaps to impress Latin America generally; having done that, the venture will be terminated; in other words, there would be no longer-term implications or consequences intended.

The main problem with this interpretation is that establishing a semi-permanent facility goes well beyond showing the flag. No Soviet leader could imagine that such a move could be passed over by an American administration.

2. It could be a move in the SALT context, to establish a presence to be bargained away for the removal of U.S. forward bases which the Soviets have pressed for in SALT.

The problem with this argument is that the prospective SALT agreement currently on the table is one that, in itself, is quite attractive to the USSR. To raise the sensitive issues of Cuba risks upsetting SALT; at a minimum, it would establish a far more belligerent atmosphere for negotiations. If the Soviets did accept a trade-off in the end, it would once again demonstrate to Castro and Latin Americans generally, that the Soviets exploited Cuba for their own strategic purposes.

3. *A deliberate confrontation.* If the above two explanations are implausible, we must assume that the Soviets are well aware of the crisis potential of their action. It is possible that the Soviets some time ago looked ahead and saw the Middle East escalating to a dangerous point. They could have reasoned that it was to their strategic advantage to widen the arena of potential conflict with the U.S., in part to put pressures on us from at least two points.

—They could foresee that these two crises would come to a head in a pre-election period, when the U.S. might be under some internal constraints.

—They lied to us as in 1962 to create an "understanding" for the record beforehand, later to be used against us in some distorted fashion.

—In this scenario, the Soviets, typically, have not thought through their tactics of a double crisis, but in their arrogance, will brazen it through.

—It could be argued that for some years, now, as their strategic power has grown, the Soviet leaders have wanted to even the score from the humiliation of 1962.

A double crisis of this magnitude, however, has always been an intriguing theory but a dangerous strategy. No one can foresee the consequences of inter-actions between two areas of contention. There is not only the danger of uncalculated escalation but the significant risk of a double defeat.

Moreover, Cuba would seem the last place the Soviets would want to invoke in a Middle East crisis. Cuba is, after all, still an area where we have immense tactical advantage.

4. *Soviet expansionism.* This interpretation fits the Cuba move into the pattern of the projection of Soviet power to various points around the globe, and expansionism symbolized primarily by a naval presence. *Under this theory the Soviets have been in the process of testing us for a reaction, and having estimated that we were relatively complacent, have decided to take a further step,* following their earlier naval visits to Cuba and flights of bomber-reconnaissance aircraft.

—The primary purpose of the Cuban move is not to create another confrontation, but to establish step-by-step the Soviet right to establish a naval presence in the area, much as they have done in the Mediterranean, the Indian Ocean, the Persian Gulf (not to mention the now-regular on-station patrolling of Y Class submarines within range of the East Coast).

—The Soviet actions are demonstrative and political for their own, not Cuban objectives, to show that the balance of power is now such that we can no longer effectively block Soviet power even in our own sphere of influence.

—The Soviets may have reasoned that it would be prudent to reaffirm the basic 1962 understanding, as a test of the limit of our permissiveness.

—The Soviets may have concluded that the Middle East crisis inhibited any forceful U.S. reaction, especially in a pre-election period.

—In this interpretation, however, there is room for tactical retreats when the Soviets judge that the temperature is rising above that of tolerable level.

My own view is that this explanation, a test of expansionism, is probably the right one. In the last six months the Soviets could have concluded they could move forward without major risks *as long as they did it piecemeal.* If they are successful, however, as the news leaks out, the Soviets can demonstrate to much of the world that the correlation of forces has shifted significantly since their defeat in Cuba almost exactly eight years ago. *In short, this is a calculated but highly significant political challenge.*

The fact that on two separate occasions the Soviets have deliberately deceived us may be an important symptom of the mood of the Soviet leaders, and an index of their assessment of us. It suggests an ominous contempt and a judgment that we are not likely to react quickly or vigorously to Soviet challenges. Why they should hold such a view, if they do, is never easy to understand. It could relate to what they may perceive as our excessive eagerness in SALT and MBFR or perhaps their view of the domestic effects of Vietnam, or their distorted views of our social-economic "crisis."

In any case, the Soviets have been moving aggressively, first in the Middle East, and now in Cuba. They are likely to continue to do so until they receive clear and unmistakable warning signals.

IV. The Cuban Angle

Why did Cuba agree to lend its territory for this purpose? What does Castro get out of it?

Conceivably Castro may have asked for such a facility to obtain a more demonstrative show of support, or the base decision could have been the result of mutual initiative based on mutually perceived advantages. However, a more plausible thesis is that this was a Soviet initiative. The Soviets clearly have the leverage to obtain Cuban cooperation—either by blackmail in threatening to stop essential economic support or by bribes in the form of more economic and military aid. This would explain a number of otherwise puzzling reports we have received over the past year or so. For example, there have been increasing reports of Soviet attempts to increase their control and influence within the Cuban regime. There have been reports of Castro's uneasiness at this, and of his alleged comments about Soviet "cold-bloodedness and ruthlessness." Failure of Castro's highly touted effort to harvest ten million tons of sugar is a heavy blow which damaged his charisma and control. The Soviets could well have felt that they could pressure him without being as concerned about his sensitivity as they have been in the past. In any event, they appear to have more influence and authority in Cuba now than at any time in recent years.

Whatever the case, the Cubans do receive—in return for use of their territory—Soviet military presence with its implicit promise of Soviet support and protection. They could conceivably use an expanded Soviet naval presence in the area to cover their clandestine subversive movements. They presumably have received expanded economic and military aid.

V. Meaning in Latin America

Existence of a Soviet base and Soviet naval power in the Caribbean is likely to be seen by Latin America as a sign of U.S. weakness, especially if seen in conjunction with the recent Chilean elections.[3] It would strengthen Soviet efforts to increase their influence in the region. It would encourage indigenous radical left elements while discouraging their opponents. It may tempt many of these American nations to become neutral vis-à-vis U.S. or to turn to the Soviets to hedge their bets.

VI. The View of the World

Most of our allies have little taste for a major confrontation with the USSR, especially in an area quite remote from Europe, and over a situation that they may not perceive as a serious strategic threat. We could expect, as in 1962, little support and considerable advice to restrain our responses. In the longer term, however, the Europeans and our other Allies could conclude that Soviet success in Cuba was an important index of the balance of power. They would assess a Soviet base as clear evidence of the decline in our power and will. Much of the world, contrasting the result with that of 1962, would see it the same way.

The main Europeans have a vested interest in the beginnings of détente. At the same time, the Soviets also have a vested interest in the new German treaty and may also be inhibited from a deliberate confrontation with us.

---

[3] On September 4, Salvador Allende Gossens was elected President of Chile.

VII. Options

If as I have suggested this is a serious political challenge, then we have no choice but to respond. In my view, our major options are:

1. *Pursue a purely diplomatic effort to get the Soviets out.* We would tell them that we know of their activity and remind them of our 1962 understandings which we expect them to respect and wait for their reply.

—The *advantages* of this course are that the chance of immediate confrontation is minimized and we might be able to strike a bargain which would get them to leave, thus solving the immediate problem. If this strategy succeeds and the Russians leave in response to an offset to which we agree, Castro may even see himself as a pawn in the USSR game and be less likely to play in the future.

—The *disadvantages* are that if we bargain to get their withdrawal the Soviets may see this kind of action as an easy route to follow for other concessions they want in the future. If they are testing us they may be willing to bargain yet engage in prolonged bargaining. Moreover, our low-key reaction may prompt them to go ahead on this project and even to make further waves in the Hemisphere or elsewhere. With the passage of time during our talks, we may end up facing Soviet submarines and weapons in Cuba—a result similar to that in 1962.

2. *Pursue a diplomatic course with Castro.* We would tell him that we cannot permit this kind of Soviet base in Cuba and that we expect him to get it out.

—The *advantages* would be similar to those above but would include also the avoidance of the need to strike a bargain with the Russians and delay further the time of confrontation. If Castro believes we are serious he may be more willing to concede than the Russians. It is Russian interests which are primarily at stake.

—The *disadvantages* are that we might have to strike some bargain with Castro which would be no less easy for us than striking one with the Soviets. Moreover, if the Soviets induced or pressured Castro into standing firm, the chances of a *fait accompli* would be great and we would face it without yet having made our position clear to the Soviets. They could take our delay in approaching them as a sign that we are unwilling to push them hard.

3. *Move decisively diplomatically, making clear at the outset we are prepared to move to confrontation.* We would tell the Russians directly and at a high level that we consider their action intolerable, that we expect them to remove the facility without delay and that we expect a prompt reply. If a satisfactory reply is not forthcoming we consider the entire 1962 understanding invalid. As a follow-up, we could call off SALT and go to the OAS—as we did in 1962—either before or simultaneously with our approach to the Soviets. Some military steps—e.g., increased surveillance, sea patrols off shore, deployment of additional tactical air to the Southeast U.S.—would signal our resolve and willingness to move to confrontation.

—The *advantages* of this course are that our resolve would be clear to the Soviets from the outset, but they could still move out without losing face (if we had not gone to the OAS). We would have made clear that we would not bargain for their withdrawal.

—The *disadvantages* are that if they are testing us, they may still not believe our determination short of an ultimatum. We will have taken more time and will still have to confront them. If they really want a base, as if they are seeking some concession from us, they may be willing to sacrifice SALT and accept confrontation as a means of getting a concession for withdrawal. If we went to the OAS and were unsuccessful in getting Soviet withdrawal we would be losing twice.

4. *Confront the Soviets immediately.* We would give them an ultimatum and take immediate military measures to emphasize our intention to prevent their use or retention of the facility. If they did not respond we would publicly demand their withdrawal and within a short time, if they did not do so, take military action against the base.

—The *advantages* of this course of action are that our intentions would be unambiguous and the consequences clear to the Soviets from the outset. It would minimize the likelihood that the base would become operational and heavily defended. It would be easier for the Soviets to withdraw now when their investment is relatively small than it might be later with a more developed facility.

—The *disadvantages* are that a crisis could be precipitated early during a period when our forces are heavily oriented toward the Middle East. A public ultimatum gives the Soviets no graceful way out and we will have played our last card and foreclosed other options.

In my view the slow diplomatic approach has serious risks. It may seem safer but most likely it would result in a gradually escalating crisis leading ultimately to confrontation. At the same time, moving immediately to military confrontation may be needlessly risky until we have probed to see what the Soviets intentions really are. But whatever our initial course, we must be prepared to move toward confrontation if this is the price of Soviet withdrawal.

I recommend that you hear out all of the views on this subject but that you do not make a decision at today's meeting.[4]

---

[4] The National Security Council met on September 22 to discuss the situation in Jordan. Nixon made limited references to Cuba. According to minutes of the meeting, "He remarked that perhaps what was needed was an additional facility in both [Greece and Turkey], not for the purpose of waging war but to underline our determination to maintain a U.S. presence and to strengthen our credibility with respect to the Soviets, especially in light of Soviet actions in Cuba." (National Archives, Nixon Presidential Materials, NSC Files, NSC Institutional Files (H-Files), Box H–109, NSC Minutes, Originals, 1970)

213. Memorandum Prepared for the President's Assistant for National Security Affairs (Kissinger)[1]

Washington, September 22, 1970.

SUBJECT

Cuba—The Problems of Soviet Intentions

While there are some fairly clear strategic advantages for the Soviets in a permanent naval base in Cuba, the incremental value to the Soviet strategic posture seems, at first glance, not to be worth much in the way of risks *to* Cuba, or in the complications in relation with the U.S. *Thus, several questions are raised:*

1. Why, at this time, do the Soviets embark on a venture that they should know has a low flashpoint in terms of American sensitivity?
2. Why, beforehand, did the Soviets seek to reaffirm the 1962 post missile crisis understanding on the flimsy pretext of the threat to Cuba?
3. Having reaffirmed the essentials of the 1962 understanding, why did the Soviets almost immediately proceed to violate the spirit if not the precise letter of that understanding?
4. Finally, how does the move into Cuba relate, if at all, to the larger posture of Soviet behavior, especially in the Middle East?

Three possible explanations can be advanced:

1. It could be that this move in Cuba is simply a self-liquidating project to show the flag, fulfill a requested gesture to Castro, and having done that, will be moved out; in other words, there are no longer-term implications or consequences involved.

—There has been a new warming trend in Cuban-Soviet relations; Castro has publicly welcomed a closer military relationship; his brother visited the USSR and talked with Marshal Grechko.

—Thus, the Cubans for some reasons, may have asked for a more demonstrative show of support from the Soviets (even in 1962 the Soviets probably gave some credence to Cuban warnings of imminent invasion).

—Under this reasoning, the diplomatic approach to the US was probably an afterthought, simply reinsurance to make sure that the 1962 noninvasion pledge still obtained; this would then be conveyed to Castro.

---

[1] Source: National Archives, Nixon Presidential Materials, NSC Files, Box 782, Country Files, Latin America, Cuba, Soviet Naval Activity in Cuban Waters (Cienfuegos), Vol. I. Secret; Sensitive. This memorandum is Tab B of a September 22 memorandum from Haig to Kissinger in preparation for the NSC meeting on Cuba held on September 23. A notation by Haig states that Hyland drafted it. Designated as "non log."

The main problem with this interpretation is that the actions of establishing a semi-permanent facility seem to go well beyond showing the flag. No Soviet leader in his right mind could imagine that such a move could be passed over by an American administration. If this explanation is implausible, then we probably must assume that the Soviets are well aware of the crisis potential of their actions. They could thus be aiming for (1) a deliberate provocation designed intentionally to create a second Cuban confrontation; or (2) a move *not* designed to become an issue of confrontation as such, but part of a longer-term pattern of Soviet expansionist policy, of which this is one important—but not decisive test.

2. *Deliberate Crisis Mongering*

It is possible that the Soviets, while Raul was in Moscow, looked ahead and saw the Middle East rapidly escalating to a dangerous point. They could have reasoned that it was to their strategic advantage to widen the arena of potential conflict with the US, in part to put pressures on us from at least two points.

—They could foresee that these two crises would come to a head in a pre-election period, when the US might be under some internal constraints.

—They sought to lie as in 1962 and create an "understanding" from the record beforehand, to be later used against us in some distorted fashion.

—In this scenario, the Soviets, typically, have not thought through their tactics of a double crisis, but in their arrogance, will brazen it through. Such a line of actions cannot be easily dismissed as totally implausible. It could be argued that for some years, now, as their strategic power has grown, the Soviet leaders have wanted to even the score from the humiliation of 1962.

Yet, from what we know of the character of the present Soviet leadership, they seem to behave with a strong element of pragmatism and prudence rather than adventurism. A double crisis has always been intriguing theory but dangerous strategy. No one can foresee the consequences of inter-actions between two areas of contention. There is not only the danger of uncalculated escalation but the significant risk of a double defeat.

But above all, Cuba would seem the last place the Soviets would want to invoke a Middle-East crisis. Cuba is, after all, still an area where we have immense tactical advantages.[2]

---

[2] It is not inconceivable that the Cuban venture is related to Chile. For example, the Soviets, if challenged, might try to extend the 1962 non-invasion pledge to include nonintervention in Chile, if in return the Soviets abjured any permanent naval facilities in the Caribbean. [Footnote in the source text.]

3. *Cuba and Soviet Expansionism*

This interpretation relates to the pattern of projection of Soviet power to various points around the globe, and expansionism symbolized primarily by a naval presence. Under this theory the Soviets have been in the process of testing us for a reaction, and having estimated that we were relatively complacent, have decided to take a further step, following their earlier naval visits to Cuba and flights of bomber-reconnaissance aircraft.

—The primary purpose of the Cuban move is not to create another roaring crisis, but to establish, step-by-step the Soviet right to establish a naval (not necessarily strategic) presence in the area, much as they have done in the Mediterranean, the Indian Ocean, the Persian Gulf (not to mention the now-regular on-station patrolling of Y Class submarines within range of the East Coast).
—Under this theory, the Soviets actions are, in the first instance demonstrative and political (for their own, not Cuban objectives); to show that the balance of power is now such that we can no longer effectively block Soviet power even in our own sphere of influence.
—This interpretation, however, would leave room for tactical retreats when the Soviets judge that the temperature is rising above that of tolerable level.
—The Soviets may have reasoned that it would be prudent to reaffirm the basic 1962 understanding, as a test of the limit of our permissiveness.[3]
—The Soviets may have concluded that our eagerness for a Middle East cease-fire *after* their involvement expanded was an indication of our fear of confrontation.
—As for the risks of a new Cuban crisis, the Soviets have left themselves the out of returning the equipment to the USSR, leaving some of it behind, but withdrawing the vessels, or negotiating for a new basic understanding (and if not challenged taking another step later, when submarines go on station).

It is difficult to argue against such possible Soviet thinking. Their ability to expand the nature and scope of activities in Cuba must have tempted them for a long time. In the last six months they could have concluded they could move forward without major risks as long as they did it piecemeal. Since the strategic increment is not a major one, and against a background of SALT beginning in about a month, a new European détente blossoming, and worldwide preoccupation with the Middle East—all would be factors conspiring against a major US reaction to the establishment of facilities that could be defended as minimal and temporary, of no immediate threat to the US.

In short, the Soviets may have embarked on a calculated risk to test whether they can break out of the spirit of the 1962 restrictions on

---

[3] The Soviets will now argue (1) that the precedence for their naval activity was established in the last two visits, without U.S. protest, and (2) that the basic 1962 understanding was reconfirmed in the knowledge that this precedent has been established. Thus, their latest move has been sanctioned. [Footnote in the source text.]

their actions. They tested the waters and decided that we would not make a major issue of their moves. And in the process, as the news leaks out, the Soviets could demonstrate to much of the world that the correlation of forces has shifted significantly since the black days of their defeat almost exactly eight years ago.

What To Do?

If the first and third explanations are close to the mark, it means we are dealing, not with a major strategic-political showdown of world-wide proportions, but with a limited challenge supported by some rational Soviet calculations (however wrong that calculation may be). The important aspect is that such a line of strategy includes, presumably, built-in lines of retreat. Once confronted with an appreciation of the limits of their actions, the Soviets can fall back on a diplomatic scenario, perhaps to renegotiate the terms of the 1962 understanding, and determine just what they can and cannot do. (A new "guarantee" for Cuba might be all they could salvage.)

If, however, the second explanation is correct, then we are confronted with a line of conduct based on entirely different and perhaps irrational calculations. If the Soviets want a deliberate crisis, they will disregard diplomacy and reinforce their own actions (more building, submarines, etc.) Such a strategy is so unpredictable that no countermoves can be prescribed to have any given effect. If we are facing this situation, however, it would be of the utmost urgency to determine it now.

My own view is that the third explanation, a test of expansionism, is probably the right one, and if faced with the consequences of their actions the Soviets will bristle and bargain but will, if permitted to do so quietly, withdraw from the Carribbean.

One Final Thought

The fact that on two separate occasions the Soviets have deliberately deceived us may be an important symptom of the mood of the Soviet leaders, and an index of their assessment of us. It suggests an ominous contempt and a judgment that we are not likely to react quickly or vigorously to Soviet challenges. Why they should hold such a view, if they do, it is never easy to understand. It could relate to excessive eagerness in SALT or perhaps their view of the domestic effects of Vietnam, or their distorted views of our social-economic "crisis" (e.g., the Arbatov article).[4]

In any case, it is reasonably clear that the Soviets have been moving aggressively, first in the Middle East, and now in Cuba. They are likely to continue to do so until they receive clear and unmistakable warning signals. Then, and only then, will they hedge their bets.

---

[4] This paragraph was highlighted and checked.

214.   Minutes of Meeting of the National Security Council[1]

Washington, September 23, 1970, 9:30 a.m.

SUBJECT

Jordan and Cuba

PARTICIPANTS

The President
Secretary of State William P. Rogers
Secretary of Defense Melvin R. Laird
Director of Central Intelligence Richard Helms
Deputy Secretary of Defense David Packard
Assistant Secretary of State Joseph Sisco
Chairman of the Joint Chiefs of Staff Admiral Thomas Moorer
Henry A. Kissinger
General Alexander M. Haig

The President opened the meeting by stating that there would be two topics on the morning's agenda—the first a review of the situation in Jordan and the second a sensitive discussion of the latest intelligence on the situation in Cienfuegos Bay in Cuba.

[Here follows an intelligence briefing and discussion on Jordan.]

He [Secretary Rogers] suggested that the group now turn from the Jordanian problem to the problem of Cuba. The President cautioned the group that the discussion on Cuba was limited to a strictly need-to-know group, pointing out that we were faced with a major election issue which opponents could seize upon for their own domestic political advantage. He cautioned each of the principals to hold the information strictly to themselves and to take equivalent action on any paperwork associated with the Cuban issue.

The President then asked Mr. Helms to present an update briefing on the Cuban situation to the group. Mr. Helms followed the prepared text at Tab A,[2] using photos. As Mr. Helms depicted the situation on the ground in Cuba through photographic evidence, Secretary Laird stated that it was important that we proceed with the [*less than 1 line of source text not declassified*] Corona. Deputy Secretary Packard commented that the only limitation on the [*less than 1 line of source text not declassified*] adding that the experience in Cuba confirmed the

---

[1] Source: National Archives, Nixon Presidential Materials, NSC Files, NSC Institutional Files (H-Files), Box H–109, NSC Minutes, Originals, 1970. Top Secret; Sensitive. The meeting took place in the Cabinet Room.

[2] Attached but not printed. For additional information about Helms' briefing, see footnote 2, Document 212.

importance of providing for the [*less than 1 line of source text not declassified*]. The President asked whether or not the [*less than 1 line of source text not declassified*] would have helped us along the Suez Canal. Secretary Packard replied, "Yes, providing it had been scheduled properly." He also pointed out that the Real-Time-Readout camera would be of great benefit [*less than 1 line of source text not declassified*]. The President asked whether or not these systems would not be an important factor in the policing of any SALT agreement. Secretary Laird confirmed that, indeed, these would be important technological assets for us. The President then stated that he wanted no more budgetary nibblings on [*less than 1 line of source text not declassified*] or the Real-Time-Readout capability and stated that these systems were too important and must be funded. He added, somewhat jokingly, that the Department of Defense could pay for these systems out of its funds.

Director Helms continued with his prepared briefing and Secretary Rogers asked when the construction in Cienfuegos and Alcatraz Island actually started. Director Helms stated that we had our first evidence this spring. He stated that in August we noted the athletic facilities and all believed that it was significant that there were no baseball fields—only soccer fields, suggesting Soviet occupation rather than Cuban. The President commented that the dates were very important and Mr. Helms replied that he would try to get a firm verification on the precise dates when various stages of the construction were initiated. Secretary Laird said that the construction had moved extremely rapidly and Admiral Moorer commented that all of the work had been done within 30 days from the period August 15 to September 15.

Admiral Moorer then commented that if the Soviets increased their SLBN levels to 41 and put a portion of them in Cuba that the Cienfuegos facility would give them what would amount to 10–12 additional submarines. The facility would also enable them to penetrate more deeply into the Gulf of Mexico and therefore enhance their targeting capabilities within the central United States. Admiral Moorer concluded that if the Cienfuegos base is, in fact, a permanent submarine support facility, it will have the effect of increasing Soviet force levels.

Admiral Moorer next stated that we are watching the situation very carefully through U–2 flights at a minimum of one every three days. He reported that the JCS are developing an attack plan and a plan for trailing Soviet submarines as well. He remarked that the Soviets themselves maintain surveillance trawlers adjacent to all U.S. bases.

Admiral Moorer then asked Mr. Helms to comment on the [*less than 1 line of source text not declassified*] which were picked up from one of the Soviet vessels. Mr. Helms stated that they had overflown with detection aircraft one of the Soviet vessels enroute to Cienfuegos and had received positive evidence of [*less than 1 line of source text not declassified*] from the vessel. However, following departure of the vessel from Cienfuegos a similar flight did not pick up such [*less than 1 line of source text not declassified*]. The President stated that this suggested that they have already stored some nuclear components in Cienfuegos.

The President then asked Admiral Moorer what additional surveillance besides U–2's we had undertaken. Admiral Moorer responded that the Navy has a destroyer right in international waters close by and stated that the Soviets are aware of its presence. Secretary Rogers asked if we have positive evidence that they have or intend to have nuclear weapons stored on shore in Cuba. The President stated that in his view whether the weapons are on the tenders or on shore, this would constitute a violation of the nebulous 1962 understanding.

Admiral Moorer replied that they have built a dock and have established permanent buoys, and that storage can be effected afloat or on shore. Secretary Rogers agreed that this would be a violation. The President stated that anyone familiar with the problem would agree that it would constitute a serious violation. Admiral Moorer stated that current Soviet tactics we have observed permit the Soviets to transfer missiles from Soviet tenders to the submarines at sea, so that storage on the tenders alone constitutes an important military asset for the Soviets.

The President then pointed out that the situation was especially serious in view of the exchange between Vorontsov and the White House in August,[3] since at that time, Vorontsov had given the U.S. assurances that they would abide by the earlier understanding and asked us to do the same. Secretary Rogers stated that his understanding of the so-called agreement was that we agreed not to invade Cuba in return for the removal of offensive missiles from Cuba. Mr. Kissinger stated that there was no agreement as such but merely a series of parallel statements. He stated that the U.S. conditions were open-ended and provided that we would not invade if adequate inspection were established whereby the removal of offensive weapons could be verified. The Soviets, in turn, never delivered on the inspection issue. Therefore, in effect, there is no binding agreement and we never gave any additional pledges.

The President asked what has been said recently on the subject. Mr. Kissinger stated that on August 4 [5], there was a scare report of a Cuban exile attack against a Soviet trawler[4] and that he, Kissinger, had assured Vorontsov that we were taking protective action in behalf of the Soviet vessel traveling to Cuba. Vorontsov, in turn, had told

---

[3] See Document 192.
[4] See Document 193.

Kissinger that the Soviets wished to use the occasion to reaffirm the understandings of 1962.

The President then asked whether or not CIA had the capability to re-institute the exile program against Cuba. Mr. Helms stated that this capability had been dismantled. The President commented that obviously there was no real understanding, and Secretary Laird confirmed this. Secretary Rogers stated that, in any event, it was a very fuzzy understanding.

Secretary Laird commented that we must now consider whether we want to reaffirm our position with respect to Cuba. The President stated that the important thing today is to think about this issue very carefully. The U.S. could consider sending a note to the Soviets but where would we go from there? The alternatives must be carefully considered. Secretary Laird stated that the whole issue will surface very shortly. He pointed out that it had come up in conference on the military authorization bill and was discussed openly. The issue added more effect to the conference, adding $25 million more for U.S. ships. He stated that the issue will surface just the same as it did in 1962 and the timing is important. The U.S. must consider and be prepared on how it will handle this issue very quickly.

Mr. Kissinger then commented that the U.S. also had to consider the international political implications of the Soviet action. Why, for example, had they chosen this point to install a base? Why also would the Soviets try to reaffirm the 1962 understandings and then 11 days later move precipitously to install strategic weapons in Cuba? What is the relationship with this action and the situation in Chile and what are its implications should Chile go Marxist? Mr. Kissinger stated that the political consequences of the Soviet action present a most serious dilemma and transcend the purely military strategic implications of the Soviet action. The real question, he stated, was why have the Soviets undertaken this move directly against the spirit, if not the letter, of the 1962 understandings?

Secretary Laird reported that they have three Y-class submarines now targeted on the U.S. and that this would increase that capability. Secretary Rogers stated that he hoped that the United States would not pull any alarm bells until after the Congressional election. He suggested that if the Soviet action leaks, then it will be necessary to low-key our response. It would be disastrous to have this break between now and elections. Therefore, it is essential that this group react very carefully to the intelligence presented. The President stated that our problem is not to react to the Soviets in a blustering way. He stated that the U.S. needs to low-key the issue for the present. We should respond with the fact that the government is aware of the situation, that we are watching it very carefully, that we consider the understandings of 1962 in effect, and that we will hold the Soviets to that. Admiral Moorer interjected that this action should be tied into the Soviets world-wide naval expansion. The President directed the WSAG to develop a suggested U.S. public response if the intelligence information breaks. He also directed the WSAG to prepare a suggested line to take officially with the Soviets.

The President then commented that, in his view, the new base would constitute a marginal strategic advantage. Therefore, it might be that the Soviets thought out the implications of this action very carefully for other political reasons. In either event, the President stated, it is desirable to keep the discussion within the group assembled in the room. That group, the President stated, knows what is actually being done by the Soviets and all understand that there can be no Soviet offensive weapons in Cuba. Mr. Kissinger stated that he regretted the necessity of playing the role of a villain on this issue. The President interrupted, stating that what he had been referring to was the public U.S. position. It was necessary, the President noted, that in private we must be very tough but that this line was to be taken privately. If we are to take a tough public stance, we will set up a great domestic clamor. Secretary Rogers reiterated that it was necessary to keep all discussions and information within this particular group. The President stated we need, in effect, two lines: (1) a public line designed to preclude a crisis atmosphere, and (2) an official line to take privately with the Soviets. It will be necessary to consider this line most seriously and it was essential that our concerns be brought forcefully to Soviet attention. In public, however, we should merely take the stance that we are aware of the situation and are watching it carefully. Dr. Kissinger stated that the important aspect of our public line is not to permit the Soviets to think that what they have done is acceptable. The President agreed, stating that it was true, that we had to be sure that the Soviets know that their acts were unacceptable.

Secretary Laird then stated again that the whole situation was soon to break and that it was important that the Soviets know our stand before it breaks publicly—not after. Secretary Rogers asked what the United States would do if the Soviets were to ignore our warning. What action could the United States take to show that it is serious? It is important that the U.S. is able to back up its words with deeds. Secretary Laird stated that we might consider moving strategic bombers into Turkey. Secretary Rogers said, "What about Cuba, itself, if we take naval action around Cuba?" Secretary Laird replied that we need more ships in the area and more surveillance.

Secretary Laird added that he did not visualize our being able to do anything in Guantanamo. The President asked if we could blockade Cuba or mine Cienfuegos Harbor. Admiral Moorer confirmed that this was possible. The President stated that he wanted us to refrain from restraining the Cuban exile community from acting against Cuba. He wanted to consider the possibility of a new blockade with surface ships and the possibility of mining the entrance to the harbor. Admiral Moorer added that we should initiate a trailing program with respect to Soviet ships traveling to and from Cuba. Secretary Laird stated he would implement this immediately.

Secretary Rogers said the important thing is how it is all done. Mr. Kissinger stated that the WSAG, which was in effect the same group as in this room, would work out a careful scenario for Presidential decision. The President stated that two problems existed—the first was the problem of our public posture. This was to be accomplished with calmness, an expression of awareness of the situation, but above all, in such a way that it is low-key. The danger would be that we would take a bellicose public stance which would force the Soviets to react in the same way. The second problem concerned the official line. The President indicated he wanted strong U.S. action. He wanted to make it clear that the U.S. could not permit the establishment of a Soviet strategic base in Cuba. In his view, the President stated, even though the strategic balance has changed drastically since 1962 the Soviets would never trade Russia for Havana.

Secretary Laird then stated again that it would be difficult to hold this any longer. He reiterated that he had been asked three times on the Hill about Cuban intelligence. Secretary Rogers suggested that we prepare a scenario without anyone knowing. Admiral Moorer commented that he could prepare one himself. The President pointed out that this was a special case with particular impact domestically. It may already be clear what the Soviets are up to. They may step up their activities world-wide and this may only be the beginning. The President stated that the group should meet again at noon the following day.

---

215. Memorandum for the Record[1]

Washington, September 24, 1970.

SUBJECT

Meeting of Senior Review Group on Cuba

---

[1] Source: National Archives, Nixon Presidential Materials, NSC Files, NSC Institutional Files (H-Files), Box H–111, SRG Minutes, Originals, 1970. Top Secret; Sensitive; Eyes Only. On September 24, Richard Kennedy sent Kissinger talking points for the meeting. (Ibid., NSC Files, Box 782, Country Files, Latin America, Cuba, Soviet Naval Activity in Cuban Waters (Cienfuegos), Vol. I)

PARTICIPANTS

    Dr. Henry A. Kissinger
    Deputy Secretary David Packard
    Under Secretary U. Alexis Johnson
    Admiral Thomas Moorer
    Director Richard Helms

The group met briefly for the purpose of discussing contingency press guidance to be used in the event that information concerning a Soviet base in Cuba became known publicly.

Dr. Kissinger began the meeting by cautioning that it was necessary to be prepared for possible press stories on the Cuban base. He suggested that the Government's public response be along the following lines:

"We are aware of the reports. The President has reviewed these reports with his senior advisors. The Soviets are well aware of the fact that establishment of a base would be of great concern to us. We are keeping the situation under constant review."

Under Secretary Johnson stated that, because of the statements made by President Kennedy in 1962, we could emphasize that the Soviets are well aware of the seriousness with which we would view such a development. He suggested that we use President Kennedy's language when he stated that we would expect that they would be kept out of this hemisphere in the future.

Dr. Kissinger commented that we wouldn't want to imply that if the Soviets stopped now, we would acquiesce in what they have done.

Director Helms then commented that we were dealing with a period of 10 days or so and asked whether we couldn't get by with reassuring reports along the lines that ever since 1962 we have been concerned about missiles in Cuba and have been checking the situation and will continue to check.

Dr. Kissinger remarked that because so many analysts were now aware of recent developments, there were two dangers: (1) it might be built into a Cuban missile crisis, and (2) on the other hand, if we kept it too low-key, then the Congress might build it up.

Director Helms indicated that he was worried about saying that the President had been briefed, feeling that this might dignify the situation. Dr. Kissinger interjected that we have to say that the President has been briefed on the situation.

Director Helms then spoke of the difference between a naval base and a naval base with special equipment. He pointed out that we know there is special equipment at Cienfuegos. Secretary Packard remarked, "But we haven't seen submarines."

Dr. Kissinger then indicated that we needed to find a happy medium that would keep the public calm and quiet and at the same time stir up the Soviets enough to get them to close down the base.

Secretary Packard commented that he wanted to see more information before drawing a final conclusion about what is actually going on in Cienfuegos. Dr. Kissinger asked him if it would be acceptable if the Soviets stopped what they were doing right where they were. Secretary Packard replied, "No." He would say he knows of reports but wants more information.

Admiral Moorer stated that the Soviets have done everything necessary to provide a base. All the fundamental elements are there now. Even if the ship leaves, the buoys and the communications are there. Dr. Kissinger then asked what we wanted the Soviets to take out. Admiral Moorer answered, "It boils down to whether we will let them use it."

Dr. Kissinger then turned to the issue of whether to mention the President in the statement or not. He suggested doing two statements which would be distributed to the principals. The President could then decide.

Admiral Moorer then stated that there should be mention in the statement of previous Soviet deployments.

Dr. Kissinger cautioned the group that nothing should be said to the Soviets until a scenario had been developed. The President wanted to have such a scenario worked out.

Dr. Kissinger closed the meeting by summarizing the consensus of the group. He asked Secretary Packard to submit what the Defense Department proposed to say limited purely to the facts of the situation. Secretary Johnson would prepare a statement along the lines outlined at the meeting and dealing with the political aspects of the question. Dr. Kissinger stated that he would blend these submissions into a composite set of instructions for the guidance of all. The guidance would be used as follows: Defense would limit itself to responses dealing with the facts of the situation but only if pressed. Any questions on the political issue or contacts with the Soviets should be handled by State or the White House as appropriate.

216.   Transcript of Telephone Conversation Between the President's Assistant for National Security Affairs (Kissinger) and the Soviet Ambassador (Dobrynin)[1]

Washington, September 24, 1970, 3:04 p.m.

D: You didn't keep your word not to organize anything during my absence.

K: Don't speak about who isn't keeping his word. You stayed away a lot longer than we thought. Let's not go into this on the phone.

D: I am calling today if it's possible to see the President about two points—The summit and things about Jordan.

K: I will talk to him. His schedule is very full. Can you talk to me?

D: Yes but the question is when I left Moscow they said [omission in the source text]. Today or tomorrow really. It could wait until tomorrow and it's not urgent.

K: I understand. I will have to ask him.

D: Understand and the timing. 20–25 mins. and then I could talk to you on a more detailed basis.

K: You understand we are leaving town next week.

D: Sunday.[2]

K: Probably, yes.

D: That's why I am calling. I just arrived late last night.

K: I will check with the President.

D: Let me know when it's possible to arrange it.

K: I will let you know. Will you be seeing others before you see the President?

D: No. Nobody. You are the first I am to call. Perhaps half an hour before I could talk with you.

K: I have no particular need to talk with you. I have to see if the President has time and if not, you may have to talk with me. Today I know is impossible.

D: Tomorrow is no problem. I am not going to see anyone before that. I will await your call.

---

[1] Source: National Archives, Nixon Presidential Materials, Kissinger Office Files, Box 128, Chronology of Cuban Submarine Base Episode, 1970–1971. No classification marking.

[2] September 27.

217. **Transcript of Telephone Conversation Between the President's Assistant for National Security Affairs (Kissinger) and the Soviet Ambassador (Dobrynin)**[1]

Washington, September 24, 1970, 7 p.m.

D: You were playing golf with the President?

K: No, I don't play. I just talked to the President[2] and he is extremely occupied tomorrow and is going to Camp David tomorrow night. What he wonders is if you could give me the messages. If there is anything warranting a personal reply from him he will see you later in the day. That's his position.

D: I have to check it with Moscow, if you don't mind.

K: No.

D: In this particular case when I left they asked me to ask for an audience with him. I would have to ask my government in this case.

K: I understand, but you recognize that he is leaving Friday night for Camp David.

D: That's why they asked me to come earlier back to Washington. But it's up to the President.

K: If a written reply is needed we will give that; if something else ... But under no circumstances will he have much time.[3] Why don't you ask Moscow if you can tell me, then we can have 15 minutes later in the day for you to get his reactions.

D: It is up to Moscow; it is not up to me. This is really the question. I can't decide myself. It is not that they don't want me to speak with you.

K: Of course, if there is something in your communication that warrants his reaction, he will, of course, see you, but not for long.

D: The question is how he will react on this, not just telling him

---

[1] Source: National Archives, Nixon Presidential Materials, Kissinger Office Files, Box 128, Chronology of Cuban Submarine Base Episode, 1970–1971. No classification marking.

[2] Kissinger spoke on the telephone with the President at 6:40 p.m. and summarized his earlier conversation with Dobrynin. Nixon responded: "Tell [Dobrynin] you would like to have a look at [the message concerning Cuba] and that you would look at my schedule. I don't think we want to appear that everytime he comes back I am going to slobber over him. Tell him if there is something substantive that would justify my seeing him, I will, but if it is just routine I can't do it." (Ibid.)

[3] Ellipsis in the source text.

the things and nothing else.

K: If it requires a significant reaction he will react, but first he wants to see what it is. Call me in the morning and see if you can give it to me; if so, I propose 10:30.

D: I will check with Moscow. When will he be back?

K: October 6.

D: He is not going anyplace after the 6th?

K: He will be in and out. We told you his schedule was very crowded for October and November. November is the political campaign and he will be taking several trips.

D: I understand, but it is a question of a 10-minute talk.

K: We don't reject the idea of a 10-minute talk. We just want to see if there's something to talk about.

D: All right. I will check with Moscow and call you tomorrow morning before 10:00 to clarify the situation from my side.

---

218.   Memorandum of Conversation[1]

Washington, September 25, 1970, 10 a.m.

PARTICIPANTS

Dr. Henry A. Kissinger and Soviet Ambassador Anatoliy Dobrynin

Circumstances of Conversation

Ambassador Dobrynin called the evening of September 24th to tell me that he had a personal message for the President from his leadership and that he wanted to have an appointment with the President the next day. In view of the newly discovered Soviet base in Cuba, the President and I thought it unwise to have such a meeting. Therefore, I told Dobrynin that he would have to deliver the note to me and only after reading it could it be judged whether it would be worthwile for him to see the President. Ambassador Dobrynin replied that his instructions were to deliver it to the President and he would consequently have to check with Moscow whether he could deliver it to me. He

---

[1] Source: National Archives, Nixon Presidential Materials, NSC Files, Box 490, President's Trip Files, Dobrynin/Kissinger, 1970, Vol. 2. Top Secret; Sensitive. The conversation was held in the Map Room at the White House.

added that this reflected no lack of trust in me and that he would, of course, be glad to chat with me for half an hour before we saw the President. I said that unfortunately it was impossible to see the President and, therefore, his choice was between delivering it to me or waiting until after the President came back from his European trip.[2] Dobrynin said he would let me know during the course of the next morning. I told him the only time I would be free would be at 10:30 a.m. The next morning at 9:30 a.m. Dobrynin called to say that he would be available at 10:30 a.m.

Summit

I met with Ambassador Dobrynin in the Map Room. After an exchange of pleasantries, he made the following point. His government had studied the proposal of a Summit with great interest and as the Soviet Government had already indicated, it was ready to proceed in principle. The Soviet Government agreed in general to the agenda outlined in our previous communication.[3] It also agreed that Ambassador Dobrynin and I should proceed with exploratory conversations. The Soviet Government wondered about the site of the conference and whether the President was perhaps thinking of Moscow. It also asked for the President's views about the best time for such a meeting and specifically whether it should be in the first half or the second half of the year. Ambassador Dobrynin added that actually it could not take place before May because of the Soviet Party Congress. I replied that given the weather conditions, what the Ambassador was really asking was whether it should be in the last half of the first half or the first half of the last half of the year—in other words, whether it should be in June or in July or September, August probably being a vacation month for both sides. Ambassador Dobrynin stated that this was essentially correct. During this portion of the discussion, Ambassador Dobrynin also informed me that Premier Kosygin would not be attending the United Nations 25th Anniversary Celebration in New York this fall. I told Ambassador Dobrynin I would let him know later about our views on a possible Summit. At this point in the conversation, Ambassador Dobrynin tried to initiate a conversation on the Middle East and other problems, but I cut him off by saying that these subjects were too complex and that too many things had happened to enable us to discuss them in a semi-social way. I added that if he wished to discuss these subjects, we should schedule a meeting and I would then be prepared to do so.

---

[2] Nixon left for Europe on September 27 and visited Italy, Yugoslavia, Spain, England, and Ireland. He returned to Washington on October 5. (Ibid., White House Central Files, President's Daily Diary)

[3] See Tab A, Document 198.

Jordan

Ambassador Dobrynin said that Moscow was struck by the fact that the U.S. had never replied to its note[4] of the previous Monday with respect to the Syrian invasion. Were we not interested in consulting with Moscow on Mideast developments? I said that certainly we were willing to discuss them with Moscow but it seemed to us that over a period of weeks every Soviet démarche had been followed by the contrary action and we simply wanted to wait to see what would happen. Dobrynin said we might not believe it but the Soviet Union had not known of the invasion of Jordan by Syria and that in any event Soviet advisors had dropped off Syrian tanks prior to crossing the frontier. I let this somewhat contradictory statement go and told Dobrynin that I would ask the President's views about consultation on Mideast issues. I added that the United States Government was always prepared to discuss the situation with the Soviet Union in times of international crises. Our ability to do so, however, was quite dependent on the degree of confidence which existed between us and our overall relationships in general. In light of Soviet violations of the ceasefire and Soviet responsibility for the violations—or what we considered Soviet responsibility for unloosening some of the forces that produced the crisis—the Jordanian situation did not provide the atmosphere for a frank exchange of views between our governments. In principle, however, we were prepared to discuss such matters with the Soviet Government. I added that the United States had no intention of launching military operations in Jordan if other outside forces stayed out of Jordan. The meeting adjourned.

---

[4] On September 21, Vorontsov presented to Sisco the Soviet reply to the U.S. request that the Soviets urge Syria to pull back from Jordan. The Soviet reply is in telegram 155169 to Moscow, September 22. According to the telegram, Sisco and Vorontsov then had the following exchange: "Sisco asked Vorontsov whether we should understand this statement to mean the Soviet Government is taking steps to bring about withdrawal of Syrian forces from Jordan. Vorontsov said he did not have information regarding the exact nature of the contacts taking place but that the Soviet Union was using all its influence in contacts with Syria." (National Archives, Nixon Presidential Materials, NSC Files, Box 713, Country Files, Europe, USSR, Vol. IX)

219.   Memorandum From William Hyland of the National Security Council Staff to the President's Assistant for National Security Affairs (Kissinger)[1]

Washington, September 25, 1970.

SUBJECT

The Cuban Dilemma

What the Soviets have done in Cienfuegos is so ambiguous that avoiding a severe political setback in dealing with it will be exceedingly difficult.

First of all, what is in place now cannot persuasively be described as an immediate or direct military risk for the United States. This installation could remain there for a year or more without much change. Indeed, the fact that something of this nature has been known to be in the works for almost a month is, in itself, a de facto evidence that we have not regarded the installation per se as a cause for serious challenge to the Soviets. Moreover, if Soviet ships or submarines do not use the installation in the next month or so, how can we, with much credibility, claim that it has suddenly become a serious matter. The only conceivable grounds for doing so is to claim that what appeared to be temporary now has become permanent, and is definitely under Soviet control.

The question arises: permanent for what?

As long as no Soviet warships or submarines visit Cienfuegos it can be credibly claimed by the USSR and Cuba that all that has happened is that the port of Cienfuegos has been slightly improved. Our claim that this is in fact a Soviet base area will not be very convincing; it rests on pictures of new barracks, and a soccer field, and the prior presence of Soviet naval ships which have now left. In other words, the time when it might have been legitimately described as a Soviet base may have passed. (The fact that the ships remaining are Soviet is still an important point.)

The dilemma is roughly this:

—Can we deny the Cubans the right to improve port facilities; can we convincingly deny the Soviets the right to make any naval visits?
—Thus, the installation in itself cannot be easily challenged.

---

[1] Source: National Archives, Nixon Presidential Materials, NSC Files, Box 782, Country Files, Latin America, Cuba, Soviet Naval Activity in Cuban Waters (Cienfuegos), Vol. I. Secret; Sensitive; Eyes Only. Sent for information and designated "non-log."

—Only certain aspects of the installation could be challenged; namely the submarine tender and the submarine nets, which are the only physical presence that can be tied directly to the USSR and which could conceivably be associated with strategic offensive weapons.

Thus, we face the possibility that the only legitimate and persuasive grounds for challenge may be the *use* of the facility by certain types of vessels, rather than the facility itself.

In effect, this means we may have to swallow a de facto Soviet base, and concentrate on denying its use in any way that would contravene the 1962 understanding.

But, if this is the outcome, we must also recognize that the Soviets will have taken an important forward step, and that much of the world will regard this as a political setback for the United States.

The alternative is to decide what specific part of the installation must be removed in order to clearly demonstrate that we are not tolerating a Soviet base.

Unfortunately, this virtually means making a crisis over three barges and one submarine tender. Thus, to be convincing we are going to have to complete a history of Soviet activities that demonstrate an expanding Soviet military presence in Cuba, of which Cienfuegos is the last straw.

Cienfuegos will have to be challenged along with flight of strategic aircraft, the guided missile ships, the Castro speeches, and the Y-Class submarines patrolling in the Atlantic. If we go this route we should recognize that we are shifting the conflict from a strict interpretation of the 1962 understanding to a larger issue of the Soviet presence, and not focussing on Cienfuegos alone. This, of course, is not necessarily a definition of the conflict that is easy to sustain, but it may be the only persuasive political ground from which to attack the rather rudimentary facilities that currently exist in Cuba.

In short, we can choose between making the issue Cienfuegos only, and restricting its usage, or on the Soviet naval presence implied by Cienfuegos.

220.   Memorandum of Conversation[1]

Washington, September 25, 1970, 5:30 p.m.

PARTICIPANTS

Dr. Henry A. Kissinger and Soviet Ambassador Anatoliy Dobrynin

Background

After consulting with the President about the answer on the Soviet Summit proposal given to me by the Soviet Ambassador that morning,[2] I called Ambassador Dobrynin to tell him that I wished to see him briefly to provide our answer on the Summit. Just after I completed this phone call, the Defense Department, due to a misunderstanding, released full details about Soviet naval activity in Cienfuegos. Interdepartmental contingency guidance had provided that minimum information would be released publicly on this subject and specific guidance had been circulated to all Departments. This unauthorized release had in turn led to my making the statement that had been agreed to as governmental guidance in event that the Soviet installations in Cienfuegos became known. Attached is that portion of my press backgrounder given earlier that afternoon dealing with Cuba.[3]

Summit

When I saw Dobrynin in the Map Room his face was ashen. I began the conversation by saying that I had the President's answer on the Summit and that the answer was as follows. In principle, the President was willing to consider a Summit. Further, the President would consider either June or September 1971 as appropriate dates and the U.S. Government was willing to consider Moscow as the site for such a meeting. Ambassador Dobrynin said this was very good news. But, he clearly had his mind on the Cuban problem.

Cuba

I then told the Ambassador that I wanted to talk to him about the press statements that had been made in both the Pentagon and at the White House earlier that afternoon. I called his attention to the fact that the announcement made in the White House had inferred that the U.S.

---

[1] Source: National Archives, Nixon Presidential Materials, NSC Files, Box 490, President's Trip Files, Dobrynin/Kissinger, 1970, Vol. II. Top Secret; Sensitive. The conversation took place in the Map Room at the White House.

[2] See Document 218.

[3] Attached but not printed.

Government did not yet know whether there was actually a submarine base in Cuba. The U.S. Government had done this deliberately in order to give the Soviet Union an opportunity to withdraw without a public confrontation. I wanted him to know that we had no illusions, that we knew already there was a submarine base in Cuba, and that we would view it with the utmost gravity if construction continued and the base remained. I added that we did not want a public confrontation and were, therefore, giving them an opportunity to pull out. But we would not shrink from other measures including public ones if forced into it. I said that the President considered the Vorontsov démarche of August 4[4] followed by the construction of the base as an act of bad faith. If the ships—especially the tender—left Cienfuegos we would consider the whole matter a training exercise. No more would be said and there would be no publicity. This is why the President had asked me to talk to him "unofficially." Otherwise, we would put matters into official channels. Ambassador Dobrynin asked whether I was telling him that this alleged base violated the understandings. I said this was a legalistic question. I did believe it violated the understandings but I wanted to remind him that in 1962 we took the most drastic action even though there was no prior understanding. To us Cuba was a place of extreme sensitivity. We considered the installation to have been completed with maximum deception and we could not agree to its continuation. Dobrynin said he would have to report to his government. And he would hope to have an answer for me soon.

The Ambassador tried to discuss other matters such as the Middle East but I cut him off and said that this was the only subject I was authorized to discuss with him. He said why do you have to give me good news and bad news simultaneously; it would be very confusing in Moscow. I said I was giving him the news that now existed. I added that the U.S. and the Soviets had reached a turning point in their relationships. It is now up to the Soviets whether to go the hard route—whether it wanted to go the route of conciliation or the route of confrontation. The United States is prepared for either. Ambassador Dobrynin said that probably the U.S. Government will start a big press campaign on this Cuban business. I said we were not going to do that but we were also determined that there would be no Soviet submarine base in Cuba since whatever the phraseology of the understanding its intent was clearly not to replace land-based by sea-based missiles in Cuba. Ambassador Dobrynin said that he would consult with Moscow and let me know.

The meeting adjourned.

---

[4] See Tab A, Document 192.

221.   Memorandum of Conversation[1]

Washington, September 29, 1970.

SUBJECT

   A Soviet Submarine Base in Cuba

PARTICIPANTS

   Senator Charles Percy
   Senator Marlowe Cook
   Senator Robert Mathias
   The Acting Secretary of State
   Mr. David Abshire
   Mr. Ronald Spiers
   Mr. Colgate Prentice

After an extended discussion of the situation in the Mediterranean, Senator Percy asked what the State Department position was on the construction of a Soviet Submarine Base in Cuba. He said that he had been asked about this subject by a newspaper reporter the previous day and was convinced that he was going to get more questions on this topic. Without official guidance, he said, Senators and Members of Congress would begin to formulate their own positions on the subject because of the pressure of public concern. He mentioned Congressman Mendel Rivers' statement as a case in point.

The other Senators strongly endorsed Senator Percy's statement and began asking questions about the nature of the Soviet installation and the USG's intended response to it. The State Department participants initially attempted to avoid a direct answer on the grounds that complete information on the nature of the installation was unavailable, and therefore a decision on our policy in this matter was premature.[2] The Senators were not satisfied with this response, however, pointing

---

[1] Source: National Archives, Nixon Presidential Materials, NSC Files, Box 782, Country Files, Latin America, Cuba, Soviet Naval Activity in Cuban Waters (Cienfuegos), Vol. I. Secret. No time indicated. Sent by Theodore Eliot on October 1 to Kissinger. An October 2 memorandum from Vaky to Haig transmitting this memorandum of conversation bears Kissinger's initials. The Acting Secretary of State on that day was Irwin. Abshire was Assistant Secretary for Congressional Relations; Spiers was Director of Politico-Military Affairs; and Prentice was Deputy Assistant Secretary for Congressional Relations.

[2] On September 26, Kissinger informed the Secretaries of State and Defense, the DCI, and the Chairman of the JCS that, "The President has directed that no comment, speculation, or backgrounding of any kind be undertaken by U.S. spokesmen or officials and that future inquiries on the subject of a possible submarine base in Cuba be responded to with the following line: 'I have nothing to add to what has already been said on this subject.'" (Ibid.)

out that they were all already under considerable pressure to take a position on this issue.

Mr. Abshire then informed the Senators that the Administration had not yet decided its position on this issue and that we had been enjoined by the President from making any further statements on the subject until his return from Europe.

The Senators then insisted that we communicate with the President and inform him of their feeling that public concern was reaching a critical stage and that without firm guidance from the Administration the President would find himself plagued with a rash of public statements, many of them unhelpful, by Senators and Congressmen. They emphasized that they were anxious to support the Administration on this issue, but could not do so without guidance and could not remain publicly silent on this subject much longer.

Mr. Abshire assured them that we would communicate their concern to Secretary Rogers.

---

222.   Memorandum of Conversation[1]

Washington, October 1, 1970.

SUBJECT

Soviet Intentions Regarding a Cuban Base

PARTICIPANTS

Mr. Yuly M. Vorontsov, Minister Counselor, Soviet Embassy
Mr. Raymond L. Garthoff, Deputy Director, Bureau of Politico-Military Affairs

In a luncheon conversation arranged to discuss procedural aspects of the forthcoming SALT talks in Helsinki, Vorontsov took the initiative in raising the subject of American agitation over a possible Soviet

---

[1] Source: National Archives, Nixon Presidential Materials, NSC Files, Box 490, President's Trip Files, Dobrynin/Kissinger, 1970, Vol. II. Secret; Nodis. Drafted by Garthoff. On October 2, Haig sent Kissinger this memorandum through Lord. Also included was a covering note from U. Alexis Johnson to Kissinger that reads: "Enclosed is a copy of a report of a very interesting conversation in which, to my knowledge, the Soviets for the first time took the initiative in bringing up the Cuban submarine base question with an American official. I particularly draw attention to the penultimate sentence in which Vorontsov said that the Soviet Government would soon 'explain fully' its position regarding the base." Copies of this note and the memorandum of conversation were also sent to Helms, Packard, and Moorer.

naval base in Cienfuegos in Cuba. He said that we could expect the subject to be mentioned at Helsinki, that Semenov would no doubt refer in more than one statement to the inconsistency of an American position opposing Soviet proposals for abolition of overseas bases and limitation on missile submarine deployment, while maintaining such bases, and then objecting to the fact that the Soviet Union might get such a base itself. Vorontsov said there was no reason for the US to be concerned. I replied that I hoped he was saying that the Soviet Union would not be establishing a submarine base at Cienfuegos. Vorontsov objected that he had not said that, nor had he said that they would do so, but that in any case there were no grounds for American objection or concern. I replied that the United States would make its own determination of what constituted a cause for concern, but that although Vorontsov chose to be vague, I still hoped that he meant that the Soviet Union would not seek to establish such a base. Vorontsov then said that the Soviet Government would "explain fully" its position regarding developments at Cienfuegos "soon." He, Vorontsov, did not want to say more in advance of the Soviet Government.

---

223. Memorandum From Viron Vaky of the National Security Council Staff to the President's Assistant for National Security Affairs (Kissinger)[1]

Washington, October 5, 1970.

SUBJECT

Cuban Exiles and the Current Cuban/Soviet Sub-Base Issue

Attached at Tab A[2] is a Canadian report from its Embassy in Havana describing alleged Cuban Government preoccupation with fears of an exile invasion. The reported concern centers on exile activity in Central America.

There is exile activity in Central America. Attached at Tab B[2] is a CIA report on this.

---

[1] Source: National Archives, Nixon Presidential Materials, NSC Files, Box 782, Country Files, Latin America, Cuba, Soviet Naval Activity in Cuban Waters (Cienfuegos), Vol. I. Secret; Sensitive; Eyes Only. Sent for information and designated "non-log."

[2] Attached but not printed are Tabs A and B.

I call your attention to other items which are related:

—Since May Castro has repeatedly declared the right of Cuba to carry the fight to the territory of any country which lends itself to the exiles' organization of invasions.

—If exiles are organizing in Central America they may be making a mistake in including Costa Rica President Figueres in their discussions, for reasons which you know about. If we should be supporting these exile plans, all the more so.

—We have wondered what the Cubans got out of agreeing to Soviet construction at Cienfuegos. Increased military assistance is probably part of the price. If Castro is worried about exiles, or if he wants some kind of capacity to project his own military strength, the Soviets may have decided to up their military aid accordingly. Exile activity in Central America might now be a convenient excuse for (a) Soviet aid, and (b) Cuban adventurism and retaliation.

—Alpha–66, a Miami-based group, has undertaken about three or four infiltration raids since May. All have been rolled up. The Agency denies they have anything to do with Alpha–66. The equipment reported captured by the Cubans when exiles were arrested include AR–18 rifles, cipher pads, and other items indicating some sophisticated support. DOD also has the capacity for clandestine support of such activity.

Our approach to the Cuban sub-base problem seems to me to require a very controlled precise approach. While in the abstract exile raids might seem useful to give Castro trouble, they are also "unguided missiles." How would such raids fit into the total picture? Are we sure of the reaction and its relation to other things? What do raids do by way of projecting signals to the Soviets and the Cubans?

In sum, do we have any well-thought-out purpose for encouraging exiles? Have we thought out the chess moves down the road? Shouldn't these be very controlled? Should they be done now?

---

224. Memorandum of Conversation[1]

Washington, October 6, 1970, 2:15 p.m.

PARTICIPANTS

Dr. Henry A. Kissinger and Soviet Ambassador Anatoliy Dobrynin

---

[1] Source: National Archives, Nixon Presidential Materials, NSC Files, Box 490, President's Trip Files, Dobrynin/Kissinger, 1970, Vol. 2. Top Secret; Sensitive. The conversation was held in the Map Room at the White House.

I received a phone call from Ambassador Dobrynin the morning of my return from the President's European trip[2] during which he stated that he would like to see me if at all possible that day. We agreed to meet at 2:15 p.m. in the Map Room. Ambassador Dobrynin greeted me by saying that he had had two communications from the Soviet Government which had come back with very great speed after our earlier conversation. He stated that Moscow's hope had obviously been to reach me before our departure for Europe but that it had been too late to do so.

The Ambassador then handed me the two communications. The first dealt with Jordan, the second with Cuba. With respect to Jordan, Dobrynin added that the note was somewhat dated but it should give us a good idea of the attitude of the Soviet Government. The two communications read as follows:

Jordan

"The Soviet Government has received with satisfaction President Nixon's communication to the effect that the United States do not contemplate any military actions in connection with the events in Jordan and that the US Government is exerting restraining influence in order to prevent interference in the events in Jordan by other foreign states.

"From the very start of the events in Jordan the Soviet side, as the US side has already been informed, has been taking steps aimed at bringing about a speedy end to the fratricidal collisions in Jordan and at preventing interference in the events therein by other states, both belonging to that area and those outside of it. This, as the US Government is aware, has produced certain results.

"The situation in Jordan still remains, however, rather complex. Therefore, we proceed from the assumption that also in the time ahead all states should exercise necessary prudence in their actions in order not to aggravate the situation but, on the contrary, to help end the conflict in Jordan.

"In Moscow it is believed that the most effective means of preventing events like those which occurred in Jordan, is a speedy attainment of a peaceful settlement in the Middle East as a whole.

"The Soviet position on questions pertaining to such settlement and, in particular, on the question of contacts between the sides through Jarring is well known to the US Government."

Cuba

"The Soviet Government has received with attention President Nixon's communication indicating some uncertainty which has appeared in

---

[2] See footnote 2, Document 218.

the President's mind in light of the understanding reached in 1962 between the USSR and US Governments on the Cuban question.

"We noted with satisfaction the reaffirmation made by President Nixon in reply to our inquiry, that the appropriate understanding reached at that time on the Cuban question remains fully in force, that is, the United States as before will not seek by the force of arms, through military means to change the existing situation in Cuba. We also noted the reaffirmation made as regards the United States's preventing such actions on the part of the Cuban counter-revolutionary exiles.

"On our part, we have already stated to President Nixon and are ready to affirm it again that in the Cuban question the Soviet Government continues to proceed from the understanding reached on this question in 1962.

"The Soviet side has not done and is not doing in Cuba now—that includes the area of the Cienfuegos port—anything of the kind that would contradict that mentioned understanding.

"The American side is well aware of the negative attitude generally on the part of the Soviet Union toward creating military bases by foreign states on the territory of other states. Moreover, the Soviet Government has introduced—both in the Committee on Disarmament and in the course of the Soviet-American strategic arms limitation talks—a proposal to limit the area of navigation for rocket-carrying submarines.

"In any case, we would like to reaffirm once more that the Soviet side strictly adheres to its part of the understanding on the Cuban question and will continue to adhere to it in the future on the assumption that the American side as President Nixon has reaffirmed, will also strictly observe its part of the understanding.

"I would like to draw your attention in connection with your remarks in our last conversation to the sometimes asserted 'right' for American atomic submarines to enter the Black Sea. Such assertions are groundless since the 1936 Convention on the status of the Black Sea Straits clearly forbids submarines of non-coastal states to enter the Black Sea."

After I had read the Cuban note, Ambassador Dobrynin added that the Soviet Government would not be able to make an agreement that Soviet submarines would never call at Cuban ports but he was prepared to state that Soviet submarines would not call there in an operational capacity. He could not say whether there might not be one submarine in six months and another one in twelve months. I told him that I considered this a forthright statement. I stated that I was concerned, however, that there might be some ambiguity about the meaning of the word "base" and, therefore, I thought it would be very unfortunate if our two governments got into a major disagreement over the issue of what actually constituted a base. Consequently, our side would have some clarifying questions to ask the Soviet Government. At the very least we would have to state our view of what constituted a base. The presence of the Soviet ships, especially the tender and barges, at Cienfuegos, was clearly inconsistent with the understanding. Ambassador Dobrynin said he would send on these questions.

Ambassador Dobrynin then tried to engage me in a discussion of the Middle East, specifically whether I thought the Deputies in New York could make some progress in negotiations. I told him that the Mideast negotiations probably had to mark some time for the moment. He then asked whether I could provide some advance information about the President's Vietnam speech.[3] I replied that it was not finished yet. He asked whether I was worried that he might give the information to their North Vietnamese allies and promised that this would not happen. I said I would not want to test your loyalty to your allies in this manner, but that I would see whether I could get him an advance copy of the President's remarks, perhaps by the next morning.

The meeting adjourned.

---

[3] On October 7, President Nixon delivered an "Address to the Nation About a New Initiative for Peace in Southeast Asia." (*Public Papers: Nixon, 1970*, pp. 825–828)

---

225.   Memorandum From William Hyland of the National Security Council Staff to the President's Assistant for National Security Affairs (Kissinger)[1]

Washington, October 7, 1970.

SUBJECT

The Soviet Reply

The Soviet reply[2] both in tone and substance is obviously intended to be conciliatory. It clearly backs away from any suggestion that the Soviets have a "right" to establish a base in Cuba, which would have been the toughest response. Rather, it specifically claims that the USSR traditionally opposes foreign bases—thus establishing a presumption

---

[1] Source: National Archives, Nixon Presidential Materials, NSC Files, Box 490, President's Trip Files, Dobrynin/Kissinger, 1970, Vol. II. Top Secret; Sensitive; Eyes Only. The memorandum is not signed. Kissinger wrote "Keep specially" in the upper righthand corner.

[2] See Document 224.

that they would not do so in Cuba (it is worth recalling, however, that Khrushchev in September 1962 publicly claimed that the USSR had no need to "transfer" its strategic missiles to any foreign bases). The note also goes to some length to pin down the understanding of 1962 and claims in particular that their activities at Cienfuegos are consistent with that understanding.

This general line, plus other possible signs strongly suggests that the Soviets are anxious to avoid a public (or private) confrontation:

—On the day following your press release, two of the Soviet vessels—the salvage and landing ship—that had been in Cienfuegos since September 9–10, departed for the USSR.

—Since then there has been virtually no change in Cienfuegos: no new construction, no significant increase in defense, no change in the use of the tender (it has apparently been at the pier since September 25–26, rather than moored at the deep basin, thought to be the submarine support area, guarded by the submarine nets).

—The Soviets have made only a minimal public acknowledgement (on September 30) and have tried to dismiss the affair as mere propaganda.

—The Soviet counselor (Vorontsov) told the UAR Ambassador in Washington that the Soviet activities were only Cuban port improvements.

The general Soviet response thus suggests that they are looking for an easy and quick end to the incident. This is consistent with the interpretation that the main purpose of the exercise has been a probe of our permissiveness, following on their earlier visits, especially the one to Cienfuegos in May, which included a cruise missile submarine. Having found that move has drawn a strong response, they probably want to resolve it by taking refuge in the 1962 agreement. In this light, the earlier conversation with Vorontsov was a form of reinsurance against the current contingency, as well as sounding us out for any reaction to what had already transpired in May and July.

Nevertheless, the Soviet response is deliberately ambiguous, a retreat but only a partial one. The note implies that, while an offensive or strategic base is not involved at Cienfuegos, the facilities could still be used from time to time in unspecified ways. Thus they are proposing a narrow definition of the 1962 agreement. The consequence could be that we might accept a de facto Soviet support base, limited only by the exclusion of ballistic submarines.

In short, the Soviet approach implies a reaffirmation of the 1962 understanding but on the basis of the status quo, i.e., the acceptance of the current facilities at Cienfuegos, and perhaps their improvement.

Next Steps

The definite commitment to the 1962 accord is an important first step toward resolving the issue on our terms. *But* there remains a gray area that should be clarified lest there be a future misunderstanding, and, most important, could signal to the Soviets we were prepared to tolerate a de facto base in Cuba.

To avoid this, *the following could be your general response:*

—You note that both sides have now reaffirmed the basic 1962 understanding.
—You also note that this applies specifically to the facilities at Cienfuegos.
—This means that Cienfuegos cannot be used to service or support missile submarines.

It remains to clarify in what way the facilities will be used.

—While we could not object to ceremonial port calls, accepted as traditional international practice, certain patterns of activity and the appearance of certain types of vessels would raise serious questions of Soviet intentions.
—In other words, our interpretation of the 1962 agreement is that the USSR should not use Cuba in any way to gain a military advantage over the US.
—The simple solution would be for the submarine tender to return to the USSR. This would be a tangible change. Otherwise it will be extremely difficult to explain to the Congress or the American public why we have not taken this up through regular diplomatic channels.
—As long as the tender remains, there will be doubts in our minds of the Soviet commitment to abide by the 1962 accords. (*Optional:* If the tender does remain, we would have to be far more concerned over any use of the Cienfuegos port by Soviet vessels.)
—Until the remaining ambiguities are resolved, we cannot consider the matter closed, and must reserve the right to shift to less confidential channels, which we would not prefer. It is in our common interest not to allow this issue to fester, and become a public confrontation.

Questions

1. What is the purpose of keeping a submarine tender in Cienfuegos, if it is not to be used? (How would the Soviets regard the stationing of a US submarine tender and nets in the Gulf of Finland?)

2. Does the Soviet Government agree that the intention of the agreements in 1962 was that the USSR would not attempt to use Cuba to gain a military advantage over the US—that is, not to change the status quo in the area?

3. Does the USSR agree that any *regular use* of Cienfuegos by *any* Soviet warships or *any* kind of submarine (ballistic, cruise or attack) would violate the basis of the understanding reached in 1962?

4. Do the Soviets agree that further construction of barracks, new communications with the USSR, storage for weapons (missiles) would change the status quo and be inconsistent with their assertion that they do not intend to establish a base in Cienfuegos?

226. Memorandum From the Joint Chiefs of Staff's Liaison at the National Security Council (Robinson) to the President's Assistant for National Security Affairs (Kissinger)[1]

Washington, October 8, 1970.

SUBJECT

Cuba

Attached at Tab A[2] is a draft response to the Soviet note concerning recent naval activity in Cuba (Tab B).[3] The proposed reply makes clear that we understand the Soviets will take no action to:

—Handle or store nuclear weapons in Cuba.
—Construct or maintain submarine or surface ship repair facilities or tenders in Cuban ports.
—Undertake visits by ballistic missile submarines.

We considered it prudent to include *all* submarine/surface ship repair facilities in our interpretation since the Soviets could convert any repair installation to one with an offensive weapon capability on short notice. Similarly, although it would be desirable to restrict visits to Cuban ports by *all* submarines and surface ships with a surface missile capability, we have not done so for several reasons:

—Their cruise-missile submarines, missile cruisers and destroyers have visited Cuba without U.S. protest on several occasions during the past 18 months. A challenge at this time might undermine the credibility of our note.
—U.S. Polaris submarines do not visit any foreign ports (other than Rota and Holy Loch). We should expect the Soviets to abide by this same restriction, but they probably would refuse to agree to a greater limitation.

One aspect of the 1962 US–USSR "Understanding" concerned the U.S. pledge of no U.S. invasion of Cuba and U.S. prevention of invasion by other countries, contingent upon verification of removal of the missiles from Cuba. Since Castro prevented on-site verification, President Kennedy never gave an unequivocal guarantee not to invade Cuba

---

[1] Source: Library of Congress, Manuscript Division, Kissinger Papers, Box TS 36, Geopolitical File, Soviet Union, 7/70–1/71. Top Secret; Sensitive; Eyes Only.

[2] Attached but not printed. The draft response to the Soviet note is virtually identical to the final version printed as Tab A, Document 228.

[3] The text of the Soviet note on Cuba is in Document 224.

(Tab C).[4] A possible Soviet ploy for removal of the base at Cienfuegos might be to have the U.S. make an explicit non-invasion guarantee. Our proposed note has not addressed this issue.

In arriving at a set of conditions acceptable to the United States, a number of activities were considered. These are enumerated at Tab D. You will note that those items which would be difficult to verify or confirm were not included in the draft note.

For your information, the nomenclature of Soviet submarines and missile-equipped surface ships is appended at Tab E.[5]

Tab D

List of Soviet Activities in Cuba[6]

Washington, undated.

Unacceptable Activity

—Facilities ashore for handling/storage of nuclear weapons.

—Facilities ashore to repair and maintain submarines or surface ships armed with nuclear-capable surface-to-surface missiles.

—Basing or extended deployment with semi-permanent facilities of tenders or other repair ships capable of repair and maintenance of submarines or surface ships armed with nuclear-capable surface-to-surface missiles.

—Facilities to transfer nuclear weapons afloat.

—Communications support facilities for submarines.

—Visits by ballistic missile submarines.

—Stockpiling of repair parts for submarines or surface ships armed with nuclear-capable surface-to-surface missiles including parts for propulsion and weapons (difficult to verify).

—Facilities for provisioning submarines or surface ships armed with nuclear capable surface-to-surface missiles to extend deployment (difficult to verify).

---

[4] Attached but not printed. See footnote 7, Document 194. After providing part of Kennedy's remarks from his November 20, 1962, press conference, Robinson added, "In the context above, and considering the current situation at Cienfuegos, the following should be considered 'offensive weapons': all submarines; nuclear missile surface warships."

[5] Attached but not printed.

[6] No classification marking.

—Presence of Soviet technicians to repair and maintain submarines or surface ships armed with nuclear-capable surface-to-surface missiles (difficult to verify if no tender present).

—Facilities ashore for submarine crew rest and crew transfer (difficult to verify if transfer occurs at sea).[7]

Acceptable Activity

—Port visits except by ballistic missile submarines.

—Harbor improvements such as placing buoys, building additional pier space, dredging to widen and/or deepen channel.

------

[7] The four previous paragraphs were bracketed with the marginal comment: "Not included in U.S. Reply to U.S.S.R. note."

------

227.   Memorandum From Thomas Latimer of the National Security Council Staff to the President's Assistant for National Security Affairs (Kissinger)[1]

Washington, October 9, 1970.

SUBJECT

CIA's Memo[2] on the Soviet Buildup on the Sino-Soviet Border

This is a comprehensive examination of the significance of the Soviet military force now deployed opposite China. Its major conclusions are as follows:

—The 37 to 41 division force structure which the Soviets have developed opposite China now exceeds what would be required to repulse any foreseeable Chinese incursion.

—The present Soviet force could probably carry out large scale raids in the border regions of China but in view of their underdevel-

------

[1] Source: National Archives, Nixon Presidential Materials, NSC Files, Box 713, Country Files, Europe, USSR, Vol. IX. Top Secret; Sensitive; Contains Codeword. Latimer handwrote "action" at the top of the memorandum. The memorandum bears Kissinger's initials and the handwritten comment, "Tell Helms excellent job." On October 28, Latimer sent Kissinger this paper and a similar report prepared by DOD (see footnote 2, Document 210) under a cover memorandum that bears Kissinger's handwritten remark, "Sum up both memos for Pres[ident] as info." (Ibid.)

[2] An attached cover memorandum to the CIA report indicates that the paper is a response to Kissinger's request, September 21, for a study on the Sino-Soviet border dispute. (Ibid.) For Kissinger's request, see Document 209.

oped service support structure they could probably not occupy and defend a significant amount of Chinese territory.

—With the divisions filled out to combat strength, a process which would take about three weeks, and provided with normal army and front level support, the Soviets would be capable of large scale offensive operations in the peripheral regions of China. Under these circumstances, the full strength Soviet force probably could seize and occupy sizable portions of territory, including Manchuria, the eastern part of Inner Mongolia, and the Dzungarian Basin in Sinkiang, using only conventional weapons.

—To date, there is no persuasive evidence of a Soviet intent to commit deliberate aggression against China. The forces now in being are not ready to undertake protracted large scale offensive operations. Were the Soviets planning to initiate a deliberate aggression, there would be a concerted effort to fill out existing understrength divisions and support units. In addition, some tactical missile units probably would be redeployed from other areas.

The CIA memorandum states that the Soviets probably had several objectives in undertaking the buildup. One objective, already realized, may have been to set the stage for discussions on the border. The Soviets also probably calculated that a credible land war threat near the China border will enhance their ability to influence events in China after the death of Mao. In addition, of course, the buildup has—from the Soviet viewpoint—put the damper on any inclination the Chinese may have to launch military forays against Soviet territory. From the standpoint of providing security for Soviet territory, the forces near the China border are not excessive when compared with Soviet forces located opposite other potential enemies.

Tab A[3]

Intelligence Report

Washington, October 1970.

THE SOVIET MILITARY BUILDUP ON THE
SINO-SOVIET BORDER

Summary

Since 1965 the Soviets have tripled their ground forces opposite China. There are now some 37 to 41 Soviet ground force divisions

---

[3] Top Secret; Ruff; Umbra; Handle via Talent–Keyhole–Comint Control Systems Jointly. According to a footnote in the source text: "Note: This report was produced solely by CIA. It was prepared by the Office of Strategic Research and coordinated with the Offices of Basic and Geographic Intelligence, Current Intelligence, and Economic Research."

deployed in the border area, about 6 of which are fully combat ready. All of the others have one or more subordinate regiments with sufficient strength to undertake combat missions. About 210,000 troops are deployed with these divisions, and nondivisional support elements bring the total to about 335,000 men. The buildup is continuing.

In 1965, when the buildup was initiated, there were only 11 or 12 divisions in the border area, and only one of these was at combat strength. All of the others were understrength and some were only cadre divisions.

Over the same period tactical air forces have increased from a single air army of 190 combat aircraft and about 40 helicopters deployed in the Vladivostok area to at least 725 combat aircraft and 300 helicopters deployed along the entire border.

Soviet strategic air defenses in the border area also have been improved in recent years, but most of this probably would have taken place even if there had been no rift with China. Most of the new missile and aircraft deployment probably results from a continuing program to strengthen air defenses throughout the USSR.

Three operational units of the 500 nautical mile Scaleboard surface-to-surface missile system—the only confirmed units in the USSR—have been deployed near the border since 1967.

Strategic ballistic missile and bomber forces have not undergone any major changes that can be attributed to the confrontation with China, other than some command and control adjustments.

The Soviet ground and tactical air forces in the border area are deployed in two essentially separate operational theaters. Most of these forces—29 to 33 divisions and nearly 700 aircraft—are located opposite northeast China in the Trans-Baikal and the Far East Military Districts and in Mongolia. The other 8 divisions and about 35 aircraft are deployed in the newly formed Central Asian Military District opposite Sinkiang.

There are, in addition, 4 divisions in the Siberian Military District and 6 in the Turkestan Military District which probably are available as reinforcements for the border area. These are located in remote areas, and except for an airborne division in Turkestan, all are at low strength. Only one, a cadre division moved into the Siberian Military District in 1969, has undergone any change since the buildup began in 1965. These divisions are not believed to be currently available for early commitment.

Other reinforcements could be obtained by redeploying divisions from the western military districts. Depending on the readiness level of the divisions to be moved and the distance to be traveled, divisions could begin arriving in the border area 10 to 17 days after the Soviets decided to reinforce.

The 37 to 41 division force structure which the Soviets have developed opposite China now exceeds what would be required to repulse any foreseeable Chinese incursion. The present force could probably also carry out large scale raids in the border regions of China, but in view of their underdeveloped service support structure they could probably not occupy and defend a significant amount of Chinese territory.

With the divisions filled out to combat strength, however, and provided with normal army and front level support, the Soviets would be capable of large scale offensive operations for objectives in the peripheral regions of China. Such a force would have about 570,000 troops, 8,200 tanks, at least 5,400 conventional artillery pieces, and some 250 missile and rocket launchers for direct nuclear support.

With their present air forces the Soviets probably could quickly establish air superiority in the peripheral regions of China. This would enable them to provide massive support to the ground forces with tactical air and medium bomber forces.

Under these circumstances, the full strength Soviet force probably could seize and occupy sizable portions of territory, including Manchuria, the eastern part of Inner Mongolia, and the Dzungarian Basin in Sinkiang, using only conventional weapons. The Soviets would probably refrain from the use of tactical nuclear weapons unless it appeared necessary for the achievement of their military objectives.

To date, however, there is no persuasive evidence of a Soviet intent to commit deliberate aggression against China. The forces now in being are not ready to undertake protracted large scale offensive operations. Were the Soviets planning to initiate a deliberate aggression there would be a concerted effort to fill out existing understrength divisions and nondivisional support units such as artillery, engineer, ponton bridge, and assault crossing units. In addition, some tactical missile units probably would be redeployed from other areas. There would also be a heavy influx of trucks to provide both divisional and rear service motor transport.

To bring the forces in the border area to full combat readiness, reservists and civilian trucks would have to be transported from centers in the central and western USSR to supplement those obtained from local mobilization. The Soviets have the resources and transportation facilities to accomplish this in about three weeks.

The availability of stocks of ammunition, POL, and general supplies in the border area is not known. Because the forces opposite China are located at the end of long and, in some areas, vulnerable supply lines, the Soviets probably have made some effort to develop their logistical base in the area. If the current rate of military traffic on the Trans-Siberian Railroad has been maintained throughout the force buildup, the Soviets could have provided the troops now in place with stocks of ammunition and POL sufficient for 90 days of combat. Unless it is interdicted, the Trans-Siberian Railroad has ample excess capacity to supply the daily tonnage of supplies needed to support the present force in combat without seriously reducing civilian traffic.

The fact that the force is still not fully combat ready after five years of buildup suggests that the immediate objective of the Soviet buildup was not to initiate hostilities against the Chinese. The pace of the buildup may have been limited by a Soviet desire to avoid drawing down forces opposite NATO or straining the civilian economy.

The personnel and equipment strengths of the developing divisions in the border area continue to increase gradually. Some divisions probably will reach combat readiness during the next year or so. Others may stabilize at less than combat strength. This would be consistent with the manner in which the Soviets have structured their forces in the USSR intended for use against NATO, where only about one-third of the divisions are kept at combat readiness during peacetime.

If the Soviets should follow this practice with the forces in the border area, it would suggest that they believe that the time it would take the relatively immobile Chinese forces to mount a serious threat would permit the Soviet forces in the border area to be filled out with re-servists and mobilized civilian trucks.

Conversely, if the Soviets continue working to bring all the forces to full combat readiness, it would indicate that they believe a large scale conflict could break out suddenly with little warning. This would reflect a more serious view of the Chinese threat than is now apparent, or it could mean that they were contemplating the initiation of offensive action themselves.

The Soviets probably had several objectives in undertaking the military buildup opposite China. One objective—already realized—may have been to set the stage for the Sino-Soviet discussions on border issues. The Soviets probably calculate that the possession of a credible land war threat near the China border will enhance their ability to influence events in China after the death of Mao. In addition, of course, the buildup has—from the Soviet viewpoint—put the damper on any inclination the Chinese may have to launch military forays against Soviet territory. From the standpoint of providing security for Soviet territory, the forces near the China border are not excessive when compared with Soviet forces located opposite other potential enemies.

The pattern of the buildup to date suggests that the Soviets are developing a force structure of at least 3 and possibly 4 army groups (potential fronts)—two or three opposite Manchuria and one opposite Sinkiang. This would imply a force of 42 to 48 divisions and 900 to 1,000 aircraft. At full strength, this force would have about 780,000 troops. Such a force would probably still not enable the Soviets to carry a conventional land war against China beyond the peripheral regions. It would, however, provide the Soviets with a capability to respond to the initiation of hostilities on a level of their own choosing, up to and including an attack to seize and hold indefinitely the most important peripheral regions of China such as Manchuria, Inner Mongolia, or large parts of Sinkiang.

[Here follows the table of contents and the body of the report with annexes and illustrations.]

228.   Memorandum of Conversation[1]

Washington, October 9, 1970, 5:30 p.m.

PARTICIPANTS

Dr. Henry A. Kissinger and Soviet Ambassador Anatoliy Dobrynin

The meeting was initialed at my request and began with my handing Dobrynin a copy of an oral note[2] dealing with the installations in Cuba. The purpose of the note was to tie down our understanding of the Soviet base. Rather than putting the issues in the form of questions they were phrased in the form of an understanding of what we considered a base.

Ambassador Dobrynin then read over the note (Tab A) and said that the only point that seemed bothersome was the point about "communica-facilities," but he would have to await further instructions from Moscow.

Ambassador Dobrynin added that Tass would soon publish a statement repeating in effect the content of the oral note of October 6[3] denying any Soviet intent to establish a base in Cuba. I said that we would judge it by the criteria of our oral note. Later in the evening Dobrynin called to inquire whether the point about repair facilities

---

[1] Source: National Archives, Nixon Presidential Materials, NSC Files, Box 490, President's Trip Files, Dobrynin/Kissinger, 1970, Vol. II. Top Secret; Sensitive. The conversation was held in the Map Room at the White House.

[2] Printed at Tab A.

[3] See Document 224.

applied to all Soviet ships or only those capable of offensive action. I replied that it applied to the ships described in the note.

We then discussed the possibility of a meeting between Soviet Foreign Minister Gromyko and the President. Ambassador Dobrynin asked whether it should take place before or after the Foreign Ministers meetings with Secretary of State Rogers. I replied that my instincts suggested that the meeting should take place afterwards. Ambassador Dobrynin then asked what date was convenient and I suggested the afternoon of October 23rd following the President's speech at the UN. Ambassador Dobrynin said that this was in general acceptable. I then told the Ambassador to make sure that during these conversations no mention would be made of the US–USSR Summit meeting or, in any event, to be sure that I received advance word in order to provide me with an opportunity to put the issue into formal channels. Ambassador Dobrynin agreed and further agreed to come to Washington before the meeting of the President and Foreign Minister Gromyko so that we could coordinate on and agree to the agenda.

Ambassador Dobrynin then turned to a general discussion of US-Soviet relations. He said it was hard to exaggerate the concern of his leadership in Moscow. Their feeling was that the United States had already decided to adopt a hard line and it was whipping up a propaganda campaign in order to get larger defense budgets and perhaps affect the election. He said that the campaign on the Mideast was out of all proportion to the provocation. He called my attention to the fact that the Soviet Union had never been part of the cease-fire. He said that when Secretary Rogers first told him about the cease-fire standstill in conjunction with the US proposal for Middle East Peace negotiations, that he had asked Secretary Rogers whether these items were linked together. Secretary Rogers had replied that it was desirable "but not" indispensable that the cease-fire and the negotiations be linked together. The Ambassador stated that, therefore, the Soviet Government did not understand why the U.S. suddenly decided to effect a linkage. Ambassador Dobrynin then said that Assistant Secretary Sisco, in the presence of Secretary Rogers, had told him there was no linkage between these elements and that, in any event, the Soviet Union had only been informed of our understanding of the cease-fire for informational purposes. The Ambassador added that the Soviet Government was seriously debating whether to start a press campaign against us along similar lines.

Ambassador Dobrynin said that he hoped that the U.S. Government did not draw the conclusion from the Middle East crisis that the Soviet Union could be intimidated by a show of United States force. He asked whether we really thought that one additional U.S. carrier in the Eastern Mediterranean would make the Soviet Union back down.

Further, Ambassador Dobrynin stated he could understand that the United States might claim for propaganda purposes that the Soviet Union controlled the Syrians but that if we really believed that to be the case then we were in bad shape. He continued that if the Soviet Union acted when its national interest was involved then it would act with great force and it would be hard to dissuade them. I replied that we were not children, that we looked at the situation with great care. Having observed Soviet military actions in the last decade and a half we knew that when the Soviet Union used its forces it did so massively. But that was not the point. The point was that we were asking the same questions about the Soviet leaders that he allegedly was asking about our leaders. I reminded him that we had offered a Summit meeting on two occasions during the summer without ever receiving a formal reply. In response there was the massive move forward of Egyptian and Soviet missiles along the canal and the massive deception in Cuba. Ambassador Dobrynin began to explain that the Cuban situation was "not clear." I interrupted saying if there is to be any sense in our meetings we must not kid one another. I added, "you know what is there and I know what is there even though we may not say it, so let us not discuss it any further."

With respect to the Egyptian missiles, Ambassador Dobrynin called my attention to the phrase that there were no Soviet personnel with the missiles in Egypt. I said that perhaps he meant "military" personnel and that they had put them into civilian clothes. He replied that the phrase was intended to mean that there were *no* Soviet personnel.

Ambassador Dobrynin then appeared to bluster stating that the Soviet Union had a lot of experience in dealing with Americans and they thought their system was more permanent than ours and therefore if things came to that point they would wait for 6 years until President Nixon was out of office. I replied that perhaps the inference that the press campaign came from us was started by people who did not know anything about American affairs. Ambassador Dobrynin said "no" it was the consensus of all their senior officials that relations with the United States had never been worse since the Cuban missile crisis. I said that I could only repeat what I had said to him previously. We were at a turning point. We recognized very well that neither side could gain anything in an arms race but if present trends continued they would force us into an enlarged military budget. He might well tell me that his leaders could wait six years and this might be true; however, President Nixon did not become President by not being persistent. Nevertheless, it did not seem sensible to exchange protestations on the issue of greater endurance. The problem was how to turn this present impasse into a more fruitful direction and, therefore, to turn our attention to that.

Ambassador Dobrynin said that it was important to discuss the Middle East and related issues. I replied again that this was not the time to do it. But that if they were ever willing to take up our offer for serious bilateral talks between Ambassador Dobrynin and me we would make every effort to proceed. The Ambassador told me that the memorandum he had handed to me, which is attached at Tab B, was written only for the President and would receive no publicity and be referred to nowhere else.

Tab A

United States Oral Note[4]

Washington, October 9, 1970.

The President appreciated the forthright reply of the Soviet Government conveying the affirmation of your government that the USSR is not and will not construct any facility in Cuba that will violate the understanding of 1962 between the USSR and US Governments on the Cuban questions. The clarification of this situation can be a significant contribution to improving US-Soviet relations.

The purpose of this memorandum is to provide the Soviet Government with what we understand by the phrase: "The Soviet side has not done and is not doing in Cuba now—that includes the area of the Cienfuegos port—anything of the kind that would contradict the mentioned understanding."

The US Government understands that the USSR will not establish, utilize, or permit the establishment of any facility in Cuba that can be employed to support or repair Soviet naval ships capable of carrying offensive weapons; i.e., submarines or surface ships armed with nuclear-capable, surface-to-surface missiles. The US Government further understands that the following specific actions will not be undertaken:

—Construction of facilities for the handling and storing of nuclear weapons and components in Cuba.
—Removal of nuclear weapons from, or transfer of nuclear weapons to, Soviet ships in Cuban ports or operating therefrom.
—Construction of submarine or surface ship repair facilities ashore in Cuba.
—Basing or extended deployment of tenders or other repair ships in Cuban ports that are capable of supporting or repairing submarines or surface ships armed with nuclear-capable surface-to-surface missiles.

---

[4] No classification marking.

—Construction of communications support facilities for Soviet submarines.

Finally, the President wishes to emphasize that the U.S. Government will observe strictly its part of the 1962 understanding as long as the Soviet Union does the same.

Tab B

Memorandum From the Soviet Leadership to President Nixon[5]

Moscow, October 9, 1970.

The attention of the Soviet leadership has been attracted to the campaign, hostile to the USSR, being waged in the US around so-called "violations of the terms of the cease-fire" in the Suez canal zone and the Soviet Union's alleged involvement in those "violations".

This anti-Soviet campaign is clearly being encouraged, and, to say more frankly, in fact inspired by American officials. How else can one judge, for example, the statement made by the Assistant Secretary of State Mr. Sisco at the press briefing in Chicago on September 16 when he, while accusing the UAR without proof of having violated the cease-fire terms, alleged in addition that all "these violations could not have taken place without the knowledge and the complicity of the Soviet Union". Speaking at the same briefing Mr. Kissinger also permitted himself to make remarks about violations of the cease-fire "by the Egyptians and the Russians". Moreover, and again with the blessing of officials, the theme was launched professing some general "credibility gap" with regard to the Soviet Union.

Clearly, in this connection the Soviet leadership cannot but raise the question as to what all this is being done for? What is the aim of the US Government in all of this? Because who else is better aware than the American Government of the complete lack of ground for the assertions that the Soviet Government had something to do with reaching the agreement on the terms of the cease-fire in the Suez Canal zone, still less—with some kind of "violations" of such agreement.

It is worthwhile to recall some facts pertaining to this question. On August 8, i.e. on the day when the cease-fire in the Suez Canal zone entered into force, the US Ambassador in Moscow, while handing to

---

[5] No classification marking.

the USSR Foreign Ministry the text of the terms of that cease-fire, already agreed upon with the Governments of the UAR and Israel, clearly and unequivocally stated that this was being done only "for the information of the Soviet Government". On August 11 transmitting to the Ministry some additional details of the terms of cease-fire, the US Ambassador said again that those clarifications had already been discussed by the US Government with the Governments of the UAR and Israel and that they were being handed to the Soviet side "just for its information".

That is how the record stands regarding involvement or, rather, non-involvement of the Soviet Union in the agreement itself on the terms of cease-fire in the Suez Canal zone.

On what basis, then, did the American side start later to present the matter in such a way as if there were some terms of cease-fire in the Suez Canal zone agreed upon between the US and USSR Governments? We have already drawn the attention of the US Government, through the American Ambassador in Moscow, in particular in the conversation with him held at the Foreign Ministry on September 15, to the fact that this kind of presentation was groundless. Nevertheless, US officials continued to distort the actual state of the matter.

Now about so-called "violations" of this agreement. It is necessary first of all to emphasize the complete lack of foundation for the attempts being made in the United States to prove that the Soviet side had something to do with such "violations". This refers, in particular, to statements alleging deployment in the Suez Canal zone of new rocket-launchers manned by Soviet personnel after August 8. That is deliberately false. Contrary to the assertions by American officials, there have not been and there are not now rocket-launchers manned by Soviet personnel in the Suez Canal zone.

What leaps into one's eye is that the American side while so unsparingly accusing the UAR of "violating" the terms of cease-fire, keeps almost complete silence with regard to actual violations made by Israel from the very first day of the cease-fire. Moreover, spokesmen of the US Government deem it appropriate to speak directly about "utmost importance for Israel to retain air superiority in the Suez Canal zone", as well as about "manoeuvrability and freedom of action in that area". Such a position hardly serves as a proof of US "impartiality". It can only mean one thing—a desire to mislead public opinion by presenting a distorted picture of the state of things and whitewashing the aggressor. All this is actually nothing but encouragement by the United States of a stubbornly obstructionist tactics of Israel, which from the very beginning and until this day has been rejecting contacts and negotiations through Ambassador Jarring, raising all sorts of far-fetched pretexts. Among them are accusations against the UAR of "violating" the terms of cease-fire. These assertions have already been refuted in an official statement made to the US representative in Cairo by the UAR Minister of Foreign Affairs M. Riad and also in M. Riad's Cairo TV address on October 6, 1970.

It should also be noted that Israel is now trying in every way to complicate and confuse the very question of cease-fire. One should recall that in American proposals of June 19 themselves negotiations between the sides through Jarring were not organicly linked to the cease-fire. That was publicly acknowledged by Mr. Sisco, who said in Chicago on September 16 that "originally the American proposals did not envisage any direct link between cease-fire and start of the talks".

However after the UAR Government accepted the American proposal on cease-fire, having thus displayed its full readiness to negotiate through Jarring, Israel started inventing new pretexts to dodge from such negotiations.

The Soviet Union has always been a sincere supporter of cease-fire, viewing it also as an important factor in creating a more favourable climate for talks between the sides. However the Soviet Union cannot ignore the attempts to deliberately complicate the question of cease-fire in order to torpedo the negotiations as is being done by Israel with the US support.

It could not but be noted in Moscow that supporting the obstructionist position of Israel the US Government itself also undertakes steps which lead to aggravation of the situation in the Middle East area. In this connection one should mention for instance the uproar created around the visit by the US President to the American 6th fleet in the Mediterranean. Among acts of this nature are the new deliveries of "Phantom" fighter-bombers and of other weapons to Israel and the reconnaissance flights by American aircraft over the territory of the UAR, a sovereign state, in gross violation of the norms of international law.

All this cannot but raise a legitimate question: where in effect is the United States leading to in the Middle East?

On our part we should like to reaffirm that the Soviet Government has been and remains a firm supporter of speedy achievement of a political settlement in the Middle East, of establishment of a durable and just peace there, on the basis of the well known resolution of the Security Council, in all its parts.

We believe that every effort should be made in order not to lose the opportunity for progress in political settlement in the Middle East which is being created by the agreement of the Arab states to negotiate through Ambassador Jarring and the actually existing state of cease-fire. We are ready to contribute to that both within the framework of our bilateral meetings and at the four-power consultations.

As for the talk about so-called "crisis of confidence" in general, the unseriousness of US officials' approach to this matter has attracted attention in Moscow. All those groundless statements indeed give reason to ask: is the US Government ready to support by its deeds what it says in the course of exchange of opinion with the Soviet Government or are those words said because of some considerations of the moment. The US position on the Middle East question and the distortion by the American side of facts pertaining to the cease-fire in the Suez Canal zone, indeed, cannot contribute to the strengthening of mutual understanding and trust in relations between our countries so needed for a fruitful development of these very relations.

---

229. Transcript of Telephone Conversation Between the President's Assistant for National Security Affairs (Kissinger) and the Soviet Ambassador (Dobrynin)[1]

Washington, October 9, 1970, 10:20 p.m.

D: You are not still in bed?

K: No.

D: Oh good, you see I would like to clarify some points beginning on the Cuba paper[2] you gave me dealing with nuclear and atomic things. One is the construction of submarines or surface repair facilities ashore in Cuba. You do not use any reference to nuclear or atomic in points covering this issue in the note. It refers in the heading to strategic systems, is that what is meant concerning repair facilities?

K: We are talking about ships in the above mentioned categories. (i.e. nuclear and atomic)

D: Just would like to be sure, they will ask me. I was under the impression that this was so but I wanted to be sure.

K: Yes, that's correct.

D: This is important. Thank you. Have a nice weekend.

---

[1] Source: National Archives, Nixon Presidential Materials, NSC Files, Box 490, President's Trip Files, Dobrynin/Kissinger, 1970, Vol. 2. No classification marking.

[2] See Tab A, Document 228.

Index

All references are to document numbers

All references are to document numbers

All references are to document numbers

All references are to document numbers

ISBN 0-16-076698-2